SECURITY EVALUATION
AND
PORTFOLIO ANALYSIS

SECURITY EVALUATION AND PORTFOLIO ANALYSIS

Edited by

EDWIN J. ELTON AND MARTIN J. GRUBER
Graduate School of Business Administration
New York University

PRENTICE-HALL, INC., Englewood Cliffs, New Jersey

Prentice-Hall International, Inc., *London*
Prentice-Hall of Australia, Pty. Ltd., *Sydney*
Prentice-Hall of Canada, Ltd., *Toronto*
Prentice-Hall of India Private Limited, *New Delhi*
Prentice-Hall of Japan, Inc., *Tokyo*

Printed in the United States of America

To Our Wives and Parents

For Their Support and Encouragement

CONTENTS

C. Relationship of Financial Data to Security Prices

BOND VALUATION

COMMON STOCK VALUATION

VALUATION OF OTHER SECURITY TYPES

D. Filter Rules and the Selection of Securities

TECHNICAL FILTER RULES

FUNDAMENTAL FILTER RULES

part two
PORTFOLIO ANALYSIS   405

PREFACE

This book is a compilation of the more important analytical articles which have appeared in the area of investments (security evaluation and portfolio analysis). The field of investments has undergone a fundamental change in the past few years, and this change has not as yet been reflected in textbooks. By bringing the important articles on investments together, we have produced a book which can be used in place of a text for an advanced course in security and/or portfolio analysis or which can be used as complementary material with a new generation of investment textbooks.

The book is intended for use in a graduate course or an advanced undergraduate course in security and/or portfolio analysis. Hopefully, it will also be of use to practicing security and portfolio analysts.

This book is divided into two parts: the first covering security analysis, and the second, portfolio analysis.

The part on security analysis is divided into four sections. The first section, covering the random walk hypothesis, deals with the efficiency of capital markets and the implications of efficient markets for our ability to predict stock prices. The second section is concerned with the predictability of earnings data as well as with the suitability of industrial classification as a basis for forecasting. The earnings variable was selected for special emphasis since it is the basis of most valuation models. The third section is concerned with the relationship between fundamental financial data and the price of securities. It answers the question, "Do financial variables affect stock prices the way in which theory would suggest?" or, "To what extent is the market rational in appraising economic differences between companies?" The fourth and last section of this part which is concerned with filter rules examines the ability of models employing both fundamental data and technical data to outperform the market. It is another way of answering the efficiency questions posed in the first part. It should be noted that the material in this section not only presents interesting and commonly used filters but also provides the theory necessary to enable a reader to formulate and test his own filter rules. Testing such selection rules involves the evaluation of groups or portfolios of securities which leads to the second section of the book.

The part on portfolio analysis is divided in to five sections. The first section lays down the basic framework for diversification and portfolio analysis. It deals with the question of finding the efficient set of portfolios for investment during a single period and the optimum set of portfolios for multi-period investment. An efficient portfolio can be defined as one with minimum risk for any given return. The second section discussed the simplifications needed to implement the theory developed in the first section and the cost and benefits from such a simplification. The third section deals with the problem of selecting portfolios which are desirable to the investor from among the efficient portfolios. The papers in this section discuss utility theory and its use in devising rules for selecting the optimum portfolio. The fourth section develops a general equilibrium theory from portfolio theory and derives a theory of asset prices under risk. The fifth and last section deals with the question of evaluating investment performance. This section deals not only with methods of evaluating the performance of two portfolios but also with the question of how well portfolio managers have performed in general. These questions can only be answered on the basis of portfolio and general equilibrium theory.

The introduction to this book presents a synthesis of the remaining material. Its purpose is to present an overall structure or framework for the individual articles as well as to highlight and hopefully clarify the contribution of each article. We suggest that the reader study this introduction before reading each section of the book and return to it to gain perspective after individual readings have been completed. In addition, a brief introduction which calls salient points in the article to the reader's attention preceeds each article in the book.

Many people have played a role in the development of this book. In particular, we would like to thank Bill Carleton, Mike Keenan, and Jerry Pogue for helpful suggestions on the manuscript. We would also like to thank Dr. Watson, whose stock selection techniques are as good as any which we have seen.

Edwin J. Elton
Martin J. Gruber

CONTRIBUTORS

David Ahlers   *Bankers Trust Company*
William Baumol   *Princeton University*
George A. Bennington   *University of Rochester*
Marshall E. Blume   *University of Pennsylvania*
William Breen   *Northwestern University*
William Carleton   *Dartmouth College*
Andrew Chen   *State University of New York at Buffalo*
Kalman Cohen   *Carnegie-Mellon University*
Edwin J. Elton   *New York University*
Eugene Fama   *University of Chicago*
Lawrence Fisher   *University of Chicago*
Myron Gordon   *University of Toronto*
Davd Green   *University of Chicago*
Martin J. Gruber   *New York University*
Frank Jen   *State University of New York at Buffalo*
Michael Jensen   *University of Rochester*
Eugene Lerner   *Northwestern University*
Burton Malkiel   *Princeton Uninversity*
Harry Markowitz   *Arbitrage Management Company, New York*
Kay Mazuy   *Boston Massachusetts*
Merton Miller   *University of Chicago*
Franco Modigliani   *Massachusetts Institute of Technology*
Marc Nerlove   *Yale University*
Joel Owen   *New York University*
Jerry Pogue   *Massachusetts Institute of Technology*
John Pratt   *Harvard University*
Richard Roll   *Carnegie-Mellon University*
Paul Samuelson   *Massachusetts Institute of Technology*
Joel Segall   *University of Chicago*
William Sharpe   *Stanford University*
John Shelton   *University of California at Los Angeles*
Seymour Smidt   *Cornell University*
L. G. Telser   *University of Chicago*
James Tobin   *Yale University*
Jack Treynor   *Financial Analyst Journal*
Roman Weil   *University of Chicago*
Stanley Zionts   *State University of New York at Buffalo*

SECURITY EVALUATION
AND
PORTFOLIO ANALYSIS

INTRODUCTION

The goal of investment analysis is to select a group or portfolio of securities which to the greatest extent possible meets a predetermined set of investor goals. These investor goals, at least in the modern literature of investment analysis, are usually expressed in terms of return (or profit) on investment and the degree of certainty about return. More return is desirable; more uncertainty is undesirable.

To obtain these goals an investor must be concerned with two problems: first, identifying and estimating relevant characteristics of individual securities, and second, finding combinations of securities (relevant characteristics) which accomplish the investor's goals.

This book is divided into two parts, security evaluation and portfolio analysis, which deal in turn with the two problems outlined above. Although these topics are discussed separately, it will become obvious to the reader that they are almost completely interdependent. For example, to evaluate success in selecting securities, one must borrow concepts of portfolio analysis, since the meaning of success can only be established within the framework of portfolio analysis. Similarly, to combine securities into desirable portfolios, one must have developed relevant information in evaluating the securities. Let us now turn to the first of these topics: security evaluation.

1. SECURITY EVALUATION

The selection of securities has traditionally progressed along two routes: the identification of price, or price and volume patterns that identify a security as a good buy (technical analysis),[1] and the identification of an intrinsic value such that when the security sells below its intrinsic value it is a good buy (fundamental analysis).[2]

[1] For example, see Edwards, Robert and John Magee, *Technical Analysis of Stock Trends,* J. Magee; Massachusetts, 1967.
[2] Graham, Benjamin, David Dodd, and Sidney Cottle, *Security Analysis,* McGraw-Hill, New York, 1962.

The first of these approaches assumes that there are certain readily discoverable price patterns that repeat themselves over time. By observing these price patterns, one can determine (depending on the theory being followed) if the market is overpriced or underpriced or if specific issues are overpriced or underpriced. For example, a chartist may plot previous prices and may buy or sell on the basis of whether or not current prices deviate significantly from the past price trend. If prices deviate on the high side, he may argue that prospects for the company have improved, that such prospects have only been partially reflected in the current price, and that purchases of the security will allow the buyer to reap the benefit of the remaining price adjustment.

The second approach assumes that information culled from a firm's balance sheet, income statement, management interviews, and economic forecasts for the industry and the economy can be combined into a number which represents the value of a security. If the security is currently selling below its value, it should outperform the market as its price approaches its "true" value. This is the method most security analysts use implicitly when they estimate future earnings and capitalize them at some predetermined price-earnings ratio. Before examining these two approaches to selecting securities, it is worthwhile reviewing the body of theoretical and empirical work which questions their validity.

A. THE THEORY OF RANDOM WALK OR LET'S ALL GO FISHING

In recent years a body of theory, first labeled "random walk" and later "a theory of efficient markets," has arisen that questions the concepts of traditional security analysis. The most extreme position taken by the random walk theorists is that all information is correctly and immediately incorporated into the price of a stock. This would suggest that both the informational content of past price changes and of all of the factors which the fundamental analyst examines are already correctly evaluated and incorporated into the present price of a firm's stock. Thus neither technical nor fundamental analysis can add new evidence, and both types of analysis are doomed to failure.[3] The more moderate adherents to a theory of efficient capital markets recognize that adjustment of price to information is neither perfect nor instantaneous, although they may still question if the imperfections are substantial enough to justify the cost of security analysis.

The articles by Fama (1) and Smidt (2) present a review of the random walk–efficient market literature. These articles review the theoretical base of the efficient market school as well as much of the major empirical research in this area. This empirical research is primarily of two types: tests to determine the statistical properties of price change and tests to determine the validity of various security selection techniques. At the very least, these articles establish a proper air of skepticism and a series of bench marks against which both fundamental and technical analysis should be judged. In addition, Smidt extends his analysis of the theory of efficient markets to outline several potential sources

---

[3] The adherents to this strong form of the theory of efficient markets would recognize monopoly access to information as the only way in which above-average returns could be earned.

of systematic price change which might, if incorporated correctly into a decision model, lead to the selection of successful investments.

We might keep in mind that findings about the inability of technical or fundamental analysis to disprove the theory of efficient markets might be due at least as much to the crude state of technical and fundamental analysis as it is to the efficiency of capital markets. In fact, Owen's article (3), in contrast to the empirical work cited by Fama, suggests that there ought to be some type of technical analysis which can produce trading profits. Owen's proof that intermediate price trends exist is one of the few pieces of evidence that runs directly contrary to a postulate of the strict form of the random walk theory, which states that the present price of a security incorporates all of the information embodied in past price movements.[4]

B. THAT ELUSIVE VARIABLE CALLED EARNINGS

Before turning to a formulation of fundamental analysis, let us examine in more detail one variable that will be found in all works on security analysis. This examination will illustrate the type of detailed analysis that can be performed with respect to each of the variables used in the remainder of this book. Elton and Gruber (4) explore, in detail, one method of forecasting earnings per share. This method is based upon first determining groups of firms which are homogeneous with respect to their earnings (growth) pattern over time and then forecasting earnings within each of the groups. Forecasts are prepared by relating growth to variables contained on the firm's balance sheet and income statement. This article demonstrates that mathematical techniques exist which, employing only historical data, can produce good earnings forecasts. In addition Elton and Gruber emphasize the importance of disaggregating data into homogeneous groups before attempting to uncover structural relationships or to prepare forecasts. The reader should be aware of this concept throughout the remainder of this book.

C. FUNDAMENTAL SECURITY EVALUATION

As stated earlier, fundamental analysis involves the combining of basic information about a company (e.g., balance sheet and income statement entries) into a measure of intrinsic value or true worth. The traditional approach to fundamental analysis has been to describe in great detail a large number of factors which should affect a firm's stock. However, the relative importance of these factors and their combination into a formula to produce a unique intrinsic value (or at least a range of intrinsic values) has always been left to the subjective judgment of the analyst. In fact, there is rarely any evidence presented that the variables discussed have any effect on price or value.

In this section we shall discuss articles that both show which variables are related to price and measure the extent of the relationship. At the most general

---

[4] The weaker form of the random walk theory will allow price trends but not of sufficient size for an investor to profit. Owen provides no evidence that the price trends are of sufficient size to be profitable.

level the value of any security can be established as the present value of a future stream of benefits.[5]

$$P = \sum_{i=1}^{n} \frac{B_i}{(1 + k)^i} \qquad (1)$$

where

> P is the value of the security,
> B_i is the cash flow or benefit that security holders expect to receive from the security in period i,
> k is the rate of return which security holders require to induce them to hold the security, and
> n is the time horizon over which they expect to receive the benefits.

The rate of return that the security holder requires (k) has two elements:

1. The rate of return he requires to delay his receipt of the money. This is often called the security holder's marginal time preference for money and is the rate of return he would require to hold a riskless security.
2. The rate of return he requires to bear the risk he perceives as being associated with the security.

From this general model (Equation 1) we can develop specific models to evaluate any type of security. This derivation involves a more exact specification of the benefit stream and risk elements which are appropriate for the security, plus a specification of the time horizon over which the investor values this benefit stream. In most of the articles contained in Section I C, regression analysis is used to determine the emphasis which the market places on each variable (regression coefficients) and the extent of association between the variables and stock price (the coefficient of determination).

Valuation of Bonds

Perhaps this derivation is easiest to see in the case of bond valuation, since the benefits which the bondholder expects to receive from holding a bond to maturity are specified. Assuming, for the sake of simplicity, that a bond pays interest once a year, we have

$$P_B = \sum_{i=1}^{n} \frac{I}{(1 + k)^i} + \frac{M}{(1 + k)^n} \qquad (2)$$

---

[5] The use of this formula involves the assumption that k is greater than the growth rate of B_i. If this is not true, a security would have an infinite value. This troublesome assumption has been handled in different ways by different authors. Gordon (8) assumes that k is an increasing function of the growth rate, thus forcing the summation to converge. Malkiel (9) assumes that the growth rate for any company will converge at some future date to an average growth rate for all companies.

where

> P_B is the market value of the bond,
> I is the interest payment at time i,
> M is the principal amount of the bond and is equal to the payment at maturity,
> n is the number of years before the bond matures, and
> k is the rate of return which bondholders desire.

Equation 2 is identical to Equation 1 except that the benefit stream has been split into two parts: interest payments and principal.

Equation 2 has two unknowns, k and P_B. If we can determine k, then we can determine P_B. As discussed earlier k should be made up of a risk element plus an element representing the bondholder's marginal time preference for money.

Fisher (6) attempts to remove the marginal time value of money by subtracting the yield on a government security of the same maturity from k. The resulting number should then be the risk premium on a corporate bond. Fisher hypothesizes that differences in this risk premium between corporate bonds should be due to differences in the risk of default on the bond and differences in marketability. Using three measures of the risk of default and one proxy for marketability, Fisher constructs a log linear regression model which is extremely stable over time and which, when applied to data from his entire sample, explains 81 percent of the difference in corporate bond risk premiums.

Starting from a firm theoretical base, Fisher has found four variables (rather than the large number usually listed in a text on security analysis) which explain almost all of the differences in the risk premiums at which bonds sell. Furthermore his regression coefficients represent the weights which the market has used in combining these variables into a bond valuation. By subtracting the yield on a government bond of the same maturity from the yield on the corporate bond, Fisher eliminates the influence of the time to maturity.

The article by Telser (5) examines this influence in detail. Telser is concerned with the issue of whether a bond with a longer maturity is more risky than one with a shorter maturity. Do investors require a liquidity premium on the longer-lived bonds because of their greater susceptibility to price changes due to a change in interest rates? The answer to this question is important not only for bond valuation but, as we shall see in the Gordon article (8), it affects the valuation of common stocks.

Valuation of Stocks

Literature on common stock valuation is more plentiful and diverse than literature on bond valuation. This is due in part to the nature of the assumptions which must be made in constructing a stock valuation model. For example, when examining bonds, both the income stream and the time horizon are well specified. When examining stocks, one can make alternative assumptions about the income stream (dividends, capital gains, and/or earnings) and the time horizon (since the stock has no maturity date). Furthermore the specification of risk variables and, in particular, the functional form these risk variables should take is open to serious question.

Let us review in some detail one of the stock-pricing models included in the book and having done so discuss the others in lesser detail. Gordon (8) begins by assuming an investor has an infinite time horizon. If we accept an infinite horizon as plausible, the benefit stream in which the stockholder is interested must be dividends. Following Gordon's assumption that the stockholder will expect dividends to grow at a specific rate each year, we have[6]

$$P = \sum_{i=1}^{\infty} \frac{D(1+g)^{i-1}}{(1+k)^{i}} \tag{3}$$

or applying the formula for the sum of a geometric progression

$$P = \frac{D}{k-g}$$

Equation 3 is identical to Equation 1 except that the benefit stream is defined more carefully. Now Gordon argues in a way that parallels the liquidity premium theory we examined in Telser's article (4) that k rather than being a constant should increase with time.[7] By assuming a plausible mathematical relationship to describe the dependency of the discount rate on time and growth, Gordon reduces the above relationship to

$$P = \alpha_5 D(1+g)^{\alpha_1}$$

where α_5 and α_1 are parameters to be estimated through regression analysis. Gordon then proceeds to add a variable reflecting the instability of earnings $(1 + \mu)$ and a size variable S to his equation. The final equation is

$$P = \alpha_5 D^{\alpha_4}(1+g)^{\alpha_1}(1+\mu)^{\alpha_2} S^{\alpha_3}$$

The parameters $\alpha_1, \alpha_2, \alpha_3, \alpha_4$, and α_5 are then estimated by regression analysis for each of four years for two industries. Gordon's article, as do the other articles in this section, serves the dual role of determining the variables that influence price and serving as a potential valuation model to be used in selecting securities.

Before examining additional full-scale pricing models, let us turn to articles concerned with the intensive examination of one of the variables used in full-scale models.

Malkiel (8) is one of the authors who was not interested in developing a full-scale pricing model but rather was interested in isolating one of the determinants of common stock price (specifically growth) for intensive analysis. Starting with the same basic assumption as Gordon, namely that the value of a share of stock is equal to the present value of all future dividends, Malkiel argues that the rate of growth of a high-growth company will approach that of a

---

[6] An even more general form of this equation will allow the rate of return that security holders require to vary over time.

[7] This assumption also avoids the famous St. Petersberg paradox that, if g is greater than k, a stock seemingly should have an infinite value.

representative or average company at some finite horizon.[8] Using these two assumptions, Malkiel shows that the multiple of earnings at which a growth stock should sell can be expressed as a function of the present dividend of the growth company, its rate of growth in dividends, and the earnings multiple at which a nongrowth stock sells. These results produce a formula useful in evaluating growth stocks as well as a set of axioms relating the performance of growth stocks to the performance of a typical share of stock. Malkiel carefully points out the similarities between his theory of stock behavior and the theory of the term structure of interest rates.

Like Malkiel, Modigliani and Miller focus on one determinant of common stock prices, the amount of debt in a firm's capital structure, for intensive analysis. Specifically, they are concerned with how the introduction of debt into a firm's capital structure affects the value of the firm and the rate of return required by its stockholders. The rate of return required by stockholders is the discount rate (k in Gordon's model) which equates the benefit stream from a share of stock with its price. Modigliani and Miller demonstrated theoretically and empirically exactly how the rate of return required by stockholders increases with an increase in the firm's debt-to-equity ratio. This implies that, if all other variables are held constant and if two firms have the same earnings per share, stock in the firm with the lower debt-to-equity ratio will sell at a higher price.

Nerlove (12) and Ahlers (11), like Gordon, present full-scale models linking fundamental data to stock prices or rate of return. Nerlove's article is interesting for several reasons. First, he formulates his dependent variable as a rate of return rather than as a stock price. His model attempts to explain the rate of return investors would earn by holding various stocks; it is not an attempt to explain the price of stocks at a point in time. Second, Nerlove tries alternative definitions of the same and similar economic phenomena. This should provide some appreciation of the sensitivity of model performance to alternative measures of the same economic phenomena; it should also demonstrate the insight that can be gained into an economic process by examining alternative variable formulations. Third, Nerlove presents tests of variables and model specifications which produced ambiguous results. Ambiguity arises when the regression coefficient associated with a variable is not significantly different from zero, when it has a sign which is inconsistent with theory, and/or when it is unstable over time. Most authors suppress these problems and present only their best results. By making the problems explicit Nerlove gives the reader an introduction to the art of model building. Furthermore these results demonstrate that some of the variables which the folklore of security analysis holds as important have effects which are far from clear. Finally, Nerlove's tests indicate that rates of return in various common stocks differ primarily "because of substantial disequilibrium in the capital market." This calls the theory advocated by most proponents of efficient capital markets into question.

Ahlers' work differs from that presented so far in his definition of variables and in his extensive testing of the model. Ahlers has done a creative job in estimating two of his independent variables (both of which are included in most valuation models). The first of these—growth—is estimated by combining an exponentially weighted average of past data with subjective estimates of future

---

[8] This assumption, like Gordon's, avoids the St. Petersberg paradox.

earnings made by security analysts. The weight placed on historical extrapolation versus that placed on the analyst's estimates is in part a function of the confidence the analyst has in his forecast. The combination of a mechanical extrapolation technique with analyst's estimates could (a) provide a better estimate of future growth, (b) provide a bench mark against which to evaluate security analysts, and (c) provide a feedback mechanism to help the analyst improve his performance over time. The second innovation in variable definition in Ahlers' model is the use of the accuracy of past earnings estimates, rather than the instability of earnings, to define risk and uncertainty. Most authors have defined risk in terms of earnings instability. Yet a company with a regular and predictable pattern of cyclical earnings is not risky *per se*. The formulation of risk in terms of the inability to predict is much more in keeping with the postulates of subjective risk assessment.

The second area in which Ahlers excels is the testing of his model. Ahlers uses his model as a filter to select under- and overvalued stocks. When the ratio of the theoretical price computed by Ahlers' valuation formula to the market price exceeds a specified number, the stock is bought; when this ratio is less than a predetermined lower limit, the stock is sold. The model was tested on a sample of 24 stocks chosen at random from the portfolio of a large Eastern bank. The return produced by the model in each of four quarters was compared with the return produced by the bank's analysts and with the Standard and Poor's 500 Stock Index. Ahlers' model outperformed the bank's analysts in each of the four quarters, it outperformed the Standard and Poor's 500 Stock Index in three of the four quarters, and it outperformed both on average for the year covered. Testing a model against a random or unmanaged portfolio is very strong evidence that the model contributes real information to the decision-making process.[9]

However, Ahlers' evidence would have been stronger had he used an unweighted average of the performance of the 24 stocks used in testing the model rather than the Standard and Poor's index. The superior performance of his model could have been because the Standard and Poor's index did not perform as well as the 24 stocks from which he made his selections rather than because of the quality of the model. His second test, demonstrating that he outperformed the bank's analysts, is significant evidence of the ability of his model to provide useful information to the portfolio manager.

Lerner and Carleton's work (10) differs from the work presented so far in its careful and detailed derivation of stock value from economic theory and in the willingness of Lerner and Carleton to derive a model which does not lend itself readily to empirical tests. Their model consists of two equations. The first relates the price of a firm's stock to stockholder expectations about variables similar to those used in the models presented earlier. The second relates management's investment plans to management's expectations about a set of similar variables. Stock price is determined by the interaction of these two equations with the equilibrium price being determined by the equalization of management

---

[9] In testing his model's performance against the Standard and Poor's index and against the banks' analysts, Ahlers should be concerned with measures of risk as well as with measures of return. His model may produce higher returns simply because he is purchasing more risk. The market relationship between risk and return is discussed in Section IID of this book.

and stockholder expectations. The strength of this model is its rigorous presentation of the types of interaction that should affect stock price and its emphasis on expectational data derived from the beliefs of management as well as the beliefs of stockholders.

The implementation problem arises because the complex nature of interdependencies contained in the model makes the empirical specification extremely difficult and because the expectational data it calls for are not directly observable. Although this model cannot as yet be used to establish the value for a security, the work is still of interest because it presents the security analyst with the type of influences he should be concerned with and points the direction that future stock-pricing models should take.

The Best of the Rest

Sections C1 and C2 discuss the valuation of pure security forms; bonds and common stock. Since there are a host of mixed security types, treatment of each in this volume would be an impossible task. It would be impossible because to treat each at a level of analysis consistent with the rest of this book would involve a work of several volumes. Furthermore it should be unnecessary to treat each in turn, for the analysis presented throughout this volume, together with a few examples of the treatment of other security forms, should allow the reader to evaluate intelligently security forms not explicitly covered in this volume. In line with this objective, we have selected three security forms for further analysis: convertible bonds, warrants, and stock splits and dividends.

Weil, Segall, and Green (13) are concerned with the difference (premium) between the price at which a convertible bond sells and the market value of the common stock into which it converts. Their analysis begins in the tradition of the present-value theory outlined above. Specifically, they assume that the premium should be equal to the present value of the difference in the cash flows accruing to a holder of a convertible bond versus the holder of the amount of common stock into which the bond converts. The authors develop a theoretically appropriate cash flow in great detail, drawing heavily on the literature of convertible bond valuation. The article is particularly interesting because it is one of the few which considers transfer costs (e.g., differences in brokerage commissions and the purchase of stocks versus bonds). Also it is one of the few articles which, having constructed a theory of valuation, finds the theory in its most complete form not susceptible to standard mathematical formulation and testing. The authors face the reformulation and simplification of theory to come up with mathematical forms which lend themselves to empirical verification.

Shelton's article on warrant valuation (14), like the previous article, attempts to relate the price of one security (warrant) to the price of another security (common stock) into which it can be converted. Shelton's article reviews most of the previous analytical literature on warrant pricing and then constructs a cross-sectional regression model. Perhaps the most significant part of this article lies in Shelton's attempt to use his model as a filter rule to select over- and undervalued securities. Shelton applies the model to a different time period from the one in which it was established. First, he notes that the model does a very good job of predicting warrant prices for this new period. This is encouraging for it suggests that the parameters of the model are stable over time. Then

Shelton uses the model as a filter rule. That is, he examines the percentage price change in overvalued warrants versus the percentage price change in warrants that are undervalued according to his model. The results are disappointing. Shelton notes that this arose because of the high sensitivity of warrant price changes to stock price changes. He then tests a rule to isolate the evaluation of his model from price changes in the stock. If a warrant is undervalued, buy the warrant and sell the stock short; if it is overvalued, buy the stock and sell the warrant short. The results are quite promising and indicate that the type of valuation model constructed by Shelton, where the price of one security is related to that of another, might have greater implications for an arbitrage strategy than it has for a pure buy or sell strategy. It would be interesting to apply the same type of filter test to the Weil, Segall, and Green (13) model to see how well it preforms.

Fama, Fisher, Jensen, and Roll (15) examine the effect of stock splits and dividends on common stock performance. This paper differs in methodology from those presented so far in that the Sharpe–Lintner general equilibrium theory is used as the basis of all tests. While the foundation of this theory is not built until Section IID, the reader at this time, knowing theoretical justification will follow, should accept the following theorem: the return on a stock should be linearly related to the return on the market with an expected deviation equal to zero. By examining the size of the residuals from this linear relationship, the reaction of stock prices to stock splits and dividends can be examined. Fama, Fisher, Jensen, and Roll performed this examination for a series of months both before and after the event took place. The conclusions of the authors that information (or at least public information) about stock splits and dividends cannot be used to increase trading profits runs contrary to much of the folklore of security analysis.

FILTER RULES

Up to this point we have been presenting models which can be used to value different types of securities. The emphasis of the articles has been on uncovering the determinants of security prices and testing the explanatory power of these determinants rather than on selecting attractive investments.[10] In this section of the introduction we shall be concerned primarily with examining the power of individual variables or sets of variables to select investments which offer a superior rate of return. The results of this section are important because they (a) demonstrate types of models that have been successful in selecting securities (b) present alternative methodologies for testing such models, and (c) provide evidence on the theory of random walks and efficient markets. The type of variables used to select under- or overvalued securities (filter rules) can be divided into two classes, fundamental and technical. We shall take each up in turn.

[10] Actually some of the articles already presented [e.g., Ahlers (11); Shelton (14); and Fama, Fisher, Jensen, and Roll (15)] have already to some extent tested their full-scale models as filter or selection devices.

Fundamental Filter Rules

All the papers in this section attempt to demonstrate that selecting stocks on the basis of one or more fundamental variables can lead to an investment performance superior to that which would be expected on the basis of chance alone. Most tests of fundamental filter rules use the methodology outlined in the previous section and the variables discussed in that section as important determinants of common stock prices.

Shelton (19) provides evidence on the efficiency of capital markets by examining the results of *The Value Line Investment Survey* contest held in 1965–66. There are really two tests of efficiency reported in this article. The first test compares the return on the portfolios selected by the 18,565 contestants to the average return on the 350 stocks from which they were allowed to choose their portfolio. The contestants outperformed the expected return by an amount greater than chance alone could account for. Although we know nothing about the selection methods used by the contestants, and indeed it is likely that the heterogeneous group of contestants used a broad spectrum of selection techniques, we have some evidence that a group of investors can select securities that outperform random selection.

The second test involves an examination of Value Line's ability to select under- and overvalued stocks. Value Line uses a valuation (regression) model similar to those discussed in the previous section to divide stocks into groups on the basis of expected performance.[11] Shelton concludes that this model can successfully rate stocks by future performance. This not only indicates that capital markets may not be totally efficient but also that modeling of the type already discussed can successfully capitalize on the inefficiencies that do exist.

The reader should be aware that Shelton's tests are not conclusive. It is possible that the Value Line contestants outperformed an average portfolio and that Value Line showed a high return because both groups picked portfolios which involved a high degree of risk. Although the evaluation of portfolios as risk–return combinations will not be discussed until Section IIE, we can state at this time that higher- risk portfolios should offer a greater return (in a perfect capital market) than low-risk portfolios. To make his tests more meaningful, Shelton should have either explicitly adjusted his results for risk, as Jensen and Bennington (17) did, or replicated the results of his experiment, as Breen (18) did.

Breen (18) investigates the performance of a fundamental selection rule defined in terms of a filter on both growth and price–earnings ratios.[12] The results indicate that the rate of return earned by applying his filter rule outperforms random portfolios of the same size. Furthermore Breen demonstrates that in a real sense his portfolios have less risk as well as a greater return than portfolios chosen at random from his population of stocks. His best filter rule produces an extraordinarily high average return that outperforms 75 percent or more of the random portfolios chosen in 13 out of the 14 years. The Breen

[11] For a discussion of the Value Line model, see Bernhard, Arnold, *The Evaluation of Common Stocks,* Simon and Schuster, New York, 1959.

[12] Several of the articles in the last section [e.g., Gordon (8) and Malkiel (9)] indicates that both earnings and growth should be major determinants of stock price.

article is even stronger proof than the Shelton article that markets are not perfectly efficient in the terms outlined by Fama (1).

The evidence presented in these articles suggests that the stock market is not perfectly efficient and that fundamental data can be employed in a way that allows investors to capitalize on the inefficiencies that exist.

Technical Filter Rules

The two papers in this section investigate whether selecting stocks on the basis of past price movements can lead to investment performance superior to that which one would expect on the basis of chance alone. Both papers test accepted trading strategies and find that these strategies do not produce superior results.

Fama and Blume (16) test a filter rule based on buying (selling short) securities when the price increases (decreases) by a specified percentage. The results indicate that when commission charges are included, this class of filter rules does not outperform a buy-and-hold strategy. This result is consistent with the random walk literature, which shows that changes in stock prices are not serially correlated.

The Jensen and Bennington article (17) provides a test of a technical filter rule and an excellent example of the correct methodology of testing filter rules. They take two filter rules based on buying and selling according to the change in stock price and simulate their performance. Their methodology is interesting for several reasons. First, they simulate the rule over samples of stocks and periods of time different from those on which it was developed and tested. This is extremely important for, if enough filter rules are tried, a rule can be found which will work on any body of data (including a series of random numbers). Anyone developing and testing filter rules should have a holdout sample on which to test the validity of the rules. Second, Jensen and Bennington explicitly introduce transaction costs into their analysis. Third, they explicitly introduce risk into the analysis in comparing the performance of the filter rules to buy-and-hold strategies. Two measures of risk are used—the standard deviation of return and Sharpe's B coefficient. These are both discussed in Section II. Furthermore Jensen computes a measure of performance which combines the risk and return characteristic of a portfolio into a single index. This measure is discussed further in Section IIE.

Both of these articles tested specific technical filter rules and found that they did not outperform a buy-and-hold strategy. While this disproves the validity of employing these two technical filter rules and is consistent with the theory of efficient markets, it should not be accepted as generalized proof that technical filter rules cannot work. In fact Owen's findings of persistent intermediate trends in stock prices suggests that a more complex filter rule based on technical analysis might well work. However, no one has as yet demonstrated a technical rule which outperforms a buy-and-hold strategy; the burden of proof is on the advocates of technical analysis.

CONCLUSION

So far we have been concerned with the analysis of individual securities. We discussed the theory of efficient markets which in its strongest form hypothesizes that stock prices adjust instantly to all information. Under this hypothesis technical analysis cannot produce returns which exceed an average return, and fundamental analysis, while capable of explaining stock prices, cannot be used to produce extraordinary returns.

After examining the prediction of earnings per share—one of the major inputs to security evaluation—we turned to a study of security evaluation models. These models, which differed in their theoretical derivations and in their variable definitions, are primarily concerned with finding the determinants of security prices or explaining security prices. Some of these models, like those of Telser, Modigliani and Miller, Malkiel, and Fama, Fisher, Jensen, and Roll, are concerned with the effect of one variable on security prices. All the other articles discussed in Section IC are concerned with constructing a full-scale valuation model. A model that explains a large percentage of security prices is useful because, at the very least, it gives the security analyst a picture of the factors which are important in explaining security prices at a point in time as well as the weight which the market places on each. The ability of a particular model to explain prices can be judged by the statistical significance of its regression coefficients, the theoretical justification for the signs and (in some cases) the magnitude of its regression coefficients, and the size of its coefficient of determination. The question remains as to whether even a model which explains security prices well can be an aid in selecting investments which offer an extraordinary return. All these models can be used to find stocks which appear undervalued (or overvalued) by determining when the theoretical price as found from the model under study is higher (lower) than the present market price of the securities. The assumption behind using the model in this way is that the actual price will adjust to the theoretical price before the theoretical price itself changes. This adjustment may not take place for two reasons:

1. Because the theoretical price (value) itself changes, due to changes in the variables determining theoretical prices or to changes in the way the market determines theoretical price (changes in the importance it places on the various variables making up value).
2. Because there are persistent or perhaps permanent differences between theoretical and actual price due to influences not contained in the model.

An example of the failure of a valuation model to spot truly under-and overvauled securities due to changes in the independent variables can be seen clearly in Shelton's article (19). His forecast of the theoretical price of a warrant depends on the market price of common stock. Apparently the market price of a common stock changes more rapidly than the true warrant price adjusts to its theoretical value; this accounts for the failure of a straightforward use of Shelton's model to produce good results.

An example of the instability of the market's preferences with respect to the determinants of common stock prices can be seen from the Gordon article (8). The influence of each variable in his model, as measured by its regression coefficient, changes from year to year.[13] These changes mean that even if the value of independent variables is stable over time, the theoretical value might change more rapidly than the price adjusts to the theoretical value.

[13] The fact that these changes are associated with macro market conditions has been demonstrated in Gruber, Martin J., *The Determinants of Common Stock Prices*, Center for Research, Pennsylvania State University, 1971.

Finally, persistent differences (usually called firm effects) between theoretical value as computed from a regression model and actual price have been noted by several authors. Ahlers' use of an "aberration factor" is an attempt to explicitly introduce these persistent differences into the valuation model.[14]

The question remains then as to whether some type of model can be used to find securities which are under- or overvalued at a point in time. The way to answer this question is to simulate security selection with the model and then to examine the risk and return of the securities it selects against selection devices utilizing no information (in general, random portfolios in the case of fundamental filter rules and buy-and-hold strategies in the case of technical filter rules). An excellent example of the procedure used in testing a filter rule is presented in the Jensen and Bennington article (17).

All of the work on evaluation models cited above can be used to develop filter rules. If a variable is important in explaining stock prices, it should be useful in differentiating between under-and overvalued securities. Not only can the valuation model itself be used as a basis of a filter rule [see Ahlers (11) and Shelton (14)] but filter rules can be developed based on the use of one or more of the variables which valuation models have shown are important [see Breen (18)]. The simulation of investment returns from the use of fundamental filter rules has resulted in such high returns and (where tested) low risk that they cast doubt on the stronger forms of the efficient market hypothesis. It appears that modeling based on fundamental factors can improve investment performance.[15]

The ability of technical analysis to increase returns above those of a "fair-game" is still open to question. The filter rules reported by Jensen and Bennington (17) and Fama and Blume (16) do not produce returns greater than a buy-and-hold strategy. Nevertheless Owen's proof (3) that intermediate-length trends exist in price movements would seem to offer hope that a more complex filter rule based on price movements alone might offer high returns.

Having presented a group of methods which should prove useful in understanding and predicting the performance of individual securities, let us turn to the problem of combining these securities into that portfolio which best meets investor goals.

2. PORTFOLIO ANALYSIS

Portfolio analysis is concerned with the best way to form combinations of securities as well as the method of evaluating alternative combinations of securities. In this section we shall present portfolio theory, discuss its implementation, and present the implication of portfolio theory for general market equilibrium and the evaluation of alternative portfolios.

---

[14] For a demonstration of the existence of firm effects as well as a detailed discussion of the statistical methodology of identifying firm effects, see Kuh, Edwin, *Capital Stock Growth: A Micro-Econometric Approach,* North-Holland, Amsterdam, 1963.

[15] However these returns may not be sufficient to cover the cost of analysis.

A. THEORETICAL STRUCTURE OF PORTFOLIO ANALYSIS

Modern portfolio analysis began with the work of Harry Markowitz (20). Markowitz made three major contributions. First, he argued that most portfolios could be dismissed from consideration because they were inefficient, in the sense of either having more risk than another portfolio of equal return or offering less return than another portfolio of equal risk. Second, Markowitz demonstrated precisely why the sum of the parts did not equal the whole, or why (and by how much) the risk of the portfolio might be less than the sum of the risks of each individual security. Third, Markowitz showed that efficient portfolios could be generated by using quadratic programming. These considerations will now be discussed in detail.

The Concept of the Efficient Frontier

To define the concept of efficiency explicitly, let us consider Figure 1. On the vertical axis we have some measure of risk, and on the horizontal axis we have some measure of return. The x's represent the return and risk we would obtain if we were to invest a fixed amount of money in various combinations of securities. The letters A, B, C, D, and E represent particular combinations of securities (portfolios).

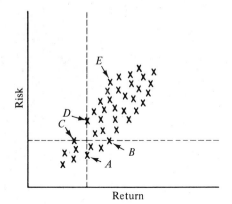

FIGURE 1

Consider the dashed line of constant risk connecting portfolio B with the vertical axis. Portfolio C is on the line. Because portfolio C lies on the line it has the same risk as portfolio B, and because it lies to the left of B it has lower return. Most people would argue that if two portfolios have the same risk the one with the higher return is preferred, and consequently portfolio C can be dismissed from further consideration. Now consider the vertical line of constant return extending upward from A. Portfolio D lies on this line. Consequently portfolio D has the same return as portfolio A and yet is riskier. Most investors faced with the choice of two portfolios yielding the same return would choose the portfolio with the lower risk; therefore we can eliminate D from consideration.[16] This discussion can be formalized into a *principle of efficiency*. A portfolio is *efficient* if

1. No other portfolio exists that has the same return and lower risk.
2. No other portfolio exists that has the same risk and a higher return.

Applying the principle of efficiency to Figure 1 allows us to construct the curve along which all efficient portfolios lie (Figure 2).

FIGURE 2

The Concept of Portfolio Risk and Return

Having presented the concept of efficiency in terms of risk and return, let us discuss how we can determine the risk and return of a particular portfolio. When we say that we expect security A to yield 10 percent, what do we mean? Usually what is meant is that security A might yield any number of different returns, but on average it will yield 10 percent. This can be stated more formally. Assume the possible returns of security A are 6 percent, 8 percent, 10 percent, 12 percent, and 14 percent, each equally likely. Then the average or expected return of security A is (6 percent + 8 percent + 10 percent + 12 percent + 14 percent)/5 = 10 percent. Let us assume that a second security B exists with an expected return of 12 percent. We might be interested in the expected return from investing a certain sum of money, say $50, in each security. In this case our expected return would be 10 percent of $50 for A plus 12 percent of $50 for B or $11. In percentage terms this is $11/$100 or 11 percent. We could have obtained the 11 percent directly by taking 50/100 of the expected return of A, plus 50/100 of the expected return of B. Let us review. If we invest $50 in A and $50 in B, the expected return in percentage terms is

1. $\dfrac{(50 \times 10\% + 50 \times 12\%)}{100}$ or equivalently

2. $\left(\dfrac{50}{100} \times 10\% + \dfrac{50}{100} \times 12\%\right)$

---

[16] Portfolios such as C or D can be eliminated because they have a higher risk than another portfolio of equal return and because they have a lower return than some portfolio of equal risk. Either of these conditions is sufficient for eliminating a portfolio.

The second formulation is more useful, and we shall now formalize it.

The expected return of a portfolio is equal to the expected return of each security in the portfolio times the percentage of the portfolio which that security constitutes. If we substitute symbols for the numbers used earlier, we have

$$\bar{r}_p = \sum_{i=1}^{N} x_i\, \bar{r}_i$$

where

$\bar{r}_p$ is the expected return of the portfolio,
x_i is the percentage of security i in the portfolio,
$\bar{r}_i$ is the expected return of security i, and
N is the number of securities in the portfolio,

In our two-security example, we have

$$\bar{r}_p = \sum_{i=1}^{N} x_i\, \bar{r}_i = x_A\, \bar{r}_A + x_B\, \bar{r}_B = \frac{50}{100}\,10\% + \frac{50}{100}\,12\% = 11\%$$

The risk of a portfolio is a little more difficult to determine because the concept is less intuitive and because the mathematical formulation is more difficult. In modern portfolio theory risk has become associated with variance or variability of return. Variability is seen as undesirable since the more variable the return, the more uncertain we are about the actual return.[17] The variance of the return of a security is defined as the average squared difference between possible and expected returns. In algebraic terms

$$\sigma_i^2 = \sum_{j=1}^{M} \left(r_i^j - \bar{r}_i \right)^2 \pi_i^j \tag{3}$$

where

r_i^j are each of the possible returns of security i (6 percent, 8 percent, 10 percent, 12 percent, 14 percent in the case of security A),
π_i^j is the probability of obtaining return r_i^j,
$\bar{r}_i$ is the expected return of security i, and
σ_i^2 is the variance of security i,
M is the number of possible returns for security i.

In the introduction we shall assume each return is equally likely. Therefore the probability of obtaining any particular return (r_i^j) is equal to one divided by the number of possible returns. If we let M equal the number of possible returns (five in the case of security A), we have the expression we shall use:

[17] It is often argued that no one would be concerned if he were to receive more than he expected, so the only variability the investor should be concerned with is variability below the expected return. This implies that semivariance might be a more appropriate measure of risk or that an investor should also measure skewness—what proportion of the returns are above or below the mean.

$$\sigma_i^2 = \sum_{j=1}^{M} \frac{(r_i^j - \bar{r}_i)^2}{M} \tag{3'}$$

For security A the variance is

$$\sigma_A^2 = \sum_{j=1}^{5} \frac{(r_A^j - \bar{r}_A)^2}{5} = \frac{(6 - 10)^2 + (8 - 10)^2 + (10 - 10)^2}{5}$$

$$+ \frac{(12 - 10)^2 + (14 - 10)^2}{5} = 8$$

We can obtain the variance of a portfolio in the same manner:

$$\sigma_p^2 = \sum_{j=1}^{M} (r_p^j - \bar{r}_p)^2 \, \pi_p^j \tag{4}$$

where

σ_p^2 is variance of the portfolio,
r_p^j are each of the possible returns of the portfolio,
$\bar{r}_p$ is the expected return of the portfolio, and
π_p^j is the probability of obtaining return r_p^j.

If each return is equally likely and if M is the number of possible returns, then Equation 4 can be rewritten as

$$\sigma_p^2 = \sum_{j=1}^{M} \frac{(r_p^j - \bar{r}_p)^2}{M} \tag{4'}$$

Let us expand Equation 4' for the two-security case.[18]

$$\sigma_p^2 = \sum_{j=1}^{M} \frac{(r_p^j - \bar{r}_p)^2}{M} = \sum_{j=1}^{M} \frac{[(x_A r_A^j + x_B r_B^j) - (x_A \bar{r}_A + x_B \bar{r}_B)]^2}{M}$$

Rearranging we have

$$\sigma_p^2 = \sum_{j=1}^{M} \frac{[(x_A r_A^j - x_A \bar{r}_A) + (x_B r_B^j - x_B \bar{r}_B)]^2}{M}$$

Squaring we have

$$\sigma_p^2 = \frac{\sum_{j=1}^{M} (x_A r_A^j - x_A \bar{r}_A)^2 + 2\sum_{j=1}^{M} (x_A r_A^j - x_A \bar{r}_A)(x_B r_B^j - x_B \bar{r}_B)}{M}$$

[18] In general the number of possible returns of a portfolio is not equal to the number of possible returns for the individual securities. We are taking some liberties here to make the derivation understandable. The reader can be assured that a more general derivation will lead to the same final expression.

$$+ \frac{\sum_{j=1}^{M} (x_B\, r_b^j - x_B \bar{r}_B)^2}{M}$$

Simplifying we have

$$\sigma_p^2 = x_A^2 \sum_{j=1}^{M} \frac{(r_A^j - \bar{r}_A)^2}{M} + 2\,x_A x_B \sum_{j=1}^{M} \frac{(r_A^j - \bar{r}_A)(r_b^j - \bar{r}_B)}{M} + x_B^2 \sum_{j=1}^{M} \frac{(r_b^j - \bar{r}_B)^2}{M}$$

Using the definition of variance we have

$$\sigma_p^2 = x_A^2 \sigma_A^2 + 2\,x_A x_B \sum_{j=1}^{N} \frac{(r_A^j - \bar{r}_A)(r_b^j - \bar{r}_B)}{M} + x_B^2 \sigma_B^2$$

The term $\sum_{j=1}^{N} \left[\frac{(r_A^j - \bar{r}_A)(r_b^j - \bar{r}_B)}{M} \right]$ is called the *covariance* between A and B and is written as σ_{AB}. Therefore we have in the two-security case:

$$\sigma_p^2 = x_A^2 \sigma_A^2 + x_B^2 \sigma_B^2 + 2\,x_A x_B\, \sigma_{AB}$$

Following this methodology we can derive an expression for the variance in the N-security case:

$$\sigma_p^2 = \sum_{i=1}^{N} x_i^2 \sigma_i^2 + 2 \sum_{i=1}^{N-1} \sum_{R=i+1}^{N} x_i x_R \sigma_{iR}$$

Now let us examine this mysterious term called the *covariance*, or the measure of common movement. The covariance between security A and B is

$$\sigma_p^2 = \sum_{j=1}^{N} \frac{(r_A^j - \bar{r}_A)(r_b^j - \bar{r}_B)}{N}$$

First note that this term will be negative if $(r_A^j - \bar{r}_A)$ has a different sign than $(r_b^j - \bar{r}_B)$. Consider the following example and assume each condition of the market is equally likely.[19]

r_A^j	r_B^j	Condition of stock market
6	16	Rotten
8	14	Poor
10	12	Average
12	10	Good
14	8	Whoopie

$\bar{r}_A = 10$ percent
$\bar{r}_B = 12$ percent

[19] For simplicity we have assumed that each stock market condition is equally likely to occur.

$$\sigma_{AB} = \frac{(6-10)(16-12) + (8-10)(14-12) + (10-10)(12-12)}{5}$$

$$\frac{+ (12-10)(10-12) + (14-10)(8-12)}{5} = -8$$

In this case, because the securities reacted in opposite fashion to changes in the market, they had a negative covariance. Now let us examine the variance of the portfolio with an equal dollar investment in securities A and B.

r_A^j	r_B^j	$r_p^j = 0.50\ r_A^j + 0.50\ r_B^j$
6	16	11
8	14	11
10	12	11
12	10	11
14	8	11

$\bar{r}_p = 11$

or using our formula

$$\sigma_p^2 = x_A^2 \sigma_A^2 + x_B^2 \sigma_B^2 + 2x_A x_B \alpha_{AB} = (0.50)^2 (8) + (0.50)^2 (8) + 2\ (0.50)$$

$$\times\ (0.50)(-8) = 0$$

This is a dramatic example of the risk of the portfolio being different from the sum of the risk of the individual securities. While each individual security was risky ($\sigma^2 = 8$), the combination of the two guarantees a certain (riskless) yield of 11 percent. Once again the reason for this is that they responded in opposite fashions to changes in the market.

We could, of course, have obtained the same results by directly computing the variance of returns on the portfolio. Since under all conditions a portfolio consisting of an equal dollar investment in both securities A and B yields a return of 11 percent, the variance of return is

$$\sigma_p^2 = \frac{(11-11) + (11-11) + (11-11) + (11-11) + (11-11)}{5} = 0$$

Now let us examine the case where the covariance between two securities is zero. This occurs when knowledge of the actual return from one security yields no information about the likely return of the second security.

Rainfall	r_A^j	r_B^j	War in Vietnam
Poor	8	16	Deescalation
Average	10	12	Average
Plentiful	12	8	Escalation

$\bar{r}_A = 10$ percent
$\bar{r}_B = 12$ percent

Consider two securities A and B. As shown in the above table, security A has three possible returns depending on the level of rainfall. Security B also has three possible returns depending on the condition of the war in Vietnam. If the level of rainfall is unrelated to the war in Vietnam, then there are nine possible portfolio returns. These returns are those associated with poor rainfall and each of the three possible conditions for the war in Vietnam, average rainfall and the three possible conditions in Vietnam, and finally, plentiful rainfall and the three possible levels of war in Vietnam.

If we assume that the three levels of rainfall are equally likely, and the three possible levels of war are equally likely, then the nine possible returns are equally likely, and we have

$$\sigma_{AB} = \frac{(8-10)(16-12) + (8-10)(12-12) + (8-10)(8-12)}{9}$$

$$+ \frac{(10-10)(16-12) + (10-10)(12-12) + (10-10)(8-12)}{9}$$

$$+ \frac{(12-10)(16-12) + (12-10)(12-12) + (12-10)(8-12)}{9}$$

$$= 0$$

Because the return of one security gave us no information about the return of the second security, there was no comovement or covariance. Let us examine the variance of the portfolio.

$$\sigma_p^2 = x_A^2 \sigma_A^2 + x_B^2 \sigma_B^2 + 2x_A x_B \sigma_{AB}$$

$$= (0.5)^2(8) + (0.5)^2(8) + 2(0.5)(0.5)(0)$$
$$= 0.25(8) + 0.25(8) \quad = 4$$

In this case the variance of the portfolio is exactly one-half the variance of each individual security. This example demonstrates a property of diversification which is not intuitively obvious. Diversification across investments which are completely unrelated leads to a reduction in risk.

Starting with the general formula for the variance of a portfolio, we can derive an expression which shows this reduction in risk.

$$\sigma_p^2 = \sum_{i=1}^{N} x_i^2 \sigma_i^2 + \sum_{i=1}^{N-1} \sum_{R=i+1}^{N} 2x_i x_R \sigma_{iR}$$

If the securities have zero covariance this reduces to

$$\sigma_p^2 = \sum_{i=1}^{N} x_i^2 \sigma_i^2$$

To clarify the meaning of this expression further, consider the case where all securities have the same variance, and we invest an equal percentage of our money in each security.

$$\sigma_p^2 = \sum_{i=1}^{N} \left(\frac{1}{N}\right)^2 \sigma^2$$

$$= N \left(\frac{1}{N}\right)^2 \sigma^2$$

$$= \frac{1}{N} \sigma^2$$

And as N approaches infinity the variance of the portfolio approaches 0. Although we had to make some simplifying assumptions to get this result, the principle is perfectly general. If we have a sufficient number of securities with zero covariance, we can make the portfolio risk arbitrarily small. Now let us examine a case where securities move together.

r_A^j	r_B^j	State of stock market
6	8	Rotten
8	10	Poor
10	12	Average
12	14	Good
14	16	Whoopie

$\bar{r}_A = 10$ percent
$\bar{r}_B = 12$ percent

$$\sigma_{AB}^2 = \frac{(6-10)(8-12) + (8-10)(10-12) + (10-10)(12-12)}{5}$$

$$+ \frac{(12-10)(14-12) + (14-10)(16-12)}{5} = 8$$

The variance of the portfolio is

$$\sigma_p^2 = (0.5)^2(8) + (0.5)^2(8) + 2(0.5)(0.5)(8) = 8$$

In this case the risk of the portfolio is identical to the risk of each individual security, and in fact a rational man would prefer security B to a portfolio of A and B since it has the same risk and a higher expected return (12 percent versus 11 percent). Note that anything less than perfect comovement would have made this risk of the portfolio lower. For example if $\sigma_{AB} = 6$ then $\sigma_p = 7$. Note also that the risk of the portfolio cannot be higher than the risk of security A or B. To convince yourself of this, examine the last table and note that we made each term in the formula for calculating the covariance as large as possible. This implies that if we have anything less than perfect comovement the risk of the portfolio is less than the average of the risk of the two securities. Hopefully we can now see why diversification is useful.

The previous discussion can be summarized graphically. Figure 3 plots two securities and portfolios of these securities in risk–return space. The securities are labeled A and B. Connecting these securities are lines which represent the risk–return characteristics of combinations of these securities with different assumptions about the degree of correlation. We can see by examining Figure 3 that, as the correlation moves from perfectly positively correlated to perfectly negatively correlated, the risk of a combination of these securities is reduced.

Mathematical Formulation of the Portfolio Problem

Recall our definition of portfolio risk and return.[20]

---

[20] Technically portfolio selection based on the mean return and the standard deviation of mean return is correct only if either one of two conditions hold. The first condition is if the mean and the standard deviation are the only two variables in the stockholder's utility function. This will be true only if the investor's utility function is quadratic.

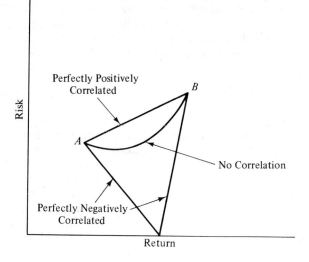

Perfectly Positively Correlated

Perfectly Negatively Correlated

No Correlation

Risk

Return

FIGURE 3

$$\sigma_p^2 = \sum_{i=1}^{N} x_i^2 \sigma_i^2 + \sum_{i=1}^{N-1} \sum_{R=i+1}^{N} 2x_i x_R \sigma_{iR}$$

$$\bar{r}_p = \sum_{i=1}^{N} x_i \bar{r}_i$$

If we combine these formulas with the principle of efficiency we can then state the portfolio problem mathematically as: minimize

$$\sigma_p^2 = \sum_{i=1}^{N} x_i^2 \sigma_i^2 + \sum_{i=1}^{N-1} \sum_{R=i+1}^{N} x_i x_R \sigma_{iR} \tag{5}$$

constrained by

$$r_p \text{ (a constant)} = \sum_{i=1}^{N} x_i \bar{r}_i \tag{6}$$

$$\sum_{i=1}^{N} x_i = 1 \tag{7}$$

This simply states that for any return (given by Equation 6) we minimize the risk (Equation 5). If we vary the constant in Equation 6 we then get the full

---

Although the quadratic utility function has been used widely and may be a useful approximation to investor's utility functions, as Pratt (27) has shown it has some undesirable properties.

The second condition for which return and standard deviation are appropriate portfolio selection criteria is when these parameters completely describe the distribution of expected returns. This will hold when the returns follow a normal distribution [see Tobin (26)].

efficient frontier. Equation 7 simply states that the sum of the fraction invested in all securities must add up to 1, or alternatively, that we must invest all of our money in the securities under consideration. As Markowitz has shown, this formulation of the problem lends itself to solution by quadratic programming. Equation 5 is a quadratic objective function, while Equations 6 and 7 are linear constraints.

COMPUTATIONAL EFFICIENCY AND REDUCTION IN DATA REQUIREMENTS

The Markowitz model requires the estimation of a large amount of input data. To use the model one must estimate the expected rate of return for each security, the expected variance of each security's rate of return, and the covariance between the returns of each pair of securities which can be formed. This last input needs more explicit explanation. If there are N securities we are considering, then we must look at the covariance between each security (N) and each of the other securities $(N-1)$. Since the covariance of security i with security j is the same as that of security j with security i there are $N(N-1)/2$ covariances.[21] In summary the input needed is

Variable name	Description	Number
σ_i^2	Variance of each security	N
$\bar{r}_i$	Mean return of each security	N
σ_{ir}	Covariance between all securities	$\dfrac{N(N-1)}{2}$
	Total	$\dfrac{N(N+3)}{2}$

If N were 100 securities, we would require 100 returns, 100 variances, and 4950 covariances.

The time and expense required to collect this data is extremely great. Furthermore, a serious organizational problem exists if analysts are to provide estimates of covariances. In most institutions analysts follow different securities. Given this structure, who provides estimates of covariances between the securities followed by different analysts? Finally, the computer time required to implement the model is large, since all the data must be manipulated to provide a solution.[22] Two suggestions have been made to reduce the data requirements and computation time. These suggestions are discussed by Sharpe (23) and Cohen and Pogue (24).[23]

Sharpe's suggestion is to assume that the only form of comovement between securities comes from a common response to a market index. In particular he assumes

---

[21] The problem can be stated simply as the number of combinations we can form from N objects taken two at a time.

[22] Technically the problem is the computational time necessary to invert the variance–covariance matrix.

[23] The single-index model discussed by Sharpe was first suggested (although not in as great detail) by Markowitz, Harry, *Portfolio Selection,* Wiley, New York, 1959.

$$R_i = A_i + B_i I + C_i$$
$$I = A_{N+1} + C_{N+1}$$

where

R_i is the return of security i,
A_i represents the unique return from security i. This is explained in more detail below,
C_i is a random variable with mean zero and variance Q_i,
I is an index such as the New York Stock Exchange Index, the Dow Jones Industrial Index, or even GNP,
A_{N+1} is an unbiased estimate of the level of the index, and
C_{N+1} is a random variable with mean zero and variance Q_{N+1},
B_i is a measure of responsiveness of the return from security i to a change in the index I.

What Sharpe has done with this formulation is to separate the return of a security into two parts, a part related to how well the market does $B_i I$ and a unique part A_i. Also he has separated the variance of a security into two parts, a unique part Q_i and a part that measures the variability in the securities return because of variability in the market index, which turns out to be $B_i^2 Q_{N+1}$. When he further specifies that the securities' unique variances (the Q_i) are unrelated to one another, Sharpe's model becomes one in which the sole comovement comes from the response to the market index. The data requirements of the Sharpe model are much less than those of the Markowitz model as shown below.

Variable name	Number
A_i	N
B_i	N
Q_i	N
A_{N+1}	1
Q_{N+1}	1
Total	$3N + 2$

Input requirements have been reduced from $N(N+3)/2$ in the Markowitz model to $3N+2$ in the Sharpe model. For 100 securities this reduction is from 5150 input variables to 302; for 500 securities this reduction is from 125,750 variables to 1502 variables. Furthermore, the Sharpe model has the important advantage of requiring analysts to provide information only for the securities they follow.

Although Sharpe's model provides a significant reduction in data requirements, the question arises as to whether this formulation is not an oversimplification. In requiring that the only form of comovement be a common response to a market index, some of the important relationships originally expressed in the covariances of the Markowitz formulation may well be lost.

Cohen and Pogue (24) present two intermediate models that are more complex and require more inputs than the Sharpe model but are less complex and require fewer inputs than the Markowitz model. These models are called the diagonal form of the multi-index model and the covariance form of the multi-index model.

The diagonal form of the multi-index model allows comovement between securities because of a common response to industry indexes. However, the industry indexes are related to one another only to the extent that these industries move with the market. This implies that securities within an industry will move together because of a common response to a market index and because of a common response to an industry index, while firms from different industries move together only because of a common response to a market index.

The covariance form of the multi-index model captures the full pattern of interaction between industry indexes rather than assuming they are only related through common movement with the market index. In this form of the model, the comovement of firms in the same industry depends on the response of the firms to their industry index. The comovement of securities from different industries depends on each firm's response to its industry average and the extent to which the industries of which they are members move together. The data requirements of the Cohen and Pogue models compared with both the Markowitz and Sharpe models are shown below.

Markowitz	$\dfrac{N(N+3)}{2}$
Multi-index covariance form	$\dfrac{3N + J(J+3)}{2}$
Multi-index diagonal form	$3N + 3J + 2$
Single-index model	$3N + 2$

N = number of securities
J = number of industries

This table ranks techniques in inverse order of computational time.[24] The saving in computational time occurs primarily because of the simplicity of the covariance matrix in the faster models rather than because there are fewer variables. In solving the portfolio problem the covariance matrix must be inverted. If this matrix has nonzero elements only along the main diagonal, such inversion is extremely simple. Since this is a characteristic of the Sharpe single-index model and the multi-index diagonal form of the Cohen and Pogue model, both models should have relatively low computational time. The covariance form of Cohen and Pogue's multi-index models should require slightly longer to solve, since in part it involves inversion of a full matrix (the past representing the covariance between indexes).[25] Finally, the computational time required for the Markowitz model is much greater than that of the other three model forms.

Which of these model forms is most useful to managers is the subject of the Cohen and Pogue article. On the basis of their tests, Cohen and Pogue conclude that the Sharpe model seems to perform about as well as any. Although these tests are extremely suggestive, the results could change with a different way of generating inputs or with a different sample of security types. For example, Cohen and Pogue suggest that one of the multi-index models might have performed better if the sample of investments had included nonequity securities. Even with the samples used, the results might have been different if a better

[24] A model might have fewer input variables and still involve greater computational time if it had a more complex structure.

[25] By partitioning techniques, the diagonal part of the matrix, which is extremely easy to invert, can be inverted separately from the covariance part. Therefore, the time required over and above the Sharpe model is just the inversion time of the covariance part.

method (than industrial classification) of selecting which firms should be related to a particular index had been used.[26]

Up to this point we have discussed two factors which should be considered in choosing between alternative models of portfolio analysis: the amount of data and the computational time required.[27]

One aspect of this problem that deserves further mention is the accuracy of data inputs and particularly the interaction between the accuracy and quantity of data inputs. Cohen and Pogue demonstrated that more efficient portfolios can be created as the number of securities examined is increased. But if expenditures are not also to be increased, some trade-off must take place between the number of securities examined and either the number of input variables estimated or the quality (cost) of each estimate.[28] For example, if we move from the Sharpe model to the Markowitz model and have a limited amount of resources to devote to locating efficient portfolios, we must either consider fewer securities or make less costly estimates of each piece of input data needed. Unfortunately the relative performance of different models operating upon different numbers of securities with different types (qualities) of input data has not been explored.

C. REDUCING THE EFFICIENT FRONTIER

Once having generated the efficient frontier by any of the methods discussed above, we are left with the problem of selecting a particular portfolio from that frontier. One way to do this is by an explicit specification of our personal risk–return trade-offs. This would yield a graph such as shown in Figure 4. Lines 1, 2, 3, and 4 indicate various levels of constant utility. That is, we are indifferent to a choice between any of the portfolios lying along the same curve.

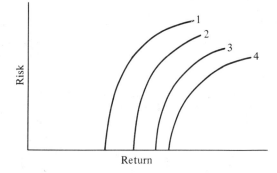

Return   **FIGURE 4**

Further, we could state that we preferred any point on a high-numbered

---

[26] For a discussion of techniques to determine industrial groupings and for some results of the use of such groupings, see Elton and Gruber (4).

[27] Another criterion which should be considered is the reasonableness of the model structure from a theoretical point of view. For example Fama (29) has shown that if the Sharpe (28) general equilibrium model holds, then the Sharpe single-index model cannot hold.

[28] All firms operate under constraints in terms of money and/or manpower in arriving at portfolio decisions.

curve to a point on a lower-numbered curve (e.g., a point on curve 4 may be preferred to a point on curve 3), for that would give us more return for the same risk or less risk for the same return. We would select the portfolio which lies at the point of tangency between the set of utility functions and the efficient frontier, since this would represent the highest level of utility which the set of possible portfolios allowed us to achieve.

Both the Pratt (27) and Tobin (26) articles deal with the specification of utility functions and the identification of desirable portfolios. It is often possible to do some preliminary reduction of the efficient frontier without fully specifying an investor's utility functions. Consider the following two portfolios. Portfolio 1 yields any of five possible returns—(4.5percent, 5percent, 5.5percent, 6percent or 6.5percent)—each equally likely. Portfolio 2 yields any of the following returns— 7percent, 10percent, or 15percent— also each equally likely. Both of these portfolios could lie on the efficient frontier, since portfolio 2 has both a higher return and a higher variance than portfolio 1. Yet any rational investor would prefer portfolio 2 to portfolio 1 for it will always provide a higher return. This is the easiest and most universally accepted criterion for eliminating part of the efficient frontier.

Now assume portfolio 1 yields the same return but portfolio 2 yields 5 percent, 6 percent, 7 percent, 8 percent, or 9 percent, each equally likely. Once again the principle of efficiency would not eliminate either portfolio, since portfolio 2 has a higher return and risk than portfolio 1. We can construct the following cumulative probability distribution.

Probability of return equaling or exceeding (percent)	Portfolio 1	Portfolio 2
4.5	1.00	1.00
5.0	0.80	1.00
5.5	0.60	0.80
6.0	0.40	0.80
6.5	0.20	0.60
7.0	0.00	0.60

Once again most rational investors would prefer portfolio 2 since the odds of achieving any particular return are always higher with portfolio 2 than portfolio 1.

Baumol (25) has still a third method of eliminating part of the efficient frontier. He argues that, if the lowest return of portfolio 2 is higher than the lowest return of portfolio 1 and portfolio 2 has a higher average return, then we should prefer portfolio 2. Since Baumol recognizes return distributions as continuous with no unique lower limit, he defines a concept analogous to a lower limit. He assumes the investor might ignore all returns K standard deviations below the mean either because he believes they really do not exist or because he is willing to expose himself to that much risk. Each individual must decide for himself the appropriate value for K. We should note that even if the return of portfolio 2, K deviations from the mean, is greater than the return of portfolio 1, it does not follow that the probability of getting any particular return is greater with 2 than with 1. For example, assume the return of portfolio 2 is normally distributed with a mean of 10.5 and a standard deviation of 3, while the return of portfolio 1 is normally distributed with a mean 8 and a standard deviation of 2. Further assume K is 2. Then, the lower limit of portfolio 2 [10.5 − 2(3) = 4.5] is greater than the lower limit of portfolio 1 [8 − 2 (2)=4]. However, the odds of getting a return of 2 or more are higher with portfolio 1 than with portfolio 2. To summarize, there are three ways of reducing the efficient frontier:

1. Eliminate those portfolios whose best return is worse than the worst of another portfolio.
2. Eliminate those portfolios which have a lower probability than a second portfolio of getting all possible returns.
3. Eliminate those portfolios with a lower mean return and a lower worst return (i.e., one K standard deviation from the mean) than a second portfolio.

After this reduction of the efficient frontier, the investor must decide on his personal risk–return trade-off and select the optimum portfolio. There is one other method of reducing the number of portfolios of risky securities that must be considered, but this will be discussed in the next section.

IMPLICATIONS OF PORTFOLIO THEORY FOR GENERAL MARKET EQUILIBRIUM

The first half of this introduction was concerned in large part with the determination of asset values. Section II of the introduction is concerned with the presentation of portfolio theory. But the two concepts are not separate and independent. As we shall demonstrate in this section, portfolio theory has major implications for the valuation of individual securities.

Assume we have two assets, one risky and one with a certain return. Let asset A, the risky asset, have a mean return of E_{RA} (expected-E, return-R asset-A) and variance of σ^2_{RA}. Let asset P (pure return) have a mean return of E_{RP} and a standard deviation of zero. Thus if we invest some fraction α in asset P and a fraction $(1-\alpha)$ in security A, our expected return of the combination E_{RC} will be

$$E_{RC} = \alpha E_{RP} + (1 - \alpha)E_{RA}$$

The variance of the combination σ_{RC} will be

$$\sigma^2_{RC} = \alpha^2 \sigma^2_{RP} + (1 - \alpha)^2 \sigma^2_{RA} + 2\sigma(1 - \alpha) Cov(RA, RP) \qquad \textbf{(7′)}$$

Since the return on RP is a constant, knowing this return can yield no information about the return on RA. Therefore Cov (RA, RP) equals zero. Since σ^2_{RP} equals zero, Equation (7′) is reduced to

$$\sigma^2_{RC} = (1 - \alpha)^2\sigma^2_{RA}$$

or

$$\sigma_{RC} = (1 - \alpha)\sigma_{RA}$$

Solving the expression for α, we have

$$\alpha = 1 - \frac{\sigma_{RC}}{\sigma_{RA}}$$

Substituting this into the expression

$$E_{RC} = \left(\frac{1 - \sigma_{RC}}{\sigma_{RA}}\right) E_{RP} + \left[1 - \left(1 - \frac{\sigma_{RC}}{\sigma_{RA'}}\right)\right] E_{RA}$$

we have by rearranging

$$E_{RC} = E_{RP} - \frac{E_{RP}}{\sigma_{RA}}(\sigma_{RC}) + \frac{E_{RA}}{\sigma_{RA}}\sigma_{RC}$$

$$E_{RC} = E_{RP} + \left(\frac{E_{RA} - E_{RP}}{\sigma_{RA}}\right)\sigma_{RC} \tag{8}$$

In this expression E_{RP}, E_{RA}, and σ_{RA} are constants since they do not depend on the amount of money invested in either the risky or risk-free portfolio. Thus Equation 8 is of the form $Y = a + bx$ or a straight line. Any combination of a risk-free asset and a risky asset (or portfolio) will lie along a straight line. Several combinations of risky and risk-free assets are shown in Figure 5.

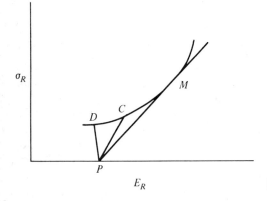

FIGURE 5

Note that all combinations containing portfolio C dominate those containing portfolio D since for any given risk they have a greater return. We can see that combinations containing portfolio M not only dominate those containing C but dominate all other individual portfolios or combinations of individual portfolios with the riskless asset. This is true regardless of the investor's risk preference. The fact that one portfolio exists (in this case M) that, in combination with a riskless asset, dominates all other portfolios is known as the *separation theorem,* this theorem was first proved by Tobin (26) and is discussed by Sharpe (28). This dominant portfolio will be at the point where a ray passing through the riskless asset is tangent to the efficient frontier. Before leaving the discussion, note the following. To obtain any portfolio on the line connecting P and M, one would invest part of the money in the risky portfolio M and part of the money in riskless asset P. These are called lending portfolios. To obtain any combination on the line above and to the right of M one must borrow and invest more than 100 percent in M. These are called the borrowing portfolios. Many researchers, while accepting the lending portfolio as reasonable, do not accept the borrowing portfolio, since the borrowing portfolios require the investor to have the ability to borrow at the risk-free rate.

Using the concept of a riskless asset also allows us to derive the equilibrium price of a risky asset. Consider Figure 6. Asset i is a risky asset that is part of portfolio M.

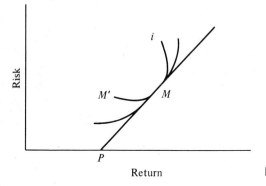

Risk

Return   **FIGURE 6**

P

It can be shown that combinations of asset i and portfolio M, which contains i, lie on the curve iMM'. The required rate of return for a risky asset can be derived by [29]

1. Determining the equation of the curve iMM' and finding its slope at G.
2. Determining the equation of the line PM and finding its slope at G.
3. Equating the equal slopes (at G) of iMM' and PM.

This equation is

$$
\begin{array}{ccc}
\text{Return of risky} & \text{Return of riskless} & \text{Covariance of risky asset} \quad \text{Excess return} \\
\text{asset} \quad = & \text{asset} \quad + & \dfrac{\text{with market portfolio}}{\text{Variance of the portfolio}} \times \text{on market portfolio}
\end{array}
$$

In symbols this is

$$ R_i = R_F + \frac{\mathrm{Cov}\,(R_i R_M)}{\sigma^2_{RM}}(R_M - R_F) \tag{9} $$

This equation states that a risky asset in equilibrium must yield the riskless rate of interest plus a premium for the amount of risk it adds to the portfolio.

Recalling our earlier discussion about ability to diversify, it should not be too surprising that the covariance is the major element for measuring the amount of risk an asset adds to the market portfolio.[30] Note also that securities with negative covariance with the market will yield less than the riskless rate. Again we see the power of diversification. A risky asset, because it reduces the risk of the overall portfolio, can yield a lower return than a riskless asset.

[29] The assumptions underlying this derivation are contained in Sharpe (28) and Fama (29).
[30] The variance sneaks in the back door by being part of the variance of the market portfolio.

EVALUATION OF INVESTMENT PERFORMANCE

The concepts developed in the previous section can be used to evaluate the performance of particular investments. Recall earlier that we derived the relationship between a riskless security and a risky portfolio. This relationship is a straight line and is

$$E_{RC} = E_{RP} + \frac{E_{RA} - E_{RP}}{\sigma_{RA}} \sigma_{RC} \tag{10}$$

Also we showed that if we had the choice of combinations of any risky portfolio shown in Figure 7 and the riskless asset, we would select portfolio C, since

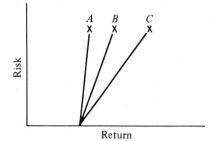

FIGURE 7

combinations of that portfolio and the riskless asset would yield a maximum return for any level of risk. Using the same reasoning, if portfolio C were unattainable, we would have preferred portfolio B, and if portfolio B were not available, we would have chosen portfolio A. A rule that will always lead to the selection of the preferred portfolio is to select that line connecting the riskless asset with a risky portfolio which has the lowest slope. This is the method of evaluating the performance of a portfolio suggested by Sharpe (30).

Recall that if we have an equation of the form $y = a + bx$, then b is the slope of the line. In this equation x is the variable on the horizontal axis and y is the variable on the vertical axis. However, Equation 10 is in the form $x = c + dy$. To change this equation to the appropriate form, we subtract c from both sides and divide through by d yielding $Y = -c/d + 1/dx$. In order to determine the desired portfolio we are minimizing the slope of $1/d$. Minimizing $1/d$ is equivalent to maximizing d or maximizing $(E_{RA}-E_{RP})/\sigma_{RA}$. This is Sharpe's portfolio evaluation rule. In words it states maximize the return over and above the return on a riskless asset $(E_{RA}-E_{RP})$ per unit of risk (σ_{RA}).

Earlier we discussed Sharpe's single-index model. It was

$$R_i = A_i + B_iI + C_i$$

Then we argued that Sharpe had split the variance of the return into two parts, one that depended on the movement of the overall market $(B_i^2Q_{N+1})$ and a unique component (Q_i). Further we argued that it was movement with the overall market that could not be diversified away. If this is true, then a measure of a fund's response to the overall market (B_i) might be a useful measure of risk. Treynor has taken advantage of this and has replaced Sharpe's overall variability of portfolio (σ_{RA}) with a measure of nondiversifiable risk or responsiveness to the overall market (B_i). Treynor's measure is $(E_{RA} - E_{RP})/B_i$. In words it states maximize the return over and above the return on a riskless asset ($E_{RA} - E_{RP}$) per unit of nondiversifiable risk (B_i).

A final measure of portfolio performance is suggested by Jensen.[31] Recall that, if the Sharpe–Lintner–Mossin general equilibrium framework holds, Equation 9 gives the return on a risky asset. Equation 9 is

$$R_i = R_F + \frac{\text{Cov}(R_i R_M)}{\sigma_{RM}^2}(R_M - R_F)$$

If we plot R_i versus $\text{Cov}(R_i R_M)/\sigma^2_{RM}$(which is Treynor's B_i) we have Figure 8. The point M represents the market portfolio. The line $R_F M$ represents all combinations of the market portfolio and the risk-free rate or put another way the naive strategy of buying the market and combining this with the riskless asset to obtain the desired level of risk. Assume we have a portfolio with return R_i and systematic risk B_i [which is $\text{Cov}(R_i R_M)/\sigma^2_{RM}$]. This portfolio is by the point (R_i, B_i) in Figure 8. The height from the line $R_F M$ to the point

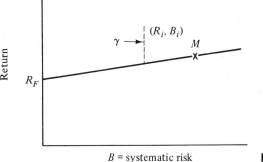

B = systematic risk   **FIGURE 8**

given (R_i, B_i) represents how much more return the manager of portfolio i earned than he would have earned if he had followed the naive strategy of buying the market and combining it with riskless asset until he obtained risk B_i. This height γ is Jensen's measure of portfolio performance.[32]

Since Jensen and Treynor's measures deal with the same variables, it might be constructive to compare them. The line $R_F M$, shown in Figure 9, is the same as in Figure 8. Treynor would call portfolios on the line $R_F H$ (and in particular A and B) equally good, and he would call all portfolios on the line

[31] See Jensen and Bennington (17).

[32] The alternative explanation of γ is to tie it directly to the market equilibrium theory and state that γ is the return that the portfolio manager has earned above (or below, for negative) that which equilibrium theory states he should have earned, given the level of risk.

$R_F L$ equally bad. Jensen, however, used the vertical distance between $R_F M$ and the portfolio as his measure of performance. In this case portfolio B would be labeled superior to portfolio A. The difference between the two arises because Jensen believes that the extra return a portfolio earns (returns above naive strategy) is an appropriate measure of performance independent of the level of risk, while Treynor believes this extra return should be expressed per unit of risk.

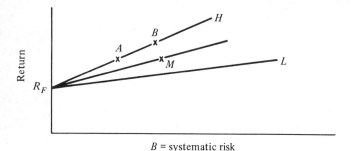

B = systematic risk

FIGURE 9

Treynor and Mazuy are concerned with measuring a different aspect of mutual fund performance. Assume the following:

1. The rate of return of mutual funds has a constant relationship with the rate of return of the market over time (in technical terms, the same B_i).
2. Mutual funds invest a constant percentage of their assets in common stock.

Given these two assumptions, if we plotted the actual rate of return of a mutual fund against the actual return of the market and the equilibrium theory discussed earlier held, we would expect the scatter of points to be a straight line. If, however, the mutual fund could anticipate market movements correctly, then the percentage of assets held in common stock might vary with anticipated levels of the market.

In this case mutual fund returns would be above the average relationship with the market whenever the market returns were very high or very low. The first case would occur because the fund would have a higher-than-normal percentage of its assets in high-return common stock, and the second case would occur because the fund shifted out of low-return common stock. Therefore, if a mutual fund anticipated market movements correctly and we plotted the rate of return of the mutual fund against the rate of the market, we would expect a curved shape. The curved shape becomes a test of the ability of mutual funds to correctly anticipate the market; this is the subject of the Treynor and Mazuy article.

CONCLUSION

This section has been concerned with modern portfolio analysis. This is a new field and as such is still in a state of flux. It has changed rapidly in the past few years, and we expect it to continue to change and improve in the future. Because of this, some comment on the future direction of research is in order.

Much of the current research is concerned with applying the Markowitz model to different periods of time. There are really two aspects to this problem. The first concerns the appropriate time horizon over which to estimate the inputs to the model. For example, the short-term outlook for a security might be extremely dim, while the long-term outlook is very good. In contrast a second security might have a very good short-term outlook and a very dim future. In short, the return of a security should really depend on the length of time rather than being considered as a unique expected value. Cutting the future into very small periods and solving the portfolio problem in each period is not the answer either, since transaction costs would be prohibitive. In fact, inclusion of transaction costs and the impact of the current portfolio has been the subject of a number of studies.[33]

The second aspect concerns the individual's choice of an optimum portfolio from the efficient frontier. How is this choice affected by the fact that the individual will be making a succession of portfolio decisions over time, and during this time his age, wealth, etc, will change? Chen, Jen, and Zionts (22) and Samuelson (21) discuss this problem.

In addition, several practical problems which have arisen in implementing the Markowitz model are likely to receive further attention. Paramount among these is the integration of the model into a firm's organizational structure so as to obtain maximum benefit both from the model and from the firm's security analysts and portfolio managers. Difficulties arise because the model requires inputs (variances and covariances) and produces outputs which are in different terms from those in which management usually think. Furthermore the model in its simplest form produces answers in only two dimensions (risk and return), while the portfolio manager is accustomed to thinking of results in a multidimensional framework (e.g., short-term capital gains, long-term capital gains, dividend income, etc.). Now that the theory has been firmly established, the process of management education along with the more detailed and realistic implementation of the theory can begin.

[33] For a discussion of how to handle this problem, see the following three sources: Cohen, Kalman and Edwin J. Elton, "Inter-Temporal Portfolio Analysis Based on Simulation of Joint Returns," *Management Science* Vol. 14 (September, 1967), pp. 5–18; Smith, Keith, "Alternative Procedures for Revising Investment Portfolios," *Journal of Financial and Quantitative Analysis* Vol. 3 (December, 1968), 371–404; and Pogue, Jerry, "An Adaptive Model for Investment Management," unpublished doctoral dissertation, Carnegic Mellon University, 1968.

part one

SECURITY ANALYSIS

A. Efficiency of Capital Markets and the Theory of Random Walks

Fama presents a nontechnical view of what he later calls a "fair-game" efficient market model. The basis of this model is that, in an efficient market, competition will on average cause new information to be incorporated correctly into price with neither a lead nor a lag. The amount of under-or overcompensation to new information, as well as the amount of time before new information is incorporated into the stock price, are both assumed to be random variables with mean zero. This implies that successive price changes are independent, that knowledge about past price changes will not help predict future price changes, and that technical analysis should not work.

It also has implications for fundamental analysis. Fundamental analysis can still work to the extent that the analyst can identify nonnegligible (random) deviations from intrinsic value and price or can predict better than others the occurrence and effect of important future events.

Fama suggests several tests for the efficiency of the stock market and outlines a procedure for testing the efficiency of any technical or fundamental trading rule.

1

Random Walks in Stock Market Prices

Eugene F. Fama*

This article is reprinted with permission from Financial Analyst Journal, *Vol. 21, No. 5 (September–October, 1965), pp. 55–59.*

For many years economists, statisticians, and teachers of finance have been interested in developing and testing models of stock price behavior. One important model that has evolved from this research is the theory of random walks. This theory casts serious doubt on many other methods for describing and predicting stock price behavior—methods that have considerable popularity outside the academic world. For example, we shall see later that if the random walk theory is an accurate description of reality, then the various "technical" or "chartist" procedures for predicting stock prices are completely without value.

In general the theory of random walks raises challenging questions for anyone who has more than a passing interest in understanding the behavior of stock prices. Unfortunately, however, most discussions of the theory have appeared in technical academic journals and in a form which the non-mathematician would usually find incomprehensible. This article describes, briefly and simply, the theory of random walks and some of the important issues it raises concerning the work of market analysts. To preserve brevity some aspects of the

*The author is indebted to his colleagues William Alberts, David Green, Merton Miller, and Harry Roberts for their helpful comments and criticisms.

This article has been reprinted as paper No. 16 in the current series of Selected Papers of the Graduate School of Business, The University of Chicago.

theory and its implications are omitted. More complete (and also more technical) discussions of the theory of random walks are available elsewhere; hopefully the introduction provided here will encourage the reader to examine one of the more rigorous and lengthy works listed at the end of this article.

COMMON TECHNIQUES FOR PREDICTING STOCK MARKET PRICES

In order to put the theory of random walks into perspective we first discuss, in brief and general terms, the two approaches to predicting stock prices that are commonly espoused by market professionals. These are (1) "chartist" or "technical" theories and (2) the theory of fundamental or intrinsic value analysis.

The basic assumption of all the chartist or technical theories is that history tends to repeat itself, i.e., past patterns of price behavior in individual securities will tend to recur in the future. Thus the way to predict stock prices (and, of course, increase one's potential gains) is to develop a familiarity with past patterns of price behavior in order to recognize situations of likely recurrence.

Essentially, then, chartist techniques attempt to use knowledge of the past behavior of a price series to predict the probable future behavior of the series. A statistician would characterize such techniques as assuming that successive price changes in individual securities are dependent. That is, the various chartist theories assume that the *sequence* of price changes prior to any given day is important in predicting the price change for that day.[1]

The techniques of the chartist have always been surrounded by a certain degree of mysticism, however, and as a result most market professionals have found them suspect. Thus it is probably safe to say that the pure chartist is relatively rare among stock market analysts. Rather the typical analyst adheres to a technique known as fundamental analysis or the intrinsic value method. The assumption of the fundamental analysis approach is that at any point in time an individual security has an intrinsic value (or in the terms of the economist, an equilibrium price) which depends on the earning potential of the security. The earning potential of the security depends in turn on such fundamental factors as quality of management, outlook for the industry and the economy, etc.

Through a careful study of these fundamental factors the analyst should, in principle, be able to determine whether the actual price of a security is above or below its intrinsic value. If actual prices tend to move toward intrinsic values, then attempting to determine the intrinsic value of a security is equivalent to making a prediction of its future price; and this is the essence of the predicitve procedure implicit in fundamental analysis.

THE THEORY OF RANDOM WALKS

Chartist theories and the theory of fundamental analysis are really the province of the market professional and to a large extent teachers of finance. Historically, however, there has been a large body of academic people, primarily economists

---

[1] Probably the best known example of the chartist approach to predicting stock prices is the Dow Theory.

and statisticians, who adhere to a radically different approach to market analysis—the theory of random walks in stock market prices. The remainder of this article will be devoted to a discussion of this theory and its major implications.

Random walk theorists usually start from the premise that the major security exchanges are good examples of "efficient" markets. An "efficient" market is defined as a market where there are large numbers of rational, profit-maximizers actively competing, with each trying to predict future market values of individual securities, and where important current information is almost freely available to all participants.

In an efficient market, competition among the many intelligent participants leads to a situation where, at any point in time, actual prices of individual securities already reflect the effects of information based both on events that have already occurred and on events which, as of now, the market expects to take place in the future. In other words, in an efficient market at any point in time the actual price of a security will be a good estimate of its intrinsic value.

Now in an uncertain world the intrinsic value of a security can never be determined exactly. Thus there is always room for disagreement among market participants concerning just what the intrinsic value of an individual security is, and such disagreement will give rise to discrepancies between actual prices and intrinsic values. In an efficient market, however, the actions of the many competing participants should cause the actual price of a security to wander randomly about its intrinsic value. If the discrepancies between actual prices and intrinsic values are systematic rather than random in nature, then knowledge of this should help intelligent market participants to better predict the path by which actual prices will move towards intrinsic values. When the many intelligent traders attempt to take advantage of this knowledge, however, they will tend to neutralize such systematic behavior in price series. Although uncertainty concerning intrinsic values will remain, actual prices of securities will wander randomly about their intrinsic values.

Of course intrinsic values can themselves change across time as a result of new information. The new information may involve such things as the success of a current research and development project, a change in management, a tariff imposed on the industry's product by a foreign country, an increase in industrial production or any other *actual or anticipated* change in a factor which is likely to affect the company's prospects.

In an efficient market, *on the average,* competition will cause the full effects of new information on intrinsic values to be reflected "instantaneously" in actual prices. In fact, however, because there is vagueness or uncertainty surrounding new information, "instantaneous adjustment" really has two implications. First, actual prices will initially overadjust to changes in intrinsic values as often as they will underadjust. Second, the lag in the complete adjustment of actual prices to successive new intrinsic values will itself be an independent, random variable with the adjustment of actual prices sometimes preceding the occurrence of the event which is the basis of the change in intrinsic values (i.e., when the event is anticipated by the market before it actually occurs) and sometimes following.

This means that the "instantaneous adjustment" property of an efficient market implies that successive price changes in individual securities will be independent. A market where successive price changes in individual securities are independent is, by definition, a random walk market. Most simply the theory of random walks implies that a series of stock price changes has no memory— the past history of the series cannot be used to predict the future in any meaningful way. The future path of the price level of a security is no more predictable than the path of a series of accumulated random numbers.

It is unlikely that the random walk hypothesis provides an exact description of the behavior of stock market prices. For practical purposes, however, the model may be acceptable even though it does not fit the facts exactly. Thus although successive price changes may not be strictly independent, the actual amount of dependence may be so small as to be unimportant.

What should be classified as unimportant depends, of course, on the question at hand. For the stock market trader or investor the criterion is obvious: The independence assumption of the random walk model is valid as long as knowledge of the past behavior of the series of price changes cannot be used to increase expected gains. More specifically, if successive price changes for a given security are independent, there is no problem in timing purchases and sales of that security. A simple policy of buying and holding the security will be as good as any more complicated mechanical procedure for timing purchases and sales. This implies that, for investment purposes, the independence assumption of the random walk model is an adequate description of reality as long as the actual degree of dependence in series of price changes is not sufficient to make the expected profits of any more "sophisticated" mechanical trading rule or chartist technique greater than the expected profits under a naive buy-and-hold policy.

EMPIRICAL EVIDENCE ON INDEPENDENCE

Over the years a number of empirical tests of the random walk theory have been performed; indeed, so many that it is not possible to discuss them adequately here. Therefore in describing the empirical evidence we limit ourselves to a brief discussion of the different approaches employed and the general conclusions that have evolved.

The main concern of empirical research on the random walk model has been to test the hypothesis that successive price changes are independent. Two different approaches have been followed. First there is the approach that relies primarily on common statistical tools such as serial correlation coefficients and analyses of runs of consecutive price changes of the same sign. If the statistical tests tend to support the assumption of independence, one then *infers* that there are probably no mechanical trading rules or chartist techniques, based solely on patterns in the past history of price changes, which would make the expected profits of the investor greater than they would be with a simple buy-and-hold policy. The second approach to testing independence proceeds by testing directly different mechanical trading rules to see whether or not they provide profits greater than buy-and-hold.

Research to date has tended to concentrate on the first or statistical approach to testing independence; the results have been consistent and impressive. I know of no study in which standard statistical tools have produced evidence of *important* dependence in series of successive price changes. In general, these studies (and there are many of them) have tended to uphold the theory of random walks. This is true, for example, of the serial correlation tests of Cootner [4],[2] Fama [5], Kendall [9], and Moore [10]. In all of these studies, the sample serial correlation coefficients computed for successive price changes were extremely close to zero, which is evidence against important dependence in the changes. Similarly, Fama's [5] analysis of runs of successive price changes of the same sign and the spectral analysis techniques of Granger and Morgenstern [8] and Godfrey, Granger, and Morgenstern [7] also support the independence assumption of the random walk model.

However, we should emphasize that, although the statistical techniques mentioned above have been the common tools used in testing independence, the chartist or technical theorist probably would not consider them adequate. For example, he would not consider either serial correlations or runs analyses as adequate tests of whether the past history of series of price changes can be used to increase the investor's expected profits. The simple linear relationships that underlie the serial correlation model are much too unsophisticated to pick up the complicated "patterns" that the chartist sees in stock prices. Similarly, the runs tests are much too rigid in their manner of determining the duration of upward and downward movements in prices. In particular: in runs-testing, a run is considered as terminated whenever there is a change in sign in the sequence of successive price changes, regardless of the size of the price change that causes the change in sign. The chartist would like to have a more sophisticated method for identifying movements—a method which does not always predict the termination of the movement simply because the price level has temporarily changed direction.

These criticisms of common statistical tools have not gone unheeded, however. For example, Alexander's filter technique [1, 2] is an attempt to apply more sophisticated criteria to the identification of moves. Although the filter technique does not correspond exactly to any well-known chartist theory, it is closely related to such things as the Dow Theory. Thus, the profitability of the filter technique can be used to make inferences concerning the potential profitability of other mechanical trading rules.

A filter of, say, 5 percent is defined as follows: if the daily closing price of a particular security moves up at least 5 percent, buy and hold the security until its price moves down at least 5 percent from a subsequent high, at which time simultaneously sell and go short. The short position is maintained until the daily closing price rises at least 5 percent above a subsequent low, at which time one should simultaneously cover and buy. Moves less than 5 percent in either direction are ignored.

It is, of course, unnecessary to limit the size of the filter to 5 percent. In fact, Professor Alexander has reported tests of the filter technique for filters ranging in size from 1 percent to 50 percent. The tests cover different time periods from 1897 to 1959 and involve daily closing prices for two indices, the Dow-Jones industrials from 1897 to 1929 and Standard and Poor's industrials from 1929 to 1959. In Alexander's latest work [2], it turns out that even when the higher broker's commissions incurred under the filter rule are ignored, the

---

[2] See References at article's end.

filter technique cannot consistently beat the simple policy of buying and holding the indices for the different periods tested. Elsewhere I have tested the filter technique on individual securities. Again the simple buy-and-hold method consistently beats the profits produced by different size filters. It seems, then. that at least for the purposes of the individual trader or investor, tests of the filter technique also tend to support the random walk model.

IMPLICATIONS OF THE RANDOM WALK THEORY FOR CHARTIST AND INTRINSIC VALUE ANALYSIS

As stated earlier, chartist theories implicitly assume that there is dependence in series of successive price changes. That is, the history of the series can be used to make meaningful predictions concerning the future. On the other hand, the theory of random walks says that successive price changes are independent, i.e., the past cannot be used to predict the future. Thus the two theories are diametrically opposed, and if, as the empirical evidence seems to suggest, the random walk theory is valid, then chartist theories are akin to astrology and of no real value to the investor.

In an uncertain world, however, no amount of empirical testing is sufficient to establish the validity of a hypothesis beyond any shadow of doubt. The chartist or technical theorist always has the option of declaring that the evidence in support of the random walk theory is not sufficient to validate the theory. On the other hand, the chartist must admit that the evidence in favor of the random walk model is both consistent and voluminous, whereas there is precious little published discussion of rigorous empirical tests of the various technical theories. If the chartist rejects the evidence in favor of the random walk model, his position is weak if his own theories have not been subjected to equally rigorous tests. This, I believe, is the challenge that the random walk theory makes to the technician.

There is nothing in the above discussion, however, which suggests that superior fundamental or intrinsic value analysis is useless in a random walk–efficient market. In fact the analyst will do better than the investor who follows a simple buy-and-hold policy as long as he can more quickly identify situations where there are non-negligible discrepancies between actual prices and intrinsic values than other analysts and investors, and if he is better able to predict the occurrence of important events and evaluate their effects on intrinsic values.

If there are many analysts who are pretty good at this sort of thing, however, and if they have considerable resources at their disposal, they help narrow discrepancies between actual prices and intrinsic values and cause actual prices, on the average, to adjust "instantaneously" to changes in intrinsic values. That is, the existence of many sophisticated analysts helps make the market more efficient which in turn implies a market which conforms more closely to the random walk model. Although the returns to these sophisticated analysts may be quite high, they establish a market in which fundamental analysis is a fairly useless procedure both for the average analyst and the average investor. That is, in a random walk–efficient market, on the average, a security chosen by a mediocre analyst will produce a return no better than that obtained from a randomly selected security of the same general riskiness.

There probably aren't many analysts (in fact, I know of none) who would willingly concede that they are no better than the "average" analyst. If all analysts think they are better than average, however, this only means that their estimate of the average is biased downward. Fortunately, it is not necessary to judge an analyst solely by his claims. The discussion above provides a natural benchmark with which we can evaluate his performance.

In a random walk–efficient market at any point in time the market price of a security will already reflect the judgments of many analysts concerning the relevance of currently available information to the prospects of that security. Now an individual analyst may feel that he has better insights than those that are already implicit in the market price. For example, he may feel that a discrepancy between market price and intrinsic value exists for some security, or he may think the intrinsic value of the security is itself about to change because of some impending piece of new information which is not yet generally available.

These "insights" of the analyst are of no real value, however, unless they are eventually borne out in the market, that is, unless the actual market price eventually moves in the predicted direction. In other words, if the analyst can make meaningful judgments concerning the purchase and sale of individual securities, his choices should consistently outperform randomly selected securities of the same general riskiness. It must be stressed, however, that the analyst must *consistently* produce results better than random selection, since, by the nature of uncertainty, for any given time period he has about a 50 percent chance of doing better than random selection even if his powers of analysis are completely non-existent. Moreover, not only must the analyst do consistently better than random selection, but he must beat random selection by an amount which is at least sufficient to cover the cost of the resources (including his own time) which are expended in the process of carrying out his more complicated selection procedures.

What we propose, then, is that the analyst subject his performance to a rigorous comparison with a random selection procedure. One simple practical way of comparing the results produced by an analyst with a random selection procedure is the following: Every time the analyst recommends a security for purchase (or sale), another security of the same general riskiness is chosen randomly. A future date is then chosen at which time the results produced by the two securities will be compared. Even if the analyst is no better than the random selection procedure, in any given comparison there is still a 50 percent chance that the security he has chosen will outperform the randomly selected security. After the game has been played for a while, however, and the results of many different comparisons are accumulated, then it will become clear whether the analyst is worth his salt or not.

In many circumstances, however, the primary concern is with the performance of a portfolio rather than with the performance of individual securities in the portfolio. In this situation one would want to compare the performance of the portfolio in question with that of a portfolio of randomly selected securities. A useful benchmark for randomly selected portfolios has been provided by Fisher and Lorie [6]. They computed rates of return for investments in common stocks on the New York Stock Exchange for various time periods from 1926 to 1960. The basic assumption in all of their computations is that at the beginning of each period studied the investor puts an equal amount of money in each common stock listed at that time on the Exchange. This amounts to random sampling where the sampling is, of course, exhaustive. Different rates of return are then computed for different possible tax brackets of the investor, first under the assumption that all dividends are reinvested in the month paid, and then under the assumption that dividends are not reinvested.

A possible procedure for the analyst is to compare returns for given time periods earned by portfolios he has managed with the returns earned for the same time periods by the Fisher–Lorie "randomly selected" portfolios. It is important to note, however, that this will be a valid test procedure only if the portfolios managed by the analyst had about the same degree of riskiness as the Fisher–Lorie "market" portfolios. If this is not the case, the Fisher–Lorie results will not provide a proper benchmark. In order to make a proper comparison between the results produced by the analyst and a random selection policy, it will be necessary to define and study the behavior of portfolios of randomly selected securities, where these portfolios are selected in such a way that they have about the same degree of riskiness as those managed by the analyst.

If the claims of analysts concerning the advantages of fundamental analysis have any basis in fact, the tests suggested above would seem to be easy to pass. In fact, however, the only "analysts" that have so far undergone these tests are open end mutual funds. In their appeals to the public, mutual funds usually make two basic claims: (1) because it pools the resources of many individuals, a fund can diversify much more effectively than the average, small investor; and (2) because of its management's closeness to the market, the fund is better able to detect "good buys" in individual securities. In most cases the first claim is probably true. The second, however, implies that mutual funds provide a higher return than would be earned by a portfolio of randomly selected securities. In a separate paper [5] I reported the results of a study which suggest that if the initial loading charges of mutual funds are ignored, on the average the funds do about as well as a randomly selected portfolio. If one takes into account the higher initial loading charges of the funds, however, on the average the random investment policy outperforms the funds. In addition, these results would seem to be consistent with those of the now famous Wharton study of mutual funds [11].

These adverse results with respect to mutual funds have tended to lead random walk theorists to feel that other financial institutions, and most professional investment advisers as well, probably do no better than random selection. Institutions and analysts can only dispel such doubts by submitting their performance to a rigorous comparison with a random selection procedure.

CONCLUSION

In sum the theory of random walks in stock market prices presents important challenges to both the chartist and the proponent of fundamental analysis. For the chartist, the challenge is straightforward. If the random walk model is a valid description of reality, the work of the chartist, like that of the astrologer, is of no real value in stock market analysis. The empirical evidence to date provides strong support for the random walk model. In this light the only way the chartist can vindicate his position is to *show* that he can *consistently* use his techniques to make better than chance predictions of stock prices. It is not enough for him to talk mystically about patterns that he sees in the data. He must show that he can consistently use these patterns to make meaningful predictions of future prices.

The challenge of the theory of random walks to the proponent of fundamental analysis, however, is more involved. If the random walk theory is valid and if security exchanges are "efficient" markets, then stock prices at any point in time will represent good estimates of intrinsic or fundamental values. Thus, additional fundamental analysis is of value only when the analyst has new information which was not fully considered in forming current market prices, or has new insights concerning the effects of generally available information which are not already implicit in current prices. If the analyst has neither better insights nor new information, he may as well forget about fundamental analysis and choose securities by some random selection procedure.

In essence, the challenge of the random walk theory to the proponent of fundamental analysis is to show that his more complicated procedures are actually more profitable than a simple random selection policy. As in the case of the chartist, the challenge is an empirical one. The analyst cannot merely protest that he thinks the securities he selects do better than randomly selected securities; he must demonstrate that this is in fact the case.

REFERENCES

1. ALEXANDER, SIDNEY S. "Price Movements in Speculative Markets: Trends or Random Walks," *Industrial Management Review,* II (May, 1961), 7–26.
2. ALEXANDER, SIDNEY S. "Price Movements in Speculative Markets: Trends or Random Walks, Number 2," *Industrial Management Review,* V (Spring, 1964), 25–46.
3. COOTNER, PAUL H. (editor). *The Random Character of Stock Market Prices.* Cambridge: M.I.T. Press, 1964. An excellent compilation of research on the theory of random walks completed prior to mid-1963.
4. COOTNER, PAUL H. "Stock Prices: Random vs. Systematic Changes," *Industrial Management Review,* III (Spring, 1962), 24–45.
5. FAMA, EUGENE F. "The Behavior of Stock Market Prices," *Journal of Business,* XXXVIII (January, 1965), 34–105.
6. FISHER, L. and LORIE, J. H. "Rates of Return on Investments in Common Stocks," *Journal of Business,* (January, 1964), 1–21.
7. GODFREY, MICHAEL D., GRANGER, CLIVE W. J., and MORGENSTERN, OSKAR. "The Random Walk Hypothesis of Stock Market Behavior," *Kyklos,* XVII (January, 1964), 1–30.
8. GRANGER, CLIVE W. J. and MORGENSTERN, O. "Spectral Analysis of New York Stock Market Prices," *Kyklos,* XVI (January, 1963), 1–27.
9. KENDALL, M. G. "The Analysis of Economic Time Series," *Journal of the Royal Statistical Society* (Series A), XCVI (1953), 11–25.
10. MOORE, ARNOLD. "A Statistical Analysis of Common Stock Prices," unpublished Ph. D. dissertation, Graduate School of Business, University of Chicago (1962).
11. "A Study of Mutual Funds," prepared for the Securities and Exchange Com-

mission by the Wharton School of Finance and Commerce. Report of the Committee on Interstate and Foreign Commerce. Washington: U.S. Government Printing Office, 1962.

Smidt carefully reviews what has been called alternatively the random walk hypothesis or the efficient market model. He devotes the majority of his time to discussing the positive contribution of the random walk theory—the establishment of a null hypothesis against which theories of stock selection should be tested. Then he reviews possible sources of nonrandom price behavior, and after reviewing some evidence of persistent price patterns, he suggests the direction which further tests should take.

2

A New Look at the Random Walk Hypothesis

Seymour Smidt

This article is reprinted with permission from the Journal of Financial and Quantitative Analysis, *Vol. III, No. 3(September, 1968), pp. 235–262.*

I. INTRODUCTION

The basic idea behind the random walk hypothesis is that in a free competitive market the price currently quoted for a particular good or service should reflect all of the information available to participants in the market that influence its present price. To the extent that future conditions of the demand or supply are currently known, their effect on the current price should be properly taken into account.

A statistical process which has the property that the expected future value of a random variable is independent of past values of the variables is said to be a Martingale process. What is generally referred to as the random walk hypothesis requires that in a perfectly competitive market, price changes should be outcomes of a Martingale process. In the last decade considerable effort has been devoted to testing hypotheses of this nature. The data most commonly used have been obtained from security markets and from commodity futures markets.

There are many different probability distributions of price changes that would be consistent with the random walk hypothesis. Similarly, there are many alternatives to randomness that would violate the hypothesis. Statistically, testing the random walk hypothesis involves testing a composite null hypothesis against a composite alternative hypothesis. The fact that a particular test fails to contradict the null hypothesis does not guarantee that another test, possibly using the same data, might not lead to a contradiction. Most tests that were used in the early stages of investigation of this hypothesis have been interpreted as being consistent with the null hypothesis. However, the first tests used were very general. That is, they were not designed to test against specific alternative hypotheses. There is always the danger that the null hypothesis will be accepted, even though it is false, because the test being used is insufficiently powerful with respect to a correct but unknown alternative hypothesis. One would have more confidence in the validity of the random walk hypothesis if it had been tested more extensively using procedures that are known to be statistically powerful against the specific alternatives that are *a priori* most likely.

Price changes that are consistent with the random walk hypothesis could occur under at least three distinct sets of circumstances. One possibility is that information that becomes available to market participants is itself random in its effect on market price (cf. Samuelson, 1965, p. 42). This is possible but it seems most unlikely. A second possibility is that all the market participants are thoroughly informed about all new information as soon as it is publicly available, and about any statistical dependencies in the information generating process. Under these conditions, for example, if an event that had a bullish influence occurred, and if it were known that future events also having a bullish influence are more likely to occur given that this event has occurred, then the price would respond both to the event that had occurred and to the increased probability of future events tending in the same direction. In this case price changes would tend to be random even though the effects of news are not random. This set of circumstances is only slightly less unlikely than the first for most markets in which empirical tests have actually been conducted. For example, in most markets, there are important groups of participants who are not as fully informed as others, or who learn about relevant new information only after a significant time lag compared to some well-informed participants. In this third set of circumstances it might still be true that the price changes would follow a random walk very closely. This requires that the well-informed market participants anticipate how lags in the information available to less well-informed participants will affect the latter's trading.

However, well-informed traders have an incentive to eliminate price dependencies only if there is sufficient non-randomness so that they can earn a competitive return by using their superior knowledge. This modified random walk hypothesis requires that the profits that can be achieved from eliminating strong systematic dependencies in price changes be sufficient to attract just enough people into this activity. Thus this set of circumstances is the one which advocates of the random walk hypothesis seem mainly to have had in mind.[1]

---

[1] For a clear statement of this point of view see Fama (1965). Although the text emphasizes lack of information, and lags in responding to information as the source of dependencies in price changes, the argument is more general. Any systematic tendencies in price changes that create opportunities for superior profits should be eliminated by traders who become aware of these systematic tendencies.

Two significant implications of this third version of the random walk hypothesis have been given insufficient attention in the literature to date. According to this version of the hypothesis, *one should expect to find some systematic dependencies in price changes*. These dependencies may result from dependencies in the underlying information generating process, the cost of transactions, the cost of acquiring and processing information and, in general, all of the frictions and lags that tend to be ignored in abstract discussions of perfectly competitive markets. Persons accepting this third version of the random walk hypothesis should be wary of interpreting a test that uncovered no dependencies as strong evidence supporting the random walk hypothesis. Rather such test results can often be interpreted more properly as indicating that the test was insufficiently powerful against relevant alternative hypcthesis.

The second implication of this version of the hypothesis is that the profits that can be generated by taking advantage of the systematic dependencies in the price changes should be at most those necessary to attract and hold resources in the activity of eliminating them. It is a violation of this requirement that would contradict the random walk hypothesis.

In practice, even when systematic dependencies in price changes have been detected, determining whether their magnitude and frequency is sufficient to constitute a violation of the random walk hypothesis is extremely difficult. The problem would be relatively simple if each type of systematic dependency could be eliminated only by a firm that must necessarily specialize in providing the service of reducing the magnitude of that type of dependency. Even then the problem is not easy, since it would involve a careful estimate of all of the costs involved, and of the return on capital required to justify the risks involved. Often, however, the relevant firms are not specialized. A firm may act in such a way that it tends to reduce the magnitude of several kinds of systematic price dependencies. The firm as a whole may earn a return that exceeds the competitive rate even though the excess return cannot be attributed to any one type of activity. To complicate matters even further, firms that act in such a way as to reduce the magnitude of some types of price dependencies may at the same time contribute to the magnitude of other types of price discrepancies.

The true significance of the random walk hypothesis is that it suggests a fruitful and sensitive though indirect means of studying aspects of economic behavior that are extraordinarily difficult to study directly. For example it is difficult to estimate from direct observations of the behavior of various categories of investors whether lags in investor response to new information have a significant impact on security prices. The random walk hypothesis provides a means of looking for the effects of such lags, because it tells us what to expect if the lags exert no effect.

Most empirical tests of the random walk hypothesis have dealt solely with sequences of price changes. However, the random walk hypothesis is more general. Since the basic idea is that the current price should reflect all relevant available information, the expected future price change should be statistically independent of such things as the volume of activity in the stock, the size of the last transaction, and the percentage change in the firm's earnings during the last quarter, provided only that this information is publicly available. If the random walk hypothesis is significant because it provides a powerful tool to help us understand how organized markets really work, then characteristics like volume and size of transactions, ought to be incorporated into the analysis more frequently than they have been in the past, since they are produced by the same market process that produces price changes.

In summary, this section has suggested that the empirical investigations of the random walk hypothesis would be most fruitful if they were conducted in the spirit of attempting to determine the size and extent of systematic tendencies that may exist in price series. Even if the largest part of a sequence of price changes may be described as following a Martingale process, it is the remaining systematic components that are the most interesting. It was also suggested that a search for systematic tendencies is likely to be more fruitful if it is guided by specific hypotheses about the characteristics of the systematic tendencies that are believed to be present. The rest of the article will consider the kinds of behavior that seem most likely to produce some residual systematic tendencies in sequences of price change. Three main sources of systematic tendencies will be considered. These result from the demand for liquidity, lags in response to new information, and inappropriate responses to new information. The empirical evidence currently available will also be evaluated. In some instances, suggestions for further research will be made.

II. THE SUPPLY SCHEDULE OF LIQUIDITY

In conducting economic affairs there is often a considerable advantage in being able to quickly exchange one asset for another. In a monetary society one of the two assets in the exchange is nearly always money. The facilities and institutions that make quick exchange possible can be thought of as producing a service. The production of this service is costly, and buyers are frequently willing to pay to have the service provided to them. Amazingly, there is no generally accepted term in economics that refers precisely to this service. In this paper, the term liquidity is used to refer to this service. [2]

If liquidity is thought of as a service, a quantitative measure of it is needed so that the quantity of liquidity demanded and its supply price can be estimated. Since liquidity is ordinarily supplied when property is exchanged for cash, it seems appropriate to measure the amount of liquidity supplied in terms of the number of units of property exchanged.

---

[2] Other writers have used other terms to refer to what in this paper is called liquidity service. Demsetz (1968) states that "On the NYSE two elements comprise almost all of transaction cost—brokerage fees and ask-bid spreads. ... The ask-bid spread is the markup that is paid for predictable immediacy of exchange in organized markets; in other markets, it is the inventory markup of retailer or wholesaler" (pp. 35–36). "Immediacy of exchange" is a good synonym for liquidity service. The cost of obtaining "immediacy of exchange" is, in our view, not the bid-ask spread, but half that amount (for the smallest unit traded). The inventory markup of most retailers and wholesalers includes payments for other services in addition to liquidity.

Holbrook Working uses the term "execution cost" to refer to the cost, in the form of price concessions, that traders must incur when they use market orders to insure prompt execution. We prefer the term costs of liquidity, because it is more general. Execution costs are the form in which the costs of liquidity are incurred in some, but not all markets.

In the absence of an actual transaction, the state of the market is represented by quoted bid and asked prices. Assuming that these quoted prices represent real commitments to buy or sell at least the smallest unit traded, it is a reasonable first approximation to define the market price as the average of the quoted bid and asked prices. If a transaction takes place because a seller is anxious to conclude his transaction immediately, the price paid for liquidity can then be defined as the market price less the price at which the transaction takes place. In this case a positive quality of liquidity is supplied, and the price of liquidity is positive. If a transaction takes place because a buyer is anxious to conclude his transaction immediately (that is, because he is anxious to reduce his liquidity by exchanging cash for some other asset), then the price paid to become illiquid can be defined as the transaction price less the market price.

If illiquidity is thought of as negative liquidity, a supply schedule of liquidity can be defined for which the amounts supplied can be either positive or negative; the price of liquidity, in this general sense, is the market price less the actual transaction price. Negative quantities of liquidity are supplied at negative prices.

A justification for treating the average of the bid and asked prices as the market price, and the difference between the market price and the transaction price as a payment for liquidity is that the initiator of the transaction can avoid buying liquidity if he so desires.[3] To do so he need only place his order as a limit order rather than as a market order. If he does so and is lucky, he may receive a payment for liquidity. If he is unlucky, his order may be executed only after a long delay, or never.

Having defined liquidity as a serivce, consider the means by which the demand and supply for liquidity is expressed in the market.

One indication of the demand for liquidity in a market is the percentage of orders to buy or sell "at the market." If there is a low level of demand for liquidity (or for illiquidity) a small fraction of the sell (or buy) orders received will be market orders. Most of the orders received in such markets will be limit orders. A market with a high ratio of limit orders should tend to exhibit a narrow spread between the bid and asked prices.

By contrast, if the demand for liquidity is high, most orders arriving in the market will be orders to buy or sell "at the market." If liquidity were supplied only through buyers and sellers willing to place limit orders, the spread between

---

[3] This discussion assumes the market price is the same before and after the transaction· However, it may happen that as a result of the transaction, or simultaneously with the transaction, there is a change in the market price. In this case, it will be convenient to define the price of liquidity in terms of the market price that prevails after the transaction, rather than before.

Liquidity, as defined above, is a noun, referring to a particular service. However, the term liquidity is often used as an adjective to describe an attribute of a particular type of property. A convenient index of liquidity for an asset is the ratio of the price that could be obtained by selling the asset to its market price. (Another way of describing this index is that it is one minus the ratio of supply price of liquidity for the asset over the market price of the asset.) A perfectly liquid asset, one that can be sold at its market price, would have an index of liquidity of one. A perfectly illiquid asset is one that has a sale price of zero. Some assets may have a negative index of liquidity. One must pay removal costs to dispose of them

bid and asked prices would tend to be large. Whether the demand for liquidity were high or low, if liquidity were supplied only by those willing to place limit orders there would be a systematic tendency for the price at which actual transactions take place to fluctuate between the bid and asked prices of the unfilled limit orders.

Depending on the gap between the bid and asked prices, the rate at which transactions took place, and other factors, the systematic tendency for transaction prices to fluctuate between the bid and asked prices might create opportunities for traders to make money by specializing in supplying liquidity.

Limit orders appear to be used as a means of supplying liquidity mostly by traders who view supplying liquidity as only a supplementary source of income. Traders who are mainly interested in supplying liquidity are characterized by their willingness to be either buyers or sellers of the asset in question provided they can make the transaction at a price sufficiently below (or above) what they consider to be the market price. Such traders might utilize limit orders, if they were not located at the point of sale. Alternatively they might wait at the point of sale and attempt to offer more favorable terms than the existing limit orders when a market order arrived for execution.

The mechanism by which liquidity is supplied by traders who specialize in supplying it depends in part on the amounts of liquidity demanded. In most organized markets there is some unit quantity, such as a 100–share lot or a 5,000-bushel contract. All regular trades take place in terms of integral multiples of this unit. Most transactions are for the unit quantity, or a small multiple of this basic unit. In so far as the quantity for which an individual decision making unit wants prompt execution is the unit quantity, or a small multiple of that unit, one can say that the discrete amount of liquidity demanded is small. The price effects of demands for small units of liquidity, the mechanism by which these price effects are produced, and the role of professional traders in supplying these demands for small units of liquidity are relatively well understood. The systematic departures from randomness produced by such small demands for liquidity have been documented for both stock exchanges and commodity futures markets. This evidence will be summarized first.

Some decision making units desire prompt execution of orders whose total amounts are many times as large as the unit of trading. The demands for large blocks of liquidity are also capable of producing systematic patterns of price movements. However, the possibility that such movements may exist has been recognized only recently. The evidence for such movements is still quite fragmentary. The price effects of the demand for such large quantities of liquidity will be discussed separately.

III. THE DEMAND FOR SMALL QUANTITIES OF LIQUIDITY

The demand for small quantities of liquidity produces a systematic tendency for transactions in which the price change is in one direction to be followed by transactions in which the price change is in the opposite direction. This characteristic of price changes from one transaction to the next has been well documented for both commodity futures markets and stock exchanges. The evidence for commodity futures is due to H. Working (1954, p. 124); for the New York

Stock Exchange, the evidence is due to Niederhoffer and Osborne (1966). Working's data are based on 143 series consisting of 100 consecutive price changes in wheat futures. In more than half of the price series, the proportion of price changes that were reversals exceeded .75. In all but two percent of the price series, the proportion of reversals exceeded 6.5. The Niederhoffer and Osborne results are based on a sample of over 10,000 transactions. Ignoring consecutive transactions in which there was no change in price, they found, for example, that the conditional probability of a price increase, given that the previous change was a decrease, was .76; by contrast the marginal probability of an increase, given only that the previous transaction was not at the same price, was .4984.

Broadly speaking the mechanism that produces these reversal tendencies is well known. The tendencies result from the fact that as orders for immediate execution arrive at that market, they tend to be executed at either the bid or asked price. Presumably there is a tendency for buy and sell orders to arrive in a random order, though this has not been documented directly, and the actual pattern may be much more complex. Demsetz (1968) also presents evidence that the bid-asked spread tends to decline as the volume of transactions increase. Working (1967, p. 22) notes that it tends to increase, if rapid price level movements take place.

With respect to the random walk hypothesis, the relevant question is not whether systematic patterns exist, but whether they provide unexploited opportunities to make above normal profits. To the author's knowledge, no direct evidence on this question is available for any organized market; nor do we know of any study that has attempted to obtain such evidence. Indirect evidence is available based on a knowlege of the institutional barriers to entry that might prohibit traders from taking advantage of opportunities for unusual profits, if they existed. Based on this indirect evidence one can be fairly confident that no such unexploited profit opportunities exist on the active commodity futures markets. However, it is not possible to make a confident judgment about either the relatively inactive futures markets, or the United States stock exchanges.

IV. THE DEMAND FOR LARGE QUANTITIES OF LIQUIDITY

In both the commodity futures and common stock markets, some participants have holdings that are many times larger than the minimum transaction size. Liquidity demands from such participants should also produce patterns of systematic changes in transaction prices. The systematic patterns produced by the acquisition or liquidation of a large position may be different from those produced when small positions are acquired or liquidated. However, the failure to detect systematic price patterns that could be attributed to demands for large quantities of liquidity would raise a question as to the sensitivity of the tests used for the random walk hypotheses.

A better understanding of the mechanisms involved in supplying liquidity in large quantities to anxious buyers and sellers under various institutional arrangements is particularly important at present. Both the increasing concentration of stock in institutional hands, and the emphasis on short-run performance have led to rapid increases in the number of large blocks traded. The possible effects of these trends on the market institutions are not well understood.

Evidence that systematic patterns of price movements are produced by attempts to acquire or liquidate a large position has only recently become available. In every case, the evidence that some systematic (non-random) patterns of price movements existed was recognized before it was realized that the pattern could be most easily interpreted as a price effect of attempts to rapidly acquire or liquidate a large position.

For a number of reasons, it is convenient to begin by discussing the evidence that pertains to commodity futures markets. Historically, the systematic price effects of attempts to acquire or dispose of large positions were first observed on such markets, and their interpretation as being due to liquidity demands is better substantiated for such markets. In addition, the exposition is simpler, because the alternatives available to an anxious buyer or seller of a large quantity of commodity futures contracts are more limited. Legally, all transactions in commodity futures must be conducted in public on the floor of the exchange during the regular trading period. Furthermore, the ticker services of such exchanges report price changes, but not volume. Thus traders not present on the trading floor can become quickly aware of the existence of a large liquidity demand (positive or negative) only through the price changes it produces.

The only alternatives available to the anxious seller (or buyer) of a large quantity of commodity futures are either to attempt to obtain execution on the entire quantity in one brief interval, or to submit a sequence of orders, thus spreading the demand over a period of time. In practice, the latter alternative seems to predominate, since it is the only alternative that can attract buying (or selling) support from traders not physically present on the trading floor.

Large liquidity demands spread over a period of days should produce a reversal pattern similar to that observed in transaction data, except that the price moves should be larger, and should be spread over a longer period of time. In a recent paper, Holbrook Working (1967) has made another signal contribution to our knowledge of organized markets. First, he has called attention to the fact that previous observations, that had not been satisfactorily explained, could be interpreted as the result of dips and bulges due to concentrated demands for large quantities of liquidity. (On commodity futures markets, such demands arise when large merchandising corporations attempt to place or to lift their hedges.) Second, he has presented significant new evidence to support his interpretation.

The previous observations, that had not been satisfactorily explained were due to Larson (1960) and Smidt (1965). Larson showed that there are small negative autocorrelations, at lags of up to three or four days, in corn futures prices, Smidt showed that a trader who used a one-cent filter on day-to-day closing prices in Soybean futures could make significant profits. The rule required selling after a price advance of one cent or more and buying after a close-to-close decline of the same magnitude. Both of these observations can be explained if one assumes that there is a systematic tendency for small day-to-day price changes in one direction to be followed by price changes in the opposite direction, spread over the next three or four days.

Working confirmed this observation by analyzing the trading record of a professional floor trader. The hypothesis that this trader profited mainly from the systematic patterns described above provided a satisfactory explanation of the trading record. Previous hypotheses, applied to the same data, had not been satisfactory. The analysis of the trading record is too complicated to summarize here.

The organized securities markets differ from commodity futures markets in some important institutional details. All the differences relevant here give the anxious buyer or seller of a large quantity of stock a wider range of means of completing his transactions. The options available involve different combinations of price concessions versus marketing effort. The initiator of a large transaction can contact interested parties to arrange a transaction that need not occur on the floor of the exchange. He can advertise his willingness to buy or sell; he can obtain the use of a sales force to contact potential buyers or sellers. To the extent that extra marketing costs of arranging a quick transaction are substitutes for price concessions, the cost of liquidity may not appear in the pattern of recorded prices.

Nevertheless, liquidity demands may produce dips and bulges in the prices on organized stock exchanges just as they do on commodity exchanges. Relevant evidence is contained in a study by Fama and Blume (1966). In this study filter trading rules were applied to the daily closing prices of the thirty stocks in the Dow-Jones average. The number of consecutive trading days per individual stocks averaged approximately 1,400. The filter used was expressed as the percentage change from the previous peak or trough. Price data were corrected for dividend payments. The filter sizes used ranged from 0.5 percent to 50 percent. The trading rule used in this study requires taking a long position in a stock when its closing price exceeds a reference trough by the size of the filter. The long position is then held until the closing price is less than a reference peak by the amount of the filter. At this point the position is switched from long to short. Short or long positions are continued until a signal to change them is reached. The reference peak (trough) is the highest (lowest) preceding closing price from the day the position was opened.

A simple buy and hold policy applied to this data yielded an annual rate of return of approximately .10. If there were no systematic patterns in this price series other than the upward drift, one would expect to earn a return of .10 during the period when long positions were open and a return of minus that amount during the period when short positions were open. The actual results for the range of filters of interest here are summarized in Table 1.

The filter rule used in this study requires a trader to be long as many times as he is short. However, it is not necessary that the number of days that long positions are held be the same as the number of days short positions are held. For this reason, as well as because of other sources of sampling error, even if the data followed the random walk hypothesis, the observed returns from long and short positions might not be identical to the expected returns.

There are four filter levels whose observed returns for both long and short positions differ in absolute magnitude by .04 or more from their expected levels. For two of these, .005 and .01, the observed returns from both long and short positions exceed the expected return. For two other filters, .045 and .050, the observed returns from both long and short positions are less than the expected returns. Deviations as large as this cannot reasonably be attributed to chance.

TABLE 1

Nominal annual rates of return before commissions by filter: Averaged over all companies.

Filter	Total transactions	Long positions only (rounded)	Short positions only (rounded)
.005	12,514	.21	.01
.010	8,660	.14	−.05
.015	6,270	.11	−.08
.020	4,784	.09	−.11
.025	3,750	.07	−.14
.030	2,994	.07	−.14
.035	2,438	.07	−.13
.040	2,013	.08	−.13
.045	1,720	.06	−.15
.050	1,484	.06	−.16
.060	1,071	.08	−.12
.070	828	.07	−.13
.080	653	.08	−.13
.090	539	.08	−.12
.100	435	.08	−.10
.120	289	.10	−.09

It is true that trader who had to pay the regular NYSE commissions could not earn normal profits if his trading was based solely on these systematic tendencies. The possibility that a member of the exchange could profitably take advantage of them will be examined later.

Whether or not this data should be interpreted as a violation of the random walk hypothesis, that is, as evidence of significant market imperfections, it would be interesting to know the source of these systematic tendencies. The hypothesis suggested here is that they represent price concessions by purchasers or sellers anxious to quickly exchange a large volume of stock. This hypothesis would be *a priori* reasonable if it could be shown that both the positive dependency indicated by the small filters, and the negative dependency indicated by the large filters could result from the occurrence of dips and bulges of the type that seem to be associated with liquidity demands on commodity markets.

To see why this suggestion is reasonable, first note that for every filter size in Table 1, the actual returns earned by the long and short positions are displaced from their expected returns by approximately the same absolute magnitude. This strongly suggests that whatever systematic pattern exists in the stock price sequence is a highly symmetric pattern. The simplest pattern that could account for this characteristic in the data is, a wave-like motion around the long-term upward trend in the data. If the waves were all of the same amplitude, then any filter size greater than the amplitude of the wave would produce no transactions. In fact, the data show that the number of transactions decreases as the filter size increases. This suggests a mixture of waves of different amplitudes. For example, the number of wave-like price movements that produce transactions with a 5 percent filter is about one-tenth the number that produce transactions with a 0.5 percent filter.

The profits produced by the trading rule studied by Fama and Blume depend on the amplitude of the wave and the size of the filter. If the amplitude of the wave is less than the filter size it produces no transactions. Such waves are filtered out and ignored. Suppose that the trough of a wave occurs when the stock is priced at \$100 per share and the peak when the stock rises to $100 + A$ dollars. The amplitude of the wave is A percent. With an I percent filter (assuming $A > I$), a buy signal will be given when the price reaches $100 + I$ dollars. A sell signal will occur when the price passes the peak and declines to $100 + A - I$ dollars. Thus the profits on this long open position will be $A - 2I$ dollars or $A - 2I$ percent before commissions. In general, the trading rule will produce gains (losses) if the average amplitude of waves that exceed the filter size is greater than (less than) twice the filter size. The data in Table 1 suggests that for the stocks in the Dow-Jones average the average amplitude of the waves detected by a one percent filter is greater than two percent. On the other hand, the average amplitude of the waves detected by a five percent filter is less than ten percent.

If these wave-like patterns are due to the demands for relatively large amounts of liquidity, the amplitude of the waves presumably results from the number of shares of stock which the anxious buyer or seller has available for exchange, and the intensity of his desire to complete the transaction rapidly. The term wave is used in a metaphorical sense. It is not suggested that if the price series were plotted that one would necessarily be able to observe a persistent wave-like pattern. The waves must be defined statistically in terms of the conditional probabilities of price changes given that the price is already in a certain relation to the previous peak or trough.

Fama and Blume argue that the statistical dependencies indicated by their data do not constitute a contradiction to the random walk hypothesis because it is not possible to profit by taking account of these dependencies. Even if this is true, it is important to identify the dependencies that exist and determine the source of deviation from strict statistical randomness.

Although Fama and Blume believe that the statistical dependencies they have uncovered are not large enough to be a potential source of trading profits, I find their logic unconvincing. A trader who was not a member of the New York Stock Exchange could not earn a normal rate of profit on his funds by trading in such a way as to take advantage solely of these systematic price patterns. However, if knowledge of these patterns were more widely publicized among such traders, it is possible they would modify their trading patterns in such a way as to increase their profits and reduce even further the degree of statistical dependence that Fama and Blume observe. An example of a situation where this seems to have occurred will be presented later.

Fama and Blume base their analysis on the 0.5 percent filter, which is appropriate, since it is apparently the most attractive for a trader who is a member of the NYSE. The average return before commissions from following this rule is 11.5 percent, assuming the trader takes both long and short positions. The clearinghouse fees from following this rule would amount to about 8.4 percent per year. (The rule requires an average of 84 transactions per security per year.) Taking only clearinghouse fees into account, the annual return is reduced to about three percent. Fama and Blume conclude that clearinghouse fees alone are "more than sufficient to push the returns from the simple filter rule below those of a buy and hold policy" (p. 238).

This calculation assumes the trader follows the rule literally. That is, he is long when the rule gives a long signal and short when the rule gives a short signal. However, a trader who wished to take advantage of the 0.5 percent filter rule might also wish to take advantage of the fact that the expected return from a long position in a security was about ten percent. He could take advantage of the expected return from a buy and hold policy by buying, say, 100 shares of stock in a given security. If in addition he wished to take advantage of the filter rule he could "trade around" this average long position. When the filter rule signaled a long position, he would increase his holding to 200 shares. When the filter rule signaled a short position, he would decrease his position to zero shares. On the average his investment would be the amount required to carry 100 shares. (His investment might average slightly more or less if the filter rule requires that a long position be open for slightly more or less than half the time.) The return on the average investment would be the sum of the return from the buy and hold policy and the return from the filter rule, or about 13 percent.

The reader may object, and with some justice, that the return should be calculated not on the average capital employed but on the total capital employed. In the example just given this is the amount required to carry 200 shares of the stock. From this point of view the pure buy and hold and the pure filter trading policies give the same results as before, ten percent and three percent, respectively. In considering the policy of trading around the trend we must ask what the trader does with the funds at his disposal when they are not invested in stock. Presumably they will be invested in some short term money instrument. Five percent is a rough indication of what can be earned this way. On the average half of his capital will be so invested. His return from trading around the trend will be (10 + 5 + 3)/2 or about nine percent. Admittedly this return is less than the expected return from a simple buy and hold policy. But a comparison of the two policies must also take risk into account. With the buy and hold policy the return is entirely from one source, and is likely to be quite variable. With the policy of trading around the trend the return comes from three sources, the long position in stock, the short-term money market, and the filter trading rule. There is likely to be much less variation in return from a policy of trading around the trend. A member of the NYSE might well find it attractive to take advantage of the statistical dependencies that Fama and Blume have so well documented.

Although the above argument is highly simplified, it does indicate the difficulties involved in estimating whether a statistically significant deviation from independence of price changes represents an economically significant deviation from the random walk hypothesis. The model of a trader as a single product firm is inadequate and misleading. The hypothetical trader described in the previous paragraph is analogous to a multi-product firm. His profits are derived from three distinct, though complementary activities, investing in common stocks, lending short-term money and filter trading. In practice, professional traders frequently engage in more than three distinct activities. Presumably during the period covered by the data it was not profitable for traders to act so as to further reduce the magnitude of the statistical dependencies discovered by Fama and Blume. Whether or not this was due to conditions of imperfect competition (such as barriers to entry) cannot be determined from the presently available data.

V. LAGS IN RESPONSE TO NEW INFORMATION

In a frictionless market, prices would respond instantaneously to new information. Furthermore, the response would, on the average, be correct and take into account any dependencies in the information generating process.[4] If frictions exist, as they undoubtedly do in the real world, then there should be some lags in the response of prices to new information (see Working ,1958, p. 195). The challenge in this instance, as in others, is to identify the lags in response to new information, and the estimate whether their magnitude is justified by the cost of reducing them even further.

The frictionless model would be violated if prices failed to respond to relevant new information, or if they responded, but not immediately. A delay in the response to new information might take the form of a rapid adjustment that occurred some time after the new information became available.[5] A delay could also take the form of a gradual adjustment of prices to the new information. In

---

[4] For an elaboration of this point of view see Fama (1965, pp. 36–39).

[5] A striking example of a rapid, but lagged response to new information is contained in the following quotation from the column by Robert Metz in The *New York Times,* Friday, August 23, 1968. Referring to the market activity in Control Data on the previous day, the column states:

> The news for the current quarter is not regarded as good. Lost in the the shuffle of the stockholders' meeting last Thursday called (to approve) the merger with Commercial Credit, was a remark that earnings in the September quarter would be significantly lower than the year-earlier quarter. *Analysts who follow the stock and heard the comment* estimated that Control Data would earn 35 to 40 cents in this quarter compared with 50 cents a share a year ago.
>
> *It seemed that the word did not reach Wall Street's performance funds until yesterday.* The stock held steady on Monday and eased 3 7/8, to 152 on Tuesday. But yesterday was a different story.
>
> Big stockholders banged out without regard to price yesterday in an effort to clean house before the earnings outlook became generally known. (Parenthetical phrase and italics added.)

The story then proceeds to describe why the mutual funds now thought the earnings prospects were below what they had been expecting, and to summarize the market action in the stock on the previous day. The price dropped $16.75 in one day on a volume of over 900,000 shares. Nearly two-thirds of the volume was accounted for by six large blocks (each in excess of 19,000 shares), including one block that was the largest in terms of dollar volume ever recorded in common stock in the history of the NYSE. The closing price of Control Data on the day of the stockholder meeting was 154 1/2. On successive trading days after that meeting the closing prices were 154 1/2, 155 7/8, 152, 135 1/4, and 128.

the latter case there should be a systematic tendency for price movements in one direction to be followed by additional movements in the same direction, a pattern that could be called a price trend. Of these alternatives, only the price trend would be detectable from an analysis of price changes alone.

In a model that allows for the fact that it is costly to obtain and evaluate data to determine if it contains any relevant new information, one would not expect that, on the average, prices would respond immediately to new information that was potentially available. One would expect a relatively long lag in cases where it is relatively costly to obtain and process data, and where the expected value of the information contained in the data is low; a relatively short lag would be expected if it is relatively easy to obtain and process new data, and if the expected value of the information contained in the data is high.[6] The available evidence is fragmentary, but it is generally consistent with this interpretation of the random walk hypothesis.

It is apparently extraordinarily difficult to detect the existence of price trends by observing only price movements. Some evidence that price trends may exist has been reported by Brinegar (1954) and Larson (1960) based on commodity futures prices, and by Cowles (1960) based on common stock price indices. However, the evidence is fragmentary and the interpretation of the evidence as being due to lagged responses to new information is open to question.

The most fruitful means of identifying price trends involves identifying specific items of new information whose date of publication can be reasonably estimated, and studying the pattern of price change on or around that date of publication. An interesting example of this approach is contained in a study by Davis (1967) which estimated the response of stock prices to the publication of sales and production data for the auto and steel industries. The example of automobile sales is most clearcut, since sales data contain more relevant information than production data, and because the data are reported separately by company. These data are reported regularly in *The Wall Street Journal* and are therefore easily and promptly available to the general public. Each report covers a recent 10–day period. Although sales are an important determinant of earnings, sales during any 10–day period are a small part of the total sales and they contain significant random variation. There is also considerable dependency in the data, since a company's market shares tend to shift when new models are introduced, and to remain relatively stable for the remainder of the marketing year. For this reason, the new information in a sales report for a 10–day period usually leads to a very small shift in stock values. These shifts are not large enough to warrant a purchase or sale solely on that account. Nevertheless, Davis was able to detect a definite though small correlation between the movement of stock prices and the information content of the sales data. The most striking conclusion of the

---

6 The Control Data incident described in the previous footnote contradicts the frictionless version of the random walk hypothesis. If one assumes, as seems likely, that the expected value of the new information an analyst could obtain from attending a stockholders meeting is low, then most interested analysts may have correctly concluded that it is not worthwhile for them to attend stockholder meetings. Only with the benefit of hindsight is it apparent that it would have been worthwhile to attend this particular meeting. Thus it is not necessarily the case that the Control Data incident contradicts a version of the random walk hypothesis that makes allowance for the costs of overcoming frictions.

study is that the adjustment of stock prices to the new information tends to be "concentrated in the two days prior to the date of publication and the three days following publication" (Davis, p. 38). Davis' study tends to strongly support the viewpoint that stock prices will respond promptly to even relatively trivial bits of new information, provided the information is easily available at low cost to a wide number of persons.

A study being conducted by Myron Scholes has developed evidence that the occurrence of secondary distributions is treated by the market as conveying information that leads to a reduction in the price of the stock. Again, the information is easily available to interested parties, and the market response to the new information is relatively prompt.

Ferber (1958) attempted to estimate the effect on stock market prices of buy and sell recommendations by four widely distributed market services. Ferber concluded that there is a small but statistically significant shift in the price of the stocks in the direction that would be expected. (That is, an increase for buy recommendations and a decrease for sell recommendations.) Most of the price change took place in the first few days immediately following the publication of the recommendations. The change apparently persisted; there was no evidence of a movement in the opposite direction for at least four weeks.

Ferber's study is consistent with the results reported by Davis and Scholes in that it indicates a very prompt market response to events that are widely publicized and therefore available to many persons at low cost.[7] Unfortunately, Ferber's study was not specifically designed to test the random walk hypothesis. It does not distinguish between recommendations based on information contained in recent data, and other recommendations based on an analysis of data that were potentially available for some time before the recommendation was published. The random walk hypothesis would suggest that the first type of recommendation would lead to greater price effects than the second.

The studies by Davis, Scholes and Ferber all deal with situations in which information, or at least data, is available at low cost to large numbers of persons. There is a need to construct more powerful tests of the random walk hypothesis by attempting to determine the speed and adequacy of response of prices to relevant data that is more costly to obtain or to process.[8]

When information is expensive to obtain and process, the speed with

---

[7] Ferber reports that the price response to the publication of a recommendation took place very promptly. By contrast publication of a recommendation about a company apparently stimulates an increase in the volume of transactions in that company's shares that continues for several weeks. J. Hass has suggested to me that this observation is consistent with the idea that only a small number of knowledgeable traders, acting promptly, are sufficient to bring about a price response to new information. A much larger group of investors may eventually wish to make some shifts in their portfolios as an eventual result of obtaining this information. It is these shifts that apparently produce the increased volume. The traders who respond quickly are presumably the "sophisticated traders" postulated by Fama (1965, pp. 37–40).

[8] Two examples of the kind of study we have in mind might be mentioned. Larson (1967) attempted to determine the extent to which speculators in egg futures were able to predict cyclical changes in egg prices. The period studied was one in which the relevant cycles were very regular. His results were inconclusive. One test indicated some forecasting ability, but another test did not. An unpublished study by Smidt and Johnson (1962) suggests that meat packers responded systematically to anticipated shifts in the supply of pork, but not to anticipated shifts in demand.

which prices can be expected to respond should depend on the economic incentives that could lead someone to devote resources to acquiring the information. The means by which one could profit from new information can be conveniently classified into three groups. First, obtaining the new information could be profitable because it is used directly by the persons who acquire it as a basis for their own investments. The securities research done by institutions managing their own portfolios is a clear example. When information is acquired for this purpose, the persons acquiring the information have an incentive to restrict its distribution, at least until they have completed whatever transactions they consider appropriate.

A second type of incentive for acquiring new information is the possibility of selling the information directly to an interested party who can make profitable use of it. Usually, but not always, the buyer will plan to use the information as a basis for his own trading. Investment counselors, and publishers of subscription market letters, are examples of firms that have an economic incentive to acquire information, with the idea of reselling it. Normally, in this case, the producer of the information has an incentive to restrict its availability to those who have agreed to pay him for it.

A third type of incentive for acquiring new information occurs if the person who acquires the new information believes he will profit by the way other people react to the new information. One example of this situation is the brokerage firm that acquires new information and passes it along to its customers in the expectation that the brokerage firm will earn commissions when customers decide to trade on the basis of the new information. Another example is contained in the following quotation:

> One of the publisher's two regular subscription services, which regularly recommended purchases of securities, had a paid circulation of 5,000 and in addition was distributed free on some occasions to as many as 100,000 nonsubscribers. During a 9-month period in 1960 the publisher traded in securities which it recommended, purchasing shortly before the recommendation and selling shortly after the publication of the recommendation, without disclosing the facts to its subscribers. . . . In one instance the publication compared two companies in the same industry. As to one where the publisher had a short position, it suggested the stock had reached its peak, while in the other, where it held call options, it recommended purchase.[9]

A more comprehensive analysis of the costs and incentives of acquiring information might reasonably be expected to suggest fruitful new approaches to testing and refining the random walk hypothesis. For example, the incentive to acquire new information about a company may vary systematically with the size of the company, the characteristics of its stockholders, the characteristics of its capital structure, etc. To what extent are there corresponding systematic

---

[9] U.S. Congress, House Committee on Interstate and Foreign Commerce, *Report of the Special Study of Securities Markets of the Securities and Exchange Commission,* House Document No. 95, Part 1, 88th Congress, 1st Session (Washington, D.C.: Government Printing Office), 1963, p. 382.

differences in the speed with which the company's share prices respond to new information?

VI. SPECULATIVE BUBBLES

Speculative bubbles are produced by an inappropriate response to new information. Since the response is inappropriate it is eventually followed by a corrective price movement.

Superficially the price pattern produced by a speculative bubble resembles the dips or bulges produced by liquidity demands, except that speculative bubbles are likely to produce larger price fluctuations and to extend over much longer periods of time. The price fluctuations caused by demands for liquidity are normally caused by the action of a single decision-making unit. Speculative bubbles, like trends, are the result of the actions of large numbers of decision-making units responding to the same information. In the case of a trend, the price reaction is appropriate in magnitude, while in the case of a speculative bubble, the price reaction is exaggerated, and eventually produces a corrective reaction in the opposite direction.

One type of speculative bubble is the result of an exaggerated response to new information. Presumably it is most often the result of exaggerated optimism, but in principle it could also be the result of exaggerated pessimism. Speculative bubbles can also result if prices responded to false or misleading information.

In a sense, the existence of speculative bubbles is hypothetical. The available information on speculative bubbles is based wholly on historical studies and similar case histories of apparent examples of this phenomenon. The South Sea Bubble, the Tulip Craze, and the bull market of the late 1920's are examples of episodes that some, at least, would classify as speculative bubbles. Of more relevance to the present paper are similar episodes that may affect the stock of a single company or industry. The danger in attempting to identify speculative bubbles solely from historical studies is that price sequences having the required characteristics can be expected to occur occasionally by chance in a time series whose changes follow precisely a random walk. The historian, examining such an episode *ex post,* may easily exaggerate the causal significance of certain events. Evidence that prices responded inappropriately to new information in particular instances is not necessarily a violation of the random walk hypothesis. In its simple version, this hypothesis requires only that the expected response should be appropriate. The random walk hypothesis would be violated if it could be shown that there is a systematic tendency for prices to respond inappropriately. For example, it would be a violation of the random walk hypothesis if it could be shown that there was a systematic tendency for security prices to rise temporarily during periods when dealers had a greater than normal incentive to sell such securities.

The fact that existing studies of the random walk hypothesis have not uncovered evidence of the existence of speculative bubbles is far from convincing. Such price patterns, if they exist, probably extend over a period of months or years. The sample sizes and the statistical techniques used in existing studies would be inadequate to detect the existence of such speculative bubbles, even if they did exist.

VII. SUMMARY

The significance of the random walk hypothesis is that it provides a fruitful null hypothesis to use in statistical studies of price behavior in organized markets. Proponents of the hypothesis should not expect to find a complete absence of systematic elements in their empirical studies. Rather, the failure to detect some degree of non-randomness sometimes can be interpreted more properly as evidence that the statistical tests used were insufficiently powerful. On the other hand, the detection of some nonrandom components is not evidence against the random walk hypothesis unless it can be shown that the systematic tendencies present unexploited opportunities to make above normal profits.

Statistical studies employing the random walk hypothesis as a null hypothesis are more likely to be fruitful if they utilize tests specifically designed to detect categories of non-randomness that are a *priori* most likely. Three sources of systematic price tendencies are considered in this paper. They are demands for liquidity, lags in response to new information, and exaggerated responses to new information. The main part of the article is devoted to describing the price patterns that could be expected from each of these sources, and to summarizing some of the most significant evidence currently available with respect to each type of systematic tendency.

REFERENCES

ALEXANDER, S. S., "Price Movements in Speculative Markets: Trends or Random Walks," *Industrial Management Review,* May 1961, *2,* pp. 7–26.
————"Price Movements in Speculative Markets: Trends or Random Walks, No. 2," *The Random Character of Stock Market Prices,* Revised Edition, P. A. Cootner, Editor (Cambridge, Mass.: M.I.T. Press), 1964, pp. 338–372.
BRINEGAR, C. S., "Statistical Analysis of Speculative Price Behavior," Unpublished Ph. D. Dissertation, Stanford University, 1954.
COWLES, A., "A Revision of Previous Conclusions Regarding Stock Price Behavior," *Econometrica,* October 1960, *28,* pp. 909–915.
DAVIS, J. V., "The Adjustment of Stock Prices to New Information," Unpublished Ph. D. Dissertation, Cornell University, 1967.
DEMSETZ, H., "The Cost of Transacting," *Quarterly Journal of Economics,* February 1968, *82,* pp. 33–53.
FAMA, E. F., "The Behavior of Stock Market Prices," *Journal of Business,* January 1965, *38,* pp. 34–105.
————and M. E. BLUME, "Filter Rules and Stock Market Trading," *Journal of Business: Special Supplement,* January 1966, *39,* pp. 226–241.
FERBER, R., "Short-Run Effects of Stock Market Services on Stock Prices," *Journal of Finance,* March 1958, *13,* pp. 80–95.
LARSON, A. B., "Measurement of a Random Process in Futures Prices," *Food Research Institute Studies,* November 1960, *1.*
————"Price Prediction on the Egg Futures Market," *Food Research Institute Studies, Special Supplement,* 1967, *7,* pp. 49–64.
LEVY, R. A., "The Theory of Random Walks: A Survey of Findings," *The American Economist,* Fall 1967, *11,* pp. 34–48.
MANDELBROT, B., "Forecasts of Future Prices, Unbiased Markets, and 'Martingale' Models," *Journal of Business: Special Supplement,* January 1966, *39,* pp. 242–255.

NIEDERHOFFER, V., "Clustering of Stock Prices," *Operations Research*, March–April 1965, *13*, pp. 258–265.

————and M. F. M. OSBORNE, "Market Making and Reversal on the Stock Exchange," *Journal of the American Statistical Association*, December 1966, *61*, pp. 897–916.

OSBORNE, M. F. M., "Brownian Motion in the Stock Market," *Operations Research*, March–April 1969, *7*, pp. 145–173.

————"Periodic Structure in the Brownian Motion of Stock Prices," *Operations Research*, May–June 1962, *10*, pp. 345–379.

————"Some Quantitative Tests for Stock Price Generating Models and Trading Folklore," *Journal of the American Statistical Association*, June 1967, *62*, pp. 321–340.

SAMUELSON, P. A., "Proof that Properly Anticipated Prices Fluctuate Randomly," *Industrial Management Review*, Spring 1965, *6*, pp. 41–50.

SMIDT, S., "A Test of the Serial Independence of Price Changes in Soybean Futures," *Food Research Institute Studies*, 1965, *5*, pp. 117–136.

————and A. JOHNSON, "Expectations and Information: A Study of Pork Inventory Behavior," Graduate School of Business and Public Administration, Cornell University, 1962. (Mimeo)

STIGLER, G. J., "Public Regulation of the Securities Market," *Journal of Business*, April 1964, *36*, pp. 117–142.

WORKING, H., "Price Effects of Scalping and Day Trading," *Proceedings of the Chicago Board of Trade Annual Symposium*, 1954, pp. 114–139.

————"A Theory of Anticipatory Prices," *American Economic Review*, May 1958, *48*, pp. 188–199.

————"Tests of a Theory Concerning Floor Trading on Commodity Exchanges," *Food Research Institute Studies, Special Supplement*, 1967, *7*, pp. 5–48.

YING, C. C., "Stock Market Prices and Volumes of Sales," *Econometrica*, July 1966, *34*, PP. 676–685.

Fama (1) cited several studies demonstrating that successive changes in stock price are independent. Owen presents clear evidence to suggest that identifiable trends exist in stock prices. Specifically, he finds that local trends (as opposed to long-term trends) of up to one year are exhibited by the Standard and Poor's 500 Stock Index. Evidence that these trends can be profitable to the investor has not yet been provided.

3

Analysis of Variance Tests for Local Trends in the Standard and Poor's Index

*Joel Owen**

This article is reprinted with permission from the Journal of Finance, *Vol. XXII, No. 3 (June, 1968), pp. 509–514.*

I. SUMMARY

In this paper, we present evidence that local trends do exist in the Standard and Poor's Index. We begin by assuming that the logarithm of the price at time t_i, say log $P(t_i)$, has an expected value which is a linear function of time. That is,

$$E \log P(t_i) = at_i + b$$

where a and b are arbitrary but fixed constants. Then we use the techniques of the analysis of variance to test whether *any* constants in the expression above satisfy the data. The tests show that these data are not explained by such an expected value. We conclude that the mean is different (certainly more complicated than $at_i + b$) over different intervals of time. The changes in expected value over these intervals are referred to as local trends. Finally, by repetition of the tests for different interval sizes, we find that the tests are significant for

*This work has been facilitated by a grant from the National Science Foundation GS-341 to Harvard University. The computer used in this work was supported by N.S.F. grant GP-2723 [see Owen (8)].

interval sizes up to approximately one year but not longer. Thus the evidence suggests that the local trends, when they occur, do not last longer than this period of time.

II. INTRODUCTION

The approaches that have been used to verify the existence of trends can be divided into two groups which we call the direct and indirect approaches. By the direct approach, we mean that some definition of trends is given; a statistic is defined; a test is performed on the statistic to determine the existence of trends. By the indirect approach, we refer to the suggested methods for playing the stock market which lead to positive monetary returns and which by implication disprove the notion of "no trends."

Much of the work done through the direct approach [A. Cowles and H. Jomes (5), A. Cowles (4), S. Alexander (1)] has involved the notion of "price rise of price fall." Whether the frequency of these events or the frequency of the succession of similar events was used, the underlying assumption is that the probability of a rise is the same as that of a fall. In terms of our expected value this means that $a = b = 0$. Alexander (1) criticizes this assumption on the grounds that the odds of a rise need not be equal to those of a fall. Thus a random walk with constant drift would still not prove anything about local trends. (In terms of the expected value, a constant drift would be $at + b$ for some values of a and b.) Alexander (1) then takes the indirect approach [along with H. Houthakker (6) and P. H. Cootner (3)] and defines a "filter rule" for playing the market. He concludes that there are trends based on the performance of the rule.

Here, we take the direct approach. In order to avoid the pitfalls already mentioned, we need a null hypothesis concerning trends which include both the zero mean function (a perfect market) and a long term linear trend. Define a weekly difference as

$$Y(i) = \log P[(i + 1)\varDelta t] - \log P[i\varDelta t]$$

If

$$E \log P[i \varDelta t] = ai \varDelta t + b$$

then

$$EY(i) = a \varDelta t$$

Then, if the sampling interval $\varDelta t$ is fixed, a perfect market would correspond to $a = 0$ and a long term trend would correspond to some fixed value of $a \neq 0$. Under either assumption, the parameter a should be constant over all the observations. If we subdivide the time interval of observation into subintervals, we should observe the same value of a in each subinterval if the market is perfect or if there is a long term trend. If, on the other hand, we conclude that the parameter a takes on different values in some subintervals, we must further conclude that the market is neither perfect nor can be described by a long term trend. Thus we wish to test the null hypothesis, "the mean value of weekly differences is the same over the subintervals considered," against the alternative hypothesis, "for some subinterval the mean value is different." We take these statements as our null and alternative hypotheses.

The analysis of variance has been used [see W. Cochran and G. Cox (2)] to test whether all "treatments" are the same in a one-way classification. Since the null hypothesis for treatments is similar to the one we wish to investigate here, we apply these techniques.

The data chosen for this investigation are the weekly values of the Standard and Poor's Index over approximately fifteen years, from 1947–1962. On the computer, we generated the logarithms of the Index values and then the weekly difference, i.e., the values $Y(i)$. These differences became the basic variables for the investigation.

We consider two kinds of tests on this data. The first, called the Binomial Test, deals with increases and decreases in the Index without regard to the magnitude of these reversals, that is, the number of times the Index rose or fell from one week to the next. The second kind of test, called the Local Sum Test, takes into account the numerical values of these changes.

III. BINOMIAL TEST

The weekly differences span a fifteen year period. To examine the local properties, we subdivide this time span into forty-five non-overlapping, consecutive time intervals. Each interval is fifteen weeks (about four months) in duration. The program produced the number of positive differences in each interval. Table 1 proceeds chronologically down the left-most column, followed by the second column, etc. For each of the forty-five intervals, the entry gives the number of increases recorded.

TABLE 1

The number of increases per interval

8	10	5	9	9
7	11	7	8	7
13	9	8	6	7
5	5	10	8	7
8	10	12	12	10
9	8	9	5	8
9	10	10	9	12
11	8	8	10	9
9	9	11	12	7

The null hypothesis that we wish to test is that all the entries in the table have the same mean value. This leads naturally to an analysis of variance. Cochran and Cox (2) have pointed out that the most crucial assumption needed for the analysis of variance is a common variance. Since the numbers in the table are the number of increases recorded per interval, the basic data are binomial in nature (a rise or a fall in the index). In their paper (7) Mosteller and Youtz point out that the variance of binomial data can be stabilized when the data are transformed by an arc sin transformation. Thus, to be conservative, we apply this transformation to the numbers of Table 1 and produce Table 2. Comparing the first number of the second table to the first number of the first table, the following relationship exists: 46.8 is the angle such that $8 = 15 \sin 46.8$, the factor 15 being the number of weekly differences in each interval.

TABLE 2

Arc Sin values per interval

46.80	54.13	35.87	50.41	50.41
43.20	58.01	43.20	46.80	43.20
66.82	50.41	46.80	39.59	43.20
35.87	35.87	54.13	46.80	43.20
46.80	54.13	62.17	62.17	54.13
50.41	46.80	50.41	35.87	46.80
50.41	54.13	54.13	50.41	62.17
58.01	46.80	46.80	54.13	50.41
50.41	50.41	58.01	62.17	43.20

We consider this table to be a one-way classification with forty-five "treatments." Proceeding with the analysis of variance, we find that the total sum of squares and thereby the error sum of squares cannot be computed. This occurs because the ordering of the fifteen samples which make up each of the table elements is lost [see (7) for a discussion of this loss]. Returning again to the work of Mosteller and Youtz (7), we find that the variance for each element in the table should be very close to $821/(n + \frac{1}{2})$. Evaluating this for $n = 15$, we have an independent value for the error sum of squares. The analysis of variance can now be performed. It is given in Table 3. The column abbreviations are respectively degrees of freedom, sum of squares, mean sum of squares and the F statistic (2).

TABLE 3

Analysis of variance for Arc Sin data

Source of variation:	d.f.	s.s.	m.s.	F
Treatments:	44	164.077	3.729	1.056
Error:	15	52.968	3.531	

The F value is not significant at the standard levels. We conclude that there is no evidence for trends when the binary data are used. This is the same conclusion reached by Alexander (1) on heuristic reasoning.

IV. LOCAL SUM TEST

Having produced no evidence for local trends using the grosser data, we procede to test the actual differences. The approach and assumptions are the same. We again use forty-five intervals. Within each interval, we form the numerical sum of weekly differences (actually the last logarithmic value minus the first). The computer produced Table 4 which is presented in the same chronological sense as before (the entries being scaled by 10).

TABLE 4

Numerical sum per interval

.094	.117	−.209	.355	.250
−.278	.477	.062	.068	.063
.707	.398	.012	−.281	−.079
−.451	−.078	.360	−.211	−.239
−.039	.440	.611	.541	.152
−.227	−.036	.494	.826	−.174
−.036	.036	.631	.009	.662
.373	.118	.280	.334	.298
.208	.023	.838	.609	.027

To test whether all the entries have the same mean, we again consider Table 4 to be a one-way classification with forty-five treatments. Since the computer could produce the total sum of squares here, we are able to proceed directly with the analysis of variance. The results are given in Table 5.

TABLE 5

Analysis of variance: Interval size 15 weeks

Source of variation:	d.f.	s.s.	m.s.	F
Treatments:	44	.342	.007772	1.414
Error:	630	3.462	.005497	
Total:	674			

The F value here is significant at the 5% level. We conclude that the assumption of "no trend" or one underlying trend does not describe the data adequately.

The analysis to this point deals with subintervals of fifteen week durations. The choice was convenient, albeit arbitrary. Obviously, any local trend that existed would not fit into this interval length exactly. On the other hand, if we choose the intervals too large, these trends may be obscured. Therefore, we now examine two other interval lengths to see if the conclusions are altered. The new interval lengths considered are thirty weeks and sixty weeks.

Applying the analysis of variance as before but making the interval length thirty weeks, produces Table 6.

TABLE 6

Analysis of variance: Interval size 30 weeks

Source of variation:	d.f.	s.s.	m.s.	*F*
Treatments:	21	.199	.009476	1.716
Error:	653	3.604	.005519	
Total:	674			

The *F* value here is still significant at the 5% level. Therefore, evidence supporting local trends remains after doubling the interval length.

TABLE 7

Analysis of variance: Interval size 60 weeks

Source of variation:	d.f.	s.s.	m.s.	*F*
Treatments:	10	.076	.007600	1.353
Errors:	664	3.729	.005616	
Total:	674			

Here the *F* value is not significant at the 5% level.

CONCLUSIONS

By using the analysis of variance we have been able to test a broader null hypothesis than was formed before. As a result of these tests, we conclude that

a. there is no evidence to suggest that the rises and falls in the Index reflect anything more than one long underlying trend;
b. there is evidence to support the notion that local trends exist when the numerical values of weekly differences are used; and
c. there is evidence to support the notion that local trends, when they occur, persist no longer than one year.

REFERENCES

1. ALEXANDER. (1961). "Price Movements in Speculative Markets: Trends or Random Walks, *Industrial Management Review*, 2.
2. W. COCHRAN, and G. COX. (1950). *Experimental Design*, John Wiley & Sons Book Co.
3. P. COOTNER. (1962). "Stock Prices: Random vs. Systematic Changes," *Industrial Management Review*, 3.
4. A. COWLES. (1960). "Revision of Previous Conclusions Regarding Stock Price Behavior," *Econometrica*, Vol. 28, 4.
5. A. COWLES and H. JOMES. (1937). "Some A Posteriori Probabilities in Stock Market Action," *Econometrica*, Vol. 5, 280.
6. H. HOUTHAKKER. (1961). "Systematic and Random Elements in Short Term Price Movements," *American Economic Review*, 51.

7. F. MOSTELLER and C. YOUTZ. (1961). "Tables of the Freeman-Tukey Transformations for the Binomial and Poisson Distributions," *Biometrika,* 48.

8. J. OWEN. (1966). "An Investor in the Stock Market," *Ph. D. Thesis,* Dept. of Statistics, Harvard Univ.

Elton and Gruber present a method of forecasting earnings per share. First, firms are placed into pseudo-industries or groups which should have the same determinants of growth in earnings. Then, earnings per share are forecasted by relating earnings growth to data taken from the firm's balance sheet and income statement. These forecasts are then compared with forecasts based solely on a firm's past earnings. These latter forecasts had previously been shown to be as accurate as those prepared by a sample of security analysts.

 This article accomplishes several purposes. First it demonstrates that type of detailed analysis which could be undertaken in estimating each of the variables which play a role in stock valuation. Second it demonstrates that forecasts (of earnings) based solely on historic data need not be worse than subjective (analyst's) forecasts. Finally it stresses the importance of disaggregating economic data into homogeneous groups. The reader should reconsider this concept as he advances through both the security valuation and portfolio analysis sections of this book.

4

Improved Forecasting Through the Design of Homogeneous Groups

*Edwin J. Elton And Martin J. Gruber**

This article is reprinted with permission from the Journal of Business, Vol. 44, No. 4 (October, 1971).

The purpose of this paper is both to discuss the need to disaggregate economic data into meaningful groups in order to better understand and forecast the future course of economic phenomena, and to illustrate with a specific example that such disaggregation can lead to improved results.

 The reasons for placing observations into homogeneous groups has already been documented by the authors (8) but will be reviewed briefly in the first section of this paper. The next section will be concerned with the general procedure for grouping observations. The remainder of the paper will discuss in some detail the improvement in forecasting ability that comes from a specific application of grouping procedures to the problem of forecasting earnings per share for a large group of manufacturing concerns. Forecasts prepared on the basis of statistically grouped data will be compared with forecasts made on data grouped on traditional industrial criteria as well as with forecasts prepared by mechanical extrapolation techniques.

 * The research for this paper was supported by grants from The Institute for Quantitative Research in Finance and by TIAA-CREF. The authors would like to thank Steve Replen for computational assistance.

THE HETEROGENEITY OF HOMOGENEOUS GROUPS

In this section we will discuss the reasons for grouping observations and will show that the grouping of observations is not unique but rather is determined by the general objective in grouping and the specific problem under study.

The reasons for grouping observations fall into two categories:

    a. to isolate homogeneous units that should act alike
    b. to isolate units which should have the same structural relationship between two or more variables.

Although, as the discussion below will make clear, these reasons are not mutually exclusive, nevertheless this dichotomy serves a useful purpose in understanding why we group.

THE NEED FOR HOMOGENEOUS GROUPS

One often tries to form groups of homogeneous units that have had or will continue to have the same value for one or more variables. For example, the SIC industrial codes can be viewed as forming groups of firms which are homogeneous with respect to end product.

SIC codes have also been used to group firms for purposes of security and portfolio analysis. Security analysts typically evaluate a stock by comparing its performance against other stocks in the same industry. For example, a company may be judged to be a good buy when its price-earnings ratio is low compared to the average price-earnings ratio for its industry. The assumption being made is that the price-earnings ratio for an industry is a good predictor of the price-earnings ratio of each stock in the industry. Similarly, the typical portfolio manager who attempts to obtain risk diversification by buying stocks from different industries is acting as if he believed that the SIC industrial classifications were homogeneous with respect to market risk.

The second reason for forming homogeneous groups is to find a sample of observations (firms) within which the same structural relationship between two or more variables exists. There are two related conditions under which the failure to properly select a sample can result in the misspecification of the relationships between two or more variables.

The first is where an omitted variable is correlated with both the dependent variable and one or more independent variables.[1] The failure to hold the effects of an omitted variable constant will result in biased regression coefficients, biased correlation coefficients, and both regression and correlation coefficients which are extremely sample sensitive.[2]

The problem of omitted variables has been recognized by several authors and the solution accepted has often been to accept SIC industrial classification as a suitable metric for homogeneity (regardless of the variable with respect to

---

[1] Often the omitted variable can not be included in the regression equation because it can not be specified exactly.

[2] For a full explanation of the source of bias see (8).

which homogeneity was being sought). For example, Modigliani and Miller (17) restricted their study of the effect of financial risk on the cost of capital to one industry in an attempt to hold business risk constant. Similarly, many of the early studies of dividend policy on cost of capital or stock price felt that they could eliminate omitted variable bias by restricting their study to a single industry.[3]

The second case where homogeneous groups are needed is where the magnitude or sign of a relationship between two variables can be affected by the value a third variable takes on. For example, suppose we were examining a sample of firms which finance their investments solely from internally generated funds. Then, one would expect a positive relationship between stock price and payout for firms which earned a low return on their marginal investment and a negative relationship for firms which earned a high return. Pooling the data could result in a multiple regression which found no relationship between payout and price, though in fact two very different relationships were present.

Once again, the way to avoid the problem of non-homogeneous relationships has typically been to accept SIC industrial classification as a suitable metric for homogeneity and so to confine regression analysis to data within one industry. This has been the practice in almost all stock pricing and cost of capital models.

These three reasons for grouping overlap to a considerable extent. For example, one may try to find a group of firms which are homogeneous with respect to risk so that security analysts can ignore risk in their analysis and so that portfolio managers can treat the group as one firm in determining appropriate diversification. Second, if risk is difficult to measure, then one may try to find a grouping that allows the relationship between the two other variables to be studied (e.g., stock price and growth) without having to worry about the effect of risk. On the other hand, if a measure of risk can be found, one might consider entering it into the regression equation as a second independent variable (rather than confining the study to a homogeneous risk group) unless the relationship between stock price and growth changes for different levels of risk. If it does change, we should group for the third reason outlined above.

HOMOGENEITY AND TRADITIONAL INDUSTRY GROUPINGS

Both the practice of security and portfolio analysis and the empirical testing of theory in finance has been based on either implicit or occasionally explicit groupings of firms. The groupings employed by almost all authors have been the same—SIC industrial classification. In other words, the assumption has been made that classification by end product is a suitable technique for grouping in almost all studies in finance.[4] But we have a host of evidence that grouping by industries in not particularly suitable for most of the purposes for which it is employed. Let us review some of the evidence.

As mentioned earlier, industry groupings are often used as a basis for comparative analysis by the security analyst. For example, the analyst will typically compare P/E ratios for a stock with the typical P/E ratio for the in-

[3] See for example, Myron Gordon (13).

[4] For example, see Gordon (13), Wippern (19), Arditti (1), Gruber (14).

dustry. Breen (4) has tested the profitability of buying high growth low P/E ratio stocks. His study defined low P/E ratios both in absolute terms and relative to the industry average P/E ratio.[5] Buying stocks with low P/E ratios relative to the industry means yielded a lower rate of return than buying stocks with a low P/E ratio relative to the overall means. This indicates that using traditional industries as a homogeneous group did not aid in formulating a strategy to produce high rates of return. This does not indicate that a proper grouping did not exist but it does indicate that the SIC industrial classifications were not appropriate.

Similar conclusions can be drawn with respect to portfolio analysis. Cohen and Pogue (6) attempted to see if introducing industry effects into the Sharpe (17) model could improve portfolio performance. Sharpe assumed that the interrelationships between the price movements of stocks could be expressed in terms of their movement with an index of general stock price movement. Cohen and Pogue added a second influence—the movement of stocks with their respective industrial average.[6] Cohen and Pogue's model did not outperform Sharpe's simple market model indicating that no new information was gained by viewing stocks as members of traditional industries.[7]

We can also question the use of industrial classification as a method of holding certain variables constant. In finance, the most common variable researchers desire to hold constant is business risk. Wippern (19) has used an analysis of variance to test differences in the stability of net operating income (his measure of business risk) within and between industries. He found that there was virtually no difference and concluded that his testing "provides clear evidence that industry groups do not provide an adequate basis on which to insure homogeneity of basic business uncertainty." If, in fact, an industry was a homogeneous risk class, then the relationships, as hypothesized by M & M, between cost of capital and financial risk should be reasonably stable across samples of firms from the same industry. Keenan (15) has demonstrated the extreme sample sensitivity of the M & M models with small random changes in a one-industry sample, indicating clearly that the industries he tested are not homogeneous risk classes. A different homogeneous group must be found in order to hold business risk constant.[8]

The normal solution to the problem of holding the effect of omitted variables constant has been to introduce additional variables (as proxies of the

[5] Since differences in growth rates were adjusted for in the Breen study, we can consider differences in P/E ratios as due to risk plus market imperfections. Adjustment by the industry average P/E can be viewed as an attempt to correct for risk differentials between industries.

[6] Cohen and Pogue actually tested two models. In the first model the industrial averages were assumed to be uncorrelated except for their common movement with the overall market. In the second, the industrial averages were assumed to have covariance above that due to movements with the general market.

[7] King (16) provides evidence that traditional industrial groupings explain part of the historical variability in the firm's rate of return. The results of his study suggest that some traditional industrial grouping might be appropriate for portfolio selection.

[8] Friend and Puckett (12) have indicated quite clearly why an industry group is not itself a satisfactory population for studying the relationship between dividends, retained earnings and stock price. They have also pointed out some models that can be used to study this relationship without resorting to homogeneous groups.

previously omitted variable) into the regression equation. Problems can still arise because some variable correlated with both the dependent and one or more independent variables has been omitted or because the nature of the relationship between some of the variables changes as the magnitude of an included variable changes. Such problems would be evidenced by extreme sensitivity of the regression parameters to changes in the sample.

Keenan (15) has used analysis of covariance in examining the models presented by Barges (2), Benishay (3), Gordon (13), and Modigliani and Miller (17). In this study, Keenan (15) has shown that the parameters of all the models which he tested are so extremely sample sensitive that the removal of one or two firms from the sample can change the sign of the regression parameter even when all firms in the sample are drawn from the same universe. A similar result is contained in Durand (7) when he demonstrated that a stock pricing model can yield statistically significant differences in parameters when it is estimated across geographical subsectors of an industry.

The purpose of this section has been both to show the necessity of finding homogeneous groups of observations and to demonstrate that one particular grouping (specifically that based on SIC industrial classification) is not an appropriate grouping for all purposes. The grouping of observations that is appropriate for any study depends on the objective of the study and the nature of the process under investigation. One must first decide on why one wants homogeneous groups, and then with that objective in mind select a variable or group of variables with respect to which homogeneity is desired. For example, in seeking a group of firms which are homogeneous with respect to business risk, one might well be content to find firms which have had the same amount of variation in past operating earnings.[9] This, rather than industrial classification, should be the basis of grouping.

In the next section of this paper we will discuss the way homogeneous groups of observations can be formed once a set of variables with which homogeneity is desired has been selected. We will then present a case study that illustrates the improvement in forecasting ability which can be obtained through the use of grouping techniques.

AN ALTERNATIVE METHOD OF FORMING HOMOGENEOUS GROUPS

An alternative to grouping on the basis of traditional industries is to group on the basis of a variable or set of variables which are deemed relevant for the problem under study. If N variables are chosen as relevant for grouping, each firm can be viewed as a point in N-dimensional space. The distance between firms can be measured by simple Euclidean Distance and firms grouped according to their distance from other points.[10] This grouping can be accomplished by using cluster analysis which in its present state of development consists of a group of heuristics for partitioning points in N-dimensional space into groups. The clustering algorithm used in this study combines points which are close together in

[9] Assuming such variation is a proxy for the basic uncertainty associated with earnings.
[10] We will take up the problem of using Euclidean Distance in the unadjusted N-dimensional space shortly.

order to minimize the sum of the squared distance between each point and its group centroid.[11]

In order for this process to yield reasonable groupings, the method of measuring interpoint distances in the N-dimensional space must be meaningful.

If we locate all firms in N-dimensional space and clustered on the basis of the Euclidean Distance between firms, then the groups that would result would depend on the scale of the orginal variables and the extent of their orthogonality. For example, the squared distance between two points is:

$$D_{jk}^2 = \sum_{i=1}^{N} (P_{ji} - P_{ki})^2 \tag{1}$$

where

D_{jk} is the Euclidean Distance between firms j and k
P_{ji} is the value of variable i for firm j

If two variables P_1 and P_2 are perfectly correlated, then it is obvious from (1) that their influence is counted first as $P_{j1} - P_{k1}$ and then as $P_{j2} - P_{k2}$ or double counted. The greater the correlation of P_1 with other variables, the greater the effect of the common influence.

Further, from (1) it is obvious that the scale of the data influences the distance measure. If each P_{j1} is in units of 1000s rather than 1,000,000s, then the influence of P_{j1} is 1000 fold higher.

Unfortunately, in most economic problems, the variables are multi-collinear and the scaling of the variables is arbitrary. It would be very un-desirable if multicollinearity and the scaling of variables affected final groupings.

Fortunately, a technique exists for decomposing a set of variables (axes) into a new set of variables that are both orthogonal and insensitive to the unit of original measurement. The first step is to perform a principal components analysis of the correlation matrix of the raw data. This produces a new set of variables (axes) which are a linear transformation of the original variables and which are uncorrelated with each other. The new variables (axes) are ordered by their ability to account for the original joint variation in the data. That is, the first principal component explains the greatest amount of variation of the original data. These new variables now define an N-dimensional space in terms of orthogonal directions.[12]

The value of any new variable for any firm can be found by simply multiplying the relevant factor loadings times the normalized value of the origi-

[11] Other objective functions assumed are maximization of the squared distance between group centroids and the minimization of average squared distance between all points within a group. These are equivalent to the one in the text. See Friedman and Rubin (11) and Elton and Gruber (8) for proofs of the equivalence. Also see Elton and Gruber (8) for a discussion of clustering techniques which assume different objective functions.

[12] One may use the information produced by the principal components analysis to decrease the dimensionality of the space in which firms are examined. The first P components where $P < N$ may explain so much of the original variation (e.g., 99 percent or more) that one is willing to assume that these P dimensions capture the relevant differences between firms.

nal variables for the firm.[13] By repeating this procedure for each new variable, we can locate any firm in an orthogonal N-dimensional space.

However, the distances defined in the principal components space will still be determined by the amount of correlation in the original data, despite the fact that the space is defined in terms of orthogonal dimensions. The variance of the values of any new variable will be a function of the ability of that component to account for the original joint variation in the data. The more highly correlated the original variables, the better a particular component can account for original variance, and so the larger the inter-point distances will be in that dimension. This again would result in the double counting of correlated variables and is likely to lead to the overpowering of important firm differences. To overcome this problem, one need only divide each new variable by its standard deviation (eigen value) across all firms.[14] This will produce a set of firm measurements and differences which are both insensitive to the correlation and scale of the original variables and so can be used to group firms.[15]

FORECASTING EARNINGS — AN APPLICATION

This section of the paper illustrates the application of grouping techniques to a particular problem and shows that these techniques can improve forecasting ability. The particular problem we chose to study was the forecasting of earnings per share for industrial corporations.

This problem was selected for several reasons:

1. Almost every valuation and cost of capital model reported in the literature employs an earnings or earnings growth variable.[16] Furthermore, the results of these models have proven to be extremely sensitive to the way the earnings or growth variable was defined.
2. We had already explored a series of more naive techniques for forecasting earnings per share and so a bench mark existed against which to judge the results of this study.
3. We felt that the determinants (forecasts) of earnings per share were not homogeneous across all companies and improvement in forecasts would result from the substitution of statistical grouping techniques for groupings based on final product.

The first steps which had to be taken in the study were the selection of criteria with respect to which we wished our groups to be homogeneous and the

---

[13] There is one set of factor loadings for each new variable.

[14] This procedure can be simplified by dividing the eigen vectors by the eigen values before computing factor scores. For more rigorous proof of the analysis in this section see Farrar (10).

[15] If all adjusted principal components are used to group firms, one can pick up and misinterpret large amounts of random noise from the last few components (which usually explain very little of the variance in the original data). To overcome this problem, one will usually use a number of principal components, which is smaller than the number of variables included in the analysis. There is no optimum way to decide on the number of components to use and the ultimate justification for our choice must rest with the usefulness of our results.

[16] Benishay (3), Gordon (13), Gruber (14), M & M (17), Wippern (19).

selection of a set of variables which could be used to forecast earnings per share within each group.

These are not really independent problems. We felt that earnings per share could be forecast by relating the change in earnings per share to corporate variables. The list of variables we used is included in Appendix B. In general, this list includes measure of the type and size of sources of funds (e. g., 1, 2, 3, 4), measures of uses of funds (e. g., 11, 12), measures of profitability (e. g., 14, 20), measures of historical growth rates (e. g., 15, 16, 17), and measures of liquidity (e. g., 6, 7, 18). While these variables should in general be good predictors of earnings per share the way in which different firms responded to change in any variable might differ. For example, a decrease in profitability for a firm with a cyclical earning pattern may mean a very different thing than a decrease in profitability for a firm which has demonstrated a steady growth in earnings.

We wanted to place firms into groups which had had the same earnings growth patterns over time. This was done because we felt that if firms have demonstrated the same pattern of growth over time (management reacted the same way to changes in economic conditions), then differences in such things as profitability or liquidity would be likely to trigger the same reaction on management's part and so have the same effect on future earnings.

Having decided on the variables to use in forming homogeneous groups for the purpose of forecasting, the next step was to design our basic sample.

The sample could have been formed by simply randomly selecting a predetermined number of firms.[17] However, it was desirable to have a large sample of firms from each of several traditional industries so that (a) the dispersion of firms from traditional industries across our homogenoeus groups could be studied, and (b) we could compare forecasts based on assuming each traditional industry is a homogeneous group with forecasts based on our pseudo-industries (statistically homogeneous groups). To accomplish this stratified sampling was employed.[18] We selected nine large four digit industry classifications at random from among those included on the compustat tape and included all firms with a suitable history from each of these traditional industries.[19] Sixty-one additional firms were then selected at random from the compustat tape. These firms were included so that we could examine whether they would cluster with traditional industries or segments of traditional industries, or whether they would remain as outliers. Our final sample consisted of 180 firms representing 44 industries. Our sample classified by both traditional and pseudo-industry is presented in Appendix A.

The next step in the study was to find homogeneous groups of firms. Annual growth rates in earnings per share were computed using earnings data for the

---

[17] Our universe is biased in favor of large firms since we restrict it to firms included on the compustat tape.

[18] All firms for which the compustat service did not record earnings in one or more years from 1953 to 1966 or which reported negative earnings from 1953 to 1962 were eliminated from the sample. This was done so that the final results could be compared with the outcome from mechanical techniques reported in an earlier paper (9). This also biases our sample in favor of large stable firms.

[19] This meant that the probability of a firm being selected in the first part of our sample was a fraction of the number of firms in the industry to which it belonged.

years 1948–1963.[20] This gave us 15 growth rates for each of our 180 companies. Principal components analysis was then performed on the correlation matrix of the raw data. The results of the principal components analysis is repeated in Appendix C. As can be seen from the eigen values in Appendix C, the first 11 principal components accounted for 84 percent of the variation of the raw data while the next 4 only accounted for 16 percent. The decision was made to cluster the data in terms of 11 orthogonal axes (principal components).[21] Each principal component was then standardized by dividing its factor loading by the standard deviation of the factor scores on that component (the square root of its eigen value) and principal component scores were calculated for each firm in terms of the standardized principal component. We now had a score for each firm on each of 11 standardized principal components. We viewed each of the 180 firms as a point in 11 dimensional orthogonal space and employed clustering techniques to group them in terms of Euclidean distance. Specifically we grouped firms by sequentially combining a firm (or a previously formed group) with the firm or group to which it was closest in terms of Euclidean distance. This sequential process was continued until further aggregation involved a "large" change in within group distances. At this point, there were 10 groups. The composition of the groups we obtained are presented in Appendix A.

THE FORECAST PROCEDURE

Having obtained pseudo-industries we are now ready to examine the usefulness of these groupings for forecasting purposes and to answer the specific question, "Do these grouping techniques yield better forecasts than aggregation along traditional industry lines?"

The first step in the experimental design was to select the method for forecasting earnings per share within each group. The specific procedure adopted involved running a cross sectional step-wise regression within each group and using the regression equations to estimate future earnings. In running the regression the dependent variable was defined as the change in earnings between the end of 1960 and 1961 while the independent variables were those presented in Appendix B calculated as of the end of 1960. Independent variables were added to the regression until no excluded variables were statistically significant at the 1 percent level.[22]

After establishing the parameters of the regression equation we forecast the value of earnings for 1964. This forecast was prepared by calculating the

[20] Data for the years 1964, 1965, 1966 were not used in the analysis for the clustering patterns obtained are to be used to test forecast accuracy for these years.

[21] The decision as to how many of the principal components to preserve must to some extent be arbitrary. Preserving all components standardized to unit variance would pick up and magnify the large amount of random fluctuations contained in the last few principal components. Using too few principal components will ignore important dimensions of the original data.

[22] Alternative procedures might be used for establishing the best forecasting equations. However, since our emphasis is on establishing the usefulness of pseudo-industries and since a large number of forecasting equations had to be established for pseudo-industries (10) and for traditional industries (9), we felt such a procedure was justified.

value of the independent variables as of 1963 substituting in the regression equations discussed above, and adding the estimated change in earnings to the actual earnings for 1963.[23]

The next step was to select a procedure for comparing forecast techniques. It was desirable both to select an external criterion against which our forecasts could be prepared and to set up a procedure for analyzing the statistical significance of results.

In an earlier study (9) the authors compared nine techniques for forecasting earnings using mechanical extrapolation techniques against each other and against analysts' estimates.[24] The results of this study showed that one technique dominated the other mechanical techniques at a statistically significant level. Furthermore the performance of this technique, an exponentially weighted moving average with an arithmetic trend, could not be differentiated from the performance of the security analysts at the three large financial institutions studied.[25] Forecasts using this technique should be a useful bench mark against which to judge the performance of our within group regression.

In order to measure differences in the performance of our three forecasting techniques (the exponentially weighted moving average with an arithmetic trend, regressions within traditional industries, and regressions within pseudo industries) we examined the frequency functions of the differences in the squared error between various pairs of forecasts. As an example, consider the determination of the frequency function used to compare the exponential with the regression within traditional industries. One observation determining this frequency function would be the squared error in the exponentially weighted forecast for company A minus the squared error for the regression forecast for company A. When we repeated this for all possible companies we have one frequency function from which we can judge the comparative performance of the two forecasting techniques. If the frequency function had all positive or all negative values, then this would indicate that one technique always had a lower

[23] The question may arise as to why we estimated earnings for 1964 rather than for 1962. Most of the independent variables used in our regressions were constructed in terms of three year averages of data (in order to dump out random fluctuations). If we had recalculated the independent variables as of 1961 in order to forecast for 1962, two out of three of the observations used in constructing the independent variables would be the same as those used in running the regression. To avoid this problem the period ending in 1963 was used in defining the independent variables. If this gap in time introduces a bias it should increase the inaccuracy of our regression results rather than work in favor of our results.

[24] The sample for this earlier study was identical to the sample used in this study. The nine forecasts were prepared in the following manner:
(1) The previous year's earnings plus the previous year's change in earnings.
(2) A four year moving average.
(3) A moving average of optimum length.
(4) A linear regression on time.
(5) A log linear regression on time.
(6) An exponentially weighted moving average with an arithmetic growth trend.
(7) An exponentially weighted moving average with a geometric growth trend.
(8) The same as (6) except an arithmetic growth in the trend was added.
(9) The same as (7) except a geometric growth in the trend was added.

[25] See (9) for a fuller description of the results and a detailed description of the procedures used to determine optimum weights for the exponential weighing.

squared error than a second technique and that dominance existed. Given the size of our sample, this would be unlikely to occur. What could and did happen is that some frequency functions had mostly postive or negative values and had a mean significantly different from zero. When the mean is significantly different from zero, we can state that it is highly unlikely that the techniques being compared forecasted equally well, and we will say that one technique is dominated by a second.[26]

The first comparisons we made were over all firms for which we had either type of within-industry forecast. Since neither the classifications by SIC industrial code or by pseudo-industries included all firms in our sample, (nor did the two classifications include the same firms), we could not directly compare pseudo-industry forecasts with forecasts using SIC industrial classifications. Instead we compared forecasts based on regressions within traditional industry groupings against mechanical forecasts for the same firms and forecasts based on regressions within our pseudo-industries against mechanical forecasts for these firms.[27]

TABLE 1

Forecasting techniques being compared	Mean difference in squared error* a-b	Standard error of mean	Significance level of the mean difference
a. Forecasts based on traditional industry groupings	.8366	.2360	1%
b. Mechanical forecasts			
a. Forecasts based on pseudo industries	–.0907	.0445	5%
b. Mechanical forecasts			

* If the number is negative, technique *a* dominates technique *b*.

The results of this are shown in Table 1. The forecast prepared using regression analysis within pseudo-industries outperforms the mechanical forecast at the 5 percent level of significance. On the other hand the forecast prepared using regression analysis within traditional industries is outperformed by the mechanical technique at the .1 percent level. The results indicate the dominance of pseudo-industry forecasts over both mechanical forecasts and forecasts prepared on the basis of traditional industries.

There is some possibility that these results arose because of differences in the pattern of earnings between firms which were selected as members of psudo-industries and firms which were members of traditional industries. For example, mechanical techniques might just work better for those firms that are

[26] From the central limit theorem we can state that the distribution of the mean of our frequency functions is normally distributed with mean equal to the mean of the frequency function and standard deviation equal to the standard deviation of the frequency function divided by the square root of the number of observations. That the frequency functions under question were derived from differencing two variables should not bother the reader. The central limit theorem states that as the number of observations increases, the distribution of the mean is normally distributed no matter what the original frequency function.

[27] Only SIC industries and pseudo-industries with 5 or more firms were included in preparing forecasts. Extremely small industries would not allow enough degrees of freedom for the regression analysis.

members of traditional industries than they do for those firms that are not members of traditional industries but are members of psuedo-industries. To avoid this possibility tests were repeated on only those firms which had been grouped as members of both traditional and pseudo-industries.[28]

TABLE 2

Forecasting techniques being compared	Mean difference in squared error	Standard error of mean	Significance level of the mean difference
a. Forecasts based on traditional industry groupings *b.* mechanical forecasts	.8862	.2546	.1%
a. Forecasts based on pseudo industries *b.* mechanical forecasts	–.1185	.0692	10%
a. Forecasts based on pseudo industries *b.* Forecasts based on traditional industry groupings	–1.0047	.2549	.1%

The results (reported in Table 2) once again support the dominance of forecasts based on pseudo-industries. Forecasts based on pseudo-industries were statistically better than forecasts based on traditional industries at the .1 percent level and forecasts based on the mechanical model at the 10 percent level. Once again the mechanical technique dominates forecasts built on traditional industries at the .1 percent level.

When the data were decomposed and forecasts prepared by each of the three methods examined for each traditional industry, the forecasts based on pseudo-industries outperformed the forecasts based on traditional industries for 8 out of the 9 traditional industries with the one reversal not being statistically significant.[29]

[28] The sample of firms that are included in both groups consists of 98 firms as seen from Appendix A.

[29] It is interesting to note the extent to which traditional industries are rearranged among pseudo-industries. Below we have noted the SIC number of the traditional industry, the number of firms in our sample from that industry, and the number of pseudo-industries into which the traditional industry split.

Traditional industry number	Number of firms in each industry	Number of pseudo-industries among which the traditional industry is split
2800	21	7
2830	15	2
2912	16	5
3000	5	3
3310	15	7
3400	4	4
3550	7	4
3560	8	3
3714	7	4

CONCLUSION

In this paper we have:

1. Discussed the need to disaggregate economic data into meaningful groups in order to both better understand and predict economic phenomena.
2. Presented a technique which can be used to partition observations into groups which are homogeneous with respect to a predetermined set of criteria.
3. Demonstrated that this technique can lead to better estimates of earnings per share than a grouping based on SIC industrial classifications. In addition the forecasts based on our statistical groupings were shown to outperform mechanical extrapolation techniques which we had previously shown perform about as well as security analysts.

REFERENCES

1. ARDITTI, F.D., "Risk and the Required Return on Equity," *Journal of Finance* XXII (March, 1967) pp. 19–36.
2. BARGES, A., *The Effect of Capital Structure on the Cost of Capital,* Englewood Cliffs, New Jersey: Prentice-Hall, Inc., 1963.
3. BENISHAY, H., *Determinants of Variability in Earnings Price Ratios of Corporate Equities,* Ph. D. Thesis, Chicago, Illinois: University of Chicago, School of Business Administration, 1960.
4. BREEN, W., "Low Price-Earnings Ratios and Industry Relatives," *Financial Analyst Journal,* Vol. 24, No. 4, July/August 1968, pp. 125–127.
5. COHEN, K. and ELTON, E., "Inter-Temporal Portfolio Analysis Based on Simulation of Joint Returns," *Management Science,* Vol. 14, No. 1 (1967), pp. 5–18.
6. COHEN, K. and POGUE, I., "An Empirical Evaluation of Alternative Portfolio Selection Models," *Journal of Business,* Vol 40, No. 1 (1967), pp. 166–193.
7. DURAND, D., "Bank Stock Prices and the Bank Capital Problem," *National Bureau of Economic Research Occasional Paper #54,* New York: National Bureau of Economic Research, 1957.
8. ELTON, E. and GRUBER, M., "Homogeneous Groups and the Testing of Economic Hypotheses, "*Journal of Financial and Quantitative Analysis,* Vol IV, January 1970, pp. 581–602.
9. ELTON, E. and GRUBER, M., "Earnings Forecasters and Expectational Data," *Management Science,* forthcoming.
10. FARRAR, D., "Multivariate Measures of Profile Similarity for the Objective Stratification of Econometric Data," Working Paper, Alfred P. Sloan School of Management, M.I.T.
11. FRIEDMAN, H. P. and RUBIN, J., "On Some Invariant Criteria for Grouping Data," *Journal of American Statistical Association,* Vol. 62, 1967, pp. 1159–1178.
12. FRIEND, I., and PUCKETT, M., "Dividends and Stock Prices," *American Economic Review,* Vol. LIV, September 1964, pp. 656–682.
13. GORDON, M., *The Investment, Financing, and Valuation of the Corporation,* Homewood, Illinois: Richard D. Irwin, Inc., 1962.
14. GRUBER, MARTIN, *The Determinants of Common Stock Prices* (College Park, Pennsylvania: Center for Research, Pennsylvania State University), 1971.
15. KEENAN, M., *Toward a Positive Theory of Equity Valuation,* Ph.D. Thesis, Carnegie Institute of Technology, 1967.
16. KING, BENJAMIN F., "Market and Industry Factors in Stock Price Behavior," *Journal of Business,* Vol. 39 (special supplement January, 1966) pp. 139–190.

17. MODIGLIANI, F. and MILLER, M., "The Cost of Capital, Corporation Finance, and the Theory of Investment," *American Economic Review* (June 1958), pp. 261–297.
18. SHARPE, W., "A Simplified Model for Portfolio Analyis, " *Management Science,* Vol. 9, No. 2 (January 1963), pp. 277–293.
19. WIPPERN, RONALD, "Financial Structure and the Value of the Firm," *Journal of Finance,* Vol. 21 (December 1966), pp. 615–633.

APPENDIX A

Standard industrial classification code		Pseudo-industry	Name of company
		Chemicals	
2800	006900	p6	Air Reduction Co.
2800	013000	p2	Allied Chemical Corp.
2800	021900	p6	American Cyanamid Co.
2800	053841		Atlas Chemical Industries Inc.
2800	131500	p5	Celanese Corp.
2800	144244		Chemetron Corp.
2800	171700	p7	Commercial Solvents Corp.
2800	215701	p2	Diamond Shamrock Corp.
2800	225000	p4	Dow Chemical
2800	229300	p3	Dupont, E. I. De Nemours & Co.
2800	236400	p3	Eastman Kodak Co.
2800	281740	p4	FMC Corp.
2800	351700	p4	Hercules Inc.
2800	359900	p4	Hooker Chemical Co.
2800	381200	p3	Interchemical
2800	413600	p8	Koppers Co.
2800	443000	p4	Mac Andrews and Forbes
2800	482800	p3	Minnesota Mining & Manufacturing Co.
2800	491010	p4	Monsanto Company
2800	512900	p5	National Lead Co.
2800	588500	p1	Pittsburgh Plate Glass Co.
2800	627900	p3	Rohm/Haas Co.
2800	734100	p6	Union Carbide Corp.
		Drugs	
2830	026000	p3	American Home Products Corp.
2830	091000	p4	Bristol-Myers Company
2830	313600	p3	Gillette Co.
2830	397700	p4	Johnson/Johnson
2830	406300	p4	Kendall Co.
2830	471000	p4	Merck & Company
2830	479000	p3	Miles Laboratories Inc.
2830	543200	p3	Norwich Pharmacal Co.
2830	565800	p4	Parke, Davis & Co.
2830	579000	p4	Pfizer Uchasco & Coct Inc.
2830	591800	p3	Plough Inc.
2830	619550	p3	Richardson-Merrell Inc.
2830	648000	p3	Searle G. D. Co.

Standard industrial classification code	Pseudo-industry	Name of company
2830 665500	p3	Smith Kline/French Laboratories Inc.
2830 693600	p4	Sterling Drug Inc.

Machinery Specialty

3550 028100		American Machine & Foundry Co.
3550 079300	p2	Black and Decker Manufacturing Co.
3550 089200	p1	Briggs/Stratton
3550 195800		Crompton Knowles Corp.
3550 252200	p1	Ex-Cell-O Corp.
3550 399200		Joy Manufacturing Co.
3550 477470	p6	Midland Ross Corp.
3550 555300	p4	Otis Elevator Co.
3550 555700	p1	Outboard Marine Corp.
3550 746200	p4	United Shoe Machinery Corp.

Machinery Industrial

3560 021000	p6	American Chain & Cable Co. Inc.
3560 081700	p2	Blaw-Knox Co.
3560 147700	p2	Chicago Pneumatic Tool Co.
3560 294800	p2	Gardner-Denver Co.
3560 378400	p2	Ingersoll-Rand Co.
3560 471900	p4	Mesta Machine Co.

Automobile Suppliers

3714 085100	p10	Borg-Warner Corporation
3714 159700	p6	Clevite Corp.
3714 203800	p6	Dana Corporation
3714 237236	p10	Eaton Yale and Towne Inc.
3714 259600	p4	Federal Mogul Corp.
3714 406000	p10	Kelsey Hayes Co.
3714 718900	p9	Timken Roller Bearing Co.

Oils

2912 053377	p8	Atlantic Richfield Co.
2912 152800	p2	Cities Service Co.
2912 187700	p4	Continental Oil Co.
2912 373250	p5	Imperial Oil Ltd.
2912 407900		Kerr McGee Corp.
2912 452180	p2	Marathon Oil
2912 583700	p4	Phillips Petroleum Co.
2912 606500	p6	Quaker State Oil Refining
2912 656500	p2	Shell Oil Co.
2912 659300	p2	Signal Oil Gas Co.
2912 662800	p2	Sinclair Oil Corp.
2912 686300	p2	Standard Oil Co. Indiana
2912 686700	p7	Standard Oil Co. Ohio
2912 699600	p2	Sun Oil Co.
2912 701220	p2	Sunray DX Oil Co.
2912 736700	p2	Union Oil Co. of California

Standard industrial classification code		Pseudo-industry	Name of company
		Tire and Rubber	
3000	047430	p4	Armstrong Rubber
3000	266300	p2	Firestone Tire and Rubber Co.
3000	317900	p4	Goodrich B. F. Co.
3000	318100	p5	Goodyear Tire & Rubber Co.
3000	738651	p2	Uniroyal, Inc.
		Steels	
3310	011600	p9	Allegheny Ludlum Steel Corp.
3310	046800	p7	Armco Steel Corp.
3310	076700	p7	Bethlehem Steel Corp.
3310	127400	p1	Carpenter Steel Co.
3310	187900	p4	Continental Steel Corp
3310	189500	p10	Copperweld Steel.
3310	214000		Detroit Steel Corp.
3310	322500	p9	Granite City Steel Co.
3310	378800	p7	Inland Steel Co.
3310	381710	p10	Interlake Steel Co.
3310	409600		Keystone Steel Wire Co. Delaware
3310	441200	p6	Lukens Steel Co.
3310	464750	p9	McLouth Steel Corp
3310	616800	p7	Republic Steel Corp.
3310	655400		Sharon Steel Corp.
3310	692700	p2	Steel Company of Canada
3310	752200	p7	U. S. Steel Corp.
3310	801700	p9	Youngstown Sheet & Tube Co.
		Machinery Fabricating	
3400	073200	p10	Belden Corp.
3400	252000		Eversharp Inc.
3400	298300	p2	General Cable Corp.
3400	516300	p6	National Standard Co.
3400	659900	p4	Signode Corp.
		Other Firms	
1042	358930	p1	Homestake Mining
1311	016400	p2	Amerada Petroleum Corp.
1311	663600	p2	Skelly Oil Co.
1311	702300	p2	Superior Oil Co.
2000	405900	p3	Kellogg Company
2052	349910	p4	Helme Products
2063	016100	p4	Amalgamated Sugar Co.
2121	298700	p2	General Cigar Co., Inc.
2200	164400		Collins Aikman Corp.
2510	226200	p4	Drexel Enterprises
2600	644600	p3	Scott Paper Co.
2700	462200	p5	McCall Corporation
2844	057610	p3	Avon Products
2899	188091	p4	Conwood Corp.
2899	232728		Eagle Picher Industries

Standard industrial classification code		Pseudo-industry	Name of company
2899	263000	p4	Ferro Corp.
2899	503230	p3	Nalco Chemical Co.
2912	048900	p2	Ashland Oil Refinery
2950	279100	p6	Flintkote Co.
3241	466600	p3	Medusa Portland Cement Co.
3321	133800	p7	Central Foundry Co.
3430	195000		Crane Company
3511	059000	p5	Babcock & Wilcox Co.
3511	169700	p4	Combustion Engineering, Inc.
3522	014600	p6	Allis Chalmers Manufacturing Co.
3522	383300	p6	International Harvester Co.
3522	788800	p3	Wickes Corp
3531	131000	p5	Caterpillar Tractor Co.
3531	156800	p10	Clark Equipment Co.
3531	617760	p6	Rex Chainbelt
3533	225900	p2	Dresser Industries, Inc.
3533	336700	p5	Halliburton Company
3540	151600		Cincinnati Milling Machine Co.
3540	488200		Monarch Machine Tool Co.
3540	504400	p1	National Acme Co.
3540	663900	p4	Skil Corp.
3540	701100		Sunstrand Corp.
3540	768800		Warner & Swasey
3569	694600	p6	Stewart Warner Corp.
3569	704900		Symington Wayne Corp.
3570	004000	p4	Addressograph-Multigraph
3570	382700	p3	International Business Machines Corp.
3570	507600	p4	National Cash Register Co.
3570	587000	p3	Pitney-Bowes Inc.
3570	798830		Xerox Corp.
3600	299800	p4	General Electric Co.
3600	359025	p3	Honeywell Inc.
3600	386100	p4	International Telephone & Telegraph
3600	608100	p6	Radio Corporation of America
3600	784700		Westinghouse Electric Corp.
3610	244900	p8	Emerson Electric Co.
3610	316200	p6	Globe Union Inc.
3610	463600	p1	McGraw-Edison Co.
3610	545800	p2	Ohio Brass Co.
3610	614500	p2	Reliance Elec Engineering
3622	202300	p2	Culter-Hammer Inc.
3622	624500	p4	Robertshaw Controls
3622	683500	p2	Square D Company
3630	461000	p4	Maytag Co.
3630	563100		Packard Bell Electronics
3630	662900	p2	Singer Co.
3670	253900		Fairchild Camera & Instrument Corp.
3670	305610	p2	General Signal Co.
3679	369705		IRC Inc.
3679	447500	p6	Mallory P R Co.
3679	682600	p1	Sprague Electric Co.

Standard industrial classification code		Pseudo-industry	Name of company
3711	303010	p1	General Motors Corp.
3713	199900	p6	Cummins Engine
3713	291100		Fruehauf Corp.
3713	787000	p9	White Motors Co.
3725	586900		Piper Aircraft Corp.
3811	039080	p2	Ametex Inc.
3811	131900	p8	Cenco Instruments
3811	627000	p6	Rockwell Manufacturing Co.
3999	338600	p5	Hammond Corp.
3999	386000		International Silver Co.
3999	628700		Ronson Corp.
3999	724300	p8	Torrinton Co. M.E

APPENDIX B

Variables*

1. $$\frac{\text{Debt } (t) - \text{Debt } (t - 1)}{\text{Total assets } (t\text{-}1)}$$

2. $$\frac{\text{Equity } (t) - \text{Equity } (t - 1) - \text{Retained earnings } (t)}{\text{Total assets } (t - 1)}$$

3. $$\frac{\text{Retained earnings } (t)}{\text{Total assets } (t - 1)}$$

4. $$\frac{\text{Preferred stock } (t) - \text{Preferred stock } (t -)}{\text{Total assets } (t - 1)}$$

5. $$\frac{\text{Depreciation } (t)}{\text{Total assets } (t - 1)}$$

6. $$\frac{\text{Cash } (t)}{\text{Current Liabilities } (t)}$$

7. $$\frac{\frac{\text{Receivables } (t) + \text{Receivables } (t - 1)}{2}}{\text{Sales } (t)}$$

8. $$\frac{\text{Long term debt } (t)}{\text{Market value stock } (t)}$$

9. $$\frac{\text{Long term debt } (t) - \text{Long term debt } (t - 1)}{\text{Market value stock } (t) - \text{Market value stock } (t - 1)}$$

10. $$\frac{\text{Preferred } (t)}{\text{Market value common } (t)}$$

11. $$\frac{\text{Total dividends } (t)}{\text{Earnings available } (t) + \text{Depreciation } (t)}$$

12. $$\frac{\text{Captial Expenditure } (t)}{\text{Change in total assets } (t) - (t - 1)}$$

13. Total assets (t)

* All variables except 15, 16, 17, 19 and 21 are defined as three year averages of the definition given above. The values of t in establishing the regression equation for 1961 were 1958, 1959, and 1960. The value for t when preparing the forecast for 1964 were 1961, 1962, and 1963.

14. $$\frac{\text{Operating income }(t)}{\text{Long term debt }(t) + \text{Preferred }(t) + \text{Book common }(t)}$$

15. 5 year average growth in earnings per share

16. 5 year average growth in sales per share

17. 5 year average of the product of retention rate and the rate of return on common equity

18. $$\frac{\text{Cash }(t)}{\text{Total assets }(t)}$$

19. STD Deviation of growth in earning over 5 years

20. $$\frac{\text{Operating income }(t)}{\text{Net sales }(t)}$$

21. Growth in market price 5 years

22. $$\frac{\text{Current liabilities }(t) - \text{Current liabilities }(t-1)}{\text{Total assets }(t-1)}$$

23. $$\frac{\text{Total assets }(t) - \text{Total assets }(t-1)}{\text{Total assets }(t-1)}$$

APPENDIX C - PRINCIPAL COMPONENT ANALYSIS

Principal component number	1	2	3	4	5	6	7	8
Eigen value	2.006	1.774	1.604	1.409	1.115	1.043	.985	.956

Principal component number	9	10	11	12	13	14	15
Eigen value	.867	.779	.664	.571	.452	.402	.375

C. Relationship of Financial Data to Security Prices
Bond Valuation

*Telser concentrates on one determinant of debt yield—time to maturity
—for analytical treatment. He is concerned with comparing evidence
which has been compiled on the two most widely accepted theories of
the term structure of interest rates: the expectations theory and the
liquidity preference theory. The first theory assumes that interest rates
for securities of different maturities depend solely on expectations as to
future interest rates. The second theory assumes that longer maturities
must offer a premium as compensation for the increased risk of price
fluctuations. Telser reviews a large amount of theoretical and empirical
work to add depth and perspective to the alternative theories.*

*The resolution of the conflict contained in these theories is
important, for it affects the formulation of full-scale bond-pricing
models [see Fisher (5)] and stock-pricing models [see Gordon (7) and
Malkiel (8)].*

5

A Critique of Some Recent Empirical Research on the Explanation of the Term Structure of Interest Rates

*L.G. Telser**

This article is reprinted with permission from the Journal of Political
Economy, *Vol. 75, No. 4, Part 2 (August, 1967), 546–561.*

INTRODUCTION

My purpose is to analyze the relevance of recent empirical research on the
term structure of interest rates in choosing among competing theories of the
determinants of the term structure. In particular, two theories have been the
subject of serious consideration. The first, known as the expectations theory,
asserts that spot interest rates of loans of different maturities depend solely on
market expectations of future interest rates. The current-term structure forecasts
the later term structure. The rival theory, known as the liquidity preference
theory, denies that the current term structure provides unbiased forecasts of
subsequent interest rates. Adherents of this theory claim that the risk aversion
of lenders makes them value the stability of principal more than the stability of

* I am grateful to Merton H. Miller for helpful discussion on this topic. I also wish to
thank Dave Fand, Harry Johnson, Bert Malkiel, and the members of the Money Workshop of the University of Chicago for their comments and criticisms. Responsibility for
all errors is mine.

income. Principal is impaired if there is an unforeseen rise in interest rates while the stability of income is reduced from a policy of successively lending a given principal for short time periods. Supporters of the liquidity premium theory conclude that as a result long-term interest rates normally exceed short-term rates. Therefore, forecasts of future rates embodied in the present term structure systematically overestimate the spot rates that materialize. It should be noted that this form of risk has nothing to do with the chance of borrowers' default; liquidity preference would exist even if bonds were guaranteed against default.

One would think that cash is the most liquid of all assets since, abstracting from changes in the price level, the principal is literally fixed. However, to explain why firms hold cash instead of lending on call, it is unnecessary to rely on a liquidity preference theory. In fact, if transactions costs were zero, then lending on call would be preferable to holding cash. Hence the holding of cash is explained by the fact that transactions costs are not zero. Therefore, transactions costs are one of the determinants of interest rates particularly important on loans of the shortest maturity. However, as far as I know, this is one of the most neglected determinants of the term structure in the formal treatments of the theory. The absence of formal analysis also explains the neglect of this factor in empirical work.

Interpretation of the empirical evidence relies on a careful study of the implications of these two explanations of the term structure. There are at least three sources of contention. First, universal risk aversion of both borrowers and lenders does not constrain the term structure in the way described by the liquidity preference theory. Risk aversion does not imply that forecasts of future interest rates are biased upward rather than downward. For example a lender can increase his risk by purchasing short-term bonds if he has long-term payment commitments because his receipts would be subject to larger random fluctuations than his payments. Similarly, a borrower can increase his risks by long-term borrowing if he has short-term payment commitments. Risk aversion of both borrowers and lenders implies they will attempt to hedge against the risk of changes in interest rates by financial transactions intended to approximately match the timing of payments and receipts. However, it does not follow that such hedging results in a bias that can be deduced a priori.

Second, it is necessary in empirical work to specify how expectations are revised or formed. This raises the troublesome question of whether the empirical evidence refutes *the* expectations theory somehow defined or some investigator's empirical version of the formation of expectations. These difficulties are heightened by the fact that the market rates of interest reflect individual differences of expectations. Hence there are no obvious criteria that enable scholars to choose among alternative expectations models. Nor is this all.

Third, individuals change their expectations in the course of time. This makes it hard to tell whether a given term structure reflects a set of widely held beliefs about future conditions that would imply higher future interest rates (such as in the 1930's when long-term rates exceeded short-term rates) or the manifestation of liquidity preference. Perhaps expectations of lower interest rates in the future during a long period of prosperity would inspire the construction of the theories of negative liquidity preference because the observed term sturcture would have higher short-term than long-term interest rates.

These three points do not question the assumption of universal risk aversion—an assumption that implies that individuals must be especially compensated for undertaking risky ventures. Yet it is well known that some individuals accept risk without special compensation, and most individuals some of the time expose themselves to risk without special compensation. Nevertheless, even if one accepts the assumption of universal risk aversion, there remains the task of deducing its empirical consequences.

II. THE ARITHMETIC OF THE TERM STRUCTURE

The link between future and present interest rates is inspired by some simple arithmetic relations implied by alternative finance programs involving the purchase and sale of bonds of different maturities. These programs show how to fix the interest rate to be paid for a loan that will commence in the future. Interest rates on such loans are called "forward" rates. An interest rate fixed in the present for a loan that begins at once is a "spot" rate. We now derive the relations between spot and forward interest rates.

To represent the interest rates involved in the pertinent financial programs of purchases and sales of bonds of different maturities, it is necessary to adopt a somewhat cumbersome notation. I shall partly follow prevailing conventions by using R to denote spot rates and r to denote forward rates. For the former, two subscripts are necessary, the first to denote the duration of the loan and the second to give the date on which the interest rate is fixed and the loan begins. An additional subscript is required for a forward rate since the date at which a forward loan can begin comes at any time specified following the time at which the interest rate is determined. Thus for the spot rate, let $R_{n,t} =$ the spot rate on an n-period loan to begin at time t. For forward rates, let $r_{n,t,s} =$ the forward rate for a loan of n periods as determined in period t, the loan to commence at time $s \geq t$. It follows that $R_{n,t} = r_{n,t,t}$.

The term structure of interest rates is the set of spot rates on loans alike in every respect save for their duation. Thus it is the sequence of spot rates as follows: $R_{1,t}, R_{2,t}, R_{3,t}, \ldots, R_{n,t}, \ldots$

One aspect of empirical research into the term structure is the adjustment of the observed interest rates in order to make them comparable in every respect except term to maturity. These adjustments are necessary because bonds can differ in their coupons, call provisions, tax advantages, default risk, eligibility as collateral for special purposes, and so forth. In theoretical analysis it is convenient to asuume that the necessary adjustments have been made so that all bonds of the same maturity are perfect substitutes. In addition, in order to avoid complicated algebra it is convenient to assume that interest is paid at the maturity date of the bonds and that transactions costs are zero.

Analysis of the forecasts of future interest rates implicit in the current term structure begins with consideration of the alternative means of finance afforded by the purchases and sale of bonds of different maturities. Since at time t it is possible to buy and sell bonds of any maturity, one can arrange for loans to begin at some future date at an interest rate presently determined. Thus if a lender at time t wishes to borrow funds for k periods to be delivered at time $t + n$ (and repaid at time $t + n + k$), he can issue a bond that matures at time $t + k + n$ and can lend the proceeds until time $t + n$ by purchasing a bond that matures in time $t + n$. This is equivalent to borrowing for k periods at the forward interest rate $r_{k,t,t+n}$. Assuming that transactions costs are zero, for the forward loan and the two transactions in the spot bonds to have the same present value it is necessary that

$$(1 + r_{k,t,t+n})^k = \frac{(1 + R_{n+k,t})^{n+k}}{(1 + R_{n,t})^n} \tag{1}$$

Formula (1) is due to Keynes (1936, chap. xiii). By means of (1) it is possible to express all spot interest rates in terms of forward interest rates for one-period loans as follows:

$$(1 + R_{n,t})^n = (1 + r_{1,t,t})(1 + r_{1,t,t+1}) \ldots (1 + r_{1,t,t+n-1}) \tag{2}$$

Formula (2) is due to Hicks (1946, p. 145); it gives a canonical form for spot interest rates.[1] There is a similar expression for forward rates on n-period loans in terms of a product of forward rates on one-period loans.

Formula (2) is sometimes (incorrectly) interpreted as an arithmetic tautology without economic content. Its value depends on the possibility that any individual can buy and sell bonds of any maturity without affecting the rates. In other words, to make any sense it must be possible to engage in the kind of arbitrage used in deriving the formula. Thus if such arbitrage is possible, we would not expect any forward interest rates to be negative, although this would be consistent with the arithmetic of (2).[2]

III. THE EXPECTATIONS THEORY

By engaging in an appropriate set of purchases and sales of bonds of various maturities, an individual can borrow or lend for arbitrary periods of time at interest rates presently determined to take effect in the future. These transactions are equivalent to allowing individuals to borrow and lend at forward rates. Alternatively, an individual who wishes funds some time in the future can postpone borrowing until the time comes and then can borrow at the going spot rate. By so doing, he exposes himself to uncertainty about the interest rates that will prevail at the time he wishes the funds. Forward borrowing eliminates uncertainty about future interest rates. The availability of both alternatives suggests that the excess demand for loans depends on $r_{1,t,s}$, the forward rate at time t for delivery of a one-period loan at time $s > t$ and expectations about $R_{1,t+s}$, the spot rate for a one-period loan at time $t + s$.

The expectations theory invents the fiction of a market expectation and claims that the forward rate is the market expectation of the spot rate that will rule in the future. This claim relies on a conceptual experiment. Suppose all individuals expect interest rates to be higher in the future than they are now,

[1] See also Lutz (1940) who credits Irving Fisher. The formulas that apply in case the bond pays a periodic coupon are given by Wallace (1964) and Wonnacott (1962). Wallace also shows that in practice the effect of the coupon is slight.

[2] Kessel (1965) cites an instance in September, 1960, during which for nine days the forward rate was negative.

although all do not necessarily expect the same rise in rates. As a result, lenders would now demand higher long-term rates because there is always the option of lending for a short time now, waiting for the appearance of the higher spot rates, and then buying bonds at the higher rates. This results in driving up long-term spot rates in the present. Conversely, if interest rates are expected to be lower in the future, borrowers would be inclined to borrow short term and wait for the lower rates to materialize in the future. As a result, the long-term interest rates now fall and reflect the expectation of lower rates to come. Thus the market responds to collective beliefs about spot rates that will prevail later on, despite individual differences of expectations.

Everyone agrees that the prevailing interest rates on loans of different maturities are equilibrium prices that clear the market in these debt instruments. To describe these rates in addition as "expectations" does not advance our understanding of the term structure. It is necessary, in addition, to demonstrate some relation between the forward rates and the subsequent spot rates. This leads to an examination of the accuracy of the forecasts provided by the forward rates. Nevertheless, although accurate forecasts would be sufficient for the validity of the expectations theory, they are not necessary since individuals can be prone to sizable errors of prophecy and still choose their actions on the basis of forward rates as expectations of subsequent spot rates.

Among the first to study the predictive accuracy of forward interest rates was Macauley. Before the establishment of the Federal Reserve, there was a pronounced seasonal in the movement of call money rates. Macauley (1938) found that time money rates did anticipate this seasonal. However, he was unable to discover evidence of successful forecasting beyond the seasonal.

Kessel (1965) repeated Macauley's test using twenty-seven-and fifty-five-day bills for the period 1959–61 and confirmed Macauley's findings that the market anticipated the seasonal in these rates.

Hickman (1943) compared the forward rates with spot rates one year hence and found a larger forecasting error than would be obtained by extrapolating the current spot rate to predict the subsequent rate. Neither Meiselman (1962) nor Kessel (1965) confirms his results; both found the current spot rate to be inferior to the forward rate as a predictor.

Kessel gives more recent evidence of forecast accuracy. For the period January, 1959–March, 1962, Kessel (1965, p. 24) compares the forward rates and the subsequent spot rates they are supposed to predict using short-term (up to six months) U.S. Treasury bills. According to his evidence, forward rates are upward-biased forecasters. His charts show that spot rates rose and fell to about their original level for the first third of the sample period and subsequently rose slightly. Moreover, when spot rates were high and rising, forward rates tended to be higher than when spot rates were nearly constant. Thus the forward rates seem to extrapolate the recent movement of spot rates. This finding is important as we shall see below.

There is another kind of somewhat qualitative evidence pertinent to the predictive accuracy of the forward rates that is implied by the cyclical behavior of interest rates. It is well known that interest rates tend to vary directly with business activity. The relation between short and long rates over the business cycle is explained by the market expectations theory in the light of the cyclical behavior of spot rates. Thus when short rates are below long rates at troughs of business activity, the market expects recovery and the rates to rise. Conversely, when short rates exceed long rates at peaks, the market anticipates decline and a fall in rates. Hence the cyclical movement of the spread between short and long rates approximately forecasts the cyclical behavior of spot rates.

In addition, short rates have a larger amplitude over the cycle than long rates. This is consistent with the market expectations theory. Long rates depend on the path of short rates that are expected over the more distant future, while the shorter rates depend on expected spot rates for shorter stretches into the future. Since the long rates represent an average of more short rates and reflect a longer horizon, the long rates should have a smaller cyclical amplitude than the short rates.

Kessel presents data for one-, five-, and twenty-year corporate bonds for the period 1901–61. The graph of interest rates in his Chart 13 approximately confirms the implications of the market expectations theory. The Great Depression, however, stands out as a unique experience. During the Great Depression the short rate remained below the long rate persistently, which implies a continuous expectation of recovery—an event that did not occur until late in the decade of the thirties. Though interest rates did rise a little from the middle of the 1930's, the rise was less than anticipated. The war intervened and with the government price-support program on bonds. Hence it is not until the middle of the 1950's that interest rates returned to the pattern common in the first three decades of the century (Kessel, 1965, p. 79).

Lutz reports the results of a comparison between short and long rates for British data spanning 1825–1938. Omitting the cases in which the two rates were close together, he reports the long rate above the short in 764 months and the short above the long in 580 months. He also reports several periods longer than twenty months in which short rates stood above long rates, and states than the longest stretch for which this occurred is forty-two months. Aside from the Great Depression, the longest stretch for which the long rate exceeded the short rate is forty-four months (Lutz, 1940).

This type of evidence implies that presently quoted forward rates roughly predict the subsequent spot rates. However, the forecast errors are often sizable and persist in one direction. Thus the market expectations implied by the forward rates tend to adjust slowly. In addition, there is some evidence that forward rates are biased forecasts of subsequent spot rates. It is Meiselman's important contribution to propose a precise model of the formation of market expectations and obtain thereby new tests of the theory.

IV. MEISELMAN'S NEW EXPECTATIONS THEORY

Drawing upon the experience of Cagan (1956), who successfully explained the demand for money during hyperinflations with a model of how price expectations are formed, and the subsequent success with which Friedman (1957) explained consumption behavior with a model of permanent income, Meiselman proposed an original hypothesis of how expectations are revised for interest rates. Like the Cagan–Friedman models, Meiselman postulated that market expectations are revised according to the size of the error between the forecast of the spot rate given by the forward interest rate and the spot rate that subsequently appeared. Thus the forecast error in period t, E_t is defined as follows: $E_t = R_{1,t} - r_{1,t-1,t}$. Recall that the first variable on the right side is the spot interest rate on a one-period loan in period t, and the second variable is the forward interest rate as quoted in period $t - 1$ for a loan to begin in period t. According to the market expectations theory, the latter forecasts the former. A measure of the change in expectations for one-period loans to begin in period $t + n$ is $r_{1,t,t+n} - r_{1,t-1,t+n}$. Meiselman (1962) postulates that to a linear approximation there is the following relation between the two:

$$r_{1,t,t+n} - r_{1,t-1,t+n} = a_n + b_n E_t, \qquad n = 1, 2, 3, \ldots \tag{3}$$

I wish to emphasize that although Meiselman's model belongs to the same family of adaptive expectations as the Cagan and Friedman models, he introduces a new feature that exploits the special fact of the market revealing its expectations in the forward rates. Meiselman correctly asserts that this model can say nothing about the *level* of expected interest rates but can only tell how expectations change. Meiselman's expected rates are the forward rates and are not weighted moving averages of past spot rates. Moreover, his model is compatible with a set of different expectations about rates to prevail at different times in the future. Thus his model implies the presence of truly extrapolative terms.

As applied to the formation of interest rate expectations, the Cagan–Friedman model gives

$$R^*_{t-1,t} = c \sum_0^\infty (1 - c)^x R_{t-1-x}, \tag{4}$$

where $R^*_{t-1,t}$, = spot rate expected to rule in period t as of period $t - 1$. Formula (4) can be generalized to show what spot rates are expected in subsequent periods as a function of past spot rates up to period $t - 1$. Moreover, the Cagan–Friedman model implies that

$$R^*_{t-1,t} = R^*_{t-1,t+1} = \ldots = R^*_{t-1,t+n} = \ldots \tag{5}$$

To prove this, observe that

$$R^*_{t-1,t+1} = c[R_t + (1 - c) R_{t-1} + (1 - c)^2 R_{t-2} + \ldots];$$
$$R^*_{t-1,t+2} = c[R_{t+1} + (1 - c)R_t + (1 - c)^2 R_{t-1} + \ldots],$$

and so forth. Since R_t, R_{t+1}, R_{t+2}, . . . are unknown as of period $t - 1$, we replace them by their expected values. This gives

$$R^*_{t-1,t+1} = c[R^*_{t-1,t} + (1 - c)R_{t-1} + (1 - c)^2 R_{t-2} + \ldots];$$
$$R^*_{t-1,t+2} = c[R^*_{t-1,t+1} + (1 - c)R^*_{t-1,t} + (1 - c)^2 R_{t-1} + \ldots].$$

Therefore,

$$R^*_{t-1,t+2} - (1 - c)R^*_{t-1,t+1} = cR^*_{t-1,t+1}$$

. . .

$$R^*_{t-1,t+n} - (1 - c)R^*_{t-1,t+n-1} = cR^*_{t-1,t+n-1},$$

which yields (5).

It is well known that (4) is equivalent to

$$R^*_{t-1,t} - R^*_{t-2,t-1} = c(R_{t-1} - R^*_{t-2,t-1}),$$

or

$$R^*_{t,t+1} - R^*_{t-1,t} = c(R_t - R^*_{t-1,t}). \tag{6}$$

Hence the Cagan–Friedman model is a hypothesis about the *level* of expectations, while the Meiselman model is a hypothesis about how expectations are *revised,* which does not give implications about the level of interest rates without additional assumptions. If forward rates are substituted for expected spot rates in (6), we obtain

$$r_{t,t+1} - r_{t-1,t} = cE_t. \tag{7}$$

This equation should be compared with (3) for $n = 1$.

The Cagan–Friedman expectations model applied to interest rates implies an asymptotically flat yield curve. This follows from (5), the substitution of forward for expected rates, and from (2). Thus from (2).

$$\log(1 + R_{n,t}) = (1/n) \sum_{j=0}^{n-1} \log(1 + r_{1,t,t+j})$$

and if

$$r_{t,t+j} = R^*_{1,t,t+j},$$

then it follows from (5) that

$$\log(1 + R_{n,t}) = (1/n) \log(1 + r_{1,t,t}) + [(n-1)/n] \log(1 + r_{1,t,t+1}).$$

Therefore

$$\lim_{n \to \infty} \log(1 + R_{n,t}) = \log(1 + r_{1,t,t+1}),$$

which proves that the Cagan–Friedman model implies an asymptotically flat yield curve. Moreover, the Cagan–Friedman model would be inconsistent with a humped or similarly non-linear yield curve. However, the statistical literature contains general models of which the Cagan–Friedman model is a very special case that would make the expected spot rate a more complicated moving average of past spot rates. The general models would be compatible with many shapes of the yield curve.[3] Since Meiselman's model gives no information about the level of rates, it is consistent with any shaped yield curve.

Equation (3) does not fully explain the revision of expectations, and it is necessary to introduce a residual variable $u_{1,t,t+n}$ to express the fact that forward rates are responsive to other factors beside the forecast error E_t. Therefore, with the introduction of the residual, (3) becomes

$$r_{1,t,t+n} - r_{1,t-1,t+n} = a_n + b_n E_t + u_{1,t,t+n}, \qquad n = 1, 2, \ldots . \qquad (8)$$

Meiselman fits (8) by least squares to annual data, 1901–54, for high-grade corporate bond yields for maturities of one to eight years, as estimated by Durand. The multiple correlations and b_n vary inversely with n. The intercepts, a_n, are close to zero and vary irregularly with term to maturity. Since b_n declines with n, it follows that expectations about more distant rates are more firmly held and less responsive to forecast error than expectations about rates closer to the present. Put otherwise, revisions of the more distant forward rates depend relatively more on the unexplained residual $u_{1,t,t+n}$ than on the forecast error E_t. Unfortunately, Meiselman does not examine the residuals to ascertain whether they show any systematic tendencies or whether they are successively independent.

His regressions have been replicated on annual British data for the period 1933–63 by Buse. Buse's findings (unpublished) are notable in one respect: the intercepts differ from zero. This finding is important for the liquidity preference theory as we shall see below. Buse's replication is important also because it refutes a claim by Grant who, using the same raw British data, rejected the market expectations theory because Meiselman's regressions gave very poor results. Both Buse and Fisher (1964) show that Grant's (1964a, 1964b) findings are largely an artifact of his peculiar method of calculating the term structure. When the British yields are calculated more accurately, these difficulties evaporate.

Wallace (1964) calculated (8) for U.S. Treasury bond rates using quarterly data for the period 1946–62. He also included a dummy variable in an attempt to account for the Federal Reserve–Treasury accord in 1951. Although Wallace found that the error term explains the revision of expectations, he also discovered that the intercepts a_n are positive and much larger than their standard

---

[3] The Cagan-Friedman model is a special case of a statistical model of time series. Let x_t be the observed value of a sequence such that $x_t = \xi_t + u_t$, where ξ_t is the "true value" and u_t is the measurement error which is uncorrelated with ξ_t. The true value is assumed to be generated by an nth order autoregression as follows: $A\ (L)\ \xi_t = v_t$, where v_t is a sequence of successively uncorrelated identically distributed random variables and $A\ (L)$ denotes an nth degree polynomial in the lag operator L (cf. n. 4). It is further assumed that the u's are also successively uncorrelated, identically distributed, and uncorrelated with the v's. Both u and v are assumed to have finite variances. This model leads to least-squares forecasts of ξ_t which are a weighted moving average of past values of the observed x's. The weights are determined from the coefficients of a rational form in L. (A rational form in L is the ratio of two polynomials, in this case derived from $A\ (L)$. In the Cagan–Friedman model it is assumed that $A\ (L) = 1 - L$, a special case of the general model.) The general model would not necessarily imply the same forecast of successive forward rates; that is, the general case does not imply an asymptotically flat-yield curve. For a complete exposition, see P. Whittle (1963, chaps. iii and viii).

errors. The residuals were found to be autocorrelated in his regressions.

Meiselman also tested whether the addition of lagged errors would improve the fit of his regressions. Actually, he had to use changes in the spot rates on bonds of thirty-year maturity to represent the revision of distant forward rates because it is not possible to calculate the actual forward rates for n greater than eight years using the Durand yield data. Fortunately, the error of using a thirty-year spot rate for this purpose is slight. Inclusion of both E_{t-1} and E_{t-2} reduces the standard error of estimate slightly. Since the addition of lagged errors would help assess the ability of the market to forecast turning points, it is a pity that this line of study has not been pursued.[4]

An interesting question about Meiselman's hypothesis concerns the consistency of the revisions of the forward rates for different n. Thus for every n there is an equation (8) that purports to describe how forward rates change in response to the forecast error. The set of n equations (8) gives $2n$ parameters, n intercepts, and n slopes. These parameters are related as follows: From the first equation (8), we obtain

$$
\begin{aligned}
r_{t,t+2} - r_{t-1,t+2} &= a_1 + b_1(r_{t,\,t+1} - r_{t-1,\,t+1}) + u_{t,\,t+2} \\
&= a_1 + b_1[a_1 + b_1(r_{t,t} - r_{t-1,t}) + \epsilon_{t,t+1}] + u_{t,t+2} \\
&= a_1(1 + b_1) + b_1^2(r_{t,t} - r_{t-1,t}) + u_{t,t+2} + b_1\epsilon_{t,t+1} \quad (9)
\end{aligned}
$$

In addition, we have from the second equation of (8) ($n = 2$),

$$
r_{t,t+2} - r_{t-1,t+2} = a_2 + b_2(r_{t,t} - r_{t-1,t}) + \epsilon_{t,t+2}. \quad (10)
$$

[4] Bierwag and Grove (in press) estimate regressions closely resembling Meiselman's tests for the presence of lagged error terms. However, they interpret their regressions differently and conclude that there are differences among traders' expectations. To deduce this result, Bierwag and Grove depart from the Meiselman model by assuming each individual trader forms his expectations as a weighted moving average of past spot interest rates. Combined with a market equilibrium condition, this makes the market expectation depend on an infinite sequence of past rates weighted in virtually an arbitrary manner.

Since their algebra is cumbersome, a concise exposition is helpful. Let L denote the lag operator and $A\,(L)$ an nth-degree polynomial in L defined as follows: $A(L) = 1 + a_1L + \ldots + a_nL^n$. Assume that individual j forms his expectations on the basis of the following: $R*_{t(j)} = B_j(L)A_j(L)^{-1} R_t$ where $B_j\,(L)$ and $A_j\,(L)$ are both polynomials in L. Bierwag and Grove argue that the market expectation, $R*_t$ is a weighted average of individual expectations. Assume there are N individuals. Then

$$
R*_t = \sum_{j=1}^{n} V_j R*_{t(j)}, \; V_j \geq 0, \sum_{j=1}^{n} V_j = 1
$$

Hence the market expectations operator is

$$
\sum_{j=1}^{n} V_j B_j\,(L)\, A_j(L)^{-1}
$$

This is a complicated function which, fortunately, can always be approximated by a rational form of the type $B(L)A(L)^{-1}$. Actually, Bierwag and Grove assume that $A_j\,(L)$ is a first-degree polynomial, omit $B_j\,(L)$ and assume that $N = 2$, calling this two poles of opinion.

Equations (9) and (10) are mutually consistent provided

$$a_2 = a_1(1 + b_1),$$

$$b_2 = b_1^2,$$

$$\epsilon_{t,t+2} = u_{t,\,t+2} + b_1\epsilon_{t,t+1}.$$

The algebra for the general case is similar and straightforward. It gives

$$a_n = a_1(1 - b_1^n) / (1 - b_1),$$

$$b_n = b_1^n,$$

$$\epsilon_{t,t+n} = u_{t,\,t+n} + b_1 u_{t,\,t+n-1} + \ldots + b_1^n \epsilon_{t,\,t+1}. \tag{11}$$

Thus the consistency of the n expectation equations implies the presence of only two basic parameters, a_1 and b_1, such that all of the others are related to these two by (11). There are, in addition, certain relations among the residuals depending on the statistical properties ascribed to the u's. For instance, if the u's are independent and identically distributed random variables, then the variances of the residuals should increase as n increases. We can determine from Meiselman's and Buse's estimates of a_n and b_n how well these parameters fit (11). Plotting b_n as a function of n shows a geometric decline as predicted by (11), but the b's do not approach zero as implied by (11). Meiselman's intercepts are approximately zero, while Buse's are positive. According to (11), the intercepts should increase and approach $a_1/(1 - b_1)$. Buse's data roughly confirms this. Although Meiselman (1962, p. 21) did attempt to relate the b_n's to n, he did not develop the implications of consistency shown in (11).

Meiselman's empirical results have been subjected to the criticism that they merely arise from a variant of the regression fallacy. Thus if the "normal" yield curve is upward sloping, meaning that short-term interest rates are less than long-term rates, and if spot interest rates are subject to independent random shocks, then the observed yield curve would bob up and down in such a way as would produce the regressions obtained by Meiselman.[5] Since it is not true that the term structure is "normal" over the past sixty years, this criticism has little force. Similar criticism can be levied against virtually any scientific hypothesis, since generally a large number of different theories are compatible with a given body of data.

Stanley Diller (1966) has taken a very interesting approach to the problem of how expectations are formed and has tested his model with the Durand and more recent data. Diller's approach is most easily described using first-order autoregressions. One may forecast spot interest rates on the basis of past spot rates by fitting autoregressions by least squares to the observed sequence of past spot rates. The autoregressions give good forecasts in the sense of minimizing the sums of squares of the deviations between actual and predicted rates. Diller postulates that the market expectations of spot rates are formed as if they were

---

[5] This criticism is due to Buse (1967).

extrapolations derived from such autoregressions. Thus for a first-order auto-regression,

$$R_t = a_0 + a_1 R_{t-1} + u_t, \tag{12}$$

the R's are the observed one-period spot rates, and u_t is a random residual. Using (12) the forecast of subsequent spot rates is based on an extrapolation from the last observed spot rate as follows:

$$R^*_{t,t+n} = a_0(1 - a_1^n) / (1 - a_1) + a_1^n R_t \tag{13}$$

It is readily verified that the forecasts satisfy the same autoregression as the observed spot rates, namely,

$$R^*_{t,t+n} - a_1 R^*_{t,t+n-1} = a_0 \tag{14}$$

If $| a_1 | < 1$, this variant of Diller's hypothesis implies that

$$\lim_{n \to \infty} R_{t,t+n} = a_0 / (1 - a_1)$$

Thus the interest rates are expected to approach a constant in the long run.

This theory also describes how expectations are revised. As of period $t - 1$, the spot rate expected to prevail in period $t + n$ is

$$R^*_{t-1,t+n} = a_0(1 - a_1^{n+1}) / (1 - a_1) + a_1^{n+1} R_{t-1} \tag{15}$$

Subtracting (15) from (13) gives the revision of the expectations as follows:

$$R^*_{t,t+n} - R^*_{t-1,t+n} = [a_0 / (1 - a_1)] \times [a_1^n (a_1 - 1] + a_1^n (R_t - a_1 R_{t-1})$$

$$= - a_1^n a_0 + a_1^n (u_t + a_0)$$

$$= a_1^n u_t \tag{16}$$

However,

$$R^*_{t-1,t} = a_0 + a_1 R_{t-1},$$
$$R_t = a_0 + a_1 R_{t-1} + u_t$$

Therefore,

$$R_t - R^*_{t-1,t} = u_t$$

which is also Meiselman's expectations error, E_t. Hence (16) implies that

$$R^*_{t,t+n} - R^*_{t-1,t+n} = a_1^n E_t \tag{17}$$

Substituting the forward rates for the expected spot rates, Diller's hypothesis for the example of a first-order autoregression explains the change in the forward rate according to (17). It is useful to compare (17) with (11), noting that (17) has no intercept. Actually, Diller claims that a seventh-order autoregression explains the revision of the forward rates in the sense of predicting the regression coefficients of the change of forward rates on the expectation errors. In addition, he uses the same approach to predict the level of the forward rates. Thus Diller attempts to explain the forward rate in terms of past spot rates where the coefficients of the past spot rates are derived from the autoregressions of spot rates that were used to predict the revision of expectations. He also assesses the accuracy of the forward rates as predictors of subsequent spot rates and finds that the residual is correlated with an index of industrial activity and stock market prices. His work opens a promising line of research into expectations that deserves additional investigation.[6]

V. THE LIQUIDITY PREFERENCE THEORY[7]

A purchaser of long-term default-free bonds incurs the risk of a rise in interest rates and a consequent fall in bond prices. Assuming bonds bear a coupon fixed in nominal terms, such a purchaser obtains a certain nominal income in partial compensation for the principal risk. A buyer of a short-term bond incurs a smaller chance of a capital loss for a given rise in interest rates because the shorter the term to maturity, the smaller is the effect on the price of a bond of a given rise in rates. However, one who purchases short-term bonds seriatim assumes the risk of fluctuations of the nominal income stream. Therefore, an individual who expects to make a payment at some unknown time in the future and considers the alternatives of buying a long-term bond to mature on the expected payment date versus buying a sequence of short-term bonds assumes a larger principal and a smaller income risk in the first case and a larger income risk but smaller principal risk in the second. The same reasoning applies, *mutatis mutandis,* to borrowers expecting receipts.

Nevertheless, some writers, notably Hicks, have argued that there is a tendency for lenders to prefer shorter- to longer-term bonds at the same interest rate, while borrowers have the opposite preference. Hicks claims there is a "congenital weakness' on the long side of the market which results in a tendency for long rates to exceed short rates. The differential is necessary to coax lenders into the purchase of long-term bonds as compensation for the greater risk of principal loss. R. F. Kahn (1954) is among the first to criticize the Hicksian argument of a congenital weakness on one side of the market. If firms in various industries commit themselves to payments over horizons of various lengths and there is universal risk aversion, then firms, who feel incompetent or are unwilling to speculate on interest rates, would hedge payment commitments by the purchase of bonds of matching maturities. There is no a priori presumption

---

[6] See Diller (1966, especially chaps. ii and iii).
[7] The major earlier references are Keynes (1936), Lutz (1940), Hicks (1946), Robinson (1951), and Kahn (1954). More recent analysis is Malkiel (1962), Meiselman (1962), Culbertson (1965), and Modigliani and Sutch (1966).

that risk aversion weakens one side of the market instead of the other.[8]

    The argument can be put in another way by considering a firm that anticipates the payment of a known amount at an unknown date in the future. The standard liquidity preference doctrine claims that if interest rates were the same for all maturities spanning the possible payment dates, then such a firm would purchase a bond to mature *before* the expected payment date, since to do otherwise would expose it to risking the loss of some of its principal. A firm, according to this theory, is induced to purchase a bond to mature on or after the expected payment date by receiving a higher interest rate on longer-term loans. Actually, the only way to secure the safety of principal *and* avoid transactions costs is to hold cash (assuming away unforeseen changes of the price level). Once a decision is made to buy a bond and given the firm's risk aversion, it does not follow on balance that the firm will choose a bond to mature before the expected date. The purchase of a bond to mature before the expected payment date exposes the firm to the risk of fluctuations of interest receipts. It does not follow from a theoretical analysis that the maturity date of the bond relative to the expected date of payment can be deduced a priori. The maturity date of the bond depends on the firm's subjective judgment about the future course of interest rates.

    Despite the logical gaps in the arguments for liquidity preference, one can still maintain that as an empirical matter the market as a whole exhibits a preference for the certainty of principal over the certainty of income. Two kinds of evidence have been offered to show that expectations alone do not explain the term structure—the bias of the forward rates as forecasts of the spot rates, and a relation between the structure of interest rates and the maturity composition of debt.

    The assertion that forward rates are unbiased estimates of future interest rates implies in Meiselman's model that the intercepts, a_n, are approximately zero. Therefore, there is no tendency for forward rates to change if the error, E_t, is zero. This condition is satisfied in Meiselman's original set of regression equations. It is not satisfied in either Buse's (unpublished) estimates for British government yields or Wallace's (1964) estimates for U.S. Treasury yields. Although I have not checked this, I suspect the special character of the sample periods. In both cases, the results may be due to the fact that the yield structure was upward sloping in most of the years—the Great Depression is included in Buse's sample and both Buse's and Wallace's samples include a large number of abnormal post-World War II years. Since Meiselman's data refer to the period 1901–54, his sample contains term structures of a wider variety of shapes more representative of long-run historical experience. It would be desirable to redo Meiselman's regressions by subperiods, 1901–32, 1933–54, to check the sensitivity to choice of period. The importance of the choice of sample period and determinant of the intercept is clearly shown in Table 10 of Meiselman's study where, using the thirty-year market rate of interest in his expectations equation, he finds a zero intercept for 1901–29 and a significant positive intercept for 1930–54.

    Both Wood (1963) and Kessel (1965) independently point out that although a zero intercept is necessary for the forward rates to forecast spot

[8] This argument seems to have been first developed by Kahn (1954).

rates unbiasedly, it is not sufficient. This is easily demonstrated. Let $R_{t,t+n} = $ the spot rate expected to rule in period $t + n$ as of period t; assume that expectations are revised according to

$$R^*_{t,t+n} - R^*_{t-1,t+n} = b_n(R_t - R^*_{t-1,t}) \qquad (18)$$

and assume that the forward rate is related to the expected spot rates as follows:

$$r_{t,t+n} = R^*_{t,t+n} + L_{t,t+n} \qquad (19)$$

where $L_{t,t+n}$ denotes the liquidity premium as of time t on a forward loan to begin in time $t + n$. It follows from these assumptions and equation (6) that

$$a_n = L_{t,t+n} - L_{t-1,t+n} - b_n L_{n-1,t} \qquad (20)$$

Hence a_n can be zero under two different circumstances. Either the liquidity premiums are themselves zero, or they satisfy the additional condition

$$L_{t,t+n} - L_{t-1,t+n} = b_n L_{t-1,t} \qquad (21)$$

This simple exercise also illustrates the general proposition that empirical results implied by a theory are necessary for the truth of the theory but they are never sufficient.

Equation (21) is a theoretical curiosum. Even if we know a_n and b_n we cannot use (21) to estimate the actual liquidity premiums except in the most trivial cases, for example, if the L's are independent of both n and t. Buse, by making the heroic assumptions, $L_{t,t+n} = L_n$, $L_n - L_{n-1} > 0$, and $L_n > 0$, was still able to determine L_n only up to an arbitrary value of L_1. Finally, equation (19) makes the liquidity premium independent of the level of interest rates. This is an assumption that Kessel himself is unwilling to accept.

Kessel claims that liquidity premiums vary directly with the level of interest rates. His argument is based on the premise that nearer-term bonds are less susceptible to risk of principal than longer-term bonds and hence provide their owners with more liquidity. At high interest rates, there is a high opportunity cost of holding money. Hence if both short-and long-term bond yields were to increase by the same amount, there would be a tendency to substitute short-term for long-term bonds to secure the greater liquidity of the former. Therefore, Kessel concludes that the spread between short-and long-term rates should widen at high interest rates.

The evidence that Kessel offers in support of his argument is as follows: He regresses the forecast error, the difference between the actual and the forward rates, on the actual rate of the preceding period. He uses two sets of data. The first set is weekly closing interest rates on 91-day Treasury bills for the period January, 1959–February, 1962. The second set uses midmonthly observations of 28-day Treasury bills for the longer period October, 1949–February, 1961. In both cases, as expected on Kessel's hypothesis, the coefficient of the previous spot rate is positive. His regressions (not published in his original study and kindly made available for this paper) are as follows:

$$R_{t+n} - r_{t,\,t+n} = -.672 + .473\,R_t$$
$$t\text{-ratios} \qquad 4.08 \qquad 8.65$$

$$R_{t+n} - r_{t,\,t+n} = -.140 + .218\,R_t$$
$$t\text{-ratios} \qquad 2.16 \qquad 6.90$$

The first regression is based on 138 weekly observations of the 91-day Treasury bill rate, January, 1959–February, 1962. The second is based on 137 monthly observations of the 28-day Treasury bill rate, October, 1949–February, 1961. In both regressions, the residuals are strongly autocorrelated. For the first, which uses data at weekly intervals, the first-to the fourth-order autocorrelations of the residuals are .79, .60, .46, and .42, respectively. For the second regression, the autocorrelation of the residual at one-month intervals is .41, which is nearly equal to the fourth-order autocorrelation coefficient for the regression using weekly data. The autocorrelation of these residuals leads me to suspect the omission of some important factors that are themselves autocorrelated. In addition, as Kessel himself admits, his tests rely on the assumption that the forecast errors are themselves independent of liquidity premiums, and he cannot estimate the actual liquidity premiums.[9]

Meiselman's original regressions indicate that a substantial amount of the revision of forward rates cannot be explained by the forecast error E_t, especially for the more distant forward rates. This leaves ample room for the introduction of other variables to explain changes in the forward rates (or, if you will, expectations). The troublesome question remains of identifying that part of the change in forward rates due to changes in the liquidity premiums and that part due to hitherto unexplored causes of changes in expectations.

A more direct analysis of liquidity premiums relates changes in the forward rates to changes in the maturity composition of all debt. Unfortunately, it is impossible to determine the direction of causation since the term structure of interest rates and the maturity composition of all debt are mutually dependent. This consideration led Neil Wallace to relate the forward rates on government securities to the composition of the federal debt, arguing that the latter is exogenously determined so that it affects the term structure of interest rates without in turn being affected by it. Wallace found that a shift in the maturity composition of the federal debt has a small effect on the term structure of interest rates in the direction predicted by the liquidity preference theory. Thus

[9] Note that Kessel's argument relating liquidity premiums to the level of interest rates raises troublesome questions about his interpretation of the intercept a_n because the latter assumes independence between liquidity premiums and the interest rates. Thus if $L_{t,t+n}$ is assumed to depend on the level of interest rates, then the presence of a_n can be due to misspecification of the equation that purports to explain the revision of expectations, for example, it may arise from the error of a linear approximation to a non-linear function. Moreover, there are functions relating the liquidity premiums to the level of interest rates that would be actually inconsistent with Kessel's interpretation of a_n. Diller (1966) makes the distinction between a liquidity trap which results from investors' reluctance to buy bonds at abnormally low interest rates for fear of a capital loss if rates should rise and liquidity preference discussed in the text. Thus the low level of short relative to long rates is evidence of a liquidity trap which, in the language of expectations theory, indicates the presence of a market expectation of a return to a normal level of rates. This phenomenon would imply an inverse relation between the forecast error and the level of rates. Van Horne (1965) attempted to demonstrate such a relation, but his work is marred by a statistical error pointed out by Roll (1966).

for a given total federal debt, an increase in its average term to maturity tends to drive up the forward interest rates. Since his regressions are not readily accessible, I reproduce them in Table 1. Despite these findings, it is consistent with the expectations theory to argue that changes in the federal debt composition can affect expectations as well as liquidity premiums (Wallace, 1964).

Modigliani and Sutch (1966) fail to find a relation between the composition of the federal debt and the term structure of rates. Using a different expectations model—one which relates the spread between long-and short-term interest rates to a weighted sum of lagged short-term rates and to the term composition of the federal debt as measured by the fraction that is short and of intermediate term—they found that the components of the debt have opposite signs and nearly equal magnitudes. This implies a trivial net effect on the term structure of rates.

VI. CONCLUSIONS AND SUGGESTIONS FOR FURTHER RESEARCH

The most challenging task for future research on the term structure of rates is the extension of the expectations model so as to incorporate the effects of other variables that might affect expectations in addition to the forecast error. In concrete terms one ought to explain more of the changes in forward rates. A preliminary approach would examine the residuals of the existing regressions with a view to finding hints of left-out expectational variables. For instance, do the residuals exhibit cycles that move in accord with business cycles? In addition, it would be desirable to try other kinds of expectation models. For instance, instead of relating the absolute change of the forward rate to the absolute forecast error, it would be interesting to relate the percentage change of the former to the forecast error expressed in percentage. This suggestion should be taken seriously if long-time series of interest rates are used and the levels of the rates widely differ.

TABLE 1

Neil Wallace's regression results testing the effect of the maturity composition of the Federal Debt on the term structure of Interest rates, quarterly, 1946–62.

$$r_{1,t,t,+n} - r_{1,t-1,t+n} = a_n + b_n E_t + c_n \left[(M_{t,t+n})/M_{tt} - (M_{t-1,t,+n})/(M_{t-1,t-1}) \right] + d_n \text{ Dummy}$$

n years	a_n	b_n	c_n	d_n	R^2	Durbin-Watson statistic
1......	.0020	.846	.009	−.0020	.94	1.37
	(.0004)	(.031)	(.004)	(.0005)		
2......	.0021	.663	.011	−.0022	.84	1.48
	(.0005)	.... (.042)	(.006)	(.0007)		
3.......	.0023	.541	.014	−.0024	.75	1.54
	(.0005)	(.043)	(.007)	(.0007)		

Note: $M_{t,t+n}$ = outstanding marketable Treasury securities at time t that mature on or after time t+n. Dummy = one for all quarterly observations from March, 1946, to March, 1951, and zero thereafter. The regressions use sixty-four observations.

The survey of the empirical research uncovers evidence in favor of both explanations of the term structure—the expectations and the liquidity preference theory. None of these results is at all decisive, and many contain errors, shortcomings, and paradoxes. In my opinion, no verdict can yet be brought, and imaginative work remains to be done in "explaining" the formation and change of expectations.

REFERENCES

BIERWAG, G.O., and GROVE, M. A. "A Model of the Term Structure of Interest Rates," *Rev. Econ, and Statis.* (in press).

BUSE, A. "The Term Structure of Interest Rates–Some British Experience," unpublished MS.

_____. "Interest Rates, the Meiselman Model and Random Numbers," *J.P.E.,* LXXY (February, 1967), 48–62.

CAGAN, PHILLIP. "The Monetary Dynamics of Hyperinflation," in Milton Friedman (ed.). *Studies in the Quantity Theory of Money.* Chicago: Univ. of Chicago Press, 1956.

CULBERTSON, J.M. "The Interest Rate Structure: Towards Completion of the Classical System," in F.H. Hahn and P.R. Brechling (eds.), *The Theory of Interest Rates.* London: Macmillian & Co., 1965.

DILLER, STANLEY. "Extrapolation, Anticipations and the Term Structure of Interest Rates," unpublished doctoral dissertation, Department of Economics, Columbia Univ., 1966.

FISHER, D. "The Structure of Interest Rates: A Comment," *Economica,* N.S., XXXI (November, 1964), 412–19.

FRIEDMAN, MILTON. *A Theory of the Consumption Function.* Princeton, N.J.: Princeton Univ. Press, 1957.

GRANT, J.A.G. "Meiselman on the Term Structure of Interest Rates," *Economica,* N.S., XXXI (February, 1964), 51–74. (*a*)

_____. "A Reply," *ibid.,* pp. 419–22. (*b*)

HICKMAN, W. BRADDOCK. "The Interest Structure and War Financing," National Bureau of Economic Research, unpublished, 1943.

HICKS, J.R. *Value and Capital.* 2d ed. Oxford: Oxford Univ. Press, 1946.

KAHN, R. F. "Some Notes on Liquidity Preference," *Manchester School Econ, and Soc. Studies,* XXII (September, 1954), 229–57.

KESSEL, RUBEN A. *The Cyclical Behavior of the Term Structure of Interest Rates.* New York: National Bureau of Economic Research, 1965.

KEYNES, J. M. *The General Theory of Employment, Interest, and Money.* New York: Harcourt, Brace & Co., 1936.

LUTZ, F. A. "The Structure of Interest Rates," *Q.J.E.,* LV (November, 1940), 36–63.

MACAULEY F. R. *The Movements of Interest Rates, Bond Yields and Stock Prices in the United States since 1856.* New York: National Bureau of Economic Research, 1938.

MALKIEL, B.G. "Expectations, Bond Prices and the Term Structure of Interest Rates," *QJ.E.,* LXXVI (February, 1962), 197–218.

MEISELMAN, DAVID. *The Term Structure of Interest Rates.* Englewood Cliffs, N.J.: Prentice-Hall, Inc., 1962.

MODIGLIANI, FRANCO, and SUTCH, RICHARD. "Innovations in Interest Rate Policy," *A.E.R.,* LVI (May, 1966), 178–97.

ROBINSON, JOAN. "The Rate of Interest," *Econmetrica,* XIX (January, 1951), 92–101.

ROLL, RICHARD. "Interest-Rate Risk and the Term Structure of Interest Rates: Comment," *J.P.E.,* LXXIV (December, 1966), 629–32.

VAN HORNE, J. "Interest-Rate Risk and the Term Structure of Interest Rates," *J.P.E.,* LXXIII (August, 1965), 344–51.

WALLACE, NEIL. "The Term Structure of Interest Rates and Maturity Composition of the Federal Debt," unpublished doctoral dissertation, Department of Economics, Univ. of Chicago, 1964.

WHITTLE, P. *Prediction and Regulation.* London: English Universities Press, 1963.

WONNACOTT, P. "The Height, Structure and Significance of Interest Rates," unpublished working paper prepared for the Royal Commisison on Banking and Finance, Canada, 1962.

WOOD, J. H. "Expectations, Error and the Term Structure of Interest Rates," *J.P.E.,* LXXI (April, 1963), 160–71.

Lawrence Fisher constructs a model to explain the risk premium at which corporate bonds sell, that is, the difference in yield between a corporate bond and a government security of the same term to maturity. Fisher believes that the risk premium can be explained in terms of the risk of default of the bond and its marketability. After defining four variables as measures of these two influences, Fisher runs a cross-sectional regression analysis relating these variables to the risk premium. These regressions were run in each of five years. Not only did Fisher's model do a good job of explaining risk premiums in each year, but unlike most models, the parameters of his model were stable over time.

6

Determinants of Risk Premiums on Corporate Bonds

Lawrence Fisher[1]

This article is reprinted with permission from the Journal of Political Economy, *Vol. 67, No. 3 (June, 1959), pp. 217–237.*

I. INTRODUCTION

Economists have long agreed that the rate of interest on a loan depends on the risks the lender incurs. But how lenders estimate these risks has been left largely to conjecture. This paper presents and tests a hypothesis about the determinants of risk premiums on corporate bonds. By risk premium is meant the difference between the market yield on a bond and the corresponding pure rate of interest.

My hypothesis is as follows: (1) The average risk premium on a firm's bonds depends first on the risk that the firm will default on its bonds and second on their marketability. (2) The "risk of default" can be estimated by a

[1] I am greatly indebted to Professor Arnold C. Harberger, who suggested that I undertake this research and guided me throughout the study. Professors Carl Christ and Phillip D. Cagan made valuable comments and criticisms, as did other members of the Research Group in Public Finance of the University of Chicago. An Earhart Foundation Fellowship facilitated the completion of this study.

This paper was read at the September, 1956 meeting of the Econometric Society in Detroit. An abstract was printed in *Econometrica*, Vol. 25 (1957), 366–67.

function of three variables: the coefficient of variation of the firm's net income over the last nine years (after all charges and taxes), the length of time the firm has been operating without forcing its creditors to take a loss, and the ratio of the market value of the equity in the firm to the par value of the firm's debt. (3) The marketability of a firm's bonds can be estimated by a single variable, the market value of all the publicly traded bonds the firm has outstanding. (4) The logarithm of the average risk premium on a firm's bonds can be estimated by a linear function of the logarithms of the four variables just listed.

For convenience, these variables will usually be designated as follows: earnings variability, x_1; period of solvency, x_2; equity/debt ratio, x_3; and bonds outstanding, x_4. Risk premium will be called x_0. Capital letters will indicate common logarithms of the variables. Earnings variability and the equity/debt ratio are pure numbers. Risk premium will be expressed in percent per annum, compounded semiannually; bonds outstanding, in millions of dollars; and the period of solvency, in years.[2]

Security analysts generally regard some form of each of these variables to be of value in appraising the "quality" of bonds. But, to the best of my knowledge, this is the first time they have been used together in an attempt to discover how much investors are influenced by various aspects of bond quality.[3]

More precise definitions of the variables will be given later, and the derivation of the hypothesis, alternative hypotheses, and statistical procedures will be explained. But first let us look at some of the main results.

II. THE MAIN RESULTS

The hypothesis was tested by least-squares regressions for cross-sections of domestic industrial corporations for five dates: December 31 of the years 1927, 1932, 1937, 1949, and 1953. The cross-sections included all firms for which I had meaningful data.[4] The cross-sections were for 71 firms in 1927, 45 firms in 1932, 89 firms in 1937, 73 firms in 1949, and 88 firms in 1953.

For each of these cross-sections the logarithms of the four variables accounted for approximately three-fourths of the variance in the logarithm of risk premium. Furthermore, I found that the elasticity[5] of risk premium with respect to each of the four variables is relatively stable over time. In view of this stability, it was possible to pool the observed variances and covariances and obtain a single set of "best" estimates of the elasticities. Figure 1 is the scatter of the 366 measured risk premiums against the risk premiums calculated by using this single set of elasticities. The regression equation from which these risk premiums were estimated is

[2] Some alternative variables will be introduced below. They will be expressed in the following units: equity, x_5, and debt, x_6—millions of dollars; annual volume of trading, x_7—millions of dollars a year; an alternative index of variability of earnings, x_8—the reciprocal of years.

[3] The study by Herbert Arkin, discussed in footnote 41, bears a superficial resemblance to this one.

[4] For the sources of data and the criteria used in selecting the firms see Section VI.

[5] Logarithmic regression coefficients are estimates of elasticities.

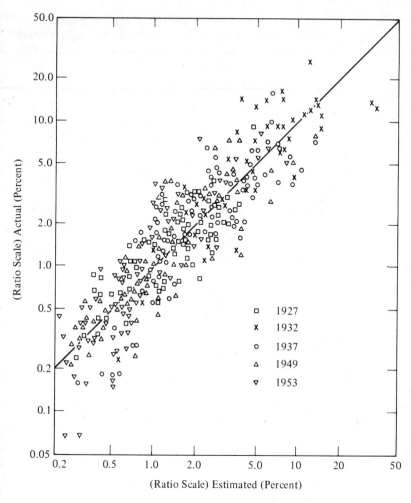

FIGURE 1

Scatter of actual risk premiums
against risk premiums estimated
from equation (1)

$$X_0 = 0.262X_1 - 0.223X_2 - 0.469X_3 - 0.290X_4 + \text{a constant} \quad (1)$$

where the constant is equal to 0.966 in 1927; 1.235 in 1932; 0.918 in 1937; 0.847 in 1949; and 0.829 in 1953. This equation accounts for 81 percent of the total variance in the logarithm of risk premium. Part of this variance, however, can be accounted for by differences in the mean of X_0 among the cross-sections. When that part of the variance is eliminated, equation (1) accounts for 74 percent of the remaining or intra-cross-section variance. To make the data strictly comparable among the cross-sections, it would have been necessary to make adjustments for such things as changes in tax rates. But, since we do not know whether the determinants of stock prices are stable and since the market value of equity was used in computing one of the variables, these adjustments were not made. Hence there was no reason to expect the constant term of this regression equation to be the same for each date, even if investor's behavior in the bond market were perfectly stable over time.[6]

Figure 2 permits us to compare the fraction of the intra-cross-section variance in the logarithm of risk premium, X_0, that is accounted for by the pooled-variance regression, equation (1), with the squares of the multiple correlation coefficients (R^2) obtained by fitting regression equations to each cross-section separately.

Figure 3 shows the estimates of elasticities and their standard errors obtained from the pooled-variance regression, equation (1), and from the regressions for the separate cross-sections. The larger bars show the estimated elasticities, η. The right ends of the small bars are at points one standard error, s, greater than the estimated elasticity; the left ends are at $\eta - s$. The estimates from equation (1) may be compared with the estimates from the separate regressions with the aid of the dashed lines. These results are summarized in Table 1, which shows the elasticities, standard errors of estimate, constant terms, and squares of the coefficients of multiple correlation.

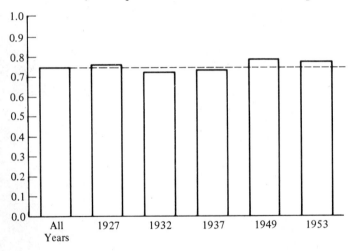

FIGURE 2

Proportion of intra-cross-section variance in the logarithms of risk premiums accunted for by the logarithms of earnings variability, period of solvency, equity/debt ratio, and bonds outstanding

---

[6] The regression equation found by keeping the constant term (as well as the elasticities) the same for all cross-sections is

$$X_0 = 0.307X_1 - 0.253X_2 - 0.537X_3 - 0.275X_4 + 0.987 \quad (R^2 = 0.75). \tag{2}$$

For a complete description of equation (2) see Table 1.

All the coefficients shown in Table 1 have the expected sign.[7] All estimated values of the elasticities are significantly different from zero at the 5 percent level or lower except the estimates for period of solvency, x_2, for 1932 and 1949.[8]

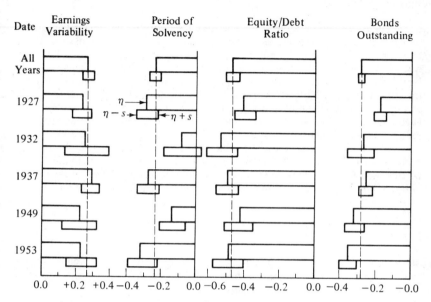

FIGURE 3

Elasticities of risk premium with respect to earnings variability, period of solvency, equity/debt ratio, and bonds outstanding estimated from cross-sections (together with standard errors of estimate).

III. THEORETICAL FRAMEWORK

The apparent cost of borrowed capital to a firm with publicly traded bonds outstanding is the market rate of return on those bonds (which generally will be the pure rate of interest plus a risk premium) plus the cost of floating the issue.[9] The determinants of the pure rate of interest have long been the subject of extensive study, both theoretical and empirical. Costs of flotation have also

[7] See Section IV.

[8] This variable, however, was not measured with any great accuracy (see Section VI). Errors in the measurement of x_2 probably had only a negligible effect on the coefficients of equation (1) (see Section VII).

[9] This is only the apparent cost because the cost of equity capital probably depends on the firm's capital structure.

been studied.[10] But the matter of what determines risk premiums has been left almost entirely to conjecture.

The basic theory of risk premiums on loans was stated by J. R. Mc-Cullough, who wrote:

> There are comparatively few species of security to be obtained in which there is no risk, either as to the repayment of the loans themselves, or the regular payment of the interest. . . . Other things being equal, the rate of interest must of course vary according to the supposed risk incurred by the lender of either not recovering payment at all, or not receiving it at the stipulated term. No person of sound mind would lend on the personal security of an individual of doubtful character and solvency, and on mortgage over a valuable estate, at the same rate of interest. Wherever there is risk, it must be compensated to the lender by a higher premium or interest.[11]
>
> Mercantile bills of unquestionable credit and having two or three months to run, are generally discounted at a lower rate of interest than may be obtained for sums lent upon mortgage, *on account of the facility they afford of repossessing the principal,* and applying it in some more profitable manner.[12]

TABLE 1

Regression equations for estimating logarithm of average risk premium on a firm's bonds as a linear function of logarithms of earnings variability, period of solvency, equity/debt ratio, and bonds outstanding

(Hypothesis that $X_0 = a_0 + a_1 X_1 + a_2 X_2 + a_3 X_3 + a_4 X_4$)

Equation	Date	No. of obser- vations	Degrees of freedom	R_2	a_0	a_1 (S_1)	a_2 (S_2)	a_3 (S_3)	a_4 (S_4)
1	All	366	357	0.811*	†	+0.262 (.032)	−0.223 (.033)	−0.469 (.029)	−0.290 (.019)
2	All	366	361	0.750	0.987	+.307 (.032)	−.253 (.036)	−.537 (.031)	−.275 (.021)
3	1927	71	66	0.756	0.874	+.233 (.048)	−.269 (.062)	−.404 (.039)	−.169 (.031)
4	1932	45	40	0.726	1.014	+.248 (.128)	−.067 (.114)	−.531 (.092)	−.286 (.071)
5	1937	89	84	0.731	0.949	+.286 (.051)	−.254 (.061)	−.491 (.060)	−.271 (.038)
6	1949	73	68	0.786	0.711	+.228 (.100)	−.124 (0.76)	−.426 (.084)	−.329 (.046)
7	1953	88	83	0.773	1.012	+.228 (.091)	−.300 (.089)	−.474 (.085)	−.363 (.043)

* *0.741 after the effects of differences in ao are eliminated.*
† *1927: 0.966; 1932: 1.235; 1937: 0.918; 1949: 0.847; 1953: 0.829.*

[10] For examples see Securities and Exchange Commission, *Costs of Flotation, 1945–1949* (Washington, 1951), and Arthur Stone Dewing, *Financial Policy of Corporations* (5th ed,; New York, 1953), II, 1131–32.

[11] *The Principles of Political Economy: With a Sketch of the Rise and Progress of the Science* (2d ed,; Edinburgh, London, and Dublin, 1830), pp. 508–9.

[12] *Ibid.,* p. 508 (italics mine).

In other words, the yields on almost all securities include compensation for risk. These risk premiums depend on lenders' estimates of the risk of default and on the ease of turning the securities into cash. Let us consider the risk of default first.

The risk premium on a bond has been defined as the difference between its market yield to maturity and the corresponding pure rate of interest. Market yield is defined as the rate of interest at which the principal and interest payments specified in the bond contract must be discounted if their present value is to equal the current market price of the bond. The corresponding pure rate of interest is defined as the market yield on a riskless bond maturing on the same day as the bond under consideration.

Risk premiums defined in this way must in general be either zero or positive if, other things being equal, bondholders prefer high incomes to low incomes. A bondholder has no expectation of receiving more than the payments called for by his bond and, since corporations have limited liability, he may receive less.[13] Hence, regardless of whether he likes or tries to avoid being in situations of uncertain income and wealth, a bondholder will demand a risk premium as compensation for holding any bond that is not certain to be paid.[14]

A lender's estimate of the "risk of default" must depend on his estimates of the probability that a default will occur[15] and of the magnitude of his loss in the event of a default.[16] Let us assume that lenders do not behave capriciously. Then our problem is to find how a rational investor can most readily estimate the probability that a bond will be defaulted. Investors' estimates must be based on information available to them. In general, if a corporation defaults on its bonds, it is because the market value of its assets is less than its liabilities. The value of its assets—that is, the value of its total capital—depends on the earning power of those assets. Hence the "risk of default" is given by the probability

---

[13] There have been cases in which creditors have received equity interests in firms through reorganizations in bankruptcy, and the firms subsequently made such large profits that the bondholders ultimately received payments larger than those called for by their bonds (but it is doubtful whether, at the time of the reorganizations, the new securities received had a market value as great as the accumulated value of the bonds). But bondholders receive such payments only after expenses of the receivership have been paid and only if the earning power of the firm is underestimated at the time of reorganization. So long as bondholders do not become stockholders, they cannot receive more than the amounts called for by their contracts. (Sinking fund and call provisions in bond indentures complicate this argument slightly, but they limit the bondholders' opportunity for capital gains; hence considering them would probably strengthen these conclusions.) We can conclude that the expectation of a bondholder's receiving more than contractual payments is negligible.

[14] That is, if a bondholder's utility is a function of his income and the first derivative of the function is positive, a dollar a year with certainty must have a greater utility than a dollar a year with probability $p < 1$ plus an amount less than one dollar a year with probability $1 - p$. This proposition is, of course, independent of the sign of the second derivative of the utility function.

[15] More precisely, the probabilities of default at each moment in time.

[16] It can easily be shown that the expected loss in the event of a default is likely to depend on two of the determinants of the probability of default—earnings variability and the equity/debt ratio. My procedure enables one to find an index of the probability of default but not to estimate the probability itself. Hence, to simplify the analysis, the magnitude of loss in the event of a default will not be discussed explicitly. Those who demand rigor may read the phrase "probability of a default" as "expected loss."

that the firm's earnings will not be large enough to meet the payments on its debts.

Recall that risk premium also depends on marketability. The theory of the determinants of risk premiums may then be restated: If investors are rational, the risk premium on any bond will depend on the probability that the issuing firm's earnings will be too small to permit it to pay its debts and on the ease with which the bondholder can turn the bond into cash before it matures.

Let us now turn to the problem of finding ways to measure these variables.

IV. AN OPERATIONAL HYPOTHESIS

Risk of Default

There are three sorts of variables that it is plausible to use together in estimating risk of default: measures of the variability of the firm's earnings, measures showing how reliable the firm has been in meeting its obligations, and measures depending on the firm's capital structure.

Variability of Earnings. In 1903, J. Pease Norton suggested the probability that a firm will fail to pay interest on its bonds in any particular year could be found by computing the coefficient of variation of the firm's income in past years, over and above the amount required for fixed charges, and by looking up the probability in a table of the normal distribution.[17] This naive procedure may be correct for non-cumulative income bonds (which are rare) but it is not correct for other types of bonds because corporations often continue to meet fixed charges during periods of losses. Nevertheless, it provides a useful point of departure.

Let us make an assumption which is implicit in Norton's procedure—that a series of observations of a firm's annual net income may be treated as a random sample from a normally distributed population of potential annual net incomes. The coefficient of variation of this series is an estimate of the coefficient of variation of the underlying population.[18] Other things being equal, a firm with a small coefficient of variation of earnings is less likely to default on its bonds than a firm with a large coefficient. Hence the variable suggested by Norton appears to be a promising one, even in analyses of bonds for which his complete procedure is invalid.

In practice, data on the earnings of a firm for its entire history are usually not available. To test the partial hypothesis that investors believe that a bond issued by a firm whose earnings have varied little is a better risk than a bond issued by a firm whose earnings have varied much, one must have comparable earnings data for the two firms. Because my tests covered a large number of firms, it was necessary to place an arbitrary limit on the number of years' earnings used in computing the coefficient of variation. Nine years was the limit

---

[17] "The Theory of Loan Credit in Relation to Corporation Economics," *Publications of the American Economic Association,* 3d ser., V (1904), 298. Cf. Irving Fisher, *The Nature of Capital and Income* (New York, 1906), p. 409.

[18] The coefficient of variation is the ratio of the standard deviation of a sample (adjusted for degrees of freedom) to the arithmetic mean of the sample.

selected. During the period considered, nine years was long enough for the earnings of most firms to fluctuate substantially.

In the abstract, one could take as "net earnings" either income after the payment of fixed charges or income after the payment of both charges and corporation income taxes. If taxes were proportional to income and tax rates did not vary during the nine-year period and if one year's losses could not be deducted from another year's profits in computing taxes, the two methods would give the same computed coefficient of variation. But tax rates do vary from year to year, and there are loss carryback and carry-forward provisions in our tax laws; neither measure is ideal. I did not use both measures together because, if I found that risk premium varied with the coefficient of variation in earnings, I wanted to measure the elasticity of risk premium with respect to this measure of the risk of default. And, since the two coefficients of variation were expected to be highly correlated with each other, a precise estimate of either elasticity could not be expected with both variables in the regression.

My choice was made on practical grounds. The appropriate measure of marketability, bonds outstanding, is highly correlated with size of firm. If both coefficients of variation in earnings are equally reliable, the measure that allows the use of the larger range of firms gives the more precise estimate of the elasticity of risk premium with respect to marketability. Issues of *Moody's Manual,* an important secondary source, give data on earnings after taxes for more firms than on earnings before taxes, particularly for very large and for small firms. Therefore, earnings after taxes ("net income") were taken as "earnings" and used in computing x_1, earnings variability.

In many studies it is necessary to adjust data for changes in the general price level. Since bond obligations are in "money" rather than "real" units, no such adjustment was necessary here.

Reliability in Meeting Obligations. The coefficient of variation in earnings computed from a "sample" is only an estimate of the coefficient of variation in the underlying population. This estimate may be either larger or smaller than the actual coefficient. But, other things being equal, the longer a firm has conducted its business without requiring its creditors to take a loss, the less likely it is that its estimated coefficient of variation in earnings is much less than the coefficient in the hypothetical underlying population of annual net incomes. Hence, a measure of the length of time a firm has met all its obligations—the length of time the firm has been solvent—provides a correction for the estimate of risk of default derived from earnings variability. This measure has been designated as x_2. In estimating a firm's period of solvency, I took the length of time since the latest of the following events had occurred: The firm was founded; the firm emerged from bankruptcy; a compromise was made in which creditors settled for less than 100 percent of their claims.

Capital Structure. Thus far, variations in a firm's earnings have been treated as though they were purely random fluctuations about some mean. Now let us modify this assumption and allow not only for these "random" fluctuations but also for shifts in the underlying mean income (or permanent earning power) of the firm, because we know that industries and firms do rise and fall over the years.

Capital assets have value only because they earn income. If investors believe that the earning power of a particular collection of assets has changed, the market value of those assets will change. When earnings variability is observed, it is impossible to distinguish between "random" fluctuations about the mean and fluctuations due to shifts in the mean itself. It is reasonable to believe that investors attribute variations in earnings to both causes. Earnings variability, then, is no longer a pure measure of random fluctuations. It also gives some information about the likelihood of future shifts in the earning power of the firm—about shifts in the value of the firm's assets. The investor will then be interested in how much the firm's assets can decline in value before they become less than its liabilities and the firm becomes insolvent. A measure of this factor is the ratio of the market value of the firm's equity to the par value of its debts. When this ratio is, say, nineteen, the firm's assets may fall 95 percent in value before it becomes insolvent. But when the equity/debt ratio is one-fourth, a default can be expected if the assets lose only 20 percent of their value. The equity/debt ratio has been designated as x_3.

MARKETABILITY

I have developed the hypothesis that investors believe that the risk that a firm's bonds will be defaulted depends on the firm's earnings variability, its period of solvency, and its equity/debt ratio. Now let us consider the measurement of the other type of risk an investor incurs by holding a corporate bond, the risk associated with the difficulty of turning the bond into cash before it matures.

If securities markets were "perfect" (in the sense that the actions of a single individual could have only an infinitesimal effect on the price of a security), it would not be necessary to take up this topic at all; turning a bond into cash would be no problem. It is true that an investor who disposes of any interest-bearing security before maturity may have to take a loss because of changes in the pure interest rate between the time he buys his bond and the time he sells it. But such losses are allowed for by defining risk premium as the difference between the yield on the bond under consideration and the yield on a bond of the same maturity which is sure to be paid, so that compensation for possible changes in the pure rate of interest is present even in the yields on riskless bonds. Thus marketability can influence the risk premium only if it measures the degree of imperfection—the effect of a single individual's action on price—in the market for a particular security.[19]

How can an investor estimate the degree of imperfection of the market for a particular security? There are several possible ways. Imperfection of the market for bonds can be expected to result in bondholders' demanding compensation for risk because it makes the price and yield of a bond at any particular moment uncertain. Ideally, one might measure this uncertainty by finding the "random" fluctuations in the price of a bond over a short period. However, the bond market is often rather inactive.[20] Bond prices are subject both to

---

[19] The holder of a risky bond may demand compensation simply because expectations about his bond may be subject to frequent change. But this type of "risk" is, I believe, merely an aspect of the risk of default itself.

[20] Total sales on the New York Stock Exchange of some of the listed issues included in

random fluctuations and to changes caused by changes in the prospects of the firm and in the pure rate of interest. If the period of observation is made so short that the non-random changes in bond prices are negligible, it will also be too short to permit much random fluctuation.

The volume of trading and the "spread" between "bid" and "ask" prices are variables sometimes suggested as measures of marketability.[21] The volume of trading can be used only for bonds listed on some securities exchange.[22] In the abstract, "spread" could be applied to both listed and unlisted securities. But published quotations for listed bonds are "inside" (actual) prices, and quotations for over-the-counter securities are generally "outside" (nominal) prices. Hence neither of these measures can be used in this study, which includes both listed and unlisted securities.

The third variable that can be used as a measure of marketability is x_4, the total market value of the publicly traded bonds the firm has outstanding. This variable was used because it is applicable to both listed and over-the-counter securities. One of the reasons for believing that it is a good measure of marketability may be summarized as follows: Other things being equal, the smaller the amount of bonds a firm has outstanding, the less frequently we should expect its bonds to change hands. The less often its bonds change hands, the thinner the market; and the thinner the market, the more uncertain is the market price. Hence, other things being equal, the larger the market value of publicly traded bonds a firm has outstanding, the smaller is the expected risk premium on those bonds.

Thus we have the proposition that risk premium depends on estimated risk of default and on marketability. Risk of default depends on earnings variability, x_1; period of solvency, x_2; and equity/debt ratio, x_3. Marketability depends on bonds outstanding, x_4.[23]

---

the cross-sections were less than $50,000—50 bonds—a year. An issue may be quoted almost every day but not traded for six months or more.

[21] Cf. Graham and Dodd, *Security Analysis* (3d ed,; New York, 1951), p. 31.

[22] For a comparison of "volume of trading" with "bonds outstanding," the measure of marketability used in this study, see Section VII.

[23] This hypothesis might, perhaps, have been derived directly from Alfred Marshall's statements on the considerations involved in determining risk premiums on loans to entrepreneurs: "It is then necessary to analyse a little more carefully the extra risks which are introduced into business when much of the capital used in it has been borrowed. Let us suppose that two men are carrying on similar businesses, the one working with his own, the other chiefly with borrowed capital.

"There is one set of risks which is common to both; which may be described as the *trade risks* [A] of the particular business in which they are engaged.

. . . But there is another set of risks, the burden of which has to be borne by the man working with borrowed capital, and not by the other; and we may call them *personal risks*. For he who lends capital to be used by another for trade purposes, has to charge a high interest as insurance against the chances of some flaw or deficiency in the borrower's personal character or ability.

"The borrower may be less able than he appears [B], less energetic, or less honest. He has not the same inducements [C], as a man working with his own capital has, to look failure straight in the face, and withdraw from a speculative enterprise as soon as it shows signs of going against him . . . " (*Principles of Economics* [4th ed.; London, 1898], p. 674; [8th ed,; New York, 1952], pp. 589–90 [italics his]).

My coefficient of variation of earnings can be identified with Marshall's "trade risks"

FORM OF THE FUNCTION

My hypothesis may now be stated as

$$x_0 = f(x_1, x_2, x_3, x_4)$$

To test the hypothesis, it was necessary to assume some form of the function.

If the influence of one independent variable on risk premium is independent of the magnitudes of the other independent variables, a linear function may be appropriate. If, however, the influence of one variable depends on the magnitudes of the other variables, then some other form is required.

It would appear that the latter is the case here. Let us again consider the two firms, one with an equity/debt ratio of 19, the other with an equity/debt ratio of one-fourth.[24] The risk of default on bonds of the first firm will probably be very small no matter how unstable its earnings may be; for in order for bondholders to suffer much of a loss if the firm's business should become unprofitable, the resale value of its assets would have to be less than 5 percent of their present value to the business as a going concern. But holders of the bonds of the second firm will be very much interested in how likely it is that the firm will continue to earn enough to meet its obligations; for if its current business should become unprofitable, its assets would probably not be worth enough to pay off the bonds in full. Hence, we should expect the influence of one variable on risk of default to depend on the magnitudes of the other variables. If the risk of default is small, an investor can be quite certain of what the equilibrium price of his bonds is. For when the risk of default is small, estimates of that risk are unlikely to change much over time.[25] Hence if an investor wants to liquidate his holdings, he exposes himself to little uncertainty by borrowing temporarily on the security of his bonds. But when the risk of default is large, his collateral does not enable the bondholder to obtain so large a loan at any given rate of interest. Thus the holder of a risky bond will have more incentive to sell quickly, at less than equilibrium price. Marketability, then, also becomes more important as the other variables indicate more risk of default.

A function which behaves in the manner implied by the preceding paragraph is given in equation (8).[25a]

$$x_0 = a_0' x_1^{q_1} x_2^{q_2} x_3^{q_3} x_4^{q_4} \tag{8}$$

This form is particularly convenient for multiple regression analysis because

[A] on the ground that the greater is the coefficient of variation, the greater are the trade risks; my period of solvency with Marshall's "the borrower may be less able than he appears" [B] on the ground that the longer a firm has operated successfully, the less likely it is that its success has been due to a run of good luck; and my equity/debt ratio directly with Marshall's "inducements" [C]. Marshall also notes the possible value of marketability (4th ed., p. 673 n,; 8th ed., p. 589 n.) and points out that investors may demand more than actuarial risk premiums (4th ed., p. 196 n.; 8th ed., p. 122 n.).

[24] These numbers are well within the range of the equity/debt ratios of firms included in the cross-sections.

[25] See any recent *Moody's Manual*, p. v.

[25a] Eqs. (1)–(7) are described in Table 1.

the method of least squares may be applied when equation (8) is transformed to

$$X_0 = a_0 + a_1X_1 + a_2X_2 + a_3X_3 + a_4X_4,$$

which is the hypothesis described in the introduction.[26]

This hypothesis was tested for cross-sections of domestic industrial corporations. The results it gave will be compared with the results given by alternative hypotheses and with the results of some other studies not directly related to this one.

V. SOME ALTERNATIVE MEASURES

The independent variables used in my hypothesis are plausible, but they were selected rather arbitrarily. Some alternatives are also plausible. The use of x_1, the coefficient of variation in earnings for the last nine years, requires the implicit assumption that investors expect the firm's average annual earnings in the future to equal the average for the last nine years. We do not know that this is true. But we do know that the market value of a firm's expected future earnings is given by the market value of the firm's equity and that this market value is highly correlated with expected future earnings. Thus an alternative to x_1, earnings variability, for measuring expected variability of earnings is the ratio of the standard deviation in earnings for the last nine years to the market value of the equity in a firm. Let us call this measure x_8.

When the equity/debt ratio is included in the function (eq. 8), the measure of marketability, x_4, becomes an inefficient measure of the size of a firm, for total debt and bonds outstanding are highly correlated. Is it not possible that investors merely prefer to invest their funds in securities issued by large firms? If the answer to this question is in the affirmative, it would be better to use a more efficient measure of firm size. When the equity/debt ratio is included, such a measure is the market value of the equity in a firm. Let us call this measure x_5.[27]

The results obtained by substituting x_8 for x_1 and x_5 for x_4 will be reported in Section VII.

VI. SUMMARY OF STATISTICAL PROCEDURES

SELECTION OF THE CROSS SECTIONS

The hypotheses presented in Sections I and V were tested on cross-sections of domestic industrial companies. The tests were restricted to firms domiciled in the United States because a lender to a foreign corporation may incur risks

---

[26] Recall that $X_i = \log_{10} x_i$.

[27] Equity is the more efficient measure because, when the equity/debt ratio is held constant, total capital of a firm and equity are perfectly correlated. In this context, total debt is an equally efficient measure of firm size.

of a kind not present in lending to domestic corporations. Only "industrial" corporations[28] were included because public utilities and transportation companies are subject to forms of regulation which prevent their maximizing profits.[29] In the event of a decline in earnings, the regulatory bodies are presumably required to relax their restrictions enough to allow earnings to return to a "fair" level. Hence there are grounds for believing that, other things being equal, if a public utility and a manufacturing or retailing firm have the same earnings variability, the public utility is less likely to default on its bonds. If this is true, public utilities and industrial firms should not be analyzed in the same cross-section.

All domestic industrial corporations were included if meaningful data for testing the hypothesis described in Section I could be obtained for them from the sources consulted. The *Commercial and Financial Chronicle* and the *Bank and Quotation Record* were the main sources for security prices, *Moody's Industrial Manual* was the chief source of other data. In general, "meaningful data" were not available for companies with any of the following characteristics:

1. The firm's risk premium could not be estimated if
   a) Price quotations were not available for at least one bond issue at each significant level of seniority
   b) The only price quotations available for a class of bonds were for issues quoted at substantially above the call price or for issues whose quotations had obviously been affected by convertibility privileges or by the issue's having been called
   c) Substantial bond issues were those of subsidiaries or affiliates and the parent firm was not responsible for their debts
   d) The firm was in or about to go into receivership
   e) The firm had defaulted or was about to default on at least one of its bond issues
2. Earnings variability could not be estimated if
   a) Substantially complete and comparable consolidated income statements were not available for either the firm's period of solvency or for nine years
   b) The firm's period of solvency was less than two years
3. The market value of the firm's equity could not be estimated if quotations were lacking for substantial stock issues

December 31, 1953, was chosen for the initial test because it was the most recent date for which data were available in *Moody's Industrial Manual* when this study was begun (May, 1955). The other dates were chosen in order to get the cross-sections spaced over time and from periods of widely differing business and financial conditions.

MEASUREMENT OF THE VARIABLES

Risk Premium, x_0. I have defined the risk premium on a bond as the difference

---

[28] For the purposes of this study, industrial firms are defined as firms which would have been included in recent issues of *Moody's Industrial Manual*. This definition includes all types of corporations except public utilities, transportation companies, financial institutions, governments, or corporations not incorporated for profit.

[29] Inclusion of financial institutions would probably require analyzing the structure of their assets.

between its market yield to maturity and the yield on a riskless bond having the same maturity date. When the coupon rate and maturity date of a bond are known, its yield may be found by finding its price and looking up the yield in a book of bond tables. In general, price was found by taking the last sale price on December 31 or the mean of the closing "bid" and "ask" quotations on December 31.[30] In computing yields, this price was adjusted by adding a quarter of a point (for 1927 and 1932) or half a point[31] (for 1937, 1949, and 1953) to allow for a buyer's transactions cost. Thus the yields I computed were estimates of yields facing potential buyers.

Hypothetical pure rates for 1949 and 1953 were obtained from yields on fully taxable United States treasury bonds. On the earlier dates, interest on government bonds was wholly or partially exempt from income taxes. Hence, yields on governments were not directly comparable with yields on industrials. For 1927, 1932, and 1937, estimates of pure rates were based on "basic yield" series compiled by the National Bureau of Economic Research for the first quarter of the year following.[32]

The average risk premium on a firm's bonds, x_0, was taken as a weighted average of the risk premiums on its individual issues.

Earnings Variability, x_1. The coefficient of variation in earnings, x_1, was generally computed from statements of consolidated net income for nine consecutive years.[33] If a firm engaged in unusual accounting practices—for example, if it had set up surplus reserves out of income or was using last-in-first-out inventory valuation—it was necessary to exclude the firm from the cross-section unless its statements could be adjusted.

Period of Solvency, x_2. The methods used to estimate this variable have been described in Section IV. It should be pointed out, however, that for many firms the information in *Moody's* permits only a very rough estimate to be made of x_2, the period of solvency.

Equity/Debt Ratio, x_3. In computing the equity/debt ratio, it was first necessary to estimate equity, x_5, and debt, x_6. Equity was taken as the total market value of all shares of stock (both preferred and common) and all warrants for the purchase of stock outstanding and in the hands of the public. In general, total debt, x_6, was taken as total par value outstanding of bonds, notes, debentures, conditional sales contracts, mortgages, and judgments for

---

[30] Bond prices are in percent of par value. Stock prices are usually in dollars a share.

[31] For bonds, a point is 1 percent of par value; for stocks, usually one dollar a share.

[32] For a description of these series see David Durand, *Basic Yields on Corporate Bonds, 1900–1942* (National Bureau of Economic Research, technical paper No. 3) (New York, 1942).

[33] If the firm's period of solvency was less than nine years, years before the beginning of the period of solvency were excluded. Except for 1949, the nine-year period ended approximately on the date for which the cross-section was taken. For 1949 the period ended near December 31, 1953. The latter date had been used for the initial cross-section; 1949 was used for the first recheck. By using the same period for the computation of x_1 for both cross-sections, much labor was saved. The partial regression coefficients of X_1 computed in this manner were identical for both cross-sections. In view of this result, it was decided not to make the effort necessary to have the data for 1949 strictly comparable with the data for the other dates.

which the firm was obligor or guarantor. Any current liabilities other than these were not counted because they often vary a great deal during the course of a firm's fiscal year. The equity/debt ratio, x_3, was then obtained by dividing x_5 by x_6.

Bonds Outstanding, x_4. Bonds outstanding, the market value of publicly traded debt, was found by multiplying the par value of each publicly traded issue included in a firm's total debt by its unadjusted price. I assumed that an issue was publicly traded if I had price quotations for it or if *Moody's* stated that the issue was listed or traded on an organized securities exchange or quoted in some financial center.

Volume of Trading, x_7. To find the volume of trading, total sales of each issue on each securities exchange were multiplied by the mean of the high and low sales price of the bond for the year preceding the date of the cross-section. The estimates of the volume of trading in each issue for the year were then added to get x_7, the volume of trading in a firm's publicly traded bonds. This variable was computed for firms which had all their bonds outstanding listed or traded on the New York Stock Exchange or the American Stock Exchange, provided that no issue had been offered or retired during the year and there was no issue whose price had obviously been affected by convertibility privileges.

Ratio of Standard Deviation in Earnings to Equity, x_8. This alternative index of the variability of earnings was computed by dividing the standard deviation of earnings, which had been used in computing x_1, by equity, x_5.

SEQUENCE IN WHICH THE TESTS WERE CARRIED OUT

Before any data were gathered for 1953, I had tentatively concluded that risk premium was a function of earnings variability, x_1, and equity/debt ratio, x_3. While these data were being collected, it became apparent to me that period of solvency, x_2, would probably be an empirically significant variable. The first test of this hypothesis was performed by finding the multiple regression of X_0 on X_1, X_2, X_5, and X_6 for December 31, 1953. All these variables were found to be significant, but it was also found that the simple correlation between X_0 and X_6 was negative and almost as great as the multiple correlation,[34] The necessity for finding a plausible explanation for this phenomenon led to the use of the hypothesis summarized in Section I and developed in Sections III and IV. No further change was made in this hypothesis. When data for the third cross-section (1937) were obtained, it was noted that twenty firms had to be excluded only because they had negative values of x_1, and no X_1 could be defined for them. The alternative index of variability of earnings, x_8, was thought of as a means of avoiding this restriction on the scope of the hypothesis.

VII. FURTHER RESULTS

The data from the five cross-sections are summarized in Table 2. This table and

---

[34] For 1953, $r_{06} = -0.76$; $R_{0.1256} = 0.89$. However, r_{06} was unstable. It was not significantly different from zero for 1932.

some simple calculations[35] reveal that, although the simple regression coefficients all have the signs which would be expected on the basis of the analysis in Section IV, these simple regression coefficients and the coefficients of simple correlation between the logarithm of risk premium, X_0, and the logarithms of the independent variables vary widely between dates.

But, as shown in Section II, both the multiple correlation coefficients and the partial regression coefficients which result from testing the hypothesis stated in the introduction are remarkably stable from cross-section to cross-section.[36] Thus we have concluded that the partial elasticities of risk premium with respect to coefficient of variation in earnings, period of solvency, equity/debt ratio, and market value of publicly traded bonds outstanding are significantly different from zero and are relatively stable over time for domestic industrial corporations.

COMPARISONS WITH ALTERNATE HYPOTHESES

Equity, x_5, was substituted for bonds outstanding, x_4, in order to use a better measure of the size of firms in the regression for each of the five cross-sections. The resulting coefficient of multiple correlation, $R_{0.1235}$, was slightly smaller than $R_{0.1234}$ for all but the 1953 cross-section, for which it was slightly

[35] The simple regression coefficients and simple correlation coefficients may be obtained from Table 2 by applying the formulas

$$b_i = \sigma_{0i}{}^2 / \sigma_i^2$$
$$r_{0i}{}^2 = b_i \sigma_{0i}{}^2 / \sigma_0^2$$

[36] An approximate test of the significance of the differences of the partial regression coefficients among the cross-sections is provided by the following:

Suppose that the estimated partial regression coefficients, b_{it}, from the separate samples $t=1 \ldots T$ are all estimates from the same population. Let s_{it} be the standard error of estimate of b_{it} and let

$$b_i{}^* = \frac{\sum_{t=1}^{T} b_{it} / s^2{}_{it}}{\sum_{t=1}^{T} 1 / s^2{}_{it}}$$

Then the statistic

$$y = \sum_{t=1}^{T} \frac{(b_{it} - b_i{}^*)^2}{s^2{}_{it}}$$

has approximately the χ^2 distribution with $T-1$ degrees of freedom. Hence an improbably high value of y is cause for rejecting the hypothesis that the partial regression coefficients are estimates from the same population. (This test was suggested by David L. Wallace.)

When the test was applied to the partial regression coefficients shown in Table 1 for $t=1927, 1932, 1937, 1949, 1953$, the results shown in the following table were obtained.

Coefficient (1)	y (2)	Probability of obtaining as large a χ^2 (3)	Accept hypothesis that all samples have the same coefficient? (4)
a_1	0.72	0.95	Yes
a_2	5.13	0.275	Yes
a_3	2.72	0.61	Yes
a_4	16.86	0.0022	No

TABLE 2

Means, variances, and covariances of the common logarithms of the variables

Variable	Date	Mean	X₀	X₁	X₂	X₃	X₄	X₅	X₈
						Variance or covariance			
X_0	1927	0.1251	0.0740	0.0554	−0.0098	−0.0868	−0.0322	−0.1132	.....
	1932	0.6997	.2008	.0871	− .0441	− .1757	− .0976	− .2130	0.1565
	1937	0.3385	.1706	.0913	− .0562	− .0936	− .1397	− .2261	.0853
	1949	0.0261	.1752	.0770	− .0970	− .0861	− .2168	− .2837	.....
	1953	−0.0811	.2058	.0907	− .0717	−.0623	− .2405	− .3071	.....
	Average	0.1783	.1650	.0808	− .0576	− .0933	−.1533	.....	.....
	Over-all	0.1783	0.2260	.1176	− .0768	− .1257	− .1684	.....	.....
X_1	1927	−0.0873	.....	.1404	.0141	− .0578	− .1086	−.0739	.....
	1932	−0.0134	.....	.1238	− .0108	− .1023	− .0044	− .0774	.1426
	1937	0.1650	.....	.2430	.0417	− .0289	− .0669	− .0929	.1384
	1949	−0.3240	.....	.0882	− .0603	− .0378	− .1010	− .1260	.....
	1953	−0.3276	.....	.1045	− .0375	− .0250	− .1208	− .1415	.....
	Average	−0.1219	.....	.1443	− .0095	− .0443	− .0696	.....	.....
	Over-all	−0.1219	.....	0.1843	− .0303	− .0554	− .0855	.....	.....
X_2	1927	1.3646	.....	.....	.0759	− .0232	.0118	− .0102	.....
	1932	1.3692	.....	.....	.1163	.0487	.0271	.0642	−.0324
	1937	1.2620	.....	.....	.1680	.0300	.0389	.0628	.0285
	1949	1.4495	.....	.....	.1529	.0464	.1349	.1694	.....
	1953	1.5717	.....	.....	.0896	.0116	.0849	.0995	.....
	Average	1.4070	.....	.....	.1219	.0208	.0624	.....	.....
	Over-all	1.4070	.....	.....	0.1344	.0257	.0716	.....	.....
X_3	1927	0.4688	.....	.....	.....	.2270	− .0735	.1419	.....
	1932	−0.0522	.....	.....	.....	.2628	.0263	.2348	−.1919
	1937	0.2942	.....	.....	.....	.1639	− .0101	.1454	−.0594
	1949	0.3510	.....	.....	.....	.1011	.0869	.1705	.....
	1953	0.4010	.....	.....	.....	.0896	.0360	.1126	.....
	Average	0.3225	.....	.....	.....	.1567	.0125	.....	.....
	Over-all	0.3225	.....	.....	.....	0.1799	.0201	.....	.....
X_4	1927	1.0117	.....	.....	.....	.....	.3218	.2473	.....
	1932	0.8624	.....	.....	.....	.....	.2819	.2703	− .0287
	1937	0.7000	.....	.....	.....	.....	.4217	.3876	− .0594
	1949	0.8541	.....	.....	.....	.....	.4249	.4858	.....
	1953	0.9830	.....	.....	.....	.....	.4692	.4967	.....
	Average	0.8792	.....	.....	.....	.....	.3972	.....	.....
	Over-all	0.8792	.....	.....	.....	.....	0.4112	.....	.....
X_5	1927	1.5265	.....	.....	.....	.....	.....	.3800	.....
	1932	0.9984	.....	.....	.....	.....	.....	.4418	−.1732
	1937	1.1259	.....	.....	.....	.....	.....	.5566	−.1399
	1949	1.3035	.....	.....	.....	.....	.....	.6366	.....
	1953	1.5691	.....	.....	.....	.....	.....	0.6360	.....
X_8	1932	0.6484	.....	.....	.....	.....	.....	.....	.2274
	1937	1.0368	.....	.....	.....	.....	.....	.....	0.1483

* *For definitions of variables see text.*

The partial regression coefficient is shown in column 1. The value of y actually obtained is shown in column 2. The probability of obtaining a value of χ^2 as large as that actually found, if the regression coefficients are independent and the differences in a_i among the cross-sections are due entirely to random errors of sampling, is shown in column 3. The decision concerning the hypothesis is indicated on column 4.

larger.[37] The largest difference between corresponding values of a_1 and $b_{01 \cdot 235}$, a_2 and $b_{02 \cdot 135}$, and a_4 and $b_{05 \cdot 123}$ was 0.035. However, the range of values for $b_{03 \cdot 125}$ was -0.149 to -0.324, while the range for a_3 was only -0.404 to -0.531. Thus bonds outstanding, x_4, appears to be the better variable. It seems to lead to better prediction of risk premiums and, when it is used, the elasticity estimates are more nearly stable. This result was confirmed when it was found that when both variables are used, although the estimates of $b_{03 \cdot 1245}$, $b_{04 \cdot 1235}$ and $b_{05 \cdot 1234}$ are all rather poor because of the multicollinearity among X_3, X_4, and X_5, the minimum ratio of $b_{04 \cdot 1234}$ to its standard error is 0.86, a value exceeded by the ratio of $b_{05 \cdot 1234}$ to its standard error in only two of the five cross-sections. However, we must distinguish between the two hypotheses chiefly on economic, rather than statistical, grounds. Both risk premium, x_0, and bonds outstanding, x_4, depend on market price. While the correlation between X_0 and X_4 from this source is undoubtedly very small, the multicollinearity among X_3, X_4, and X_5 is so great that the influence of the autocorrelation on $b_{04 \cdot 1235}$ may not be negligible. On economic grounds, X_4 is clearly superior to X_5. Large corporations, we find, are able to borrow at lower cost than small corporations, other things being equal. Variable X_4 offers an explanation; X_5 merely repeats the statement.

My tests of the ratio of the standard deviation of earnings to equity, x_8, as an alternative to the coefficient of variation of past earnings, x_1, are also somewhat inconclusive.[38] For 1932, X_8 appears to be a slightly better variable. For 1937, X_1 appears to be a considerably better variable. Of the two, X_8 has meaning for the larger number of firms, but X_8 is more highly correlated with X_2, X_3, and X_4 than is X_1.[39] It would appear that the market value of the equity in a firm depends not only on the expectation of the firm's earnings but also on the other factors which determine the risk premiums on the firm's bonds. Since the use of X_1 is based on the arbitrary assumption that investors expect the future average annual earnings of a firm to equal the arithmetic mean of the last nine years' earnings and since neither X_1 nor X_8 is clearly superior to the other, I am sure that an index of expected future earnings can be found that is better than that used in computing either X_1 or X_8. Such a variable could probably best be found in a study of the determinants of market value of equity organized along lines similar to those followed in this study.

The major reason for using X_8, however, was to test the applicability of the general hypothesis to firms whose net earnings have been negative. Figure 4 shows the scatter of 1937 risk premiums for the 89 firms included in regression equation (10), Table 3, and for 20 firms with negative mean earnings not included in that regression, plotted against values of x_0 estimated from that re-

---

Although a_4 the coefficient of bonds outstanding, appears to vary significantly, the effects of this variation are small. The root mean-square standard error of estimate of X_0 from the regressions for the separate cross-sections is 0.2076. For the pooled-moments regression (eq. [1]) it is only 0.2094—less than 1 percent greater.

[37] The difference between the R's for this sample was the third largest of five.

[38] Compare equations (9) and (10) (Table 3) with equations (4) and (5) (Table 1).

[39] Other things being equal, the standard errors of partial regression coefficients increase as certain elements of the inverse of the variance-covariance matrix of the independent variables increase. These elements depend in part on the collinearities among the independent variables. For 1932 and 1937, five out of six such elements were greater when X_8 was used than the corresponding elements when X_1 was used.

TABLE 3

Regression equations under the hypothesis that

$$X_0 = d_0 + d_8 X_8 + d_2 X_2 + d_3 X_3 + d_4 X_4$$

Equation	Date	No. of firms	Degrees of freedom	R^2	d_0	d_8 (s_8)	d_2 (s_2)	d_3 (s_3)	d_4 (s_4)
9	1932	45	40	0.738	1.186	+0.295 (.123)	−0.060 (.112)	−0.415 (.117)	−0.272 (.069)
10	1937	89	84	0.693	1.304	+.326 (0.080)	−.254 (0.067)	−.423 (0.072)	−.261 (0.042)

gression equation. It is obvious from Figure 4 that these 20 risk premiums are predicted with about as much precision as the 89.

Thus it appears that, where applicable, the variables of the main hypothesis, specified in Section I, are superior to the alternative variables suggested in Section V for the purpose of estimating the elasticities of risk premium with respect to factors indicating risks incurred by lenders.

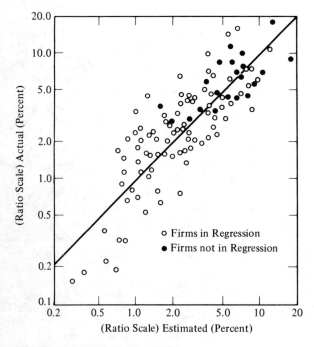

FIGURE 4

Scatter of December 31, 1937, risk premiums against risk premiums estimated from equation (10)

POSSIBLE SOURCES OF ERROR

When X_0, the logarithm of risk premium, is estimated from equation (1), its standard error of estimate is 0.2094, which indicates that approximately two-thirds of the estimates of x_0, risk premium, are between 62 percent and

162 percent of the measured values. Let us consider the possible reasons for the errors in these estimates. If the variables I have used are proper ones and the form of the function I have used is correct, these errors must be due to four causes: errors in the measurement of risk premium; errors in the measurement of the independent variables; omission of relevant variables from the hypothesis; and randomness of bond prices or imperfect adjustment of the market prices of securities to their "equilibrium" values.

Errors in Risk Premiums. Errors in the measurement of risk premium exist for two reasons. There are errors in the yields of bonds, and there are errors in the "pure rate of interest." Errors in the yields of the bonds arose because for many firms I had to rely on the mean of "bid" and "ask" prices. Since these two prices are not the same, one can observe only a range within which the true yield of a bond must lie. Given the "spread" (difference between the bid and ask prices), this uncertainty in the bond yield becomes more serious (since the logarithm of risk premium is used in the regression equations) the nearer the yield is to the pure rate and the shorter the time until the bond matures.

I believe that the errors in X_0, the logarithm of risk premium, introduced by the "random" errors in prices are, in general, uniformly distributed over the range of risk premiums. For the spread in price quotations generally narrows as a bond approaches maturity and as its market yield approaches the pure rate. That part of the standard error of estimate of X_0 which is due to the uncertainty of bond prices is perhaps 0.05 (or about 11 percent of the value of x_0). Elimination of random errors of this magnitude would raise the squares of the coefficients of multiple correlation by only about 0.02. Not much of the error in estimating risk premium can be due to this cause.

Errors in the pure rate of interest introduce both random and systematic errors in the values of X_0. Errors in the "pattern" of rates may introduce random errors in X_0. But errors in the general level of the pattern can produce non-linearities in the function, for an error of given magnitude in the pure rate will cause a larger error in the logarithm of a small risk premium than it will cause in the logarithm of a large risk premium. Overestimating the level of pure interest rates may be the cause of the slight nonlinearities of the scatter in Figure 1 for 1937 and 1953. Since I do not know the errors in the pure rates, I cannot estimate the effects of such errors on the correlation coefficients. It is interesting to note, however, that the multiple correlation coefficients for the dates before World War II are less than the multiple correlation coefficients for the postwar dates. For the former dates basic yield series of the National Bureau of Economic Research were used in estimating pure rates—these series are hypothetical; for the latter dates yields on United States government bonds were used—these series were actually observed.

Errors in Independent Variables. The errors in the measurement of all independent variables except X_2 are believed to be neglibible. Random errors in X_2 resulting in a standard error of estimate of X_2 of 0.0791 (20 percent of the period of solvency, X_2) would have a negligible effect on equation (1). A standard error of 0.176 (two-thirds of observed values of x_2 between 2/3 and 3/2 times the the actual values) would have decreased R^2 by about 0.02, a_1 by 0.005, and a_2 by 0.088 and increased a_3 by 0.012 and a_4 by 0.014 (all in absolute magnitude) from their "true" values.[40] I believe that 0.176 is larger than the actual standard error of estimate of X_2. Furthermore, it would appear that the errors in X_2 are negatively correlated with the actual values. Such errors would tend to increase the absolute magnitude of a_2. Hence it appears that the estimates of elasticities in equation (1) can be taken at their face value.

Omission of Variables. The problem of the omission of relevant variables is a difficult one. Possible omitted variables are of two kinds: those which would indicate the probability of default and expected loss in the event of a default, and those which take account of the differences in the ways in which interest income and capital gains are taxed.

The latter is a less serious problem. If a bond is bought for par or above, all income from the bond is taxed as ordinary income if the investor holds the bond until maturity. If, however, the investor buys the bond below par, only the interest payments on the bonds are taxed as ordinary income. The difference between the purchase price and the amount for which the bond is redeemed is a capital gain. This difference in tax is difficult to take into account. One would expect the market yield on a bond with a high coupon rate to be higher than the yield on a bond with a low coupon rate because the former is more likely to sell above par if other things are equal. But bonds with the highest coupon rates will tend to be issued by the firms most likely to default. Hence one would expect to find the coupon rate correlated with other independent variables. Another effect also tends to obscure any effect of a high coupon rate. The investor in such a bond will get his income somewhat sooner than the investor in an equivalent bond with a low coupon rate—the high-coupon-rate bond has a shorter "duration." If the term-structure of interest rates is higher for long-term securities than for short-term securities, the high-coupon-rate bond will tend to have the lower yield—the tax and duration effects will largely offset each other. Long-term rates were substantially higher than short-term rates for all dates in this study except December 31, 1927.

Other variables that might have been taken into account are various terms contained in the bond indenture. These terms relate to the type of lien the bondholders have; the conditions, if any, under which the firm may issue additional bonds having the same or a higher lien; restrictions on dividends and sale of assets; conditions under which the indenture may be modified; sinking-fund and call provisions; the ratio of current assets to liabilities which the firm must maintain; and possibly other provisions.

One would expect that, if these provisions were included in the regressions, much of their effect on risk premiums would be obscured; for the compaincs least likely to default usually borrow without incurring many restrictions on their future operations. Even where this is not the case, it is difficult to appraise the effects of many indenture proivisions on risk premium. Perhaps an indenture can be modified if holders of two-thirds of the issue consent, or perhaps there is no provision for modification. If the company must extend its bonds to avoid receivership, some bondholders will be better off if the indenture can be modi-

---

[40] For a method of finding biases in partial regression coefficients when one independent variable is subject to (known) random error, see Gregory C. Chow, "Demand for Automobiles in the United States" (Doctoral dissertation in the University of Chicago Library), Appendix 1.

fied; others may consider themselves worse off. Hence, it is difficult to say whether a provision permitting modification will tend to raise or lower risk premium. This is an illustration of difficulties of taking indenture provisions into account. I am not a professional security analyst and was forced to neglect these provisions largely because of my lack of knowledge.[41]

RELATIONSHIP BETWEEN x_4 AND x_7

Some attempt was made to compare bonds outstanding, x_4, with volume of bonds traded, x_7. For each of the prewar cross-sections a correlation coefficient of about 0.8 was found between the logarithms of these variables; for the postwar cross-sections a correlation coefficient of about 0.7 was found. The annual volume of trading was about 10 percent of bonds outstanding for the prewar years, but only about I percent for the postwar years. Furthermore, the data for x_7 appear to be poor. For many issues different publications showed rather different volumes of trading. Moreover, there appears to be no relationship between residual risk premiums estimated from equation (1) and residual volume of trading estimated from bonds outstanding. These results, which show lower correlations in years of inactive markets, are consistent with the argument advanced in Section IV for bonds outstanding, as a measure of marketability.

STABILITY ON THE LEVEL OF RISK PREMIUMS

This study was not designed to measure whether the level of the regression equation is constant between cross-sections, since to do so we would have to know whether the determinants of stock prices are stable. Nevertheless, it appears that investors' behavior in the bond market is more stable than one would infer merely from inspecting the spreads between Moody's Aaa and Baa indexes of corporate bond yields. These spreads are shown in Table 4.

The coefficient of variation of the differences between Moody's Baa and Aaa indexes is 0.76. The similar coefficient for the implied indexes is only 0.365. If these spreads are assumed to be normally distributed over time, one must reject the hypothesis that the spreads between Moody's indexes are at least as stable as the spreads between the implied indexes if one uses the 10 percent level of significance, even though each series shown in Table 4 has only four degrees of freedom. The spreads, however, are highly correlated. The coefficient of correlation between the values in columns 4 and 7 of Table 4 is 0.924, which is significantly different from zero at the 2.5 percent level, even

[41] Herbert Arkin, in "A Statistical Analysis of the Internal Factors Affecting the Yields on Domestic Corporate Bonds" (Doctoral dissertation, Columbia University [Hewlett, N.Y., 1940]), attempted to measure the influence on bond yields of factors that are almost all specified by the bond contract. He could account for only 23 percent and 13 percent of the variance in yields of industrials at year-end 1927 and mid-year 1932, respectively. Since Arkin did not take the chief determinants of risk premiums into account (only coupon rate was significant in both of his industrial samples), it is difficult to say what the real importance of indenture provisions is. Arkin's is the only previous study I have found in which multiple regression analysis was used in attempting to discover how market prices of bonds are determined.

TABLE 4

Comparison of Moody's daily indexes of yields on industrial bonds with similar indexes implied by this study

Dec. 31 (1)	Moody's daily indexes (percent)			Indexes implied by this study (percent)		
	Aaa (2)	Baa (3)	Difference (4)	High grade (5)	Medium grade (6)	Difference (7)
1927	4.60*	5.50*	0.90*	4.59	5.71	1.12
1932	4.53	7.22	2.69	4.27	6.81	2.54
1937	2.95	4.64	1.69	2.60	4.20	1.60
1949	2.51	2.87	0.39	2.48	3.68	1.20
1953	3.07	3.64	0.57	3.03	4.42	1.39

Sources: Moody's Indexes: Moody's Investment Survey and Moody's Bond Survey. Implied indexes: Yields on bonds of firms with risk premiums implied by equation (1) (1953 constant term) of less than 0.40 percent for high grade and between 1.00 percent for medium grade.
* *Read from a graph, not strictly comparable with other dates.*

though this regression has only three degrees of freedom. However, if the values of x_1 and x_3 were adjusted to take changes in corporation income tax rates into account, the spread in the implied indexes for 1932 would almost certainly be reduced.

The problem of whether or not the level of risk premiums, given the showing risks incurred by investors, is stable over time cannot be answered conclusively on the basis of this study. If the variables I have used should prove to give the most nearly stable level of risk premiums over time, then it is clear that investors' behavior could not be deemed stable over time. For the improvement of the estimates of risk premium which occurs when one goes from equation (2), which assumes both a stable level and stable elasticities, to equation (1), which does not assume a stable level, is clearly significant.

CONCLUSION

This study shows that economic and statistical methods are applicable to security analysis. Although by its design it could not show whether investor behavior is rational or even stable, we know that, at least in the bond market, elasticities are reasonably stable over time.

Modigliani and Miller construct and test a hypothesis concerning the effect of the amount of debt in a firm's capital structure on the value of the firm, the cost of equity capital, and the overall cost of capital. The article is of particular interest because of its definitions and its use of perfect capital market conditions to derive propositions with respect to the behavior of actual capital markets. The detailed consideration of the risk–return characteristics of earnings stream together with the illustration of the ability of individuals to change the characteristics of a security by holding a combination of securities has implications for the valuation of any type of security.

7

The Cost of Capital, Corporation Finance and the Theory of Investment; Corporate Income Taxes, and the Cost of Capital: A Correction

Franco Modigliani and Merton H. Miller*

These articles are reprinted with permission from the American Economic Review, *Vol. XLVIII(June, 1958), pp. 261–297 and Vol. LIII, No. 3 (June, 1963), pp. 433–443. Parts of the first article have been deleted by the editors.*

What is the "cost of capital" to a firm in a world in which funds are used to acquire assets whose yields are uncertain; and in which capital can be obtained by many different media, ranging from pure debt instruments, representing money-fixed claims, to pure equity issues, giving holders only the right to a pro-rata share in the uncertain venture? This question has vexed at least three classes of economists: (1) the corporation finance specialist concerned with the techniques of financing firms so as to ensure their survival and growth;

* This article is a revised version of a paper delivered at the annual meeting of the Econometric Society, December 1956. The authors express thanks for the comments and suggestions made at that time by the discussants of the paper, Evsey Domar, Robert Eisner and John Lintner, and subsequently by James Duesenberry. They are also greatly indebted to many of their present and former colleagues and students at Carnegie Tech who served so often and with such remarkable patience as a critical forum for the ideas here presented.

(2) the managerial economist concerned with capital budgeting; and (3) the economic theorist concerned with explaining investment behavior at both the micro and macro levels.[1]

In much of his formal analysis, the economic theorist at least has tended to side-step the essence of this cost-of-capital problem by proceeding as though physical assets—like bonds—could be regarded as yielding known, sure streams. Given this assumption, the theorist has concluded that the cost of capital to the owners of a firm is simply the rate of interest on bonds; and has derived the familiar proposition that the firm, acting rationally, will tend to push investment to the point where the marginal yield on physical assets is equal to the market rate of interest.[2] This proposition can be shown to follow from either of two criteria of rational decision-making which are equivalent under certainty, namely (1) the maximization of profits and (2) the maximization of market value.

According to the first criterion, a physical asset is worth acquiring if it will increase the net profit of the owners of the firm. But net profit will increase only if the expected rate of return, or yield, of the asset exceeds the rate of interest. According to the second criterion, an asset is worth acquiring if it increases the value of the owners' equity, i e., if it adds more to the market value of the firm than the cost of acquisition. But what the asset adds is given by capitalizing the stream it generates at the market rate of interest, and this capitalized value will exceed its cost if and only if the yield of the asset exceeds the rate of interest. Note that, under either formulation, the cost of capital is equal to the rate of interest on bonds, regardless of whether the funds are acquired through debt instruments or through new issues of common stock. Indeed, in a world of sure returns, the distinction between debt and equity funds reduces largely to one of terminology.

It must be acknowledged that some attempt is usually made in this type of analysis to allow for the existence of uncertainty. This attempt typically takes the form of superimposing on the results of the certainty analysis the notion of a "risk discount" to be subtracted from the expected yield (or a "risk premium" to be added to the market rate of interest). Investment decisions are then supposed to be based on a comparison of this "risk adjusted" or "certainty-equivalent" yield with the market rate of interest.[3] No satisfactory explanation has yet been provided, however, as to what determines the size of the risk discount and how it varies in response to changes in other variables.

Considered as a convenient approximation, the model of the firm constructed via this certainty—or certainty-equivalent—approach has admittedly

---

[1] The literature bearing on the cost-of-capital problem is far too extensive for listing here. Numerous references to it will be found throughout the paper though we make no claim to completeness. One phase of the problem which we do not consider explicitly, but which has a considerable literature of its own is the relation between the cost of capital and public utility rates. For a recent summary of the "cost-of-capital theory" of rate regulation and a brief discussion of some of its implications, the reader may refer to H. M. Somers [20].

[2] Or, more accurately, to the marginal cost of borrowed funds since it is customary, at least in advanced analysis, to draw the supply curve of borrowed funds to the firm as a rising one. For an advanced treatment of the certainty case, see F. and V. Lutz [13].

[3] The classic examples of the certainty-equivalent approach are found in J. R. Hicks [8] and O. Lange [11].

been useful in dealing with some of the grosser aspects of the processes of capital accumulation and economic fluctuations. Such a model underlies, for example, the familiar Keynesian aggregate investment function in which aggregate investment is written as a function of the rate of interest—the same riskless rate of interest which appears later in the system in the liquidity-preference equation. Yet few would maintain that this approximation is adequate. At the macroeconomic level there are ample grounds for doubting that the rate of interest has as large and as direct an influence on the rate of investment as this analysis would lead us to believe. At the microeconomic level the certainty model has little descriptive value and provides no real guidance to the finance specialist or managerial economist whose main problems cannot be treated in a framework which deals so cavalierly with uncertainty and ignores all forms of financing other than debt issues.[4]

Only recently have economists begun to face up seriously to the problem of the cost of capital *cum* risk. In the process they have found their interests and endeavors merging with those of the finance specialist and the managerial economist who have lived with the problem longer and more intimately. In this joint search to establish the principles which govern rational investment and financial policy in a world of uncertainty two main lines of attack can be discerned. These lines represent, in effect, attempts to extrapolate to the world of uncertainty each of the two criteria—profit maximization and market value maximization—which were seen to have equivalent implications in the special case of certainty. With the recognition of uncertainty this equivalence vanishes. In fact, the profit maximization criterion is no longer even well defined. Under uncertainty there corresponds to each decision of the firm not a unique profit outcome, but a plurality of mutually exclusive outcomes, which can at best be described by a subjective probability distribution. The profit coutcome, in short, has become a random variable and as such its maximization no longer has an operational meaning. Nor can this difficulty generally be disposed of by using the mathematical expectation of profits as the variable to be maximized. For decisions which affect the expected value will also tend to affect the dispersion and other characteristcs of the distribution of outcomes. In particular, the use of debt rather than equity funds to finance a given venture may well increase the expected return to the owners, but only at the cost of increased dispersion of the outcomes.

Under these conditions the profit outcomes of alternative investment and financing decisions can be compared and ranked only in terms of a *subjective* "utility function" of the owners which weighs the expected yield against other characteristics of the distribution. Accordingly, the extrapolation of the profit maximization criterion of the certainty model has tended to evolve into utility maximization, sometimes explicitly, more frequently in a qualitative and heuristic form.[5]

[4] Those who have taken a "case-method" course in finance in recent years will recall in this connection the famous Liquigas case of Hunt and Williams [9, pp. 193–96] a case which is often used to introduce the student to the cost-of-capital problem and to poke a bit of fun at the economist's certainty-model.

[5] For an attempt at a rigorous explicit development of this line of attack, see F. Modigliani and M. Zeman [14].

The utility approach undoubtedly represents an advance over the certainty or certainty-equivalent approach. It does at least permit us to explore (within limits) some of the implications of different financing arrangements, and it does given some meaning to the "cost" of different types of funds. However, because the cost of capital has become an essentially subjective concept, the utility approach has serious drawbacks for normative as well as analytical purposes. How, for example, is management to ascertain the risk preferences of its stockholders and to compromise among their tastes? And how can the economist build a meaningful investment function in the face of the fact that any given investment opportunity might or might not be worth exploiting depending on precisely who happen to be the owners of the firm at the moment?

Fortunately, these questions do not have to be answered; for the alternative approach, based on market value maximization, can provide the basis for an operational definition of the cost of capital and a workable theory of investment. Under this approach any investment project and its concomitant financing plan must pass only the following test: Will the project, as financed, raise the market value of the firm's shares? If so, it is worth undertaking; if not, its return is less than the marginal cost of capital to the firm. Note that such a test is entirely independent of the tastes of the current owners, since market prices will reflect not only their preferences but those of all potential owners as well. If any current stockholder disagrees with management and the market over the valuation of the project, he is free to sell out and reinvest elsewhere, but will still benefit from the capital appreciation resulting from management's decision.

The potential advantages of the market-value approach have long been appreciated; yet analytical results have been meager. What appears to be keeping this line of development from achieving its promise is largely the lack of an adequate theory of the effect of financial structure on market valuations, and of how these effects can be inferred from objective market data. It is with the development of such a theory and of its implications for the cost-of-capital problem that we shall be concerned in this paper.

Our procedure will be to develop in Section I the basic theory itself and to give some brief account of its empirical relevance. In Section II, we show how the theory can be used to answer the cost-of-capital question and how it permits us to develop a theory of investment of the firm under conditions of uncertainty. Throughout these sections the approach is essentially a partial-equilibrium one focusing on the firm and "industry." Accordingly, the "prices" of certain income streams will be treated as constant and given from outside the model, just as in the standard Marshallian analysis of the firm and industry the prices of all inputs and of all other products are taken as given. We have chosen to focus at this level rather than on the economy as a whole because it is at the level of the firm and the industry that the interests of the various specialists concerned with the cost-of-capital problem come most closely together. Although the emphasis has thus been placed on partial equilibrium analysis, the results obtained also provide the essential building blocks for a general equilibrium model which shows how those prices which are here taken as given, are themselves determined. For reasons of space, however, and because the material is of interest in its own right, the presentation of the general equilibrium model which rounds out the analysis must be deferred to a subsequent paper.

I. THE VALUATION OF SECURITIES, LEVERAGE, AND THE COST OF CAPITAL

A. THE CAPITALIZATION RATE FOR UNCERTAIN STREAMS

As a starting point, consider an economy in which all physical assets are owned by corporations. For the moment, assume that these corporations can finance their assets by issuing common stock only; the introduction of bond issues, or their equivalent, as a source of corporate funds is postponed until the next part of this section.

The physical assets held by each firm will yield to the owners of the firm—its stockholders—a stream of "profits" over time; but the elements of this series need not be constant and in any event are uncertain. This stream of income, and hence the stream accruing to any share of common stock, will be regarded as extending indefinitely into the future. We assume, however, that the mean value of the stream over time, or average profit per unit of time, is finite and represents a random variable subject to a (subjective) probability distribution. We shall refer to the average value over time of the stream accruing to a given share as the return of that share; and to the mathematical expectation of this average as the expected return of the share.[6] Although individual investors may have different views as to the shape of the probability distribution of the return of any share, we shall assume for simplicity that they are at least in agreement as to the expected return.[7]

This way of characterizing uncertain streams merits brief comment. Notice first that the stream is a stream of profits, not dividends. As will become clear later, as long as management is presumed to be acting in the best interests of the stockholders, retained earnings can be regarded as equivalent to a fully subscribed, pre-emptive issue of common stock. Hence, for present purposes, the division of the stream between cash dividends and retained earnings in any period is a mere detail. Notice also that the uncertainty attaches to the mean value over time of the stream of profits and should not be confused with vari-

---

[6] These propositions can be restated analytically as follows; The assets of the ith firm generate a stream:

$$X_i \ (1), X_i \ (2) \ \ldots X_i \ (T)$$

whose elements are random variables subject to the joint probability distribution:

$$\chi_i \ [X_i \ (1), X_i \ (2) \ \ldots X_i \ (t) \ ]$$

The return to the ith firm is defined as:

$$X_i = \lim_{T \to \infty} \frac{1}{T} \sum_{t=1}^{T} X_i(t)$$

X_i is itself a random variable with a probability distribution $\Phi_i(X_i)$ whose form is determined uniquely by χ_i. The expected return $\bar{X}_i$ is defined as $\bar{X}_i = E(X_i) = \int \chi_i X_i \ \Phi_i \ (X_i) dX_i$. If N_i is the number of shares outstanding, the return of the ith share is $x_i = (1/N) \ X_i$ with probability distribution $\phi_i(x_i) dx_i = \phi_i(N x_i) d(N x_i)$ and expected value $\bar{x}_i = (1/N) \ \bar{X}_i$.

[7] To deal adequately with refinements such as differences among investors in estimates of expected returns would require extensive discussion of the theory of portfolio selection. Brief references to these and related topics will be made in the succeeding article on the general equilibrium model.

ability over time of the successive elements of the stream. That variability and uncertainty are two totally different concepts should be clear from the fact that the elements of a stream can be variable even though known with certainty. It can be shown, furthermore, that whether the elements of a stream are sure or uncertain, the effect of variability per se on the valuation of the stream is at best a second-order one which can safely be neglected for our purposes (and indeed most others too).[8]

The next assumption plays a strategic role in the rest of the analysis. We shall assume that firms can be divided into "equivalent return" classes such that the return on the shares issued by any firm in any given class is proportional to (and hence perfectly correlated with) the return on the shares issued by any other firm in the same class. This assumption implies that the various shares within the same class differ, at most, by a "scale factor." Accordingly, if we adjust for the difference in scale, by taking the *ratio* of the return to the expected return, the probability distribution of that ratio is identical for all shares in the class. It follows tht all relevant properties of a share are uniquely characterized by specifying (1) the class to which it belongs and (2) its expected return.

The significance of this assumption is that it permits us to classify firms into groups within which the shares of different firms are "homogeneous," that is, perfect substitutes for one another. We have, thus, an analogue to the familiar concept of the industry in which it is the commodity produced by the firms that is taken as homogeneous. To complete this analogy with Marshallian price theory, we shall assume in the analysis to follow that the shares concerned are traded in perfect markets under conditions of atomistic competition.[9]

From our defintion of homogeneous classes of stock it follows that in equilibrium in a perfect capital market the price per dollar's worth of expected return must be the same for all shares of any given class. Or, equivalently, in any given class the price of every share must be proportional to its expected return. Let us denote this factor of proportionality for any class, say the kth class, by $1/\rho_k$. Then if p_j denotes the price and $\bar{x}_j$ is the expected return per share of the jth firm in class k, we must have:

$$p_j = \frac{1}{\rho_k}\bar{x}_j; \tag{1}$$

or, equivalently,

$$\frac{\bar{x}_j}{p_j} - \rho_k \text{ a constant for all firms } j \text{ in class } k. \tag{2}$$

---

[8] The reader may convince himself of this by asking how much he would be willing to rebate to his employer for the privilege of receiving his annual salary in equal monthly installments rather than in irregular amounts over the year. See also J. M. Keynes [10, esp. pp. 53–54].

[9] Just what our classes of stocks contain and how the different classes can be identified by outside observers are empirical questions to which we shall return later. For the present, it is sufficient to observe: (1) Our concept of a class, while not identical to that of the industry is at least closely related to it. Certainly the basic characteristics of the probability distributions of the returns on assets will depend to a significant extent on the product sold and the technology used. (2) What are the appropriate class boundaries will depend on the particular problem being studied. An economist concerned with

The constants ρ_k (one for each of the k classes) can be given several economic interpretations: (a) From (2) we see that each ρ_k is the expected rate of return of any share in class k. (b) From (1) $1/\rho_k$ is the price which an investor has to pay for a dollar's worth of expected return in the class k. (c) Again from (1), by analogy with the terminology for perpetual bonds, ρ_k can be regarded as the market rate of capitalization for the expected value of the uncertain streams of the kind generated by the kth class of firms.[10]

B. DEBT FINANCING AND ITS EFFECTS ON SECURITY PRICES

Having developed an apparatus for dealing with uncertain streams we can now approach the heart of the cost-of-capital problem by dropping the assumption that firms cannot issue bonds. The introduction of debt-financing changes the market for shares in a very fundamental way. Because firms may have different proportions of debt in their capital structure, shares of different companies, even in the same class, can give rise to different probability distributions of returns. In the language of finance, the shares will be subject to different degrees of financial risk or "leverage" and hence they will no longer be perfect substitutes for one another.

To exhibit the mechanism determining the relative prices of shares under these conditions, we make the following two assumptions about the nature of bonds and the bond market, though they are actually stronger than is necessary and will be relaxed later: (1) All bonds (including any debts issued by households for the purpose of carrying shares) are assumed to yield a constant income per unit of time, and this income is regarded as certain by all traders regardless of the issuer. (2) Bonds, like stocks, are traded in a perfect market, where the term perfect is to be taken in its usual sense as implying that any two commodities which are perfect substitutes for each other must sell, in equilibrium, at the same price. It follows from assumption (1) that all bonds are in fact perfect substitutes up to a scale factor. It follows from assumption (2) that they must all sell at the same price per dollar's worth of return, or what amounts to the same thing must yield the same rate of return. This rate of return will be denoted by r and referred to as the rate of interest or, equivalently, as the capitalization rate for sure streams. We now can derive the following two basic propositions with respect to the valuation of securities in companies with different capital structures:

Proposition 1. Consider any company j and let $\bar{X}_j$ stand as before for the expected return on the assets owned by the company (that is, its expected profit before deduction of interest). Denote by D_j the market value of the debts of the company; by S_j the market value of its common shares; and by $V_j \equiv S_j + D_j$

---

general tendencies in the market, for example, might well be prepared to work with far wider classes than would be appropriate for an investor planning his portfolio, or a firm planning its financial strategy.

[10] We cannot, on the basis of the assumptions so far, make any statements about the relationship or spread between the various ρ's or capitalization rates. Before we could do so we would have to make further specific assumptions about the way investors believe the probability distributions vary from class to class, as well as assumptions about investors' preferences as between the characteristics of different distributions.

the market value of all its securities or, as we shall say, the market value of the firm. Then, our Proposition I asserts that we must have in equilibrium:

$$V_j = (S_j + D_j) = \bar{X}_j / \rho_k, \text{ for any firm } j \text{ in class } k. \tag{3}$$

That is, the *market value of any firm is independent of its capital structure and is given by capitalizing its expected return at the rate ρ_k appropriate to its class.*

This proposition can be stated in an equivalent way in terms of the firms' "average cost of capital," $\bar{X}_j/V_j$, which is the ratio of its expected return to the market value of all its securities. Our proposition then is

$$\frac{\bar{X}_j}{(S_j + D_j)} \equiv \frac{\bar{X}_j}{V_j} = \rho_k, \text{ for any firm } j, \text{ in class } k. \tag{4}$$

That is, *the average cost of capital to any firm is completely independent of its capital structure and is equal to the capitalization rate of a pure equity stream of its class.*

To establish Proposition I we will show that as long as the relations (3) or (4) do not hold between any pair of firms in a class, arbitrage will take place and restore the stated equalities. We use the term arbitrage advisedly. For if Proposition I did not hold, an investor could buy and sell stocks and bonds in such a way as to exchange one income stream for another stream, identical in all relevant respects but selling at a lower price. The exchange would therefore be advantageous to the investor quite independently of his attitudes toward risk.[11] As investors exploit these arbitrage opportunities, the value of the overpriced shares will fall and that of the underpriced shares will rise, thereby tending to eliminate the discrepancy between the market values of the firms.

By way of proof, consider two firms in the same class and assume for simplicity only, that the expected return, $\bar{X}$, is the same for both firms. Let company 1 be financed entirely with common stock while company 2 has some debt in its capital structure. Suppose first the value of the levered firm, V_2, to be larger than that of the unlevered one, V_1. Consider an investor holding S_2 dollars' worth of the shares of company 2, representing a fraction α of the total outstanding stock, S_2. The return from this portfolio, denoted by Y_2, will be a fraction α of the income available for the stockholders of company 2, which is equal to the total return X_2 less the interest charge, rD_2. Since under our assumption of homogeneity, the anticipated total return of company 2, X_2, is, under all circumstances, the same as the anticipated total return to company 1, X_1, we can hereafter replace X_2 and X_1 by a common symbol X. Hence, the return from the initial portfolio can be written as:

$$Y_2 = \alpha(X - rD_2) \tag{5}$$

---

[11] In the language of the theory of choice, the exchanges are movements from inefficient points in the interior to efficient points on the boundary of the investor's opportunity set; and not movements between efficient points along the boundary. Hence for this part of the analysis nothing is involved in the way of specific assumptions about investor attitudes or behavior other than that investors behave consistently and prefer more income to less income, *ceteris paribus.*

Now suppose the investor sold his αS_2 worth of company 2 shares and acquired instead an amount $s_1 = \alpha\,(S_2 + D_2)$ of the shares of company 1. He could do so by utilizing the amount αS_2 realized from the sale of his initial holding and borrowing an additional amount αD_2 on his own credit, pledging his new holdings in company 1 as a collateral. He would thus secure for himself a fraction $s_1/S_1 = \alpha(S_2 + D_2)/S_1$ of the shares and earnings of company 1. Making proper allowance for the interest payments on his personal debt αD_2, the return from the new portfolio, Y_1, is given by:

$$Y_1 = \frac{\alpha(S_2 + D_2)}{S_1}X - r\alpha D_2 = \alpha\frac{V_2}{V_1}X - r\alpha D_2 \qquad (6)$$

Comparing (5) with (6) we see that as long as $V_2 > V_1$ we must have $Y_1 > Y_2$, so that it pays owners of company 2's shares to sell their holdings, thereby depressing S_2 and hence V_2; and to acquire shares of company 1, thereby raising S_1 and thus V_1. We conclude therefore that levered companies cannot command a premium over unlevered companies because investors have the opportunity of putting the equivalent leverage into their portfolio directly by borrowing on personal account.

Consider now the other possibility, namely that the market value of the levered company V_2 is less than V_1. Suppose an investor holds initially an amount s_1 of shares of company 1, representing a fraction α of the total outstanding stock, S_1. His return from this holding is:

$$Y_1 = \frac{s_1}{S_1} X = \alpha X.$$

Suppose he were to exchange this initial holding for another portfolio, also worth s_1, but consisting of s_2 dollars of stock of company 2 and of d dollars of bonds, where s_2 and d are given by:

$$s_2 = \frac{S_2}{V_2}s_1, \qquad d = \frac{D_2}{V_2}s_1. \qquad (7)$$

In other words the new portfolio is to consist of stock of company 2 and of bonds in the proportions S_2/V_2 and D_2/V_2, respectively. The return from the stock in the new portfolio will be a fraction s_2/S_2 of the total return to stockholders of company 2, which is $(X - rD_2)$, and the return from the bonds will be rd. Making use of (7), the total return from the portfolio, Y_2, can be expressed as follows:

$$Y_2 = \frac{s_2}{S_2}(X - rD_2) + rd = \frac{s_1}{V_2}(X - rD_2) + r\frac{D_2}{V_2}s_1 = \frac{s_1}{V_2}X = \alpha\frac{S_1}{V_2}X$$

(since $s_1 = \alpha S_1$). Comparing Y_2 with Y_1 we see that, if $V_2 < S_1 \equiv V_1$, then Y_2 will exceed Y_1. Hence it pays the holders of company 1's shares to sell these holdings and replace them with a mixed portfolio containing an appropriate fraction of the shares of company 2.

The acquisition of a mixed portfolio of stock of a levered company j and of bonds in the proportion S_j/V_j and D_j/V_j respectively, may be regarded as an operation which "undoes" the leverage, giving access to an appropriate fraction of the unlevered return X_j. It is this possibility of undoing leverage which prevents the value of levered firms from being consistently less than those of unlevered firms, or more generally prevents the average cost of capital $\bar{X}_j/V_j$ from being systematically higher for levered than for nonlevered companies in the same class. Since we have already shown that arbitrage will also prevent V_2 from being larger than V_1, we can conclude that in equilibrium we must have $V_2 = V_1$, as stated in Proposition I.

Proposition II. From Proposition I we can derive the following proposition concerning the rate of return on common stock in companies whose capital structure includes some debt: the expected rate of return or yield, i, on the stock of any company j belonging to the kth class is a linear function of leverage as follows:

$$i_j = \rho_k + (\rho_k - r)D_j / S_j \tag{8}$$

That is, *the expected yield of a share of stock is equal to the appropriate capitalization rate ρ_k for a pure equity stream in the class, plus a premium related to financial risk equal to the debt-to-equity ratio times the spread between ρ_k and r.* Or equivalently, the market price of any share of stock is given by capitalizing its expected return at the continuously variable rate i_j of (8).[12]

A number of writers have stated close equivalents of our Proposition I although by appealing to intuition rather than by attempting a proof and only to insist immediately that the results were not applicable to the actual capital markets.[13] Proposition II, however, so far as we have been able to discover is new.[14] To establish it we first note that, by definition, the expected rate of return, i, is given by:

$$i_j \equiv \frac{\bar{X}_j - rD_j}{S_j} \tag{9}$$

---

[12] To illustrate, suppose $\bar{X}=1000$, $D=4000$, $r=5$ per cent and $\rho_k=10$ per cent. These values imply that $V=10,000$ and $S=6000$ by virtue of Proposition I. The expected yield or rate of return per share is then:

$$i = \frac{1000 - 200}{6000} = .1 + (.1 - .05)\frac{4000}{6000} = 13\tfrac{1}{3} \text{ per cent}$$

[13] See, for example, J. B. Williams [21, esp. pp. 72–73]; David Durand [3]; and W. A. Morton [15]. None of these writers describe in any detail the mechanism which is supposed to keep the average cost of capital constant under changes in capital structure. They seem, however, to be visualizing the equilibrating mechanism in terms of switches by investors between stocks and bonds as the yields of each get out of line with their "riskiness." This is an argument quite different from the pure arbitrage mechanism underlying our proof, and the difference is crucial. Regarding Proposition I as resting on investors' attitudes toward risk leads inevitably to a misunderstanding of many factors influencing relative yields such as, for example, limitations on the portfolio composition of financial institutions. See below, esp. Section I.D.

[14] Morton does make reference to a linear yield function but only " . . . for the sake of simplicity and because the particular function used makes no essential difference in my conclusions" [15, p. 443, note 2].

From Proposition I, equation (3), we know that:

$$\bar{X}_j = \rho_k(S_j + D_j)$$

Substituting in (9) and simplifying, we obtain equation(8).

C. SOME QUALIFICATIONS AND EXTENSIONS OF THE BASIC PROPOSITIONS

The methods and results developed so far can be extended in a number of useful directions, of which we shall consider here only two: (one) recognizing the existence of a multiplicity of bonds and interest rates; and (two) acknowledging the presence of market imperfections which might interfere with the process of arbitrage.[15]

Effects of a Plurality of Bonds and Interest Rates. In existing capital markets we find not one, but a whole family of interest rates varying with maturity, with the technical provisions of the loan and, what is most relevant for present purposes, with the financial condition of the borrower.[16] Economic theory and market experience both suggest that the yields demanded by lenders tend to increase with the debt-equity ratio of the borrowing firm (or individual). If so, and if we can assume as a first approximation that this yield curve, $r = r(D/S)$, whatever its precise form, is the same for all borrowers, then we can readily extend our propositions to the case of a rising supply curve for borrowed funds.[17]

Proposition I is actually unaffected in form and interpretation by the fact that the rate of interest may rise with leverage; while the average cost of borrowed funds will tend to increase as debt rises, the average cost of funds from *all* sources will still be independent of leverage (apart from the tax effect). This conclusion follows directly from the ability of those who engage in arbitrage to undo the leverage in any financial structure by acquiring an appropriately mixed portfolio of bonds and stocks. Because of this ability, the ratio of earnings (*before* interest charges) to market value—*i.e.,* the average cost of capital from

---

[15] The Tax section of this article has been deleted by the editors.

[16] We shall not consider here the extension of the analysis to encompass the time structure of interest rates. Although some of the problems posed by the time structure can be handled within our comparative statics framework, an adequate discussion would require a separate paper.

[17] We can also develop a theory of bond valuation along lines essentially parallel to those followed for the case of shares. We conjecture that the curve of bond yields as a function of leverage will turn out to be a nonlinear one in contrast to the linear function of leverage developed for common shares. However, we would also expect that the rate of increase in the yield on new issues would not be substantial in practice. This relatively slow rise would reflect the fact that interest rate increases by themselves can never be completely satisfactory to creditors as compensation for their increased risk. Such increases may simply serve to raise r so high relative to p that they become self-defeating by giving rise to a situation in which even normal fluctuations in earnings may force the company into bankruptcy. The difficulty of borrowing more, therefore, tends to show up in the usual case not so much in higher rates as in the form of increasingly stringent restrictions imposed on the company's management and finances by the creditors; and ultimately in a complete inability to obtain new borrowed funds, at least from the institutional investors who normally set the standards in the market for bonds.

all sources—must be the same for all firms in a given class.[18] In other words, the increased cost of borrowed funds as leverage increases will tend to be offset by a corresponding reduction in the yield of common stock. This seemingly paradoxical result will be examined more closely below in connection with Proposition II.

A significant modification of Proposition I would be required only if the yield curve $r = r(D/S)$ were different for different borrowers, as might happen if creditors had marked preferences for the securities of a particular class of debtors. If, for example, corporations as a class were able to borrow at lower rates than individuals having equivalent personal leverage, then the average cost of capital to corporations might fall slightly, as leverage increased over some range, in reflection of this differential. In evaluating this possibility, however, remember that the relevant interest rate for our arbitrage operators is the rate on brokers' loans and, historically, that rate has not been noticeably higher than representative corporate rates.[19] The operations of holding companies and investment trusts which can borrow on terms comparable to operating companies represent still another force which could be expected to wipe out any marked or prolonged advantages from holding levered stocks.[20]

Although Proposition I remains unaffected as long as the yield curve is the same for all borrowers, the relation between common stock yields and leverage will no longer be the strictly linear one given by the original Proposition II. If r increases with leverage, the yield i will still tend to rise as D/S increases, but at a decreasing rather than a constant rate. Beyond some high level of leverage, depending on the exact form of the interest function, the yield may even start to fall.[21] The relation between i and D/S could conceivably take the form

[18] One normally minor qualification might be noted. Once we relax the assumption that all bonds have certain yields, our arbitrage operator faces the danger of something comparable to "gambler's ruin." That is, there is always the possibility that an otherwise sound concern—one whose long-run expected income is greater than its interest liability—might be forced into liquidation as a result of a run of temporary losses. Since reorganization generally involves costs, and because the operation of the firm may be hampered during the period of reorganization with lasting unfavorable effects on earnings prospects, we might perhaps expect heavily levered companies to sell at a slight discount relative to less heavily indebted companies of the same class.

[19] Under normal conditions, moreover, a substantial part of the arbitrage process could be expected to take the form, not of having the arbitrage operators go into debt on personal account to put the required leverage into their portfolios, but simply of having them reduce the amount of corporate bonds they already hold when they acquire underpriced unlevered stock. Margin requirements are also somewhat less of an obstacle to maintaining any desired degree of leverage in a portfolio than might be thought at first glance. Leverage could be largely restored in the face of higher margin requirements by switching to stocks having more leverage at the corporate level.

[20] An extreme form of inequality between borrowing and lending rates occurs, of course, in the case of preferred stocks, which cannot be directly issued by individuals on personal account. Here again, however, we would expect that the operations of investment corporations plus the ability of arbitrage operators to sell off their holdings of preferred stocks would act to prevent the emergence of any substantial premiums (for this reason) on capital structures containing preferred stocks. Nor are preferred stocks so far removed from bonds as to make it impossible for arbitrage operators to approximate closely the risk and leverage of a corporate preferred stock by incurring a somewhat smaller debt on personal account.

[21] Since new lenders are unlikely to permit this much leverage (cf. note 17), this range of

indicated by the curve *MD* in Figure 2, although in practice the curvature would be much less pronounced. By contrast, with a constant rate of interest, the relation would be linear throughout as shown by line *MM'*, Figure 2.

The downward sloping part of the curve *MD* perhaps requires some comment since it may be hard to imagine why investors, other than those who like lotteries, would purchase stocks in this range. Remember, however, that the yield curve of Proposition II is a consequence of the more fundamental Proposition I. Should the demand by the risk-lovers prove insufficient to keep the market to the peculiar yield-curve *MD*, this demand would be reinforced by the action of arbitrage operators. The latter would find it profitable to own a pro-rata share of the firm as a whole by holding its stock *and* bonds, the lower yield of the shares being thus offset by the higher return on bonds.

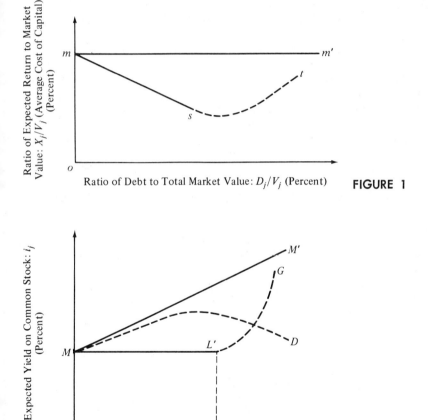

FIGURE 1

FIGURE 2

the curve is likely to be occupied by companies whose earnings prospects have fallen substantially since the time when their debts were issued

Although the falling, or at least U-shaped, cost-of-capital function is in one form or another the dominant view in the literature, the ultimate rationale of that view is by no means clear. The crucial element in the position—that the expected earnings-price ratio of the stock is largely unaffected by leverage up to some conventional limit—is rarely even regarded as something which requires explanation. It is usually simply taken for granted or it is merely asserted that this is the way the market behaves.[22] To the extent that the constant earnings-price ratio has a rationale at all we suspect that it reflects in most cases the feeling that moderate amounts of debt in "sound" corporations do not really add very much to the "riskiness" of the stock. Since the extra risk is slight, it seems natural to suppose that firms will not have to pay noticeably higher yields in order to induce investors to hold the stock.[23]

A more sophisticated line of argument has been advanced by David Durand [3, pp. 231–33]. He suggests that because insurance companies and certain other important institutional investors are restricted to debt securities, nonfinancial corporations are able to borrow from them at interest rates which are lower than would be required to compensate creditors in a free market. Thus, while he would presumably agree with our conclusions that stockholders could not gain from leverage in an unconstrained market, he concludes that they can gain under present institutional arrangements. This gain would arise by virtue of the "safety superpremium" which lenders are willing to pay corporations for the privilege of lending.[24]

The defective link in both the traditional and the Durand version of the argument lies in the confusion between investors' subjective risk preferences and their objective market opportunities. Our Propositions I and II, as noted earlier, do not depend for thier validity on any asumption about individual risk preferences. Nor do they involve any assertion as to what is an adequate compensation to investors for assuming a given degree of risk. They rely merely on the fact that a given commodity cannot consistently sell at more than one price in the market; or mero precisley that the price of a commodity representing a "bundle" of two other commodities cannot be consistently different from the weighted average of the prices of the two components (the weights being equal to the proportion of the two commodities in the bundle).

An analogy may he helpful at this point. The relations between $1/\rho_k$, the price per dollar of an unlevered stream in class k: $1/r$, the price per dollar of a

[22] See *e.g.*, Graham and Dodd [6, p. 466].

[23] A typical statement is the following by Guthmann and Dougall [7. p. 245]: "Theoretically it might be argued that the increased hazard from using bonds and preferred stocks would counterbalance this additional income and so prevent the common stock from being more attractive than when it had a lower return but fewer prior obligations. In practice, the extra earnings from 'trading on the equity' are often regarded by investors as more than sufficient to serve as a 'premium for risk' when the proportions of the several securities are judiciously mixed."

[24] Like Durand, Morton [15] contends "that the actual market deviates from [Proposition 1] by giving a changing over-all cost of money at different points of the [leverage] scale" (p. 443, note 2, inserts ours), but the basis for this contention is nowhere clearly stated. Judging by the great emphasis given to the lack of mobility of investment funds between stocks and bonds and to the psychological and institutional pressures toward debt portfolios (see pp. 444–51 and especially his discussion of the optimal capital structure on p. 453) he would seem to be taking a position very similar to that of Durand above.

sure stream, and $1/i_j$, the price per dollar of a levered stream j, in the kth class, are essentially the same as those between, respectively, the price of whole milk, the price of butter fat, and the price of milk which has been thinned out by skimming off some of the butter fat. Our Proposition I states that a firm cannot reduce the cost of capital—i.e., increase the market value of the stream it generates—by securing part of its capital through the sale of bonds, even though debt money appears to be cheaper. This assertion is equivalent to the proposition that, under perfect markets, a dairy farmer cannot in general earn more for the milk he produces by skimming off some of the butter fat and selling it separately, even though butter fat per unit weight, sells for more than whole milk. The advantage from skimming the milk rather than selling whole milk would be purely illusory; for what would be gained from selling the high-priced butter fat would be lost in selling the low-priced residue of thinned milk. Similarly our Proposition *II*—that the price per dollar of a levered stream falls as leverage increases—is an exact analogue of the statement that the price per gallon of thinned milk falls continuously as more butter fat is skimmed off[25]

It is clear that this last assertion is true as long as butter fat is worth more per unit weight than whole milk, and it holds even if, for many consumers, taking a little cream out of the milk (adding a little leverage to the stock) does not detract noticeably from the taste (does not add noticeably to the risk). Furthermore the argument remains valid even in the face of institutional limitations of the type envisaged by Durand. For suppose that a large fraction of the population habitually dines in restaurants which are required by law to serve only cream in lieu of milk (entrust their savings to institutional investors who can only buy bonds). To be sure the price of butter fat will then tend to be higher in relation to that of skimmed milk than in the absence of such restrictions (the rate of interest will tend to be lower), and this will benefit people who eat at home and who like skim milk (who manage their own portfolio and are able and willing to take risk). But it will still be the case that a farmer cannot gain by skimming

[25] Let M denote the quantity of whole milk, B/M the proportion of butter fat in the whole milk, and let p_M, p_B, and p_a, denote, respectively, the price per unit weight of whole milk, butter fat, and thinned milk from which a fraction α of the butter fat has been skimmed off. We then have the fundamental perfect market relation:

$$p_a (M-\alpha B)+p_B\alpha B=p_M M, \quad 0 \geq \alpha \leq 1. \tag{a}$$

stating that total receipts will be the same amount $p_M M$, independently of the amount αB of butter fat that may have been sold separately. Since p_M corresponds to $1/\rho$, p_B to $1/r$, p_a to $1/i$, M to $\bar{X}$ and αB to rD, (a) is equivalent to Proposition I, $S+D=\frac{\bar{X}}{\rho}$ From (a) we derive:

$$p_a=p_M \frac{M}{M-\alpha B} - p_B \frac{\alpha B}{M-\alpha B} \tag{b}$$

which gives the price of thinned milk as an explicit function of the proportion of butter fat skimmed off; the function decreasing as long as $p_B > p_M$. From (a) also follows:

$$1/p_a=1/p_M+(1/p_M-1/p_B) \frac{p_B\alpha B}{p_a(M-\alpha B)} \tag{c}$$

which is the exact analogue of Proposition II, as given by (8).

some of the butter fat and selling it separately (firm cannot reduce the cost of capital by recourse to borrowed funds).[26]

Our propositions can be regarded as the extension of the classical theory of markets to the particular case of the capital markets. Those who hold the current view—whether they realize it or not—must assume not merely that there are lags and frictions in the equilibrating process—a feeling we certainly share,[27] claiming for our propositions only that they describe the central tendency around which observations will scatter—but also that there are large and *systematic* imperfections in the market which permanently bias the outcome. This is an assumption that economists, at any rate, will instinctively eye with some skepticism.

In any event, whether such prolonged, systematic departures from equilibrium really exist or whether our propositions are better descriptions of long-run market behavior can be settled only by empirical research. Before going on to the theory of investment it may be helpful, therefore, to look at the evidence.

II. IMPLICATIONS OF THE ANALYSIS FOR THE THEORY OF INVESTMENT

A. CAPITAL STRUCTURE AND INVESTMENT POLICY

On the basis of our propositions with respect to cost of capital and financial structure (and for the moment neglecting taxes), we can derive the following simple rule for optimal investment policy by the firm.

Proposition III. If a firm in class k is acting in the best interest of the stockholders at the time of the decision, it will exploit an investment oportunity if and only if the rate of return on the investment, say ρ^*, is as large as or larger than ρ_k. That is, *the cut-off point for investment in the firm will in all cases be ρ_k and will be completely unaffected by the type of security used to finance the investment.* Equivalently, we may say that regardless of the financing used, the marginal cost of capital to a firm is equal to the average cost of capital, which is in turn equal to the capitalization rate for an unlevered stream in the class to which the firm belongs.[28]

[26] The reader who likes parables will find that the analogy with interrelated commodity markets can be pushed a good deal farther than we have done in the text. For instance, the effect of changes in the market rate of interest on the over-all cost of capital is the same as the effect of a change in the price of butter on the price of whole milk. Similarly, just as the relation between the prices of skim milk and butter fat influences the kind of cows that will be reared, so the relation between i and r influences the kind of ventures that will be undertaken. If people like butter we shall have Guernseys; if they are willing to pay a high price for safety, this will encourage ventures which promise smaller but less uncertain streams per dollar of physical assets.

[27] Several specific examples of the failure of the arbitrage mechanism can be found in Graham and Dodd [6, *e.g.,* pp. 646–48]. The price discrepancy described on pp. 646–47 is particularly curious since it persists even today despite the fact that a whole generation of security analysts has been brought up on this book!

[28] The analysis developed in this paper is essentially a comparative-statics, not a dynamic analysis. This note of caution applies with special force to Proposition III. Such

To establish this result we will consider the three major financing alternatives open to the firm—bonds, retained earnings, and common stock issues—and show that in each case an investment is worth undertaking if, and only if, $\rho^* \geqq \rho_k$.[29]

Consider first the case of an investment financed by the sale of bonds. We know from Proposition I that the market value of the firm before the investment was undertaken was:[30]

$$V_0 = \bar{X}_0 / \rho_k \tag{10}$$

and that the value of the common stock was:

$$S_0 = V_0 - D_0. \tag{11}$$

If now the firm borrows I dollars to finance an investment yielding ρ^* its market value will become:

$$V_1 = \frac{\bar{X}_0 + \rho^* I}{\rho_k} = V_0 + \frac{\rho^* I}{\rho_k} \tag{12}$$

and the value of its common stock will be:

$$S_1 = V_1 - (D_0 + I) = V_0 + \frac{\rho^* I}{\rho_k} - D_0 - I \tag{13}$$

or using equation 11,

$$S_1 = S_0 + \frac{\rho^* I}{\rho_k} - I. \tag{14}$$

Hence $S_1 \gtreqless S_0$ as $\rho^* \gtreqless \rho_k$ [31]

---

problems as those posed by expected changes in r and in ρ_k over time will not be treated here. Although they are in principle amenable to analysis within the general framework we have laid out, such an undertaking is sufficiently complex to deserve separate treatment. *Cf.* note 17.

[29] The extension of the proof to other types of financing, such as the sale of preferred stock or the issuance of stock rights is straightforward.

[30] Since no confusion is likely to arise, we have again, for simplicity, eliminated the subscripts identifying the firm in the equations to follow. Except for ρ_k the subscripts now refer to time periods.

[31] In the case of bond-financing the rate of interest on bonds does not enter explicitly into the decision (assuming the firm borrows at the market rate of interest). This is true, moreover, given the conditions outlined in Section I.C, even though interest rates may be an increasing function of debt outstanding. To the extent that the firm borrowed at a rate other than the market rate the two I's in equation (14) would no longer be identical and an additional gain or loss, as the case might be, would accrue to the shareholders. It might also be noted in passing that permitting the two I's in (14) to take on different values provides a simple method for introducing underwriting expenses into the analysis.

To illustrate, suppose the capitalization rate for uncertain streams in the kth class is 10 percent and the rate of interest is 4 per cent. Then if a given company had an expected income of 1,000 and if it were financed entirely by common stock we know from Proposition I that the market value of its stock would be 10,000. Assume now that the managers of the firm discover an investment opportunity which will require an outlay of 100 and which is expected to yield 8 per cent. At first sight this might appear to be a profitable opportunity since the expected return is double the interest cost. If, however, the management borrows the necessary 100 at 4 per cent, the total expected income of the company rises to 1,008 and the market value of the firm to 10,080. But the firm now will have 100 of bonds in its capital structure so that, paradoxically, the market value of the stock must actually be reduced from 10,000 to 9,980 as a consequence of this apparently profitable investment. Or, to put it another way, the gains from being able to tap cheap, borrowed funds are more than offset for the stockholders by the market's discounting of the stock for the added leverage assumed.

Consider next the case of retained earnings. Suppose that in the course of its operations the firm acquired I dollars of cash (without impairing the earning power of its assets). If the cash is distributed as a dividend to the stockholders their wealth W_0, after the distribution will be:

$$W_0 = S_0 + I = \frac{\bar{X}_0}{\rho_k} - D_0 + I \qquad (15)$$

where $\bar{X}_0$ represents the expected return from the assets exclusive of the amount I in question. If however the funds are retained by the company and used to finance new assets whose expected rate of return is ρ^*, then the stockholders' wealth would become:

$$W_1 = S_1 = \frac{\bar{X}_0 + \rho^*I}{\rho_k} - D_0 = S_0 + \frac{\rho^*I}{\rho_k} \qquad (16)$$

Clearly $W_1 \gtreqless W_0$ as $\rho^* \gtreqless \rho_k$ so that an investment financed by retained earings raises the net worth of the owners if and only if $\rho^* > \rho_k$. [32]

Consider finally, the case of common-stock financing. Let P_0 denote the current market price per share of stock and assume, for simplicity, that this price reflects currently expected earnings only, that is, it does not reflect any future increase in earnings as a result of the investment under consideration.[33] Then if N is the original number of shares, the price per share is:

$$P_0 = S_0 / N \qquad (17)$$

---

[32] The conclusion that ρ_k is the cut-off point for investments financed from internal funds applies not only to undistributed net profits, but to depreciation allowances (and even to the funds represented by the current sale value of any asset or collection of assets). Since the owners can earn ρ_k by investing funds elsewhere in the class, partial or total liquidating distributions should be made whenever the firm cannot achieve a marginal internal rate of return equal to ρ_k.

[33] If we assumed that the market price of the stock did reflect the expected higher future earnings (as would be the case if our original set of assumptions above were strictly

and the number of new shares, M, needed to finance an investment of I dollars is given by:

$$M = \frac{I}{P_0}. \tag{18}$$

As a result of the investment the market value of the stock beomes:

$$S_1 = \frac{\bar{X}_0 + \rho^* I}{\rho_k} - D_0 = S_0 + \frac{\rho^* I}{\rho_k} = NP_0 + \frac{\rho^* I}{\rho_k}$$

and the price per share:

$$P_1 = \frac{S_1}{N + M} = \frac{1}{N + M}\left[NP_0 + \frac{\rho^* I}{\rho_k}\right] \tag{19}$$

since by equation (18) $I = MP_0$, we can add MP_0 and subtract I from the quantity in bracket, obtaining:

$$P_1 = \frac{1}{N + M}\left[(N + M)P_0 + \frac{\rho^* - \rho_k}{\rho_k}I\right]$$

$$= P_0 + \frac{1}{N + M}\frac{\rho^* - \rho_k}{\rho_k}I > P_0 \text{ if,}$$

and only if, $\rho^* > \rho_k$.

Thus an investment financed by common stock is advantageous to the current stockholders if and only if its yield exceeds the capitalization rate ρ_k.

Once again a numerical example may help to illustrate the result and make it clear why the relevant cut-off rate is ρ_k and not the current yield on common stock, i. Suppose that ρ_k is 10 per cent, r is 4 per cent, that the original expected income of our company is 1,000 and that management has the opportunity of investing 100 having an expected yield of 12 per cent. If the original capital structure is 50 per cent debt and 50 per cent equity, and 1,000 shares of stock are initially outstanding, then, by Proposition I, the market value of the common stock must be 5,000 or 5 per share. Furthermore, since the interest bill is $.04 \times 5,000 = 200$, the yield on common stock is $800/5,000 = 16$ per cent. It may then appear that financing the additional investment of 100 by issuing 20 shares to outsiders at 5 per share would dilute the equity of the original owners since the 100 promises to yield 12 per cent whereas the common stock is currently yielding 16 per cent. Actually, however, the income of the company would rise to 1,012; the value of the firm to 10,120; and the value of the common stock to 5,120. Since there are now 1,020 shares, each would be worth 5.02 and the wealth of the original stockholders would thus have been increased. What has happened is that the dilution in expected earnings per share (from .80

followed) the analysis would differ slightly in detail, but not in essentials. The cut-off point for new investment would still be ρ_k, but where $\rho^* > \rho_k$ the gain to the original owners would be larger than if the stock price were based on the pre-investment expectations only.

to .796) has been more than offset, in its effect upon the market price of the shares, by the decrease in leverage.

Our conclusion is, once again, at variance with conventional views, [34] so much so as to be easily misinterpreted. Read hastily, Proposition III seems to imply that the capital structure of a firm is a matter of indifference; and that, consequently, one of the core problems of corporate finance—the problem of the optimal capital structure for a firm—is no problem at all. It may be helpful, therefore, to clear up such possible misunderstandings.

B. PROPOSITION III AND FINANCIAL PLANNING BY FIRMS

Misinterpretation of the scope of Proposition III can be avoided by remembering that this Proposition tells us only that the type of instrument used to finance an investment is irrelevant to the question of whether or not the investment is worthwhile. This does not mean that the owners (or the managers) have no grounds whatever for preferring one financing plan to another; or that there are no other policy or technical issues in finance at the level of the firm.

That grounds for preferring one type of financial structure to another will still exist within the framework of our model can readily be seen for the case of common-stock financing. In general, except for something like a widely publiciz-ed oil-strike, we would expect the market to place very heavy weight on current and recent past earnings in forming expectations as to future returns. Hence, if the owners of a firm discovered a major investment opportunity which they felt would yield much more than ρ_k, they might well prefer not to finance it via common stock at the then ruling price, because this price may fail to capitalize the new venture. A better course would be a pre-emptive issue of stock (and in this connection it should be remembered that stockholders are free to borrow and buy). Another possibility would be to finance the project initially with debt. Once the project had reflected itself in increased actual earnings, the debt could be retired either with an equity issue at much better prices or through retained earnings. Still another possibility along the same lines might be to combine the two steps by means of a convertible debenture or preferred stock, perhaps with a progressively declining conversion rate. Even such a double-stage financing plan may possibly be regarded as yielding too large a share to outsiders since the new stockholders are, in effect, being given an interest in any similar op-portunities the firm may discover in the future: If there is a reasonable prospect that even larger opportunities may arise in the near future and if there is some danger that borrowing now would preclude more borrowing later, the owners might find their interests best protected by splitting off the current opportunity into a separate subsidiary with independent financing. Clearly the problems involved in making the crucial estimates and in planning the optimal financial strategy are by no means trivial, even though they should have no bearing on the basic decision to invest (as long as $\rho^* \geq \rho_k$) [35]

---

[34] In the matter of investment policy under uncertainty there is no single position which represents "accepted" doctrine. For a sample of current formulations, all very different from this, see Joel Dean [2, esp. Ch. 3], M. Gordon and E. Shapiro [5], and Harry Roberts [17].

[35] Nor can we rule out the possibility that the existing owners, if unable to use a financing plan which protects their interest, may actually prefer to pass up an otherwise profitable

Another reason why the alternatives in financial plans may not be a matter of indifference arises from the fact that managers are concerned with more than simply furthering the interest of the owners. Such other objectives of the management—which need not be necessarily in conflict with those of the owners—are much more likely to be served by some types of financing arrangements than others. In many forms of borrowing agreements, for example, creditors are able to stipulate terms which the current management may regard as infringing on its prerogatives or restricting its freedom to maneuver. The creditors might even be able to insist on having a direct voice in the formation of policy.[36] To the extent, therefore, that financial policies have these implications for the management of the firm, something like the utility approach described in the introductory section becomes relevant to financial (as opposed to investment) decision-making. It is, however, the utility functions of the managers per se and not of the owners that are now involved. [37]

In summary, many of the specific considerations which bulk so large in traditional discussions of corporate finance can readily be superimposed on our simple framework without forcing any drastic (and certainly no systematic) alteration of the conclusion which is our principal concern, namely that for investment decisions, the marginal cost of capital is ρ_k.

III. CONCLUSION

With the development of Proposition III the main objectives we outlined in our introductory discussion have been reached. We have in our Propositions I and II at least the foundations of a theory of the valuation of firms and shares in a world of uncertainty. We have shown, moreover, how this theory can lead to an operational definition of the cost of capital and how that concept can be used in turn as a basis for rational investment decision-making within the firm. Needless to say, however, much remains to be done before the cost of capital can be put away on the shelf among the solved problems. Our approach has been that of static, partial equilibrium analysis. It has assumed among other things a state of atomistic competition in the capital markets and an ease of

venture rather than give outsiders an "excessive" share of the business. It is presumably in situations of this kind that we could justifiably speak of a shortage of "equity capital," though this kind of market imperfection is likely to be of significance only for small or new firms.

[36] Similar considerations are involved in the matter of dividend policy. Even though the stockholders may be indifferent as to payout policy as long as investment policy is optimal, the management need not be so. Retained earnings involve far fewer threats to control than any of the alternative sources of funds and, of course, involve no underwriting expense or risk. But against these advantages management must balance the fact that sharp changes in dividend rates, which heavy reliance on retained earnings might imply, may give the impression that a firm's finances are being poorly managed, with consequent threats to the control and professional standing of the management.

[37] In principle, at least, this introduction of management's risk preferences with respect to financing methods would do much to reconcile the apparent conflict between Proposition III and such empirical findings as those of Modigliani and Zeman [14] on the close relation between interest rates and the ratio of new debt to new equity issues; or of John Lintner [12] on the considerable stability in target and actual dividend-payout ratios.

access to those markets which only a relatively small (though important) group of firms even come close to possessing. These and other drastic simplifications have been necessary in order to come to grips with the problem at all. Having served their purpose they can now be relaxed in the direction of greater realism and relevance, a task in which we hope others interested in this area will wish to share.

The purpose of this communication is to correct an error in our paper "The Cost of Capital, Corporation Finance and the Theory of Investment" (this *Review,* June 1958). In our discussion of the effects of the present method of taxing corporations on the valuation of firms, we said (p. 272):

> The deduction of interest in computing taxable corporate profits will prevent the arbitrage process from making the value of all firms in a given class proportional to the expected returns generated by their physical assets. Instead, it can be shown (by the same type of proof used for the original version of Proposition 1) that *the market values of firms in each class must be proportional in equilibrium to their expected returns net of taxes (that is, to the sum of the interest paid and expected net stockholder income).* (Italics added.)

The statement in italics, unfortunately, is wrong. For even though one firm may have an *expected* return after taxes (our $\bar{X}^r$) twice that of another firm in the same risk-equivalent class, it will not be the case that the *actual* return after taxes (our X^r) of the first firm will always be twice that of the second, if the two firms have different degrees of leverage.[1] And since the distribution of returns after taxes of the two firms will not be proportional, there can be no "arbitrage" process which forces their values to be proportional to their expected after-tax returns.[2] In fact, it can be shown—and this time it really will be shown—that "arbitrage" will make values within any class a function not only of expected after-tax returns, but of the tax rate and the degree of leverage. This means, among other things, that the tax advantages of debt financing are somewhat greater than we originally suggested and, to this extent, the quantitative difference between the valuations implied by our position and by the traditional view is narrowed. It still remains true, however, that under our analysis the tax advantages of debt are the *only* permanent advantages so that the gulf between the two views in matters of interpretation and policy is as wide as ever.

I. TAXES, LEVERAGE, AND THE PROBABILITY DISITRIBUTION OF AFTER-TAX RETURNS

To see how the distribution of after-tax earnings is affected by leverage, let us

---

[1] With some exceptions, which will be noted when they occur, we shall preserve here both the notation and the terminology of the original paper. A working knowledge of both on the part of the reader will be presumed.

[2] Barring, of course, the trivial case of universal linear utility functions. Note that in deference to Professor Durand (see his Comment on our paper and our reply, this *Review,* Sept. 1959, *49, 639–69*) we here and throughout use quotation marks when referring to arbitrage.

again denote by the random variable X the (long-run average) earnings before interest and taxes generated by the currently owned assets of a given firm in some stated risk class, k.[3] From our definition of a risk class it follows that X can be expressed in the form $\bar{X}Z$, where $\bar{X}$ is the expected value of X, and the random variable $Z = X/\bar{X}$, having the same value for all firms in class k, is a drawing from a distribution, say $f_k(Z)$. Hence the random variable X^τ, measuring the after-tax return, can be expressed as:

$$X^\tau = (1-\tau)(X-R) + R = (1-\tau)X + \tau R = (1-\tau)\bar{X}Z + \tau R \qquad \text{(1)}$$

where τ is the marginal corporate income tax rate (assumed equal to the average), and R is the interest bill. Since $E(X^\tau) \equiv \bar{X}^\tau = (1-\tau)\,\bar{X} + \tau R$, we can substitute $\bar{X}^\tau - \tau R$ for $(1-\tau)\,\bar{X}$ in (1) to obtain:

$$X^\tau = (\bar{X}^\tau - \tau R)Z + \tau R = \bar{X}^\tau\left(1 - \frac{\tau R}{\bar{X}^\tau}\right)Z + \tau R. \qquad \text{(2)}$$

Thus, if the tax rate is other than zero, the shape of the distribution of X^τ will depend not only on the "scale" of the stream X^τ and on the distribution of Z, but also on the tax rate and the degree of leverage (one measure of which is $R/\bar{X}^\tau$). For example, if $\text{Var}(Z) = \sigma^2$, we have:

$$\text{Var}(X^\tau) = \sigma^2(\bar{X}^\tau)^2\left(1 - \tau\frac{R}{\bar{X}^\tau}\right)^2$$

implying that for given $\bar{X}^\tau$ the variance of after-tax returns is smaller, the higher τ and the degree of leverage.[4]

II. THE VALUATION OF AFTER-TAX RETURNS

Note from equation (1) that, from the investor's point of view, the long-run average stream of after-tax returns appears as a sum of two components: (1)

[3] Thus our X corresponds essentially to the familiar EBIT concept of the finance literature. The use of EBIT and related "income" concepts as the basis of valuation is strictly valid only when the underlying real assets are assumed to have perpetual lives. In such a case, of course, EBIT and "cash flow" are one and the same. This was, in effect, the interpretation of X we used in the original paper and we shall retain it here both to preserve continuity and for the considerable simplification it permits in the exposition. We should point out, however, that the perpetuity interpretation is much less restrictive than might appear at first glance. Before-tax cash flow and EBIT can also safely be equated even where assets have finite lives as soon as these assets attain a steady state age distribution in which annual replacements equal annual depreciation. The subject of finite lives of assets will be further discussed in connection with the problem of the cut-off rate for investment decisions.

[4] It may seem paradoxical at first to say that leverage *reduces* the variability of outcomes, but remember we are here discussing the variability of total returns, interest plus net profits. The variability of stockholder net profits will, of course, be greater in the presence than in the absence of leverage, though relatively less so than in an otherwise

an uncertain stream $(1 - \tau)\bar{X}Z$; and (2) a sure stream τR.[5] This suggests that the equilibrium market value of the combined stream can be found by capitalizing each component separately. More precisely, let ρ^τ be the rate at which the market capitalizes the expected returns net of tax of an unlevered company of size $\bar{X}$ in class k, i.e.,

$$\rho^\tau = \frac{(1 - \tau)\bar{X}}{V_U} \quad \text{or} \quad V_U = \frac{(1 - \tau)\bar{X}}{\rho^\tau} \quad \text{[6]}$$

and let r be the rate at which the market capitalizes the sure streams generated by debts. For simplicity, assume this rate of interest is a constant independent of the size of the debt so that

$$r = \frac{R}{D} \quad \text{or} \quad D = \frac{R}{r} \quad \text{[7]}$$

Then we would expect the value of a levered firm of size $\bar{X}$, with a permanent level of debt D_L in its capital structure, to be given by:

$$V_L = \frac{(1 - \tau)\bar{X}}{\rho^\tau} + \frac{\tau R}{r} = V_U + \tau D_L \quad \text{[8]} \tag{3}$$

In our original paper we asserted instead that, within a risk class, market value would be proportional to expected after-tax return $\bar{X}^\tau$ (cf. our original equation [11]), which would imply:

comparable world of no taxes. The reasons for this will become clearer after the discussion in the next section.

[5] The statement that τR—the tax saving per period on the interest payments—is a sure stream is subject to two qualifications. First, it must be the case that firms can always obtain the tax benefit of their interest deductions either by offsetting them directly against other taxable income in the year incurred; or, in the event no such income is available in any given year, by carrying them backward or forward against past or future taxable earnings; or, in the extreme case, by merger of the firm with (or its sale to) another firm that can utilize the deduction. Second, it must be assumed that the tax rate will remain the same. To the extent that neither of these conditions holds exactly then some uncertainty attaches even to the tax savings, though, of course, it is of a different kind and order from that attaching to the stream generated by the assets. For simplicity, however, we shall here ignore these possible elements of delay or of uncertainty in the tax saving; but it should be kept in mind that this neglect means that the subsequent valuation formulas overstate, if anything, the value of the tax saving for any given permanent level of debt.

[6] Note that here, as in our original paper, we neglect dividend policy and "growth" in the sense of opportunities to invest at a rate of return greater than the market rate of return. These subjects are treated extensively in our paper, "Dividend Policy, Growth and the Valuation of Shares," *Jour Bus.*, Univ. Chicago, Oct. 1961, 411–33.

[7] Here and throughout, the corresponding formulas when the rate of interest rises with leverage can be obtained merely by substituting $r(L)$ for r, where L is some suitable measure of leverage.

[8] The assumption that the debt is permanent is not necessary for the analysis. It is employed here both to maintain continuity with the original model and because it gives an upper bound on the value of the tax saving. See in this connection footnote 5 and footnote 9.

$$V_L = \frac{\bar{X}^\tau}{\rho^\tau} = \frac{(1-\tau)\bar{X}}{\rho^\tau} + \frac{\tau R}{\rho^\tau} = V_U + \frac{r}{\rho^\tau}\tau D_L \qquad (4)$$

We will now show that if (3) does not hold, investors can secure a more efficient portfolio by switching from relatively overvalued to relatively undervalued firms. Suppose first that unlevered firms are overvalued or that

$$V_L - \tau D_L < V_U$$

An investor holding m dollars of stock in the unlevered company has a right to the fraction m/V_U of the eventual outcome, i.e., has the uncertain income

$$Y_U = \left(\frac{m}{V_U}\right)(1-\tau)\bar{X}Z$$

Consider now an alternative portfolio obtained by investing m dollars as follows: (1) the portion,

$$m\left(\frac{S_L}{S_L + (1-\tau)D_L}\right)$$

is invested in the stock of the levered firm, S_L ; and (2) the remaining portion,

$$m\left(\frac{(1-\tau)D_L}{S_L + (1-\tau)D_L}\right)$$

is invested in its bonds. The stock component entitles the holder to a fraction,

$$\frac{m}{S_L + (1-\tau)D_L}$$

of the net profits of the levered company or

$$\left(\frac{m}{S_L + (1-\tau)D_L}\right)[(1-\tau)(\bar{X}Z - R_L)]$$

The holding of bonds yields

$$\left(\frac{m}{S_L + (1-\tau)D_L}\right)[(1-\tau)R_L]$$

Hence the total outcome is

$$Y_L = \left(\frac{m}{S_L + (1-\tau)D_L}\right)[(1-\tau)\bar{X}Z)$$

and this will dominate the uncertain income Y_U if (and only if)

$$S_L + (1-\tau)D_L \equiv S_L + D_L - \tau D_L \equiv V_L - \tau D_L < V_U.$$

Thus, in equilibrium, V_U cannot exceed $V_L - \tau\, D_L$, for if it did investors would have an incentive to sell shares in the unlevered company and purchase the shares (and bonds) of the levered company.

Suppose now that $V_L - \tau\, D_L > V_U$. An investment of m dollars in the stock of the levered firm entitles the holder to the outcome

$$Y_L = (m \,/\, S_L)[(1 - \tau)(\bar{X}Z - R_L)]$$
$$= (m \,/\, S_L)(1 - \tau)\bar{X}Z - (m \,/\, S_L)(1 - \tau)R_L$$

Consider the following alternative portfolio: (1) borrow an amount (m/S_L) $(1-\tau)\,D_L$ for which the interest cost will be $(m/S_L)\,(1 - \tau)\,R_L$ (assuming, of course, that individuals and corporations can borrow at the same rate, r); and (2) invest m plus the amount borrowed, i.e.,

$$m + \frac{m(1 - \tau)D_L}{S_L} = m\frac{S_L + (1 - \tau)D_L}{S_L} = (m \,/\, S_L)[V_L - \tau D_L]$$

in the stock of the unlevered firm. The outcome so secured will be

$$(m \,/\, S_L) \left(\frac{V_L - \tau D_L}{V_U}\right)(1 - \tau)\bar{X}Z$$

Subtracting the interest charges on the borrowed funds leaves an income of

$$Y_U = (m \,/\, S_L) \left(\frac{V_L - \tau D_L}{V_U}\right)(1 - \tau)\bar{X}Z - (m \,/\, S_L)(1-\tau)R_L$$

which will dominate Y_L if (and only if) $V_L - \tau D_L > V_U$. Thus, in equilibrium, both $V_L-\tau\, D_L > V_U$ and $V_L - \tau\, D_L < V_U$ are ruled out and (3) must hold

III. SOME IMPLICATIONS OF FORMULA (3)

To see what is involved in replacing (4) with (3) as the rule of valuation, note first that both expressions make the value of the firm a function of leverage and the tax rate. The difference between them is a matter of the size and source of the tax advantages of debt financing. Under our original formulation, values within a class were strictly proportional to expected earnings after taxes. Hence the tax advantage of debt was due solely to the fact that the deductibility of interest payments implied a higher level of after-tax income for any given level of before-tax earnings [i.e., higher by the amount τR since $\bar{X}^\tau = (1 - \tau)$ $\bar{X} + \tau R$]. Under the corrected rule (3), however, there is an additional gain due to the fact that the extra after-tax earnings, τR, represent a sure income in contrast to the uncertain outcome $(1-\tau)\,\bar{X}$. Hence τR is capitalized at the more favorable certainty rate, $1/r$, rather than at the rate for uncertain streams, $1/\rho^\tau$ [9]

Since the difference between (3) and (4) is solely a matter of the rate at which the tax savings on interest payments are capitalized, the required changes

---

[9] Remember, however, that in one sense formula (3) gives only an upper bound on the value of the firm since $\tau R/r = \tau D$ is an exact measure of the value of the tax saving only

in all formulas and expressions derived from (4) are reasonably straightforward. Consider, first, the before-tax earnings yield, i.e., the ratio of expected earnings before interest and taxes to the value of the firm.[10] Dividing both sides of (3) by V and by $(1 - \tau)$ and simplifying we obtain:

$$\frac{\bar{X}}{V} = \frac{\rho^\tau}{1 - \tau}\left[1 - \tau\frac{D}{V}\right] \qquad\qquad \textbf{(31.c)}$$

which replaces our original equation (31). The new relation differs from the old in that the coefficient of D/V in the original (31) was smaller by a factor of r/ρ^τ.

Consider next the after-tax earnings yield, i.e., the ratio of interest payments plus profits after taxes to total market value.[11] This concept was discussed extensively in our paper because it helps to bring out more clearly the differences between our position and the traditional view, and because it facilitates the construction of empirical tests of the two hypotheses about the valuation process. To see what the new equation (3) implies for this yield we need merely substitute $\bar{X}^\tau - \tau R$ for $(1 - \tau) \bar{X}$ in (3) obtaining:

$$V = \frac{\bar{X}^\tau - \tau R}{\rho^\tau} + \tau D = \frac{\bar{X}^\tau}{\rho^\tau} + \tau\frac{\rho^\tau - r}{\rho^\tau} D, \qquad\qquad \textbf{(5)}$$

from which it follows that the after-tax earnings yield must be:

$$\frac{\bar{X}^\tau}{V} = \rho^\tau - \tau(\rho^\tau - r)D / V. \qquad\qquad \textbf{(11.c)}$$

This replaces our original equation (11) in which we had simply $\bar{X}^\tau/V = \rho^\tau$. Thus, in contrast to our earlier result, the corrected version (11.c) implies that even the after-tax yield is affected by leverage. The predicted rate of decrease of $\bar{X}^\tau/V$ with D/V, however, is still considerably smaller than under the naive traditional view, which, as we showed, implied essentially $\bar{X}^\tau/V = \rho^\tau - (\rho^\tau - r) D/V$. See our equation (17) and the discussion immediately preceding it.[12] And, of course, (11.c) implies that the effect of leverage on $\bar{X}^\tau/V$

---

where both the tax rate and the level of debt are assumed to be fixed forever (and where the firm is certain to be able to use its interest deduction to reduce taxable income either directly or via transfer of the loss to another firm). Alternative versions of (3) can readily be developed for cases in which the debt is not assumed to be permanent, but rather to be outstanding only for some specified finite length of time. For reasons of space, we shall not pursue this line of inquiry here beyond observing that the shorter the debt period considered, the closer does the valuation formula approach our original (4). Hence, the latter is perhaps still of some interest if only as a lower bound.

[10] Following usage common in the field of finance we referred to this yield as the "average cost of capital." We feel now, however, that the term "before-tax earnings yield" would be preferable both because it is more immediately descriptive and because it releases the term "cost of capital" for use in discussions of optimal investment policy (in accord with standard usage in the capital budgeting literature).

[11] We referred to this yield as the "after-tax cost of capital." Cf. the previous footnote.

[12] The $i_k{}^*$ of (17) is the same as ρ^τ in the present context, each measuring the ratio of net profits to the value of the shares (and hence of the whole firm) in an unlevered company of the class.

is *solely* a matter of the deductibility of interest payments whereas, under the traditional view, going into debt would lower the cost of capital regardless of the method of taxing corporate earnings.

Finally, we have the matter of the after-tax yield on *equity* capital, i.e., the ratio of net profits after taxes to the value of the shares.[13] By subtracting D from both sides of (5) and breaking $\bar{X}^\tau$ into its two components—expected net profits after taxes, $\bar{\pi}^\tau$, and interest payments, $R = rD$—we obtain after simplifying:

$$S = V - D = \frac{\bar{\pi}^\tau}{\rho^\tau} - (1 - \tau)\left(\frac{\rho^\tau - r}{\rho^\tau}\right)D \qquad (6)$$

From (6) it follows that the after-tax yield on equity capital must be:

$$\frac{\bar{\pi}^\tau}{S} = \rho^\tau + (1 - \tau)[\rho^\tau - r]D / S \qquad \textbf{(12.c)}$$

which replaces our original equation (12) $\bar{\pi}^\tau/S = \rho^\tau + (\rho^\tau - r) D/S$. The new (12.c) implies an increase in the after-tax yield on equity capital as leverage increases which is smaller than that of our original (12) by a factor of $(1 - \tau)$. But again, the linear increasing relation of the corrected (12.c) is still fundamentally different from the naive traditional view which asserts the cost of equity capital to be completely independent of leverage (at least as long as leverage remains within "conventional" industry limits).

IV. TAXES AND THE COST OF CAPITAL

From these corrected valuation formulas we can readily derive corrected measures of the cost of capital in the capital budgeting sense of the minimum prospective yield an investment project must offer to be just worth undertaking from the standpoint of the present stockholders. If we interpret earnings streams as perpetuities, as we did in the original paper, then we actually have two equally good ways of defining this minimum yield: either by the required increase in before-tax earnings, $d\bar{X}$, or by the required increase in earnings net of taxes, $d\bar{X}$ $(1 - \tau)$.[14] To conserve space, however, as well as to maintain continuity with the original paper, we shall concentrate here on the before-tax case with only brief footnote references to the net-of-tax concept.

Analytically, the derivation of the cost of capital in the above sense amounts to finding the minimum value of $d\bar{X}/dI$ for which $dV = dI$, where I denotes the level of new investment.[15] By differentiating (3) we see that:

---

[13] We referred to this yield as the "after-tax cost of equity capital." Cf. footnote 9.

[14] Note that we use the term "earnings net of taxes" rather than "earnings after taxes." We feel that to avoid confusion the latter term should be reserved to describe what will actually appear in the firm's accounting statements, namely the net cash flow including the tax savings on the interest (our $\bar{X}^\tau$). Since financing sources cannot in general be allocated to particular investments (see below), the after-tax or accounting concept is not useful for capital budgeting purposes, although it can be extremely useful for valuations as we saw in the previous sections.

[15] Remember that when we speak of the minimum required yield on an investment we are

$$\frac{dV}{dI} = \frac{1 - \tau}{\rho^\tau} \frac{d\bar{X}}{dI} + \tau \frac{dD}{dI} \geq 1 \qquad \text{if } \frac{d\bar{X}}{dI} \geq \frac{1 - \tau \dfrac{dD}{dI}}{1 - \tau} \rho^\tau \qquad (7)$$

Hence the before tax required rate of return cannot be defined without reference to financial policy. In particular, for an investment considered as being financed entirely by new equity capital $dD/dI = 0$ and the required rate of return or marginal cost of equity financing (neglecting flotation costs) would be:

$$\rho^S = \frac{\rho^\tau}{1 - \tau}$$

This result is the same as that in the original paper (see equation [32], p. 294) and is applicable to any other sources of financing where the remuneration to the suppliers of capital is not deductible for tax purposes. It applies, therefore, to preferred stock (except for certain partially deductible issues of public utilities) and would apply also to retained earnings were it not for the favorable tax treatment of capital gains under the personal income tax.

For investments considered as being financed entirely by new debt capital $dI = dD$ and we find from (7) that:

$$\rho^D = \rho^\tau \qquad (33.c)$$

which replaces our original equation (33) in which we had:

$$\rho^D = \rho^S - \frac{\tau}{1 - \tau} r. \qquad (33)$$

Thus for borrowed funds (or any other tax-deductible source of capital) the marginal cost or before-tax required rate of return is simply the market rate of capitalization for net of tax unlevered streams and is thus independent of both the tax rate and the interest rate. This required rate is lower than that implied by our original (33), but still considerably higher than that implied by the traditional view (see esp. pp. 276–77 of our paper) under which the before-tax cost of borrowed funds is simply the interest rate, r.

Having derived the above expressions for the marginal costs of debt and equity financing it may be well to warn readers at this point that these expressions represent at best only the hypothetical extremes insofar as costs are concerned and that neither is directly usable as a cut-off criterion for investment planning. In particular, care must be taken to avoid falling into the famous "Liquigas" fallacy of concluding that if a firm intends to float a bond issue in some given year then its cut-off rate should be set that year at ρ^D; while, if the next issue is to be an equity one, the cut-off is ρ^S. The point is, of course, that no investment can meaningfully be regarded as 100 per cent equity financed if the

---

referring in principle only to investments which increase the *scale* of the firm. That is, the new assets must be in the same "class" as the old. See in this connection, J. Hirshleifer, "Risk, the Discount Rate and Investment Decisions," *Am. Econ. Rev.,* May 1961, *51* 112–20 (especially pp. 119–20). See also footnote 16.

firm makes any use of debt capital—and most firms do, not only for the tax savings, but for many other reasons having nothing to do with "cost" in the present static sense (cf. our original paper pp. 292–93). And no investment can meaningfully be regarded as 100 per cent debt financed when lenders impose strict limitations on the maximum amount a firm can borrow relative to its equity (and when most firms actually plan on normally borrowing less than this external maximum so as to leave themselves with an emergency reserve of un-used borrowing power). Since the firm's long-run capital structure will thus contain both debt and equity capital, investment planning must recognize that, over the long pull, *all* of the firm's assets are really financed by a mixture of debt and equity capital even though only one kind of capital may be raised in any particular year. More precisely, if L^* denotes the firm's long-run "target" debt ratio (around which its actual debt ratio will fluctuate as it "alternately" floats debt issues and retires them with internal or external equity) then the firm can assume, to a first approximation at least, that for any particular investment $dD/dI = L^*$. Hence, the relevant marginal cost of capital for investment plann-ing, which we shall here denote by ρ^*, is:

$$\rho^* = \frac{1 - \tau_L{}^*}{1 - \tau}\, \rho^\tau = \rho^S - \frac{\tau}{1 - \tau}\, \rho^D L^* = \rho^S(1 - L^*) + \rho^D L^*$$

That is, the appropriate cost of capital for (repetitive) investment decisions over time is, to a first approximation, a weighted average of the costs of debt and equity financing, the weights being the proportions of each in the "target" capital structure.[16]

V. SOME CONCLUDING OBSERVATIONS

Such, then, are the major corrections that must be made to the various formulas and valuation expressions in our earlier paper. In general, we can say that the force of these corrections has been to increase somewhat the estimate

[16] From the formulas in the text one can readily derive corresponding expressions for the required net-of-tax yield, or net-of-tax cost of capital for any given financing policy. Specifically, let $\bar\rho(L)$ denote the required net-of-tax yield for investment financed with a proportion of debt $L=dD/dI$. (More generally L denotes the proportion financed with tax deductible sources of capital.) Then from (7) we find:

$$\bar\rho(L) \to (1 - \tau)\, \frac{d\bar X}{dI} = (1-L\tau)\rho^\tau \tag{8}$$

and the various costs can be found by substituting the appropriate value for L. In particular, if we substitute in this formula the "target" leverage ratio, L^* we obtain:

$$\bar\rho^* \equiv \bar\rho(L^*) = (1-\tau L^*)\,\rho^\tau$$

and $\bar\rho^*$ measures the average net-of-tax cost of capital in the sense described above. Although the before-tax and the net-of-tax approaches to the cost of capital provide equally good criteria for investment decisions when assets are assumed to generate perpetual (i.e., non-depreciating) streams, such is not the case when assets are assumed to have finite lives (even when it is also assumed that the firm's assets are in a steady state age distribution so that our X or EBIT is approximately the same as the net cash flow before taxes). See footnote 3 above. In the latter event, the correct method for determining the desirability of an investment would be, in principle, to discount the

of the tax advantages of debt financing under our model and consequently to reduce somewhat the quantitative difference between the estimates of the effects of leverage under our model and under the naive traditional view. It may be useful to remind readers once again that the existence of a tax advantage for debt financing—even the larger advantage of the corrected version—does not necessarily mean that corporations should at all times seek to use the maximum possible amount of debt in their capital structures. For one thing, other forms of financing—notably retained earnings—may in some circumstances be cheaper still when the tax status of investors under the personal income tax is taken into account. More important, there are, as we pointed out, limitations imposed by lenders (see pp. 292–93), as well as many other dimensions (and kinds of costs) in real-world problems of financial strategy which are not fully comprehended within the framework of static equilibrium models, either our own or those of the traditional variety. These additional considerations, which are typically grouped under the rubric of "the need for preserving flexibility," will normally imply the maintenance by the corporation of a substantial reserve of untapped borrowing power. The tax advantage of debt may well tend to lower the optimal size of that reserve, but it is hard to believe that advantages of the size contemplated under our model could justify any substantial reduction, let alone their complete elimination. Nor do the data indicate that there has in fact been a substantial increase in the use of debt (except relative to preferred stock) by the corporate sector during the recent high tax years.[17]

As to the differences between our modified model and the traditional one, we feel that they are still large in quantitative terms and still very much worth trying to detect. It is not only a matter of the two views having different implications for corporate financial policy (or even for national tax policy). But since the two positions rest on fundamentally different views about investor behavior and the functioning of the capital markets, the results of tests between them may have an important bearing on issues ranging far beyond the immediate one of the effects of leverage on the cost of capital.

REFERENCES

1. F. B. ALLEN, "Does Going into Debt Lower the 'Cost of Capital'?", *Analysts Jour,*. Aug. 1954, 10, 57–61.
2. J. DEAN, *Capital Budgeting.* New York 1951.
3. D. DURAND, "Costs of Debt and Equity Funds for Business: Trends and Problems of Measurement," in Nat. Bur. Research, *Conference on Research in Business Finance.* New York 1952, pp. 215–47.

---

net-of-tax stream at the net-of-tax cost of capital. Only under this net-of-tax approach would it be possible to take into account the deductibility of depreciation (and also to choose the most advantageous depreciation policy for tax purposes). Note that we say that the net-of-tax approach is correct "in principle" because, strictly speaking, nothing in our analysis (or anyone else's, for that matter) has yet established that it is indeed legitimate to "discount" an uncertain stream. One can hope that subsequent research will show the analogy to discounting under the certainty case is a valid one; but, at the moment, this is still only a hope.

[17] See, e.g., Merton H. Miller, "The Corporate Income Tax and Corporate Financial Policies," in *Staff Reports to the Commission on Money and Credit* (forthcoming).

4. W. J. EITEMAN, "Fanancial Aspects of Promotion," in *Essays on Business Finance* by M. W. Waterford and W. J. Eiteman. Ann Arbor, Mich. 1952, pp. 1–17.

5. M. J. GORDON and E. SHAPIRO, "Capital Equipment Analysis: The Required Rate of Profit," *Manag. Sci.,* Oct. 1956, 3, 102–10.

6. B. GRAHAM and L. DODD, *Security Analysis,* 3rd ed. New York 1951.

7. G. GUTHMANN and H. E. DOUGALL, *Corporate Financial Policy,* 3rd ed. New York 1955.

8. J. R. HICKS, *Value and Capital,* 2nd ed. Oxford 1946.

9. P. HUNT and M. WILLIAMS, *Case Problems in Finance,* rev. ed. Homewood, Ill. 1945.

10. J. M. KEYNES, *The General Theory of Employment, Interest and Money.* New York 1936.

11. O. LANGE, *Price Flexiblity and Employment.* Bloomington, Ind. 1944.

12. J. LINTNER, "Distribution of Incomes of Corporations among Dividends, Retained Earnings and Taxes," *Am. Econ. Rev.,* May 1956, 46, 97–113.

13. F. LUTZ and V. LUTZ, *The Theory of Investment of the Firm.* Princeton 1951.

14. F. MODIGLAINI and M. ZEMAN, "The Effect of the Availability of Funds, and the Terms Thereof, on Business Investment," in Nat. Bur Econ. Research, *Conference on Research in Business Finance.* New York 1952, pp. 263–309.

15 W. A. MORTON, "The Structure of the Capital Market and the Price of Money," *Am Econ. Rev.,* May 1954, 44, 440–54.

16. S. M. ROBBINS, *Managing Securities.* Boston 1954.

17. H. V. ROBERTS, "Current Problems in the Economics of Capital Budgeting," *Jour. Bus.,* 1957, 30 (1), 12–16.

18. D. T. SMITH, *Effects of Taxation on Corporate Financial Policy.* Boston, 1952.

19. R. SMITH, "Cost of Capital in the Oil Industry," (hectograph). Pittsburgh: Carnegie Inst. Tech. 1955.

20. H. M. SOMERS, " 'Cost of Money' as the Determinant of Public Utility Rates," *Buffalo Law Rev.,* Spring 1955, *4,* 1–28.

21. J. B. WILLIAMS, *The Theory of Investment Value.* Cambridge, Mass. 1938.

22. U. S. Federal Communications Commission, *The Problem of the "Rate of Return" in Public Utility Regulation.* Washington 1938.

In this article Gordon presents and tests a full-scale valuation model. This model is based on the theory that the value of a share of stock is equal to the present value of all future dividends and risk increases as a function of futurity (as in the liquidity premium theory). The model demonstrates one of the highest levels of association between its dependent and independent variables of any cross-sectional model reported in the literature. The reader might question what the changes in the size of each regression coefficient across the years mean in terms of changes in market preferences and changes in intrinsic value.

8

The Savings Investment and Valuation of A Corporation

Myron J. Gordon

This article is reprinted with permission from the Review of Economics and Statistics, *Vol. XLIV (February, 1962), pp. 37–51.*

In the neo-classical theory of a firm's investment, the objective of the firm is to maximize its value. Its value is a function of its future income and its future income is a function of its investment. As Lutz and Lutz [8] admirably demonstrated in their standard work on the subject, given the behavior postulate and these two functions, the investment and value of a firm may be determined. Unfortunately, however, the numerous models they constructed assume the future is known with certainty and with minor qualifications that the firm can freely lend or borrow at a given rate of interest. These conditions are not realized in fact, the data of their models cannot be observed, and the models stand as elegant intellectual exercises of limited usefulness.[1] A consequence is

* The research reported here was supported by a grant from the Sloan Research Fund, School of Industrial Management, Massachusetts Institute of Technology, and the computations were carried out at the Computation Center, M.I.T. Discussions with Professors Chow, Kuh, and Solow and comments by Professor Modigliani on an earlier draft of this paper have been of considerable assistance to the writer. The advice of Ramesh Gangolli on problems of statistical inference was most helpful. I am especially indebted to Henry Y. Wan, Jr., for his unflagging energy and painstaking care in collecting the data and programming the computations.

[1] In the last half of their book the Lutzes withdraw the assumption that the future is certain, but this material is largely a well written distillation of the qualitative statements contained in textbooks on finance.

that the literature concerned with testable propositions on the investment and the valuation of the firm makes little or no reference to the neo-classical theory. Further, empirical theories of investment, for example, those discussed in Meyer and Kuh [10], refer to the valuation of the firm only in passing, and theories of valuation such as Durand [3] make no reference to the investment of the firm. Only the normative literature, including in a sense Modigliani and Miller [11] relates the investment and value of a firm, but this literature continues to provide little empirical information on the investment and financing that maximize the value of a firm.

The purpose of this paper is to present a theory of the investment and valuation of a corporation analogous to the neo-classical theory without the assumptions that the future is certain and that funds are freely available at a given rate of interest. Specifically, the initial statement is that the value of a firm is a function of its expected future income. The future income is then represented by a function of the corporation's investment to obtain an expression in which a share's price is the dependent variable, the investment function provides the independent variables, and the parameters represent the corporation's cost of capital. In general structure the model parallels those of neo-classical theory, and similarly it may be solved to find the investment that maximizes the value of the firm. The difference is that the variables are observable and the parameters may be estimated from sample data.

The model is developed under restrictive assumptions with respect to the financing policies of corporations and the form of the return on investment function. These assumptions are irritating from a theoretical point of view, but they are of limited material significance as will be evidenced by the empirical results to be presented. Work currently under way and to be reported later, however, will make the model considerably more general.

The theory will be tested here as a valuation model and not as an investment model. That is, the ability of the model to explain the differences in price among common stocks will be tested, and it will be seen that under a variety of considerations the model performs better than previous efforts in this direction. By the statement that the theory will not be tested as an investment model, I mean that no attempt will be made to establish whether or not the investment of the corporation is determined by the objective of maximizing its value.

Under the functional form of the stock price model established, a corporation's cost of capital is an increasing function of the rate of growth in its dividend. An inference from this theorem is that the price of a share is not independent of the distribution of the corporation's income between dividends and retention.[2] Strictly speaking the statistical findings do not test the theorem. However, the deductive argument leading to its adoption, and the general quality of the empirical results may be considered evidence in support of the theorem. In addition, it will be shown that the theorem is true under a plausible set of assumptions with respect to behavior.

---

[2] This position is generally rejected by economists. For instance, Modigliani and Miller stated " . . . the division of a (income) stream between cash dividends and retained earnings in a period is a mere detail" ([11], 266).

THE GENERAL THEORY

Most of the terms to be used in what follows are defined below:

$Y_t =$ Income a share of stock is expected to earn in period t.
$D_t =$ Dividend a share of stock is expected to pay in period t.
$B_t =$ Investment in the corporation or common equity per share of stock at the end of period t.
$b =$ Fraction of income the corporation is expected to retain.
   $b = (Y_t - D_t)/Y_t, t = 1,2, \ldots$
$r =$ Average return the corporation is expected to earn on the common equity investment of $bY_t, t = 1, 2, \ldots$
$P_o =$ The price of a corporation's stock at the end of $t = 0$.
$k =$ The rate at which the corporation's future dividends are discounted at the end of $t=0$ to arrive at their present value.

The fundamental proposition of capital theory is that the value of an investment opportunity is the expected future receipts its ownership provides discounted at the rate of profit required on the investment. In the case of a share of stock, the expected future receipts are the dividends, so that

$$P_o = \int_0^\infty D_t e^{-kt} dt. \tag{1}$$

In a system where capital gains are not subject to preferential tax treatment, this statement is true regardless of whether the share is purchased for dividends or for price appreciation, since the price at any future date is expected to be the discounted value of the subsequent dividends.[3] It will be seen shortly that the theory explicitly recognizes growth or price appreciation and the market's valuation of it in the price of a share. If capital gains receive preferential tax treatment, the deductive argument and the interpretation of the empirical price model are modified, but the conclusions reached are not materially changed, and the elaboration of the theory on an after-tax basis will not be undertaken here.

It has been shown [4] [6] that if a corporation issues no new shares, maintains a constant debt equity ratio, retains a fraction b of its income, and earns a rate of return r on investment, then the dividend will grow at a rate br. If the initial level of income is Y_o, then $D_o = (1 - b)Y_o$, and with continuous growth the dividend in period t will be

$$D_t = Y_o(1 - b)e^{rbt}. \tag{2}$$

Substituting (2) for D_t in (1) results in

[3] It has been widely believed that earnings and not dividends are the relevant variable in the valuation of a share. However, Bodenhorn [1] has shown that the investor does not discount expected future earnings in arriving at the value of a share. It will be shown in what follows that what the advocates of the earnings hypotheses must maintain is that dividends are what investors buy, but that price of a share is independent of the dividend rate.

$$P_o = \int_0^\infty Y_0(1 - b)e^{brt}e^{-kt}dt. \tag{3}$$

P_0 is finite and the integration may be carried out if $k > br$. The result is

$$P_o = \frac{Y_0(1 - b)}{k - br}. \tag{4}$$

The value of a share is the current dividend divided by the difference between the rate of profit on the stock investors require and the rate of growth in the dividend.

On the four assumptions necessary for (4), the first three deal with financing policy. In defense of the first, it is well known that corporations, particularly those engaged in manufacturing, undertake relatively little outside equity financing. On debt financing, a recent study by the writer [5] provides considerable evidence that apart from short-term inventory financing requirements, the maintenance of a stable debt equity ratio is a widely practiced policy on the part of corporations.[4] To put the matter differently, it is quite reasonable to assume that in estimating a corporation's future dividends investors do not consider the possible future stock sales by a corporation as being material and that they expect the corporation to maintain its existing debt equity ratio.

On the third assumption it is clear that a corporation will not retain the fraction b of its income in every future period, but we are not really interested in what a corporation actually will do. Rather, what a corporation is expected to do by investors is relevant. If investors behave rationally, they estimate what b, and r also, will be in the future, or they formulate expectations that contain implicit estimates of b and r.[5] Whether or not the expectations are adequately represented by the assumption that b will be the same in every future period is a question of fact that can in part be resolved by the statistical work. Support for the assumption is provided by the work of Lintner [9] and others which indicates that corporations are widely recognized to follow a policy of paying a stable fraction of their normal income in dividends.

The consequence of these three assumptions is that an investor's estimate of b, a corporation's retention rate, implies an estimate of its investment rate. That is, if q is the ratio of a corporation's debt to its equity and b is the fraction of income it retains, bY_t will be the addition to the corporation's equity in period t, and $(1 + q) bY_t$ will be its investment in the period.

The view that dividend policy is irrelevant to the investment and valuation of a corporation has been so widely accepted that some reflection on the previous argument is desirable. First, we have cited evidence that a very common practice among corporations is to maintain a stable debt equity ratio. Year to year changes cancel out for the most part. Second, we assume that investors estimate

---

[4] Debt is here defined as short-term and long-term liabilities net of monetary-type assets and short-period inventory movements. An increase in debt to finance an increase in government bonds is clearly of no significance for a theory of investment in real assets. For a further discussion of this point see [5], 476–479.

[5] The rational investor values a share on the basis of the future payments it provides. and he therefore performs some operations on the data available to him to arrive at such estimates.

a retention rate b and a debt equity rate q that they *expect* the corporation to maintain for the indefinite future. Third, the corporation is not expected to engage in outside equity financing. The last two assumptions may not be empirically true, but under them it logically follows that the investment a corporation is expected to undertake in a future period t is $(1 + q) bY_t$. Further, with q given we may use the terms investment rate and retention rate interchangeably, since one is a constant multiple of the other.[6]

The last assumption, that a corporation's return on investment is expected to be r in every future period is probably the most objectionable. The assumption is that given b, the investment rate, investors expect the return on investment to be r. It does not exclude the possibility that the value of r expected for a corporation in every future period will vary depending on the value of b. It does exclude the case where for a given b, r is expected to take on different values over time. Here again we are not concerned with what the value of the variable actually will be. Our speculation in support of the assumption is, if investors were polled on the change they expect in the rate of profit a corporation will earn, the typical result will be a frequency distribution with mean zero and a small standard deviation. The quality of the empirical results will turn in large measure on the accuracy of this speculation.

This defense of the four assumptions, of course, does not deny the advantages in theoretical elegance as well as improved accuracy and scope of the empirical findings in having a theory not restricted by the above assumptions. The defense does, I believe, indicate that the assumptions have enough correspondence with reality to justify the empirical investigation of a theory that reflect them.

INTERPRETATION AND EMPIRICAL FORMULATION OF THE THEORY

Thus, reviewing the development of (4), we began with the statement that the value of a share is the present value of its expected future dividends. It was then shown that under empirically relevant assumptions this dividend expectation is given by the corporation's current income, Y_0, the return on investment the corporation is expected to earn on the common equity investment, and the retention rate b the corporation is expected to maintain. Given the return on investment investors require, k, the value of a share was found to be

$$P_o = \frac{Y_o(1 - b)}{k - br}.\tag{4}$$

The model may be used to find the investment rate that maximizes the share's value with the character of the solution depending on the assumptions with respect to the behavior of r and k as b varies.

For instance, if it is assumed that r and k are independent of b, we simply take the derivative of P with respect to b and find that

---

[6] In what follows we will assume $q=o$, but the conclusions reached apply with no qualifications for a corporation with $q\neq o$.

$$\frac{\partial P}{\partial b} = (r - k)\frac{Y_0}{(k - rb)^2}. \tag{5}$$

If $r = k$, $\partial P/\partial b = 0$, or a share's price is independent of the retention rate. If r is greater (less) than k, price rises (falls) as b is increased. The important feature of this result is that it agrees perfectly with the conclusions reached by those who maintain that dividend policy per se has no influence on share price.

In the above conclusion we first assumed that k is a constant. Under this assumption the price of a share is independent of the corporation's retention and investment, if the rate of return the corporation can earn on investment is the same as the rate of return stockholders require. If $r \gtrless k$, the price of the share will rise or fall with b, but this is due to the profitability of investment and not the financing of it by retention. The variation in price with b is due simply to the fact that it is the sole method of finance under consideration.

Of course, with $r \gtrless k$, price will not rise or fall indefinitely with b, because the rate of return is not a constant. A plausible hypothesis is that r falls, or if there are indivisibilities in the firm's investment opportunities, r rises and then falls as b increases. In this event,

$$\frac{\partial P}{\partial b} = [-k + rb - (1 - b)(-r - b\frac{\partial r}{\partial b})]\frac{Y_0}{(k - rb)^2}$$

$$= [r - k + b(1 - b)\frac{\partial r}{\partial b}]\frac{Y_0}{(k - rb)^2}. \tag{6}$$

This expression yields a maximum price at a finite investment rate. The value of a share is maximized at $b > 0$ if $r > k$ at $b = 0$. As b increases, r falls, and $b(1 - b) \partial r/\partial b$, which is negative because $\partial r/\partial b$ is negative, increases in absolute amount. Therefore, there is some value of b at which $\partial P/\partial b = 0$, and the price of the share is maximized at this investment rate.

It may be noted that at $b = 1$ we have $P = 0$ regardless of the values of k and r. The interpretation of this statement is that regardless of how profitable a corporation is, its stock has a zero value if it is expected that the corporation will never pay a dividend. What this implies is that investors do not believe a corporation will never pay a dividend.[7]

We see, then, that if the management's objective is to maximize the value of a corporation under certain financial constraints, the theory provides a solution to a corporation's investment as well as to its value. To be able to use solution, however, we must be able to observe the values of the variables in (4). For Y_0, r, and b we may be able to derive estimates from historical data, but what do we do for k? Furthermore, can we be sure that k is independent of r and b?

If the answer to the last question is in the affirmative we could proceed as follows. Write (4) in the form

$$\frac{Y_0(1 - b)}{P_0} = k - br. \tag{7}$$

---

[7] If a corporation has not been paying a dividend, stockholders expect a change in management policy or a change in management. It is evident, however, that our model is not the most effective means of dealing with this type of situation since stockholders may expect no dividend for a number of years.

The left side is d, a corporation's dividend yield *based on its current dividend*. Take a sample of corporations that is homogeneous with respect to risk and other attributes that might influence k (the homogeneity achieved by sample selection or the introduction of other variables), and use the sample to estimate the parameters of

$$d = \alpha_0 - \alpha_1 br. \tag{8}$$

α_0 is an estimate of k, and we would expect to find $\alpha_1 = 1$.

However, α_1 would undoubtedly turn out to be significantly less than one.[8] And the more we look at (8), the more uncomfortable we get about the assumption that k is independent of br. If k is a constant, for a sufficiently high growth rate, d becomes negative and a share's price goes through infinity.

It may be argued that $br > k$ is unlikely on the following grounds. An extraordinarily high value of r is necessary for $br > k$, but contrary to our assumption investors are not likely to expect this state to continue forever. Further, a corporation with r very large should undertake additional outside financing. Hence $br > k$ becomes possible only under the restrictive assumptions of the theory. On the other hand, there are corporations that are expected to earn extraordinary rates of return for a very long time (forever is not necessary with the future discounted), many of them do not engage in other financing, and they still sell at finite prices.

An alternative explanation of why shares sell at finite prices, one that is very attractive empirically, is provided by the assumption that k is an increasing functionof br. In support of it, common sense as well as the mathematics of our model suggest that as br, the rate of growth in the dividend, rises, the required yield based on the current dividend should fall—not in a one to one ratio but by decreasing amounts, so that d asymptotically approaches zero. An expression that satisfies this requirement is

$$d = \alpha_0(1 + br)^{-\alpha_1}. \tag{9}$$

The alternative functions for d are illustrated in Chart 1.

Substituting (9) for $k - br = d$ in (4), the latter becomes

$$P = Y_0(1 - b)\frac{1}{\alpha_0}(1 + br)^{\alpha_1}. \tag{10}$$

When $b = 0$, the price of a share is its dividend $Y_0(1 - b)$ multiplied by $1/\alpha_0$. As b increases, the multiplier rises to $(1/\alpha_0)(1 + br)^{\alpha_1}$. Given $Y_0(1 - b)$, the current dividend, the larger the value of br, its expected rate of growth, the higher the price investors are willing to pay for a share. The only restriction on the parameters of (10) is that they be positive.

Although (10) may be attractive empirically, some may consider its

[8] The empirical work reported in Gordon [4] may be reasonably interpreted to provide evidence in support of this conclusion.

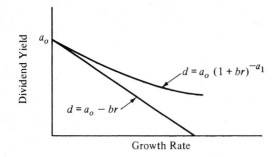

CHART 1

Variation in dividend yield with expected rate of growth in the dividend

theoretical implications sheer heresy. To justify it theoretically we must assume that a corporation's cost of capital is an increasing function of the rate of growth in its dividend expectation. To see this, note that

$$k - br = d = a_0(1 + br)^{-\alpha_1} \qquad (11)$$

implies that

$$k = a_0(1 + br)^{-\alpha_1} + br \qquad (12)$$

and

$$\frac{\partial k}{\partial br} = -\alpha_1 a_0(1 + br)^{-(1+\alpha_1)} + 1$$

$$= 1 - \frac{\alpha_1 a_0}{(1 + br)^{1+\alpha_1}} . \qquad (13)$$

The product $\alpha_0\alpha_1$ should be about equal to one.[9] What this means is that if $\alpha_0\alpha_1 > 1$, k will fall over some interval of b starting with $b = 0$. However, as b and br rise, $\partial k/\partial br$ becomes positive and remains so.

To interpret the definition of k provided by (12), a_0 is a corporation's cost of capital when $b = 0$. As br rises the second term on the right side of (12) rises, but the first term falls and moderates the rise in k with br, Further, the larger the absolute value of α_1 the smaller the rise in k with br. Hence, α_1 may be looked on as the price investors are willing to pay for growth in the dividend. If α_1 is large, investors are willing to pay a lot for dividend growth, and vice versa.

What this means is that the value of a share depends on the corporation's dividend and investment rates. The value should, of course, change with investment due to the return on investment, but we now have an independent influence. Note $k = \alpha_0$ when $br = 0$. If we set $r = \alpha_0$, a share's price will change with b because k changes. Formerly with k a constant and $r = k = \alpha_0$, price was independent of b.

An interesting feature of the assumption that $\partial k/\partial br > 0$ is that with r a constant the resultant stock value model yields an optimum price for a finite dividend rate. The optimum dividend or retention rate is found by taking the

[9] Plausible values are $\alpha_0 = .08$ and $\alpha_1 = 12$.

derivative of (10) with respect to b and finding the value of b that satisfied $\partial P/\partial b = 0$. If r is independent of b, P_0 is maximized by the retention rate

$$b = \frac{\alpha_1}{\alpha_1 + 1} - \frac{1}{r(\alpha_1 + 1)}. \tag{14}$$

The plausible result is that the optimum retention rate is an increasing function of r, the profitability of investment, and of α_1, the price the market is willing to pay for growth in the dividend.

It should be noted that having k an increasing function of br does not imply share price is a decreasing function of br. Reflection on (10) reveals that for given b, P_o always rises with r, and for given r and α_1, P_o rises and then falls with b.

A RATIONALE OF THE CRITICAL PROPOSITION

The proposition that the rate of profit investors require in placing a value on a dividend expectation is an increasing function of its rate of growth conflicts with widely held views on the cost of capital. Our main defense of the theorem is that a model based on the proposition does a remarkably good job of explaining the valuation of shares by investors. However, before presenting the empirical results, it may be useful to present a theoretical rationale of the proposition. We will not prove the proposition is true. We will state a set of assumptions under which the proposition proves to be true. Some may find these assumptions reasonable. More important, this rationale may provide insights for new theorems on observable phenomena that contribute to their explanation, and prediction.

The basic postulate of our model is that the value of a share is the present value of its expected future dividend payments. An investor may be *represented* as arriving at the present value of the expected payment in some future period, say $t = n$, by one of two methods. Under the "certainty equivalent method" he proceeds as follows. Let D_n, the dividend during n, be a random variable with expected value $\bar{D}_n$ and standard deviation σ_n. The investor uses σ_n as an index of the uncertainty of D_n,[10] and he arrives at the certainty equivalent of D_n by multiplying $\bar{D}_n$ by some function of σ_n. If this function is $f(\sigma_n)$ and i is the pure rate of interest, the present value of the dividend expectation in period n is

$$PV_n = \frac{\bar{D}_n f(\sigma_n)}{(1 + i)^n}. \tag{15}$$

Under the "profit rate method" he simply discounts $\bar{D}_n$ at a rate k_n that reflects its risk; that is, k_n is also a function of σ_n. It is clear that there is some number k_n such that

$$PV_n = \frac{\bar{D}_n}{(1 + k_n)^n}. \tag{16}$$

[10] For some purposes a relative measure of variation should be used, but everything that is established in what follows holds equally when a relative measure such as the coefficient of variation is used.

Both of the above representations of an investor's behavior are plausible and neither method is inherently superior to the other.

What can we say about the uncertainty of D_t as t goes from one to infinity? If there is no growth expected in the dividend we might assume that at the end of $t = 0$, $D_0 = \bar{D}_1 = \bar{D}_2 = \ldots = \bar{D}_n \ldots$. In this event we would also expect that at the end of $t = n - 1$, $\bar{D}_n = D_{n-1}$ If the variance at the end of $n-1$ of $D_n - D_{n-1}$ is independent of n, equal to σ^2 say, the successive dividends over time are an additive process with stationary independent increments and the variance at $t = 0$ of D_n increases with n. It is $n\sigma^2$ and the standard deviation of D_n is $\sigma\sqrt{n}$.

The hypothesis that $\bar{D}_t = D_{t-1}$ may not be correct. The entire dividend history may influence $\bar{D}_t$ and subsequent expectations. Regardless of the nature of how expectations are formed, however, it is most likely that the uncertainty of an item in a dividend series increases with its time in the future. Hence, we may accept with great confidence that $\sigma_{n+1} > \sigma_n$ and $f(\sigma_{n+1}) < f(\sigma_n)$.

We will examine now the relation between k_n and k_{n+1} for a dividend expectation with $D_0 = \bar{D}_n = \bar{D}_{n+1}$. Let

$$PV_n = \frac{\bar{D}_n f(\sigma_n)}{(1 + i)^n} = \frac{\bar{D}_n}{(1 + k_n)^n} \tag{17}$$

and

$$PV_{n+1} = \frac{\bar{D}_{n+1} f(\sigma_{n+1})}{(1 + i)^{n+1}} = \frac{\bar{D}_{n+1}}{(1 + k_{n+1})^{n+1}}. \tag{18}$$

Dividing PV_n by PV_{n+1} we obtain

$$\frac{\bar{D}_n f(\sigma_n)(1 + i)}{\bar{D}_{n+1} f(\sigma_{n+1})} = \frac{\bar{D}_n(1 + k_{n+1})^{n+1}}{\bar{D}_{n+1}(1 + k_n)^n}. \tag{19}$$

Simplifying, and recalling that $f(\sigma_n) > f(\sigma_{n+1})$ we have

$$1 < \frac{f(\sigma_n)}{f(\sigma_{n+1})} = \frac{(1 + k_{n+1})^{n+1}}{(1 + k_n)^n(1 + i)}. \tag{20}$$

What restrictions does the above equality place on the possible values of k_n and k_{n+1}? Absolutely none! Since $i < k_n$ we may have the equality satisfied given $f(\sigma_n)$ and $f(\sigma_{n+1})$ with $k_n \geq k_{n+1}$. If the uncertainty of the dividend increases only slightly with time and if aversion to risk is small, $f(\sigma_n)/f(\sigma_{n+1})$ is only slightly greater than one and $k_{n+1} < k_n$. [11] Under the opposite conditions $k_{n+1} > k_n$. *The important point to note, however, is that there is nothing to guarantee that k_t is a constant for all values of t. The behavior of k_t is a question of fact that cannot be settled by deductive argument.*

It will be shown next that if it is true that k_t is an increasing function of t, a corporation's cost of capital is an increasing function of the rate of growth in its dividend. First, however, let us recall the assumptions which brought us

---

[11] For example, let $f(\sigma_n) = u_0\sigma_n^{-1/\mu_1}$. If u_1 is a large number, $f(\sigma_n)$ falls very slowly as σ_n increases. If we also have σ_t increasing very slowly with t, it is likely that k_t falls as t increases.

where we are. We assumed only that investors have an aversion to risk and that other things remaining the same, the uncertainty of each element in a series of payments generated by an asset increases with the payments time in the future. These assumptions seem quite reasonable.

In developing our valuation theory, the value of a share was arrived at by discounting a firm's entire dividend expectation at a single rate k. As long as no growth is expected in the dividend and it is an infinite series, this is of no consequence. Nothing is lost by being oblivious of the fact that the single k used to discount the series is in fact an average of the k_t.

However, this is not true when the dividend is expected to grow. Let a designate a share of stock for which the dividend is expected to grow at the rate g_a. At $t = 0$, the expected value of the dividend in $t = n$ is $\bar{D}_{n,a} = D_0 (1+g_a)^n$. The value of the share is

$$P_a = D_0 \left[\frac{1 + g_a}{1 + k_1} + \frac{(1 + g_a)^2}{(1 + k_2)^2} + \cdots + \frac{(1 + g_a)^n}{(1 + k_n)^n} \cdots \right]. \tag{21}$$

There is some average of the k_t, $\bar{k}_a$ such that the above price

$$P_a = D_0 \sum_{t=1}^{\infty} \frac{(1 + g_a)^t}{(1 + \bar{k}_a)^t}. \tag{22}$$

Now let β designate another share. β has the same initial dividend as a, but the dividend on β is expected to grow at the rate g_β, and $g_\beta > g_a$. The two shares have the same degree of risk or relative variance, so that $\bar{D}_{n,a}$ and $\bar{D}_{n,\beta}$ are both discounted at the same rate k_n. Discounting the series $\bar{D}_{t,\beta}$ at the rate k_t, $t = 1$, $2, \ldots, \infty$, results in a value P_β for the share β. There is some average of the k_t, $\bar{k}_\beta$ which satisfies

$$P_\beta = D_0 \sum_{t=1}^{\infty} \frac{(1 + g_\beta)^t}{(1 + \bar{k}_\beta)^t}. \tag{23}$$

Both $\bar{k}_a$ and $\bar{k}_\beta$ are weighted averages of the same k_t series. However, since $g_\beta > g_a$, the weights of $\bar{k}_\beta$ are relatively greater for the large k_t in the distant future and relatively smaller for the smaller k_t in the near future. The consequence is that $\bar{k}_\beta > \bar{k}_a$ if the k_t increases with t.[12] A rigorous proof of this statement has been derived by Ramesh Gangolli and is provided in Appendix A.

DERIVATION OF THE EMPIRICAL MODEL

Our purpose in this section is to arrive at an estimating equation and rules for observing its variables that may be used to establish how well (10) explains the differences in price among common stocks.

It is widely accepted that the price an investor is willing to pay for a dividend expectation will vary depending on its uncertainty. As it stands (10)

---

[12] It is evident that $P_\beta > P_a$, but the difference is smaller than it would be if $\bar{k}_\beta = \bar{k}_a$ were true.

assumes that all corporations have the same degree of risk, and hence, estimates of its parameters from a random sample of corporations would be inefficient. Since risk may vary among industries, there is some advantage in using sample data stratified by industry. With this in mind samples of 48 food and 48 machinery corporations were used and sample data were obtained for the years 1954–1957.[13] Obtaining sample results for a given industry over a number of years is desirable for reasons that will become evident later.

With an industry, corporations will differ in risk, and investor evaluation of a corporation's risk should in some measure be related to observable properties of the corporation. Specifically, it may be thought that the more unstable a corporation's past earnings, the more uncertain its future earnings and dividends. Further, stability is associated with size so that regardless of its actual historical performance, investors may have more confidence in a large than in a small corporation. Accordingly, (10) enlarged to recognize the variation in a share's price with these two variables and with $\alpha_5 = 1/\alpha_0$ is

$$P_o = \alpha_5 Y_o (1 - b)(1 + br)^{\alpha_1} (1 + u)^{\alpha_2} S^{\alpha_3}. \tag{24}$$

S is an index of the corporation's size, and u is an index of the instability of its earnings. When $br = o$ a corporation's cost of capital is

$$\alpha_0 (1 + u)^{-\alpha_2} S^{-\alpha_3} \tag{25}$$

and when $br > 0$, k is obtained by substituting the above expression for α_o in (12). We expect $\alpha_2 < 0$ and $\alpha_3 > 0$.

The most difficult problem in testing and using (24) is the observation of the variables, particularly b and r. They are expectations and not exactly specified historical data. Investors may be presumed to form expectations out of the history available to them, and an essential hypothesis in the empirical formulation of the theory is a statement of how investors arrive at the expectation variables.

We know that earnings and to a lesser degree dividends fluctuate from one year to the next so that the actual values for the current year need not be what an investor considers a suitable basis for formulating expectations. We will assume that investors take an exponentially weighted average of a corporation's past dividends to arrive at D_o', the normalized current dividend and of past earnings to arrive at Y_o', the normalized current earnings.[14] Further, it is assumed that the return a corporation is expected to earn on investment is the

---

[13] The corporations included in the sample are from the indicated industry groups of The Value Line Investment Survey [13] at the end of 1958. A firm was excluded: (1) if its dividend and earnings data did not extend back to 1947; (2) if there was an abnormal market interest in its shares (e.g., Fairbanks Morse was excluded on the grounds that Penn-Texas was buying its stock over most of the period); and (3) if its dividend fell below two per cent of its book value in two or more years of the period 1951–58. The larger sample, 1951–58, is to be used in another study. An objective in these conditions was to include in the sample only those corporations with an historical record that could be interpreted to provide estimates of the corporation's dividend expectation.

[14] For a discussion of exponentially weighted averages of past values of a variable as an estimate of its normalized value, see Brown [2].

normalized return it has been earning on its existing assets. Accordingly, the variables of (10) are defined as follows

$$Y_o(1 - b) = D'_o; r = Y'_o/B_o; \quad b = 1 - \frac{D'_o}{Y'_o};$$

$$rb = \frac{Y'_o - D'_o}{B}$$

In the above, B_0 is the actual net worth or book value per share of stock at the end of $t = o$.

The two variables introduced in (24) are not so important as the others and their measurement is not so critical. The size S of a corporation is defined as the sum of its net plant account and working capital.[15] The instability index for a corporation's earnings is an absolute average of the year to year difference in the rate of return (earnings divided by book value) from 1947 through the current year. Here, more sophisticated definition and measurement of the variable might materially improve the results, but the computations involved can be quite formidable, and were not considered justified at this stage in the empirical work.

Returning to D'_t and Y_t', our definitions of these variables are

$$D'_t = \beta D_t + (1 - \beta)D'_{t-1};$$

and

$$Y'_t = \lambda Y_t + (1 - \lambda)Y'_{t-1}.$$

D'_t and Y'_t were assigned arbitrary initial values for 1947 equal to .05 and .08 times the end of 1947 book value respectively. The above equations yielded the value in each subsequent year with the qualification that D'_t was always taken as the higher of the actual dividend or two per cent of B_t.[16]

The final problem to be solved was the values to be assigned to the smoothing constants β and λ. On the basis of an analysis discussed in Appendix B the smoothing constants adopted were $\beta = .6$ and $\lambda = .5$.[17]

THE EMPIRICAL FINDINGS

In the logs (24) is linear, and least squares estimates of its parameters may be obtained from the expression

$$LnP = ln\,\alpha_5 + \alpha_4\,lnD' + \alpha_1\,ln\,(1 + br)$$
$$+ \alpha_2\,ln\,(1 + u) + \alpha_3\,lnS. \qquad (26)$$

[15] Other definitions such as the market value of its outstanding securities might seem superior on some counts, but the statistical findings should not differ materially.

[16] Also, if inspection of the quarterly dividend payments up through the end of a year indicated a different dividend than that actually paid during the year, the former was used. For instance, if the regular dividend was raised in the second quarter, the higher quarterly figure was annualized in arriving at the figure for the year.

[17] Due to certain computation problems this was not exactly true for the machinery sample. The variable br was based on the above weights, but D' was determined with $\beta=.8$. This undoubtedly did not materially influence the findings.

Notice the form of the model does not force $\alpha_4 = 1$, but obtains an estimate of the coefficient from the sample data.

Table I presents the sample estimates of the parameters, their standard errors, the multiple correlation coefficient and the means and standard deviations of the variables. The coefficient of the dividend turns out to be very close to one in all eight samples, ranging from .82 to .93. However, its standard error is so small that it must be considered significantly less than one, particularly since it is below one for every sample. What this means is that a doubling of the dividend with everything else unchanged does not double the price of a share. A possible explanation is that everything else remaining the same, high priced shares sell at lower prices (relative to the dividend) than low priced shares. Another possible explanation is that there is some normal level for the dividend and investors believe a low dividend is more likely to rise than a high dividend.[18]

TABLE I

Stock price model variable and regression statistics, food and machinery samples, 1954–1957

	Food sample				Machinery sample			
	1954	1955	1956	1957	1954	1955	1956	1957
LnP	3.70	3.69	3.59	3.54	3.53	3.62	3.67	3.36
S.D.	.57	.59	.54	.52	.47	.51	.55	.52
$Ln\alpha_5$	2.55	2.56	2.62	2.49	2.42	2.57	2.41	2.23
S.E.	.15	.13	.14	.12	.22	.19	.17	.17
LnD′	.671	.672	.654	.600	.609	.619	.553	.557
S.D.	.494	.503	.500	.488	.412	.465	.518	.518
α_4	.83	.93	.92	.83	.88	.83	.82	.85
S.E.	.06	.05	.05	.05	.09	.07	.05	.05
Ln (1+br)	.039	.040	.042	.042	.047	.045	.054	.055
S.D.	.021	.021	.020	.018	.025	.022	.024	.021
α_1	11.80	9.87	8.76	9.87	4.16	6.07	7.68	3.91
S.E.	1.49	1.29	1.34	1.25	1.32	1.39	1.12	1.25
Ln (1+u)	.031	.029	.027	.026	.035	.035	.035	.033
S.D.	.024	.022	.020	.019	.023	.020	.019	.017
α_2	−5.49	−4.28	−4.44	−6.21	−1.97	−2.32	1.77	−4.52
S.E.	1.31	1.23	1.35	1.20	1.61	1.48	1.40	1.50
LnS	4.36	4.41	4.47	4.51	3.68	3.76	3.87	3.98
S.D.	.85	.84	.84	.85	.73	.75	.77	.81
α_3	.071	.055	.027	.065	.122	.093	.116	.149
S.E.	.036	.032	.032	.026	.045	.039	.034	.033
Mult. Corr.	.951	.965	.955	.965	.894	.932	.955	.945

[18] Some evidence in support of this hypothesis, with the dividend a percentage of book value as the variable, is presented in Gordon [4].

It is also possible that error in the measurement of the dividend has produced some downward bias in the estimate of its coefficient.

The most striking aspect of the statistical findings is the high statistical significance and the small range of fluctuation in successive samples over time in the dividend and the growth rate coefficients. The dividend coefficient, as stated earlier, had a low of .82 and a high of .93, and it typically is over ten times its standard error. The growth coefficients vary from 8.8 to 11.8 for the food sample and are at least seven times their standard errors. The machinery sample does not perform as well with a coefficient range of 3.9 to 7.7, but they are all well within the one per cent level of significance. The somewhat poorer results for the machinery sample might be expected on the grounds that investors are less confident that machinery companies will realize the expected rate of growth in their dividends than will food companies. If so, they would pay less for the stock.[19] On the other hand, it may also be true that the historical record is a less reliable source of information on the expected growth rate for machinery companies.

These results are striking by comparison with the results obtained in earlier attempts to explain the variation in price among stocks. Typical practice in these models is to include every variable, particularly dividends, earnings, and book value, that investors are supposed to consider in pricing a share. Due to a number of reasons, including in particular the high intercorrelation among the independent variables, the coefficients have large standard errors and fluctuate violently from one sample to the next. (Cf. Durand [3], 53 and Gordon [4], 102). These models do not permit reliable statements on how price will vary with one of the independent variables. The superior results obtained with the present model are, in part, due to the use of exponentially weighted averages for the independent variables, but averaging has been used with other models, and the results must be attributed in part to the functional form of the relation among price, dividend, earnings, and book value derived from our theory.

Turning to the other two variables, positive results were obtained for them also. The instability of the earnings coefficient is highly significant for every food sample. It is significant at the five per cent level for only one machinery sample, but in view of the fact that it has the right sign and exceeds its standard error for every sample, is safe to say that for machinery companies, stock prices vary inversely with earnings instability. The size coefficient behaves like the instability of earnings coefficient with the roles of the two industries reversed. The coefficient is highly significant for every machinery sample and fails at the 5 per cent level for two food samples. The sign is correct for every food sample.

In the previous discussion the reliability of the coefficient estimates obtained was evaluated by reference to the size of each in relation to its standard error and the variation in a coefficient among samples. Other tests were employed but before the results of these tests are presented a methodological observation is in order. When a sample is drawn from a large population, and when the sampling procedure and the data satisfy certain conditions, statistical theory may be used to make probability statements about the population

---

[19] A result that may or may not be coincidental is that at the end of 1956, a high point in market optimism, the machinery growth coefficient was at its highest and the food coefficient was at its lowest. The stability of the food industry makes its stocks good defensive issues.

parameters. It is clear, however, that the corporations with the wide investor interest and other attributes necessary for inclusion in an industry category of the *Value Line Investment Survey* do not represent a random sample from a large population. Also, the independent variables are not free of error in the sense, for instance, that we are not certain the value of *br* obtained for a corporation is the value that investors expect. For these and other reasons, the statistical analysis of the sample data *strictly speaking* cannot be used to make probability statements about the parameters. It is believed, nonetheless, that such analysis contributes to our knowledge on the performance of the model and the reliability of the coefficient estimates.

When time series data are used to test a theory, the residuals are examined for the presence of serial correlation, since correlation between the residuals in successive periods suggests that a different model may provide a better explanation of the variation in the dependent variable. With cross-section data of the sort used here, the existence of correlation between the squares of the residuals and an independent variable impairs the reliability of the coefficient estimates. For the food samples, the correlation between the squares of the residuals and the two important variables, growth rate and dividend, was computed and not found to be significant.

Kuh [7] has shown that when the same sample of firms is used in successive cross sections over time the residuals may be examined to discover whether "firm effects" influence the determination of the value of the dependent variable. That is, if the average of the residuals for a firm over the n cross section regression equations departs significantly from zero, one or more independent variables excluded from the model and peculiar to the firm in question may have a significant influence on the dependent variable. When firm effects are present, the variance in the estimate of the dependent variable is larger than it otherwise would be, and there is a possibility that the parameter estimates for the included independent variables are biased. The analysis of variance test employed by Kuh ([7], 202) to test the significance of firm effects was used with the food sample, and the firm effect was found to be highly significant. Different measurement rules for the independent variables or the inclusion of additional variables may eliminate the large firm effects.

Alternatively, it may be possible to deal with them directly, that is, include among the independent variables in some way. The techniques by which this may be accomplished are still in the exploratory stage, and it would not be appropriate to deal with the problem further in this paper. It will be observed only that the resolution of the problem will result in closer correspondence between actual and predicted value for share prices and possibly in revised estimates of the model's parameters.[20]

THE OPTIMUM DIVIDEND RATE

An interesting use of the theory and the data is to examine the quantitative statements they yield with respect to a corporation's optimum dividend rate.

---

[20] A paper by Walter [14] presents an approach to the differentiation among shares according to quality, and his approach may be useful for the isolation of the firm effect.

Alternative stock price models either exclude the dividend on the grounds that it is irrelevant or include it in a manner that implies a share's price is a monotonic increasing function of the dividend with earnings given. The present model states that there is an optimum dividend rate and it is finite.

The theory does more than that. For a corporation that engages in no outside equity financing and maintains a given debt equity ratio as a matter of policy, the model provides the investment and retention that maximizes the value of its stock. Therefore, we can set up a "representative corporation" and find its optimum retention rate. Most corporations retain between .20 and .60 of their normal income, and if our representative corporation fell outside of these bounds, we might wonder at the results. If the corporation is representative, possible explanations are that the theory is wrong, that parameter estimates from the sample data are wrong, that corporations do not set their retention rates to maximize the price of their stock, and that the argument underlying this application of the theory is incorrect. If the data indicated that the representative corporation should retain and invest nothing, it would be difficult to reject the suggestion that the theory is wrong or the parameter estimates are seriously in error. On the other hand, the theory would seem to justify further consideration if the normative statements obtained from the parameter estimates proved to be within the bounds of reason.

Our stock price model in its final form is

$$P = \alpha_5[Y'(1 - b)]^{\alpha_4}(1 + br)^{\alpha_1}(1 + u)^{\alpha_2} S^{\alpha_3}. \tag{27}$$

The most plausible assumption with respect to r is that it is a function of b, and on the further assumption that indivisibilities in investment opportunities are not important, a simple function we may use is

$$r = w(1 + b)^{-1}. \tag{28}$$

When $b = 0$, a corporation's average return on investment is w. As b rises, r falls, and for $b = 1$, $r = w/2$. Inspection of the sample data for b and r suggests that $w = .20$ is representative of a profitable corporation, $w = .15$ of an average corporation, and $w = .10$ of an unprofitable one.

To find the retention rate that maximizes the price of a share we substitute (28) for r in (27), obtain numerical values for the parameters and the variables, and compute the share's price for various values of b. Actually, if we are only interested in the b that maximizes P and not the resultant value of P, we need only know α_1, α_4, and w. For the food samples the five year averages of the parameter estimates are $\alpha_4 = .88$ and $\alpha_1 = 10.1$. Using these values, when $w = .20$ the price of a share is maximized at $b \sim .28$. On the basis of reasonable values for the other variables and parameters and $Y = \$2.00$, the price of a share is \$25.65 when $b = 0$.[21] By comparison when $b = .28$, $D = \$1.44$, $r = .156$, $br = .0437$, and $P = \$29.59$. With $b = .5$ we have $D = \$1.00$, $r = .133$, $br = .667$, and $P = \$26.73$. Variation in price with the retention rate is both within the bounds of reason and fairly material.

[21] We used $ln\alpha_0 = 2.555$, $\alpha_2 = -5$, $in (1+u) = .028$, $\alpha_3 = .05$, and $ln S = 4.4$ for the other variables and parameters.

For an average corporation, one with $w = .15$, the optimum retention rate falls to $b \sim .20$, while for an unprofitable corporation the optimum retention rate barely exceeds $b = 0$. Food corporations typically retain larger fractions of their incomes than our model suggests they should. However, the differences are not alarming. It is possible that maximizing the value of its stock is not the sole concern of these corporations. Also, our parameter estimates may be in error for a number of reasons, among which are errors in the measurement of the independent variables, and the failure of the model to include other forms of financing. However, these empirical findings do not suggest there is something radically wrong with the theory or the data.

Turning to the machinery sample we have a different story. The sample estimates of α_1 vary over such a wide range, there is some question as to whether a meaningful number is obtained by averaging them. Doing so we have $\alpha_1 = 5.5$ and $\alpha_4 = .85$. For a profitable corporation the optimum retention rate is $b \sim .10$. Both an average and an unprofitable corporation should at the minimum distribute all of its income in dividends. We must conclude that for one reason or another the parameter estimates for the machinery sample are seriously in error.

SUMMARY AND CONCLUSIONS

Since this paper already is quite long, the summary and conclusion will be brief. Our two fundamental assumptions were (1) that the purchaser of a share of stock buys a dividend expectation, and (2) that in placing a value on the expectation, the rate of profit he requires is an increasing function of the rate of growth in the dividend. The first assumption is quite reasonable, and it has been shown that the second is not beyond the pale of reason. In order to arrive at an operational stock price model we then made a set of assumptions with respect to investor expectations that are clearly unattractive. Among these assumptions those that made it possible to ignore a corporation's leverage and outside equity financing are not too serious in that it is likely that the theory can be enlarged to recognize the variation in the dividend expectation and its valuation with the variables. The more troublesome assumptions were that investors expect a corporation's retention rate and (given its retention rate) its rate of return on investment to be the same in every future period. There are no theoretical problems involved in withdrawing these assumptions, but it is difficult to see how one can have an operational model for explaining stock prices without them. With these assumptions there are likely to be firms for which the performance of the model is far from satisfactory.

The interesting point is that under assumptions we proceeded directly to an operational stock price model that can be interpreted to yield the functional relation between price and investment rate. The central problem of capital theory on the level of the firm has been to establish the investment that maximizes the value of the firm. Neo-classical theory solved the problem under certainty. In our world of uncertainty we have three practically independent classes of theories—investment theories, valuation theories, and finance theories—for the guidance of businessmen. The promise of the research described in the preceding pages is an integrated theory of investment, financing, and valuation that can be used to make both normative and descriptive empirical statements on the subject.

Notwithstanding the restrictive nature of the financing and valuation assumptions on which our stock value model was based, it did a very creditable job of explaining the variation in price among common stocks. The significance of these results cannot be emphasized too strongly. They make it very likely that further research will give rise to models that allow very accurate statements on the relations among the variables. Further research will take the form of refinements in the theory to allow withdrawing the restrictive assumptions and improvements in the measurement rules for the variables. The research will benefit from the interaction of theory and evidence due to the operational character of the theory, and it is even possible that the research will modify or disprove the fundamental propositions. For instance, it may turn out that the price of a share is independent of the rate of growth in the corporation's dividend.

REFERENCES

1. BODENHORN, DIRAN, "On the Problem of Capital Budgeting," *The Journal of Finance,* XIV (December 1959), 473–492.
2. BROWN, ROBERT G., *Statistical Forecasting for Inventory Control* (New York, 1959).
3. DURAND, DAVID, *Bank Stock Prices and the Bank Capital Problem* (New York, 1957).
4. GORDON, MYRON J., "Dividends, Earnings, and Stock Prices," this *Review,* XLI (May 1959), 99–105.
5. GORDON, MYRON J., "Security and a Financial Theory of Investment," *The Quarterly Journal of Economics,* LXXIV (August 1960), 472–492.
6. GORDON, MYRON J. and ELI SHAPIRO, "Capital Equipment Analysis: The Required Rate of Profit," *Management Science,* III (October 1956), 102–110.
7. KUH, EDWIN, "The Validity of Cross-Sectionally Estimated Behavior Equations in Time Series Applications," *Econometrica,* XXVII (April 1959), 197–214.
8. LUTZ, FREDERICK and VERA LUTZ, *The Theory of Investment of the Firm* (Princeton University Press, 1951).
9. LINTNER, J., "Distribution of Incomes of Corporations Among Dividends, Retained Earnings and Taxes," *American Economic Review,* XLVI (May 1956), 97–113.
10. MEYER, JOHN R. and EDWIN KUH, *The Investment Decision: An Empirical Study* (Cambridge, Mass., 1957).
11. MODIGLIANI, FRANCO and M. H. MILLER, "The Cost of Capital, Corporation Finance and the Theory of Investment," *The American Economic Review,* XLVIII (June 1958), 261–297.
12. MODIGLIANI, FRANCO, and M. H. MILLER, "The Cost of Capital, Corporation Finance and the Theory of Investment: Reply," *The American Economic Review,* XLIX (September 1959), 655–668.
13. *The Value Line Investment Survey* (New York: Arnold Bernhard and Co., Inc.).
14. WALTER, JAMES E., "A Discriminant Function for Earnings-Price Ratios of Large Industrial Corporations," this *Review* XLI (February 1959).

Malkiel examines the effect of one variable—growth—on the price of common stock. His assumption that extraordinary growth rates approach an average growth rate at some future horizon allows him to (1) derive a valuation formula for growth stocks and (2) formulate a set of propositions regarding the price behavior of growth stocks over time. A point of interest in the article is the demonstration that expressing the price of a share of stock as the present value of all future dividends is equivalent to expressing its price in terms of the present value of its dividends over a finite period of years plus the present value of its price at the end of this period.

9

Equity Yields, Growth, and the Structure of Share Prices

*Burton G. Malkiel**

This article is a modified version of the one which appeared in the American Economic Review, *Vol. LIII, No. 5 (December, 1963), pp. 1004–1031; it is reprinted with the permission of the* American Economic Review.

The first half of 1962 witnessed one of the most precipitous declines in stock market prices in recent history. In terms of the volume of trading and the magnitude of the daily erosion of stock values, one must look back to the crashes of 1929 and 1937 to find parallels. Moreover, the decline was not confined to U. S. stock prices, for a world-wide revaluation of equity values was transmitted from New York.

For most professional financial observers of these developments, two aspects of the decline served as the foci of their analysis. There was first the sharp drop in the *level* of share prices. Second, and perhaps more interesting,

* The author is a professor of economics at Princeton University. He is indebted to W. J. Baumol, L. V. Chandler, and R. E. Quandt who assisted through several formative drafts of this paper and made valuable suggestions which led to considerable improvements in the verbal and algebraic presentation of the argument. He has also profited from the later, useful criticism of F. Machlup, J. W. Land, and P. A. Tinsley as well as the members of the Princeton University Seminar on Research in Progress. Finally, acknowledgement is made to the National Science Foundation whose grant to the study "Dynamics of the Firm" helped to complete of this paper.

there was a marked change in the *structure* of share prices, i.e., the relationships among equities of different characteristics. We can illustrate the revaluation in the level of stock prices by noting that from December 12, 1961, the date of the pre-1962 peak level of stock prices, to June 26, 1962, the date of the 1962 trough, the Dow-Jones Industrial Average, an average of 25 very high-quality shares, declined from 734 to 539, a drop of 26.6 per cent. During the same period the Standard and Poor 425 Industrial Stock Average, a broader and more heterogeneous grouping of stocks, declined from 76.69 to 54.80, a drop of 28.5 per cent. This decline of more than 25 per cent we take as illustrative of the drop in the level of stock prices.

Perhaps the most interesting and conspicuous change in the structure of share prices was what the financial press called "the revaluation of 'growth stocks.' " Much steeper price declines were suffered by those companies whose extraordinary earnings growth had gained them far higher price-earnings ratios than those applied to the standard list of industrial stocks. For example, an index of five high-quality growth stocks[1] declined in the same period from 78.60 to 37.60, a drop of 52.2 per cent, almost double that suffered by the standard group. Even the *ne plus ultra* of growth stocks, International Business Machiens Corporation, declined in the same period from 580 to 320, a loss of 44.8 per cent.

In the setting of the 1962 market adjustment, this paper will attempt to analyze the relationship of "growth stocks" to standard equities. First we will present a brief historical summary and critique of security analysis since the Great Depression. This is both necessary for explaining how the late 1961 structure of stock prices developed and useful for understanding the types of criteria long used by practical men to value common shares. Next we will construct a model designed to throw light on the "proper" relationships among equity groups that differ in their earnings and dividend growth. Several theorems from the model will be used to demonstrate the precise relationship between warranted share prices and the relevant determinants of valuation. But perhaps even more important than providing a valuation model, the analysis will serve as a conceptual scheme by which we can explain the change in the structure of share prices which occurred.

There is a remarkable similarity between the problems of building a theory of the term structure of interest rates and attempting to formulate the principles underlying the structure of equity prices with respect to issues differing in their growth characteristics. For example, we know that long-term bonds have wider price fluctuations than short issues for a given change in interest rates. Similarly, we shall find that nondividend-paying growth stocks are inherently more volatile than standard issues in response to a change in the capitalization rate applied to equities in general. Moreover, this volatility is an increasing function of the duration of growth expected. As dividends are paid on the growth stocks, however, we will find that, in response to a change in the general level of share prices, the volatility of the shares is reduced. Thus, the ingredients will be furnished for a beginning to the type of analysis based on expectations and the mathematics of price movements which I have previously [12] attempted in a study of the term structure of interest rates. Finally, we shall note that several

---

[1] The construction of the index, as well as the criteria for selection of the shares included, will be explained later.

awkward difficulties arise peculiar to the valuation of shares, and thus the limitations as well as the applications of our model will be stressed.

I. A BRIEF HISTORY OF SECURITY ANALYSIS SINCE THE GREAT DEPRESSION

After its publication in 1934, Graham and Dodd's *Security Analysis* [8] became the classic training manual and reference work for the generation of security analysts who picked over the debris left by the 1929 crash in a search for hidden earning power and hidden assets. The work was a thorough and critical survey of the existing methods and techniques of analysis and was of uniformly high quality. Many of the methods of analysis described in the text remained unexceptionable even throughout the 1950's. The central idea of the work, however, was increasingly criticized in the postwar period, and it is this, its philosophy of valuation, with which we are chiefly concerned.

The fundamental proposition of security analysis advanced by Graham and Dodd is that any common share may be valued by capitalizing its indicated "earning power" by some suitable multiple. The concept of earning power combines a statement of actual earnings shown over a period of years with the expectation that these past earnings will be approximated in the future, unless extraordinary conditions supervene [8, pp. 418–19]. It is both in the earning-power concept and in the problem of selecting an appropriate multiple of these earnings that security analysts of the 'fifties broke sharply with Graham and Dodd. In the first place Graham and Dodd severely admonished the analyst against unduly emphasizing the past trend in earnings of any company, particularly when the trend is upward. "It must be remembered that the automatic or normal economic forces militate against the indefinite continuance of a given trend. Competition, regulation, the law of diminishing returns, etc., are powerful foes to unlimited expansion . . ." [8, p. 422]. But, and here is the crucial distinction, even if after qualitative study the analyst is convinced that the favorable trend will continue, "the analyst's philosophy must still impel him to base his investment valuation on an assumed earning power *no larger than the company has already achieved* in some year of normal business. Investment values can be related only to demonstrated performance . . ." [8, pp. 422–23, italics mine].

Later Graham and Dodd admit that the earnings of companies which have enjoyed above-average growth may be capitalized more liberally, but the absolute maximum suggested was a multiple 20 per cent higher than that accorded the securities in the Dow-Jones group [8, p. 458]. *Security Analysis* repeatedly warns against the special dangers inherent in overvaluing the earnings of growth stocks [8, pp. 388–89, 396–400, 458]. To buttress their argument they adduce the thesis of Mead and Grodinsky that all industries after a period of growth face an inexorable decline which once begun is rarely reversed [13, pp. 708–09]. Thus the security analyst who strictly followed the tenets of Graham and Dodd would view indulgently no more than a very limited premium for the earnings of a growth stock, and the entire flavor of the Graham and Dodd valuation approach would make him uneasy about even this compromise.

The opposing school of security analysis, which we shall describe as the growth-stock school, also had its beginnings in the Great Depression. It is deffilcult to acsribe to any one individual the credit for originating the application of the "present value" technique to growth stocks. S. Eliot Guild [9] is often given this distinction, although the classic development of the technique and particularly the nuances associated with it were worked out by John B. Williams [16] in 1938.

This theory argues that it is nonsense to claim that there must exist some arbitrarily defined maximum earnings multiple which should apply to a security no matter what its growth prospects. Surely, the warranted earnings multiple must be related to these prospects if any sense is to be made of the structure of share prices. The growth-stock approach to valuation can be illustrated by a recent variant of the approach suggested by Clendenin and Van Cleave [3]. Utilizing the basic Williams valuation formula (i.e., the present worth of a share is the summation of all dividends expected to be received from it, discounted to present value at an appropriate rate of interest) [16, p. 55], the authors have constructed tables showing the present value of a stock now paying $1.00 per share with varying assumptions concerning the growth rate and the growth period. The important point to be gained from the analysis is that, depending on the growth assumptions made, the investor may be justified in paying double or triple the price for growth shares compared with those which enjoy little or no growth [3, Table 4, p. 371]. Or to put the proposition somewhat differently, if the market values of shares corresponded roughly to the Graham and Dodd measure of central value, then an investor who purchased the shares of "growth companies" would receive an extraordinarily large effective return. Therefore, the search was on for those shares expected to enjoy above-average growth. This search and the concomitant bidding-up of the prices of such shares roughly characterized the major change in the structure of share prices in the 1950's.

While the basic idea of the growth-stock school was both correct and a necessary addition to the Graham and Dodd techniques of security analysis, there were several difficulties with the approach. In the first place, much of the theoretical valuation work focused entirely on dividend payments as the exclusive source of value. It has been argued recently [11] [14] that dividend payments may under certain assumptions be totally irrelevant. Furthermore, the search for an appropriate discount rate had led, at best, to the arbitrary choice of a single rate or, at worst, to the choice of several discount rates where dividends more distant in time are discounted at progressively higher discount rates [3, Table 5, p. 373] [6, pp. 41–43]. This type of technique is not only capricious, but it also suffers from what Miller and Modigliani call the "bird-in-the-hand fallacy."[2] In addition, an extremely long (60-year) horizon is utilized. This has the advantage of seemingly avoiding estimates of future dividend-price relationships. Unfortunately, it has the great disadvantage of resting on the unrealistic assumption that investors are actually able to make estimates for that long a period; if, indeed, it is meaningful even to speak of growth rates compounded over 60 years. Thus we must conclude that these techniques really offer no satisfactory solution to the growth-stock valuation problem.

[2] Miller and Modigliani [14, p. 424 n.] argue that the attempt to use a purely subjective discount rate to derive uncertainty-valuation formulas is to commit an error analogous to deriving certainty-valuation formulas for shares through the use of marginal rates of time preference.

Another difficulty is inherent in the proposition that the long-term growth rate of dividends may exceed the discount rate. This leads to a very awkward situation. Depending upon how many years one wishes to include in his horizon, one may be justified in paying any amount one wishes for the securities of those companies. Indeed, if perpetual growth at a rate greater than the discount rate is expected, the present value of the shares is infinity [3, pp. 368–69]. David Durand [5] has pointed out the remarkable analogy between this problem and the famous St. Petersburg Paradox of Bernoulli. But the common-stock buyers of the late 1950's were not troubled by the subtleties of these difficulties. Instead, it seemed logical that the investor should not worry about the price he paid for the shares of growth stocks—all that mattered was to find those securities which were experiencing the largest rates of growth. As a corollary to this "new investment maxim," the growth-stock philosophy believed that it had finally solved the age-old investment problem of timing. "The time to buy a growth stock is now. The whole purpose in such an investment is to participate in future larger earnings, so *ipso facto* any delay in making the commitment is defeating" [2, p. 122].

Graham and Dodd's *Security Analysis,* the erstwhile bible of the security analyst, had lost touch with the realities of the new "new era" of common-stock valuation. The search for growth became the main preoccupation of the security analyst [17]. "Growth" took on an almost mystical significance, and to question the propriety of such analysis became, as in a generation past, heretical. The structure of share prices existing in late 1961 is understandable only against this background of the recrudescence of these "new-era concepts" in security analysis. This structure of prices represented the illogical extension of a procedure that was designed by Guild and Williams as simply an ancillary technique to the main body of security analysis, not its replacement.

II. THE LEVEL OF COMMON-STOCK PRICES

How then should one decide the appropriate prices for those securities which enjoy a superior rate of growth in earnings per common share? To attempt to answer this question we next begin the construction of a valuation model which, initially, will be presented in terms of perfect certainty. Later we shall introduce some elements of uncertainty into the analysis. In theory, the valuation of any common stock can be reduced to a very simple relationship. Assuming that the investor has a finite horizon, the value of any common stock can be expressed simply as the sum of the present values of both the dividends to be received over the years included in the horizon and the terminal price of the common shares at the end of the horizon period. But immediately a whole host of problems arise: how can one determine the future stream of dividends to be received? How can one solve the valuation formula without first dealing with the problem of how the common shares will be valued at the end of the horizon period? What is the appropriate discount rate to use? And so forth. We might first note that we shall set ourself a task that will be somewhat simplified by the nature of our investigation. Our initial problem will be to deal soley with the structure of stock prices in a certainty setting where we abstract from taxes and market imperfections. The question we shall ask is what is the proper relationship between a given price level for a representative or standard security and the price of a security whose prospects for growth are above average. Then we shall seek to determine the effect of a *ceteris paribus* change in the standard price level on the price of a growth stock. But throughout the discussion we shall abstract from investor expectations concerning future movements of the prices of standard issues. Thus our first job will be to define what is meant by the level of stock prices.

When we refer to the level of stock prices, we have in mind whether equities in general seem to be high or low. In practice, financial people usually take the level of stock prices simply to be the index number associated with the popular market averages of standard securities. The difficulty with such a measure, wholly apart from the index-number problems involved, is the its information content is unsuitable for our purposes. A general price-level index cannot distinguish between a change in its value that results only from a change in the earnings and dividends of standard issues and a change that reflects a difference in the capitalization rate applied to constant earnings and dividends. In this paper, which is addressed to the problem of the determination of the "real value" of a share, the appropriate measure is clearly one that deals with capitalization rates, not with absolute prices. Consequently, we shall find it useful to define the level of share prices as the price commanded by a dollar of earnings for a representative share. This "normalized" price is identical with the price-earnings-ratio concept used by financial men to describe the ratio of the price paid per share of stock (P) to the earnings per share (E). The price-earnings multiple (ratio) for any share (m) is simply the inverse of the rate of capitalization of earnings, i.e.,

$$m \equiv \frac{P}{E}. \tag{1}$$

Our choice of this normalized price m instead of the absolute price P is also necessitated because we will want to make comparisons between the values of different securities. Clearly, the ratio of the absolute price of two stocks is a matter of the denominations in which they are issued. It is only the ratio between their price-earnings mutiples which can indicate the way in which the two securities are regarded by the market.

We may now briefly outline the development of the model that follows. We shall first use the theoretical construct of a representative standard share in order to find the objective market-determined discount rate that will be employed in valuing other issues. Next we will find the relationship between the discount rate and the earnings multiple of the standard share. It will be seen that a given standard earnings multiple uniquely determines this rate. The growth-stock valuation model will then be introduced. This model will evaluate for any standard earnings multiple (and the discount rate that it implies) the warranted earnings multiple for a growth stock. Since the earnings multiples for both growth and standard shares can be considered normalized prices, we will then have determined a structure of comparable share prices for issues that differ in their earnings and dividend growth rates.

Assuming the investor could buy a share of a representative standard security, what yield would he receive if he knew with certainty the future dividends and the future valuation of the composite share? Assuming the dividend, earnings, and price per share grow at the same percentage rate, it is easy to make a marginal-efficiency-of-investment calculation and solve for the effective yield. We shall find that it equals the current dividend rate per share (i.e., the dividend payment to be received for the year expressed as a percentage of existing market price)[3] plus the percentage annual growth in earnings per share, which, by assumption, is equal to the annual growth in the dividend and the price of each share as well.

The above proposition may be demonstrated most easily if we begin with the simplest possible case and utilize the Williams valuation formula. We define the value of the representative standard share as the present value of the dividends to be received by each share in all future periods. Since, by assumption, last year's dividend payment per representative standard share (D_s) is conveniently expected to grow at a constant growth rate (g_s), over time, the price per share (P_s) will equal:

$$P_s = \sum_{i=1}^{\infty} D_s \left(\frac{1+g_s}{1+r}\right)^i. \tag{2}$$

Summing the geometric progression and solving for r we obtain:

$$r = \frac{D_s(1+g_s)}{P_s} + g_s, \tag{3}$$

i.e., the marginal efficiency of the investment is equal to the current year's dividend rate (the dividend to be paid at the end of the current year as a percentage of the existing market price) plus the growth rate. It can also easily be shown that the same result follows if, instead of discounting the future stream of dividends in perpetuity, we utilize a finite time period and discount back for the dividends and the price of the standard share as of any future date. Assuming that investors continue to be willing to capitalize the earnings of the share at the same rate, the price of the representative share also grows at the rate g_s, and the valuation formula becomes:

$$P_s = \sum_{i=1}^{N} D_s \left(\frac{1+g_s}{1+r}\right)^i + P_s\left(\frac{1+g_s}{1+r}\right)^N \tag{4}$$

Summing the progression and rearranging terms we get:

$$P_s\left[1 - \left(\frac{1+g_s}{1+r}\right)^N\right] = \frac{D_s(1+g_s)}{r-g_s}\left[1 - \left(\frac{1+g_s}{1+r}\right)^N\right]$$

which (after solving for r) reduces to (3). Thus we see that the time horizon chosen for valuing the representative security is irrelevant under the assumptions postulated.

[3] In financial circles this expression is often called the dividend yield. We shall use the term "rate" to avoid confusion with the total yield or marginal efficiency. It should be noted that Gordon and Shapiro [7] have previously developed an expression identical to (3) for the yield of a (standard) security, although the application made of their model is different from our own.

We shall call r the "apparent marginal efficiency" of the representative standard share. Now we will demonstrate how r uniquely can be determined once the standard earnings multiple, m_s, is known. First, we will find the general relationship between the r and m_s, Let the dividend rate, d_s. be defined as:

$$d_s \equiv \frac{D_s(1 + g_s)}{P_s} \qquad (5)$$

d_s is related to r by (3), $r - g_s = d_s$. By (1) $P_s = m_s E_s$, Substituting this expression into (5) and solving for m_s, we have:

$$m_s = \frac{D_s(1 + g_s)}{E_s} \Big/ d_s. \qquad (6)$$

In this expression,

$$\frac{D_s(1 + g_s)}{E_s}$$

is simply the payout ratio (based on next year's dividend), which we assume to be known and constant through time, as is implied by our prior assumption that dividends and earnings would grow at the same rate. Therefore, we are able to determine the price-earnings ratio, m_s, from (6). Alternatively, we can view the price-earnings multiple as determining r. Given a fixed payout ratio for standard shares, then any m_s, will uniquely determine the dividend rate (d_s). Since g_s is also taken to be a constant, we can then immediately find the apparent marginal efficiency.[4] Thus our construct describing the determination of the level of normalized share prices (i.e., the earnings multiple for a representative standard share) can provide us with a necessary building block for the construction of our valuation model. It uniquely determines an objective market rate of discount which we may then apply to the valuation of growth stocks. Moreover, we shall see that it provides both a method of capitalizing the earnings of these stocks when their period of extraordinary growth is concluded and a standard of comparison of value.

III. MODEL FOR THE VALUATION OF GROWTH STOCKS

The term "growth stock" as used in the financial community is a term of approbation to describe those common shares which have enjoyed (or are expected to enjoy) in some sense above-average earnings growth. We shall use the term to

---

[4] But note that if the dividend payout ratio for the standard share is zero (i.e., no dividends are paid) then $r=g_s$. which is, of course, independent of m_s. Alternatively, we might say that the price-earnings ratio is indeterminate. This is so because, given the assumption that investors will continue to be willing to capitalize the earnings of the share at the same rate, any price-earnings ratio is consistent with (3). A, say, 5 per cent rate of growth in earnings will produce a 5 per cent capital appreciation per year (and hence a 5 per cent internal rate of return) regardless of what earnings multiple the standard share commands. Once any dividend is paid, however, this problem disappears.

describe any equity security that meet both of the following conditions: first,

$$d + g > d_s + g_s, \tag{7}$$

the dividend rate plus the growth rate of the growth stock (the absence of the subscript s always indicates a growth stock) must exceed the dividend plus growth rate for the representative standard share or, what is the same thing, its apparent marginal efficiency. Second, we require that

$$g > g_s, \tag{8}$$

the growth rate of the growth stock must exceed the standard growth rate. This avoids considering as growth stocks securities which merely pay unusually high dividends. In the event that the growth security pays no dividends, then the growth-stock definition simply requires:

$$g > r. \tag{9}$$

Moreover, we expect that the above conditions must have been satisfied on the average, say, for the past three years and are expected to be satisfied for at least the next two years. However, we reject the possibility that a growth rate will exceed r in perpetuity.[5] This particular definition of a growth stock has been chosen to permit applicability of the model to the maximum number of shares. If these conditions are not met, the following model is not appropriate.[6]

We begin with the fundamental proposition that the "market" will tend to equalize the net yield obtainable form all securities. Since the stream of receipts from the growth stock and the representative standard issue are both expected with certainty, then we can use the apparent marginal efficiency of the standard issue as the interest rate appropriate for discounting the future stream of receipts. Let us now recapitulate the symbols to be used:[7]

$E=$earnings per common share of the growth stock in the fiscal year just past. Again we remind the reader that when the subscript s appears with E, we refer to the earnings of the standard share.

$D=$dividends per share in the past fiscal year. Dividends are assumed to be paid out annually at the end of each fiscal year.

$g=$the expected growth rate of earnings per share and dividends per share over the next N years.[7]

[5] This of course would lead us into the "growth stock paradox" again. But as Modigliani and Miller point out [15, p. 664 n.] this possibility must be rejected as a curiosum devoid of economic significance. Assuming that there must be a finite value for all shares, then r (a variable in a general equilibrium setting) would have to rise to restore equilibrium to the capital markets should the rate of earnings growth of some shares be perpetually greater than r. Nevertheless, it is both possible and plausible that the rate of growth of many firms over some finite period may exceed r by a wide margin.

[6] See footnote 9.

[7] Underlying the projection of a particular growth rate are, of course, specific assumptions concerning the investment opportunities of the firm and its investment and financial policies. In my view these assumptions are better left implicit in a model which for this discussion addresses itself only to the problem of share valuation. However, in much of the recent work in this area (e.g., Gordon, and Miller and Modigliani) these assumptions are integrated explicitly into the models.

$m \equiv P/E =$ the price-earnings ratio of the share today.
$d \equiv D(1+g)/Em =$ the dividend rate based on next year's dividend payment.
$P =$ the present value of the future stream of receipts, i.e., the value of the common share today.
$r =$ the apparent marginal efficiency of the representative standard share.

   In our valuation formula we shall assume that both the dividends and earnings per share of the growth stock grow at a rate g for a period of N years. After that period, the security enjoys only the average growth expected of the standard list of securities (and therefore is able to pay the average dividend of the standard composite security).[8] Accordingly, we postulate that the price-earnings multiple of the shares to be valued falls to that multiple which the market is applying to standard issues. This acknowledges that above-average earnings growth can continue only for a limited period. Furthermore, the price-earnings ratio is expected to recede to the standard level thus avoiding the mistake of "counting the same trick twice," i.e., continuing to value growth stocks at extraordinarily high price-earnings ratios after the extraordinary rate of earnings growth has already occurred [8, pp. 459–60].[9]
   Assuming that each year's dividend is paid at the end of the year and that valuation is to be made at the beginning of the year, our valuation formula becomes:

$$ P = \frac{D(1 + g)}{(1 + \bar{r})} + \frac{D(1 + g)^2}{(1 + \bar{r})^2} + \cdots + \frac{D(1 + g)^N}{(1 + \bar{r})^N} + \frac{\bar{m}_s E(1 + g)^N}{(1 + \bar{r})^N}. \quad (10) $$

The numerator of the last term of (10) represents the market price of the security at the end of year N. The earnings in year N, $E(1+g)^N$, are capitalized by applying the standard earnings multiple, m_s, This assumes that the growth stock, in effect, takes on the characteristics of a standard issue after the period of extraordinary growth is completed. Moreover, we assume that no change occurs in the standard multiple at the end of the growth period (i.e., the level of share prices remains constant). This terminal value we discount to the present and add to the sum of the present values of the stream of dividend receipts.[10] Summing (10) and dividing through by E, we can solve for the price-earnings ratio, m, of the share:

$$ m = \frac{D(1 + g)}{E(\bar{r} - g)} - \frac{D(1 + g)^{N+1}}{E(\bar{r} - g)(1 + \bar{r})^N} + \frac{\bar{m}_s(1 + g)^N}{(1 + \bar{r})^N}. \quad (11) $$

[8] Alternatively, the shares could grow at a rate r and retain all earnings. In fact, any combination of $g+d$ which equals r is permissible. See (A3) below.

[9] This assumption renders the model inapplicable for securities not meeting our conditions for growth. It is one thing to argue that, after a period of abnormal growth, the multiple applied to the shares will fall back to the standard ratio. It is quite another matter to invoke this condition for shares where the historical record has been substandard. In the latter case there is no reason to assume that the issue could, for example, grow at the standard rate and have the same dividend payout ratio as does the standard issue.

[10] It should be noted that the investor need not hold his security for N periods to obtain the yield r. Assuming that the standard security continues to be valued at the same rate (i.e., the level of share prices remains constant), then the investor may sell his security at any intermediate time and realize the holding-period yield r.

It will now be useful to review three well-known theorems concerning growth stocks.[11] First, we should note that the warranted price-earnings ratio, m, that can be paid for a growth stock will always exceed the standard multiple, $\bar{m}_s$. Second, it is clear that the premium over the standard earnings multiple is an increasing function of the growth rate, g. Finally, the valuation premium is also an increasing function of the number of years that the issue continues to meet our criteria of growth. While the form of valuation equation (10) would also seem to indicate that $\partial m / \partial D > 0$, such a conclusion is not justified. Our formula omits the relationship between dividend payments per share and the ability to achieve future earnings growth per share. It could well be that $\partial m / \partial D = 0$ because, while the effect of a large dividend per share would bend to increase m, the lower terminal value *per share* might reduce m by an exactly equal amount.[12]

Let us turn now to the special case of the growth stock that pays no dividends at all. This case is an important one since this condition characterizes a number of securities normally considered growth stocks.

Here the valuation formula reduces to:

$$P = \bar{m}_s E \frac{(1 + g)^N}{(1 + \bar{r})^N}, \quad \text{or} \tag{12}$$

$$m = \bar{m}_s \frac{(1 + g)^N}{(1 + \bar{r})^N}. \tag{13}$$

We are thus able to express the normalized price of a nondividend-paying growth stock as some multiple of the price-earnings ratio for the representative standard share.

We shall now examine the effect of a *ceteris paribus* change in the standard price level on the normalized prices of growth stocks, that is, a change in the standard earnings multiple not associated with a change in the market's estimate of g_s or in any of the other variables of the model. Such a change might occur in response to a change in the level of interest rates. But, while we allow for such a change to occur, we shall posit that investors have formed no expectations concerning the likelihood of the general level of equity prices moving either up or down. Thus, whatever the level of standard share prices is, the model asserts that a structure of share prices is formed which assumes the perpetuation of the present level. Given this assumption, it follows that nondividend-paying growth

---

[11] Formal proof of these theorems is offered in the Appendix.

[12] Miller and Modigliani [14, p. 414], for example, have argued that when a company pays a cash dividend it simply puts in the share-owner's left-hand pocket what it has taken from his right. Given the investment decision, dividend payments to current shareholders merely reduce the value of their claim in the enterprise. This is so because additional equity shares in the business (representing an amount equal to the dividend payment) must be sold in order to finance the predetermined level of capital expenditures. The worth of the enterprise is accordingly affected, not by "how the fruits of the earning power are 'packaged' for distribution," but only by the "real" variables of the company's earning power and investment opportunities. Looked at in this way, a cash dividend is just as irrelevant as a stock dividend. Of course, this argument abstracts, as does ours, from tax considerations, market imperfections, etc. However, for uncertainty counterarguments to the Miller–Modigliani position, see W. J. Baumol [1] and John Lintner [11].

stocks are inherently more volatile than standard issues. Moreover, the greater is the number of years for which the extraordinary growth is expected, the more widely will the shares fluctuate in price as the level of share prices changes. However, the volatility of the price-earnings ratio is invariant with respect to the *rate* of growth expected.

While formal proof is offered in the Appendix, these findings can be understood easily if one simply examines equations (12) and (13). When the level of share prices falls, the price-earnings ratio, m_s, of the standard list falls, and therefore the warranted price-earnings ratio of the shares to be valued tends to fall *pari passu* with m_s, But a falling level of share prices also implies that the dividend yield on standard shares tends to rise. Therefore, the discount rate used to convert the future value of the growth stock to present worth increases. The result is that m falls *a fortiori*. Hence, *ceteris paribus*, the price-earnings ratios of nondividend-paying growth stocks may be expected to fall by a greater percentage rate than those of ordinary shares. Furthermore, since the discount factor $(1+r)$ is raised to the Nth power, the decline will be greater, the larger N is, i.e., the longer the period is over which the shares are expected to continue their superior growth record.

Returning to the case of dividend-paying growth stocks, the above results do not, in general, hold. The relevant elasticity expression for dividend-paying shares is, unfortunately, rather unpleasant, and I was unable to deal with it analytically. Instead I was forced to examine ranges of representative values of the function for different values of the variables to determine their effects. Specifically, the value of ϵ_m (the elasticity of the price-earnings ratio) was calculated for all the relevant ranges of m_s, D/E, g, and for N.[13] The following propositions are suggested by these calculations:

$$\frac{\partial \epsilon_m}{\partial (D/E)} < 0. \tag{14}$$

The larger is the dividend paid on the growth stock, then, *ceteris paribus*, the less volatile will it be. The computations also suggest that a necessary, but not a sufficient, condition for this elasticity to be less than unity is for the growth stock to have a payout ratio $(D/E) > (D_s/E_s)$. It also appears that

$$\frac{\partial \epsilon_m}{\partial g} > 0 \quad \text{for} \quad N \geq 2 \quad \text{and} \quad \frac{\partial \epsilon_m}{\partial g} = 0 \quad \text{for} \quad N = 1. \tag{15}$$

Thus for all horizons greater than one year, the volatility of dividend-paying growth stocks increases with the growth rate. Finally, we conjecture that

[13] The calculations were performed on the Institute for Defense Analysis CDC 1604 computer. m_s was allowed to vary from 8 to 25 in intervals of 1, D_s/E_s was set at 0.6, and g_s was held constant at 2 per cent. These values were chosen as being historically relevant in accordance with the empirical analysis which follows. For each m_s (and the r it uniquely determines) a set of warranted growth-stock price-earnings ratios and corresponding elasticities was calculated. Over 17,000 hypothetical growth stocks representing all combinations of payout ratios from 0 to 100 per cent, growth rates up to 40 per cent, and growth horizons up to 15 years were considered in each set. It can also be shown that these volatility relationships hold (within the hypothesized range of parameters even when m_s varies only in response to equiproportionate changes in all growth rates. I am greatly indebted to R. E. Quandt for programming the calculation.

$$\frac{\partial \epsilon_m}{\partial N} > 0 \quad \text{for} \quad \epsilon_m > 1 \quad \text{when} \quad N = 1. \tag{16}$$

The volatility increases with N whenever the stock is more volatile than the standard issue to begin with. Thus in the dividend-paying case the following generalization appears to be valid: a dividend payment tends *ceteris paribus* to decrease the volatility of a growth stock. Nevertheless, unless the dividend payout ratio is larger than that for standard issues, these shares will still be more volatile than standard shares and an increase in the growth horizon will, as before, increase their volatility. Finally, the volatility of dividend-paying growth stocks (in contrast to nondivdidend-paying shares) increases with the growth rate for all horizons longer than one year.

We conclude, then, that in one important respect growth stocks are intrinsically different from standard issues. When the level of share prices changes, the prices of growth stocks must fluctuate more than proportionately if the sturcture of share prices is to remain unchanged. Thus, growth stocks are inherently more volatile than standard issues. When the level of share prices drops sharply, as was the case during the first six months of 1962, a significantly larger fluctuation in the prices of growth stocks is to be expected as a normal concomitant. Thus at least a part of the "revaluation of growth stocks" experienced in early 1962 may not have been revaluation at all, but rather a predictable result of the relevant functional relationship.

IV. APPLICATION ON THE MODEL

Before turning to the application of our model we must find some operational definition for the level of share prices and establish the conditions under which the certainty analysis may be used to approximate the world of uncertainty.[14] As the empirical counterpart to our construct of the representative standard share, we shall choose the index number associated with the Standard and Poor 425 Industrial Stock Average (425ISA).[15] This index number can be considered to be the price of a standard composite industrial share. The price-earnings ratio applicable to the composite share we will take to be the normalized price, i. e., the level of share prices.

Recall that we found by (3) that the apparent marginal efficiency of the representative standard share was composed of the sum of its dividend rate and its growth rate. If we assume that the recent rate of growth of earnings of the S & P composite share will continue at a constant rate into the future, we can,

---

[14] We shall make no attempt in this paper to develop a full uncertainty model of share valuation. However, we shall indicate in several places during the following discussion the kinds of considerations that are relevant for such an extension to uncertainty.

[15] The problems associated with any index number are well known in the economic literature. The peculiar difficulties associated with the popular market averages are particularly discouraging. Nevertheless, we know of no alternative to attempting to describe the level of share prices in terms of one of the standard lists of equities. We do assert, however, that the S & P 425ISA gives the broadest and fairest available representation of standard industrial shares.

at any time, actually assign an internal rate of return to the stock average. Over the past five years (1957 through 1962) the 425ISA has achieved a compounded earnings growth of 1.9 per cent per annum. By taking different periods it is possible to find both higher and lower growth rates. If, for example, 1929 is taken as a base, the annual growth rate rises to 3.8 per cent. However, if the recent high-profit year of 1955 is used, the growth rate of earnings is negligible. The growth of dividends has exceeded the growth rate of earnings in recent years, but the two have been roughly similar for longer periods. We shall use, for illustrative purposes only, a rate of 2 per cent as an empirical approximation to what, in the certainty analysis, would be the anticipated (with certainty) annual percentage increase in earnings and dividends per share. This rate roughly conforms to past experience as adjusted for the less favorable recent earnings performance.[16] The price-earnings ratio of the composite share and the dividend yield that it determines are, of course, matters of record. At the December 12, 1961 market peak, the 425ISA sold at a price-earnings multiple m_s of 20.3 and had an apparent marginal efficiency, r, of approximately 43/4 per cent.[17] The relevant figures for the June 26, 1962 trough are $m_s = 15.5$ and $r = 5.9$ per cent.

It is important to note here that in the operational counterpart to our theoretical construct, we have strayed from the protection of perfect certainty. Our empirical internal rate of return is not a "pure" yield, for it includes an allowance for the risk inherent in holding a standard industrial share. This discount rate can be applied appropriately only to growth issues for which the risk is in some sense equal to the of standard securities, for all stocks will not tend to have the same yield regardless of risk. However, we do postulate that there should be no clear risk-premium difference between growth and ordinary shares. That is, for two securities which are equally risky in all other respects, we will ignore any risk differences resulting solely from the fact that the expected yield from one may come largely from capital appreciation, whereas the yield from the second is expected to be derived largely from dividend payments.[18]

---

[16] Some support for our choice of 2 per cent as the rate of anticipated earnings growth can be found by examining long-term data. Using the Cowles Commission All-Stock Index [4, p. 59], annual gains of 1.8 per cent were experienced from just after the Civil War to the middle of the 1930's.

Nevertheless, the choice of an appropriate growth rate is not an obvious one and the reader may wish to substitute his own. Moreover, in a world of uncertainty, the market's estimate of g_s is unlikely to remain constant over time.

[17] The dividend yield, based on the anticipated next year's dividend rate, was 2.75 per cent, and 2 per cent was the projected growth rate of earnings per share.

[18] For support of this position in the context of an argument concerning the relevancy or irrelevancy of dividend payments, see Lintner [11, p. 255] and Miller and Modigliani [14, pp. 426–32]. Their demonstration, however, is consistent with a view that growth stocks may still be more risky than standard issues. While there is undoubtedly some justification for this frequently voiced position, its importance can be overstated. It is easy to imagine cases where the risk for a company continuously investing large amounts may actually be less than the normal risk of a business doing little investing. Moreover, one can point to a large class of growth companies which derive a substantial share of their earnings from rental and service revenues. In these cases, the companies not only enjoy a stable source of revenue and profit but also grow as the result of each new sale.

There is, however, one respect in which we can say unambiguously that most growth stocks are riskier than standard securities. The former have been shown to be inherently more volatile than representative standard issues. It could be maintained that because of this greater volatility, a higher discount rate should be applied than the apparent marginal efficiency of the standard list. The investor, according to this argument, should be given a risk premium to compensate him for assuming the risks of larger price fluctuations. Thus, by a process akin to "normal backwardation" in the futures markets, growth stocks would have to sell at a discount from their certainty value, which is calculated by abstracting from changes in the level of share prices. But if one subjects this argument to careful examination, one finds a Pandora's box of difficulties. Surely, if investors expect that the level of share prices will rise, then growth stocks should be expected to sell at a premium vis-a-vis ordinary shares since they would offer greater possibilities for capital appreciation. Thus a thorough uncertainty model of share valuation would contain precisely the same considerations as make up the expectational theory of the term structure of interest rates. At times, more volatile issues should sell at a premium and at other times at a discount, from their certainty valuation precisely because of their inherent mercurial qualities. While we shall not extend this discussion further, these implications may indicate a few of the considerations which need to be included in a full-uncertainty model of share valuation.

We may now proceed to apply the model to recent periods of stock market history. In particular, we shall examine the recent market "adjustment" in the United States, where both the level and the structure of share prices underwent an unusually extensive metamorphosis. Using the formulas developed above, we shall first compute the theoretically justifiable price-earnings ratios for securities with differing growth characteristics. We then may compare the "warranted" normalized prices at recent peak and trough dates with those which actually existed. Table 1 treats nondividend-paying shares, and, consequently valuation formula (13) is used. The numbers enclosed in the boxes are the warranted price-earnings multiples appropriate for two different levels of share prices. They represent normative valuations, assuming that the listed rate of growth of earnings is to occur for N years.[19] After this, the security loses its extraordinary growth characteristics and becomes valued as a typical standard issue.[20] The greater volatility of the shares compared with standard issues is immediately revealed.

Thus, it is not self-evident, when comparing issues of roughly the same quality, why the security analyst would necessarily be less confident of his forecast of earnings growth than his appraisal of the viability of an established yearly dividend. Indeed, any number of counterexamples may be found. Moreover, if we introduce tax considerations, most investors should be expected, if anything, to prefer growth stocks because their ultimate yield would be taxed at substantially lower rates than the shares of standard issues paying higher dividends. This is not to deny, however, that many growth companies, particularly those which invest in completely new areas of endeavor, may indeed be riskier than standard issues.

[19] Of course, the model could easily be modified to allow for a diminution in the growth rate in later years of the growth horizon or the continuation of a more moderate growth rate after the end of N years.

[20] A similar and independent analysis has recently been performed by Charles C. Holt [10]. However, Holt neglects the dependence of the standard yield on the earnings

TABLE 1

Warranted price-earnings ratios at peak and trough levels of share prices

No. of years ahead discounted N	7.5 Peak	7.5 Trough	15 Peak	15 Trough	20 Peak	20 Trough	25 Peak	25 Trough	35 Peak	35 Trough	Per cent decline peak to trough for all g
2	21.38	15.97	24.47	18.28	26.64	19.90	28.91	21.60	33.72	25.19	25.3
3	21.94	16.21	26.86	19.85	30.52	22.55	34.49	25.49	43.45	32.11	26.1
4	22.52	16.46	29.49	21.55	34.96	25.55	41.16	30.00	56.00	40.93	26.9
5	23.11	16.71	32.37	23.41	40.05	28.96	49.12	35.52	72.17	52.18	27.7
7	24.34	17.22	39.02	27.60	52.56	37.18	69.95	49.48	119.88	84.80	29.3

Peak (December 12, 1961) equation:

$$m = 20.3 \frac{(1+g)^N}{(1.0475)^N}$$

Trough (June 26, 1962) equation:

$$m = 15.5 \frac{(1+g)^N}{(1.059)^N}$$

Percent decline in standard multiple (m_s): 23.6%.

We shall now look at the actual price-earnings multiples that existed for certain well-known nondividend-paying growth shares. We can then reverse the analysis. Instead of asking what the warranted earnings multiple should be, we can instead determine from our model what growth is implicitly being anticipated and is already discounted in the market prices of the shares. Then we can ask whether the past history of earnings growth of these companies suggests that the rate of growth required to justify their current prices is reasonable. What follows is perhaps a very rough and, in large measure, an impressionistic attempt to select a sample of growth stocks that are no riskier than those issues included in the standard list. We wish to insure that the apparent marginal efficiency of the standard list is the rate of return relevant for discounting. It would, of course, be impossible to formulate rigorous criteria for equal riskiness without developing a full-uncertainty valuation model. Nevertheless, we would argue that our method of choosing securities insures that our certainty model gives a good approximation to what might be considered warranted valuations.[21]

Our procedure will be to compute a mean (compounded) growth rate for each company. As has become abundantly clear in much of the recent work in uncertainty analysis, it may very well be that higher moments are of very significant inportance to decision-making investors. Thus our insistence on relatively consistent growth will insure that the standard deviation of the mean growth rate is very low. It is necessary that higher moments of the total expected yield for any growth security be essentially similar to those applicable for standard issues. Similarly, we require an investment grade status comparable to standard issues in order to screen out those securities whose past records would suggest that a discount rate higher than r be applied. While a full-uncertainty analysis would include several modifications of this procedure, I do not believe they would materially affect the valuation results we have derived.

We now reach the denouement of our story. In Table 2 the price-earnings ratios existing at the recent market peak and trough are compared with the growth rates and growth periods that were implicitly assumed by their prices. We find that to justify the market prices for these issues at the market peak, an investor would have to expect extraordinary rates of growth (typically larger than had ever been achieved in the past) for a very long period of years.

To appraise this finding, it is necessary to make two observations, one bordering on the obvious, the other on the metaphysical. Our first comment is simply a reminder that the maintenance of a long-run high level of compounded earnings growth implies an ever increasing arithmetic growth of earnings. If a company which has enjoyed a 25 percent annually compounded growth rate over the past five years is to continue its same rate of growth in the next five

---

multiple applied to standard issues. Therefore, his analysis suggests (incorrectly) that relative earnings ratios are invariant with respect to the general level of share prices.

[21] Our five sample nondividend-paying growth stocks have been selected on the basis of the following criteria: (1) that the company has been established in business for at least ten years (we want to exclude speculative new companies without sufficient past history to indicate future prospects); (2) that the company has been profitable in each of the past five years; (3) that the company has met the requirements of the definition of a growth stock in at least four of its last five fiscal years preceding the date of valuation; and (4) that the shares be considered of "investment grade" as evidenced by ratings applied by the investment advisory services and by widespread inclusion in the portfolios of the leading investment companies specializing in common-stock investments.

years, then it will have to triple its absolute *increase* of earnings.[22] When we consider that we are discussing earnings *per share,* it is obvious that the difficulties are increased significantly. The actual growth rate of total earnings must in most cases be even larger to overcome the dilution effects of new shares issued.

TABLE 2

Growth-Stock valuations (Growth rates and periods implicitly assumed)

Growth stock	Market peak December 12, 1961					
	Price P	Earnings multiple m	Years[a] of growth at rate historic needed to justify current price N	Growth rate (g) needed to justify current price		Historic growth rate g (based on past 5 years)
				3-year horizon $N=3$	4-year horizon $N=4$	
	(1)	(2)	(3)	(4)	(5)	(11)
Automatic Retailers	64	98.5	8	77%	55%	28%
Howard Johnson	60	33.5	4	24%	19%	18%
Litton Industries	161	63.9	6	53%	40%	28%
Perkin Elmer	61	54.0	4	45%	34%	37%
Varian Associates	47	64.4	5	53%	40%	31%
Average of five growth stocks	79	62.9	6	53%	39%	28%

Growth stock	Market Through June 26, 1962					
	Price P	Earnings multiple[b] m	Years[a] of growth at historic rate needed to justify current price N	Growth rate (g) needed to justify current price		Historic growth rate g (based on past 5 years)
				3-year horizon $N=3$	4-year horizon $N=4$	
	(6)	(7)	(8)	(9)	(10)	(11)
Automatic Retailers	29	25.2	$2\frac{1}{2}$	24%	20%	28%
Howard Johnson	32	16.4	$\frac{1}{2}$	8%	7%	18%
Litton Industries	78	24.8	$2\frac{1}{2}$	24%	19%	28%
Perkin Elmer	26	24.5	2	23%	19%	37%
Varian Associates	23	33.8	$3\frac{1}{2}$	37%	29%	31%
Average of five Growth stocks	38	24.9	$2\frac{1}{2}$	24%	19%	28%

[a] *Rounded to nearest half-year. Thus there are minor rounding inconsistencies in the table.*
[b] *Based on latest 12-months' earnings to each period.*

[22] If the company earned a dollar a share at the beginning of the first period, it must earn over three dollars at the end of the fifth year (a two-dollar increase) and over nine dollars at the end of the tenth year (a six-dollar increase over year five).

Finally, we should note that most "growth companies" were able to achieve the spectacular growth rates of Table 2 only because of the very low earnings base from which they started. Thus we must conclude on a priori grounds that it is highly unlikely that these companies will continue such rapid rates of growth for more than perhaps one year or, at best, a very few years.

Our second comment concerns the horizon over which the valuation is based. A strong a priori case can be made for the use of a relatively short horizon. I believe that ordinarily five years should realistically be considered the maximum for the investment horizon and, for the reasons given above, growth rates of 20 per cent or more should be viewed very suspiciously if projected for more than three years. Usually a corporation's investment prospects can be forecast intelligently only for the shorter three-year period. The five-year period represents, to my knowledge, the maximum budgeting horizon used by corporations themselves and by financial analysts in attempting an analytical forecast of earnings. An attempt to project industrial growth rates further (except in the most unusual circumstances) seems completely unjustified.[23] But no matter how questionable, precisely these kinds of projections seem to have been made and indeed, as Table 2 indicates, the structure of share prices in late 1961 can be rationalized only on that basis. Thus we would argue that in the world of uncertainty, the time horizon for discounting is one of the most important variables for determining equity values. The difficulty is that while there may be a priori reasons for setting a maximum to the discounting period (and for concluding that these issues were overvalued), there is no *one* reasonable horizon. I believe there is only a *putatively reasonable horizon,* a variable characteristic of market sentiment at any time. That the putatively reasonable horizon may undergo rapid shifts is obvious when we compare columns 3 and 8 of Table 2. At the trough, the wheel had turned full circle. Market prices implied more moderate rates of growth (usually well below the past performance of the companies) for periods well under the five-year "maximum" horizon. Even if one argues that part of the revaluation of growth stocks represented a growing distrust of projecting the high growth rates of the past into the future, this explanation is not complete. There was also a definite reduction in the putatively reasonable horizon used by investors in the valuation process. We might also note that to the extent that one could rely on continued good rates of growth for these companies (even if more moderate than in the past), the existing structure of share prices tended to undervalue growth stocks during June 1962, just as it had overvalued them in December 1961.

Our discussion of the use of the model would be incomplete without reference to the valuation of International Business Machines' shares. No other security is so synonymous with growth in the minds of investors as is IBM.

---

[23] By utilizing a *limited* horizon period over which extraordinary growth may be projected, we are introducing a type of finite-horizon method for dealing with uncertainty. Economists have pointed out that this technique leaves much to be desired for, among other things, it usually ignores any prospective receipts after the cut-off date and can be shown in some circumstances to lead to rather absurd rankings of investment projects. But the growth-stock model employs a finite-horizon device that is rather less crude. If investors' horizons are limited as a practical matter to five years, this does not imply that all receipts to the shareholders after the horizon period are ignored. All that is implied is that only normal growth is projected after the cut-off period.

Perhaps the most salient feature of IBM's past growth is its remarkable steadiness. Computing compounded growth rates, using each of the past ten years as a basis, one finds that the growth rate in earnings per share was 20 per cent, or slightly above, for each year. Despite IBM's deserved reputation as the ideal growth stock, we should nevertheless be very suspicious if the growth rate implied by the price of the shares should exceed that rate which has been achieved in the past decade. Indeed, as we remarked earlier, we would be surprised to see it continue, particularly considering the size of the company.[24]

Table 3 presents a series of valuation estimates for IBM under differing assumptions as to future growth rates and growth periods. Since IBM pays dividends, formula (11) has been used for the calculation. In addition, we have introduced one innovation into our valuation principle. We may well be accused of being too conservative in assuming that after the period of abnormal growth is completed the shares will sell at the same price-earnings ratio as do standard shares. Indeed, would it not be plausible to assume that the shares of a company such as IBM would still be able to command a premium over ordinary shares both because of its extraordinarily high quality and because the company's growth prospects may still appear to be above average? To be as liberal as possible, we have made a separate calculation making the (arbitrary) assumption that the residual price-earnings multiple for the shares will be 50 per cent higher than the multiple applied to standard securities. The calculations are presented below.

TABLE 3

Valuation of IBM common stock

Hori-zon N	Market peak December 12, 1961				Market through June 26, 1962			
	$g=20\%$		$g=15\%$		$g=20\%$		$g=15\%$	
	Residual earnings multiple		Residual earnings multiple		Residual earnings multiple		Residual earnings multiple	
	20. 3	30	20. 3	30	15. 5	23	15. 5	23
3	31.5	46.1	27.5	40.3	23.6	34.5	20.5	30.1
5	42.0	61.1	33.5	49.0	31.0	45.0	24.5	35.8
7	55.7	80.8	40.7	59.4	40.4	58.4	29.3	42.7

At the market peak, IBM shares sold at 580, a multiple of 64 times the most recent 12-months' earnings.[25] Particularly in light of our previous dis-

[24] IBM's total revenues are now running at an annual rate of approximately $2 billion. To keep up a long-term 20 per cent growth rate (we assume earnings and revenues must expand at the same rate) then the revenue growth from year seven to eight would equal $1.4 billion, the revenue volume of 1960. To push the argument to the absurd, if the growth rate continued for an additional 22 years, IBM's revenues would exceed the U.S. national income in 1962.

[25] As estimated by the author. Reported earnings in all cases have been adjusted to include unremitted foreign income.

cussion on the implications of extending a growth rate of 20 per cent for a period of seven years and beyond, we can assert unequivocally that IBM shares were overvalued relative to the standard list of securities. In the words of a favorite Wall Street aphorism "share prices were discounting not only the future but also the here-after." At the trough, IBM shares sold at 320, a multiple of 32 times the latest 12-months' earnings. While the case for considering IBM shares undervalued is not as clear-cut as the overvaluation at the December peak, it is easy to find justification for believing that the shares of IBM were probably slightly on the low side of a reasonable valuation vis-a-vis the level of share prices.[26]

SUMMARY AND CONCLUSION

It will be useful now to review the ground we have covered and to appraise the results we have achieved. We attempted to explain the December, 1961 peak structure of share prices as a phenomenon understandable only against a background of the history of security analysis since the Great Depression. We described the shifts in the central interest of security analysis from an analysis of balance sheet values through an emphasis on earning power and finally to the elevation of growth analysis as the *sine qua non* of profitable investment. Concomitantly, we observed that fashions of equity investment determine a structure of share prices which, at various times, has put varying degrees of premium on these values.

Next we introduced and developed a simple model by which we might determine a warranted structure of share prices on a certainty basis. In addition to demonstrating its potential usefulness in detecting cases of over-and under-valuation of growth shares, the model could serve as a conceptual scheme for analyzing the change in the structure of share prices which took place. In the first place, we showed that a part of the much larger percentage decline in growth stocks was to be expected from a stable functional relationship, just as when interest rates rise, long-term bonds can be expected to suffer a sharper decline in price. Next, we analyzed the revaluation in terms of investors' reluctance to continue to accept the plausibility of projections of past rates of growth into the future and their uneasiness with the very long horizons implicit in share prices. Moreover, we showed that precisely because some stocks were being valued on the basis of a long growth horizon, their volatility, given a change in the level of share prices, was increased. Finally, in our modification to the IBM valuation model, we suggested that the expected residual price-earnings ratio applied to the shares at the termination of their period of extraordinary growth could also be an important variable. In a world of uncertainty, where company prospects beyond the very immediate future become increasingly fuzzy, there may be room for a considerable range of residual valuations for the same security.

---

[26] Assuming a growth rate of 15 per cent could be achieved for three years and that the residual multiple of earnings be a modest 23, the price-earnings multiple is (approximately) justified.

But perhaps even more important than these considerations, our analysis has at once demonstrated what an ephemeral process valuation is and underlined the very severe limitations by which any model of security valuation must necessarily be beset. There is no self-evident appropriate horizon for the projection of growth rates, only a putatively reasonable one. The history of share-price behavior demonstrates ineluctably that investors are at some times willing to take a much longer view than at others. At the beginning of the present decade of the "soaring 'sixties" it did not seem unreasonable to anticipate with some degree of confidence a decade of substantial growth. At the 1962 market trough investors were unwilling to pay a substantial premium for any growth that was not expected to occur over the fairly immediate future. We have demonstrated the very large magnitude of difference in warranted prices that can result from such a change in the growth horizon. Moreover, it is enormously difficult to determine the growth rates that should be used in the valuation formulas, if, indeed, it is even admissible (except for simplification of analysis) to project compounded growth rates for earnings per share. It is very difficult to be neutral about things so uncertain as future growth rates. At times of great optimism it is easy to accept the idea that even some acceleration of past growth rates is possible, given the exorbitant claims that were made for the economy during the decade of the 'sixties. At times of great pessimism it seems implausible to believe that any but the most modest rates of growth are sustainable for companies which now must grow on a far larger base of sales and earnings than was the case in years past, when their historic growth records were made. The problem, of course, is that it is easy for investors to convince themselves of the credibility of either of these positions.

The Keynesian analogy of the newspaper contest is by now a classic statement of the problems which we face. It is immaterial to the contestant what his personal criteria of beauty may be. What is important is rather what the average opinion considers the relevant criteria to be, or rather, what the average opinion believes the popular criteria to be, etc. Similarly, it is less important in determining market values to pick, let us say, four years as the objectively proper period over which growth can be discounted, when the relevant period for discounting is determined by that period which the average opinion believes to be proper. This I believe to be at the heart of the problem of valuation. However, this is not to be construed as implying that market values are necessarily determined by the irrationality of some sort of perpetual tulip-bulb craze. On the contrary, I am convinced that actual market values oscillate around a structure of prices that does a reasonably good job at attempting to equalize net yields, given the often very limited amount of information available to the investing community. But styles and fashions have a habit of changing drastically for considerable periods of time, so that the Keynesian admonition about the long run must always be kept in mind. Therefore, we must always accept an uncomfortably large degree of indeterminacy in economic models that attempt to determine objectively a structure of warranted stock prices. Nevertheless, it seems to me that both economists and those closest to the financial markets can benefit from this kind of conceptual scheme which, if nothing more, can describe quantitatively the market valuations that exist at any time.

APPENDIX

Theorem 1: The normalized price, m, that can be paid for a growth stock will always exceed the standard multiple, m_s.

Proof: Substituting d for $D(1 + g)/mE$ in (11) and solving for $\bar{m}_s/m$ we obtain:

$$\frac{\bar{m}_s}{m} = \frac{(1 + \bar{r})^N}{(1 + g)^N} - \frac{(1 + \bar{r})^N}{(1 + g)^N}\left(\frac{d}{\bar{r} - g}\right) + \left(\frac{d}{\bar{r} - g}\right) \qquad \text{(A1)}$$

Now it can be shown that the quantity $\bar{m}_s/m < 1$ for a growth stock. Assume $g < r$. Then

$$\frac{(1 + \bar{r})^N}{(1 + g)^N} > 1 \quad \text{and} \quad \frac{d}{\bar{r} - g} > 1$$

from (7), the definition of a growth stock. It can then be seen that

$$\frac{(1 + \bar{r})^N}{(1 + g)^N}\left[1 - \left(\frac{d}{\bar{r} - g}\right)\right] < \left[1 - \left(\frac{d}{\bar{r} - g}\right)\right] \quad \text{or} \quad \frac{\bar{m}_s}{m} < 1, \qquad \text{(A2)}$$

the price-earnings multiple of the growth stock is greater than the standard multiple. A similar demonstration applies to the case of $g > r$. If $g = r$, then utilizing (10) we have:

$$m - \bar{m}_s = N\left(\frac{D}{E}\right) > 0. \qquad \text{(A3)}$$

But note when

$$d = r - g, \quad m = \bar{m}_s.$$

Theorem 2: The warranted price-earnings multiple for a growth stock is an increasing function of the growth rate expected.

Proof: Substituting mE for P in (10) and differentiating we obtain:

$$\frac{\partial m}{\partial g} = \frac{D}{E(1 + \bar{r})} + \frac{2D(1 + g)}{E(1 + \bar{r})^2} + \cdots + \frac{ND(1 + g)^{N-1}}{E(1 + \bar{r})^N}$$

$$+ \frac{N\bar{m}_s(1 + g)^{N-1}}{(1 + \bar{r})^N} > 0. \qquad \text{(A4)}$$

Of course, this proposition holds even in the absence of the convenient assumption of constant growth, as the formulation of (A4) makes abundantly clear.

Theorem 3: The warranted earnings multiple is an increasing function of the number of years for which the security is expected to continue its extraordinary rate of growth.

Proof: Differentiating (11) and simplifying we obtain:

$$\frac{\partial m}{\partial N} = \ln\left[\frac{(1+g)}{(1+\bar{r})}\right]\left[\frac{(1+g)}{(1+\bar{r})}\right]^N\left[\bar{m}_s - \frac{D}{E}\frac{(1+g)}{(\bar{r}-g)}\right]. \tag{A5}$$

If

$$g > \bar{r}, \ln\left[\frac{1+g}{1+\bar{r}}\right] > 0 \text{ and } -\frac{D}{E}\frac{(1+g)}{(\bar{r}-g)} > 0 \text{ so that } \frac{\partial m}{\partial N} > 0.$$

If

$$g < \bar{r}, \ln\left[\frac{1+g}{1+\bar{r}}\right] < 0, \text{ but } \left[\bar{m}_s - \frac{D}{E}\frac{(1+g)}{(\bar{r}-g)}\right] < 0 \text{ also.}$$

To show

$$\bar{m}_s < \frac{D}{E}\frac{(1+g)}{(\bar{r}-g)}$$

we divide both sides by $m > 0$ and obtain

$$\frac{\bar{m}_s}{m} < \frac{d}{(\bar{r}-g)}$$

This holds since

$$\frac{\bar{m}_s}{m} < 1 \text{ by (A2) and } \frac{d}{(\bar{r}-g)} > 1 \text{ by (7).}$$

Theorem 4: Nondividend-paying growth stocks are more volatile than standard issues. For a given (percentage) change in the level of share prices, m_s, m will vary more than in proportion.

Proof: Utilizing expression (3) for r and substituting $m_s \bar{E}_s$ for P_3, we can restate (13) as

$$m = m_s\frac{(1+g)^N}{\left[1 + g_s + \frac{\bar{D}_s(1+g_s)}{m_s\bar{E}_s}\right]^N}. \tag{A6}$$

Now letting m_s vary (i.e., allowing the general level of share prices to change) and differentiating m with respect to m_s, we have:

$$\frac{\partial m}{\partial m_s} = \tag{A7}$$

$$\frac{\left[1 + \bar{g}_s + \frac{\bar{D}_s(1+\bar{g}_s)}{m_s\bar{E}_s}\right]^N[1+g]^N + m_s[1+g]^N N\left[1 + \bar{g}_s + \frac{\bar{D}_s(1+\bar{g}_s)}{m_s\bar{E}_s}\right]^{N-1}\left[\frac{\bar{D}_s(1+\bar{g}_s)}{E_s m_s^2}\right]}{\left[1 + g_s + \frac{\bar{D}_s(1+\bar{g}_s)}{m_s\bar{E}_s}\right]^{2N}}$$

Multiplying through by m_s/m to convert (A7) into an elasticity formulation (where we use expression (A6) for m), we have:

$$\frac{\partial m}{\partial m_s} \cdot \frac{m_s}{m} = 1 + \frac{Nd_s}{1+r} > 1. \tag{A8}$$

Theorem 5: The volatility of nondividend-paying growth stocks increases with the number of years included in the time horizon but is invariant with respect to the rate of growth expected.

Proof: Letting $\epsilon_M \equiv \partial_M / \partial_{Ms} \cdot Ms / M$ represent the elasticity of the price-earnings ratio and differentiating (A8), we have:

$$\frac{\partial \epsilon_m}{\partial N} = \frac{d_s}{1 + r} > 0 \tag{A9}$$

and

$$\frac{\partial \epsilon_m}{\partial g} = 0. \tag{A10}$$

REFERENCES

1. WILLIAM J. BAUMOL, "Comment on Dividend Policy, Growth and the Valuation of Shares," *Jour. Business,* Jan. 1963, *36,* 112–15.
2. J F. BOHMFALK, JR., "The Growth Stock Philosophy," *Financial Analysts Jour.,* Nov.-Dec. 1960, *16,* 113–23.
3. JOHN C. CLENDENIN AND MAURICE VAN CLEAVE, "Growth and Common Stock Values," *Jour. Finance,* Dec. 1954, *60,* 365–76.
4. A. COWLES, *et al., Common-Stock Indexes, 1871-1957,* Cowles Commission on on Research in Economics, Monograph No. 3. Bloomington 1938.
5. DAVID DURAND, "Growth Stocks and the St. Petersburg Paradox," *Jour. Finance,* Sept. 1957, *12,* 348–63.
6. MYRON J. GORDON, "The Savings Investment and Valuation of a Corporation," *Rew, Econ. Stat.,* Feb. 1962, *44,* 37–51.
7. ———and ELI SHAPIRO, "Capital Equipment Analysis: The Required Rate of Profit," *Management Science,* Oct. 1956; reprinted in Ezra Solomon, ed., *The Management of Corporate Capital,* Glencoe 1959.
8. B. GRAHAM AND D. L. DODD WITH C. TATHAM, JR., *Security Analysis,* New York 1951
9. S. E. GUILD, *Stock Growth and Discount Tables,* Boston 1931.
10. C. C. HOLT, "The Influence of Growth Duration on Share Prices," *Jour. Finance,* Sept. 1962, *17,* 465–75.
11. JOHN LINTNER, "Dividends, Earnings, Leverage, Stock Prices, and the Supply of Capital to Corporations," *Rev. Econ. Stat.,* Aug. 1962, *44,* 243–69.
12. BURTON G. MALKIEL, "Expectations, Bond Prices and the Term Structure of Interest Rates," *Quart. Jour. Econ.,* May 1962, *76,* 197–218.
13. E. S. MEAD AND J. GRODINSKY, *The Ebb and Flow of Investment Values,* New York 1939.
14. MERTON H. MILLER AND FRANCO MODIGLIANI, "Dividend Policy, Growth and the Valuation of Shares," *Jour. Business,* Oct. 1961, *34,* 411–33.
15. FRANCO MODIGLIANI AND MERTON H. MILLER, "The Cost of Capital Corporation Finance and the Theory of Investment: Reply," *Am. Econ. Rev.,* Sept. 1959, *44,* 655–69.
16. J. B. WILLIAMS, *The Theory of Investment Value,* Cambridge 1938.
17. "Growth-The Hottest Word in Wall Street" (an editorial), *Financial Analysts Jour.,* Sept.-Oct. 1960. *16,* 3, 38.

Lerner and Carleton explain stock prices in terms of a set of two simultaneous equations. The first equation resembles those presented earlier, in that stock price is related to stockholder expectations about a set of firm variables. The second equation (the LC function) relates management's investment plans to management's expectations about a set of similar variables. Stock price is determined by the interaction of these two equations with the equilibrium price being determined by the equalization of management and stockholder expectations.

10

Financing Decisions of the Firm

*Eugene M. Lerner and Willard T. Carleton**

This article is reprinted with permission from the Journal of Finance, *Vol. XXI, No. 2 (May, 1966), pp. 202–214.*

There is general agreement among economists and financial analysts that share price (stockholder wealth) maximization is the appropriate normative model for corporate behavior.[1] However, no professional consensus has been reached about the apparatus for achieving this maximization.[2]

In a recent article, we suggested that the theoretical stalemate over the apparatus for achieving share price maximization may have arisen from the general failure to recognize explicitly that the corporate financial decisions take

* New York University, Graduate School of Business Administration.

[1] David Durand was the first to show that this criterion possesses different consequences and is preferable to the alternative of profit maximization. See his "Cost of Debt and Equity Funds for Business: Trends and Problems of Measurement," *Conference on Research in Business and Finance* (New York: National Bureau of Economic Research, 1952,) p. 216.

[2] Modigliani and Miller have presented a strong case that, at least in a world of no taxes and perfect capital markets (and in which stockholders are indifferent to the dividend decision) the total value of the corporation is invariant with respect to capital structure, and, as a consequence, the capital budget cut-off point is the critical financial decision. See their "The Cost of Capital, Corporation Finance, and the Theory of Investment," *American Economic Review,* June 1958, pp. 261–298; "Dividend Policy, Growth, and the Valuation of Shares," *Journal of Business,* October, 1961; and "Corporate Cost of Capital: A Correction," *American Economic Review,* July, 1963, pp. 433–443.

place within a constraint given by the prevailing conditions in the product market in which the firm sells its output and the factor market in which it buys its inputs.[3] When this constraint is recognized, it becomes transparent that corporate decision making must take place jointly on several frontiers if share prices are to be maximized.

The constrained share price maximization model that we presented, however, was incomplete, for it did not face up to the problems of corporate borrowing and uncertainty. This paper is an attempt to extend the framework of our earlier study and in so doing to gain a new perspective on some of the important issues in financial theory. Toward this end Section I sketches a purely formal framework of the corporate financial decision problem without specifying the forms of the functions involved. The classification of variables (e.g., stochastic and nonstochastic) as well as the existence and properties of any solution are discussed. Section II introduces a dividend capitalization valuation model of the sort made popular by Gordon and Lintner. Section III develops a profit opportunities schedule for the corporation for the class of investments which increase the scale rather than the diversity of the firm. Finally, in Section IV, a solution is presented to the price maximization problem for a firm facing constraints in its product and factor markets as well as in the financial market.

I. GENERAL STATEMENT OF THE PROBLEM

Let the corporation's objective (share price) function,† be given in terms of its potential decision variables:

$$P = P(r, b, i, L \mid E) \tag{I.1}$$

where: r = average rate of return on assets before interest and taxes, b = retention rate,[4] L/E = ratio of liabilities to equity, both variables measured at

On the other hand, M. Gordon, *The Investment, Financing, and Valuation of the Corporation* (Homewood: Richard D. Irwin, 1962) and J. Lintner, "Dividends, Earnings, Leverage, Stock Prices and the Supply of Capital to Corporations," *Review of Economics and Statistics,* August, 1962, pp. 243–269 and "Optimum Dividends and Corporate Growth Under Uncertainty," *Quarterly Journal of Economics,* February, 1964, pp. 49–95, have argued most persuasively that under realistic economic conditions the dividend and capital structure decisions are vital to stock price maximization. Theory aside, the weight of empirical evidence would appear to support Gordon and Lintner, See, for example, G. Donaldson, *Corporate Debt Capacity* (Boston: Harvard University 1861) and J. Lintner, "Distribution of Income of Corporations Among Dividends, Retained Earnings, and Taxes," *American Economic Review,* May, 1956, pp. 97–114. The avoid needless misunderstanding we admit at the outset that our conclusions are at variance with the several findings of Modigliani and Miller because we adopt model specifications which seem to us to be closer approximations to corporate reality than those of M and M. For a discussion of the implications of the M and M assumptions, see Lerner and Carleton, *A Theory of Financial Analysis* (New York: Harcourt, Brace and World, 1966), Ch. 10.

[3] Lerner and Carleton, "The Integration of Capital Budgeting and Stock Valuation," *American Economic Review,* September, 1964, pp. 683–703.

† We wish to thank Prof. John Bossons for pointing out a notational error in the draft presented at The American Finance Association meetings.

[4] A firm can raise additional equity through either retained earnings or the sale of

book value,[5] and $i =$ the interest rate that the firm pays for borrowed funds. The form of this function will be specified in Section II.[6]

Shareholders are assumed to consider each of these variables as expected normal values, i.e., when a shareholder pays a particular price for a share of stock, he believes that the corporation will continue to earn an expected normal rate of return r, maintain an expected normal capital structure, L/E, and so forth. The valuation of a security takes place, of course, at a moment in time.

---

additional stock. The sale of additional stock, however, usually involves a heavy transaction cost: the total cost of floating a fully underwritten public offering of securities consists of the investment banker's commission, or gross spread (the difference between the price paid by the buyer and the amount received by the issuing corporation) and the expenses incurred by the issuer, including stamp taxes, printing and engraving expenses, and registration fees. These costs can amount to as much as 10 percent of the gross proceeds realized.

If there were no transaction costs and no tax considerations, a firm would, in principle, be indifferent between retaining a portion of its earnings and distributing the rest in dividends or distributing all of its earnings as dividends and selling additional shares to raise the equity capital needs for expansion. If a corporation pursues the latter course and sells the new shares on a pre-emptive rights basis, that is, sells the new shares to existing shareholders in amounts proportionate to their existing holdings, the corporation in effect allows each stockholder to determine for himself the retention rate that he considers optimal. (The individual can, of course, determine his own retention rate even in the absence of subscriptions for new equity by marginal purchases and sales of stock). Moreover, if the new stock is offered to existing stockholders at less than the market price, the right to subscribe to the new shares will have a marketable value. Since these rights can be sold, they represent, in a sense, an attempt by the corporation to give the stockholders the necessary funds to pay the personal income taxes that are incurred on the dividends received from their holdings.

It should be emphasized at this point that the ability of an individual stockholder to create his own retention rate cannot be aggregated to find the corporation's retention rate. That is, the total of funds retained or acquired for use in the firm is independent of changes in the portfolios of individual stockholders. The price of the company's stock, furthermore, will presumably reflect a balancing of such individual stockholder preferences. But this is not to deny that such an aggregate balance might take place at a different (higher or lower) share price if some other retention rate were adopted by the firm. The retention decision defined as optimal will be optimal with respect to existing and potential stockholders to avoid the non-operation conclusions that whatever is, is optimal.

Throughout this study, b, the retention rate, is also defined to include both retained earnings and outside equity. Thus, let b_e be the percentage of earnings that the firm seeks to obtain by selling additional shares of stock and b_r, be the percentage of earnings that are retained. Then $b = b_e + b_r$, the sum of b_e and b_r, must be less than one, other things equal, or the security will represent a net drain of funds to shareholders rather than a positive source of income. "Other things equal," it should be stressed, is an important part of this proposition since shifts in the profit opportunities schedule can give rise to shifts in stockholder growth expectations, and then to the retention rate. In such cases an historically calculated b might well exceed one.

[5] Under the assumption that a firm's entire debt is continuously refinanced, the book and market value of the debt become one and the same. Moreover, if the firm depreciates its assets at a rate such that the book value of the asset represents the present value of the asset's future stream of earnings, the book value of the equity will represent its liquidating value.

[6] In addition to these four variables, the valuation equation that will be developed in Section II utilizes three parameters. These parameters, which lie outside the range of influence of the individual corporate manager, are T, the tax rate, α, the interest rate on risk-free securities and s, a market risk aversion factor.

Should an unanticipated event, either favorable or unfavorable, take place, shareholders will revalue their expected normal rate of return, retention rate, capital structure, and interest rate and the price of the security will change.

Let the corporation's profit opportunities schedule, hereafter referred to as the LC function, be given by:

$$LC(r, b, i, L \mid E) = 0 \qquad \textbf{(I.2)}$$

where the variables are defined in the same way as they were above. The precise form of this function will be specified in Part III.[7]

Though the entire profit opportunities schedule may shift from time to time, it is assumed to be fixed at a moment in time. As the firm grows more rapidly, and exploits additional opportunities, it therefore moves downward along a given LC function. To finance this growth, the firm may either use equity (by raising b) or debt (by maintaining or raising the ratio of L/E).

By setting equation (I.2) equal to zero, we assume that the corporation is efficient, i.e., that it operates along its profit opportunities frontier. Monsen and Downs have argued that corporate managers, seeking to maximize their own lifetime earnings, may not choose to operate along the firm's maximum LC function.[8] Rather, they may prefer to operate along a lower (less efficient) LC function. The periodic movements within each corporation toward greater or lesser efficiency will be treated like any one of the several events that can cause the entire profit opportunities schedule to shift.

Finally, let the financial constraint facing a firm link the interest rate that a corporation pays for borrowed funds to its debt equity ratio:[9]

$$FC(i, L \mid E) = 0 \qquad \textbf{(I.3)}$$

The problem facing the corporation seeking to maximize the wealth of its shareholders can now be simply stated: it is to maximize the objective price equation (I.1) subject to two constraints. These constraints are, first, the LC function (I.2), which summarizes conditions in the firm's product and factor markets and secondly, the FC function (I.3), which summarizes conditions in the financial markets facing the firm.

In order to simplify the exposition, we specify (I.3) as

$$i = \delta L / E \qquad \textbf{(I.3)}'$$

and substitute into (I.1) and (I.2) to eliminate the interest rate.[10]

$$P = P(r, b, L \mid E) \qquad \textbf{(I.1)}'$$

$$LC(r, b, L \mid E) = 0 \qquad \textbf{(I.2)}'$$

---

[7] In addition to these four variables, the LC function which will be specified in Section II utilizes two parameters: r_0, which is a function of the national income and firm's level of assets and r_1, which measures the change in the average rate of return that results from a change in the firm's growth rate.

[8] R. Joseph Monsen, Jr. and Anthony Downs, "A Theory of Large Managerial Firms," *Journal of Political Economy*, June 1965, pp. *221–237*.

[9] As was true of the valuation and LC functions, the financial constraint can be drawn parametric to other values. The most important of these is the interest rate that lenders can earn on government bonds.

[10] More complex forms of (I.3)' could be used which would generate similar solutions but

The mathematics of share price maximization then becomes a straight-forward matter assuming that second order conditions can be satisfied over some reasonable range of r, b and L/E.

Even at this incomplete state, a number of comments can be made about this approach to the share price valuation problem. First, while imperfect capital markets require a constraint such as (I.3) and imperfect product and factor markets require a constraint such as (I.2) whether or not a price maximization is sought, the valuation of common stocks typically has been explored with a price equation alone.

One school of practicing analysts, popularized by the writing of Arnold Bernhard[11] simply fits a multiple regression between measured stock prices and earnings, dividends, book values, lagged prices, and similar variables. In this approach the choice of the independent variables is essentially arbitrary. It might be noted that the traditional practice of security analysis can be described as the more intuitive use of this same procedure.

A second school, exemplified by Myron Gordon (*op. cit.*) utilizes an internally consistent, but inadequately constrained, valuation equation. The question as to whether a unique maximum share price exists depends upon the specification of this equation and the empirical meaning attached to the concept of uncertainty.

The only explicit recognition which we have been able to find of the effects that constraints such as (I.2) or (I.3) have upon the valuation equation is by Lintner first in 1963 and later in his 1964 article.[12]

The second comment about this approach to the valuation problem is that the existence of a binding constraint such as (I.2)′ implies that when the corporation operates jointly on any two of its three decision variables, r, b, and L/E, the third is then determined. Freedom to vary all of the variables simultaneously is not possible for the system will then be overdetermined. A two-dimensional analogy to this condition can be drawn from the theory of the firm. A monopolist is free to set either his price or his output, but not both. Given a demand function, the determination of either one implies the other. Here a firm can set the values of two variables; the third is then given by the LC function.

If the firm sets any two of the three variables at an arbitrary level, however, the corporation's stock will not in general be maximized. Rather, to maximize the wealth of shareholders, the corporate managers must select the particular values of two of the values, say r and L/E so that both $\partial p/\partial r$ and $\partial P/\partial(L/E)$ are equal to zero simultaneously.

Third, each of the arguments of (I.1)′ and (I.2)′ is a potential decision variable and each is potentially stochastic. However because of the constraint, only two of the values can be set by the firm: the third will therefore be a

messier mathematics. For example, $i = i_g = \delta L/E$ where i_g is the government bond rate. Inasmuch as (I.3)′ is an explicit recognition of the capital market imperfections and/or lender risk aversion, it should be noted that will differ among corporations.

[11] Arnold Bernhard, "The Valuation of Listed Securities," reprinted from the *Financial Analysts Journal* in *Readings in Financial Analysis and Investment Management,* E. M. Lerner, ed. (Homewood, Ill.: Richard D. Irwin, 1963), pp. 235–245.

[12] John Lintner, "The Cost of Capital and Optimal Financing of Corporate Growth," *Journal of Finance,* May, 1963, pp. 292–310. Gordon refers to a constraint, *op. cit.,* pp. 49–50, but does not effectively integrate it into his analysis.

stochastic variable. For example, if the firm sets both r and L/E, b is a stochastic variable; if it sets b and L/E, r is stochastic. This observation will be more fully articulated in Section III.

Finally, if a corporation's cost of capital is a function of the firm's rate of return, capital structure, retention rate or some combination of these variables, such as the growth rate, then the exact cost of capital can only be known in solution (*ex post*). Phrased differently, if the cost of capital is a schedule, the precise point along this schedule where the firm operates, and hence its *ex post* cost of capital, is known only after the solution to the share price maximization problem is in hand, not before the problem is even approached.

To summarize this section then, a corporation striving to maximize shareholder wealth faces two constraints. One is in the product and factor market (*LC*), the other in the financial market (*FC*). Corporations are free to select any two of the three financial variables that influence share prices: the rate of return, the retention rate, and the capital structure. The selection of any two variables, through the constraint (I.2), implies the third. If a lending institution, for example, dictates both the capital structure and the dividend policy (retention rate), the efficient firm is left with no degree of freedom.[13] The two variables that are fixed by the firm are nonstochastic; the remaining variable is stochastic. Finally, if the cost of capital is a function of the three financial variables, its precise value can only be known *ex post,* i.e., after the value of these variables is known.

THE DIVIDEND CAPITALIZATION FUNCTION

The price of a share of stock, like the price of any asset, is defined as the present value of its future return. We adopt the Gordon–Lintner definition that dividends constitute the shareholder's returns.[14] If, at time period $t,$ dividends are expected to grow at a rate g[15] and are discounted at a rate $k,$ then the capitalization model can be stated as:

$$P_0 = \int_0^\infty D_0 e^{E(g)t} e^{-kt} dt = \frac{D_0}{k - E(g)} \qquad \textbf{(II.1)}$$

$D_0,$ $k,$ and $E(g)$ must now be specified so as to include the effects of corporate

---

[13] This statement is strictly true only if the firm is restricted to straight debt or straight equity issues. If it has the option to sell preferred stock, convertible bonds, or other such hybrids, it has some remaining degrees of freedom.

[14] Lintner (1962) has shown that over a large class of problems earnings and dividend capitalization models lead to equivalent results and do not require capital gains calculations. Capital gains are ignored because an infinite time horizon is postulated. If some shorter horizon is postulated, the question of what determines the price of the stock on some future date (the date of the sale) must be answered. If this future price is determined by the expected stream of dividends from that point forward, the statement that return is given by the infinite stream of dividends is equivalent to the statement that return is equal to dividends plus expected capital gain.

[15] As noted above, shareholders at a particular moment in time expect g to continue indefinitely. If some new and unanticipated development unfolds, the expected value of g will change and the new rate will then be expected to continue indefinitely.

taxes, borrowing and the uncertainty surrounding the growth rate expectation before it can be applied to serious financial problems.

THE DIVIDEND PAYMENT AND THE GROWTH RATE

The most straightforward definition of dividends is that they are expected to be a fixed percentage of after tax profits. Thus, if T = tax rate and π_t = expected profits at period t, then the corporation's expected dividend for period t, D_t, can be written as:

$$D_t = (1 - b)(1 - T)\pi_t \qquad \textbf{(II.2)}$$

where b is the retention rate.

Profits are defined as

$$\pi_t = rAt - iL_t \qquad \textbf{(II.3)}$$

where r and i are defined as above and A_t and L_t are book values of assets and liabilities at t respectively. In calculating book values of assets, it is assumed that accounting depreciation charges accurately reflect economic depreciation, and replacements are continually made to restore the steady state assets (steady state earning power at the equilibrium value of r). [16]

By letting r be the pre-tax rate of return on assets, the operating problem of the firm (how efficiently it manages its assets) is clearly separated from the financing problem of the firm (the sources of funds used to purchase the assets). Two firms, identical in all respects save the way in which they financed their assets would show the same r but different π_t for each time period.

Using (II.3) and the balance sheet identity, $A = L + E$, equation (II.2) can be written as: [17]

$$D_t = (1 - b)(1 - T)[r + (r - i)L \,/\, E]E_t \qquad \textbf{(II.4)}$$

Note that E as well as L and A are recorded at book value, not market value. Second, if the solution or equilibrium values of r, b and L/E are used in (II.4) the time subscript can be dropped. This tactic of focusing on r, b and L/E as variables fixed in solution (or fixed in mean value) accords with both empirical practice and customary theoretical treatment, [18] and if T and $L/E = 0$, equation (II.4) collapses into expressions made familiar by Gordon and Lintner.

---

[16] This definition of corporate asset valuation is of course consistent with a long run expected rate of return. See Modigliani and Miller, 1961, p. 434 and footnotes. Within the context of an earnings opportunities schedule, however, it can be demonstrated that all that is required to permit analysis is that the firm adopt a consistent accounting depreciation policy over time. See Lerner and Carleton, *A Theory of Financial Analysis* (New York: Harcourt, Brace and World, 1966), ch. 4.

[17] Since $\pi = rA = iL$
$$= r(E + L)\, iL$$
$$= rE - (r - i)\, L \text{ and hence the result in the text.}$$

[18] A. Sametz, "Trends in the Volume and Composition of Equity Finance," *Journal of Finance*, September 1964, p. 431.

Finally, at least three different price equations can be derived from (II.4), depending on the kind of equilibrium model assumed. For example, if at $t = 0$, the dividend is assumed fixed, then $D_0 = D_0^*$. Alternatively, if at $t = 0$, profits are given, then $D_0 = (1 - b)(1 - T)\pi_0$. Finally, in a full equilibrium context, only E_0 is fixed and the current dividend is assumed to reflect equilibrium values of r, b, i and L/E_0. $D = (1 - b)(1 - T)[r + (r - i)L/E]E_0$. In developing the theory, we will adopt this latter model, but a word of caution is in order: existence of a theoretical maximum price in the case of the first two models will presuppose that the LC and FC constraints and discount rate k have been appropriately specified.

It can be seen that the expected rate of growth of dividends equals the rate of growth of retained earnings:

$$E(g) = \frac{dD}{D} = \frac{dE}{E} = (1 - T)b[r + (r - i)L/E] \qquad \textbf{(II.5)}$$

Moreover, since L/E will be fixed in solution, the rate of growth of debt as well as assets will also be at this rate.

THE DISCOUNT RATE

The discount rate that a shareholder applies to his future stream of earnings will be specified as consisting of two components. The first, α, is the risk-free alternative open to investors.[19] The second is associated with the riskiness[20] of the growth rate and can be specified as $s\,\mathrm{Var}\,(g)$ where s is a parameter reflecting the investor's risk aversion preferences.[21]

If $\qquad\qquad\qquad\qquad k = \alpha + s\mathrm{Var}(g) \qquad\qquad\qquad\qquad$ **(II.6)**

[19] To the extent that common stocks are imperfect substitutes for risk-free securities (e.g., a long term government bond) α can be thought of as $\alpha = (1 = M)\alpha_0$ where α_0 is the return on the government bond and M is a constant reflecting the market in which the security is traded. For example, if securities in the over-the-counter market are even more imperfect substitutes for government bonds than securities traded on the New York Stock Exchange, M_{otc} will be greater than M_{nyse}.

[20] In a certain world, k, the rate of discount, is a pure riskless interest rate satisfying only the investors' time preference function. In an uncertain world, several alternatives have been proposed, the most popular of which is the solution of (II.6): $k = D/P = E(g)$. Solomon, for example, stresses this as a measure of the cost of capital. *The Theory of Financial Management* (New York: Columbia University Press, 1963), p. 34. Since this expression merely defines what k must be at any equilibrium share price P, uses of such a discount rate as the cost of capital for decision purposes are obviously tainted with circularity.

[21] Lintner (1964) has developed a discount function along these lines for a no-debt, no-taxes model, utilizing a hyperbolic investor utility function. Lintner's formulation possesses some advantages but we imply a quadratic utility function in our discount function on the grounds that it has better known properties. Other variants on the form of (11.6) include: (1) Var (g) = a constant, in which case k = a constant (the well-known fixed cost of capital model); and (2) $k = \alpha +$ standard deviation (g), which under specifications to be made as to the LC function implies a discount function linear in $E(g)$. The aggregation problem is admittedly severe, whatever form and micro-justification is given to the market discount function.

the denominator of the valuation equation becomes:

$$k - E(g) = \alpha + s \ \text{Var}(g) - E(g)$$

This denominator, which is the rate at which the current dividends of a corporation are discounted, can also be expressed in terms of the firm's certainty equivalent growth, $CE \ (g)$.

If
$$CE(g) = E(g) - s \ \text{Var}(g)$$

the discount rate applied to a corporation's current dividend is:

$$k - E(g) = \alpha - CE(g)$$

Thus, the dividends of a common stock are discounted at the same rate as the interest stream of a risk-free bond less the dividend's stream's certainty equivalent growth rate.

To summarize this section then, if (II.4), (II.5) ,and (II.6) are substituted into (II.1), the valuation equation at period 0 becomes:

$$P_0 = \frac{\{(1 - t)[r + (r - i)L/E] - E(g)\} E_0}{\alpha + s\text{Var}(g) - E(g)} \qquad \textbf{(II.1)}'$$

Two bounds which have to be placed on this equation are immediate: (1) $r > i$; the corporation will not borrow if there is no internal gain to leverage; and (2) $\alpha + s \ \text{Var} \ (g) > E \ (g)$; we rule out the possibility of a growth stock paradox.

Equation (II.1)', which we believe captures most of what analysts would consider essential in a valuation equation, can be viewed as generating a family of iso-price lines. Furthermore, any given P can be obtained by an infinite number of $r, b, L/E$ combinations. The problem that remains therefore is to specify the region of $r, b,$ and L/E values open to the corpoartion. We do this in the next section.

III. THE PROFIT OPPORTUNITES SCHEDULE

The region of obtainable, $r, b,$ and L/E values open to a corporation will be controlled by the demand and cost schedules for a company's products. Assume for the moment that the corporation produces a single product and that income, tastes, and the prices of competitive and complementary goods remain constant. Then both the price of the product and its average cost can be specified as proportionate to both the level of output and to rate of change of output.[22]

[22] The demand and cost curves are specified in this form rather than in the more conventional form because of the rather widely held belief that for the large publicly held corporations that are of concern to the shareholder, prices and costs are more sensitive to the relative changes in output than the absolute changes in output. More importantly, the stock valuation model is itself a growth model and hence the profit opportunities function must also be expressed in comparable units.

$$p_t = \alpha_0 + \alpha_1 Q_t + \alpha_2 \frac{d \ln Q}{dt} \tag{III.1}$$

and

$$c_t = \beta_0 + \beta_1 Q_t + \beta_2 \frac{d \ln Q}{dt} \tag{III.2}$$

where both α_1 and $\alpha_2 \leq 0$ and β_1 and $\beta_2 \geq 0$.

If the firm produces under perfect competition, both α_1 and α_2 equal zero. Similarly if the company purchases its inputs in competitive markets and encounters no diminishing returns as it expands output, both β_1 and β_2 equal zero. To the extent that the firms have some monopoly and monopsony power,

$$\alpha_1, \alpha_2 < 0 \text{ and } \beta_1, \beta_2 > 0.$$

The profits of the firm at time t can be represented as:

$$\pi_t = (p_t - c_t)Q_t = (\alpha_0 - \beta_0)Q_t + (\alpha_1 - \beta_1)Q_t^2 + (\alpha_2 - \beta_2)\frac{d \ln Q}{dt}Q_t \tag{III.3}$$

If capacity is proportionate to assets,[23] and firms strive to operate at a fixed percentage of capacity,[24] then output will be proportionate to assets and the growth of output will be proportionate to the growth of assets.

$$Q_t = \lambda A_t \tag{III.4}$$

and

$$\frac{d \ln A}{dt} = \frac{d \ln Q}{dt} \tag{III.5}$$

Substitute (III.4) and (III.5) into (III.3) and divide by the level of assets:

$$r_t = \frac{\pi_t}{A_t} = (\alpha_0 - \beta_0)\lambda + (\alpha_1 - \beta_1)\lambda^2 A + (\alpha_2 - \beta_2)\frac{d \ln A}{dt}\lambda \tag{III.6}$$

The rate of return, r_t, under the assumption that national income, tastes, and the prices of competitive and complementary goods remain fixed at time t is therefore seen to depend upon both the level of assets at time t and the rate of growth of assets. Since $(\alpha_1 - \beta_1)\lambda^2 < 0$ the average rate of return will fall from period to period as the asset base rises. If the assumptions of fixed national income and consumer tastes are relaxed however, r need not have a secular

---

[23] If the accounting measures of assets reflect the underlying economic value of assets, as assumed previously, this statement is a truism. To the extent that the accounting statements fail to measure economic reality, capacity will not be effectively measured by the accounting statement.

[24] Hickman has developed an imaginative measure to express excess capacity by nothing the deviation of output from such a percentage. See "On a New Method of Capacity Estimation," *Journal of the American Statistical Association,* Vol. 59, No. 306, pp. 529–550.

decline. In order to focus on decisions concerning continuing growth, we
assume that profits at t are a linear homogeneous function of A_t and dA/dt,

$$\pi_t = \gamma_0 A_t + \gamma_1 \frac{dA}{dt} \tag{III.6'}$$

or

$$r = \frac{\pi_t}{A_t} = \gamma_0 + \gamma_1 \frac{dA}{A} \tag{III.7}$$

where $\gamma_0 > 0$ reflects the effect of $(\alpha_0 - \beta_0)\lambda + (\alpha_1 + \beta_1)\lambda^2 A_t$ plus the
period by period shift in the schedule to make the intercept a constant. γ_1 of
course is less than zero. Under these conditions the rate of return depends upon
the rate of growth of assets and if this is set at some (to be determined) solution
value, we can describe a steady state r and drop the t subscript.[25]

Equation (III.7) can be readily generalized to incorporate the gross effects
of changes in the output of competitive and complementary firms.[26] An obvious
extension yields:

$$r = \gamma_0 + \gamma_1 \left(\frac{dA}{A}\right)_1 + \gamma_2 \left(\frac{dA}{A}\right)_2 + \ldots + \gamma_n \left(\frac{dA}{A}\right)_n \tag{III.8}$$

where $\gamma_j = (\alpha_j - \beta_j)\lambda_i \lambda_j$.

Because the rate of growth of substitute and complementary firms will
influence a firm's rate of return, equation (III.7) must therefore be amended
to recognize its stochastic character.[27]

[25] An (expectationally) stationary rate of return opportunities schedule is in fact required
in order to secure an expectationally constant solution r. Functions similar to (III.7)
have as a consequence been adopted by many writers. For example, see Lintner, 1964,
pp. 56–58 and references cited in footnote 7 therein. We have simply demonstrated the
kinds of assumptions which might be made to justify (III.7).

[26] An extension of still another sort may be made. Consider the corporation at a moment
of time to possess a set of investment alternatives rather than a single option of changing
the scale of activity it is presently engaged in. Such an extension forms an obvious
continuity with the capital budgeting literature. Unfortunately, it introduces internal
asset mix (internal portfolio) considerations which require an analysis of the internal
covariance matrix, but the formulation of (III.8) would require that attention be given
to a conditional covariance matrix, conditional upon the investment behavior of at
least some of the firm's competitors. Rather than to broaden the analysis of this paper
beyond its intended scope by considering the internal diversification problems, we
restrict our attention to that class of investments which increase the scale of the firm.
In this respect we follow Modigliani and Miller (1964), p. 440, footnote 15 and the
reference therein to J. Hirshleifer, "Risk, the Discount Rate, and Investment Decision,"
American Economic Review, May, 1961, pp. 112–120.

[27] In a general equilibrium model, r would be completely determinate. The stochastic
character of r in (III.7)' is simply a reflection of the fact that a corporation's rate of
return depends upon a host of "ifs" which cannot be unambiguously determined by the
corporation, much less by the stockholder. Worse yet, each stockholder will consider a
different set of dA/A's and subjectively assign his own values both to them and to the
γ_j's. The final effect of these diverse stockholder judgments on observed share prices is
moot. The simplified discount function of (II.6) assumed that the aggregate effect of
such stockholder beliefs was stable in the form given.

Thus:

$$r = r_0 + r_1\left(\frac{dA}{A}\right) + u \qquad \text{(III.7)}'$$

Further, it is assumed that $E(u) = 0$. No bias is involved in considering the firm in isolation. The variance of u is specified as:

$$\text{Var}(u) = c\left(\frac{dA}{A}\right)^2 \qquad \text{(III.9)}$$

When a corporation is expected to grow rapidly it may, on the one hand find new firms entering the industry and old firms expanding their output. The higher the rate of return, the more vulnerable the firm will be to vigorous competition for any given state of barriers to entry. Alternatively, firms producing complementary goods may be induced to increase their output. As a consequence, the variance of u will be specified as proportionate to the square of the growth rate itself.

IV. THE SOLUTION

For widest generality, maximization of (II.1)' subject to some form of the LC constraint should be handled by Lagrangian multipliers. This tactic would not force the choice of which variables are to be considered independent. However, the mathematical problem of maximizing share prices subject to a constraint is slightly more manageable if we proceed by elimination of b. This procedure will yield identical results. It can be justified on the following grounds: when the ratio of debt to equity is fixed by management as its solution value, the LC function can then be written either as:[28]

$$r = \frac{r_0 - r_1(1-T)b\delta(L/E)^2 + u}{1 - r_1(1-T)b(1+L/E)} \qquad \text{(III.7)}''$$

or

$$b = \frac{r - r_0 - u}{r_1(1-T)[r + (r-i)L/E]} \qquad \text{(III.7)}'''$$

In the former case b is considered fixable with certainty; in the latter case, r is considered fixable with certainty. Which of these two alternatives should be selected? The discount function in the valuation equation contains the term $\text{Var}(g)$. Since $\text{Var}(g) = \text{Var}\{(1-T)b[r(1+L/E) - \delta(L/E)^2]\}$, substituting either form of the LC function into this expression will eliminate one of the variables. In one case $\text{Var}(g)$ becomes a function of b and L/E, in the other, of r and L/E. We adopt the latter for it leads to a more tractable mathematical solution.[29]

---

[28] Recall that $g = dA/A = (1-T)b[r + (r-i)L/E]$ and that $i = \delta L/E$, (II.5) and (1.3)' respectively.

[29] If the firm's borrowing costs were stochastic, and its LC function were fixed, both the

Substitute (III.7)''' into (II.5),

$$g = \frac{r - r_0 - \mu}{r_1}$$

and

$$E(g) = \frac{r - r_0}{r_1} \qquad \textbf{(IV.1)}$$

Therefore,

$$\text{Var}(g) = \frac{\text{Var}(u)}{r_1{}^2}$$

Since Var (u) was specified in (III.9) as proportional to the square of the growth rate,

$$\text{Var}(g) = \frac{c}{r_1{}^2} \left(\frac{r - r_0}{r_1} \right)^2 \qquad \textbf{(IV.2)}$$

By substituting (IV.1) and (IV.2) into the valuation equation, it becomes a function of only two variables.

$$P = \frac{\left\{ (1 - T)[r + (r - \delta L / E)L / E] \left(\frac{r - r_0}{r_1} \right) \right\}}{\alpha + \frac{\psi}{r_1{}^2} \left(\frac{r - r_0}{r_1} \right)^2 - \left(\frac{r - r_0}{r_1} \right)} E_0 \qquad \textbf{(II.1)''}$$

where s, the risk aversion coefficient and c, the factor of proportionality have been combined to form a single constant.

The maximum[30] obtainable share price is found by solving $\partial p / \partial r = 0$ and $\partial p / \partial (L/E) = 0$ for r and L/E.[31]

In Figure 1 a graphic solution is presented.

The vector $\partial p / \partial (L/E) = 0$ is a straight line[32] through the origin with the slope of 28. This vector can be interpreted as meaning that the price of the stock is maximized with respect to L/E if its L/E ratio is chosen such that the

---

growth rate and its expected value would be different. See Lerner and Carleton, "The Corporate Structure Problem of a Regulated Public Utility," *op. cit.* To completely generalize the system, both the financial constraint and the *LC* function should be treated as if they were stochastic. This has not been done because we have not as yet discovered a convenient and plausible way to handle the complex problem of the covariance between the two functions.

[30] It should be observed again that alternative assumptions as to forms of the discount function and as to what is controllable at $t = 0$ lead to alternative decision rules. Thus, if the numerator of (II.1)'' is fixed, then the constrained maximization of P becomes equivalent to the constrained minimization of dividend yield. Alternatively, one might regard π_0 fixed, in which case earnings yield is minimized.

[31] Second order conditions are satisfied at this point if $(1-T)(4\delta\phi + 2\phi r_0 + r_1 3) - 4\delta\phi/r_1 > 0$. This is essentially a requirement that the slope of the *LC* function not be too large.

[32] This result follows from specifying the financial constraint as $i = \delta L/E$. Had a different specification been used, a different result would follow. See footnote 10 above.

rate of return that this corporation earns on its assets is twice the interest rate it pays on borrowed funds.

The second vector $\partial p / \partial r = 0$ is a more complicated function whose position and slope will depend upon the parameters, α, r_0, r_1, ψ, β and T. Movements along this vector can be translated as meaning that the price of the stock is maximized with respect to the rate of return if the corporation chooses (for each L/E) a rate of return regarded as optimal. The alternatives are to choose a higher (lower) rate of return, larger (smaller) present dividends, and smaller (larger) rate of growth for any capital structure that shareholders would prefer.

The only point that satisfies both conditions and thereby assures a unique maximum price is r_0 and $(L/E)_0$. Substituting these values back into the LC function assures a unique value of b, and into (II.1)″ the maximum P_0.[33]

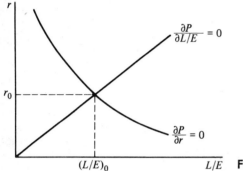

$$\frac{\partial P}{\partial L/E} = 0$$

$$\frac{\partial P}{\partial r} = 0$$

$(L/E)_0$ L/E **FIGURE 1**

Suboptimum cases may also be analyzed in terms of Figure 1. The principal lessons remain clear however:

(1) Corporate financial decisions to maximize stockholder wealth must be made jointly, and
(2) Once the market imperfections within which the firm operates are considered as explicit constraints, these financial decisions cease to be trivial.

[33] While we have not drawn boundaries of the available r, L/E set in Figure 1, it is assumed that r_0, $(L/E)_0$ are within limits previously established: $r \le r_0$(for $b = 0$), $r \ge \delta \ L/E$, and $r \ge r_0/ [1 - r_1 (1 - T)]$ (for $b \to 1$ and $L/E = 0$).

Ahlers presents a valuation model which in based on the way security analysts value stocks rather than on a theoretical derivation. Nevertheless, the independent variables used are similar to those used by Gordon. The model is of particular note for its (1) use of a combination of historical extrapolation techniques and subjective estimates for forecasting growth and (2) identification of risk with a failure to predict future earnings rather than variability in past earnings. The article also explicitly tests the ability of the model to select stocks both against the performance of stocks in general and against the performance of a group of analysists.

11

SEM : A Security Evaluation Model

David M. Ahlers

This article is reprinted with permission from Cohen and Hammer, Analytical Methods in Banking, *Irwin, Homewood, Ill., pp. 305–336. Parts of the original article have been deleted by the editors.*

1. OBJECTIVES

1.1. FORMALIZED FORECASTING OF SECURITY PERFORMANCE

The security analyst, when faced with the problem of making a buy, hold, or sell decision, must first evaluate the past performance of the security and then, coupled with his personal experience, predict its future performance and relative market position. The detailed data available to the analyst for this task far exceeds his human capabilities of assimilation. The analyst, therefore, will normally base his predictions on several basic attributes of the security and modify these results in the light of his intuitive beliefs. While this process may be generally successful, its intuitive segments make the evaluation of errors and improvements of this technique very difficult, if not impossible.

In production-oriented industries, where sales forecasts are needed to plan production schedules, formalized forecasting techniques to predict future sales based upon past sales data have been used successfully. Yet, the security analyst when presented with a similar problem very rarely implements any of the existing forecasting tools. The first objective of this paper, therefore, is to demonstrate that existing formalized forecasting techniques can be modified into a form which will be applicable to security analysis.[1]

1.2. OPERATIONAL TOOL

Underlying the development of the forecasting model is the second objective of this paper: current operationality of the model. If the model is to be accepted by security analysts, it must, at a minimum, possess the following properties:

- 1.21 Sensitivity to the beliefs of the analyst.
- 1.22 Adaptiveness to changes in the security and the market.
- 1.23 Provision for estimates of the error in the model's forecasts.
- 1.24 Reasonableness to the analyst. This reasonableness includes the method and cost of forecasting, as well as insuring that the analyst is able to interpret, in his own language, the full implications and meaning of the model's results.

1.3. IMPLICATIONS FOR PORTFOLIO SELECTION MODELS

Several approaches toward the problem of Portfolio Selection have been translated into computer programs and are currently available to security analysts.[2] The operationality, however, of these programs has been severely limited by the extensive requirements for subjective data from the security analysts. This restriction may be eased by substituting historical patterns for the analysts' subjective beliefs, but only at a cost of the analysts' confidence in the final results. Although a complete Portfolio Selection procedure is beyond the immediate scope of this paper, its third objective is to provide input data which might substantially reduce the cost of implementing a Portfolio Selection Program without reducing the analysts' confidence in the results.

2. ENVIRONMENT OF THE MODEL

In an effort to develop an operational model which would be accepted by security analysts, the goals of the model and the form of its results were designed to correspond as closely as possible to current practices in the field of security analysis.[3]

---

[1] The author is indebted to the management and staff of a large Eastern bank for providing market data, analysts' forecasts and continuing suggestions, comments, and personal time toward the development of the model. Professor Kalman J. Cohen of the Carnegie, Institute of Technology was also extremely helpful, both by critically evaluating the model and constructively suggesting new avenues for research.

[2] In particular the models of Harry M. Markowitz, *Portfolio Selection: Efficient Diversification of Investments* (New York: John Wiley & Sons, Inc., 1959); and William F. Sharpe, "A Simplified Model for Portfolio Analysis," *Management Science,* Vol. 9, No. 2 (January, 1963), pp. 277–93, both of which have been coded in FORTRAN II.

[3] An excellent description of the specific decisions involved in security analysis may be found in Geoffrey P. E. Clarkson, *Portfolio Selection: A Simulation of Trust Investment* (Englewood Cliffs, N.J.: Prentice-Hall, Inc., 1962), pp. 110–11.

The fundamental goal of the security analyst is to outperform the market. Outperforming the market is defined to mean that each security selected should have a greater return (dividends plus price appreciation) than a selected market index. Or, rephrasing, the security analyst plans to perform, not necessarily optimally, but at least better than average without incurring an unreasonable amount of risk. This goal is also the one chosen for the model developed in this paper. While such a goal is clearly not the last step in employing analytical techniques in security analysis, accomplishing it with a computer model should greatly increase security analysts' interest in and acceptability of more refined techniques.

A simplified version of the security analysis decision process can be generalized in the following manner. Initially the analyst poses the question, "If the Dow-Jones price-earnings ratio in (say) three months were (say) 19, what would be the price-earnings ratio and the earnings per share of the XYZ company?" After making these estimates, he then multiplies the price-earnings ratio times the earnings per share to obtain an estimated price for XYZ, i.e., (P/E) $E = P$. Comparison of this forecasted price with the current price enables him to compute an estimated rate of return by which all securities may be ranked. The selection of securities to purchase or sell can then be made cognizant of this ranking with its inherent variability and the diversification requirements of the investment firm.[4]

Although investment firms are continually trying to improve their performance, very little emphasis has been placed on evaluating just how well this forecasting process works and on developing a systematic method for its improvement.

3. SEM: THE SECURITY EVALUATION MODEL

The Security Evaluation Model, SEM, consists of three basic parts; the determination of parameters and initial forecasts of earnings per share for each security, the market evaluation of securities, and the feedback and control analysis. An empirical test of SEM is presented in section 4.

3.1 DETERMINATION OF PARAMETERS AND INITIAL FORECASTS

Although many attributes of a firm and the performance of its securities come to bear in the prediction of future security performance, the earnings per share of the firm, in general, appears to be the dominant attribute of company, and hence of security, performance. Security analysts tend to rely heavily on earnings performance and the trade literature in the field reflects this importance of earnings in evaluating securities.[5]

---

[4]   This is a generalization of the security analysis procedure and is not intended to reflect the investment strategy of any particular financial institution.

[5]   Michael Kourday, "A Method of Outperforming the Market," *Financial Analysts Journal*, Vol. 19 (November–December, 1963), pp. 35–44. A conflicting view may be found in Myron. J. Gordon, *The Investment Financing and Valuation of a Corporation*

An exponentially weighted moving-average system was chosen to predict quarterly earnings per share for several reasons. Such a system is computationally very convenient and inexpensive to operate, requiring a minimum of computer storage and running time. Security analysts are familiar with moving averages. The introduction of exponentially weighted moving averages is an extension of an accepted concept and not the introduction of a new and radical approach. Finally, this system is sensitive to new observations in the determination of forecasts.

The forecasting system used is, with two important changes, the exponentially weighted moving-average system developed by Winters[6] for forecasting with ratio seasonals and a linear trend. First, the analyst's subjective beliefs concerning future values of earnings may be incorporated into the model. Secondly, the Winters procedure allows trend effects to be distributed over seasonal factors. SEM, however, maintains a separation between seasonal and trend effects.

3.11 The Winters Forecasting Model. The steady state or "normalized" component of earnings is given in the Winters formulation by[7]

$$SE_t = WE\left(\frac{CE_t}{F_j^{t-1}}\right) + (1 - WE)(SE_{t-1} + R_{t-1}) \tag{1}$$

Where: $0 \leq WE \leq 1$.
CE_t is the quarterly earnings per share in period t.
F_j^t is the seasonal adjustment factor for season j as of period t.
SE_t is the steady state value of quarterly earnings per share as of period t.
R_t is the quarterly trend in SE as of period t.
L is the number of periods per cycle.
j is the current season in L corresponding to t.

Equation (1) simply states that the new estimate for the constant component of earnings SE_t is an average of the current observed earnings CE_t adjusted by the most current seasonal factor F_j^{t-1} and the previous estimate SE_{t-1} increased by the most recent estimate of the trend R_{t-1}. The effect of past data will vary inversely with the magnitude of the weight parameter WE.

Continuing Winters' formulation, a new seasonal factor F_j^t may be computed by[8]

$$F_j^t = WF\left(\frac{CE_t}{SE_t}\right) + (1 - WF)F_j^{t-1} \tag{2}$$

(Homewood, Ill.: Richard D. Irwin, Inc., 1962). Gordon, however, does not consider earnings to be relevant, but relies on the yearly dividend and the retention rate (1-payout ratio) as two of the independent variables in his model. The notion of payout ratio will be considered in 3.22, and because of current practices and the ease of predicting one rather than two variables, quarterly earnings per share is forecasted by this phase of the model.

[6]   Peter R. Winters, "Forecasting Sales by Exponentially Weighted Moving Averages," *Management Science,* Vol. 6 (April, 1960), pp. 324–42.

[7]   *Ibid.,* p. 329.

[8]   *Ibid.,* p. 330.

where $0 \leq WF \leq 1$.

Each new F_j^t, therefore, is an average of the current seasonal effect (CE_t/SE_t) and the value attained over $t-1$ periods of F_j^{t-1} for the jth season.

Similarly, a new value R_t for the trend is found by[9]

$$R_t = WR(SE_t - SE_{t-1}) + (1 - WR)R_{t-1} \qquad (3)$$

where $0 \leq WR \leq 1$.

The new trend R_t is an average of the current observable trend in the steady state component $(SE_t - SE_{t-1})$ and the previous estimate R_{t-1}.

A forecast of earnings per share i periods from t is given by[10]

$$FE_i^t = (SE_t + i \cdot R_t)F_j^t. \qquad (4)$$

where:

> FE_i^t is the forecasted earnings per share i periods from t.
> j is the season in L corresponding to $t + i$.

The forecast FE_i^t is, therefore, determined by adding i trend effects to the current steady state SE_t and adjusting the result by F_j^t.

3.12. SEM: Forecasting. One difficulty arises, however, if the model described by the Winters equations is used to predict future values FE_i^t. If the seasonal cycle is L periods long, and if the seasonal factors F_j^t are to measure only the seasonal allocations and not the level or growth of earnings, then

$$\sum_{j=1}^{L} F_j^t \equiv L.$$

Even if

$$\sum_{j=1}^{L} F_j^0 \equiv L,$$

(2) does not imply that

$$\sum_{j=1}^{L} F_j^1 \equiv 1.$$

The following procedure describes a correction technique for this problem.

Let

$$\sum_{j=1}^{L} F_j^{t-1} \equiv L \quad \text{and} \quad \sum_{j=1}^{L} F_j^t = L + d.$$

In period t, which corresponds to the kth season, the only F_j^t which is recomputed is F_k^t. Then

$$d = F_k^t - F_k^{t-1}. \qquad (5)$$

---

[9]   *Ibid.*, p. 330.
[10] *Ibid.*, p. 330.

By scaling each seasonal factor by $L/(L + d)$,

$$F_j^t = \frac{L}{(L + d)} F_j^t \quad \text{and} \quad \sum_{j=1}^{L} F_j^t \equiv L. \qquad (6)$$

SEM, therefore, begins at $t = 1$ with a set of estimated seasonal factors which are equal to L. In each succeeding period, SEM satisfies the constraint

$$\sum_{j=1}^{L} F_j^t \equiv L$$

by normalizing the current set of seasonal factors.

This normalization process, however, changes the forecast FE_i^t computed from (4) by a factor of $L/(L + d)$. Consequently, the second constraint imposed upon the SEM forecasting method is that the value of the forecast FE_i^t be unaltered by the correction process. This final constraint is satisfied by multiplying the factors within the parentheses in (4) by $(L + d)/L$ or $(1 + d/L)$. The steady state level of earnings is now given by

$$SE_t = \left(1 + \frac{d}{L}\right) SE_t. \qquad (7)$$

The trend component is computed by multiplying the results of (3) by $(1 + d/L)$

$$R_t = [WR(SE_t - SE_{t-1}) + (1 - WR)R_{t-1}]\left(1 + \frac{d}{L}\right) \qquad (8)$$

The exponential forecasting system employed in SEM operates in the following sequence.

1. A current value of earnings CE_t is is given to the system.
2. (1) computes an unadjusted SE_t.
3. (2) computes F_k^t
4. (5) determines d, over the L period seasonal cycle, caused by the new value F_k^t.
5. (6) normalizes all F_j^t to L.
6. (8) computes and adjusts R_t.
7. (7) adjusts SE_t.
8. (4) forecasts values of E of for i periods ahead.

Winters defines the "best" values for WE, WF, and WR as those values for which the standard deviation of forecast errors over a given observed number of periods is a minimum.[11] The $t + 1$ forecast error is given by

$$FE_{t+1} - CE_{t+1} = e_{t+1} \qquad (9)$$

(the forecast made in period t for 1 period ahead minus the actual value in that period). Winters describes an iterative procedure over past data, based on the

[11]   *Ibid.*, p. 332.

assumption that the best parameter solutions are convex in nature, to select values for *WE, WF,* and *WR*. The SEM model extends this iterative process to include the analyst's subjective beliefs.

The analyst's beliefs are essentially treated as an extension of the observable past data. The analyst's forecast of earnings per share is made on a yearly basis. This must first be converted to a quarterly estimate before the estimated forecast errors can be calculated.

Let *ATE* be the analyst's forecast of total earnings over an *L*-period cycle (*L* is 4 for quarterly earnings data). Then if *AE* is the current steady state quarterly earnings implied by the analyst's forecast and *SE, F,* and *R* are the current values of the steady state, seasonal, and trend components as determined by SEM, then by (4)

$$ATE = \sum_{i=1}^{L} (AE + i \cdot R)F_j$$

or

$$ATE = AE \left(\sum_{j=1}^{L} F_j\right) + R\left(\sum_{i=1}^{L} i \cdot F_j\right)$$

or

$$AE = \frac{ATE - R\left(\sum_{i=1}^{L} i \cdot F_j\right)}{L} \qquad (10)$$

where *j* is the season *i* periods from the current period.

The sum of the squared error e_a introduced by including the analyst's adjusted forecast as observed data is

$$\sum_{i=1}^{L} e_{ai}^2 = \sum_{i=1}^{L} [(SE + i \cdot R)F_j - (AE + i \cdot R)F_j]^2$$

or

$$\sum_{i=1}^{L} e_{ai}^2 = (SE - AE)^2 \sum_{j=1}^{L} F_j^2 .$$

or

$$\sum_{i=1}^{L} e_{ai}^2 = \left\{ SE - \left[\left(ATE - R\left(\sum_{i=1}^{L} i \cdot F_j\right)\right) / L\right]\right\}^2 \sum_{j=1}^{L} F_j^2 . \qquad (11)$$

With the inclusion of the above error term, the procedure followed by SEM to determine the best exponential weights parallels Winters' approach and consists of the following steps.

1. An initial portion of the observed CE_t containing *H* observations is used to calculate starting values for SE_1, R_1, and F_1. These values are averages over the *H* periods and are calculated exactly in the same manner as the corresponding variables in the Winters model.[12]

---

[12]   *Ibid.*, p. 335 and p. 338. Note that the F_t's are normalized to *L* rather than 12.

2. The forecasting model is applied to the CE_t data from period 1 through period H, but no record of single period forecast errors is maintained. This double simplementation of the first H periods tends to "wash out" initial bias in the starting values.
3. Forecasts are continued from period $H + 1$ through the total number of observations, D. A running sum-of-square forecast errors is computed during this portion of the forecasting.

$$\sum_{i=H+1}^{D} e_{0i}^2 = \sum_{j=H}^{D-1} (FE_j{}^t - CE_{j+1})^2. \tag{12}$$

4. Forecasts, based upon data through period D, are made for each quarter through the date of the analyst's forecast of yearly earnings. The total error for any complete forecasting cycle is the sum of the observed errors from (12) plus the approximate error introduced by the analyst forecast (11) weighted by the analyst's confidence, $CONFD$, in his forecast.[13]

$$\text{Total Error} = \sum_{i=H+1}^{D} e_{0i}^2 + (CONFD) \cdot \sum_{i=1}^{L} e_{ai}^2 \tag{13}$$

5. All possible combinations of $WE, WR,$ and WG within specified upper and lower bounds and by specified increments between these bounds are tried to discover the particular combination resulting in the lowest Total Error. The convex nature of the solution permits local improvement on an initial solution with tighter constraints on the parameter ranges in subsequent runs.[13]

6. The ability of the forecasting model to predict future values of earnings may be measured by computing the standard deviation of forecast errors σ and an estimate $CVAR$ of the coefficient of variation. In computing σ only the squared error over the observed data is considered.

$$\sigma = \left[\sum_{i=H+1}^{D} e_{0i}^2/(D - H - 1) \right]^{1/2} \tag{14}$$

$CVAR$ is computed by

$$CVAR = \sigma / \left(\sum_{i=H+1}^{D} CE_i(D - H) \right) \tag{15}$$

where the denominator is just the average CE_t over the forecast range. The value of σ is a criterion by which successive narrowing of the iterative limits on the exponential weights may be evaluated. $CVAR$, on the other hand, permits a comparison among securities of the relative variability of forecast errors.

In summary, the first phase of SEM establishes, by an iterative procedure, a forecasting model for each security, based upon both the observed data of the past and the analyst's subjective beliefs of future performance. This model not only has the capability to predict future earnings within an error range $CVAR$

[13] *Ibid.*, p. 339.

but also provides current estimates for normalized earnings, the trend in normalized earnings and seasonal adjustments.

3.2. MARKET EVALUATION

Although the forecasts made in phase 1 of SEM of future quarterly earnings are valuable for control and analysis purposes[14] they do not solve the analyst's problem of evaluating and ranking securities. The analyst, who has at his disposal only past data, must forecast the future relative performance of each security. Relationships between the price of a security and its attributes (growth in dividends, instability of earnings, etc.) at a given point in time have been developed,[15] but to forecast price and then to compute relative performance requires first forecasting each of the securities' attributes. A forecasting system better suited to the analyst's problem would be one in which currently available data could be employed to rank securities by anticipated relative performance. A system of this type has been developed by investment analysts Whitbeck and Kisor of the Bank of New York.[16]

3.21. The Whitbeck and Kisor Model. The Whitbeck and Kisor model utilizes a security's growth rate in earnings, payout ratio, and variability of earnings as independent variables in a regression model to determine whether the security is undervalued or overvalued in the *current* market.[17] The relevant variables are defined and calculated in the following manner:

$$\ln (EPS_{it}) = a_i + g_i t + \epsilon_i \text{ for the } i\text{th security} \qquad (16)$$

where

a_i is a constant.
g_i is the growth rate (regression coefficient).
t is the year ($1 \leq t \leq 15$ for the study).
ϵ_i is a random error term.

Equation (16) is determined by standard regression techniques.[18]

$$POR = \left(\sum_{t=1}^{10} DIVIDENDS_t \Big/ \sum_{t=1}^{10} EPS_t \right) + ADJ \qquad (17)$$

where

POR is the payout ratio.
ADJ is the analyst's adjustment for trend effects in POR.

The POR as can be seen from (17) is simply the current ten-year average

14 See section 3.3. of original article, *eds.*
15 Cf. Gordon. *op. cit.*
16 Volkert S. Whitbeck and Manown Kisor, Jr., "A New Tool in Investment Decision-Making," *Financial Analysts Journal,* Vol. 19 (May–June, 1963), pp. 55–62.
17 *Ibid.,* p. 58.
18 *Ibid.,* p. 55.

adjusted by the analyst's subjective beliefs.[19]

$$TPE_i = b_0 + b_1(g'_i) + b_2(POR_i) + b_3(\sigma_{ei}) + \epsilon_i \qquad (18)$$

where

TPE_i is the computed theoretical price-earnings ratio for the ith security.
g'_i is g_i adjusted by the analyst's beliefs to estimate the growth rate for the next five years.
σ_{ei} is the standard error of the ith equation of the form $EPS_i = a_0 + a_1 t$.
b_j are the regression coefficients.

Equation (18) represents a least-squares fit to the market's evaluation of the selected attributes. The signs of the b_j's are indicative of market desires concerning the corresponding attributes. The coefficient b_1 would logically be expected to be greater than zero implying a positive valuation for growth, while similarly a $b_3 < 0$ would be logically indicative of a negative valuation on increasing earnings instability. The observed data for the TPE_i were the actual price earnings ratios APE_i. These ratios were computed by dividing the current actual market price AP by a normalized (mid-cycle) earnings estimate NE.

$$PR = \frac{TPE_i}{APE_i} = \frac{TP / NE}{AP / NE} = \frac{TP}{AP} \qquad (19)$$

where for the ith security:

NE is the normalized earnings per share.
TP is the theoretical price.
AP is the actual price.
PR is the price ratio.

Equation (19) combined with the following assumption is the crux of the Whitbeck and Kisor model.

"Given the theoretical or normal price of any stock, we assume that the market price of the stock will seek this level faster than the theoretical price itself will change."[20]

The PR of a security is a ratio of its theoretical price TP determined by considering the market's evaluation of the security's attributes and its actual price AP in the market. If the security is neither undervalued nor overvalued this ratio will be 1. If, however, $PR > 1$ this implies that $TP > AP$ or that the security is undervalued and selling for less than the market evaluation (18) indicates that it should. The assumption quoted above, rephrased, states that in the undervalued case the actual price will rise to meet the theoretical price faster than the theoretical price will itself change. A similar argument holds for overvalued securities when $PR < 1$.

The PR, therefore, is a dynamic concept enabling the analyst to rank securities in terms of anticipated performance.

[19] *Ibid.*, p. 62.
[20] *Ibid.*, p. 60.

3.22. SEM: Market Evaluation.
SEM retains the basic philosophy of the Whitbeck and Kisor model, but reformulates (18) into (20) utilizing results from the first phase of SEM.

$$\ln(TPE_i) = b_0 + b_1\ln[(R_i/SE_i) + 1] + b_2\ln(YD_i/AP_i) + b_3\ln(CVAR_i) + \epsilon_i \tag{20}$$

where

YD_i is the current yearly dividend for the ith security and all other variables are as previously defined for the ith security in period t.

The SEM growth rate R_i/SE_i was chosen in lieu of the Whitbeck and Kisor g' for several reasons. First the SEM growth rate is a readily available by-product of the forecasting process in phase 1. This growth factor measures the rate of growth in normalized rather than historical earnings. As each new quarter is observed, estimates of R_i and SE_i are revised according to the "best" weights established in phase 1. While such a procedure for updating g' might also be constructed,[21] the selection criterion for weighting new and past observations would remain a problem. The analyst's beliefs have also been incorporated into the SEM growth factor by considering the analyst's forecast in selecting the "best" exponential weights of phase 1.

The current yield rate YD_i/AP_i was selected instead of the payout ratio POR to account for the market's desire for dividend yield. The POR is not a relative measure between securities when considering the return to investors.[22] This substitution was made, therefore, to preserve the relative nature of (20).

Again, $CVAR$ was selected rather than σ_e due to the direct availability of $CVAR$ from phase 1. There is, however, an important conceptual difference between $CVAR$ and σ_e. The standard error σ_e measures the variability from the trend of actual earnings. Much or none of this variation may be explainable by seasonal or cyclical patterns which are not considered in determining the σ_e's. The assumption is made here that investors are more concerned with the unexpected portion of earnings variability than with the total variability. If phase 1 of SEM is assumed to be forecasting as a rational investor when it makes allowance for seasonal variations, the normalized level of earnings and the analyst's beliefs of the future, then $CVAR$ is an estimate of an unexpected error in a rational forecast.

Finally, the terms in the market evaluation equation have been changed from additive to multiplicative. This transformation may be more clearly seen by rewriting (20) in its equivalent form without logarithms:

$$TPE_i = b'_0 \cdot [(R_i/SE_i) + 1]^{b1}(YD_i/AP_i)^{b2}(CVAR_1)^{b3} \cdot \epsilon'_i \tag{21}$$

[21] A technique for efficiently re-estimating the growth coefficient g may be found in Robert Goodell Brown, *Smoothing, Forecasting and Prediction of Discrete Time Series* (Englewood Cliffs, N.J.: Prentice-Hall, Inc., 1962), chap. xi.

[22] Consider two securities A and B with the same payout ratio POR, price P, variation $CVAR$, and growth R/SE. Clearly the level of actual earnings may be different for A and B and hence the dividend yield may be different.

where

$$b'_0 = e^{b0}.$$

$$\epsilon'_i = \ln \epsilon_i.$$

The addition of a plus one to the growth rate term solves two problems. First, it maintains the sign effect of the growth rate term. If, for example, $(R / SE) < 0$ then $[(R_i/SE_i) + 1] < 1$ and $\ln[(R_i/SE_i) + 1] < 0$. Similarly, the value of the logarithmic term will be positive whenever the growth rate is positive. Secondly, since the nature of the data limits negative values of the growth rate to be greater than minus one, the addition of a plus one will always result in a non-negative term. This effectively eliminates the possibility of trying to compute the logarithm of a negative number.

The multiplicative form of the market evaluation equation was suggested by the considerable success that Gordon has had with equations consisting of multiplicative terms.[23] Initially the model was tested for both forms (18) and (20) of the market evaluation equation. The performance of (20), however, proved to be superior to the performance of (18) and consequently (20) was selected as the equation form to be used by SEM.[24]

In conjunction with the selection of (20), the price ratio PR was redefined in logarithmic terms. Price ratios are computed by

$$PR_i = (\ln TPE_i) / (\ln APE_i). \tag{22}$$

Price ratios determined by (22) will be equivalent to those computed by (19) with respect to being less than or greater than one. The relative rankings of securities, however, may not be the same. Consider two securities A and B such that the following ocnditions hold:

$$TPE_A = K \cdot TPE_B$$

$$APE_A = K \cdot APE_B \text{ where } K > 1.$$

Then by (19)

$$PR_A = TPE_A / APE_A = (K \cdot TPE_B) / (K \cdot APE_B) = TPE_B / APE_B = PR_B.$$

However, by (22)

$$PR_A = \ln TPE_A / \ln APE_A = \ln(K \cdot TPE_B) / \ln(K \cdot APE_B) \text{ or}$$

$$PR_A = (\ln TPE_B + \ln K) / (\ln APE_B + \ln K) \neq \ln TPE_B / \ln APE_B = PR_B.$$

The equation above illustrates that the logarithmic PR (22) in comparing two securities also takes into account the magnitudes of the price earnings ratios

[23]   Gordon, *op. cit.*, p. 169.
[24]   Total undervalued yield over the simulation was 6.83% for the additive model versus 8.40% for the multiplicative model. The additive model made only 28 correct valuations as opposed to 46 made by the multiplicative model.

which the linear *PR* (19) does not consider. This new form of the *PR* will, therefore, shift toward one from both the undervalued and overvalued sides as the price-earnings ratios become larger. This shifting is consistent with the beliefs of security analysts who, when securities are undervalued will prefer, all other things being equal, lower price-earnings ratios, and when securities are overvalued will hold higher price-earnings ratios on a quality basis.

The Whitbeck and Kisor study incorporated a sample of 135 common stocks which were compared with respect to price performance[25] against the Standard and Poor 500-common-stock index. The under- or overvaluation of stocks, however, is determined in the 135-stock market and not in the market considered by the index. In samples as large as the one in the Whitbeck and Kisor study this apparent translation problem should be negligible. In smaller samples, however, a correction factor is needed to maintain the consistency of the index comparison.

Although security analysts frequently joke about being unable to "buy" the index, the bench marks of index performance, price, earnings, and dividends are reported as though such a security actually did exist.[26] SEM, therefore, forecasts the index's earnings, treating the index as an existing security. The index is not included, however, in determining the regression coefficients of the sample market. The *PR* of the index *XPR* is computed from the values of the index attributes and the sample market regression coefficients. All PR_j's for stocks in the sample are revised to the index level by

$$PR'_i = PR_i \,/\, XPR. \tag{23}$$

Clearly since the rankings do not change, the total effect of the index correction is to alter the under-over-valued cutoff point. The final effect on the performance of selected securities will depend on the investment strategy followed.

4.1. EMPIRICAL TEST DATA

The necessary data for this test were provided for 24 common stocks and the Standard and Poor 425-Stock Index by the investment analysis division of a large Eastern bank. The decisions of the analyst in the simulation are the decisions made by the investment analysis division as a whole and reflect the performance of this organization rather than the performance of a particular security analyst. The common stocks selected were chosen randomly from the bank's present portfolio. Earnings per share for each stock and the index begin with the first quarter of 1958. The beginning date of the simulation is the first quarter of 1964 and the ending date is the fourth quarter of 1964. A hold range factor of .8, which is similar to the .15 employed by Kisor and Whitbeck for the same purpose, was chosen for the test.[27]

[25] A slightly different criterion of success is employed by SEM. See section 3.33.

[26] Security analysts do not normally forecast earnings for the index. SEM, therefore, does not consider forecasted earnings by the analyst when it determines the "best" exponential weights for the index.

4.2. SIMULATION OF SEM

The best exponential weights for each stock and the index were determined by a two-stage process. Initially a lower bound of .00, an upper bound of 1.0 and an increment of .20 were tried for all stocks and the index. Narrow ranges, usually ± .10, about the initial best weights were then examined by a subsequent run of the program.[28]

Subsequent to determining the "best" exponential weights for each security, SEM ranks each security ranging from the most undervalued to the most overvalued. The first ranking was computed using the data available through the last quarter of 1963. The next report generated by SEM is for the end of the first quarter in 1964 and summarizes the results of the buy-hold-sell decisions made at the end of 1963 by both the analyst and the model.

4.3. YIELD PERFORMANCE

While the model provides a considerable amount of valuable detailed information for the analyst, the foremost questions at this point are "How well did the model perform?" and "What is the nature of the maximum performance that one might expect?" In the context of this simulation an understanding of the second question is necessary prior to answering the first question.

Clearly, the greatest per dollar return over the simulated year would be obtained by selecting only the stock with the greatest yield in each quarter. While this would provide an upper limit on the return inherent in the data, such a criterion is unrealistic in its total lack of any diversification. The market depth as computed by SEM is a measure of the actual group yield of under-and overvalued stocks. For example, the undervalued market depth is the combined yield of all the stocks which were actually undervalued in the preceding quarter. If the model or the analyst exceeds this undervalued market depth in a particular quarter, it is indicative of an ability to select the "better" of the "good" buys.

Figure 4–1 represents a summary of the undervalued or buy decisions by SEM and the analyst for the year 1964. The most pertinent observation is that SEM outperformed the analyst in every quarter and the index in three of the four quarters. In addition, SEM was also able to select the "better" undervalued securities in three of the four quarters, while the analyst was able to do this only in the last quarter of 1964.

Both SEM and the analyst were able, for the overall simulation and for three of the four simulated quarters, to properly label groups of stocks which subsequently performed less than the index yield as overvalued. A summary of the overvalued decisions for 1964 is presented in Figure 4–2.

---

[27] Whitbeck and Kisor, *op. cit.,* p. 60. The multiplicative form of the model and the nature of the hold range computation account for this difference. The average standard error of the market evaluation equations is somewhat lower than had been anticipated and the corresponding Whitbeck and Kisor range is actually about .10.

[28] Winters, *op. cit.,* p. 340. The convex nature of the solution permits a more advanced search technique other than complete enumeration. The enumeration scheme employed by SEM was chosen for programming convenience and not for computational efficiency.

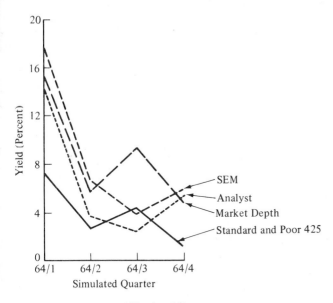

Simulated Quarter

Cumulative Yield Results for 1964

Market Depth	8.89%
SEM	8.40%
Analyst	6.52%
Standard and Poor 425	3.82%

FIGURE 4–1

Undervalued yield

4.4. CORRECT DECISIONS

Although the yield results are the most relevant outcome to the overall performances of both the analyst and SEM, it is also appropriate to examine the success of under- or overvalued predictions. Figure 4–3 summarizes the number of correct under-and overvaluations (irrespective of hold conditions) made by the analyst, SEM, and the analyst and SEM jointly. Several points are worth noting about these results.

First, the analyst and SEM had 31 and 46 correct decisions respectively; together, however, they agreed on only 20 of these. A possible implication is that each is strong in a part of the problem area where the other is weak. Or, rephrasing, the model appears to do well when the analyst does poorly and the analyst does well when the model does poorly. If further research is able to reconcile these differences, the trading of information between SEM and the analyst should improve the performance of both.

Secondly, the results of Figure 4–3 are pertinent only to those stocks for which buy and sell decisions or under-and overvaluations were made. SEM, for the hold range chosen, had about 25 percent fewer hold stocks than the

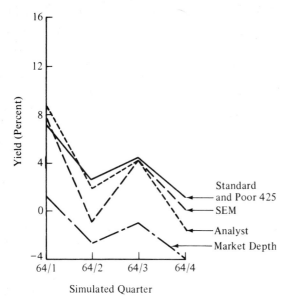

Simulated Quarter

Cumulative Yield Results for 1964

Standard and Poor 425	3.82%
Analyst	3.34%
SEM	2.88%
Market Depth	−1.68%

FIGURE 4–2

Overvalued yield

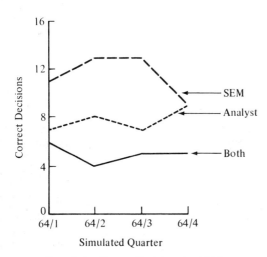

Simulated Quarter

Cumulative Correct Decisions for 1964

	Undervalued	Overvalued	Total
SEM	15	31	46
Analyst	11	20	31
Both	7	13	20

FIGURE 4–3

Number of correct decisions

analyst. In order to compare the ability of the analyst and SEM to predict correctly the following percentages were determined:

	Analyst	SEM
Percentage of occurrences for which the stock was labeled undervalued (buy) or overvalued (sell) and this decision was correct.....	51%	61%
Percentage of occurrences for which the stock was labeled undervalued (buy) and this decision was correct.	52%	75%*

* *Significantly greater than 50% at a 2.5% significance level.*

From the above results, it is evident that SEM's primary advantage lies in its ability in this test to identify undervalued stocks with a better than even chance of success.

4.5. MARKET EVALUATION EQUATION STATISTICS

The market evaluation equation (20) was used in all quarters except the last, when its form was changed to (34) to include the aberration factor. The logarithmic form of both equations and scale differences among the variables may cause some confusion in the interpretation of the effect of changes in the independent variables upon the theoretical price earnings ratio TPE.[29] In the table, 4.51 below, the effect on the TPE for an increase in the value of an independent variable is presented, therefore, rather than the actual sign of the corresponding regression coefficient.

4.51. *Regression Statistics.* In interpreting the effects of an increase in the aberration factor, it is helpful to recall that this factor will be positive whenever the stock has been consistently incorrectly overvalued. This type of overvaluation error results whenever the stock has a TPE which is too low and, conse-

Qtr	R^2	Growth	Yield	Variation	Aberration
63/4	.60	+#	+ *	−*	na
64/1	.56	+	+ *	−*	na
64/2	.46	−	+ *	−*	na
64/3	.59	−*	+ *	−*	na
64/4	.66	−	+ *	−#	+*

*, # *Coefficient is significantly different from zero at respectively a 5%, 10% significance level.*

[29]   The theoretical price-earnings ratio, TPE, while not presented explicitly by SEM is computed internally and does have several applications in security analysis beyond the immediate scope of this paper. For example, the product TPE · SE is equal to the theoretical price, P_T, of the stock. If the stock has been determined to be undervalued, then P_T is clearly an upper limit on the price that should be paid for it during the next quarter. A method to estimate the duration of growth for a stock, which could be easily included in SEM, has been proposed by Charles C. Holt, "The Influence of Growth Duration on Share Prices," *Journal of Finance*, Vol. 17, No. 3 (September, 1962), pp. 465–75. Without discussing the details of this analysis, the growth duration time, t, in quarters would be computed by

$$t = \frac{\ln (TPE_i/TPE_x)}{\ln [(1+R_i/SE_i+YLD_i)/(1+R_x/SE_x+YLD_x)]}$$

where i is the particular security and x is the index.

quently, less than the actual price-earnings ratio. The positive correction effect indicated in the table is, therefore, in the logical direction.

The signs of the yield and variation terms are consistent with the notion that the market values a good yield rate and discounts unpredictable variation in earnings.

The negative signs of the growth term are inconsistent with present beliefs in security analysis. This apparent inconsistency and the lack of significance in the growth rate term is probably due to the following conditions under which the simulation was performed. First, the small size of the sample precluded a sufficient number of "growth stocks." The majority of the stocks in the simulation were not growth stocks and growth rates were probably not significant in discriminating among them. Secondly, the development of large (over 3) tracking errors in the forecasting of earnings, beginning with 64/2, would have a considerable erroneous effect on the growth rate employed in the market evaluation equation.

4.6. OPERATING COSTS

The final important aspect of SEM is its low operating cost. The feedback and control report for 24 stocks required on the average 12 seconds of computation time and the *PR* determination and ranking required 7 seconds. Thus the total quarterly computer cost was approximately 6.25 cents per second times 19 seconds or about $1.19. The data collection and preparation costs added another $10.00 to the total quarterly costs.

The initial collection of earnings history and best fit determination similarly averaged about $6.00 per stock or $150.00 for the 24 stocks and the index.

In both the initial and quarterly analyses, costs should increase at most linearly with the number of securities considered.

5. CONCLUSION

The Security Evaluation Model, SEM, developed in this paper approaches the problem of security analysis from the viewpoint of practicing security analysts. The model is sensitive to the beliefs of the analyst and adaptive to changes in the market as well. Alterations in the underlying structure for a particular security are quickly reflected in the associated error terms.

In a conversation with the author one security analyst made the statement "Sure the problem is tough, but we have to solve it anyway." SEM is intended as a *first* step from an operational standpoint toward the solution of the security analysis problem. SEM's results are familiar to security analysts and can be obtained with a reasonable amount of effort and at low cost. The stocks selected as under-or overvalued by SEM do not, of course, determine optimal portfolios. Yet the results of SEM are dynamic in nature and provide a reasonable data base from which portfolio selection methods might proceed.

Nerlove tests a model to explain differences in both the short-run and the long-run rates of return on common stocks. The article is interesting because Nerlove's attempt to find alternative empirical measures of the same and similar economic influences and because he reports the results and discusses the meaning of variables which have little or no explanatory significance, as well as those which have a clear and significant relationship. In addition, Nerlove draws significant conclusions as to the efficiency of capital markets.

12

Factors Affecting Differences Among Rates of Return on Investments in Individual Common Stocks

Marc Nerlove*

This article is reprinted with permission from the Review of Economics and Statistics, *Vol. L, No. 3 (August, 1968), pp. 312–331.*

"You may call it "nonsense' if you like," she said, "but *I've* heard nonsense, compared with which [this] would be as sensible as a dictionary."

Through the Looking-Glass

I. INTRODUCTION, SUMMARY AND CONCLUSIONS

That rates of return tend, *ceteris paribus,* to equality in different employments of capital, both human and nonhuman, is one of the most fundamental theorems of classical economics:

*The research on which this article is based was done, in part, at the Cowles Foundation for Research in Economics at Yale University with the financial support of the National Science Foundation, and, in part, during the author's tenure as the Frank W. Taussig Research Professor, 1967–1968, at Harvard University with the financial support of the Harvard Economics Department.
The author is greatly indebted to Donald Hester for his constant criticism and advice,

"The whole of the advantages and disadvantages of the different employments of labor and stock must, in the same neighborhood, be either perfectly equal or continually tending to equality. If in the same neighborhood, there was any employment evidently either more or less advantageous than the rest, so many people would crowd into it in the one case, and so many would desert it in the other, that its advantages would soon return to the level of other employments. This at least would be the case in a society where things were left to follow their natural course, where there was perfect liberty and where every man was perfectly free. . ." [17, p. 99]

More recently Stigler [18, p. 54] has emphasized the social implications of this classical proposition:

"There is no more important proposition in economic theory than that, under competition, the rate of return on investment tends toward equality in all industries. Entrepreneurs will seek to leave relatively unprofitable industries and enter relatively profitable industries, and with competition there will be neither public nor private barriers to these movements. This mobility of capital is crucial to the efficiency and growth of the economy. . . "

Such empirical evidence as exists, however, suggests large and persistent differences among rates of return observed in the real world.

As Hirshleifer [5, p. 77] has pointed out, there are essentially two schools of thought concerning the reasons for large and persistent differences among observed rates of return. Eckstein [2, p. 493] suggests that the evidence indicates ". . . the capital market to be imperfect, to be rife with rationing, ignorance, differential tax treatments, reluctance to finance investment from external funds, slow adjustment processes, etc., which destroy the normative significance of actual rates found in the market." At the other extreme, it might be argued that much of the diversity reflects differences among alternatives important to efficient allocation of resources. In this paper, some preliminary results of a study designed to account for differences among observed rates of return on investments in various individual common stocks over varying periods of time are reported. Although far from unambiguous, these initial findings suggest that imperfections in allocative efficiency, at least over the relatively short periods considered in this investigation, play an extremely important role in explaining the differences among rates of return. This is not to deny the importance of factors connected with risk and uncertainty which play a legitimate role in both the determination of differential rates of return and in the allocation of resources. Broadly speaking, the findings presented here are consistent with the following hypothesis:

Rates of return on investments in different common stocks differ, in some measure because of differences in riskiness, but much more im-

which he gave freely despite his misgivings concerning the basic approach. Professor Meyer, Lintner, and Marris, as well as other members of the Seminar on Quantitative Economics at Harvard, also made a large number of helpful comments on an earlier draft. Mrs. E. Bockelman assisted in programming the calculations. The author alone is responsible for any errors of commission or omission.
This article is a condensation and revision of a longer study [14]. The author is indebted to Otto Eckstein for his comments on the longer study.

portantly because of substantial disequilibrium in the capital market. Not only is external capital severely rationed, but investors in stocks share the imperfect recognition of profitable expansion with other suppliers of capital. Dim perception of opportunities which appear to be especially prevalent in rapidly expanding firms (or at least those firms which take advantage of the opportunities they have), is responsible for lower prices initially. As, however, the great profitability of internal investment is realized, prices rise resulting in substantial capital gains. Over long periods of time, firms with considerable internal investment potential, which they realize through high high retention of earnings, pay out high or increased dividends which contribute importantly to a high rate of return on investments in the common stock of such firms. (Sed the definition of rate of return below.) Retained earnings, however, coupled with profitable opportunities for investing them, remain the most important single source of high rates of return on investments in individual ocmmon stocks.

In the course of the present investigation the following findings, subject to certain qualifications, have emerged:

1) The most important variables explaining differences among rates of return over both short and long periods are sales growth and retention of earnings.
2) Growth in earnings appears to be of considerably lesser importance than either growth in sales or retention of earnings.
3) Dividends are quite important in determining differences among rates of return over long periods but not over short periods. In any event, dividends are of considerably less quantitative significance than retained earnings.
4) Over long periods, leverage is positively associated with the rate of return, as one would expect since highly levered common stock is a more risky investment than a stock in a firm with little long-term debt or preferred stock. On the other hand, leverage has little effect over short periods.
5) Other variables such as asset growth, inventory turnover, cash flow, share turnover, and such standard measures as quick or current ratios, apparently have little or no effect on relative rates of return.
6) When firms are classified by the general nature of their final products, highly significant differences among these groups in the rates of return emerge.
7) Over long periods of time firms with a large proportion of fixed plant among their total assets show inexplicably low rates of return. It may be shown that the effect of this variable is not due to industry differences in performance which are attributed in the statistical analysis to the proportion of fixed plant.

II. IMPERFECTIONS IN THE STOCK MARKET

What we observe are *ex post* rates of return, not the *ex ante* rates which direct the flow of capital from one line of enterprise to another. If all future events were correctly anticipated, the *ex post* and *ex ante* rates would coincide. Furthermore, with perfect foresight, no posibility of disequilibrium could exist in the absence of absolute impediments to the flow of capital. However, when the future events are foreseen only imperfectly and when there are frictions or temporary impediments to the free flow of capital, unanticipated events may create differences among *ex post* rates of return on alternative forms of investment. While the stock market may appear to be one of the most perfect devices attainable by man for the transfer of financial capital among a limited number of alternative forms of investment, there are, in fact, three important sources of friction:

First, transfer of capital among investments in common stock and from common stock to other forms of investment is far from costless. Brokerage commissions may amount to 1 per cent or more of the price in a round-lot transaction.[1] The transactions cost in percentage terms, of investment and disinvestment in a given security may easily exceed the rate of return over very short periods of time, and may be greater than differences among rates of return over moderate periods. Over very long periods, of course, transactions costs become negligible except in cases where rates of return are extremely small in absolute value.

Second, information is not costless, nor is it possible to obtain some information without a considerable lag. Full company reports are issued only annually, although many companies supply a substantial amount of information on a quarterly basis.[2] Furthermore, because it may take a large number of observations to establish the causes and significance for the prospects of a given firm of changes affecting it, the tendency to equality of rates of return may

---

[1]According to [12], commissions on round-lot transactions on the New York Stock Exchange (NYSE) average about one per cent of the market value of the securities involved in the transaction. The commission schedule for nonmembers on the NYSE was as follows at the time of writing:

Money involved per round lot	Commission
Under $100.00	As mutually agreed
$100,00–$399.99	2% plus $3
$400,00–$2,399.99	1% plus $7
$2,400.00–$4,999.99	1/2% plus $19
$5000.00 and over	1/10% plus $39

Minimum: $6, when the amount involved is $100 or more.
Maximum: $75.

The rate on odd lots is 2 dollars less than on round, but there is 12 1/2 cents or 25 cents per share odd-lot differential, for shares of under and over 40 dollars per share price, respectively, which makes such transactions considerably more expensive. The following table shows how these rates work out as a percentage of the purchase price of 100 shares at various prices per share:

Price per share (dollars)	Commission as a percentage of the total investment (percent)
10	1.70
25	1.26
40	0.975
50	0.88
75	0.62
100	0.49
150	0.36

There were rate changes in 1953 and in 1958. See [4, pp. 323–332].

[2]Graham, Dodd, and Cottle [3, pp. 79–82] give a convenient summary of the Securities and Exchange Commission (SEC) reporting requirements, including the requirements for interim reports.

be evident only over relatively long periods of time due to induced lags in the flow of financial capital.

Third, although tax rates are markedly lower on long-term capital gains than on short-term gains or ordinary income, they are not negligible. The differential between rates applicable to short-term and long-term gains provides a powerful incentive for holding securities and other assets longer than six months. Many motives for accumulation, such as the bequest, retirement, and "rainy day" motives, lead to optimal holding periods of even greater duration and thus to further impediments to the free flow of financial capital among investments with different rates of return, differences which may be perceived only dimly.

There is evidence that investors in common stock tend to hold their investments for relatively long periods of time. Lengthy holding periods cannot, by themselves, be evidence of market imperfections, because rates of return could be equilibrated in the absence of any transactions whatsoever and only one transaction in any period of observation would be sufficient for an outside observer to determine that this was the case. However, long holding periods do suggest that investors recognize the imperfections in their knowledge and various transactions costs and tax considerations which do, in fact, prevent equilibration of *ex post* rates of return. Furthermore, an *ex post* rate of return may be calculated only on the assumption that a share is held for a given period of time and then sold; in other words, the rates of return, differences among which this study seeks to explain, can be calculated only for specified holding periods. While it is of considerable interest to examine differences among rates of return on the same security held for different periods of time, some notion of the actual holding periods on average is clearly relevant.

Good information on holding periods is difficult to come by; however, rather imperfect estimates of the holding periods for investments in corporate stock may be obtained from the stratified random sample of 1962 returns showing transactions in such stock in that year [6, pp. 112–113].[3]

Table 1 shows the mean and median holding periods in months as computed from information presented in a special report of the Internal Revenue Service for 1962 tax returns.[4] When such allowance as is possible is made for the peculiarities of 1962, the findings reported suggest that a holding period of five years or more on the average is not an unreasonable estimate of the time

---

[3] I am indebted to Vito Natrella for calling these data to my attention.

[4] It is greatly to be regretted that 1962 is the only year for which the information on holding periods for corporate stock which is available from individual income tax returns has been tabulated. A single observation on such an important magnitude would in itself be cause for concern, but even more to the point is the distinctly atypical nature of 1962. The reader may recall that May 28–31, 1962, was a period of sharply declining prices and heavy volume. Prices had risen substantially over the preceding months and did not recover from the decline until well over a year later. So reminiscent of 1929 were the events of May, 1962, and so great was the evidence of panic among the substantial number of small investors drawn into the market by the preceding boom, that public concern set in motion the now famous *Special Study of the Securities Markets* by the Securities and Exchange Commission [16]. Chapter 13 of the special study report gives a detailed description and analysis of the market break, the events leading up to it, and the following months. That there was considerable "panic" selling in 1962 is suggested both by the large number of securities sold in that year held less

TABLE 1

Mean and median holding periods by adjusted-gross-income-reported class

Adjusted-gross-income-reported Class	Mean[a]	Median[b]
	months	months
All returns	61.9	15
Taxable returns under $10,000	40.7	10
Taxable returns $10,000 to $49,999	50.6	12
Taxable returns $50,000 to $99,999	74.7	20
Taxable returns $100,000 or more	130.7	67
Nontaxable returns	43.9	10

Source: Based on [6, pp. 112–113, table 12].
[a] *Computed as a weighted average of midpoints of closed holding-period ranges, treating "short-term, period not reported" as six months and aggregating "20 years or more" and "long-term, period not reported" and treating both together as 30 years.*
[b] *Treating "short-term, period not reported" and "long-term, period not reported" as aobve.*

period over which it is relevant to calculate rates of return. Median holding periods in 1962 were, to be sure, considerably shorter than this, but a great deal of stock was held for periods much longer and one might expect the median to be rather severely affected by the peculiarities of the year. In any case, the stability of our findings with respect to variations in the holding period is examined in detail below.

III. RATES OF RETURN

The data used in this study were taken from Standard and Poor's "Compustat" tape.[5] This tape provides data on stock prices, dividends, and important income statement and balance sheet items for a very large number of companies from 1946 to the present date.[6] Our tape contained some data on 899 industrial

---

than one month and by the heavy losses sustained by taxpayers of all income classes but the highest in that year on sales of securities held less than 3 to 5 years. (See table 12 [6, pp. 112-113].) Those with incomes over $100,000 in 1962 lost very little and then only on sales of securities held for six months or less. Since heavy losses reduce income, there is, to be sure, some difficulty in the interpretation of the income classes, which are based on the adjusted gross income reported on the return. It is clear that holding periods are probably substantially understated by the 1962 data for all income classes. Furthermore, the lower income groups contain a higher proportion of those who would be in the upper groups in a more normal year (or in 1962 had they refrained from selling). What is not so clear is to what extent the data are affected and what other abnormalities arise from the peculiarity of the single observation available.

[5] Supplied to Yale University by Standard Statistics Company, Inc., New York, solely for educational and research purposes. I am indebted to Mr. Peter Maggi, Assistant Manager for "Compustat" for helpful assistance at a crucial point in our use of the tape.

[6] The March, 1966 update tape has been used exclusively in this study. Since many items are not available for 1965 on this update, we have chosen 1964 as our terminal date. 1950 was our initial date for the bulk of our investigations for a variety of reasons explained in the text.

corporations but sufficient information for our purposes was not available for all 899 firms in all years since 1946. Consequently, our study was restricted to a smaller number of companies and fewer years than the total.

Because of the substantial unavailability of data for many companies in the early years covered by the "Compustat" tape, it was decided to begin the analysis with the year 1950. In addition, we felt that the period 1946–1949 was one of rather severe disequilibrium due to the readjustment of the market to the disruptions of the second world war. The period ends with the year 1964 only because the tape that has been used, although updated early in 1966, contains many missing items in 1965.

Differences between the data on the tape and those available in company reports and financial records, or derivable therefrom, frequently occur because one of the important aims of "Compustat" is to achieve as much comparability among companies as possible given the restrictive accounting framework adopted. Thus adjustments and recombinations are frequent. Furthermore, some material is taken from the Securities and Exchange Commission and other outside sources which is not available in corporation records. Some important modifications are as follows:

The number of shares outstanding is stated after subtracting treasury stock (not always the case in corporation records when stock is held for a profit sharing fund), and is adjusted for all stock splits and dividends (usually adjustment is made in corporation records only for stock dividends of more than 10 per cent). Prices per share and cash dividends per share are adjusted for all stock splits and dividends occurring during the year in question.

Net income figures in "Compustat" are before nonrecurring income and expense items which are net of applicable income taxes. Company treatment of such items varies greatly.

In case of a merger, reported data are used for years prior to the merger for the surviving company in general. Pooled data are used in the year in which the merger occurred. However, in the event a merger is extremely far-reaching and changes radically the size and character of the surviving company, no data are reported prior to the year of the merger.

The treatment of mergers has, perhaps, the most important implications for our results. Merger activity in the United States economy during the postwar period has been very great and is considered by some to have been one of the most important aspects of the growth of large firms.[7] By deleting firms with a past history of important merger activity which has substantially altered the characters of the firms in question, we have removed some of the most important observations related to determinants of relative rates of return among investments in alternative common equities. It is likely that average rates of return are lowered. In addition the effects of various measures of growth upon relative rates of return may be reduced, since many of the firms deleted from the sample will have been among the most rapidly expanding. Despite this fact, one of the findings reported below, namely, the importance of the rate growth of net sales, suggests that some of what has been noted by other observers is reflected in our truncated sample.

Rates of return were calculated for each firm for various time periods

7Penrose [15, pp. 153–196]; Nelson [13].

according to the following scheme: Let d_{it} be the dividends per share paid by the ith firm in the tth year and let P_{it} be the "price." The meaning of this last quantity is ambiguous and, indeed, two alternative measures have been examined in many of the analyses. In one case I have used closing and in the other, an arithmetic average of the high and low prices during the year in question. Some evidence that latter may be a good measure of the "average price during the year" is provided by Marris and Singh [9]. [8]The analyses provide some additional evidence that it is also a better measure in the sense of leading to more readily interpretable statistical results. Whichever concept is used, however, the rate of return for firm i over period of years 0, 1, . . ., T is computed as that rate of discount which will equate the discounted value of the flow of dividends during the period and the price at the end of the period to the initial price. That is r_i for the period 0, 1, . . ., T is defined as the root of the polynomial

$$P_{i0} - \sum_{t=0}^{T-1} \frac{d_{it}}{(1+r)^{t+1}} - \frac{P_{iT} + d_{iT}}{(1+r)^{T+1}} = 0$$

closest to zero. Two other rates of return were also calculated, but the results were either rather close to r_i calculated as above, or rather implausible: The two alternatives tried were: (1) The rate of return is calculated as that rate of discount which equates the discounted value of the total holding at the end of the period to the beginning-of-period price per share assuming that all dividends are reinvested. And (2), the rate of return is that rate of discount which equates the beginning of period price per share to the discounted value of the stream of dividends plus capital gains each year (positive or negative) to the end-of-period holding (assumed by this method to equal the beginning-of-period price per share).[9] Method (1) is equivalent to finding the geometric average of the one-period rates of return for the overall period of interest and has recently been recommended for various reasons by Arditti [1]. Our calculations suggest, however, that it is nearly the same as the rate used in our study in most cases. In a few cases, however, it was wildly different due to the apparently greater sensitivity of the reinvested-dividend rate to fluctuations in security prices.[10] Method

---

[8] "Average price during the year" is placed in quotes because, although we can know the price at very short intervals of time, we cannot, in fact, know how many shares are exchanged at each price. Marris and Singh actually average once-a-month closing prices for comparison with average annual highs and lows.

[9] Formulae for these two rates of return are as follows:

$$\rho_i \text{reinv} = \left[\left(1 + \frac{d_{i0}}{P_{i1}}\right) \left(1 + \frac{d_{i1}}{P_{i2}}\right) \cdots \left(1 + \frac{d_{iT-1}}{P_{iT}}\right) \left(\frac{P_{iT} + d_{iT}}{P_{i0}}\right) \right]^{\frac{1}{T+1}} - 1,$$

and $\rho_i$const. inv. the root closet to zero of the polynomial

$$\rho_{i0} - \sum_{t=0}^{T-1} \frac{(d_{it} + p_{it+1} - p_{it})(p_{i0}/p_{it})}{(1+r)^{t+1}} - \frac{(p_{iT} + d_{iT})(p_{i0}/p_{iT})}{(1+r)^{T+1}} = 0$$

[10] Michael Gort has suggested reinvesting dividends, not in the stock under consideration, but at an "average" rate for all securities listed on the NYSE, to the end of the holding period under consideration. Such average rates have been computed by Lawrence Fisher of the University of Chicago. Such a procedure might certainly be expected to eliminate the problem of extreme outliers, whether it might also reduce the strong positive association between rates of return and earnings retention reported below, as Gort suggests, is an issue which can only be decided by further investigation.

(2) produced results very similar to the method finally adopted, but does not have much theoretical justification.

Dividends per share, used in the calculation, represents all dividends paid during the year, adjusted for all stock splits and stock dividends that occurred during that year excluding payments in preferred stock and the value of spin-offs. The prices, high, low, and close, represent the absolute high, low and close transactions during the year for companies on national stock exchanges and bid prices for companies whose stock is traded over the counter. Prices are adjusted for all stock splits and dividends during the calendar year in question except for companies reporting on a fiscal year basis which have declared stock splits or dividends of stock between the end of the fiscal year and the end of the calendar year. Such splits are included in the adjustment to the subsequent year's price quotations. Inasmuch as companies reporting on a fiscal year and those reporting on a calendar year basis are not distinguished, we have been unable to ascertain the importance or effect of this difference in treatment in the "Compustat" figures.

Some idea of the extent of variation in rates of return may be obtained from Table 2, which reports mean rates of return and coefficients of variation for such rates for samples of firms over various periods. Rates of return have been calculated as that rate of discount which equates the discounted value of the end-of-period price and the flow of dividends within a period to the beginning-of-period price. Both average high-low prices in beginning and ending years and closing prices were used in these calculations. It can be seen that the dispersion of rates of return is quite substantial ranging from a low coefficient of variation of roughly 40 per cent of a mean rate for 456 firms for the full 15-year period to a coefficient of more than one for those same firms for the recent period 1960–1964 and still more if all firms are considered for which data for that period are available. The evidence suggests that dispersion among rates has been increasing at the same time as the average level has been falling.

TABLE 2

Means and coefficients of variation of rates of return calculated using either closing or average high and low prices in each year, various periods and various numbers of firms

Period	Number of firms	Based on average of high and low prices in each year		Based on closing prices in each year	
		Mean (percent)	Coefficient of variation	Mean (percent)	Coefficient of variation
1950–54	456	14.7	0.63	14.1	0.63
1955–59	456	12.6	0.76	13.3	0.88
1960–64	456	7.7	1.28	9.2	1.13
1950–64	456	13.8	0.40	12.8	0.42
1055–59	571	13.9	0.81	13.4	0.94
1960–64	717	7.7	1.46	8.9	1.35

A number of the analyses carried out used rates of return computed on the basis of both average and closing prices as the dependent variable to be explained. Results obtained for regressions using a rate of return computed on the basis of average prices were not greatly different from those using a rate of return based on closing prices, but, where differences occurred, the former results were more plausible theoretically. Hence, all of the analyses reported in this paper use a rate of return computed on the basis of average prices.

IV. EXPLANATORY VARIABLES

As anyone who has attempted extensive empirical analysis in economics will testify, it is rare indeed that one's initial formulations prove to be satisfactory, either theoretically or empirically. Nonetheless, the insights of earlier analyses provide the basis for further work. It would be less than honest, if I did not now confess that my initial formulations differed from the formulations reported below. Eleven explanatory variables, as well as certain dummy variables based on the Standard and Poor industry classification, were used in various combinations in regressions designed to explain differences among rates of return for various time periods. Of these eleven, five were dropped or modified and replaced by a number of other variables. A second list of sixteen explanatory variables and a substantially revised industry classification resulted from the preliminary analyses. This list, in turn, was shortened. Full details and a "blow-by-blow" description of the investigation are reported in [14] upon which this article is based. Here I report only a small number of the final statistical analyses and descriptions of the explanatory variables used in those analyses. Reference, however, is made to certain of the earlier results where appropriate.

The explanatory variables used in the analyses reported here were as follows:

1) *Rate of Growth of Net Sales:* The value of this variable was computed for each firm by taking the regression of net sales on a simple linear trend for the period under consideration and dividing the slope of time in the regression by mean net sales for the period in question. Two consecutive missing observations during any five-year period were sufficient to remove a firm from our sample; fewer missing observations, however, were interpolated from adjacent values. The sales variable on the "Compustat" tape represents gross sales and other operating revenues less discounts, returns, and allowances.

Rapidly growing firms, particularly those growing by expansion into new markets or different lines of activity, are more likely to be in a disequilibrium position vis-a-vis the capital market, than are firms with a less rapid growth. Thus, one might expect higher rates of return, *ceteris paribus,* on investments in such companies due to slow adjustments in the supply of capital to such firms. This assumes, of course, that on the whole rapid expansion ultimately proves profitable and, indeed, more profitable than slower expansion either because of the nature of the management of the firms undertaking it or because of the nature of their business, and further that such increased profitability is not offset by increased risk due to rapid growth, or at least not entirely so. A highly significant positive coefficient for this variable could be taken as evidence of considerable imperfections in the operation of the market.

2) Rate of Growth of Earnings Available for Common: The value of this variable was computed in a similar fashion to the rate of growth of net sales above. Earnings available for common represent net income less preferred dividend requirements, which are typically the same as preferred dividends declared. Net income equals operating income less depreciation and amortization less fixed charges less income taxes less net nonrecurring expense; operating income represents net sales less cost of sales and operating expenses before deducting depreciation, etc.[11]

If one were to take the popular financial press at face value, the role of earnings and growth of earnings in the determination of equity values would assume paramount importance. However, we are here attempting to explain, not equity prices, but rather rates of return. To the extent that earnings growth is correctly anticipated, prices will tend to be adjusted accordingly, and rates of return should be affected little or not at all. Past earnings growth might be used by investors to project future growth; if such projections overestimate actual growth, and future prices are based upon current earnings, then this variable might be expected to show a negative association, *ceteris paribus,* with *ex post* rates of return. On the other hand, if such projections tend to understate actual growth under similar circumstances, we would expect this variable to show a positive association, *ceteris paribus,* with rates of return. Additionally, earnings, or better cash flow, provide the primary source of investment funds for many firms which finance expansion and replacement (often involving technical change) largely through internally generated funds, either by choice or necessity. Thus, a positive association of this variable with rates of return may suggest only imperfections in the supply of capital to the firms in our sample. To some extent this effect of earnings may be mitigated by including variables reflecting the rate of growth and level of cash flow. The importance of earnings as a source of internal financing might then be minimized.

Despite the seemingly greater relevance of cash flow, when either the rate of growth of cash flow or mean cash flow per dollar of total assets (or per dollar of gross plant) or both variables are incorporated in regressions explaining the rate of return, the effects of these variables appear either statistically insignificant or highly erratic with respect to variations in the period of analysis.[12]

---

[11] While these items retain their usual accounting significance on the "Compustat" tape, several points are worth mentioning: Depreciation and amortization includes depletion allowances and, for oil and gas companies, dry holes, retirements, abandonments, and other intangible drilling costs. For airlines amortization of deferred costs is included. Income taxes, tax carry-backs and tax carry-forwards are netted against current taxes. Prior years' tax adjustments are included. Net income is stated before appropriations for general contingencies; such appropriations are treated as adjustments to surplus.

[12] When both the rate of growth of earnings and the rate of growth of cash flow are included in regressions explaining differences among rates of return over the fifteen-year period, 1950–1964, and three five-year subperiods, 1950–1954, 1955–1959, and 1960–1964, the coefficient of the rate of growth of earnings is consistently positive and significant in each of the three five-year subperiods but, surprisingly, fails to emerge as significant in the full-period regressions. On the other hand, the rate of growth of cash flow, the coefficient of which behaves quite erratically in the five-year subperiods, emerges as highly significant in the overall period. Since the simple correlation between the rate of growth of cash flow and the rate of growth of earnings is only 0.28 for the period 1950–1964 and even smaller for shorter periods, this result cannot be due to a high degree of collinearity between the two. In the regressions reported here, the rate

3) *Mean Retained Earnings Per Dollar of Total Assets:* Retained earnings are computed for each year and each firm by deducting common dividends from earnings available for common. The variable used in the analyses was the arithmetic mean value over the period in question. Again, up to two consecutive missing observations for firms retained in the sample were essentially ignored, the mean being computed from the available figures. Common dividends include dividends declared in the stock of other corporations, including spinoffs, and dividends in preferred stock, but exclude common stock dividends and subsidiary dividends. Thus this figure, on a per share basis, differs from the dividend figure used to compute the rate of return by including dividends in preferred stock and spin-offs, etc.

Total assets represents current assets plus net plant plus other noncurrent assets (including intangible assets and deferred items). Current assets are cash and other assets which, in the next twelve months, are expected to be realized in cash or used up in the production of revenue. Gross plant represents tangible fixed property (generally at cost) such as land, buildings, and equipment. Net plant represents gross plant minus accumulated reserves for depreciation, amortization, etc. Intangibles are excluded from net plant, but included in total assets.

The desirability of treating retained earnings and dividends as separate variables rather than examining total earnings and the payout ratio is discussed below. Deflation by total assets is a device to avoid attributing differences in rates of return to simple differences in the size of the earnings figure. For the group of firms included in this study, size alone should have no effect on the rate of return. This hypothesis will be tested in subsequent investigations. The effects of variation in the payout ratio may be ascertained by comparing the coefficient of retained earnings with that of dividends.

Earnings retained given an indication, not so much of the possibilities for internal investment, but of their realization. It is a widely held view that a dollar of retained earnings is of less economic value to the stockholders than a dollar of dividends.[13] This view has been persuasively questioned by Modigliani and Miller, [10] and [11], who argue that under certain conditions the retention rate is irrelevant. It is doubtful, however, whether such conditions as it is necessary to assume would characterize the world from which our sample of firms comes, nor indeed is it likely that Modigliani and Miller would deny this.[14] Both the view and the question as to its validity under idealized circumstances

---

of growth of cash flow is not used as an explanatory variable; the coefficient of the rates of growth of earnings is consistently positive and significant when the same five-year subperiods and the overall period are examined. Slight changes, however, in the period considered produce rather large changes in the size and significance of the coefficient of this variable. Some of these difficulties may be due, however, to the inclusion of one rather unusual firm in the sample of 456 upon which the initial regressions were based. This firm was not included in the sample of 371 firms used in the regressions reported here due to lack of data on certain variables appearing in these regressions.

[13] See, for example, Graham, Dodd, and Cottle [3, p. 486]. Their famous dictum that a dollar of dividends "is worth" about four dollars of retained earnings is a related matter. However, it should be noted that the dictum has to do with the effect on market price, not the rate of return.

[14] See Lintner [7].

refer, not to rates of return, but to stock prices. Even if a high payout ratio results in higher security prices than a low payout ratio, it does not follow that the stock of a firm which retains only a small fraction of its earnings will show a higher rate of return than the stock of a firm retaining a higher proportion. To the extent that the firm can earn a higher rate of return on internal investment than the stockholder can, retention should confer positive benefits to the stockholder, which, however, may be expected to be reflected equally in the current and future prices in relation to the dividend stream so that the relative rates of return on investments in low-payout vs. high-payout securities should be affected only by tax considerations and the fact that a dollar of dividends now is more certain than a capital gain later. Since capital gains are less highly taxed than dividends for the majority of investors, we might expect high retention, to the extent that it is in fact associated with capital gains, to result in *lower* before tax rates of return. On the other hand, the greater uncertainty of capital gains works in the opposite direction.

4) *Mean Dividends Per Dollar of Total Assets:* Dividends paid on common stock were divided by total assets and averaged in the same manner as retained earnings.

In a world in which internal rates of return to investment are insufficently appreciated outside of the firm and in which retained earnings are the main source of finance, it might be expected that on balance high rates of retention would be associated with high rates of return. However, to arrive at a firm conclusion on this point, the association of retained earnings, *ceteris paribus,* should be compared with the effect of dividends, or at least with total earnings.

The desirability of treating retained earnings and dividends separately rather than the payout ratio and earnings or dividends, arises from the fact that earnings can well be negative or zero; thus, the payout ratio could be negative or undefined. Avoidance of such situations, especially when dealing with a mass of data, is a desideratum of the first order.

The results reported below confirm the exceptional importance of retained earnings and the relative unimportance of dividends in the determination of relative rates of return. The coefficient of retained earnings per dollar of total assets is more than eight times as large as the coefficient of dividends.

5) *Mean Reciprocal of Leverage:* Because common equity might conceivably be negative as well as positive and thus, on occasion, zero, it was decided not to attempt to use leverage as ordinarily defined, but rather its reciprocal. Thus the total of long-term debt, preferred stock, and common equity was divided into equity for each firm and year. The results were arithmetically averaged over the period under consideration. Common equity represents common stock at par plus surplus plus surplus reserves less unamortized debt revenues plus deferred income taxes plus capital stock premium less treasury stock less intangibles less unamortized debt discount and expense less capital stock expense less accumulated unpaid preferred dividends. Preferred stock represents the net number of shares outstanding at year-end times the involuntary liquidating value per share. Unpaid accumulated dividends are included. Long-term debt represents debt obligations due after one year.

Since this variable is the reciprocal of leverage rather than leverage itself we would expect it to have a negative association, *ceteris paribus,* with the rate of return since greater leverage entails greater risk. Indeed, for relatively long periods leverage does have the expected positive association with the rate of return. However, for shorter periods the association appears to be insignificant.

6) *Mean Inventory Turnover:* The ratio of cost of goods sold to inventories was averaged arithmetically over the period under consideration. Inventories represent merchandise bought for resale and materials and supplies purchased for use in the production of revenue. Specifically excluded are supplies and pre-paid expenses for companies that lump these items together. (The effect of this noncomparability is unknown.) Cost of goods sold includes all costs directly allocated by the company to production such as material labor, direct overhead, etc. Specifically excluded are depreciation and amortization.

This variable may reflect industry differences and/or price effects in certain periods, in which case the direction of influence upon the rate of return is indeterminate in short periods and it is probably negligible over a long period, or it may reflect differences in risk. Since a high turnover might be expected to be associated with less risk, we expect a negative association between turnover and rate of return on this account. The results presented below show, however, that whatever independent effect inventory turnover has is probably swamped by its association with industry differences in *ex post* rates of return.

7) *Mean Share Turnover:* This variable was the mean ratio of the number of common shares traded during a year of the period under consideration to the number of common shares outstanding at year-end (excluding treasury shares). Both of these variables were adjusted, in the manner described previously in connection with the calculation of rates of return, for all stock splits and stock dividends.

The purpose of this variable was to reflect in some way the marketability or "liquidity" of an investment in the stock in question.[15] The variable chosen for this purpose was share turnover. Among other things, this variable gives some measure of the market and, hence, of the liquidity of a stock. The greater the share turnover, the less the rate of return we should expect to observe. On the

---

[15] Originally, an attempt was made to get at this same thing through a variable based on prices. For each year and each firm we took the difference between the high and low price during each year and divided it by the average of the two. The resulting figures were then averaged arithmetically over the years during the period under consideration. The idea is simply that if a stock fluctuates a great deal in price about a fixed or even rising level, it is illiquid in the sense that an investor who needs to sell his securities at a certain point in time may find their prices temporarily low. To be sure, in a more perfectly functioning capital market, he could always borrow using his shares as collateral, but it is unrealistic to assume that such options will be open to the majority of investors. Hence, we might expect stocks with highly fluctuating prices to show above average rates of return.

The problem is that there is another reason to expect a positive association between the variable we have chosen to measure price variability, namely, the arithmetic mean of high-low differences as a fraction of their average for each year of the period in question. Over relatively short periods of time, much of the return that we measure is in fact due to capital gains or losses. Firms, on whose stock there are such gains or losses, will typically show large differences between the high and low prices for one or more years and, in short periods, these differences dominate the mean. Since high-low is always positive, these considerations would lead us to expect a positive association in short periods dominated by capital gains, a negative association in short periods dominated by capital losses, and little or no association in long periods where neither large gains or losses during a year in the period are likely to dominate.

In analyses not reported here, the coefficient of this variable behaved erratically,

other hand, to the extent that a speculative nature and a high turnover are found together share turnover and rate of return will tend to be positively associated. The net effect may be slight and/or variable from period to period. Over short periods the positive association may perhaps dominate, but over longer periods, the negative association is more likely to prevail. Although the evidence is weak, our results support this expectation to a mild degree. It is likely that turnover reflects largely visibility, institutional interest, and similar factors, in addition to the "thickness" or "thinness" of the market. The inconclusive results obtained with this variable may thus be due simply to the large number of different effects encompassed.

8) *Mean Gross Plant Per Dollar of Total Assets:* Gross plant divided by total assets was averaged in the manner described above. Theoretically, it is supposed to measure the "fixity" of assets. It may also differentiate among industries. To the extent the former effect is dominant, we should expect a positive association between this variable and the rate of return. To the extent the industry effect dominates, it is not clear in which direction the association will run. As noted earlier, the coefficient of this variable is not only significantly *negative,* but introduction of industry dummies does not affect the result, so that it becomes difficult to argue that the variable really differentiates "heavy" industries, which have grown slowly, from others, such as electronics, which have grown fast.

9) *Industry Dummies:* In addition to the above, twenty-one dummy variables, representing twenty-one industry groupings were also introduced into a few of the regressions. The industry groupings were obtained by a careful examination of the descriptions of the 371 compaines contained in *Moody's Industrials,* 1965. Generally speaking, an attempt was made to group firms by the nature of their final products rather than by the nature of the productive process used. The resulting groups did not correspond closely to the industry grouping on the "Compustat" tape; in addition, about 10 per cent of the 371 firms examined to be misclassified by Standard and Poor even according to their own grouping criteria. Quite a number of firms produced products in a considerable diversity of lines; when the descriptions in *Moody's Industrials* suggested that a significant portion of the products produced fell outside the main industry group into which the firm had been classified, the firm was designated as "significantly conglomerate." Anoter dummy variable was introduced to reflect this distinction. Finally, in those instances when Moody's descriptions were too vague to make a proper classification of the firm, it was noted as "possibly misclassified." A final dummy variable was introduced to reflect this designation.

The twenty-one industry groupings of the 371 firms and the names of the firms included in each are given in the appendix.

Ideally, one would like to explain differences among rates of return solely by means of objectively measurable variables, preferably derivable from balance sheet or income statement items. Unfortunately, the world is not so simple that it can be adequately summarized within the traditional accounting framework.

---

changing sign between the period 1955–1959 and 1960–1964 (on both occasions highly significant), and was positive in the period 1950–1954 (significant when no industry dummies are included and insignificant when they were). It is interesting to note that this variable was never significant for the explanation of 15-year rates of return (as anticipated), and it did not in fact make a great deal of difference if it was omitted from the regressions.

Industry groupings may play a key role in summarizing a multitude of other factors not captured by the accounts. The significance of the industry dummies in the analyses reported below strongly suggests that this is the case.

10) *Other Variables:* In addition to the variables described above and used in the analyses reported here, a number of other variables were tried either in combination with some of those referred to above or in place of them. Here, we mention these briefly:

Rate of growth of cash flow and mean cash flow per dollar of gross plant were tried with no success.[16]

Mean sales per dollar of net plant or per dollar of long-term debt plus preferred stock plus common equity was introduced, without success, in an attempt to get at industry differences.[16]

Rates of growth of total and net assets were also tried (but not simultaneously) as explanatory variables in regressions explaining rates of return. These variables were never used in the same analysis together, the correlation between the two being quite high in all periods considered.[17]

The reason for considering variables such as these is that growth of assets, rather than of sales or earnings, is treated as the central variable in Marris's theory of the firm [8, p. 119].[18] Although it is by no means clear, it is plausible that growth of assets represents, in effect, the *realization* of investment opportunities, while growth of sales and to a lesser extent earnings represents the

---

[16] These variables have composite effects. They reflect the extent to which the capital of a firm is short-or long-lived. Short life is associated with less risk and thus lower rates of return. On the other hand, since cash flow provides the funds for internal gross investment, then, in a world in which investors do not fully appreciate the high profitability of such investments, a large cash flow, as suggested above, should tend to be associated with high rates of return. Alternatively, short-and long-lived plant differences may simply be associated with industry differences. To the extent this effect dominates, the *ceteris paribus* relation between cash flow and rate of return may vary from period-to-period.

[17] For example,

1950–51:	0.92
1955–59:	0.92
1960–64:	0.85
1950–64:	0.95

[18] Marris does emphasize, however, that in the long run, his concept of "balanced" or "sustainable" growth requires growth in sales at an equal rate. In this connection, it is interesting to note that not only are the mean rates of growth of sales and of assets quite different over some periods for our sample of 371 firms, but the simple correlations are lower than one might have expected. The correlations between the rate of growth of net sales and that of total assets and of net assets are as follows:

Period	Total asset	Net assets
1950–54	.68	.51
1955–59	.78	.68
1960–64	.69	.56
1950–64	.87	.78

Only in the full fifteen-year period do the simple correlations approach anticipated levels. When asset growth is included with sales growth in explaining rates of return in the analyses reported below, little additional explanatory power is obtained. In the long period, however, the asset growth variable appears to rob the sales growth variable of its significance.

presence of partially *unrealized* investment opportunities to the firm. Consequently, one might expect rates of return, particularly insofar as returns are largely the result of capital gains, to be affected more by sales growth and earnings growth than by growth of assets. This expectation is borne out to some extent by results presented in [14]. While it turned out that over the long-term (15–year period), growth was significant and sales growth was not when the two were included together, there was further evidence that replacement of sales by asset growth was in part an industry effect. In any event, sales growth is the preferred variable since it works well in both long and short periods.

In addition to introducing retained earnings and dividends deflated by total assets, these variables were also tried in slightly different form,—deflated by net common equity. This proved to be a mistake. The results showed greater instability over time, and the coefficient of the reciprocal of leverage became quite implausible as well as highly unstable.

An unsuccessful attempt was made to test a standard hypothesis in the security analysis literature by including either the "current" or the "quick" ratio.[19] The former is the ratio of current assets to current liabilities; the latter is the ratio of cash plus receivables to current liabilities. According to the hypothesis, a high value for either of these two ratios is indicative of low risk. Consequently, given general risk aversion, the rate of return might be expected to be somewhat lower for firms with high current or quick ratios. To the extent that capital is rationed to most firms, those with great internal investment opportunities, unperceived by those outside the firms in question, will tend to have relatively low ratios of current assets (including or excluding inventories) to current liabilities sinces, holding cash and other relatively liquid assets will tend to be costly for such firms in terms of foregone opportunities. Hence, low quick or current ratios should tend to be associated with high rates of return. Unfortunately, the hypothesis is not particularly well supported in analyses reported in [14].[20] Nonetheless, further investigation appears called for because of the partial evidence for the hypothesis.

V. STATISTICAL RESULTS

Table 3 presents the squared multiple correlation coefficient, the coefficients of the eight independent variables described above, and the ratios of those coefficients to their standard errors, i.e., the so-called *t*-ratios. The regressions re-

[19] See Graham, Dodd, and Cottle [3, p. 219].

[20] Neither the current nor the quick ratio proves to be significant except in the period 1960–1964 when both have a significant and unexpected positive coefficient. When industry dummies are introduced the current ratio has the expected negative sign in 1950–1954 and 1955–1959 but is never significant except in the 1960–1964 period, when again it is positive and highly significant. Thus, it is not likely that the unexpected result is due to industry effects. Nor does there appear to be any peculiarity in the simple correlations among these two variables and other independent variables in the period 1960–1964 as compared with other periods. The positive association appears in the simple correlation with the rate of return in this period as contrasted with other periods. One may perhaps conjecture that very conservatively managed companies held up somewhat better during this period during which the market experienced one of its sharpest breaks in history. To establish this hypothesis as more than mere conjecture, however, would require extensive further investigation.

ported are based on data for a sample of 371 firms, the names of which are given in the appendix. For so many degrees of freedom, the t-ratio is approximately normally distributed on the usual assumptions made concerning the disturbance in the regression equation. The point at which the area under the standard normal density exceeds 95 per cent is approximately 1.65; t-ratios in excess of this figure, positive or negative, have been marked with an asterisk.

Sales growth proves to be a highly significant variable in all subperiods as well as the overall period, despite the inclusion of the earnings growth variable.[21] The size of the coefficient, however, varies substantially in absolute terms, being more than twice as large in the period 1960–1964 than in 1950–1954. Over long periods one might expect the past growth rates of sales and earnings both to have a lesser bearing on realized rates of return because imperfections in the capital market are of lesser effect in the long run. Earnings growth is highly

TABLE 3

Regression results. Coefficients, t-ratios, R^2. 1950–1964 and five-year subperiods. 371 firms

R^2 and independent variable	Period			
	1950–1954	1955–1959	1960–1964	1950–1964
R^2	0.425	0.515	0.280	0.493
1. Rate of growth of sales	0.196	0.336	0.469	0.157
	3.54*	6.56*	6.33*	2.74*
2. Rate of growth earnings	0.076	0.032	0.015	0.0094
	4.28*	3.26*	3.20*	2.64*
3. Retained earnings per dollar of total assets	2.105	2.075	1.253	2.022
	10.20*	10.20*	5.06*	12.26*
4. Dividends per dollar of total assets	0.278	0.240	0.226	0.225
	1.72*	1.18	1.03	1.95*
5. Reciprocal of leverage	–0.046	–0.020	–0.061	–0.066
	2.05*	0.75	1.90*	3.98*
6. Inventory turnover	–0.0017	–0.00056	0.0024	–0.0003
	4.08*	1.25	2.85*	0.96
7. Share turnover	0.044	0.138	–0.021	0.0035
	2.13 *	6.38*	0.85	0.25
8. Gross plant per dollar of total assets	0.010	–0.060	–0.0034	–0.028
	0.90	4.92*	0.24	4.14*
9. Constant	0.076	0.064	0.052	0.130
	4.03*	2.72*	1.82*	9.06*

Source: Regression results for 371 firms (see appendix).
* The point at which the area under the standard normal density exceeds 95 per cent is approximately 1.65; t-ratios in excess of this figure, positive or negative, are marked with asteristks.

[21] When the rate of growth of total assets is included in the regression, the rate of growth of sales becomes insignificant in the 15-year period, but retains its significance in the shorter five-year subperiods. This result perhaps gives some support to the Marris treatment of asset growth as a central variable (see footnote 18 above). Given a more-or-less constant capital-output ratio, sales and asset growth should, of course, exactly match over the long run although substantial short-run deviations may occur. Since typical holding periods appear to be shorter than fifteen years and since the sales variable works as well as the asset variable when the latter is excluded, it seems simplest to use that explanatory variable which works well in both long and short periods.

significant throughout, although its influence or rate or return falls in later periods as compared with earlier ones and in the full 15–year period as compared with the five-year subperiods.

Both the significance and decline in the size of these coefficients as the period of analysis is lengthened is further documented below.

Retained earnings per dollar of total assets is clearly the most significant variable in the explanation of relative rates of return except in the period 1960–1964 when sales growth assumes a more important role. Note that the coefficient of this variable is close to two in all periods, both short and long, except 1960–1964. This means that an increase of one percentage point in the retention of earnings as a percentage of total assets results in a two-percentage point increase in the rate of return on average. Since the rate of return averages about 12 per cent and earnings retention as a percentage of total assets about 3 per cent, this result implies an elasticity of one-half. A more detailed examination of the behavior of this coefficient is attempted below; while the stability of the coefficient is not as great as these results might suggest, it is considerably more stable than a number of other coefficients and always of great significance in the explanation of relative rates of return.

The effect of retained earnings contrast sharply with that of dividends.[22] The coefficient of divdends is only about one-eighth of the coefficient of retained earnings and it assumes statistical significance at conventional levels of significance only in the long period, 1950–1964, and in the period 1950–1954.

The unimportance of dividends over short periods as contrasted with retained earnings and their moderate importance over long periods is consistent with the hypothesis that considerable opportunities for internal investment exist in many firms that are only gradually perceived by those outside the firm. Thus, a firm with such opportunities may retain a substantial portion of its earnings, and will be able to realize even greater future earnings some of which will eventually be reflected in higher dividends. Only gradually will market price reflect these profitable reinvestments of earnings; thus, substantial capital gains may be realized by investments in the common stock of such firms. Over long periods dividends of such firms will play a more important role in determining the observed rate of return and may well be larger per dollar of assets than for firms with lesser opportunity for profitable internal investment and consequent lesser retention of earnings.

Leverage has the expected positive association with the rate of return for all subperiods of the full fifteen-year period. Furthermore, the effect of leverage is moderately stable and significant in all but the period 1955–1959. This finding persists when industry dummies are introduced and when a more detailed examination over time is made.

The coefficient of inventory turnover is highly variable. It is statistically

---

[22] This finding strongly rejects the well-known security analysts' rule that a dollar of dividends is "worth" about four dollars of retained earnings (Graham, Dodd, and Cottle [3, pp. 486–487]). Note, however, this principle is enunciated on the basis of findings referring to the prices of common stocks at a point in time rather than to rates of return over time. The Modigliani-Miller result is also not supported by this evidence; however, the reader should bear in mind that the tentative explanation of the results presented here involves a direct contradiction to one of the key assumptions of the Modigliani-Miller argument.

significant in two subperiods, 1950–1954 and 1960–1964, but not in the overall period or in 1955–1959. There is some evidence, which is not very convincing, that these results are due to industry effects. Earlier results suggest that a small number of firms with extreme inventory turnover values may be responsible for the changes in the signs, sizes, and significance of the observed coefficients.

Share turnover proves to be an even more disappointing variable. If the "liquidity" effect predominates, the variable should be negatively assoicated with the rate of return, yet it is positively associated in 1950–1954 and 1955–1959 and significantly so. This finding is not consistently maintained, however, in regressions containing different combinations of variables or industry dummies. Furthermore, detailed analysis of the behavior of this coefficient for periods of different length reveals exceptionally erratic behavior. It is likely that share turnover represents largely some measure of what might be called "speculative interest," special visibility, and the like, in addition to the "size" of the market. As such, there is no reason for any particular association with the rate of return and every reason to suspect that the particular results obtained may be due to a small number of outliers.[23]

Gross plant per dollar of total assets reveals a significant negative association with the rate of return in the two regressions, 1955–1959 and 1950–1964. Introduction of industry dummies strengthens this finding and in one instance makes the variable highly significant in most periods. Detailed examination of the behavior of the coefficient of this variable for periods of varying length reveals similar behavior and considerable stability once the length of the period exceeds six years. Nor can the behavior of this coefficient be explained by the high correlation of gross plant per dollar of total assets with some other variable. While "heavy" industries tend to grow slowly and require little management, the industry dummies should have accounted for this effort. The matter must therefore be left to subsequent investigation.

As indicated above, one of the major purposes of the present investigation was to discover whether a meaningful industry classification of rates of return could be constructed. It appears this purpose has been fulfilled. The twenty-one groups into which the 371 firms have been classified are listed in the appendix. The same regressions as described in Table 4 were run including the twenty-one industry dummies plus two additional variables designed to reflect a significantly conglomerate nature and/or the possibility of industry misclassification. These are reported in Table 4.

The substantial increase in the R^2's (we have 371 degrees of freedom to start with) indicates the great significance of the industry dummies.[24] In addition, the t-ratios for many of the dummies are extremely large, so that one may say that the dummies are not only highly significant as a group, but many are individually significant. However, the attempts to allow for significant conglomeration and/or possible misclassification were less successful; these variables were individually insignificant.[25] This was to be expected, given the highly subjective nature of these detrminations.

---

[23] Detailed examination of the 371 firms might be expected to reveal whether this was the case, but such an examination has not yet been made.

[24] F-test statistics may easily be computed, but are obviously unnecessary.

[25] No test was made to see if they were collectively significant.

The main conclusions of our previous analyses are not altered by the inclusion of industry dummies. Sales and earnings growth remain quite significant. Retained earnings per dollar of total assets is now clearly the more significant explanatory variable, including industry classification, in every period. Leverage is uniformly positively associated with the rate of return and significantly so in the periods 1950–1954 and 1950–1954. The effects of share and inventory turnover are still mixed. Gross plant per dollar of total assets has a uniformly negative association with the rate of return and is significant in three out of the four periods considered, strongly so in 1950–1964.

TABLE 4 Regression results. Industry dummies included. Coefficients, t-ratios, R^2. 1950–1964 and five-year subperiods. 371 firms

R^2 and independent variable	Period			
	1950–1954	1955–1959	1960–1964	1950–1954
R^2	.518	.587	.431	.581
1. Rate of growth of sales	.166	.357	.389	.166
	2.71*	6.65*	5.27*	2.81*
2. Rate of growth of earnings	.079	.032	.012	.0082
	4.44*	3.33*	2.65*	2.36*
3. Retained earnings per dollar of total assets	2.027	1.966	1.405	1.876
	9.15*	9.35*	5.78*	10.96*
4. Dividends per dollar of total assets	.180	.253	.305	.251
	1.11	1.24	1.43	2.21*
5. Reciprocal of leverage	−.055	−.021	−.032	−.077
	2.35*	.76	.71	4.71*
6. Inventory turnover	−.0001	.0010	−.0004	−.0002
	.15	1.66*	.34	.50
7. Share turnover	.0061	.143	−.0048	−.027
	.28	6.16*	.19	1.84*
8. Gross plant per dollar of total assets	−.011	−.044	−.029	−.042
	.77	2.81*	1.69*	4.84*
Industry dummies (constant terms)				
9. Sugar and confectionery, food processing and retailing, beverages, soap and detergents	.08605	.04159	.07167	.1445
	4.02*	1.64	2.42*	9.49*
10. Tobacco	.05426	.06975	.07448	.1368
	2.17*	2.36*	2.17*	8.05*
11. Nonferrous mining, metal and fabrication	.1410	.01913	.04921	.1609
	5.24*	.64	1.46	9.16*
12. Coal	.09117	.09750	.06511	.1791
	2.09*	2.05*	1.21	6.67*
13. Textiles, shoes, apparel, synthetic fibers, home furnishings, retail apparel	.08035	.01617	.07622	.1317
	3.22*	.58	2.35*	7.94*
14. Lumber, paper, containers, publishing	.1132	.03923	.06313	.1634
	4.71*	1.40	1.99*	9.80*
15. Chemicals, sulphur, potash, fertilizers	.1003	.02704	.05149	.1456
	3.93*	.91	1.51	8.38*
16. Drugs	.04295	.1088	−.01196	.1349

TABLE 4   (CONTINUED)

R² and independent variable	Period			
	1950–1954	1955–1959	1960–1964	1950–1964
	1.55	3.31*	.31	7.07*
17. Oil, oil field equipment	.1202	.02725	.1253	.1737
	3.87*	.81	3.32*	8.81*
18. Building materials, heating,	.1013	.01726	.03560	.1539
air-conditioning, plumbing	3.56*	.54	.99	8.29*
19. Steel and blast furnaces	.1264	.08314	.02731	.1784
	4.61*	2.65*	.78	9.98*
20. Agricultural, construction	.1247	.04488	.02863	.1563
and materials handling	4.40*	1.40	.77	8.50*
machinery				
21. Machine tools	.1224	.04606	.06058	.1750
	4.37*	1.47	1.70*	9.46*
22. Office and business equipment,	.1106	.05350	−.01719	.1569
electronic and electrical	4.10*	1.84*	.52	8.80*
equipment and controls				
23. Autos, trucks and components,	.1366	.05398	.04800	.1733
tires and rubber	5.37*	1.84*	1.43	10.06*
24. Aerospace and aircraft	.1281	.02238	−.003406	.2000
	3.84*	.64	.09	9.77*
25. Railroad equipment, ship	.1300	.04877	.05580	.1978
building	3.82*	1.30	1.32	9.15*
26. Air transport	.001941	−.08702	.2329	.1566
	.04	2.11*	5.16*	5.95*
27. Retail-general	.07947	.04454	.08933	.1474
	3.14*	1.55	2.70*	8.69*
28. Miscellaneous-manufacturing	.1350	.04417	.01057	.1632
	5.05*	1.47	.31	9.15*
29. Miscellaneous-other	.1777	.05288	.03337	.2071
	5.01*	1.37	.74	9.21*
30. Significantly conglomerate	−.005277	.01373	−.01100	−.004007
	.65	1.59	1.12	.85
	−.01375	.01408	.005907	.000627
31. Possibly misclassified	1.18	1.15	.42	.09

Source: Regression results of 371 firms (see appendix).
* *The point at which the area under the standard normal density exceeds 95 per cent is approximately 1.65; t-ratios in excess of this figure, positive or negative, are marked with asterisks.*

As a final test of these conclusions, the stability of the sign, significance and size of the coefficients of the final set of variables selected is examined as the period of the analysis is increased, in steps of one period, from three to fifteen years. Note that all analyses are essentially cross-sectional but that the periods over which rates of return, rates of growth, and mean values of certain variables are computed vary. The object of the regressions reported in Table 5 was to examine the behavior of the regression coefficients as this period was steadily increased. Three years was considered to be the minimal period for which meaningful results could be obtained. Part I of Table 5 reports regressions not including industry dummies; Part II reports results when such dum-mies are included as well as the two additional dummy variables described above.

Sales growth and earnings retention per dollar of total assets are positively associated with the rate of return and highly significant, irrespective of industry dummies. The coefficient of sales growth rises to a peak at a period of six years and then declines, more or less steadily as the period of analysis is lengthened. The coefficient of retained earnings behaves more erratically but generally shows a rising tendency as the period of analysis is lengthened.

The rate of growth of earnings has a highly erratic coefficient, albeit one which is always positive and is significant in only three periods when no industry dummies are included and five when they are, These results suggest that one may substanitally discount the importance of earnings growth in the determination of relative rates of return.

Dividends per dollar of total assets fare somewhat better than earnins–growth on these criteria. The coefficient of this variable shows a roughly rising trend with increasing length of period and increasing statistical significance. The results are even better when industry dummies are included. Thus one may accept the hypothesis that dividends are important to the determination of relative rates of return over fairly long periods of time, although not over short periods and very much less important than retained earnings.

Leverage too has a more or less steadily increasing effect on the rate of return which becomes increasingly significant. It appears that this variable like dividends exerts its effects largely over moderate or long periods of time. In the case of dividends it is intuitively clear why this should be so since dividends play a greater role in the total returns on an investment in longer than in shorter periods. It is less clear why leverage should be more important over long periods than short but the effect is none the less quite marked.

Inventory turnover appears to be important in the regressions reported in Table 5 only when industry dummies are excluded. Share turnover has an erratic and generally insignificant effect.

The behavior of the coefficient of gross plant per dollar of total assets is more regular and interesting. This coefficient falls rather steadily with increasing period until a period of 13 years at which point it begins to rise slightly. The significance of the coefficients follows an opposite pattern, increasing steadily until a period of 13 years then dropping off slightly. As indicated above, it has not been possible to account for the regular behavior of this coefficient or, especially, for its sign which is negative in all regressions based on periods of more than three or four years.

VI. A FINAL CAVEAT

The principal conclusions of this investigation are summarized in section I. Here, I consider briefly the question which must ultimately occur to any mo-derately intelligent reader of a study dealing with the stock market. If the conclusions of this study are valid, why has the author published the results instead of using them to make money? The answer, I think, must be that the

TABLE 5

Regression results: Coefficients, t-ratios, R^2, various periods three to fifteen years. Industry dummies excluded and included

	Period												
	1962–1964	1961–1964	1960–1964	1959–1964	1958–1964	1957–1964	1956–1964	1955–1964	1954–1964	1953–1964	1952–1954	1951–1964	1950–1964
					I. Industry dummies excluded								
R^2	0.274	0.236	0.280	0.348	0.399	0.435	0.448	0.479	0.480	0.483	0.503	0.512	0.493
1. Rate of growth of sales	.273	.397	.469	.509	.487	.454	.484	.389	.330	.218	.170	.161	.159
	4.72*	5.74*	6.33*	7.26*	7.25*	6.48*	7.55*	6.61*	5.64*	3.69*	3.09*	2.97*	2.74*
2. Rate of growth of earnings	.0021	.0096	.0149	.0022	.0011	.0067	.0068	.0018	.0034	.0163	.0121	.0019	.0094
	0.94	1.58	3.20*	0.75	0.50	0.89	1.40	0.39	1.59	2.42*	1.55	0.87	.264*
3. Retained earnings per $ of total assets	1.684	1.183	1.253	1.278	1.567	1.618	1.270	1.553	1.755	2.034	2.024	2.061	2.020
	6.43*	4.51*	5.06*	5.88*	7.47*	7.56*	6.38*	8.90*	10.28*	11.80*	12.55	13.00	12.26*
4. Dividends per $ of total assets	.210	.0948	.226	.256	.217	.225	.358	.373	.284	.282	.249	.296	.226
	0.88	0.41	1.03	1.33	1.20	1.24	2.15*	2.56*	2.02*	2.04*	2.01*	.53*	1.95*
5. Reciprocal of leverage	-.0476	-.0217	-.0610	-.0445	-.0605	-.0568	-.0374	-.0520	-.0600	-.0746	-.0730	-.0696	-.0637
	1.24	0.61	1.90*	1.61	2.38*	2.23*	1.61	2.55*	3.07*	3.87*	4.23	4.22*	3.98*
6. Inventory turnover	.0033	.0037	.0024	.0014	.00137	.0072	.00116	.00041	.00016	.00041	.00034	.00012	-.00030
	2.91*	3.74*	2.85*	1.98*	2.31	3.06*	2.33*	1.00	0.42	1.07	1.01	0.39	.096
7. Share turnover	.0686	.0023	-.0214	-.0495	-.0189	.0104	.00481	-.00064	.00540	.00540	-.00777	-.0103	.00347
	2.62*	0.087	0.85	2.34*	0.96	0.51	0.25	0.038	0.34	0.34	0.53	0.74	0.25
8. Gross plant per $ of total assets	.0582	.0283	-.0034	-.0318	-.0490	-.0682	-.0706	-.0569	-.0498	-.0458	-.0514	-.0432	-0.283
	3.47*	1.83*	0.24	2.66*	4.42 *	6.24*	7.08*	6.55*	6.01*	5.65*	7.12	6.30*	5.15
9. Constant	-.0039	-.0319	.0521	.0560	.1087	.1206	.0949	.1017	.1266	.1466	.1457	1.291	.1300
	0.12	1.02	1.82*	2.28*	4.79*	5.38	4.64*	5.65*	7.30*	8.58*	9.52*	8.93*	9.06*

II. Industry dummies included

	1962–1964	1961–1964	1960–1964	1959–1964	1958–1964	1957–1964	1956–1964	1955–1964	1954–1964	1953–1964	1952–1954	1951–1964	1950–1964
R^2	.442	.400	.431	.455	.476	.520	.524	.529	.523	.541	.574	.595	.581
1. Rate of growth of sales	.230	.316	.389	.432	.419	.371	.406	.365	.347	.233	.172	.168	.166
	4.13*	4.62*	5.27*	5.94*	5.93*	5.07*	5.93*	5.60*	5.42*	3.67*	2.97*	3.00*	2.81*
2. Rate of growth of earnings	.0018	.0058	.0116	.0027	.0018	.0079	.0079	.0023	.0032	.0168	.0129	.0011	.0082
	.91	1.00	2.65*	.94	.84	1.02	1.67*	.50	1.48	2.54*	1.70*	.55	2.36*
3. Retained earnings per $ of total assets	1.543	1.256	1.405	1.440	1.760	1.878	1.426	1.598	1.734	1.908	1.989	1.983	1.876
	6.18*	4.93*	5.78*	6.55*	8.11*	8.48*	6.84*	8.52*	9.34*	10.35*	11.64*	11.94*	10.96
4. Dividends per $ of total assets	.180	.154	.305	.319	.314	.325	.428	.459	.359	.329	.330	.374	.251
	.79	.68	1.43	1.66*	1.71*	1.80*	2.56*	3.05*	2.45*	2.32*	2.65*	3.22*	2.21*
5. Reciprocal of leverage	–.00018	.0110	–.0232	–.0119	–.0401	–.0365	–.0254	–.0519	–.0618	–.0761	–.0773	–.0793	–.0774
	.00	.31	.71	.41	1.49	1.40	1.06	2.43*	3.00*	3.82*	4.42*	4.83*	4.71*
6. Inventory turnover	.00024	.00088	–.00036	–.0012	–.00057	.00020	.00019	.00014	.00012	–.00013	–.000061	.000080	–.00022
	1.8	.70	.34	1.38	.75	.28	.30	.25	.22	.24	.13	.18	.50
7. Share turnover	.0230	–.0104	–.0048	–.0287	–.0050	.0427	.0347	.0187	–.0074	–.0161	–.0221	–.0294	–.0268
	.88	.40	.19	1.30	.24	2.00*	1.70*	1.02	.42	.92	1.40	1.98*	1.84*
8. Gross plant per $ of total assets	.0069	–.0049	–.0293	–.0357	–.0440	–.0516	–.0553	–.0549	–.0542	–.0565	–.0551	–.0463	–.0422
	.34	.26	1.69	2.35*	3.06*	3.69*	4.30*	4.80*	4.90*	5.30*	5.89*	5.29*	4.84*
9. Sugar and confectionery, food processing and retailing, beverages (inc. alcoholic), soap and detergents	.0184	–.0167	.0717	.0674	.106	.115	.0939	.103	.124	.154	.153	.136	.145
	.54	.52	2.43*	2.59*	4.31*	4.84*	4.30*	5.24*	6.48*	8.32*	9.36*	8.89*	9.49*
10. Tobacco	–.0177	–.0280	.0745	.0661	.102	.125	.115	.122	.142	.156	.149	.141	.137
	.44	.74	2.17*	2.20*	3.61*	4.53*	4.58*	5.45*	6.54*	7.49*	8.12*	8.23*	8.05*

	1962–1964	1961–1964	1960–1964	1959–1964	1958–1964	1957–1964	1956–1964	1955–1964	1954–1964	1953–1964	1952–1954	1951–1964	1950–1964
11. Nonferrous mining metal and fabrication	.0581 / 1.47	.0048 / .13	.0492 / 1.46	.0208 / .70	.0667 / 2.38*	.0496 / 1.83*	.0253 / 1.01	.0638 / 2.84*	.114 / 5.24*	.155 / 7.35*	.141 / 7.54*	.130 / 7.39*	.161 / 9.16*
12. Coal	–.0136 / .21	–.0295 / .49	.0651 / 1.21	.0634 / 1.34	.0982 / 2.21*	.0776 / 1.79*	.0828 / 2.09*	.147 / 4.16*	.183 / 5.38*	.201 / 6.15*	.178 / 6.19*	.167 / 6.19*	.179 / 6.67*
13. Textiles, shoes, apparel, synthetic fibers, home furnishings, retail apparel	.0483 / 1.29	.0275 / .78	.0762 / 2.35*	.0657 / 2.30*	.129 / 4.79*	.121 / 4.65*	.0855 / 3.56*	.0910 / 4.23*	.120 / 5.76*	.142 / 7.04*	.141 / 7.84*	.124 / 7.39*	.132 / 7.94*
14. Lumber, paper containers, publishing	.0402 / 1.10	.00016 / .00	.0631 / 1.99*	.0415 / 1.48	.0846 / 3.20*	.0881 / 3.42*	.0665 / 2.81*	.0899 / 4.22*	.124 / 5.96*	.174 / 8.63*	.167 / 9.34*	.151 / 9.00*	.163 / 9.80*
15. Chemicals, sulphur, potash, fertilizers	.0566 / 1.43	–.0094 / .25	.0515 / 1.51	.0346 / 1.15	.0849 / 2.99*	.0772 / 2.81*	.0577 / 2.28*	.0828 / 3.66*	.112 / 5.12*	.146 / 6.91*	.134 / 7.18*	.122 / 7.00*	.146 / 8.38*
16. Drugs	–.0360 / .81	–.0807 / 1.93*	–.0120 / .31	–.0015 / .05	.0488 / 1.54	.0725 / 2.36*	.0881 / 3.12*	.108 / 4.31*	.130 / 5.38*	.155 / 6.66*	.132 / 6.42*	.113 / 5.87*	.135 / 7.07*
17. Oil, oilfield equipment	.0873 / 1.99*	.0536 / 1.29	.125 / 3.32*	.0783 / 2.35*	.0992 / 3.15*	.0776 / 2.54*	.0729 / 2.59*	.111 / 4.40*	.136 / 5.57*	.169 / 7.12*	.151 / 7.16*	.146 / 7.36*	.174 / 8.81*
18. Building materials, heating, air conditioning, plumbing	.0214 / .51	–.0344 / .87	.0356 / .99	.0275 / .87	.0772 / 2.59*	.0755 / 2.61*	.0529 / 1.99*	.0788 / 3.30*	.120 / 5.17*	.163 / 7.29*	.152 / 7.61*	.143 / 7.16*	.154 / 8.29*
19. Steel and blast furnaces	.0327 / .79	–.0322 / .83	.0273 / .78	.0104 / .34	.0816 / 2.81*	.0769 / 2.73*	.0634 / 2.45*	.103 / 4.45*	.154 / 6.85*	.193 / 8.91*	.177 / 9.29*	.155 / 8.68*	.178 / 9.98*
20. Agricultural, construction and materials handling machinery	.0602 / 1.37	–.0080 / .19	.0286 / .77	–.00049 / .02	.0603 / 1.98*	.0453 / 1.54	.0265 / .98	.0773 / 3.21*	.119 / 5.08*	.151 / 6.71*	.136 / 6.88*	.138 / 7.46*	.156 / 8.50*

	1962–1964	1961–1964	1960–1964	1959–1964	1958–1964	1957–1964	1956–1964	1955–1964	1954–1964	1953–1964	1952–1954	1951–1964	1950–1964
21. Machine tools	.0435	.0058	.0606	.0219	.0818	.0592	.0506	.0954	.128	.173	.170	.159	.175
	1.05	.15	1.70*	.70	2.76*	2.06*	1.91*	4.02*	5.52*	7.75*	8.62*	8.58*	9.46*
22. Office and business equipment, electronics, electrical equipment and controls	−.0204	−.0723	−.0172	−.0048	.0595	.0607	.0566	.0762	.112	.156	.151	.144	.157
	.54	2.02*	.52	.17	2.15*	2.26*	2.28*	3.41*	5.13*	7.38*	8.00*	8.11*	8.80*
23. Autos and trucks and components, tires and rubber	.0637	.0238	.0480	.0347	.105	.0969	.0789	.0990	.134	.168	.162	.157	.173
	1.62	.64	1.43	1.17	3.73*	3.57*	3.16*	4.42*	6.15*	8.04*	8.78*	9.04*	10.06*
24. Aerospace and aircraft	−.0300	−.0707	−.0034	.0094	.0681	.0501	.0448	.0795	.131	.198	.185	.182	.200
	.69	1.72*	.09	.28	2.16*	1.62	1.57	3.08*	5.16*	8.12*	8.51*	8.86*	9.77*
25. Railroad equipment, shipbuilding	.0201	−.0291	.0558	.0525	.106	.0961	.0779	.112	.158	.202	.197	.189	.198
	.40	.62	1.32	1.41	3.00*	2.82*	2.49*	4.00*	5.82*	7.75*	8.54*	8.72*	9.15*
26. Air transport	.329	.214	.233	.164	.195	.146	.0986	.100	.130	.199	.167	.135	.157
	6.32*	4.24*	5.16*	4.18*	5.23*	4.03*	2.95*	3.21*	4.08*	6.49*	6.10*	5.18*	5.95*
27. Retail-general	.0318	.0091	.0893	.0863	.138	.136	.101	.110	.139	.170	.160	.138	.147
	.83	.25	2.70*	2.95*	5.01*	5.10*	4.09*	4.97*	6.47*	8.19*	8.74*	8.10*	8.69*
28. Miscellaneous-manufacturing	−.0024	−.0535	.0106	.0167	.0786	.0669	.0531	.0791	.113	.154	.154	.144	.163
	.06	1.42	.31	.55	2.76*	2.42*	2.08*	3.45*	5.06*	7.14*	8.06*	8.04*	9.15*
29. Miscellaneous-other	−.0014	−.0462	0.334	.0693	.123	.125	.0940	.0994	.144	.200	.213	.199	.207
	.03	.92	.74	1.77*	3.37*	3.53*	2.92*	3.46*	5.17*	7.37*	8.88*	8.84*	9.21*
30. Significantly conglomerate	−.0181	−.0130	−.0110	−.0071	−.0047	−.0032	−.0021	−.0012	−.000007	−.0037	−.0042	−.0035	−.0040
	1.54	1.19	1.11	.82	.58	.41	.29	.19	.00	.64	.82	.73	.84
31. Possibly misclassified	.0078	.0091	.0059	.0074	.0138	.0178	.0149	.0156	.0146	.0083	.0018	−.00060	.00063
	.46	.58	.42	.60	1.20	1.60	1.46	1.73*	1.69*	1.01	.25	.09	.09

Source: Regression results for 371 firms (see appendix).

* The point at which the area under the standard normal density exceeds 95 per cent is approximately 1.65; t-ratios in excess of this figure, positive or negative, are marked with asterisks.

conclusions of the present study suggest not how to choose investments wisely but rather why it is not possible to do so in general on the basis of information contained in the past balance sheets and profit and loss statements of corporations. An attempt has been made to show that a great part of the variability of *ex post* rates of return is due to disequilibrium in the capital market. Both suppliers of capital to the firm and investors in common stock share an imperfect and dim perception of the profitable opportunities for investment open to the firm. As these opportunities are realized by a management which recognizes them and through retention of earnings, their profitability is eventually perceived by the market. Thus one might say that the "special situation," at least in some long-run sense, dominates relative rates of return. Successful and wise investors have known this for years. Recent justifications of the "random walk" theory of stock prices are derived from the same source, and the emphasis many mutual funds and investment trusts currently place on "in-depth" analysis of the companies in which they invest lends additional support to these conclusions. The existence of relatively high *ex post* rates of return on some investments requires a great deal of ignorance on the part of a great many people and only a little ability to learn on the part of a few. Who can count himself among the perceptive few?

REFERENCES

1. ARDITTI, F. D., "Risk and the Required Return on Equity," *Journal of Finance,* 22 (March 1967) 19–36.
2. ECKSTEIN, O., "A Survey of the Theory of Public Expenditure Criteria, Reply," pp. 493–494 in Conference of the Universities-National Bureau Committee for Economic Research, *Public Finance: Needs, Sources, and Utilization* (Princeton: Princeton University Press, 1961).
3. GRAHAM, B., D. L. DODD, and S. COTTLE, *Security Analysis,* 4th ed. (New York: McGraw-Hill, 1962).
4. HAZARD, J. W., and M. CHRISTIE, *The Investment Business: A Condensation of the SEC Report* (New York: Harper and Row, 1964).
5. HIRSHLEIFER, J., "Efficient Allocation of Capital in an Uncertain World," *American Economic Review, Papers and Proceedings,* 54 (May 1964), 77–85.
6. Internal Revenue Service, Statistics Division, *Statistics of Income, 1962, Supplemental Report: Sales of Capital Assets Reported on Individual Income Tax Returns,* Publication No. 458 (Washington: U.S. Government Printing Office, 1966) 10–66.
7. LINTNER, J., "Dividends, Earnings, Leverage, Stock Prices and the Supply of Capital to Corporations," this REVIEW, 44 (Aug. 1962) 243–269.
8. MARRIS, R., *The Economic Theory of 'Managerial' Capitalism* (New York: The Free Press of Glencoe, 1964).
9. MARRIS, R., and A. SINGH, "A Measure of a Firm's Average Share Price," *Journal of the Royal Statistical Society,* Series A, 129: 74–97 (1966).
10. MODIGLIANI, F., and M. H. MILLER, "The Cost of Capital, Corporation Finance, and the Theory of Investment" *American Economic Review,* 48 (June 1958) 261–297.
11. MODIGLIANI, F., and M. H. MILLER, "Dividend Policy, Growth and the Valuation of Shares," *Journal of Business,* 34 (Oct. 1961) 411–433.
12. National Observer, *A Report in Depth on the Stock Market* (New York: Dow, Jones and Co., 1965).

13. NELSON, R. L., *Merger Movements in American Industry, 1895–1956* (Princeton: Princeton University Press, 1959).
14. NERLOVE, M., "Preliminary Results on Factors Affecting Differences Among Rates of Return on Investments in Individual Common Stocks," *Discussion Paper No. 23, Harvard Institute of Economic Research* (Apr. 1968).
15. PENROSE E. T., *The Theory of the Growth of the Firm* (New York: John Wiley and Sons, 1959).
16. Report of the Special Study of the Securities Markets of the Securities and Exchange Commission, 88th Congress, 1st Session, House Document No. 95, 1963.
17. SMITH, A., *An Inquiry into the Nature and Causes of the Wealth of Nations,* Modern Library Edition (New York: Random House, 1937).
18. STIGLER, G. J., *Capital and Rates of Return in Manufacturing Industry* (Princeton: Princeton University Press, 1963).

Weil, Segall, and Green construct a theory of convertible bond prices. First, they define the premium at which a convertible bond sells as the difference between the market price of the bond and the market price of the stock into which it is convertible. Second, they relate this premium to differences in the cash flow and risk that would accrue to holders of the convertible bond versus holders of the stock. Of particular interest is the simplification of this theory to obtain a mathematical structure that is amenable to testing. The authors should be commended in explicitly describing rather than camouflaging this simplification.

13

Premiums on Convertible Bonds

Roman L. Weil, Jr., Joel E. Segall, David Green, Jr.*

This article is a modified version of the one which appeared in the Journal of Finance, *Vol. XXIII, No. 3 (June, 1968), pp. 445–464 and is reprinted with the permission of the* Journal of Finance.

Convertible bonds seldom sell at their conversion parity (i.e., the number of common shares into which the bond can be exchanged times the price per share), and the difference between the bond's market price and this conversion parity—usually labeled the premium—has been discussed in several recent papers.[1] None of these pretends an exhaustive listing of all possible determinants of the premium, nor do we. The premium should be the difference between the present values of the individual expected cash streams. Thus the concept of the premium seems simple and plaudsible; it is not, however, operational. To make it operational requires specification of the expected interest and dividend payments, duration of the bond including the likelihood of call, the likelihood and extent of dilution of the conversion option, appropriate discount rates, the value of the option, and the configurations over time of all these variables.

* We thank Lester Lave, Eugene Fama, Lawrence Fisher, Richard Roll, David Duvel, and Hodson Thornber for comments, and the Ford Foundation which, through its grant to the Graduate School of Business of The University of Chicago, supported this research. An earlier version was presented to the Seminar on the Analysis of Securities Prices of the Center for Research in Security Prices (sponsored by Merrill Lynch, Pierce, Fenner and Smith, Inc.), May 11, 1967 at the University of Chicago.

[1] E.g., Baumol, Malkiel, and Quandt [1966], Brigham [1966], and Poensgen [1965–66].

The concept turns out to be monstrously difficult to implement. It is not surprising that writers on convertible bonds take a less global view of the premiums and confine their work to rough proxy variables. This paper devotes Section I to a review and summary of the variables suggested by others. Section II describes the tests we have employed to examine these variables for their importance in determining premiums. Section III contains the meager conclusions reached and the Appendix suggests an analytical framework for further reasearch.

I. THE DETERMINANTS OF THE PREMIUM

As we interpret the literature, the premium may be explained by the following factors.

1. *Transaction Costs.* Broker's commissions are lower on bonds than on stocks. The commission for a bond is $2.50; to buy equivalent stock, the commission is likely to be at least $15 and may be as much as $75.[2] For example, if the bond is convertible into 100 shares of stock and has no premium, the investor who desires 100 shares of stock could save by buying the bond and converting it. The bond deserves a premium to reflect this saving.

2. *Income Differences.* The owner of a convertible bond (CB) is promised a specific interest stream and principal repayment, although he may expect something less than the promised stream. The owner of the equivalent stock is promised nothing but maintains some expectation about a dividend stream or increasing share prices. If the present value of expected bond income exceeds the present value of expected stock income, bonds should merit a premium on that account and vice versa. Negative premiums are, of course, limited by arbitrage possibilities which are discussed below.

3. *Financing Costs.* The Federal Reserve Board margin requirements currently permit borrowing of 30 per cent of the cost of a stock purchase while current banking practices allow borrowing of 70 to 90 per cent of the bond purchases. Kleine [1966] and Hershey [1966] argue that CBs deserve a premium for this additional borrowing capacity.

4. *Anti-dilution Clauses.* Kaplan [1965] points out that CBs do not have uniform anti-dilution clauses. Among the many ways in which the CB holder's interest may be diluted and his security cheapened are:

   a. the sale of common stock below market price,
   b. the payment of stock dividends (a particular form of (a) where the sale price is zero),
   c. the distribution of "capital" in the form of large dividends or partially liquidating dividends, and
   d. the issuance of options, rights, warrants, or other convertible securities.

---

[2] As the price of the stock rises, the commission paid to buy the stock rises (to a limit of $75 per hundred shares), but that paid to buy the bond remains a constant $2.50. The approximate transaction cost difference of buying a bond rather than the equivalent stock selling currently at prices of $10, $20, $30, $40, $50, or $100 can be estimated from Table 5 (constructed for another purpose) by subtracting $5.00 from the appropriate entry of the first row. The estimate obtained in this fashion will be exact only if the number of shares into which the bond is convertible is 100, i.e., a conversion price of $10.

To protect the bondholder, various anti-dilution clauses are usually provided. Kaplan reports a surprising variance in these provisions. All modern convertibles include provisions for stock splits and stock dividends above some small per centage, but the provisions for the more subtle forms of potential dilution vary greatly. Consequently, the premium should reflect the strength and coverage of the anti-dilution clause.

5. *Price Floors.* It is widely accepted that the CB has a safety feature which the equivalent stock does not have. The CB pays a relatively certain coupon and has a relatively certain value of $1000 at maturity. It has, therefore, a value as a bond which is in some measure independent of the value of the conversion feature. If the stock price falls, the bond price may also fall but only to a price somewhat above the prices of nonconvertible bonds of similar quality. This minimum price is regarded as the *floor* for the CB. Since there is no such floor for the stock, the CB warrants a premium. The floor is the more valuable the closer it is to the bond price. The premium, then, should be inversely related to the difference between the floor and the bond price.

6. *Volatility of Price.* It has been alleged that the larger the variance in the price movements of the stock, the more valuable will be the conversion option on the bond; and the more valuable the conversion option, the greater will be the premium on the bond.[3] Also, the more volatile the price of the stock, the more likely is the bond floor to be reached, and the more relevant the floor, the higher will be the premium.

7. *Duration.* In general, the longer the life of an option the more valuable it must be. Therefore, the premium should be positively associated with time to maturity or expected time to call or, perhaps, expected time to dilution.[4] Some bonds may be exchanged for successively fewer shares of stock over time according to a schedule set forth in the indenture. For such bonds, duration must incorporate changes in the exchange ratio.

These seven variables are alleged to be important in the determination of premiums on convertible bonds; preliminary investigation, intuition, and convenience have persuaded us to disregard or at least defer consideration of four of these.

Financing costs seem quantitatively unimportant. Changes in margin requirements appear to have little impact on stock prices even though changes in margin requirements are assoicated with marked changes in the volume of stock market credit.[5] Apparently, substitute credit sources are readily aviailable at small differences in cost. On statistical grounds, too, a financing cost variable is exceptionally difficult to interpret. Assume that a trader may borrow 30 per cent of a stock purchase and 80 per cent of a bond purchase. The gross financing cost difference (*FCD*) will be:

---

[3] Poensgen [1965–66] demonstrates that the value of the conversion option is an increasing function of the bond price variance. Poensgen's "value of the conversion option" is not identical with our premium, but his statement is the only one we can find in the scholarly literature.

[4] Brigham [1966] reports that 23 per cent of the firms in his sample follow a policy of encouraging conversion by increasing common stock dividends. We have described this policy earlier as dilution.

[5] See, e.g., Moore [1966].

$$FCD = B(.2I_p + .8I_m) - S(.7I_p + .3I_m) \tag{1}$$

where

B is the cost of the convertible bond,

S is the cost of the same amount of stock as can be obtained from converting the bond into stock,

I_p is the cost of capital of the individual trader or the rate of interest he charges himself for money, and

I_m is the interest rate the trader must pay his banker or broker to borrow.

Now define $\varDelta$ so that $I_p = I_m + \varDelta$; that is, $\varDelta$ is the difference between the two interest rates. We expect that $\varDelta$ is greater than zero for most individuals but the following analysis is independent of the sign of $\varDelta$. Substituting $I_m + \varDelta$ for I_p in (1) we obtain

$$FCD = I_m(B - S) + \varDelta (.2B - .7S)$$

or

$$FCD = (I_m + .2\varDelta)(B - S) - .5 \varDelta S. \tag{2}$$

At any time $(I_m + 2\varDelta)$ is approximately the same for all stock–bond pairs.[6] Observe that the coefficient of $(I_m + .2\varDelta)$ on the right-hand side of (2) is $B - S$, exactly the premium that we are concerned with. If $\varDelta$ were zero, the FCD would be exactly proportional to the premium we wish to predict or explain. Even as $\varDelta$ becomes different from zero, the FCD is by its definition almost proportional to the premium. In preliminary studies we found that as $\varDelta$ ranged from zero to .06, the simple correlation between FCD and the premium dropped only from 1. to. 85. Since such a large component of the financing cost difference is proportional to the premium itself, we cannot hope to infer the impact of holding costs on the premium. A different methodology or a different form of the variable might yield more reliable inferences about the sign of financing costs. We do not yet have a suitable methodology or form.

We believe that *anti-dilution* clauses are relatively unimportant in the determination of the premium. In a more formal analysis, the strength and coverage of these clauses would be incorporated in an expected income variable; indeed, some sources of dilution, e.g., stock dividends, are automatically captured in any sensible measure of income accruing to stockholders. Still, it could be helpful to quantify the existence of anti-dilution clauses. Unfortunately, such quantification is costly, inconvenient, and we have no notion of either the correct form of the variable or, given the form, what a reasonable coefficient might be. Accordingly, we do not treat anti-dilution clauses in this paper.

The standard analysis of *price volatility* seems faulty; if it is corect to regard a stock price as the present value of some expected cash stream, and if the market is not indifferent to price volatility, an allowance for that volatility is

---

[6] At least one New York brokerage firm, Garvin Bantel and Co., charges different rates of interest depending upon the security. In the quotations we have seen, the spread between the largest and smallest rates is only .0075.

incorporated in the stock price, presumably through the rate used to discount the cash stream. But if the bond price is influenced mainly by the stock price, then the bond price will also incorporate an allowance for volatility and there should be no additional premium on the bond. If the bond price is influenced mainly by the floor (i.e., the premium is very high), volatility can be very important since only a volatile stock will provide a large probability that the bond price will move above the floor. We conclude that for bonds whose prices are close to the floor, the more valuable bonds will be those whose underlying stocks are the more volatile. For such bonds, the premium will be positively associated with volatility. But bond prices can be well above the floor only because they reflect the value of the underlying stock. Such bond prices will already include the volatility allowance and we should expect no association between the premium and volatility. For reasons to be explained below, our sample consists only of bonds selling well above the floor and so volatility will not enter the analysis.

The possibility remains that volatility is important even for bonds selling well above the floor because volatility makes the floor more likely to be called into play. Preliminary tests involving a regression of the premium on the floor *and* a measure of volatility suggest that volatility is unimportant. Table 8 shows another preliminary test of the volatility notion. Data for the test are those reported in Table 2. For each of the 18 observation dates the premiums for the bonds in the sample data were ranked and for each bond in the data a measure of volatility of the underlying stock price was calculated. This measure is the coefficient of variation of stock price relatives over the last n months for n = 3, 6, 12, 24, 60, and as many months back to January 1, 1926 as are available.[7] These measures were ranked and the Spearman rank correlation coefficient computed for the two sets of ranks, one on premiums and the other on volatility. The coefficients are shown in the table for each of the six time periods and for bond premiums measured both in dollars and as a percentage of bond price. We conclude that we do not find a significant over-all relationship between volatility and premium and we do not further consider the volatility variable.[8]

The *duration* of the conversion privilege seems of great importance, but we find that we can do very little with specifying the empirical counterpart. Ideally, duration would be measured by the length of time traders of CBs expect the privilege to last. Although the privilege expires with maturity or call or other forced or encouraged conversion, maturity dates and call provisions provide little information. All bonds in our sample were callable and all matured at least six years after the relevant dates—a longer period than is generally contemplated

---

[7] The volatility index is constructed as in the following example for $n = 6$. Suppose the closing prices of the stock in the last six months were

100	120	80	100	75	100

Then the price relatives (price at time t divided by price at time $t-1$) are

6/5	2/3	5/4	3/4	4/3

The mean price relative is 1.04. The standard deviation of the stock price relative is about .277 and the coefficient of variation is about .277/1.04 or about .27.

[8] We recognize a danger in this treatment. Volatility could be important once the other relevant variables are taken into account. The simple rank correlations are sufficiently unimpressive, though, to suggest that the danger is more apparent than real.

for the investor's horizon.[9] There is some information on the conversion policies of issuing firms,[10] but nothing that would enable us to assign a duration value to each of the CBs. With regret, we abandon the duration variable.

We also have grave doubts as to the standard analysis of the price floor for the bonds, but preliminary tests do not allow us to dismiss that variable completely. Since the premium is expected to vary inversely with the difference between the bond floor and the bond price, and since the floor does not increase equally with the bond price, we should expect the premium to be inversely related to the bond price. Table 1 shows bonds from two dates, February 11 and November 13, 1963, ranked from lowest premium to highest premium. Also shon are the bond price and the rank of the bond price for these bonds. The rank-correlation coefficient is $-.60$; the size of the premium is significantly inversely correlated with the absolute bond price.

We have no similar doubts about the income and transaction cost differences; thus three variables are left with which we shall try to explain the premiums.

II. THE TESTED VARIABLES

THE DATA

The data of Table 2 were employed in our tests. These data include all New York Stock Exchange CBs that

a. are listed in the odd-numbered months, 1961–1963, in *Moody's Bond Survey,* "Convertible Bonds,"
b. have actual transaction prices rather than bid prices shown in the *Bond Survey,*
c. do not require additional cash payments to convert the bond,[11] and
d. have a conversion value (market value of the stock into which the bond is convertible) greater than par.

Summary figures concerning these data are shown in Table 3.

The last criterion, d, requires further explanation. Typically, publicly sold CBs are offered at about par, the conversion ratios set so that the conversion value is less than par value at time of issue, and the coupon rate is lower than the yield on nonconvertible debt issues of similar quality.[12] This set of circumstances implies a trade off between the ratio of conversion value to par and the ratio of nonconvertible yields to CB coupon rates. The actual ratios

---

[9] Cf. Baumol, Malkiel, and Quandt [1966].

[10] Cf. Brigham [1965].

[11] Bladen [1966] points out that securities such as the United Air Lines 4s of 1990, which require an additional cash payment to convert, provide the bondholder with an advantage in the form of an interest-free loan and a reduced likelihood of a margin call. This kind of convertible bond carries an additional premium, Bladen says, because of its added attractiveness and is, therefore, excluded from our sample. During the time from which our data are gathered, there were less than six such bonds.

[12] Cf. Brigham [1965].

TABLE 1

Array of bond premiums (in the nearest whole dollar) and bond prices (and ranks) for two selected dates in 1963

	Bond price decimals represent eighths	Rank of bond price	Bond premium Feb. 11	Bond premium Nov. 13
Macy	5–77	180.0	41	–59	
Int. T & T	4 (7/8–83	269.0	48		–26
Gardner Denver	4 (1/4–76	147.5	29		–23
Central Ill Lt	4 (1/4–74	144.0	25	–19	
Natl Airlines	6–76	248.2	47		–18
Cons Pwr	4 (3/8–75	169.5	35	–15	
Cons Pwr	4 (3/8–75	175.5	39		–15
Lock Air	3 (3/4–80	212.5	43		–11
Gen T & Elec	4–71	170.0	36		–6
Pan Am Air	4 (7/8–79	175.2	38		–6
Gen T & Elec	4 (1/2–77	175.0	37		–2
Scott Paper	3–71	146.0	27		–1
Intl Silver	5–81	145.7	26	9	
Balt G & E	4 (1/4–74	147.0	28	12	
Scott Paper	3–71	129.0	14	14	
Grace	3 1/2–75	165.0	34	15	
Am Opt	4.40–80	129.5	15		17
Natl Airlines	6–76	160.2	33	19	
Int T & T	4 (7/8–83	246.0	46	21	
Gen T & Elec	4 (1/2–79	159.0	32	23	
Int Dep Str	4 (5/8–81	179.0	40		24
Avco	5–79	211.2	42		26
Lock Air	3 (3/4–80	219.0	45	27	
Aldens	5–80	132.0	17	28	
Dow	3–82	140.1	23		32
U.S. Freight	5–81	143.0	24		36
Richfield Oil	4 (3/8–83	130.2	16		38
Gen T & Elec	4–71	156.5	31	38	
Northrop	5–79	127.5	12	48	
Sym Wayne	4 (3/4–82	117.0	4		51
Libby McN	5–76	115.0	2		52
Richfield Oil	4 (3/8–83	128.0	13	58	
Am T & T	4 (1/4–73	376.0	49	59	
Avco	5–79	213.5	44	59	
Intl Silver	5–81	135.0	21		71
Dow	3–82	132.5	18	71	
Int M & C	3.65–77	122.7	9		75
Northrop	5–79	123.4	10		91
U.S. Freight	5–81	134.7	20	93	
Hal Xerox	4 (1/2–81	156.0	30	113	
Am T & T	4 (1/4–73	412.0	50		119
Gt West Fnl	5–74	137.0	22	120	
Sym Wayne	4 (3/4–82	117.0	4	125	
Aldens	5–80	117.2	6		129
Nopco	4 (3/4–87	117.0	4	134	
Am Opt	4.40–80	123.5	11	145	
Int Dep Str	4 (5/8–81	120.0	8	150	
Metro Bdcast	6–75	134.0	19	155	
Union Oil	4 (1/4–91	117.6	7	172	
Ox Paper	4 (3/4–78	109.5	1		319

Spearman rank-correlation coefficient $= .60$

TABLE 2

Calculated bond premiums where stock price exceeds conversion price, bimonthly, 1961–1963

(for $1000 bonds)

		1961						1962						1963					
		1/9	3/13	5/8	7/10	9/11	11/13	1/8	3/12	5/14	7/9	9/10	11/12	1/3	3/11	5/13	7/8	9/9	11/11
Aldens	5-80	112	44	14	−3	73	−6	*	−18	−18	57	119	64	56	*	20	101		129
Am Dist	4 3/8-86	−	−				11/1ⁱ	157	*	86	127	125		130ⁱ	*	113	86	*	15
Am Op	4.40-80			203	55	132	136	60					−	2/21		107			
Ashland Oil	3 7/8-93								135	−	−	−	−						
Atl Ref	4 1/2-87	160	121	126	−38	137	120	135	*	−28	−7	−26	−10	37		−11	−35	*	*
Avco	5-79	96	5	46	*	3	56	*	*	−12	14	6	−22	4	*	*	−23	1	25
Balt G & BE	4 1/4-74	*	10	*	−23	−9	−27	−12	13						4	*			*
Boeing	4 1/2-80			195	155	335	368	149											
Bruns Corp	4 1/2-81	N	355	440	*														
Burroughs	4 1/2-81						208	208	166	152									
Chad Goth	5.90-71xw			29	*	41	60	*	35	−41	54	59							
Chad Goth	6-74xw			39	54	*	55	*	20	−71	*	*							
City Pdts.	5-82	−							200									*	
Comb Eng	3 3/8-81		6/14ⁱ	106	53	109	154												
Cons Electro	4 1/2-84	38	17	*	13	34	23	20	26	43	*	*	−44	−126	−39	4	44	63	32
Crow Coll	5-83	*	*	*	*	*	*	*	*	5	*	119	55	43	*	5/13ⁱ	149	64	107
Det Ed	3 3/4-71	14	*	*	*	*	*	*	*	43	*	*	−44	−126	−39	123	149	64	107
Dow	3-82	91	2	−1	−4	−24	−7	20	26	5	119	55	43		*	4	44	12	32
Fan Stl	4 3/4-76		19	*	*	232	77	*	*	93	119								
Food Fair	4-79					37	37	*	128	60									
Gardner Denver	4 1/4-76	*	32	*	−27	−47	*	*	*	77	*	25	*	*	*	−28	*	7	−23
Gen Am Oil	4 3/4-84									93	*	−20	3	N	*	N	N	N	N
Gen Am Tr	4-81	10	*	*	*	*	*	*	*	35	25	55	68	26	*	N	*	N	−6
Gen T & Elec	4-71	3	−26	36	93	93	174	*	35	−4	43	87	74	41	6	8	51	−11	−11
Gen T & Elec	4 1/2-77	19	−26	61	28	84	13	23	22	*	−3	11	−7	−8	6	22	57	−11	−2
Grace	3 1/2-75		81	14	23	−1	32	37	8								3	2	*
Grand Union	4 1/8-78		73	42	−18	32													
Gt West Fnl	5-74	47	5/8ⁱ	*	*	−74	−4	−58	*	−88								148	*
Hal Xerox	4 1/2-81			*	*	*	*	*	*	*	60	122	171	196	135	*	97		
Hunt Food	4 3/8-86	−	−	7/14	54	44	135	135	193	113	317	166	189	152	175	136	58	*	11/29ᶜ

TABLE 2 (CONTINUED)

	1961						1962						1963					
	1/9	3/13	5/8	7/10	9/11	11/13	1/8	3/12	5/14	7/9	9/10	11/12	1/3	3/11	5/13	7/8	9/9	11/11
Int Min & Chem 3. 65-77	—	—	—	7/3^i	—	260	235	121										
Int Silver 5-81	14	-16	57	-11	-40	16	-62	70	4	95	83	102	27	77	*	*	*	76
Int T & T 4 7/8-83								-34	-45	*	-63	142	-13	-15	*	*	-35	71
Int Dept Str 4 5/8-81		49	41	8/17^i	148	8	23	-10	-26	60	142	126	108	61	61	66	13	-26
Kayser Roth 5 1/2-80				3	39	18	42	43	-45	*	109	N	2/1^c					24
Libby McN 5-76								113			177		*			87	112	52
Lionel 5 1/2-80	56	204	192	*	-51	*	*											
Lock Air 3 3/4-80	*	13	*	-32	9	-38	7	11	-8	-24	*	4	-20	-12	-3	-3	5	-11
Macy 5-77	*	-7	*	*				-88	-23	*	-19	-26	*	-26	*	*	*	*
Metro Brd 6-75	—	*	*	*								160	*	-3			5	*
National Airlines 6-76	*	5/15^i	*	-5	-7	7	38	200	70		73			-8	-13	-13	-8	-18
Natl Tea 3 1/2-80		102	33	12	61	3	144	178	27	10	34	50	42	66			75	91
Northrop 4-75	71	-2		6/19^c														
Northrop 5-79		73																
Ox Paper 4 3/4-78													69		49		2	-1
Pan Am Air 4 7/8-79	-20	-45	*		-70	11/15^c												
Phillips 4 1/4-87	98	58	103	*	49	35	48	33	91	115	81	103	125		110		65	
Potomac El Pw 3 3/4-73	55	54	-3	21	23	53	55	48	79			76	30		51		3	
Richfield Pil 4 3/8-83		127	-38	-1	*	*	49	40	85	79	103	103	34	30		51	3	38
Rohr 5 1/4-77	-11	-39	-26	16	-4	-27	-30	-6	-9	32	57	70	61	3	-3	5	-11	18
Scott Paper 3-71									*								5	
Smith Corona 5/14-79									5/21^i			124	145					
Spiegel 5-84	5	-27	13	7	134	158	124	149		*	57	*	160	160	164	164	175	61
Sym Wayne 4 3/4-82									*			35	*	*		81	86	*
Talcott 5-79	8	203	-40	*	-25	*	*	-40										
Thom Ramo 4 7/8-82			6/10^i	62	172	203	168	186			165	165	115	115	64	64	*	-6
Union Oil 4 1/4-91	*	187	48			201	201	79	49	142	142	204	128	128	7/29^c	7/29^c		
United Airl 4 7/8-85		4/1^i		173	93	124	121	79	49	129	129	37	24	-1	12	12	4	36
U.S. Freight 5-81		280	285			335												
Vendo 4/12-80			179															

* No market transaction on observation date
i Issued   c Called   – Not outstanding

N Not on Moody's List
Blank space when stock price below conversion price
Sources: Moody's Bond Survey, "Convertible Bonds," various dates

TABLE 3

Average bond prices and premiums for the eighteen observation dates

Date	No. of bonds observed	Bond price	Premium In $	Premium As a % of bond price
1/9/61	18	1,488	39	3.0
3/13/61	29	1,531	66	5.0
5/8/61	27	1,520	69	5.0
7/10/61	28	1,494	36	2.9
9/11/61	30	1,579	46	3.6
11/13/61	33	1,565	77	5.9
1/8/62	30	1,485	76	6.0
3/12/62	35	1,477	74	5.9
5/14/62	28	1,416	25	2.3
7/9/62	16	1,332	61	4.8
9/10/62	20	1,424	64	5.0
11/12/62	23	1,476	66	4.9
1/3/63	25	1,527	60	4.8
3/11/63	16	1,603	62	4.4
5/13/63	27	1,567	47	3.7
7/8/63	23	1,500	54	4.3
9/9/63	22	1,570	35	2.9
11/11/63	22	1,579	31	2.5

are said to be determined in light of market preferences for the relatively certain interest income and the relatively less certain capital gain. The burden of this exposition is that the premiums on many CBs will be determined primarily by the terms of issue, most notably the issuer's choice of trade off between coupon rate and conversion value. If the market value rises above par, however, the analysis ceases to be valid; the premium will be less sensitive to the terms of issue and more sensitive to the intrinsic differences between the asset forms. We may put this issue differently: a cross-section of *all* CBs will include many CBs whose premiums differ mainly because of differences in issuing terms; if the cross-section includes only those CBs whose conversion value exceeds par, premiums will tend to be smaller and the impact of the happenstance of issue terms will be reduced; hence, criterion d.

Ideally, the data employed for this study should be derived from simultaneous bond and stock transactions. The prices shown in the *Bond Survey* closing prices and are not likely to be simultaneous. Table 4 shows the import of this problem. The premiums as calculated from the *Bond Survey* data of February 11, 1963 are shown next to premiums calculated in the following way: for each of the twenty bonds for which data are available we look at tranaction prices quoted in *The Wall Street Journal* for the 5 business days preceding February 11 and for the 5 business days following February 11; we pick the one day when the price range over which the stock traded is the smallest; we calculate the premium for the bond from the prices quoted on that day and call it the "Near Date" premium. "Near Date" premiums are less sensitive to the

TABLE 4

Comparison of the Feb. 11, 1963 calculated premiums with those calculated from the near date with minimum stock price fluctuation

	Premiums in dollars		Premiums as percent of closing bond price on	
	Near date	Feb.11	Near date	Feb.11
Balt G & E	−10	12	−.67	.82
Int T & T	6	21	.24	.85
Natl Airlines	8	19	.48	1.19
Scott Paper	14	14	1.09	1.09
Intl Silver	17	9	1.19	.62
Richfield Oil	46	58	3.61	4.53
Gen T & Elec 4 1/2s	47	23	3.01	1.45
Avco	49	59	2.25	2.76
Northrop	56	48	4.41	3.76
Gen T & Elec 4s	58	38	3.75	2.43
Dow	68	71	5.13	5.36
Aldens	75	28	5.60	2.12
U.S. Freight	85	93	6.25	6.90
Int Dep Str	98	150	8.28	12.50
Hal Xerox	120	113	7.50	7.24
Sym Wayne	120	125	10.43	10.68
Nopco	134	134	11.45	11.45
Union Oil	154	172	13.29	14.62
Metro Bdcast	165	155	12.22	11.57
Gt West Fnl	187	120	13.17	8.76
	1497	1462		
Rank correlation coefficient	.902		.925	

simultaneity problem and are more accurate estimates of the true premium, although the "Near Date" premiums are not necessarily calculated from transactions closer together in time. The differences in calculated premiums suggest the extent of the unreliability of our basic data. Since we have only a rough estimate of the "true" premiums we cannot expect a highly satisfactory statistical explanation.

Some negative premiums may be noted in Table 2. A negative premium implies the existence of an arbitrage possibility: the investor could buy the bond, sell short the underlying stock, and then convert the bond to stock in order to cover the short sale. The negative premiums in the data are anomalies reflecting either nonsimultaneous transactions or transaction costs too large to warrant the arbitrage operation. In Table 5 we show the transaction costs per bond, exclusive of transfer taxes, to effect the arbitrage operation. The numbers in this table show the magnitude of negative premiums which are not exploitable by the outside buyer. Floor traders, of course, pay no commissions and could be expected to exploit arbitrage opportunities that are unprofitable for the outside buyer. At least some of the negative premiums result from observation error.

TABLE 5

Anti-arbitrage shield transactions cost per $1,000 bond to buy, convert, and sell assuming sufficient bonds acquired to convert to 100 shares ignoring tansfer taxes

No. of shares per bond	Stock prices					
	10	20	30	40	50	100
100	19.50	29.50	36.50	41.50	46.50	51.50
50		16.00	19.50	22.00	24.50	27.00
33 1/3			13.83	15.50	17.17	18.83
25				12.25	13.50	14.75
20					11.30	12.30
16 2/3						10.67
14 2/7						9.36
12 1/2						8.63
11 1/9						7.94
10						7.40

THE EQUATIONS

A general form of the equation employed is:

$$\frac{P}{B} = f(F) + \beta\frac{Y_d}{B} + \gamma\frac{T}{B} + \delta\frac{1}{B} \tag{3}$$

where

P = calculated premium,

B = bond price,

F = floor variable; the difference between the bond price and the straight debt value of the bond as reported in the *Bond Survey;* the form of the floor variable is not yet specified,

Y_d = difference in current income streams; bond income (coupons) less stock income (dividends per share multiplied by number of shares into which the bond is convertible); we would prefer the present value of the expected income difference over the expected life of the bond; for obvious reasons, we settled for current income difference,

T = transaction cost difference; cost to buy the stock into which the bond is convertible less cost to buy the bond including all transfer taxes.

To reduce the effect of measurement errors all variables are divided by the bond price. For any one bond–stock pair, this transformation is neutral, but when the transformation is applied to two or more the measurements are placed on the same basis.

THE FORM OF THE FLOOR VARIABLE

The extant theory on the floor variable implies that the premium is inversely but nonlinearly related to the floor. That is, as the price of the bond rises above the straight debt value, the value of the floor declines[13] but the value of the floor declines less the higher the increase in the bond price. Thus, as a bond price rises from 1,000 to 1,250 the insurance value of the bond decreases more than when the bond price rises from 2,000 to 2,250 (the same absolute increase) or even to 2,500 (the same percentage increase).

This analysis suggests that the premium is a monotonically decreasing function of the floor variable. Our test of this suggestion was as follows: the observations of the floor variable were divided into 10 ranges, [0–10], (10–20], (20–30], (30–40], (40–50], (50–75], (75–100], (100–150], (150–200], and (above 200)—the square bracket indicates inclusion of the end point of the range and the parenthesis indicates exclusion of the end point. Ten dummy variables were specified, one for each of the 10 ranges: the ith dummy variable for a given bond observation is set equal to 1 if the floor variable of that observation falls in the ith range while all other dummy variables for that observation are set equal to zero. For example, if a bond with a straight debt value of 95 sells for 130, the floor variable is 35; thus the fourth dummy variable is set to equal 1 and all other dummy variables are set equal to zero. This standard technique is often used to test a variable which is hypothesized to affect a regression model in some unspecified nonlinear fashion. For the results of this test to be fruitful, R^2 s at least as high as in the other tests, significant coefficients, and coefficients which decrease in some pattern over the 10 ranges are required. That is, we excpect the coefficient of the first dummy floor variable [0–10] to be the largest, the coefficient of the last dummy variable (above 200) to be the smallest with a pattern of more or less decreasing coefficients in between to justify the hypothesis that the smaller the floor variable, the larger the premium on that account. The slight pattern of the floor dummy variables showed increases over the range, not decreases. Ideally, a complete nonlinear regression analysis on (3) is required to determine the best nonlinear function for $f(F)$, but aside from the analysis above, our investigation was confined to the following forms: $1/F^2$, B/F^2, B^2/F^2, $1/BF^2$. The from $1/BF^2$ gave the best initial results; therefore we examined $1/BF^n$ for n between 1.5 and 16. Since the best fit was obtained for n almost equal to 2, $f(F)$ was taken to be $1/BF^2$, [14] and the equation becomes

$$\frac{P}{B} = \frac{\alpha}{BF^2} + \beta\frac{Y_d}{B} + \gamma\frac{T}{B} + \delta\frac{1}{B}. \tag{4}$$

THE TESTS

Test I. The data consist of 452 observations on the convertible bond prices for 18 different dates over the three-year period. We split the data into two sets using a random-number series. Then one-half of the data were used to find the

---

[13] The floor probably increases as the value of the common stock increases since the debt-equity ratio declines with an increase in the value of the common stock. Alternatively, the floor increases with the value of the stock because the promised cash flow of the bond becomes more certain. The upper limit to the floor will be reached when the floor is sufficiently high to make the cash flow equivalent to the pure rate of interest. We shall ignore changes in the floor arising from changes in the value of the common stock.

[14] In the full study of all 18 sets of data we tried both the form B/F^2 and $1/F^2$ and found little difference in the results.

coefficients of equation (4) and the other half of the data were tested using the coefficients we had estimated. If the theory is valid, then we ought to be able to find the estimate of the true parameters α, β, γ and δ using part of the data and demonstrate that the estimates are good ones by using them to predict the premiums on other bonds which were not included in the sample used to estimate the coefficients. Since the 18 sets of data represent 18 different dates and since market conditions in general are not constant, we used 18 constant terms, one for each month rather than one as indicated in equation (4). The first equation fitted was

$$\frac{P}{B} = \frac{\alpha}{BF^2} + \beta \frac{Y_d}{B} + \gamma \frac{T}{B} + \frac{1}{B} \sum_{i=1}^{18} \delta_i m_i \qquad (5)$$

where m_i for each observation was equal to one if the observation were from the ith set and was equal to zero otherwise.[15] The results of this regression are shown in Table 6, column 1; R^2 was .57. After the coefficients were estimated, they were used to predict the premiums on the observations in the other, "held-out," sample and the quasi-R^2 was .36. As should be expected, the estimated coefficients did not perform as well on the test data as they did on the data from which they were derived, but they are clearly not useless. Observe from the t-values that all the coefficients except that for the floor are significantly different from zero. We ran a similar regression omitting the floor variable:

$$\frac{P}{B} = \beta \frac{Y_d}{B} + \gamma \frac{T}{B} + \sum_{i=1}^{18} \frac{1}{B} \delta_i m_i. \qquad (6)$$

The results of this regression are shown in Table 6, column 3; again the estimated coefficients did not do as well in predicting the premiums for the test data as they did in predicting the premiums for the data from which they were derived but the results are as good on the test data as when the floor variable was included. Columns 2 and 4 of Table 6 are included to help delimit the power of the 18 dummy variables in equations (5) and (6). For the two regressions shown in these columns there is but one constant term for all bonds—no distinction is made between bonds of different periods. The R^2s are slightly worse but the predictive power of the coefficients is as good with one constant term as with 18 dummy variable constants.

The results of Test I are not particularly conclusive; we have been only moderately successful in predicting premiums in the test data.

Test II. As a further test, we split the data into 18 sets, each set including all the observations for a given data, and fit equation (7) to each set.

$$\frac{P}{B} = \frac{\alpha}{BF^2} + \beta \frac{Y_d}{B} + \gamma \frac{T}{B} + \delta \frac{1}{B}. \qquad (7)$$

Consider equation (7): if the extant theory is valid, the 18 α coefficients from the 18 regressions will be significant, and more or less the same; similarly, the

---

[15] The m_i, commonly called dummy variables, are in this context interpreted as constants for each month.

TABLE 6

Results of regressions

1. $P/B = \alpha/BF^2 + \beta Y_d/B + \gamma T/B + 1/B \sum_{i=1}^{18} \delta_i M_i$
2. $P/B = \alpha/BF^2 + \beta Y_d/B + \gamma T/B + \delta B$
3. $P/B = \beta\ Y_d/B + \gamma T/B + 1/B \sum_{i=1}^{18} \delta_i M_i$
4. $P/B = \beta Y_d/B + \gamma T/B + \delta/B$

Using one-half of observations and the resulting coefficients to predict the other half

	Regression coefficients (t-values)			
	1.	2.	3.	4.
FLOOR (α)	589.89	269.22	–	–
	(1.37)	(0.66)		
YDIFF (β)	1.62	1.73	1.70	1.76
	(8.77)	(9.43)	(9.56)	(10.01)
TRCDF (γ)	-6.84	-6.78	-7.11	-6.88
	(9.65)	(9.58)	(10.41)	(10.00)
CONSTANT (δ)	–	12.80	–	13.15
		(11.94)		(14.23)
MONTH 1 (δ_1)	8.52	–	9.38	–
	(4.46)		(5.19)	
MONTH 2 .	14.27		14.83	
	(8.09)		(8.62)	
MONTH 3 .	9.79		10.60	–
	(5.16)		(5.86)	
MONTH 4 .	11.06	–	11.72	–
	(6.62)		(7.31)	
MONTH 5 .	10.57	–	11.24	–
	(6.39)		(7.11)	
MONTH 6 .	15.90	–	16.46	–
	(9.41)		(10.01)	
MONTH 7 .	12.45	–	13.27	–
	(7.08)		(8.01)	
MONTH 8 .	15.47	–	16.09	–
	(9.52)		(10.29)	
MONTH 9 .	11.05	–	12.29	–
	(5.89)		(7.47)	
MONTH 10 .	13.16	–	14.17	–
	(6.27)		(7.18)	
MONTH 11 .	15.47	–	16.49	–
	(7.69)		(8.80)	
MONTH 12 (δ_{12})	15.49	–	16.27	–
	(7.87)		(8.62)	
MONTH 13 .	14.72	–	15.45	–
	(7.47)		(8.12)	
MONTH 14 .	11.66	–	12.48	–
	(5.35)		(5.94)	
MONTH 15 .	12.03	–	12.91	–
	(6.48)		(7.39)	
MONTH 16 .	13.09	–	14.03	–
	(6.88)		(7.89)	
MONTH 17 .	11.51	–	12.91	–
	(4.97)		(6.21)	
MONTH 18 (δ_{18})	11.55	–	12.30	–
	(5.69)		(6.29)	
FIRST HALF: R^2	.57	.50	.57	.50
SECOND HALF: QUASI- R^2	.36	.37	.35	.36

$(1-b/a$ where a is variance of p/B and b is residual variance)

TABLE 7

Results of fitting regressions

$$1.\ P/B = \alpha/BF^2 + \beta Y_d/B + \gamma T/B + \delta B$$
$$2.\ P/B = \beta Y_d/B + \gamma T/B + \delta/B$$

Separately for each of the observation dates and testing the stability of the coefficients over time

| | | Observation | | | | | | | | | | Degree of freedom for F | |
| | | 1. With floor | | | | | 2. Without floor | | | | | | |
Row	Date	R^2	α (t)	β (t)	γ (t)	δ (t)	R^2	β (t)	γ (t)	δ (t)		F^*	n_1/n_2
1.	1/16/61	.70	2570. (1.42)	1.30 (2.34)	1.79 (.74)	-1.04 (.26)	.65	1.26 (2.18)	-.37 (.18)	3.57 (1.46)		—	—
2.	3/20/61	.69	2164. (1.35)	2.54 (3.54)	-3.94 (1.27)	7.64 (1.68)	.67	2.50 (3.43)	-5.51 (1.88)	11.18 (2.95)		2.07	3/44
3.	5/15/61	.59	130. (.04)	1.98 (2.41)	-8.00 (2.85)	13.48 (3.59)	.59	2.00 (2.77)	-7.99 (2.92)	13.54 (3.85)		1.25	1/71
4.	7/17/71	.52	27.63 (1.08)	1.61 (2.32)	-5.81 (2.56)	7.94 (2.23)	.50	1.72 (2.47)	-6.22 (2.77)	10.18 (3.50)		.98	9/99
5.	9/18/61	.55	-2267. (.83)	2.01 (2.83)	-6.04 (2.53)	12.03 (3.15)	.54	1.85 (2.72)	-5.47 (2.41)	10.14 (3.34)		.75	12/129
6.	11/20/61	.62	1116. (.64)	2.08 (2.53)	-7.62 (2.70)	14.73 (3.41)	.62	2.06 (2.53)	'8.16 (3.06)	16.32 (4.69)		.92	15/162
7.	1/15/62	.73	-125. (.10)	1.86 (2.07)	-6.15 (2.20)	14.01 (3.25)	.73	1.88 (2.21)	-6.07 (2.32)	13.77 (4.04)		.94	18/192

TABLE 7 (CONTINUED)

Row	Date	Observation										Degree of Freedom for F	
		1. With floor					2. Without floor						
		R^2	α (t)	β (t)	γ (t)	δ (t)	R^2	β (t)	γ (t)	δ (t)		F	n_1/n_2
8.	3/19/62	.86	776. (.87)	2.20 (5.41)	-9.28 (5.72)	16.57 (6.78)	.85	2.22 (5.49)	-9.83 (6.59)	17.90 (9.45)		1.10	21/227
9.	5/21/62	.65	854. (1.11)	.54 (1.33)	-7.17 (3.92)	11.32 (3.54)	.63	.62 (1.54)	-8.19 (5.16)	13.86 (6.16)		1.42	24/255
10.	7/16/62	.85	-757. (.44)	1.97 (3.74)	-9.85 (5.03)	18.63 (5.03)	.85	1.92 (3.85)	-9.75 (5.18)	17.57 (6.47)		1.35	27/271
11.	9/17/62	.84	-467 (.29)	1.93 (3.44)	-6.22 (3.38)	14.75 (5.22)	.84	1.84 (3.98)	-6.26 (3.51)	14.45 (5.66)		1.36	30/291
12.	11/19/62	.82	2244. (1.58)	1.97 (4.33)	-3.26 (1.44)	8.06 (2.16)	.80	1.99 (4.20)	-4.56 (2.09)	11.88 (4.02)		1.35	33/214
13.	1/21/63	.88	4839. (2.98)	1.67 (4.08)	-5.07 (2.84)	8.99 (2.83)	.83	1.97 (4.29)	-6.97 (3.59)	15.13 (5.38)		1.34	36/339
14.	3/18/63	.71	3819. (1.52)	1.24 (2.18)	-2.70 (.92)	5.40 (.95)	.65	1.19 (2.00)	-4.66 (1.69)	11.31 (2.59)		1.30	39/355
15.	5/20/63	.85	3637. (3.46)	1.13 (3.11)	-4.60 (2.88)	7.98 (3.01)	.77	1.09 (2.49)	-7.26 (4.28)	14.38 (6.24)		1.28	42/382
16.	7/15/63	.79	1893. (2.18)	.60 (1.35)	-2.81 (1.50)	7.53 (2.64)	.73	.88 (1.93)	-3.86 (1.97)	10.73 (4.02)		1.27	45/405
17.	9/16/63	.63	1185. (1.74)	.61 (.99)	-2.24 (.72)	5.72 (1.21)	.56	1.16 (2.13)	-4.77 (1.65)	10.52 (2.61)		1.23	48/427
18.	11/18/63	.62	1091. (1.17)	.47 (.90)	-1.37 (.81)	4.75 (1.83)	.59	.80 (1.82)	-1.38 (.80)	5.66 (2.27)		1.30	51/449

* Null hypothesis for F shown on row i: $\beta_1 = \beta_2 = \ldots \beta_i$, $\gamma_1 = \gamma_2 = \ldots = \gamma_i$ and $\delta_1 = \delta_2 = \ldots = \delta_i$. The numbers in this column show that none of the seventeen null hypotheses can be rejected.

TABLE 8

Spearman rank-correlation coefficient of bond premiums (in $ and %) and coefficient of variation of monthly stock price relatives over selected numbers of months

Observation Dates	$	(n)	3 Months			6 Months			21 Months			24 Months			60 Months			Maximum Number of Observations
			%	$	(n)	%	$	(n)	%	$	(n)	%	$	(n)	%	$	(n)	%
1961																		
1/16	-0.10	(18)	-0.10	-0.19	(18)	-0.22	0.03	(17)	0.00	0.22	(17)	0.20	0.46*	(17)	0.45*	0.46*	(18)	0.43*
3/20	-0.00	(28)	-0.01	0.18	(29)	0.17	0.15	(28)	0.14	0.21	(28)	0.20	0.38*	(28)	0.38*	0.35*	(29)	0.35*
5/15	0.21	(27)	0.25	0.27	(25)	0.23	0.49**	(25)	0.46*	0.37**	(24)	0.34*	0.28	(24)	0.27	0.33*	(27)	0.33*
7/17	-0.04	(28)	-0.03	-0.05	(27)	-0.01	-0.03	(27)	0.01	0.03	(26)	0.07	0.16	(26)	0.20	0.18	(28)	0.22
9/18	-0.29	(30)	-0.27	-0.01	(30)	0.03	0.13	(29)	0.17	0.39*	(28)	0.41*	0.43*	(28)	0.45**	0.41*	(30)	0.43*
11/20	0.04	(33)	0.05	0.26	(33)	0.27	0.39*	(29)	0.38*	0.30	(29)	0.28	0.37*	(29)	0.35*	0.32*	(33)	0.30*
1962																		
1/15	0.04	(30)	-0.02	0.15	(30)	0.07	0.25	(30)	0.20	0.42*	(29)	0.31*	0.50**	(29)	0.43*	0.20	(30)	0.18
3/19	-0.14	(35)	-0.16	-0.15	(35)	-0.18	0.00	(34)	-0.02	0.04	(32)	0.01	0.27	(32)	0.24	0.25	(35)	0.24
5/21	-0.11	(28)	-0.08	-0.16	(28)	-0.16	-0.42*	(27)	-0.44*	-0.27	(25)	-0.29	-0.10	(24)	-0.11	-0.32*	(28)	-0.32*
7/16	-0.09	(16)	-0.05	0.06	(16)	0.02	0.30	(15)	0.28	0.07	(14)	0.06	-0.08	(13)	-0.08	0.25	(16)	0.28
9/17	0.23	(20)	0.17	0.28	(20)	0.25	0.64**	(20)	0.56**	0.40**	(18)	0.34	0.43*	(17)	0.41	0.27	(20)	0.25
11/19	0.62**	(23)	0.56**	0.55**	(23)	0.51**	0.64**	(23)	0.58**	0.38*	(22)	0.36*	0.37*	(21)	0.32	0.47*	(23)	0.42*
1963																		
1/21	0.32	(25)	0.34*	0.46*	(25)	0.44*	0.43*	(24)	0.40*	0.33	(23)	0.31	0.19	(22)	0.18	0.26	(25)	0.28
3/18	-0.12	(16)	-0.10	0.31	(16)	0.33	0.57*	(16)	0.56	0.50*	(15)	0.47*	0.41	(14)	0.38	0.69*	(16)	0.69*
5/20	0.14	(27)	0.16	-0.00	(27)	0.02	0.24	(26)	0.19	0.21	(25)	0.19	0.06	(24)	0.04	0.19	(27)	0.17
7/15	-0.02	(23)	-0.07	-0.01	(23)	-0.08	0.29	(23)	0.22	0.16	(22)	0.15	0.05	(20)	0.10	0.31	(23)	0.29*
9/16	-0.14	(22)	-0.20	0.23	(22)	0.18	-0.05	(22)	-0.12	0.14	(21)	0.08	-0.01	(19)	-0.03	0.46	(22)	0.41
11/18	0.06	(20)	0.09	0.04	(20)	0.05	0.18	(20)	0.21	0.23	(20)	0.28	0.00	(19)	0.03	0.27	(20)	0.29

* *Significant at 5% level.*
** *Significant at 1% level.*

18 β coefficients and the 18 γ coefficients will be significant and more or less equal. The δ coefficients need not remain constant over all dates because of variable market conditions, in particular market rates of interest.

The results of fitting equation (7) to the 18 sets of observations are shown in Table 7, regression 1.

THE RESULTS

Income Differences. The extant theory does not explicitly predict the size of the coefficients but some reasonable guesses can be made. We expect the coefficient of the income difference to be positive, a number equal to the present value at some appropriate discount rate of an uncertain annuity of $1 to be received for as long as the bond is held. We would not be surprised at a coefficient within the range, say, 1 to 10. The actual coefficients, ranging from 1.6 to 1.8, do not, therefore, surprise us, but they are on the low side of our range. *Transaction Costs.* The sign of the coefficient of the transaction cost difference is hypothesized positive since it costs more to buy the stock than the bond.[16] One hypothesis is that the coefficient of the transaction cost difference should be nearly $+1$, reflecting an expectation of buying the bond, later converting it to stock, and then selling the stock so that transaction cost difference is realized exactly one. A coefficient between 1 and 2 would be a reflection of the reasonable possibility of sometimes once realizing the difference and sometimes twice. In both tests the coefficient of the transaction cost difference is not even close to its "reasonable" value; indeed, the sign is negative.[17] One seemingly relevant aspect of the transaction cost difference is not, to our knowledge, discussed in the literature: the spread between bid and asked prices for both the bond and the stock. Since the trader buys at approximately the bid and sells at approximately the asked, the greater the spread the greater the transaction cost. The spreads on the bonds and the underlying stocks were computed for the 17 bonds for which quotations were available from market data[18] on November 11, 1963. The difference between the stock spread and the bond spread was divided by two to approximate a one-way (either purchase *or* sale) trading cost and so make the spread component of the transaction cost consistent with the commission and taxes component of the transaction cost. The spread component was added to the transaction cost as previously defined to form a new transaction cost variable and the regression was recomputed for the 17 bonds. If the spreads were useful in explaining the premium, the coefficient of the redefined

---

[16] The transaction cost difference variable is measured as the cost of buying the stock minus the cost of buying the bond. This variable is positive and the larger it is, the greater the advantage of buying the bond.

[17] As discussed below, the floor variable really adds nothing to the regression. It is empirically demonstrable and theoretically understandable that there is a strong inverse relation between the actual price of the bond and the size of the premium. (This is shown in Table 1.) As bond price gets higher, the premium gets lower. As bond price gets higher, the transaction cost savings get larger. The negative coefficient on the transaction cost variable may indicate only that the higher the bond price the lower the premium.

[18] The data came from Francis Emory Fitch, Inc., *Stock Quotations on the New York Stock Exchange* and *Bond Quotations on the New York Stock Exchange.* The Stock quotations are reported at 11:30 A.M. and the bond quotations at 11:00 A.M.

transaction cost variable would conform more closely to what a "reasonable" coefficient might be and R^2 would not fall. The coefficient does become more "reasonable," 1.14 as compared to –3.11 for the old transaction cost variable, but the t-value was such that the coefficient is not significantly different from zero; coefficients of other variables are reduced in significance, and R^2 drops from .69 to .63. The addition of the spread adds nothing to the explanation of the premium.

The Floor Variable. As noted under Test I, the floor variable adds little to the results obtained. In Test II, with three exceptions, the coefficients of the floor variable are not significantly different from zero.[19] Sixteen of the other fifty-four coefficients are not significantly different from zero. When the floor variable is omitted, however, the results shown in Table 7, regression 2, are very much more encouraging. The R^2s are only slightly smaller than in the regression with the floor variable and of the fifty-four coefficients, only ten are not significantly different from zero. Furthermore, when the null hypotheses that all $\beta, \gamma,$ and δ for all the observation dates up to and including a given date are equal, the hypotheses cannot be rejected.[20]

III. CONCLUSIONS

It seems clear that our tests do not strongly support our interpretation of the received theory of the premium on CBs. This result could arise because of the nonsimultaneous transactions from which the data are gathered, from insufficiently refined tests, from a mistaken interpretation of the theory, or from a faulty theory. We blush to do so, but we blame the theory.

The most commonly stated source of the premium, in theory, is the price floor. Brigham [1966], for example, asserts

---

[19] One should not be misled by the magnitudes of the coefficients for the floor variable. Although these coefficients are sometimes 1,000 times as large as the coefficient of the income difference variable, the coefficient of the income difference variable can be significantly different from zero while the coefficient of the floor variable is not. The "*t*-value" is used to test the significance of a coefficient. Each coefficient in our results is shown with its *t*-value. Unless that *t-value* is as large as or larger than 2, the associated coefficient is not significantly different from zero. By reference to standard statistical tables of *t*-values, the reader can ascertain the exact size the *t*-value must exceed in order for the associated coefficient to be different from zero for a given significance level.

[20] There are actually 17 different null hypotheses tested in Table 7 for regression 2. For example, the fourth null hypothesis is that

$$\beta_1 = \beta_2 = \beta_3 = \beta_4 = \beta_5$$
$$\gamma_1 = \gamma_2 = \gamma_3 = \gamma_4 = \gamma_5$$
$$\delta_1 = \delta_2 = \delta_3 = \delta_4 = \delta_5$$

where $\beta_1, \gamma_1, \delta_1$ are the coefficients in the ith row of the table. None of the seventeen null hypotheses is rejected by the F test. If only the βs and γs are simultaneously tested for equality, the Fs are even smaller; most in fact are less than one. (In general, the smaller the Fs, the more likely is the null hypothesis.) The F tests are not shown for regression 1 in Table 7 because they are irrelevant in view of the unimportance of the floor variable.

. . . the convertible bond usually commands a premium over its conversion value because, by holding convertibles, an investor is able to reduce his risk exposure. To illustrate, suppose a particular bond is convertible into 20 shares of stock with a market price of $70, giving a conversion value of $1,400. If the stock market turns sharply down and the stock price falls to $35 per share, a stock investor suffers a 50 per cent loss in value. Had he held a convertible bond, its price would have fallen from $1,400 to the bond value floor . . . which is probably well above $700. Hence, holding the convertible entails less risk than holding common stock, and this causes convertibles to sell at a premium above their conversion value.

Similarly, Baumol, Malkiel, and Quandt [1966] observe

But our security holder also knows (assuming he has not actually converted his security in the interim) that if it turns out that his forecast was mistaken and that stock price has in fact fallen sharply, he has the option of disposing of a security whose market price will be largely governed by its value as a bond rather than a stock. Thus the "bond value" of the convertible may provide a cushion limiting the risk assumed by the convertible holder vis-a-vis the outright owner of common shares. Consequently, the determination of the value of a convertible comes down to the analysis of the values of these two components—the expected value of the security and the insurance value of the convertibility features.

Both papers recognize that the higher the price of the bond, the less important is the floor since the higher the price the lower is the likelihood of a fall to the floor. But even so, the importance of the floor is exaggerated. The owner of one $1,400 bond convertible into 20 shares of stock now selling at $70 has a floor of, say, $1,000 and the owner of 20 shares of stock worth $1,400 does not; but establishing an identical floor for the stockholder is easy and the cost seems trivial. A stop–sell order at $50 for 20 shares is an obvious device.[21] It is true that stop–sell orders are sometimes not executed at the trigger price, but then the cost of the floor per share becomes only the difference between the stop–sell trigger price and the price at which the order is finally executed plus commissions and the other transactions costs—all multiplied by the probability of a price fall to $50 and the probability of the market price going through the stop–sell price. A second way for the stockholder to establish a floor for himself might be the purchase of a put for 20 shares at $50 of the same duration as the conversion privilege. Such an option could be costly, but it also conveys more possibilities for gain to the purchaser than does the simple floor. We think it appropriate, then, to regard the owner of one $1,400 convertible bond as standing in the same position vis-a-vis the floor as the owner of 20 shares of stock with a stop order at the straight-debt value.[22] Since a stop order is cheap, the floor should play little role in determining the premium. We show in the Appendix that the only difference between the present value of the stock and the bond, other than that accounted for by the difference between transaction costs and income streams, is the present value of an option to sell the stock into which the bond is convertible for $1,000 at the terminal date of the bond's existence.

[21] We are indebted to Eugene F. Fama for his suggestions in this area.

[22] More precisely, if S is the straight-debt value and N the number of shares into which a bond is convertible, the stop order should be placed at S/N.

This terminal date is the date the bond is called or matures, whichever comes first.

Indeed, the notion of a floor for the bond may be entirely without merit even when the price of the stock is less than its conversion price. Suppose the price of the stock in our example were $40 and the price of the bond $1,000. A bondholder has little or no downside risk, but will gain from an increase in the price of the stock. Now consider the owner of $1,000 worth of stock (25 shares) with a stop–loss order at, say, $39.50. He, too, has little downside risk and will gain even more than the bondholder from an increase in the price of the stock. It seems to us that a convertible bond is almost completely described as a claim to a fixed and relatively certain cash stream plus an option to exchange that claim for another claim to a variable and relatively uncertain cash stream. There is no place in this description for a floor any larger than the expected cost of executing a stop–sell order. The determination of the premium depends, we suggest, entirely on the differences in the expected cash streams, but the calculation of the expected cash streams must be the subject of another paper.

APPENDIX

The assertion above that the premium depends only on the differences of expected cash streams requires that the principal repayment of the bond be treated as a component of the cash stream accruing to the bondholder. But the principal repayment may be differentiated from the coupon payments and valued separately. We show below that the principal repayment is the equivalent of an option to sell, much like a put.

Assume without loss of generality that the bond is convertible into one share of stock.

Let $f(p, t)$ be the probability that the stock has a price of p at time t;

   $h(p, t)$ be the premium that the bond buyer must pay at time t when the stock is p; at time t the stock costs p and the bond costs $p + h(p, t)$;[23]

   P_0 be the price of the stock at time $t = 0$;

   Y_S, Y_B be the income streams from the stock and the bond, respectively;

   C_B, C_S be the transaction costs to buy the stock and the bond, respectively;

   $PV(\cdot)$ be the present value operator.

The horizon for this derivation is T, the time the bond matures.[24] The expected value at T of holding the convertible bond is represented by[25]

$$B_T = \int_0^{1000} 1000 f(p,T)\, dp + \int_{1000}^{\infty} pf(p,T)\, dp$$

[23] It is recognized (see, for example, Harbaugh [1963]) that the premium is dependent upon the time until the bond matures as well as the price of the stock.

[24] The bond may be called by the company before it matures. This possibility slightly complicates the expression for B_T but does not alter the essential conclusion of the analysis.

[25] This analysis was first suggested to us by David Duvel in an unpublished manuscript.

where the first integral represents the value of the bond if the stock price is below \$1,000 and the second integral represents the bond value for stock prices above \$1,000.

$$B_T = \int_0^{1000} 1000f(p,T)\,dp + \int_0^\infty pf(p,T)\,dp - \int_0^{1000} pf(p,T)\,dp$$

$$= \int_0^\infty pf(p,T)\,dp + \int_0^{1000} (1000 - p)f(p,T)\,dp.$$

The first integral above is just the value of the stock at T and the second integral is the value of an option to sell the stock for \$1,000 at T. Thus we can write

$$B_T = E[\text{stock}] + E[\text{option}].$$

The bond buyer pays

$$P_0 + h(P_0,t_0) + C_B \tag{1}$$

and his expected present value from horizon T is

$$PV(E[\text{stock}] + E[\text{option}]) + PV(Y_B). \tag{2}$$

The stock buyer pays

$$P_0 + C_S \tag{3}$$

and his expected present value from horizon T is

$$PV(E[\text{stock}]) + PV(Y_S). \tag{4}$$

The difference between what the buyer of the stock and the buyer of the bond pays is (1) − (3) or

$$h(P_0,t_0) + C_B - C_S \tag{5}$$

and the difference between the expected present value of their wealth at T is

$$PV(E[\text{option}]) + PV(Y_B - Y_S). \tag{6}$$

Equating (5) and (6) we see that

$$h(P_0,t_0) = PV(E[\text{option}]) + PV(Y_B - Y_S) + (C_S - C_B).$$

Thus the premium the bond buyer expects to pay at any time is the present value of the difference in income streams plus the difference in transaction costs plus the present value of an option to sell the stock for \$1,000 at maturity.[26]

[26] When the possibility of call is allowed, this put becomes the present value of a put at the call price at time t multiplied by the probability of call at t plus the probability of the bond's maturing multiplied by the value of the put for \$1,000 at T.

REFERENCES

1. BAUMOL, W. J., MALKIEL, B. G., and QUANDT, R. E. "The Valuation of Convertible Securities," *Quarterly Journal of Economics,* LXXX, No. 1 (February, 1966), 48–59.
2. BLADEN, ASHBY. "Time to Buy?" *Barron's,* October 10, 1966, 9ff.
3. BRIGHAM, EUGENE F. "An Analysis of Convertible Debentures: Theory and Some Empirical Evidence," *Journal of Finance,* XXI, No. 1 (March 1966), 35–54.
4. HARBAUGH, ALLAN W. *Operations Research in the Stock Market.* El Sequndo, Calif.: Computer Sciences Corporation (650 N. Sepulveda Blvd.), 1963. (Multilith.)
5. HERSHEY, ROBERT D. "Bond Men Start Hunting," *The New York Times,* August 21, 1966, Section F, p. 1.
6. KAPLAN, STANLEY A. "Piercing the Corporate Boilerplate: Antidilution Clauses in Convertible Securities," *University of Chicago Law Review,* XXXIII, No. 1 (Autumn, 1965), 1–30.
7. KLEINE, ALEXANDER E. "Address to the Illinois Society of Certified Public Accountants," June 30, 1966. (Distributed by Harris, Upham and Company, Chicago.)
8. MOORE, THOMAS GALE. "Stock Market Margin Requirements," *Journal of Political Economy,* LXXIV, No. 2 (April, 1966), 158–167.
9. POENSGEN, OTTO H. "The Valuation of Convertible Bonds," *Industrial Management Review,* VII, No. 1 (Fall, 1965), 77–92, and *ibid.,* No. 2 (Spring, 1966), 83–98.

Shelton examines the value of a security which is convertible into common stock. He does an excellent job of reviewing the relevant literature and relating his theory to earlier ones. Shelton tests his final model both in terms of its ability to explain warrant prices and its ability to produce trading profits.

14

The Relation of the Price of a Warrant to the Price of Its Associated Stock

John P. Shelton*

These articles are reprinted with permission from the Financial Analysts Journal, *Vol. 23, No. 3 (May–June, 1967), pp. 134–151 and Vol. 23, No. 4 (July–August, 1967), pp. 88–100. Parts of both articles have been deleted by the editors.*

PART I

A. INTRODUCTION: GOALS AND SUMMARY CONCLUSIONS

The goals of this paper and its subsequent installment in the next issue of the *Financial Analysts Journal* are threefold:

1) To summarize references to the major papers that have been written about warrant evaluation. Much of the literature on warrants has, unfortunately for anyone who tried to trace it, been published in the form of private monographs or in journals that are obscure. This two-installment article, which contains references to all the papers on warrants uncovered by the author, constitutes

* The author is indebted to Mr. Benjamin Graham and the Western Data Processing Center for their important contributions to this paper, and to the Division of Research at the U.C.L.A. Graduate School of Business Administration for financial support.

papers on warrants uncovered by the author, consitutes a bibliography of the large majority of warrant studies. Hopefully, this, in itself, is a worthwhile contribution to the subject.

2) To test the factors influencing warrant prices and make statistically valid generalizations about the major variables determining a warrant's price.

3) To develop a reasonably simple yet accurate formula for evaluating warrants by investors who do not have access to an electronic computer.

These purposes call for a lengthy paper. The study's length and complexity are further enlarged by a discussion of the statistical methodology that underpin the conclusions. Furthermore, technical aspects arising from the nature of warrants have to be clarified to make the mechanics of the statistical approach understandable to analysts who may wish to evaluate or apply the proposed method. The major empirical highlights established by my research are set forth below. The analysis and details supporting the conclusions are developed in the body of the paper.

1. The single most important factor in determining the future price change of a warrant is the future price change of its underlying common stock. This means there is no simple, mechanical way to invest in warrants that eliminates the necessity for careful analysis of the common stock itself.

2. Percentage-wise, warrants almost always show greater gains or losses than the underlying common stock.

3. The market typically makes only a slight downward adjustment in the price of a warrant as it maturity shortens. It is in fact negligible so long as the warrant has three years or more before expiration. Most of the reduction in premium occurs in the last two years.

4. All things being equal, warrants listed on the American Stock Exchange carry a slightly higher premium than those traded over-the-counter.

5. The premium on a warrant is reduced to some extent when it is associated with common stock that pays a dividend.

6. Several other factors that might be associated with the outcome for warrants prices such as the prior history of the common stock price-gains, or the volatility of the common stock did not appear to be significantly important in determining the price of the warrant.

B. THE ZONE OF PLAUSIBLE WARRANT PRICES

The first step in comparing the price of a warrant with the price of its associated stock is to establish a value-range that is wide enough to include virtually all warrants, and also to provide a logical justification for the existence of such a zone.

The lower edge of the price-zone for a warrant is the price of the common minus the option price, but the price-zone can't fall below zero. If the warrant fell below this minimum by enough to cover transaction costs. arbitrage would ensue until the warrant rose at least to its exercise value. Defining the lower edge of the price zone for warrants adds nothing to the state of the art of warrant-pricing since the minimum value has been generally discussed in the literature.

Heretofore the only upper limit that was mentioned was the fact that a warrant should not sell for more than the common. (Of course, a short "squeeze" could result in a higher price in a cornered market.) This ceiling is so high that it provides no useful guidance for actual warrant valuation. *The keystone in the structure of this analysis is the assumption that the price of the warrant will equal its exercise value (i.e., the lower limit of the zone) if the stock sells for four times its option price or more.* For example, this means that if a stock sells at $80 and the warrant carries the right to buy one share of stock for $20, the warrant will sell for $60, which is its exercise value ($80 minus $20 = $60). Beyond that, according to this model, if the stock price moves up, the warrant will be supported at its exercise value: if the stock sells for $95, e.g., the warrant will sell for $75. The zone of plausible warrant prices, with its lower and upper limits, is shown in Figure 1.

The assumption that the price of the warrant will seldom trade above its exercise value, if the stock sells at four (or more) times the option price, is supported by empirical observations and logical considerations. Of the 157 observations relating the price of a warrant to the price of its stock, shown in Figure 1, all were resting very close to the exercise value when the stock price approached four times its option price. A logical explanation for this empirical observation follows: by the time a stock reaches a price four times its option there is little difference in the proportional gain that might develop from owning the warrant or the stock, because both are going to be fairly high-priced, and at prices not far from each other. In the second place, by the time a stock has risen to four times the option price (which is typically placed high enough when the warrant is issued to represent a good future advance for the stock) it is likely to be paying dividends and the warrant-holder is deprived of dividend income. The absence of dividends for the warrant-holder tends to offset the greater percentage gain possible from owning the warrant if it is priced at its exercise value and the stock continues to rise.

Again, numbers may be useful to explain this. If we assume the stock cited in the illustrative example rose from $80 to $100 over a period of a few years, the holder of the stock would get a 25% gain, whereas the holder of the warrant would get a 33% increase as the warrant rose from $60 to $80. However, during that period the warrant-holder would have no dividend income, and he also would have taken the risk of a larger percentage drop in case the stock went down instead of up.

The Samuelson Study

Paul Samuelson, in his mathematically rigorous paper entitled "Rational Theory of Warrant Pricing" demonstrates that even for a perpetual warrant the price must coincide with its exercise value at some point, given the reasonable assumption that investors would not buy warrants unless they offer greater potential return than the common stock. This reasonable assumption derives from two considerations: The common stock may be paying a dividend, or will be expected to pay a dividend sometime in the future, so the common stock-holder receives not only any potential stock price gain but also a dividend yield; to provide only an equal yield the warrant growth would have to exceed the common stock capital gain by the amount of the dividend yield. Furthermore, since warrants are more volatile than common stock the investor should want a higher return from warrants than can be obtained from common stock.

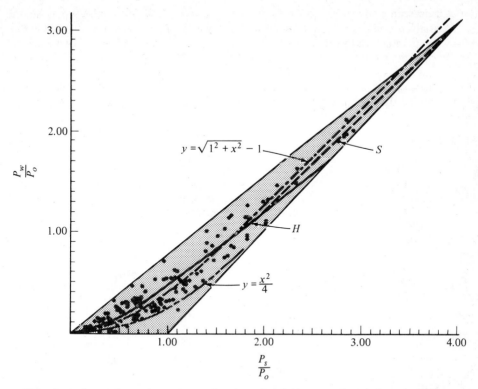

This chart shows observed warrant-stock price relationships on selected dates in 1959, 1960, 1961 and 1962, including days of individual high and low prices for 1962. Note that most observations fall within the shaded "Zone of Plausible Prices." The hatched lines show predicted values for different models:

$Y = \sqrt{1^2 + X^2} - 1$ refers to Kassouf; $Y = \frac{X^2}{4}$ refers to Giguère; H refers to Harbaugh. The latter is based on the following values: six-year longevity; option price of \$20; investor discount rate of 6%. S refers to Samuelson's perpetual warrant when the common pays no dividends and the ratio between the desired rate of return on the warrant and the expected growth of the common stock price is 16/9. The Samuelson values coincide so closely to Harbaugh's they can't be shown separately on the scale of this Figure below P_s/P_o of 2; for higher P_s/P_o the Samuelson values are demarked. P_s stands for the price of the stock; P_w designates the price of the warrant; P_o is the warrant's option price.

FIGURE 1

The zone of plausible prices

Warrants with a limited life approach their exercise value also as they come closer to expiring.

    Samuelson shows that in a specific case, viz., that of a perpetual warrant related to a non-dividend paying stock where the probable distribution of the logarithm of future price changes is normally distributed, the warrant price will converge on the exercise value when the stock price is three or four times its option price (given reasonable estimates for the relation between the expected rate of return on the common stock and the warrant). Though the research for this study was done prior to the publication of Samuelson's paper, so the analysis could not have been influenced by Samuelson's work, it is notable that the data studied in this paper led to the empirical observation that virtually all warrants would be resting on their exercise value when the stock price reached four times its option price. The Samuelson paper provides welcome theoretical support for the empirical observation of this study, as this study provides useful empirical evidence relating to Samuelson's theoretical constructions. [1]

The Upper Limit

Accepting the fact that warrants seldom sell above their exercise value when the stock is priced at four or more times its option price, *this juncture of the upper and lower limits of the zone can be used to develop a logical upper limit for the entire range of warrant prices.* The logic goes thusly: if the stock is not expected to pay dividends (ergo, the warrant-holder is not being deprived of any dividend income), and if the warrant has a perpetual life, then the investor could be indifferent between the warrant and the stock so long as the percentage gain or loss in the warrant would equal the percentage gain or loss if he owned the stock. Returning to the example, assume the investor believes the warrant (with an option price of $20) will sell for $60 if the stock gets to $80; the stock (non-dividend paying) is selling for $40; and the warrant is a perpetual warrant. The investor could afford to pay up to $30 for the warrant, for if the stock doubles in value to $80, then the warrant will also double in value to $60. By the same line of reasoning, if the stock were priced at $20, the warrant could be advantageously purchased up to $15, because if the stock eventually gets to $80 (a 300% increase), the warrant-holder would get an equal percentage gain buying for $15 and selling for $60. The upper limit of the zone of value is indicated in Figure 1. Prices along this line represent equal percentage gain or loss to the holder of either the warrant or the stock, assuming the warrant will sell at its exercise value when the stock rises to four times the option price. As the previous discussion presumably made clear, the equal-percentage-gain-or-loss relationship requires the upper bound of the zone to be a straight line, which is 3/4 the price of the stock. (It should be noted here that the major reason for placing the juncture of the "maximum value of the zone of plausible prices" and the "exercise value" at four times the option price was to have the theoretical ceiling of $3/4P_S$ be high enough to include virtually all observations in the sample. No warrants were observed priced so high as $4P_O$; a few, however, were priced around $3/4P_S$ and it was desired to make the zone of plausible prices broad enough to cover virtually all warrants.)

The maximum line described above provides a fairly realistic upper limit to the price of warrants. This fact is observed by noting how few of the 157 observations shown in Figure 1 appear above the zone of plausible prices.

To summarize the analysis thus far: the "four times option price" axiom postulates that even perpetual warrants will sell close to their exercise (or minimum) value if the stock reaches four or more times the option price. A verbal explanation for this phenomenon was presented earlier in this paper; a mathe-

---

[1] Samuelson, Paul, "Rational Theory of Warrant Pricing," *Industrial Management Review*, Volume 6, No. 2 (Spring 1965), p. 29.

matical proof is given for a particular situation by Samuelson. From this axiom, a logical justification is presented for a maximum price of a warrant at any stock price less than four times the option price. This maximum price is the "equal-gain, equal-loss" line, which turns out to be 3/4 of the price of the stock. Combining this maximum with the obvious minimum value that arbitrage will maintain (referred to in this paper as the "exercise value") creates a zone of value whithin which warrant prices should prevail. Observation of a wide sample of prices lends credence to the hypothesized value-zone.

Using symbolic notation, the range of value described here and pictured in Figure 1 can be stated as:

$$(P_s - P_o) < P_w < 3/4P_s \text{ if } P_s < 4(P_o)$$
$$P_w = (P_s - P_o) \qquad \text{if } P_s \geq 4(P_o)$$

Where:

P_s = Price of the stock
P_w = Price of the warrant
P_o = Option price

(The formulas above assume an option to purchase only *one* share. If the warrant is linked to more than one share, the option price and the warrant price are divided by the exchange ratio.)

Anyone buying or selling warrants needs a technique for valuing them. This may be especially helpful when there is no market quotation; such a situation arises when an underwriter receives stock warrants as part of his compensation for floating securities. The Internal Revenue Service requires the value of the warrants to be treated as ordinary income for tax purposes, which is obviously proper. The rub, so far as underwriters are concerned, is that I.R.S. rulings, while allowing the option to be taxed when granted if it can be valued at that time, in practice make it extremely difficult to value the warrant at the time of issue. In that case, the income from the warrants is taxed when the underwriter exercises it; in many cases the value then includes a component of capital gain even though the total is taxable as ordinary income. Underwriters have argued that the option should be valued when it is granted, and that the I.R.S. regulations are unduly restrictive. To the extent the research described in this paper succeeds in determining the true value of a warrant, it will help underwriters shift the valuation of warrants to the time the option is granted, rather than when it is sold.

C. OTHER STUDIES

The Giguère Parabola

Before discussing the empirical findings of this research it is useful to consider other analyses of the proper relation between the price of a warrant and its stock. One that lends itself to a direct comparison with the range of values hypothesized in this study is entitled "Warrants, A Mathematical Method of Evaluation" by Guynemer Giguère. Mr. Giguère hypothesized that, "The relationship between the price of a [perpetual] warrant [entitling the holder to buy one share] and its related stock is given by a parabola with its vertex at (0,0) whose equation is:

$$W = \frac{P^2}{4A}$$

where:

W = Price of the warrant measured along the vertical axis;
P = Price of the stock measured along the horizontal axis to the same scale;
A = Option price."[2]

He justifies his formula partly because it describes warrant prices rising curvilinearly so that the warrant price increases exponentially as long as the stock price rises (until the stock gets to be two times its exercise value). As the author states, "The basic premises of the relationship are the following:

(A) A perpetual warrant is always worth something, even when the price of the stock is relatively very low.
(B) At some point the relationship must be defined by the equation, $W = P - A$.

The function defining W should therefore give very small values for W when P is near O, increasing gradually to meet $W = P - A$ in such a way that the transition onto the straight line is gradual."[3]

Giguère also plots the values of six warrants at different times in their market history and finds the warrant-stock price relationships fit his formula closely enough to satisfy him of its merit.

For warrants with a life less than one year, Giguère suggests the best thing to do is to estimate the price of the stock on the date of expiration. For warrants with a life of one to five years, he has a modified form of his basic equation which lowers the values by the amount $A/16$.

Specifically, the equation is[4]

$$W = \frac{P^2}{4A} - \frac{A}{16}$$

For warrants with a life longer than five years he recommends the same formulation as for perpetual warrants.

Giguère's formulation differs from the analysis to be presented in this paper in various ways. For one thing, his formula has the warrant resting on its exercise value at two times the subscription price, instead of four times as contended in this paper. (Giguère's formula, as he acknowledges, cannot apply when $P > 2A$, because it would price the warrant below its exercise value, so if the stock has risen beyond that point he merely has the warrant rest on its exercise value.) Giguère's formula also ignores whether the warrant is listed, or traded over-the-counter, and the value of dividends foregone by holding the warrant instead of the stock. Finally, Giguère's formula leads to values that were lower than actually observed for most of the quotations observed in this

---

[2] Giguère, Guynemer, "Warrants, A Mathematical Method of Evaluation," *Analysts Journal*, Vol. 14, No. 5 (November 1958), p. 17.

[3] Ibid., p. 19.

[4] Ibid., p. 25.

research, as can be seen from Figure 1. Samuelson also notes that Giguère's formula postulates warrant prices that are generally too low[5]. On the other hand, some of Giguère's concepts are consistent with the analysis of this paper: the realization that at some stock price the warrant will rest on its exercise value, and the observation that warrants with more than five years life are valued as if they were almost perpetual.

The Kassouf Warrant Evaluation

Another mathematical evaluation of the price of a warrant in relation to the price of its common stock is offered by S. T. Kassouf in a monograph entitled, "Evaluation of Convertible Securities." He defines the normal value of the warrant in relation to the stock as

$$Y = \sqrt{A^2 + X^2} - A,$$

Six steps for Valuing Warrants

If one wishes to use the statistically developed formula described in this paper to determine a reasonable market price for a warrant he should use the following procedure, illustrated by data for Allegheny Corporation and Martin Marietta warrants, as of May 4, 1967. Before beginning this step-by-step explanation, however, two warnings are offered. First, this "cook-book" explanation tends to make the technique seem unduly ad hoc; this inference should be tempered by consideration of the fairly elaborate statistical analysis that generated the formula. Second, the technique may seem complicated, but much of the complexity arises from the unavoidably complex nature of warrants. They often exchange for odd numbers of shares; the option price may be changed at future dates; the option prices and maturities differ between warrants; even the manner of quoting the option price and the exchange ratio is not standardized, so confusion can easily arise in merely trying to understand the terms of a warrant. Because this formula is developed to apply to all warrants, much of its apparent complexity arises from the need to convert a uniform analysis to the specific terms of each warrant.

(a) Multiply the price of the stock by 75%. This is the upper edge of the zone of plausible price. Using May 4, 1967 closing prices, the values are as follows:

Allegheny: (.75) ($11.00) = $8.25
Martin Marietta: (.75) ($21.13) = $15.85

(b) Obtain the option price and subtract it from the price of the stock. This establishes the warrant's minimum value that arbitrage will permit, and is the lower edge of the zone of plausible prices. Since the warrant cannot fall below zero, even if the option price is greater than the price of the stock, the lower edge is still zero. The calculations of the minimum values are:

Allegheny: $11.00 − $3.75 = $75.2
Martin Marietta: $21.13 − $16.48 = $4.65

(Martin Marietta was specifically used in this explanation because it illustrates one of the technical problems in evaluating warrants. One M-M warrant entitles the holder to purchase 2.73 shares for $45.00. In order to analyze such a warrant it is necessary to reduce it to the equivalent of a warrant that carries the right to purchase *one* share; then as the final step of the calculation, the estimated value has to be multiplied by the appropriate factor—2.73 in the case of M-M—in order to match the actual price. Thus, the option price of Martin Marietta is given as $16.48, which is $45.00 divided by 2.73, instead of $45.00.)

[5] Samuelson, *op. cit.*, p. 30.

where $Y =$ Price of warrant, $A =$ Exercise price, and $X =$ Price of common.[6] This, like Giguère's formula has a warrant valuation that rises from zero at an increasing rate, but Kassouf's normative line never drops to the exercise value.

A valuation line derived from Kassouf's formula is also plotted on Figure 1 and it comes closer, in general, to the data observed in this study than does Giguère's formula. Kassouf justifies his equation partly because he considers that it fits, to a closeness that is satisfactory to him, at least 20 warrant-stock price relationships plotted in his monograph. Furthermore, he thinks the owner of a warrant should require a leverage factor of about 2 as a fair compensation for the risks inherent in warrants. His equation implies that a warrant would appreciate 1.7 times the rate of the common if the common is selling at its option value; if the common is selling at half the option value, the warrant would appreciate twice as fast as the common.

Kassouf's formulation differs from the one presented in this paper in at least two respects. His warrant prices never rest on the exercise value, no matter

---

(c) The warrant price should fall somewhere between the lower and upper edges of the zone of plausible prices.

For Allegheny, the price will be between:

$8.25 and $7.25

For Martin Marietta, the price will be between:

$15.85 and $4.65

(d) To determine where in the zone of plausible prices the warrant should be priced, use the formula:

$$\left(\sqrt[4]{\frac{M}{72}}\right)(.47 - .425Y + .17\ L)$$

where $M =$ the months of remaining longevity, $Y =$ the dividend yield of the common stock, and L signifies whether the warrant is listed on the American Stock Exchange. If the warrant is listed, L is given the value of 1; otherwise L is valued at zero. In the case of any warrant with longevity in excess of 10 years (e.g., Allegheny's warrant has a perpetual life), the longevity (M) is arbitrarily assumed to be 120 months.

To illustrate how this formula is used, consider each half. The longevity adjustment involves calculating the fourth root of 72 for Allegheny and 18 ÷ 72 for Martin, which expires November 1, 1968. (A partial reason for using the fourth root is that it can be calculated by first taking the square root of a number, then the square root of the square root.) For Allegheny (and all other warrants with longevity equal to or greater than 10 years), the fourth root of 120 ÷ 72 = 1.135. For Martin Marietta, the fourth root of 18 ÷ 72 .705.

The next half of the formula involves determining the yield foregone by holding the warrant instead of the common stock. In Allegheny's case, the dividend for 1967 was assumed to be 20c, so the dividend yield was .018 ($11.00 divided into 20c). For Martin the dividend yield was .0473 ($21.13 divided into $1.00). Both were multiplied by—4.25, giving products of—.08 for Allegheny and −.20 for Martin Marietta. Since both were listed on the American Exchange, a value of .17 times 1 was added to the constant value of .47. (If the warrant is traded over-the-counter, nothing is added.)

For Allegheny the sum of the three factors is:

.47 − .08 + .17 = .56

[6] Kassouf, S. T., *Evaluation of Convertible Securities* (Analytic Investors, Inc.: Maspeth, New York, 1962), p. 26.

how high the stock price rises; the data observed in researching this paper and Samuelson's theoretical analysis cast doubt on the precision of any formula that does not require the warrant price to rest eventually on its exercise value. Like Giguère, Kassouf does not deal explicitly with such considerations as dividends foregone or whether the warrant is listed or unlisted. Kassouf does not consider the longevity of the warrant explicitly, though he does state that the life span of the warrant, the dividend rate of the common, and the potential dilution of the common stock resulting if all warrants are exercised should be considered (in a non-specified fashion) in evaluating deviations from his norm-value. Aside from the fact that Kassouf does not specify how such factors should be weighted in calculating deviations from his norm, it is not theoretically clear why the potential dilution of the common stock should be considered at all. The valu- ation of the stock itself should clearly be influenced by the prospective dilution, but the formula of Kassouf, as in all the other analyses in this paper, develops a value of the warrant *in relation to* the price of the stock. The stock price is accepted as a given; any downward pressure exerted by the potential dilution from exercised warrants is presumably already considered by investors. To decrease further the value of the warrant would seem to be either counting opponents' tricks twice, or assuming the investing public is not well enough informed to consider, in advance, the effect on an issue of common stock of whatever dilution may result.

D. FACTORS INFLUENCING THE WARRANT-STOCK PRICE RELATIONSHIP

This section of the paper gives the results of statistical tests to determine the extent that relevant factors influenced the position of a warrant within the value-zone. The reader, looking at Figure 1, may say to himself, "Yes, virtually all the warrants are priced within the value-zone, but some are near the top and some are near the bottom. Can anything explain the position of a warrant in the

---

For Martin Marietta the sum is:
$$.47 - .20 + .17 = .44$$

(e) Multiply both components of the equation to determine what percentage of the width in the zone should be added (as a premium) to the minimum exercise value of the warrant.
For Allegheny: The longevity adjustment (1.135) multiplied by the sum of the other three factors (.56) equals .64.
For Martin Marietta: .705 (longevity adjustment) $\times$ .44 (other factors) equals .31.

(f) For Allegheny the zone was $1.00 wide at the particular price of the common stock, being bounded by $8.25 (the upper edge) and $7.25 (the lower edge, or exercise value). From step 5, above, it is determined that the market would typically add to the exercise value a premium of 64% of that zone, or 64c.
For Martin the zone is $11.20 wide ($15.85—$4.65); this is multiplied by 31% (as calculated in step 5) to find the premium to be added to the $4.65 minimum value.
For Allegheny the estimated market price was: $7.25 $\times$ 64c = $7.89. This price is quite close to the May 4 closing price of $8.00.
For Martin the estimated price is:
$$\$4.65 + (.31 \times \$11.20) = \$4.65 + \$3.47 = \$8.12$$
In this case, the value has to be multiplied by 2.73 to reflect the terms of the warrant. That gives a final estimate of 2.73 $\times$ $8.12 = $22.17. (The May 4 closing price was $24.63.)

zone?" The research behind this paper shows that answers to the question are hard to specify completely, but considerable insight can be obtained.

Presumably many factors could push a warrant price up near the top edge of the plausible-price-zone or down toward its lower limit, the exercise value. The research sought to answer the question: can these factors be specified and can their relative importance be weighed?

The statistical technique used in seeking such answers was stepwise multiple regression, and the basic concepts of the research are explained in the next few paragraphs. However, the actual processing of the data in order to analyze each warrant in a comparable fashion is sufficiently complex to make a full explanation unduly tedious except for someone who was deeply interested in replicating or using the analysis. For those who need to understand exactly how the research was designed and who want to evaluate the appropriateness of the research model used, an appendix that details the research is attached; in the main part of the paper, however, only the basic concepts are explained.

Price were obtained for all warrants (and their related stocks) quoted in

---

One of the severest tests for any statistical forecasting technique is to see how well it performs. Using the formula developed in this paper, the following estimated prices were calculated on randomly selected days removed by several years from the time period when the data were gathered to develop the formula. For comparison, the actual closing prices of the warrants are shown.

JULY 1, 1966

	Year expires	Estimated price	Actual price
Allegheny Corporation	Perpetual	$ 7.89	$ 7.88
Martin Marietta	1968	33.28	31.00
General Acceptance	1969	6.59	5.75
Atlas Corporation	Perpetual	1.77	1.88
Hitlon Hotels	1971	6.46	7.50
Sperry Rand	1967	10.09	10.50
T.W.A.	1973	69.06	71.63
Tri-Continental	Perpetual	38.40	38.00
General Tire & Rubber	1967	77.60	80.00 (Bid)

MAY 4, 1967

	Year expires	Estimated price	Actual price
Atlas Corporation	Perpetual	$ 2.04	$ 2.25
Cooper Tire & Rubber	1969	25.32	20–22
General Tire & Rubber	1967	70.98	68–70
Hilton Hotels	1971	20.08	18.63
Indian Head	1990	17.31	13.88
Mid-America Pipeline	1972	7.34	8.63–9.13
National General	1974	4.83	4.50
Pacific Petroteum	1968	3.72	3.50
Sperry Rand	1967	12.86	9.73
T.W.A.	1973	56.23	55.88
Tri-Continental	Perpetual	45.47	41.38
Del Webb	1975	1.43	1.88–2.13
General Acceptance	1969	7.56	6.25 (Bid)
McCrory (Old warrants)	1976	5.73	5.25

Standard and Poor's Stock Guide at five points in time: the last trading day of the year in 1959, 1961, and 1962; November 30, 1960; and August 31, 1962. In addition, to make sure the observations covered a full range of prices, the warrant and stock prices were collected as of the date of the highs and lows (for stock and for warrant) during 1962, a year of rather formidable price fluctuations. In all, 157 stock-warrant price relations were plotted to see if they fell within the zone of plausible prices. Those that were chosen at 1962 high or low prices merely to test extreme values of the zone were then eliminated from the subsequent statistical processing since the statistical analysis was used to establish normative relationships; the number of warrant-stock-relationships used for this purpose was 99.

Next the location of each of the 99 warrants in the zone was calculated as a percentage: if the warrant was at the lower edge of the zone, it was scored as zero percent; if it was priced at the upper limit of the range of values, it scored 100%. As a by-product of tabulating the warrant price in terms of its percentage location in the range of values, further confirmation was obtained of the basic hypothesis that warrant prices could be fairly described as falling within the specified range. The 99 warrant prices used in the statistical analysis were located, on the average, 49% of the distance between the lower and upper limits; in short, the mean value for a warrant was practically at the middle of the plausible zone. If this sample of 99 warrant-stock price relationships is representative, the odds are 19 to 1 that the true mean for all warrants would be between 45% and 53% of the spread between the maximum and minimum values of the zone of plausible prices.

Basically, the next step was to see what factors influenced the amount of premium-over-exercise value for a specific warrant. Independent variables that would seem, a priori, to have a reasonable relation to warrant valuation were selected and tested, by single and multiple regression, to see how much, if at all, the various warrant-stock price locations in the band could be "explained" by relating each one to its associated variables. Six independent variables were selected for trial: the longevity of the warrant (measured in months with an arbitrary truncation for perpetual warrants); the dividend yield on the related stock (current dividend divided by price at the time observed); whether the warrant was listed on the American Stock Exchange or traded over-the-counter (none are traded on the New York Stock Exchange); whether the warrant sold for more or less than $5.00 because below that price most member firms will not extend margin; the past volatility of the common stock (measured by averaging the ratios of annual high divided by annual low for each of the three preceding years); and the recent trend of the stock price (measured by the percentage change of the stock price over the past year). Each variable was tested against the percentage location in the band (which was the dependent variable) by single regression; also the independent variables were tested by single regression against each other to see if there was so much collinearity between any of them that one should be excluded. There was virtually no collinearity between the independent variables, so the multiple regression proceeded by selecting the variable that explained most of the dispersion in the zone first, then adding variables in order of their explanatory value.

The 99 observations used in the multiple regression were first analyzed separately for each of the five time periods. The variables that contributed most to the explanation of the warrant prices were found to be consistent over time, so all observations were finally evaluated in one regression analysis because this enlarged the sample size and increased the accuracy of the weight assigned to each variable.

One contribution of this research was to find that half the independent variables selected by a priori reasoning contributed almost nothing to explaining whether a warrant would be high or low in the zone of plausible prices. To the extent that the 99 observations are representative of all warrants, the statistics permit us to generalize that warrant-stock price relationships are probably not influenced by the past volatility or price trend of the associated stock, or by the fact that the warrant may sell for more or less than $5.00.

The variables that were statistically significant (using an "*F*" test and a probability of 99% that the relationship was not spurious) were, in order of importance: The foregone dividend yield of the associated stock; whether the warrant was listed; and the longevity of the warrant. In each case, the influence exerted by these factors was indicated (by the sign of the coefficient) to be in a logical direction; the higher the foregone dividend yield, the lower the warrant in the price zone; the warrant is higher in the zone the longer its life, and if it is listed.

Another fact about warrant pricing can be deduced from the multiple regression analysis. When these three factors were used, a multiple correlation value of .61 was achieved; this is statistically significant, but it still means that more than half the variation observed in· the scatter of prices in the plausible zone must be explained by factors not included in the test. Since every quantifiable factor that the researchers expected, a priori, to influence the warrant price in relation to its stock was tested, a factor not included in the model, probably speculative emotions, appears to play a large role in determining warrant prices.

The next step in the research involved a judgmental decision. The multiple regression equation, using the three variables—foregone yield, listing, and longevity—would show an expected value for a warrant above its minimum exercise price even when the warrant was about to expire. This arose from the perfectly reasonable fact that few of the warrants observed were on the brink of expiring, so the data used could hardly be expected to reveal the influence of extremely short life on the price of the warrants. Furthermore, the researchers doubted, that the influence of longevity was linear: a warrant life of 10 years, e.g., would not be considered by investors as being twice as valuable as a life of 5 years. However, since the multiple regression equation revealed that longevity was significant in locating a warrant in the plausible price zone and because warrants invariably sell at, or very close to, the exercise value when expiring, it was decided to apply this variable in a special way. The location of a warrant in the price zone was estimated using the multiple regression equation for the two variables: yield and listing; then the influence of warrant longevity was superimposed on this equation by a multiplicatory factor that was selected partly by judgment and partly by trying various values to see which gave the best fit. It was finally decided to reflect the effect of longevity by multiplying the values obtained from the two-variable equation by the fourth root of the longevity measured in months divided by 72* (i.e., six years). It should be kept in mind the value mentioned now is the premium above exercise price.

* The justification for this particular value is that 72 months was the average longevity

The dashed, smoothed curve indicates how the premium is affected by the "fourth root" adjustment used

in the equation $\left(\sqrt[4]{\frac{M}{72}}\right)(0.47 - 4.25Y + 0.17L)$

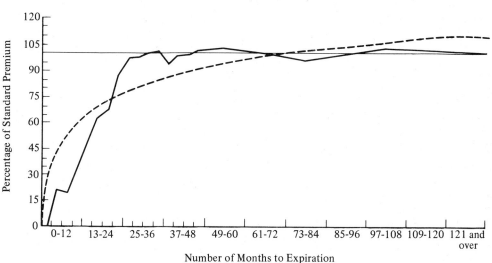

This chart shows the reduction of premium associated with diminishing life span of a warrant as calculated by the "fourth-root adjustment" (smoothed, dashed curve), and as reported in an Investment Bankers Association-sponsored study (heavy, solid line). The IBA study indicates very little reduction in the normal premium occurs earlier than three years before expiration of the warrant; the "fourth-root adjustment", which was determined separately from the IBA study, closely approximates, in a smoothed pattern, the results observed by the IBA.

FIGURE 2

Analysis of effect of approaching expiration: median percentage of standard premiums at which warrants were valued by the market by number of months to expiration

    The decision to adjust the amount of premium by the fourth root of the remaining longevity was supported by the evidence reported in a private study prepared for the Investment Bankers Association in connection with legal matters arising from determination of the taxable value of warrants issued as

---

of the warrants studied (as adjusted with the maximum longevity treated as 10 years). Thus, if the longevity were 72 months, the multiplicatory factor would be 1; for shorter warrants it would decline slowly to zero at time of expiration.

part of underwriting fees.[7] Figure 2, which is taken directly from that study, shows the observed pattern by which the premium disappears as the warrant approaches maturity. The smoothed, dashed curve superimposed on the graph plots the way premium is adjusted by the "fourth-root" calculation used in this paper. The close fit of the "fourth-root" adjustment to the reported data provides visual support for its use in the formula presented in this paper.

As a result of the winnowing process of the research, the following equation was selected to explain wherein the zone of plausible prices a warrant value will fall:

$$Y = \left(\sqrt[4]{\frac{\text{Longevity}}{72}} \right)(.47 - 4.25 \text{ yield} + .17 \text{ if listed})$$

How can the above equation be interpreted? It says that an investor who wants to estimate where in the price zone depicted in Figure 1 a warrant should be located would start by placing it 47% of the distance from top to bottom of the vertical slice of the zone associated with the price of the stock. Then he would subtract percentage points if the associated stock is paying dividends. (To be specific, he would multiply the yield by 4.25 and subtract that amount; e.g., if the stock is yielding 5%, he would subtract 21% from the base figure.) Then he would add 17% if the warrant is traded on the American Exchange. Finally the resulting sum is multiplied by the fourth root of the length-of-life-for-the-warrant-divided-by-72. For purposes of calculation, perpetual warrants and any warrant with a life of more than 10 years have been arbitrarily treated in this research as if they had only a 10-year life span, so M never exceeds 120. This and other data-defining problems are explained in more detail in the appendix.

Statistical results tend to generate an aura of precision that is seldom justified in economic affairs, so no one should assume the above is a magic formula for evaluating warrant prices. Nonetheless, some evidence resulting from the statistical research seems so strongly documented that unless further statistical data are presented to refute it, the following statements can be made about the way warrant prices are actually determined for stocks selling below four times the option price: (1) Virtually all warrant prices (adjusted, if necessary, to relate one warrant to one share of stock) will fall within the plausible price zone, the lower limit of which is the exercise value and the upper limit of which is 3/4 the price of the stock; (2) Warrant prices may be located anywhere within this zone, but they will, on average, be near the middle of it; (3) Variations within the zone are not explained by some factors that could have been expected to have been relevant. Specifically, the following three elements had little ascertainable influence on the warrant-stock price relation: volatility, trend of the associated common stock, and whether the warrant was so low-priced that margin trading was restricted. (4) The dividend yield foregone by owning the warrant instead of the stock is the most significant factor in explaining location in the zone. This has a depressing force on the price of the warrant, in relation to the stock; presumably this is the case not only because the warrant-holder is foregoing dividend income but also because stocks with high dividend

---

[7] This is a privately circulated study prepared for the Investment Bankers Association. Authorship and title are not given.

yields are likely to appreciate less rapidly, and warrant-holders focus on growth in the common stock's market price. The validity of the statistical analysis is reinforced by the fact that theoretical considerations suggest that dividend yield should have been quite significant.[8] (5) Being listed on the American Exchange makes a warrant more valuable. (6) Longevity has an influence which in the limit is controlling, i.e., as the expiration date nears, the warrant price loses any premium. But in the sample studied here, as is true of warrants at any given time, few were on the verge of expiring; consequently longevity was revealed as having only a slight influence on the warrant price. Close observers of warrant prices have felt that the stock market behaved as if a warrant with a life of three years was nearly as good as a perpetual warrant; this study and the one prepared for the Investment Bankers of American give empirical support to that belief. For example, using the adjustments incorporated in the formula developed in this paper, any warrant with 10 or more years life has only 36% more premium than an identical warrant with three years longevity.

One of the implications of the equation is that, all other things being equal, warrants are a better buy when the stock is close to its option price. In this context, the warrant is considered a better buy because it would magnify an upward movement more than it would magnify an equal downward movement in the stock. If the market is wise it will react to such an "elbow" in the price pattern of warrants by favoring warrants at that point, thus pushing their price up enough to eliminate the non-symmetric volatility. Consequently, there was some doubt whether this implication was actually true or a misleading result of the particular statistical technique used. To check on this question, the data were transformed to logarithmic values and the relationship recalculated. The basic conclusion still prevailed: The market did not seem to anticipate completely the potential price growth of warrants after the stock reaches its option price, thus, when the common stock is near its option price appears to be a slightly favorable time to purchase the warrant. This conclusion is qualified by the fact that the observations were much more widely scattered around the slope of the line of best fit below the option price than above; consequently the "bend" in the slope at the option price is only moderately convincing.

E. VALIDITY TESTS

Most investors, even those familiar with the inferences that can be drawn from statistical results, would prefer to see tests that have more practical overtones. One way to test the general value of the equation, which is based on observations during the 1959–62 period, is to test it against prices at another period. This was done for 20 widely traded warrants as of November 18, 1963. The results are shown on Table 1.

The closeness of the predicted prices to actual warrant prices outside the 1959–62 period for which the data were gathered is the best single test of the validity of the foregoing analysis. Most observers would feel that the predicted prices calculated by the equation were close enough to the actual prices to

[8] Samuelson, *op. cit.*, p. 19.

support the belief that the model explains, with reasonable satisfaction, the factors that determine warrant prices. Or, to put it another way, the relationships observed in the 1959–62 period appear to be reasonably stable over time.

The close fit between the equation-calculated values and the actual warrant prices for November 18, 1963 (and for July 1, 1966 and May 4, 1967—both cited in the "how-to-do-it" section) may seem surprising in light of the fact that the multiple correlation coefficient of .61 indicated that a sizable portion of the variation in zone location could not be explained by the model but might be attributed to speculation or market ignorance. Two factors reconcile the moderate precision implied by the multiple regression score with the fairly high degree of accuracy when the model was used to estimate values on November 18, 1963, July 1, 1966 and May 4, 1967.

TABLE 1

Identification of warrant	Closing price of stock, 11/18/63	Option price 11/18/63	No. of shares obtainable per warrant	Dividend yield	Remaining life of warrant (in months)	Traded on American Exchange (A)or over Counter (OC)	Value predicted by Equation	Actual market price
Allegheny	$10.00	$ 3.75	1	1.1%	120*	A	$ 7.09	$ 6.63
Armour	39.38	20.00	1	3.5%	13	A	22.62	22.00
Atlas	3.12	6.25	1	Nil	120*	A	1.70	1.38
Coastal States Gas	34.00	10.67	1	Nil	42	OC	24.21	23.75
Alabama Gas	36.00	35.00	1	4.7%	12	OC	5.41	2.88
General Acceptance	18.62	20.00	1	5.4%	71	A	5.69	4.50
General Tire and Rubber	24.38	8.81	3.12	2.0%	46	OC	51.46	49.50
Hilton Hotels	15.25	46.00	1	Nil	74	A	7.35	3.50
Kerr-McGee Oil '67	37.00	39.22	2.04	2.7%	43	OC	17.45	16.75
Mack Truck (9/1/66)	37.00	33.94	1.4	4.7%	22	A	15.56	17.25
Mack Truck (4/1/71)	37.00	46.00	1	4.7%	88	OC	7.75	8.63
Martin Marietta	20.12	16.48	2.73	4.8%	59	A	22.86	21.13
McCrory	11.25	20.00	1	6.9%	120*	A	3.31	2.38
National General	11.38	3.38	1/4	Nil	70	OC	.98	.75
Sperry Rand	17.00	23.15	1.08	Nil	46	A	7.28	7.75
Symington-Wayne	18.38	15.00	1	4.8%	54	OC	5.91	7.00
Teleregister	7.12	17.00	1	Nil	17	A	2.38	2.75
Textron	37.50	25.00	1	3.7%	120*	A	21.04	11.25
TWA	28.75	20.00	1	Nil	95	A	17.52	12.50
Pacific Petroleum	10.75	19.00	1	Nil	52	A	4.75	5.88

* *For warrant longevity over 10 years, the value is arbitrarily taken to be 120 months. For warrants with increasing option prices, the current option price is used and the length of life of the warrant is shortened as specified by a relationship described in the appendix.*

First, the model begins by establishing a zone to which all results are confined; and at stock prices much above the option price, say above two times the option price, the zone gets fairly narrow in absolute values. The regression analysis was used only to place warrant prices in the zone. If the zone is only $3.00 wide, say, then the difference between being 35% or 50% between the top and bottom of the zone is small in terms of final price. Also the longevity variable in the multiple regression equation was removed in the final model and was applied in a fashion that judgment and testing indicated would lead to better results.

Perusal of Table 1 suggests that the formula presented in this paper should be considered as most applicable to warrants with a life of more than one year; for less than 12 months the "fourth-root" adjustment may not reduce the premium sufficiently. Probably the best advice when evaluating warrants with a life of less than one year is to forecast the stock price during the coming months. In this approach, Morrison's formula, cited in the previous installment, may be useful for deciding the relative attractiveness of the stock or warrant. Another way to view a short-lived warrant is to compare its price to that of a similar "call."

Near the end of a warrant's life, allowance should be made for artificial values caused by technical aspects such as potential "short-cornering." What happened to the Molybdenum warrants in their final year is a classic example of this situation.

For the practical investor, however, another test of the validity of the model is likely to occur. It is natural to note that some of the prices predicted by the equation differ from the actual prices by more than 25%, especially Textron and TWA. The tempting thought arises: Are warrants priced below the computed value likely to rise, and are those that are apparently "overvalued" likely to fall? The data for 1959–62 were tested to answer this question, and the results were only mildly encouraging. The main reason the formula seems to be more successful in predicting what warrant price is likely to prevail at a given point in time than in predicting what direction a warrant price will move is simply that the major element in determining the future price of a warrant is the future price of its stock. The analysis in this paper focuses solely on the concomitant relationship between a warrant's price and the price of its associated stock. Even if a warrant is shown to be "overpriced" in relation to its stock at a given time, the warrant will almost certainly rise if the stock rises in the subsequent year; conversely if the stock falls, the warrant will drop. The evidence is strong that if one wants to know whether the price of a warrant is likely to rise or fall, the answer hinges predominantly on the question: What will the stock do?

The close relation between the price change of a warrant and that of its stock is shown in Table 2, which specifies the percentage profit or loss for 14 periods between 1956 and 1962 if an investor had taken a long position of $1,000 in every warrant cited in the *Standard and Poor's Stock Guide* and also in its associated stock.

Even though it should be clear that if one wants to forecast the price trend of a warrant his most important step is to foresee the future price of its stock, it may still be useful to have some idea whether a warrant is fairly valued in relation to the stock's current price. For one thing, if the stock is expected to remain close to its current price, the warrant might be expected to drift toward the normative value described by the model. Furthermore, it might be reasoned that if "undervalued" warrants are likely to rise more, or fall less, than their related stocks, an investor should go along on an "undervalued" warrant instead of the stock if he contemplates buying either, or conversely, go short on the "overvalued" warrant instead of shorting the stock. (In practice, it is not

TABLE 2

Percentage change in price of stocks and associated warrants for selected periods (Percentages determined by weighting as if equal amounts were invested in each security)

Period	Percentage change for all warrants	Percentage change for related stocks
Periods Approx.		
3 Years Long		
12/31/56–12/31/59	+148%	+54%
12/31/57–11/30/60	+159	+72
12/31/58–12/31/61	+26	+17
Periods Approx.		
2 Years Long		
12/31/56–12/31/58	+45	+18
12/31/57–12/31/59	+223	+127
12/31/58–11/30/60	+19	+26
12/31/59–12/31/61	+28	+35
Periods Approx.		
1 Year Long		
12/31/56–12/31/57	−35	−31
12/31/57–12/31/58	+62	+51
12/31/58–12/41/59	+26	+16
12/31/59–12/30/60	−26	−2
11/30/60–12/31/61	+60	−22
12/31/61–12/31/62	−33	−19
11/30/61–8/31/62	−28	−21

* *This table illustrates two facts about warrants: their price change almost always goes in the same direction as the price change of the associated stock and moves in greater magnitude than the stock.*

recommended that an investor take a non-hedged, pure short position on stock; even for a speculator this is a dubious operation.)

Several ways of testing the predictive power of the model in this comparative sense were tried: (A) The number of times an "undervalued" warrant outperformed its associated stock was calculated as was the number of times an "overvalued" warrant did correspondingly worse than its stock; (B) The comparative profitability of going long on "undervalued" warrants compared to going long on the stock, and of shorting "overvalued" warrants vs. shorting the stocks was estimated. This differs from (A) in that the results are scored on the basis of profitability instead of quantity; (C) The results from going long on all "undervalued" warrants and short on all "overvalued" warrants were calculated, on the reasoning that when enough situations were considered the dominating effect of upward or downward changes in the stock prices would wash out. The net results of these tests indicated that the model has some normative significance but its discriminatory power is imperfect.

Perhaps the test that comes closest to matching what the shrewd investor might do if he wanted to utilize the results of the research embodied in this model starts by selecting the 10 most "undervalued" and the 10 most "overvalued" warrants among the 99 observations in the 1959–62 period. This group approximately represents those that deviated from the "formula value" by more than one standard deviation; the degree of undervaluation or overvaluation was determined by comparing the theoretical, formula-calculated value against the actual price. Realizing the dominance of future stock prices on changes in warrant prices, the decision was to go an equal dollar amount long on each undervalued warrant, then hedge this with an equivalent dollar investment short in each related stock. The rationale is: If the stock price remains constant, the undervalued warrant should rise; if the stock rises, the warrant should rise more; if the stock falls and generates a profit from the short position, the warrant will fall proportionately less. For overvalued warrants the policy was just the reverse: short the warrant and hedge by going long on the related stock. The position, in either case, was closed out in one year.

Consider two specific examples. Among the 10 most undervalued were the Hilton Hotel warrants on November 30, 1960; the warrants were purchased at $5.38, and the stock was shorted at $31.13. One year later the warrants were selling at $10.13 (a gain of 88%), and the stock had risen to $32.13 (a loss of 3%). Assuming $1,000 had been invested in each position, the net profit, excluding brokerage costs, would have been $850, or 42.5% on the total, hedged investment. Among the 10 most overvalued were Molybdenum warrants as of December, 1961. They were shorted at $16.25, and an equal dollar amount was placed long on the stock at $27.88. One year later the positions were closed out with a 20% loss in the stock and a 42% profit from the shorted warrant, or a net gain of 22%; this amounts to 11% annual rate of profit on the total investment.

This simulation of twenty hedges showed an annual average profit rate of 21.68%, but the profit is overstated because brokerage costs have been excluded. Since 44% of the transactions involved securities priced at $5.00 or less, where brokerage fees run 2.5 to 6% of investment outlays, it is probable the average brokerage cost on all trades probably would have been as high as 3%; for the round trip of buying and selling, transaction costs in the order of 6% must be subtracted from the simulated profit.

F. CONCLUSION AND SUMMARY

The first installment of this study presented the hypothesis that warrant prices should fall within a range determined at the minimum by the exercise value (or zero) and at the maximum by an amount equal to 3/4 the price of the stock until the stock reaches four times the option price. In the relatively few situations where warrants exist with stocks selling at more than four times the option price, the hypothesis is that warrants will sell for their exercise value. This *zone of plausible prices* has theoretical justification and considerable empirical support. Of 99 observations selected on five arbitrary days between 1959 and 1962, the warrants were priced on the average, at 49% of the height of the range, i.e., very close to the mid-point between the limits. Even when other observations were included to test extreme values by selecting dates of annual highs and lows for the warrants and their stocks, few observations were found outside the zone.

The second installment reports on a statistical analysis using stepwise multiple regression to determine the factors that influence the point where, in the zone of plausible values, the warrant would be priced. Essentially this is a technique for determining the appropriate premium-over-arbitrage-value to place on a warrant. All variables that could be expected to have any substantial influence on the relationship between warrant and stock price were analyzed. Three were found to be important: the dividend yield foregone, whether the warrant is traded on the American Exchange or over-the-counter, and the longevity of the warrant.

The following factors were found to have statistically insignificant influence: whether the warrant sold at or below $5.00 (in fact all price levels for the warrant were tested, and none were found to have significant infleuence on the warrant-stock price relation); the past trend; and the past volatility of the stock.

After several tests, the following formula was considered to be most effective for calculating the actual location of a warrant in the zone. The percentage of the distance from top to bottom of the appropriate slice in the zone can be estimated by

$$\left(\sqrt[4]{\frac{M}{72}}\right)(.47 - 4.25Y + .17L)$$

where M = number of months of warrant longevity, Y = the dividend yield, as a percentage, on the related common stock, and L has values of 1 or 0, depending on whether the warrant is listed on the American Exchange or traded over-the-counter.

Finally, the formula was tested to see if it could be useful to the warrant trader. For one thing, it was used to estimate warrant prices for November 18, 1963, July 1, 1966, and May 4, 1967—dates subsequent to the period during which the data were gathered. The estimated warrant prices compared closely to the actual price. Then the formula values were tested, over the 1959–62 period, to see if the equation had predictive value in being able to discriminate between warrants that will rise or fall, or at least do relatively better or worse than their stock. The most important element in determining the future price of a warrant was found to be the future price of its stock, but the formula provided guidelines that, even though not accurate in all cases, were generally correct, as shown by a simulated hedging operation.

Finally, this research and the other analyses of warrant values cited in these two papers provide a foundation that should make warrant valuation at least as precise as common stock valuation.

APPENDIX

Explanation of the Statistical Processes Used in the Research

The statistical analysis underlying this paper is difficult to explain simply. It can be most clearly understood if the rationale behind the statistical approach is explained step-by-step. The first thought was to test the price of a warrant as a function of the price of its associated stock. Immediately, though, it is apparent that factors other than the price of the stock influence the price of the warrant:

e.g., the remaining life of the warrant, the option price of the warrant, whether the warrant was listed on the American Exchange or traded over-the-counter, etc. This indicated that the price of the warrant might be tested by multiple regression. The next step in designing the research was to recognize that the influence of some variables would certainly be non-linear: the price of the stock means one thing for warrant valuation when stock is priced below the option price and has a far different impact when above the option price.

This led to the next step in the analysis, viz., determining the premium paid for the warrant rather than the price of the warrant. Consideration of actual relationships showed that the premium was affected by the ratio of the stock price to the option price: the higher the stock price/option price ratio, the lower the premium. This led to a refinement that narrowed the range of warrant price valuation and provided an appropriate situation for using multiple regression to place the warrant price within the zone of reasonable premium (called the Zone of Plausible Prices in the body of the paper).

The statistical technique essentially was to use multiple regression to determine the weight assigned to various factors that determine the location in a zone of plausible premium. Adding the premium thus determined to the minimum exercise value of the warrant establishes a typical market price for the warrant.

But even when the statistical analysis was reduced to the stage of a multiple regression, judgment was still involved. The first element of judgment involved choosing the factors to include in the multiple regression; the second element involved choosing the warrant-stock observations to include in the cross section of observations that provided the basic observation to be analyzed in the multiple regression. The author was completely cognizant of the dangers associated with using more than one observation from any particular warrant; on the other hand, the number of warrants available for which price quotations on the warrant and the stock could be readily obtained was less than forty. Furthermore, a cross section analysis at one period of time might reveal only a relationship peculiar to that point of time. As a matter of fact, the analysis was first made by using a cross section of warrants at separate time periods. Only after it was determined that the values of the coefficients were reasonably stable over the different periods was it decided to use all warrant stock price observations at various intervals of time, thus providing a sample much larger than any single sample and in all probability more representative.

The second issue was whether to determine the variables to include in the multiple regression in advance, or to make the analysis based on those that stood out as empirically significant after testing many variables that might seem important. Such after-the-fact model building runs the danger that the variables found to be important over the period tested may not be important at other times, and the conclusions drawn may be unduly influenced by circumstances peculiar to the test period. This potential weakness, however, was faced by using the data developed in the testing period for predicting warrant prices in a subsequent period, which is one of the most penetrating ways to test the validity of a model. There would be even more confidence in the equation if the variables, and the weight assigned to each, had *a priori* theoretical justification. Nonetheless, strong support is provided the model because its independent variables have a logical basis, and when the equation was used to predict warrant prices in a period several years removed from the period used in the basic analysis, the predicted warrant prices were close to the actual prices.

Given the above research design, the only thing that remains to be explained is the mechanics by which the various warrants were treated so they could be comparable to others. This would have been simple if every warrant were exchangeable for stock on the same basis, e.g., a 1-to-1 exchange ratio between the warrant and the stock, and had identical option prices. Unfortunately, however, one warrant may have an option price of $7.50, another of $17.66; one warrant may entitle the owner to buy one share of stock, another two shares, and a third 1.08 shares of stock, etc.

In order to analyze all warrants as plotted on Figure 1, a way had to be found to convert the various warrants to directly comparable values. For example, General Tire & Rubber had outstanding in 1962 warrants that entitled the holder to buy 3 shares of General Tire common at $8.81 per share. In order to deal with those warrants within the framework of Figure 1 (where each warrant is treated as if it carried the right to buy only one share), the market price of the warrant was divided by 3. Specifically, the observations that dealt with August 31, 1962 showed the warrant priced at $39.50 while the stock was priced at $20.75. If a warrant carries the right to buy only one share it would not sell for more than the stock (barring some unusual situation, such as a corner on the warrants); therefore the price of this warrant reflects the fact that three shares can be purchased through one warrant. If the General Tire warrant carried the right to buy only one share instead of 3, it would sell for $39.50 ÷ 3, or $13.17. After this adjustment, the procedure is the same as with warrants that convert 1-for-1, viz., the adjusted price of the warrant ($13.17) was divided by the option price ($8.81) to get the price of the warrant as ratio of the option price (1.495). This is plotted against the vertical axis of Figure 1.

Figure 1 and the calculations described in this paper are based on adjusted prices, i.e., neither the actual price of the stock nor the warrant is used; "normalized" prices are used instead. The preceding paragraph explained the adjustments made to the warrant prices in order to analyze them on a comparable basis, viz., as if they all carried the same option price and converted 1-for-1. Because it was necessary to normalize the warrant prices, it became necessary also to normalize the stock prices. This was accomplished by dividing the stock prices by the option price. Since the purpose of this analysis is to show the *relationship* between warrant and stock prices, the *relationship* is not affected when both variables are divided by the same number (the option price). The "normalized" stock prices constitute the horizontal axis of Figure 1. It is interesting to note that Samuelson used exactly the same technique of normalization in his paper.

Another problem arose in quantifying the longevity of warrants. Many warrants change their option price before they expire. For example, Textron warrants had an option price of $25 until April 30, 1964, then $30 for the next five years, $35 for the five years from 1969 to 1974, $40 for the following half decade, and finally $45 until they expire in April 1984. It would be inaccurate as of 1963 to say the option price was $45 and the warrant had about 21 years to maturity, but it would also be wrong to claim its option price was $25 and maturity only about 1 year. A reasonable compromise between these two extremes was based on a study of the typical pattern for changing warrant prices.

The life of the warrant was reduced, for statistical comparisons, by 2.5% for every 1% increase in the option price. For example, if a warrant had an option price of $20 until December 1964, then $22 until it finally expired in December 1966, the 10% increase in option price would be acknowledged by reducing the final two years by 25% (2 1/2 times 10%) and processing the warrant as if it stayed at $20 until June 1966. Admittedly, this is only an approximation of the net effect of two factors: the increased price and the longer maturity. But, since the longevity of a warrant apparently has only slight influence on the price, the adjustment is not believed to be crucial to the evaluation.

Another technical adjustment was required when the research moved to the stage of multiple regression. One of the variables was longevity of the warrant, counted in months, but no figure could be used for perpetual warrants. As stated in the main body of the paper, longevity was only a slight factor at best, and statistical analysis showed there was virtually no difference in warrants with five years or more longevity, so no warrants were assigned a maturity of greater than 10 years (120 months) for purposes of statistical processing.

Fama, Fisher, Jensen, and Roll examine the effect of stock splits and dividends on the price of common stocks. They show that stock splits and dividends by themselves have little influence on the stock price and, therefore, that extraordinary profits cannot be earned by buying stocks which have announced splits or dividends. In addition, this article re-presents an interesting application of the Sharpe–Lintner general equilibrium theory to test a hypothesis relating to firm valuation. Equilibrium theory is discussed in Part II of this book.

15

The Adjustment of Stock Prices to New Information

Eugene F. Fama, Lawrence Fisher, Michael C. Jensen, and Richard Roll

This article is reprinted with permission from the International Economic Review, *Vol. 10, No. 1 (February, 1969), pp. 1–21.*

1. INTRODUCTION

There is an impressive body of empirical evidence which indicates that successive price changes in individual common stocks are very nearly independent.[2] Recent papers by Mandelbrot [11] and Samuelson [16] show rigorously that independence of successive price changes is *consistent* with an "efficient" market, i.e., a market that adjusts rapidly to new information.

It is important to note, however, that in the empirical work to date the

---

[1] This study way suggested to us by Professor James H. Lorie. We are grateful to Professors Lorie, Merton H. Miller, and Harry V. Roberts for many helpful comments and criticisms.

The research reported here was supported by the Center for Research in Security Prices, Graduate School of Business, University of Chicago, and by funds made available to the Center by the National Science Foundation.

[2] Cf. Cootner [2] and the studies reprinted therein, Fama [3], Godfrey, Granger, and Morgenstern [8] and other empirical studies of the theory of random walks in speculative prices.

usual procedure has been to *infer* market efficiency from the observed independence of successive price changes. There has been very little actual testing of the speed of adjustment of prices to *specific kinds* of new information. The prime concern of this paper is to examine the process by which common stock prices adjust to the information (if any) that is implicit in a stock split.

2. SPLITS, DIVIDENDS, AND NEW INFORMATION: A HYPOTHESIS

More specifically, this study will attempt to examine evidence on two related questions: (1) Is there normally some "unusual" behavior in the rates of return on a split security in the months surrounding the split?[3] and (2) if splits are associated with "unusual" behavior of security returns, to what extent can this be accounted for by relationships between splits and changes in other more fundamental variables?[4]

In answer to the first question we shall show that stock splits are usually preceded by a period during which the rates of return (including dividends and capital appreciation) on the securities to be split are unusually high. The period of high returns begins, however, long before any information (or even rumor) concerning a possible split is likely to reach the market. Thus we suggest that the high returns far in advance of the split arise from the fact that during the pre-split period these companies have experienced dramatic increases in expected earnings and dividends.

In the empirical work reported below, however, we shall see that the highest average monthly rates of return on split shares occur in the few months immediately preceding the split. This might appear to suggest that the split itself provides some impetus for increased returns. We shall present evidence, however, which suggests that such is not the case. The evidence supports the following reasoning: Although there has probably been a dramatic increase in earnings in the recent past, in the months immediately prior to the split (or its announcement) there may still be considerable uncertainty in the market concerning whether the earnings can be maintained at their new higher level. Investors will attempt to use any information available to reduce this uncertainty, and a proposed split may be one source of such information.

In the past a large fraction of stock splits have been followed closely by dividend increases—and increases greater than those experienced at the same

---

[3] A precise definition of "unusual" behavior of security returns will be provided below.

[4] There is another question concerning stock splits which this study does not consider. That is, given that splitting is not costless, and since the only apparent result is to multiply the number of shares per shareholder without increasing the shareholder's claims to assets, why do firms split their shares? This question has been the subject of considerable discussion in the professional financial literature. (Cf. Bellemore and Blucher [1].) Suffice it to say that the arguments offered in favor of splitting usually turn out to be two-sided under closer examination—e.g., a split, by reducing the price of a round lot, will reduce transactions costs for some relatively small traders but increase costs for both large and very small traders (i.e., for traders who will trade, exclusively, either round lots or odd lots both before and after the split). Thus the conclusions are never clear-cut. In this study we shall be concerned with identifying the factors which the *market* regards as important in a stock split and with determining how market prices adjust to these factors rather than with explaining why firms split their shares.

time by other securities in the market. In fact it is not unusual for the dividend change to be announced at the same time as the split. Other studies (cf. Lintner [10] and Michaelsen [14]) have demonstrated that, once dividends have been increased, large firms show great reluctance to reduce them, except under the most extreme conditions. Directors have appeared to hedge against such dividend cuts by increasing dividends only when they are quite sure of their ability to maintain them in the future, i.e., only when they feel strongly that future earnings will be sufficient to maintain the dividends at their new higher rate. Thus dividend changes may be assumed to convey important information to the market concerning management's assessment of the firm's long-run earning and dividend paying potential.

We suggest, then, that unusually high returns on splitting shares in the months immediately preceding a split reflect the market's anticipation of substantial increases in dividends which, in fact, usually occur. Indeed evidence presented below leads us to conclude that when the information effects of dividend changes are taken into account, the apparent price effects of the split will vanish.[5]

3. SAMPLE AND METHODOLOGY

a. The data. We define a "stock split" as an exchange of shares in which at least five shares are distributed for every four formerly outstanding. Thus this definition of splits includes all stock dividends of 25 per cent or greater. We also decided, arbitrarily, that in order to get reliable estimates of the parameters that will be used in the analysis, it is necessary to have at least twenty-four successive months of price-dividend data around the split date. Since the data cover only common stocks listed on the New York Stock Exchange, our rules require that to qualify for inclusion in the tests a split security must be listed on the Exchange for at least twelve months before and twelve months after the split. From January, 1927 through December, 1959, 940 splits meeting these criteria occurred on the New York Stock Exchange.[6]

b. Adjusting security returns for general market conditions. Of course, during this 33 year period, economic and hence general stock market conditions were far from static. Since we are interested in isolating whatever *extraordinary* effects a split and its associated dividend history may have on returns, it is necessary to abstract from general market conditions in examining the returns on securities during months surrounding split dates. We do this in the following way: Define

[5] It is important to note that our hypothesis concerns the information content of dividend changes. There is nothing in our evidence which suggests that dividend *policy* per se affects the value of a firm. Indeed, the information hypothesis was first suggested by Miller and Modigliani in [15, (430)], where they show that, aside from information effects, in a perfect capital market dividend policy will not affect the total market value of a firm.

[6] The basic data were contained in the master file of monthly prices, dividends, and capital changes, collected and maintained by the Center for Research in Security Prices (Graduate School of Business, University of Chicago). At the time this study was conducted, the file covered the period January, 1926 to December, 1960. For a description of the data see Fisher and Lorie [7].

P_{jt} = price of the j-th stock at end of month t.

P'_{jt} = P_{jt} adjusted for captal changes in month $t+1$. For the method of adjustment see Fisher [5].

D_{jt} = cash dividends on the j-th security during month t (where the dividend is taken as of the ex-dividend data rather than the payment date).

R_{jt} = $(P_{it}+D_{jt})/P'_{j,t-1}$ = price relative of the j-th security for month t.

L_t = the link relative of Fisher's "Combination Investment Performance Index" [6, (Table Al)]. It will suffice here to note that L_t is a complicated average of the R_{jt} for all securities that were on the N.Y.S.E. at he end of months t and $t-1$. L_t is the measure of "general market conditions" used in this study.[7]

One form or another of the following simple model has often been suggested as a way of expressing the relationship between the monthly rates or return provided by an individual security and general market conditions.[8]

$$\log_e R_{jt} = \alpha_j + \beta_j \log_e L_t + u_{jt} \tag{1}$$

where α_j and β_j are parameters that can vary from security to security and u_{jt} is a random disturbance term. It is assumed that u_{jt} satisfies the usual assumptions of the linear regression model. That is, (a) u_{jt} has zero expectation and variance independent of t; (b) the u_{jt} are serially independent; and (c) the distribution of u_j is independent of $\log_e L$.

The natural logarithm of the security price relative is the rate of return (with continuous compounding) for the month in question; similarly, the log of the market index relative is approximately the rate of return on a portfolio which includes equal dollar amounts of all securities in the market. Thus (1) represents the monthly rate of return on an individual security as a linear function of the corresponding return for the market.

c. Tests of model specification. Using the available time series on R_{jt} and L_t, least squares has been used to estimate α_j and β_j in (1) for each of the 622 securities in the sample of 940 splits. We shall see later that there is strong evidence that the expected values of the residuals from (1) are non-zero in

[7] To check that our results do not arise from any special properties of the index L_t, we have also performed all tests using Standard and Poor's Composite Price Index as the measure of market conditions; in all major respects the results agree completely with those reported below.

[8] Cf. Markowitz [13, (96–101)], Sharpe [17, 18] and Fama [4]. The logarithmic form of the model is appealing for two reasons. First, over the period covered by our data the distribution of the monthly values of $\log_e L_t$ and $\log_e R_{jt}$ are fairly symmetric, whereas the distributions of the relatives themselves are skewed right. Symmetry is desirable since models involving symmetrically distributed variables present fewer estimation problems than models involving variables with skewed distributions. Second, we shall see below that when least squares is used to estimate α and β in (1), the sample residuals conform well to the assumptions of the simple linear regression model.

Thus, the logarithmic form of the model appears to be well specified from a statistical point of view and has a natural economic interpretation (i.e., in terms of monthly rates of return with continuous compounding). Nevertheless, to check that our results do not depend critically on using logs, all tests have also been carried out using the simple regression of R_{jt} on L_t. These results are in complete agreement with those presented in the text.

months close to the split. For these months the assumptions of the regression model concerning the disturbance term in (1) are not valid. Thus if these months were included in the sample, estimates of α and β would be subject to specification error, which could be very serious. We have attempted to avoid this source of specification error by excluding from the estimating samples those months for which the expected values of the residuals are apparently non-zero. The exclusion procedure was as follows: First, the parameters of (1) were estimated for each security using all available data. Then for each split the sample regression residuals were computed for a number of months preceding and following the split. When the number of positive residuals in any month differed substantially from the number of negative residuals, that month was excluded from subsequent calculations. This criterion caused exclusion of fifteen months before the split for all securities and fifteen months after the split for splits followed by dividend decreases.[9]

Aside from these exclusions, however, the least squares estimates $\hat{\alpha}_j$ and $\hat{\beta}_j$ for security j are based on all months during the 1926–60 period for which price relatives are available for the security. For the 940 splits the smallest effective sample size is 14 monthly observations. In only 46 cases is the sample size less than 100 months, and for about 60 per cent of the splits more than 300 months of data are available. Thus in the vast majority of cases the samples used in estimating α and β in (1) are quite large.

Table 1 provides summary descriptions of the frequency distributions of the estimated values of α_j, β_j, and r_j where r_j is the correlation between monthly rates of return on security j (i.e., $\log_e R_{jt}$) and the approximate monthly rates of return on the market portfolio (i.e., $\log_e L_t$). The table indicates that there are indeed fairly strong relationships between the market and monthly returns on individual securities; the mean value of the r_j is 0.632 with an average absolute deviation of 0.106 about the mean.[10]

TABLE 1

Summary of frequency distributions of estimated coefficients for the different split securities

Statistic	Mean	Median	Mean absolute deviation	Standard deviation	Extreme values		Skewness
$\hat{\alpha}$	0.000	0.001	0.004	0.007	–0.06,	0.04	Slightly left
$\hat{\beta}$	0.894	0.880	0.242	0.305	–0.10*,	1.95	Slightly right
$\hat{r}$	0.632	0.655	0.106	0.132	–0.04*,	0.91	Silghtly left

* *Only negative value in distribution.*

[9] Admittedly the exclusion criterion is arbitrary. As a check, however, the analysis of regression residuals discussed later in the paper has been carried out using the regression estimates in which no data are excluded. The results were much the same as those reported in the text and certainly support the same conclusions.

[10] The sample average or mean absolute deviation of the random variable x is defined as where x is the sample mean of the x's and N is the sample size.

Moreover, the estimates of equation (1) for the different securities conform fairly well to the assumptions of the linear regression model. For example, the first order auto-correlation coefficient of the estimated residuals from (1) has been computed for every twentieth split in the sample (ordered alphabetically by security). The mean (and median) value of the forty-seven cofficients is –0.10, which suggests that serial dependence in the residals is not a serious problem. For these same forty-seven splits scatter diagrams of (a) monthly security return versus market return, and (b) estimated residual return in month $t+1$ versus estimated residual return in month t have been prepared, along with (c) normal probability graphs of estimated residuals returns. The scatter diagrams for the individual securities support very well the regression assumptions of linearity, homoscedasticity, and serial independence.

It is important to note, however, that the data do not conform well to the normal, or Gaussian linear regression model. In particular, the distributions of the estimated residuals have much longer tails than the Gaussian. The typical normal probability graph of residuals looks much like the one shown for Timken Detroit Axle in Figure 1. The departures from normality in the distributions of regression residuals are of the same sort as those noted by Fama [3] for the distributions of returns themselves. Fama (following Mandelbrot [12]) argues that distributions of returns are well approximated by the non-Gaussian (i.e., infinite variance) members of the stable Paretian family. If the stable non-Gaussian distributions also provide a good description of the residuals in (1), then, at first glance, the least squares regression model would seem inappropriate.

Wise [19] has shown, however, that although least square estimates are not "efficient," for most members of the stable Paretian family they provide estimates which are unbiased and consistent. Thus, given our large samples, least squares regression is not completely inappropriate. In deference to the stable Paretian model, however, in measuring variability we rely primarily on the mean absolute deviation rather than the variance or the standard deviation. The mean absolute deviation is used since, for long-tailed distributions, its sampling behavior is less erratic than that of the variance or the standard deviation.[11]

In sum we find that regression of security returns on market returns over time are a satisfactory method for abstracting from the effects of general market conditions on the monthly rates of return on individual securities. We must point out, however, that although (1) stands up farily well to the assumptions of the linear regression model, it is certainly a grossly over-simplified model of price formation; general market conditions alone do not determine the returns on an individual security. In (1) the effects of these "omitted variables" are impounded into the disturbance term u. In particular, if a stock split is associated

$$\frac{\sum_{t=1}^{N} |x_t - \bar{x}|}{N}$$

[11] Essentially, this is due to the fact that in computing the variance of a sample, large deviations are weighted more heavily than in computing the mean absolute deviation. For empirical evidence concerning the reliability of the mean absolute deviation relative to the variance or standard deviation see Fama [3, (94–8)].

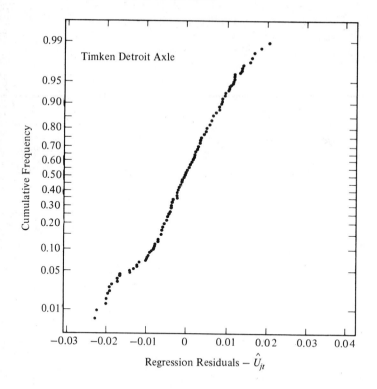

The lower left and upper right corners of the graph represent the most extreme sample points. For clarity, only every tenth point is plotted in the central portion of the figure.

FIGURE 1

Normal probability plot of residuals

with abnormal behavior in returns during months surrounding the split date, this behavior should be reflected in the estimated regression residuals of the security for these months. The remainer of our analysis will concentrate on examining the behavior of the estimated residuals of split scurities in the months surrounding the splits.

3. "EFFECTS" OF SPLITS ON RETURNS: EMPIRICAL RESULTS

In this study we do not attempt to determine the effects of splits for individual companies. Rather we are concerned with whether the process of splitting is in general associated with specific types of return behavior. To abstract from the eccentricities of specific cases we can rely on the simple process of averaging;

we shall therefore concentrate attention on the behavior of cross-sectional averages of estimated regression residuals in the months surrounding split dates.

a. Some additional definitions. The procedure is as follows: For a given split, define month 0 as the month in which the effective date of a split occurs. (Thus month 0 is not the same chronological date for all securities, and indeed some securities have been split more than once and hence have more than one month 0.)[12] Month 1 is then defined as the month immediately following the split month, while month -1 is the month preceding, etc. Now define the average residual for month m (where m is always measured relative to the split month) as

$$u_m = \frac{\sum_{j=1}^{Nm} \hat{u}_{jm}}{N_m}$$

where $\hat{u}_{jm}$ is the sample regression residual for security j in month m and n_m is the number of splits for which data are available in month m.[13] Our principal tests will involve examining the behavior of u_m for m in the interval $-29 \leq m \leq 30$, i.e., for the sixty months surrounding the split month.

We shall also be interested in examining the cumulative effects of abnormal return behavior in months surrounding the split month. Thus we define the behavior in months surrounding the split month. Thus we define the cumulative average residual U_m as

$$U_m = \sum_{k=-29}^{m} u_k.$$

The average residual u_m can be interpreted as the average deviation (in month m relative to the split month) of the returns of split stocks from their normal relationships with the market. Similarly, the cumulative average residual U_m can be interpreted as the cumulative deviation (from month -29 to month m); it shows the cumulative effects of the wanderings of the returns of split stocks from their normal relationships to market movements.

Since the hypothesis about the effects of splits on returns expounded in Section 2 centers on the dividend behavior of split shares, in some of the tests to follow we examine separately splits that are associated with increased dividends and splits that are associated with decreased dividends. In addition, in order to abstract from general changes in dividends across the market, "increased" and "decreased" dividends will be measured relative to the average dividends paid by all securities on the New York Stock Exchange during the relevant time periods. The dividends are classified as follows: Define the dividend change ratio as total dividends (per equivalent unsplit share) paid in the twelve months after the split, divided by total dividends paid during the twelve

---

[12] About a third of the securities in the master file split. About a third of these split more than once.

[13] Since we do not consider splits of companies that were not on the New York Stock Exchange for at least a year before and a year after a split, n_m will be 940 for $-11 \leq m \leq 12$. For other months, however, $n_m < 940$.

months before the split.[14] Dividend "increases" are then defined as cases where the dividend change ratio of the split stock is greater than the ratio for the Exchange as a whole, while dividend "decreases" include cases of relative dividend decline.[15] We then define u_m^+, u_m^- and U_m^+, U_m^- as the average and cumulative average residuals for splits followed by increased" (+) and "decreased" (−) dividends.

These definitions of "increased" and "decreased" dividends provide a simple and convenient way of abstracting from general market dividend changes in classifying year-to-year dividend changes for individual securities. The definitions have the following drawback, however. For a company paying quarterly dividends an increase in its dividend rate at any time during the nine months before or twelve months after the split can place its stock in the dividend "increased" class. Thus the actual increase need not have occurred in the year after the split. The same fuzziness, of course, also arises in classifying dividend "decreases." We shall see later, however, that this fuzziness fortunately does not obscure the differences between the aggregate behavior patterns of the two groups.

b. *Empirical Results.* The most important empirical results of this study are summarized in Tables 2 and 3 and Figures 2 and 3. Table 2 presents the average residuals, cumulative average residuals, and the sample size for each of the two dividend classifications ("increased," and "decreased") and for the total of all splits for each of the sixty months surrounding the split. Figure 2 presents graphs of the average and cumulative average residuals for the toal sample of splits and Figure 3 presents these graphs for each of the two dividend classifications. Table 3 shows the number of splits each year along with the end of June level of the stock price index.

Several of our earlier statements can now be substantiated. First, Figures 2a, 3a and 3b show that the average residuals (u_m) in the twenty-nine months prior to the split are uniformly positive for all splits and for both classes of dividend behavior. This can hardly be attributed entirely to the splitting process. In a random sample of fifty-two splits from our data the median time between the announcement date and the effective date of the split was 44.5 days. Similarly, in a random sample af one hundred splits that occurred between 1/1/1946 and 1/1/1957 Jaffe [9] found that the median time between announcement date and effective date was sixty-nine days. For both samples in only about 10 per cent of the cases is the time between announcement date and effective date greater than four months. Thus it seems safe to say that the split cannot account for the behavior of the regression residuals as far as two and one-half years in advance of the split date. Rather we suggest the obvious—a sharp improvement, relative to the market, in the earnings prospects of the company sometime during the years immediately preceding a split.

---

[14] A dividend is considered "paid" on the first day the security trades ex-dividend on the Exchange.

[15] When dividend "increase" and "decrease" are defined relative to the market, it turns out that dividends were never "unchanged." That is, the dividend change ratios of split securities are never identical to the corresponding ratios for the Exchange as a whole. In the remainder of the paper we shall always use "increase" and "decrease" as defined in the text. That is, signs of dividend changes for individual securities are measured relative to changes in the dividends for all N.Y.S.E. common stocks.

TABLE 2

Analysis of residuals in months surrounding the split

(1)	Splits followed by dividend "increases"			Splits followed by dividend "decreases"			All splits		
Month m	(2) Average u_m^+	(3) Cumulative U_m^+	(4) Sample size N_m^+	(5) Average u_m^-	(6) Cumulative U_m^-	(7) Sample size N_m^-	(8) Average u_m	(9) Cumulative U_m	(10) Sample size N_m
−29	0.0062	0.0062	614	0.0033	0.0033	252	0.0054	0.0054	866
−28	0.0013	0.0075	617	0.0030	0.0063	253	0.0018	0.0072	870
−27	0.0068	0.0143	618	0.0007	0.0070	253	0.0050	0.0122	871
−26	0.0054	0.0198	619	0.0085	0.0155	253	0.0063	0.0185	872
−25	0.0042	0.0240	621	0.0089	0.0244	254	0.0056	0.0241	875
−24	0.0020	0.0259	623	0.0026	0.0270	256	0.0021	0.0263	879
−23	0.0055	0.0315	624	0.0028	0.0298	256	0.0047	0.0310	880
−22	0.0073	0.0388	628	0.0028	0.0326	256	0.0060	0.0370	884
−21	0.0049	0.0438	633	0.0131	0.0457	257	0.0073	0.0443	890
−20	0.0044	0.0482	634	0.0005	0.0463	257	0.0033	0.0476	891
−19	0.0110	0.0592	636	0.0102	0.0565	258	0.0108	0.0584	894
−18	0.0076	0.0668	644	0.0089	0.0654	260	0.0080	0.0664	904
−17	0.0072	0.0739	650	0.0111	0.0765	260	0.0083	0.0746	910
−16	0.0035	0.0775	655	0.0009	0.0774	260	0.0028	0.0774	915
−15	0.0135	0.0909	659	0.0101	0.0875	260	0.0125	0.0900	919
−14	0.0135	0.1045	662	0.0100	0.0975	263	0.0125	0.1025	925
−13	0.0148	0.1193	665	0.0099	0.1074	264	0.0134	0.1159	929
−12	0.0138	0.1330	669	0.0107	0.1181	266	0.0129	0.1288	935
−11	0.0098	0.1428	672	0.0103	0.1285	268	0.0099	0.1387	940
−10	0.0103	0.1532	672	0.0082	0.1367	268	0.0097	0.1485	940
−9	0.0167	0.1698	672	0.0152	0.1520	268	0.0163	0.1647	940
−8	0.0163	0.1862	672	0.0140	0.1660	268	0.0157	0.1804	940
−7	0.0159	0.2021	672	0.0083	0.1743	268	0.0138	0.1942	240
−6	0.0194	0.2215	672	0.0106	0.1849	268	0.0169	0.2111	940
−5	0.0194	0.2409	672	0.0100	0.1949	268	0.0167	0.2278	940
−4	0.0260	0.2669	672	0.0104	0.2054	268	0.0216	0.2494	940
−3	0.0325	0.2993	672	0.0204	0.2258	268	0.0289	0.2783	940
−2	0.0390	0.3383	672	0.0296	0.2554	268	0.0363	0.3147	940
−1	0.0199	0.3582	672	0.0176	0.2730	268	0.0192	0.3339	940
0	0.0131	0.3713	672	−0.0090	0.2640	268	0.0068	0.3407	940
1	0.0016	0.3729	672	−0.0088	0.2552	268	−0.0014	0.3393	940
2	0.0052	0.3781	672	−0.0024	0.2528	268	0.0031	0.3424	940
3	0.0024	0.3805	672	−0.0089	0.2439	268	−0.0008	0.3416	940
4	0.0045	0.3851	672	−0.0114	0.2325	268	0.0000	0.3416	940
5	0.0048	0.3898	672	−0.0003	0.2322	268	0.0033	0.3449	940
6	0.0012	0.3911	672	−0.0038	0.2285	268	−0.0002	0.3447	940
7	0.0008	0.3919	672	−0.0106	0.2179	268	−0.0024	0.3423	940
8	−0.0007	0.3912	672	−0.0024	0.2155	268	−0.0012	0.3411	940
9	0.0039	0.3951	672	−0.0065	0.2089	268	0.0009	0.3420	940
10	−0.0001	0.3950	672	−0.0027	0.2062	268	−0.0008	0.3412	940
11	0.0027	0.3977	672	−0.0056	0.2006	268	0.0003	0.3415	940

TABLE 2 (continued)

(1)	Splits followed by dividend "increases"			Splits followed by dividend "decreases"			All splits		
Month m	(2) Average u_m^+	(3) Cumulative U_m^+	(4) Sample size N_m^+	(5) Average u_m^-	(6) Cumulative U_m^-	(7) Sample size N_m^-	(8) Average u_m	(9) Cumulative U_m	(10) Sample size N_m
12	0.0018	0.3996	672	−0.0043	0.1963	268	0.0001	0.3416	940
13	−0.0003	0.3993	666	0.0014	0.1977	264	0.0002	0.3418	930
14	0.0006	0.3999	653	0.0044	0.2021	258	0.0017	0.3435	911
15	−0.0037	0.3962	645	0.0026	0.2047	258	−0.0019	0.3416	903
16	0.0001	0.3963	635	−0.0040	0.2007	257	−0.0011	0.3405	892
17	0.0034	0.3997	633	−0.0011	0.1996	256	0.0021	0.3426	889
18	−0.0015	0.3982	628	0.0025	0.2021	255	−0.0003	0.2423	883
19	−0.0006	0.3976	620	−0.0057	0.1964	251	−0.0021	0.3402	871
20	−0.0002	0.3974	604	0.0027	0.1991	246	0.0006	0.3409	850
21	−0.0037	0.3937	595	−0.0073	0.1918	245	−0.0047	0.3361	840
22	0.0047	0.3984	593	−0.0018	0.1899	244	0.0028	0.3389	837
23	−0.0026	0.3958	593	0.0043	0.1943	242	−0.0006	0.3383	835
24	−0.0022	0.3936	587	0.0031	0.1974	238	−0.0007	0.3376	825
25	0.0012	0.3948	583	−0.0037	0.1936	237	−0.0002	0.3374	820
26	−0.0058	0.3890	582	0.0015	0.1952	236	−0.0037	0.3337	818
27	−0.0003	0.3887	582	0.0082	0.2033	235	0.0021	0.3359	817
28	0.0004	0.3891	580	−0.0023	0.2010	236	−0.0004	0.3355	816
29	0.0012	0.3903	580	−0.0039	0.1971	235	−0.0003	0.3352	815
30	−0.0033	0.3870	579	−0.0025	0.1946	235	−0.0031	0.3321	814

Thus we conclude that companies tend to split their shares during "abnormally" good times—that is, during periods of time when the prices of their shares have increased much more then would be implied by the normal relationships between their share prices and general market price behavior. This result in doubly interesting since, from Table 3, it is clear that for the exchange as a whole the number of splits increases dramatically following a general rise in stock prices. Thus splits tend to occur during general "boom" periods, and the particular stocks that are split will tend to be those that performed "unusually" well during the period of general price increase.

It is important to note (from Figure 2a and Table 2) that when all splits are examined together, the largest positive average residuals occur in the three or four months immediately preceding the split, but that after the split the average residuals are randomly distributed about 0. Or equivalently, in Figure 2b the *cumulative* average residuals rise dramatically up to the split month, but there is almost no further systematic movement thereafter. Indeed during the first year after the split, the cumulative average residual changes by less than one-tenth of one percentage point, and the total change in the cumulative average residual during the two and one-half years following the split is less than one percentage point. This is especially striking since 71.5 per cent (672 out of 940) of all splits experienced greater percentage dividend increases in the year after the split than the average for all securities on the N.Y.S.E.

TABLE 3

Number of splits per year and level of the stock market index

Year	Number of spjits	Market index* (End of June)
1927	28	103.5
28	22	133.6
29	40	161.8
1930	15	98.9
31	2	65.5
32	0	20.4
33	1	82.9
34	7	78.5
35	4	73.3
36	11	124.7
37	19	147.4
38	6	100.3
39	3	90.3
1940	2	91.9
41	3	101.2
42	0	95.9
43	3	195.4
44	11	235.0
45	39	320.1
46	75	469.2
47	46	339.9
48	26	408.7
49	21	331.3
1950	49	441.6
51	55	576.1
52	37	672.2
53	25	691.9
54	43	818.6
55	89	1190.6
56	97	1314.1
57	44	1384.3
58	14	1407.3
59	103	1990.6

* *Fisher's "Combination Investment Performance Index" shifted to a base January, 1926 = 100. See [6] for a description of its calculation.*

We suggest the following explanation for this behavior of the average residuals. When a split is announced or anticipated, the market interprets this (and correctly so) as greatly improving the probability that dividends will soon be substantially increased. (In fact, as noted earlier, in many cases the split and dividend increase will be announced at the same time.) If as Lintner [10] suggests, firms are reluctant to reduce dividends, then a split, which implies an increased expected divdend, is a signal to the market that the company's directors are confident that future earnings will be sufficient to maintain divdend payments at a higher level. If the market agrees with the judgments of the

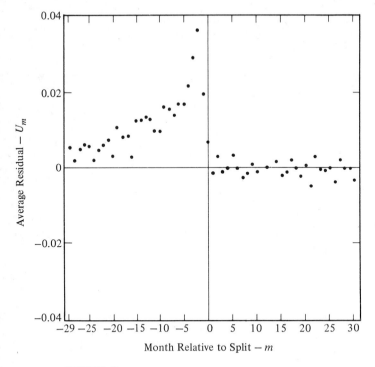

FIGURE 2a

Average residuals—all splits

directors, then it is possible that the large price increases in the months immediately preceding a split are due to altering expectations concerning the future earning potential of the firm (and thus of its shares) rather than to any intrinsic effects of the split istelf.[16]

If the information effects of actual or anticipated divdend increases do indeed explain the behavior of common stock returns in the months immediately surrounding a split, then there should be substantial differences in return behavior subsequent to the split in cases where the dividend increase materializes and cases where it does not. In fact it is apparent from Figure 3 that the differences are substantial—and we shall argue that they are in the direction predicted by the hypothesis.

The fact that the cumulative average residuals for both dividend classes

---

[16] If this stock split hypothesis is correct, the fact that the average residuals [where the averages are computed using all splits (Figure 2)] are randomly distributed about 0 in months subsequent to the split indicates that, on the average, the market has *correctly* evaluated the implications of a split for future dividend behavior and that these evaluations are fully incorporated in the price of the stock by the time the split occurs. That is, the market not only makes good forecasts of the dividend implications of a split, but these forecasts are fully impounded into the price of the security by the end of the split month. We shall return to this point at the end of this section.

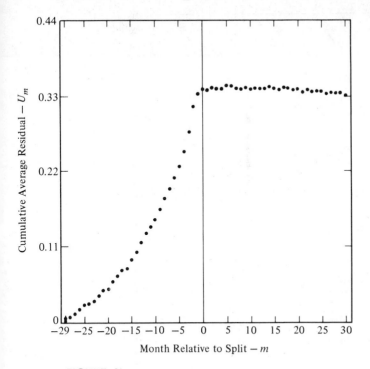

FIGURE 2b

Cumulative average residuals—all splits

rise sharply in the few months before the split is *consistent* with the hypothesis
that the market recognizes that splits are usually associated with higher dividend
payments. In some cases, however, the dividend increase, if it occurs, will be
declared sometime during the year after the split. Thus it is not suprising that the
average residuals (Figure 3a) for stocks in the dividend "increased" class are in
general slightly positive, in the year after the split, so that the cumulative average
residuals (Figure 3c) drift upward. The fact that this upward drift is only very
slight can be explained in two (complementary) ways. First, in many cases the
dividend increase associated with a split will be declared (and the corresponding
price adjustments will take place) before the end of the split month. Second,
according to our hypothesis when the split is declared (even if no dividend
announcement is made), there is some price adjustment in anticipation of future
dividend increases. Thus only a slight *additional* adjustment is necessary when the
dividend increase actually takes place. By one year after the split the returns
on stocks which have experienced dividend "increases" have resumed their
normal relationships to market returns since from this point onward the
average residuals are small and randomly scattered about zero.

The behavior of the residuals for stock splits associated with "decreased"
dividends, however, provides the strongest evidence in favor of our split hypothesis. For stocks in the dividend "decreased" class the average and cumulative
average residuals (Figures 3b and 3d) rise in the few months before the split but

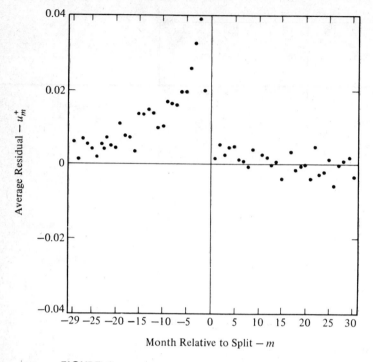

FIGURE 3a

Average residuals for dividend "increases"

then plummet in the few months following the split, when the anticipated dividend increase is not forthcoming. These split stocks with poor dividend performance on the average perform poorly in each of the twelve months following the split, but their period of poorest performance is in the few months immediately after the split—when the improved dividend, if it were coming at all, would most likely be declared.[17] The hypothesis is further reinforced by the observation that when a year has passed after the split, the cumulative average residual has fallen to about where it was five months prior to the split which, we venture to say, is probably about the earliest time reliable information concerning a possible split is likely to reach the market.[18] Thus by the time it has become clear that the anticipated dividend increase is not forthcoming, the apparent effects of the split seem to have been completely wiped away, and the stock's

---

[17] Though we do not wish to push the point too hard, it is interesting to note in Table 2 that after the split month, the largest negative average residuals for splits in the dividend "decreased" class occur in months 1, 4, and 7. This "pattern" in the residuals suggests, perhaps, that the market reacts most strongly during months when dividends are declared but not increased.

[18] In a random sample of 52 splits from our data in only 2 cases is the time between the announcement date and effective date of the split greater than 162 days. Similarly, in the data of Jaffe [9] in only 4 out of 100 randomly selected splits is the time between announcement and effective date greater than 130 days.

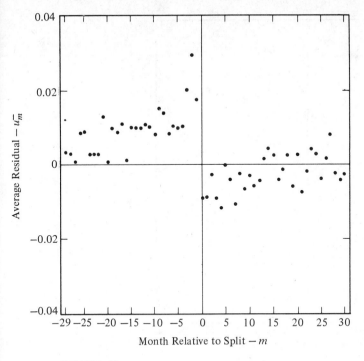

FIGURE 3b

Average residuals for dividend "decreases"

returns have reverted to their normal relationship with market returns. In sum, our data suggest that once the information effects of associated dividend changes are properly considered, a split *per se* has no net effect on common stock returns.[19]

Finally, the data present important evidence on the speed of adjustment of market prices to new information. (a) Although the behavior of post-split returns will be very different depending on whether or not dividend "increases" occur, and (b) in spite of the fact that a substantial majority of split securities *do* experience dividend "increases," when all splits are examined together (Figure 2), the average residuals are randomly distirbuted about 0 during the year after the split. Thus there is no net movement either up or down in the cumulative average residuals. According to our hypothesis, this implies that on the average the market makes unbiased dividend forecasts for split securities and these forecasts are fully reflected in the price of the security by the end of the split month.

[19] It is well to emphasize that our hypothesis centers around the information value of dividend changes. There is nothing in the empirical evidence which indicates that dividend policy *per se* affects the market value of the firm. For further discussion of this point see Miller and Modigliani 15, (430).

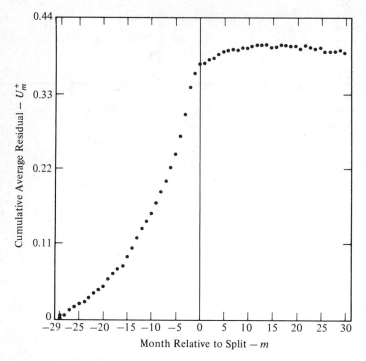

FIGURE 3c

Cumulative average residuals for dividend "increases"

5. SPLITS AND TRADING PROFITS

Although stock prices adjust "rapidly" to the dividend information implicit in a split, an important question remains: Is the adjustment so rapid that splits can in no way be used to increase trading profits? Unfortunately our data do not allow full examination of this question. Nevertheless we shall proceed as best we can and leave the reader to judge the arguments for himself.

First of all, it is clear from Figure 2 that expected returns cannot be increased by purchasing split securities after the splits have become effective. After the split, on the average the returns on split securities immediately resume their normal relationships to market returns. In general, prices of split shares do not tend to rise more rapidly after a split takes place. Of course, if one is better at predicting which of the split securities is likely to experience "increased" dividends, one will have higher expected returns. But the higher returns arise from superior information or analytical talents and not from splits themselves.

Let us now consider the policy of buying splitting securities as soon as information concerning the possibility of a split becomes available. It is impossible to test this policy fully since information concerning a split often

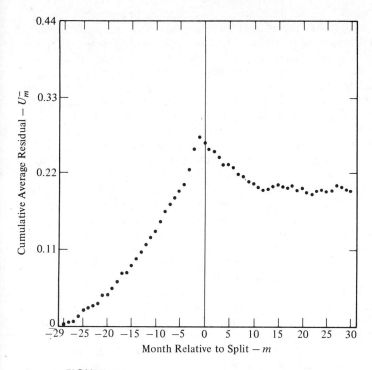

FIGURE 3d

Cumulative average residuals for dividend "decreases"

leaks into the market before the split is announced or even proposed to the shareholders. There are, however, several fragmentary but complementary pieces of evidence which suggest that the policy of buying splitting securities as soon as a split is *formally announced* does not lead to increased expected returns.

First, for a sample of 100 randomly selected splits during the period 1946–1956, Bellemore and Blucher [1] found that in general, price movements associated with a split are over by the day after the split is announced. They found that from eight weeks before to the day after the announcement, 86 out of 100 stocks registered percentage price increases greater than those of the Standard and Poor's stock price index for the relevant industry group. From the day after to eight weeks after the announcement date, however, only 43 stocks registered precentage price increases greater than the relevant industry index, and on the average during this period split shares only increased 2 per cent more in price than nonsplit shares in the same industry. This suggests that even if one purchases as soon as the announcement is made, split shares will not in general provide higher returns than nonsplit shares.[20]

---

[20] We should note that though the results are Bellemore and Blucher's, the interpretation is ours.

Since in the vast majority of cases prices rise substantially in the eight weeks prior to

Second, announcement dates have been collected for a random sample of 52 splits from our data. For these 52 splits the analysis of average and cumulative average residuals discussed in Section 4 has been carried out first using the split month as month 0 and then using the announcement month as month 0. In this sample the behavior of the residuals after the announcement date is almost identical to the behavior of the residuals after the split date. Since the evidence presented earlier indicated that one could not systematically profit from buying split securities after the effective date of the split, this suggests that one also cannot profit by buying after the announcement date.

Although expected returns cannot in general be increased by buying split shares, this does not mean that a split should have no effect on an investor's decisions. Figure 4 shows the cross-sectional mean absolute deviations of the residuals for each of the sixty months surrounding the split. From the graph it is clear that the variability in returns on split shares increases substantially in the months closest to the split. The increased riskiness of the shares during this period is certainly a factor which the investor should consider in his decisions.

In light of some of the evidence presented earlier, the conclusion that splits cannot be used to increase expected trading profits may seem a bit anomalous. For example, in Table 2, column (8), the cross-sectional average residuals from the estimates of (1) are positive for at least thirty months prior to the split. It would seem that such a strong degree of "persistance" could surely be used to increase expected profits. Unfortunately, however, the behavior of the *average* residuals is not representative of the behavior of the residuals for *individual securities;* over time the residuals for individual securities are much more randomly distributed about 0. We can see this more clearly by comparing the average residuals for all splits (Figure 2a) with the month by month behavior of the cross-sectional mean absolute deviations of residuals for all splits (Figure 4). For each month before the split the mean absolute deviation of residuals is well over twice as large as the corresponding average residual, which indicates that for each month the residuals for many *individual* securities are negative. In fact, in examining residuals for individual securities the following pattern was typical: Prior to the split, successive sample residuals from (1) are almost completely independent. In most cases, however, there are a few months for which the residual are abnormally large and positive. These months of large residuals differ from security to security, however, and these differences in timing explain why the signs of the *average* residuals are uniformly positive for many months preceding the split.

Similarly, there is evidence which suggests that the extremely large positive average residuals in the three or four months prior to the split merely reflect the fact that, from split to split, there is a variable lag between the time split information reaches the market and the time when the split becomes effective. Jaffe [9] has provided announcement and effective dates for the 100 randomly chosen splits used by herself and Bellemore [1]. The announcement dates occur as follows: 7 in the first month before the split, 67 in the second and third months, 14 in the fourth month, and 12 announcements more than four months before

---

the announcement date, Bellemore and Blucher conclude that if one has advance knowledge concerning a contemplated split, it can probably be used to increase expected returns. The same is likely to be true of all inside information, however.

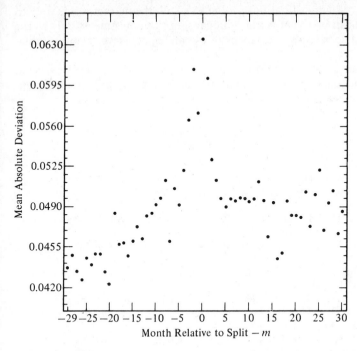

FIGURE 4

Cross-sectional mean absolute
deviation of residuals—all splits

the split. Looking back at Table 2, column (8), and Figure 2a we see that the largest average residuals follow a similar pattern: The largest average residuals occur in the second and third months before the split; though smaller, the average residuals for one and four months before the split are larger than those of any other months.

    This suggests that pattern of the average residuals immediately prior to the split arises from the averaging process and thus cannot be assumed to hold for any particular security.

6. CONCLUSIONS

    In sum, in the past stock splits have very often been associated with substantial dividend increases. The evidence indicates that the market realizes this and uses the announcement of a split to re-evaluate the stream of expected income from the shares. Moreover, the evidence indicates that on the average the market's judgements concerning the information implications of a split are fully reflected in the price of a share at least by the end of the split month but most probably almost immediately after the announcement date. Thus the results of the study lend considerable support to the conclusion that the stock market is "efficient" in the sense that stock prices adjust very rapidly to new information.

The evidence suggests that in reacting to a split the market reacts only to its dividend implications. That is, the split causes price adjustments only to the extent that it is associated with changes in the anticipated level of future dividends.

Finally, there seems to be no way to use a split to increase one's expected returns, unless, of course, inside information concerning the split or subsequent dividend behavior is available.

REFERENCES

1. BELLEMORE, DOUGLAS H. and Mrs. LILLIAN BLUCHER (JAFFE), "A Study of Stock Splits in the Postwar Years," *Financial Analysts Journal,* XV (November, 1956), 19–26.
2. COOTNER, PAUL H., ed., *The Random Character of Stock Market Prices* (Cambridge, Mass.: M.I.T. Press, 1964).
3. FAMA, EUGENE F., "The Behavior of Stock-Market Prices," *Journal of Business,* XXXVIII (January, 1965), 34–105.
4. ———, "Portfolio Analysis in a Stable Paretian Market," *Management Science,* XI (January, 1965), 404–19.
5. FISHER, LAWRENCE, "Outcomes for 'Random' Investments in Common Stocks Listed on the New York Stock Exchange," *Journal of Business,* XXXVIII (April, 1965), 149–61.
6. ———, "Some New Stock Market Indexes," *Journal of Business,* XXXIX (Supplement, January, 1966), 191–225.
7. ——— and JAMES H. LORIE, "Rates of Return on Investments in Common Stocks," *Journal of Business,* XXXVII (January, 1964), 1–21.
8. GODFREY, MICHAEL D., CLIVE W. J. GRANGER and OSKAR MORGENSTERN, "The Random Walk Hypothesis of Stock Market Behavior," *Kyklos,* XVII (1964), 1–30.
9. JAFFE (BLUCHER), LILLIAN H., "A Study of Stock Splits, 1946–1956," Unpublished Master's Thesis, Graduate School of Business Administration, New York University (1957).
10. LINTNER, JOHN, "Distribution of Incomes of Corporations Among Dividends, Retained Earnings and Taxes," *American Economic Review,* XLVI (May, 1956), 97–113.
11. MANDELBROT, BENOIT, "Forecasts of Future Prices, Unbiased Markets, and 'Martingale' Models," *Journal of Business,* XXXIX (Supplement, January, 1966), 242–255.
12. ———, "The Variation of Certain Speculative Prices," *Journal of Business,* XXXVI (October, 1963), 394–419.
13. MARKOWITZ, HARRY, *Portfolio Selection: Efficient Diversification of Investments* (New York: Wiley, 1959).
14. MICHAELSEN, JACOB B., "The Determinants of Dividend Policies: A Theoretical and Empirical Study," Unpublished Doctoral Dissertation, Graduate School of Business, University of Chicago (1961).
15. MILLER, MERTON H. and FRANCO MODIGLIANI, "Dividend Policy, Growth and the Valuation of Shares," *Journal of Business,* XXXIV (October, 1961), 411–33.
16. SAMUELSON, PAUL A., "Proof That Properly Anticipated Prices Fluctuate Randomly," *Industrial Management Review* (Spring, 1965), 41–49.
17. SHARPE, WILLIAM F., "Capital Asset Pricing: A Theory of Market Equilibrium under Conditions of Risk", *Journal of Finance,* XIX (September, 1964), 425–42.

18. ———, "A Simplified Model for Portfolio Analysis," *Management Science*, IX (January, 1963), 277–93.

19. WISE, JOHN, "Linear Estimators for Linear Regression Systems Having Infinite Variances," paper presented at the Berkeley–Stanford Mathematical Economics Seminar (October, 1963).

The Fama and Blume article is a continuation of the well-known filter tests performed by Alexander and is based on whether last period's price change exceeds a predetermined amount. Fama's results indicate quite clearly that filters formulated in terms of a previous change is stock price cannot outperform a buy-and-hold strategy when dividends and transaction costs are considered.

16

Filter Rules and Stock-Market Trading

*Eugene F. Fama and Marshall E. Blume**

This article is reprinted with permission from the Journal of Business, *Vol. 39, No. 1 (January, 1966), pp. 226–241.*

I. INTRODUCTION

In the recent literature there has been a considerable interest in the theory of random walks in stock-market prices. The basic hypothesis of the theory is that successive price changes in individual securities are independent random variables. Independence implies, of course, that the past history of a series of changes cannot be used to predict future changes in any "meaningful" way.

What consitutes a "meaningful" prediction depends, of course, on the purpose for which the data are being examined. For example, the investor wants to know whether the history of prices can be used to increase expected gains. In a random-walk market, with either zero or positive drift, no mechanical trading rule applied to an individual security would consistently outperform a policy of simply buying and holding the security. Thus, the investor who must choose between the random-walk model and a more complicated model which assumes the existence of an excessive degree of either persistence

* In preparing this paper the authors have benefited from discussions with Professors Lawrence Fisher, Benoit Mandelbrot, Merton Miller, Peter Pashigian, and Harry Roberts of the University of Chicago.

(positive dependence) or reaction (negative dependence) in sccessive price change should accept the theory of random walks as the better model if the actual degree of dependence cannot be used to produce greater expected profits than a buy-and-hold policy.[1]

On the other hand, the statistician has different though equally pragmatic notions of what constitutes an important violation of the independence assumption of the random-walk model. He will typically be interested in whether the degree of dependence in successive changes is sufficient to account for some particular property of the distribution of price changes or whether the dependence is sufficient to invalidate the results produced by statistical tools applied to the data. For example, price changes may be one variable in a regression analysis and the statistician will want to determine whether dependence in the series might produce serial dependence in the residuals. If the amount of dependence is low, he will probably conclude that it will not seriously damage his results. From the investor's point of view, however, the dependence may make the expected profits from some mechanical trading rule greater than those of a simple buy-and-hold policy.

It is important to note, however, that though a strict definition of "important dependence" is always specific to the case at hand, the ultimate criterion is always practical. In an encounter with a more complicated alternative, the theory of random walks is overthrown only if the alternative leads to a better atcion than the random-walk theory would have sugested.

Previously the independence assumption of the random-walk model has been tested primarily with standard statistical tools, and in most cases the results have tended to uphold the model. This is true, for example, of the serial correlation tests of Cootner [3], Fama [4], Kendall [8], and Moore [11]. In these

---

[1] Although independence of successive price changes implies that the history of a price series cannot be used to increase expected gains, the reverse proposition does not hold. It is possible to construct models where successive price changes are dependent, yet the dependence is not of a form which can be used to increase expected profits. In fact, Mandelbrot [9] and Samuelson [12] show that, under fairly general conditions, in a market that fully "discounts" all available information prices will follow a "martingale" which may or may not have the independence property of a pure random walk. In particular, the martingale property implies only that the *expected values* of future prices will be independent of the *values* of past prices; the distributions of future prices, however, *may* very well depend on the values of past prices. In a martingale, though price changes may be dependent, the dependence cannot be used by the trader to increase his expected profits. A random walk is a martingale, but a martingale is not necessarily a random walk.

Unfortunately, however, most empirical work on the behavior of stock-market prices came about before the theoretical importance of the martingale model was established. Thus empirical work is usually concerned with the theory of random walks. In practice, this is not serious, since in most cases it is probably impossible to distinguish a series that follows a martingale with some dependence from a series that follows a random walk. In most cases the degree of dependence shown by a martingale will be so small that for practical purposes it will not do great violence to the independence assumption of the random-walk model.

The terminology used in this paper will be that of the more familiar theory of random walks rather than the more general (but perhaps simpler) theory of martingale processes. The reader will note, however, that the bulk of our discussions remain valid if the word "martingale" is substituted for "random walk" and the words "the martingale property" are substituted for "independence."

studies the sample serial correlation coefficients computed for successive daily, weekly, and monthly price changes were extremely close to zero—evidence against "important" dependence in price changes. Similarly, Fama's [4] analysis of runs of successive price changes of the same sign and the spectral analysis techniques of Granger and Morgenstern [7], and Godfrey Granger, and Morgenstern [6], also lend support to the independence assumption of the random-walk model.

Nevertheless, it is difficult to determine whether these results indicate that the random-walk model is adequate for the investor. For example, there is no obvious relationship between the magnitude of a serial correlation coefficient and the expected profits of a mechanical trading rule. Moreover, the market professional would probably object that common statistical tools cannot measure the types of dependence that he sees in the data. For example, the simple linear relationships that underlie the serial correlation model are much too unsophisticated to identify the complicated "patterns" that the "chartist" sees in stock prices. Similarly, runs tests are too rigid in determining the duration of upward and downward movements in prices. A run is considered terminated whenever there is a change in sign in the sequence of successive price changes, regardless of the magnitude of the price change that causes the reversal in sign. The market professional would require a more sophisticated method to identify movements—a method that does not always predict the termination of the movement simply because the price level has temporarily changed direction.

Not all the published empirical tests of independence have employed standard statistical models, however: Most notable, for example, is the work of Sidney S. Alexander [1, 2]. Professor Alexander's filter technique is a mechanical trading rule which attempts to apply more sophisticated criteria to identify movements in stock prices. An x per cent filter is defined as follows: If the daily closing price of a particular security moves up at least x per cent, buy and hold the security until its price moves down at least x per cent from a subsequent high, at which time simultaneously sell and go short. The short position is maintained until the daily closing price rises at least x per cent above a subsequent low at which time one covers and buys. Moves less than x per cent in either direction are ignored.

Alexander formulated the filter technique to test the belief, widely held among market professionals, that prices adjust gradually to new information.

> The professional analysts operate in the belief that there exist certain trend generating facts, knowable today, that will guide a speculator to profit if only he can read them correctly. These facts are assumed to generate trends rather than instantaneous jumps because most of those trading in speculative markets have imperfect knowledge of these facts, and the future trend of price will result from a gradual spread of awareness of these facts throughout the market [1, p. 7].

For the filter technique, this means that for some values of x we would find that "if the stock market has moved up x per cent it is likely to move up more than x per cent further before it moves down by x per cent" [1, p. 26].

In his earlier article [1, Table 7] Alexander reported tests of the filter technique for filters ranging in size from 5 to 50 per cent. The tests covered different time periods from 1897 to 1959 and involved closing "prices" for two indexes, the Dow-Jones Industrials from 1897 to 1929 and Standard and Poor's Industrials from 1929 to 1959. In general, filters of all different sizes and for all the different time periods yielded substantial profits—indeed profits significantly greater than those of the simple buy-and-hold policy. This led Alexander to conclude that the independence assumption of the random-walk model was not upheld by his data.

Mandelbrot [10, pp. 417–18] pointed out, however, that Alexander's computations incorporated biases which led to serious overstatment of the profitability of the filters. In each transaction Alexander assumed that his hypothetical trader could always buy at a price exactly equal to the low plus x per cent and sell at the high minus x per cent. In fact, because of the frequency of large price jumps,[2] the purchase price will often be somewhat higher than the low plus x per cent, while the sale price will often be below the high minus x per cent.

In his later paper [2, Table 1] Alexander reworked his earlier results to take account of this source of bias. In the corrected tests the profitability of the filter technique was drastically reduced.

However, though his later work takes account of discontinuities in the price series, Alexander's results are still very difficult to interpret. The difficulties arise because it is impossible to adjust the commonly used price indexes for the effects of dividends. This will later be shown to introduce serious biases into filter results.

II. THE FILTER RULE AND TRADING PROFITS

Alexander's filter technique has been applied to series of daily closing price for each of the individual securities of the Dow-Jones Industrial Average. The initial dates of the samples vary from January, 1956, to April, 1958, but are usually about the end of 1957. The final date is always September 26, 1962. Thus there are thirty samples with 1,200 to 1,700 observations per sample.

Twenty-four different filters ranging from 0.5 per cent to 50 per cent have been simulated. Table 1 shows, for each security and filter size, the annual returns, adjusted for dividends but not for brokerage fees, under both the filter technique and a simple buy-and-hold policy. For each security and filter size, buy-and-hold returns are computed only for the period during which active positions are open under the filter rule, which requires that multiple buy-and-hold figures be reported for each security. The exact procedure used to compute the returns is discussed in the note to Table 1.

Table 1 presents only a small fraction of the results of this study. For example, returns under the filter technique have been computed in many different ways: gross and net of brokerage fees, with and without dividends, etc. Since presenting all the empirical work would require a small book of tables, we shall be constrained to concentrate on summary versions of the results—summarized by security and by filter size. Table 1 presents the most important of the basic results in full detail, however, and permits the reader to verify conclusions that will be drawn from the summary statistics.

---

[2] The point is of central theoretical importance for the stable Paretian hypothesis. For additional discussion and empirical evidence, see Fama [4].

TABLE 1

Comparison of rates of return, before commissions, under the filter technique (F) and under a buy-and-hold policy (B)

Security	Filter size															
	0.005		0.010		0.015		0.020		0.025		0.030		0.035		0.040	
	F	B	F	B	F	B	F	B	F	B	F	B	F	B	F	B
Allied Chemical	.155	.068	.087	.069	.042	.063	.030	.066	-.105	.069	.008	.066	-.002	.064	-.010	.051
Alcoa	.401	.025	.308	.023	.318	.016	.330	.021	.241	.022	.303	.025	.270	.008	.182	.006
American Can	.121	.085	-.065	.075	-.123	.075	-.088	.078	-.057	.074	-.129	.072	-.201	.071	-.226	.070
Amer. Tel & Tel	.150	.189	.146	.189	.158	.189	.133	.185	.135	.182	.131	.180	.143	.176	.076	.182
Amer. Tobacco	.165	.170	.019	.168	.018	.172	.012	.168	-.057	.170	-.080	.168	.002	.163	.048	.162
Anaconda	.288	.047	.101	.049	-.012	.046	-.048	.042	-.038	.059	-.005	.057	-.030	.055	-.019	.055
Beth. Steel	.082	.032	.051	.033	.033	.036	-.004	.038	-.038	.054	-.128	.052	-.250	.049	-.169	.044
Chrysler	.031	.004	-.090	-.002	-.090	.002	-.183	.016	-.234	.015	-.152	.015	-.082	.012	.029	.012
Dupont	.152	.107	.125	.106	.087	.108	.100	.105	.032	.097	.054	.097	.084	.098	.058	.103
Eastman Kodak	.078	.194	.025	.195	.005	.189	.057	.185	.085	.183	.009	.183	.032	.178	.133	.175
General Elec.	.080	.078	.046	.075	-.015	.075	-.016	.069	.013	.069	-.052	.069	.011	.072	-.010	.070
General Foods	.122	.257	.122	.256	.146	.257	.028	.251	.084	.250	.062	.246	.112	.250	.080	.250
General Motors	.107	.088	.108	.091	.065	.091	.048	.094	-.063	.093	-.101	.098	-.151	.099	-.171	.095
Goodyear	-.229	.086	-.195	.083	-.151	.085	-.109	.076	-.092	.070	.048	.077	-.013	.077	.076	.112
Int. Harvester	-.088	.180	-.082	.177	-.206	.176	-.112	.174	-.142	.170	-.113	.178	-.036	.175	-.018	.178
Int. Nickel	.218	.148	.170	.136	.118	.136	.077	.137	.005	.155	.088	.148	.105	.147	.041	.160
Int. Paper	.205	.010	.156	.007	.095	.005	.063	.003	.034	.010	.026	.011	.014	.011	-.013	.015
Johns Manville	.021	.094	-.016	.093	-.162	.087	-.159	.085	-.070	.077	-.194	.072	-.204	.074	-.157	.074
Owens-Illinois	.008	.113	-.036	.116	-.043	.115	-.130	.119	-.120	.120	-.112	.120	-.091	.124	-.037	.106
Procter & Gamble	.315	.210	.290	.212	.221	.206	.176	.208	.130	.212	.066	.212	.015	.219	.100	.222
Sears	.337	.258	.249	.256	.225	.252	.167	.252	.196	.251	.181	.255	.238	.247	.203	.241
Std. Oil (Calif.)	.076	.093	.052	.090	-.079	.094	-.106	.099	-.124	.099	-.123	.094	-.117	.097	-.158	.098
Std. Oil (N.J.)	.036	.077	-.072	.067	-.094	.067	-.093	.070	-.084	.068	-.083	.064	-.084	.057	-.086	.056
Swift & Co.	.010	.047	.002	.042	-.026	.037	.016	.035	-.044	.037	-.115	.037	-.052	.034	-.060	.031
Texaco	.172	.188	.165	.192	.105	.189	.095	.188	.109	.186	.166	.184	.144	.183	.115	.178
Union Carbide	.290	.052	.124	.052	.144	.049	.097	.050	.067	.049	.028	.047	.038	.038	.089	.037
United Aircraft	-.025	.054	-.020	.052	-.023	.054	-.110	.059	-.134	.053	-.089	.048	-.025	.049	-.026	.046
U.S. Steel	.101	.014	-.039	.010	.036	.014	.049	.027	.077	.028	.072	.035	.027	.030	.032	.025
Westinghouse	.008	.038	-.103	.040	-.047	.038	-.215	.054	-.216	.048	-.097	.049	-.083	-.051	-.015	.047
Woolworth	.068	.128	.012	.132	.088	.131	.029	.129	-.058	.131	-.076	.132	-.052	.141	-.061	.140
Average	.115	.104	.055	.103	.028	.102	.002	.103	-.016	.103	-.017	.103	-.008	.102	.001	.101

TABLE 1—(CONTINUED)

Security	Filter size 0.045 F	B	0.050 F	B	0.060 F	B	0.070 F	B	0.080 F	B	0.090 F	B	0.100 F	B	0.120 F	B
Allied Chemical	.026	.050	-.038	.052	-.073	.056	-.018	.066	-.163	.069	-.049	.069	.055	.056	.083	.126
Alcoa	.221	.009	.037	.025	.108	.023	-.085	.020	-.083	.023	-.170	.018	-.157	.005	-.135	-.011
American Can	-.212	.069	-.125	.059	-.133	.062	-.047	.059	.048	.058	.019	.060	.090	.059	.100	.066
Amer. Tel. & Tel	.133	.176	.135	.174	.169	.181	.118	.190	.087	.186	.119	.183	.083	.195	.157	.198
Amer. Tobacco	-.016	.159	-.020	.157	.021	.150	.196	.161	.211	.171	.217	.170	.197	.164	.197	.148
Anaconda	.024	.052	-.027	.050	-.119	.050	-.167	.045	.153	.041	-.109	.034	-.045	.031	.134	.043
Beth. Steel	-.113	.038	-.153	.038	.027	.034	-.037	.022	-.094	.025	-.039	.018	-.042	.010	-.006	.014
Chrysler	-.004	.018	-.060	.020	.054	.010	.064	.009	.069	.013	.017	.011	.090	-.025	-.058	-.020
Dupont	.058	.099	.076	.096	.003	.079	.003	.079	.035	.071	.112	.074	.071	.074	.081	.072
Eastman Kodak	.121	.171	.099	.170	.110	.168	.029	.169	.080	.168	.009	.170	.074	.164	-.004	.170
General Elec.	.010	.070	.054	.060	.042	.061	.050	.057	-.001	.052	-.062	.051	-.116	.051	-.086	.044
General Foods	.058	.256	.061	.265	.070	.280	.073	.276	.217	.258	.249	.254	.226	.252	.326	.239
General Motors	-.134	.099	-.117	.099	-.215	.095	-.098	.094	-.058	.097	-.017	.096	.025	.100	.055	.080
Goodyear	-.285	.120	-.341	.125	.062	.095	.036	.088	.072	.090	.050	.085	.018	.078	-.026	.088
Int. Harvester	-.036	.169	.054	.163	-.006	.163	-.070	.164	-.094	.163	-.176	.173	-.024	.169	-.066	.165
Int. Nickel	.024	.160	.047	.154	.019	.158	.040	.154	-.050	.148	-.025	.147	.019	.136	.061	.125
Int. Paper	-.055	.013	-.026	.014	.044	.013	.000	.012	-.032	.027	-.039	.029	.001	.070	.068	.038
Johns Manville	-.107	.060	-.065	.069	-.075	.069	.001	.062	-.023	.069	-.022	.094	-.074	.082	-.112	.087
Owens-Illinois	-.026	.095	.043	.096	.094	.088	.142	.092	.130	.090	.057	.090	.062	.089	-.068	.084
Procter & Gamble	.151	.222	.133	.226	.163	.222	.176	.215	.121	.222	.190	.223	.156	.226	.169	.217
Sears	.220	.246	.200	.247	.192	.231	.101	.234	.078	.232	.191	.229	.163	.229	.136	.233
Std. Oil (Calif.)	-.128	.096	-.134	.089	-.055	.083	-.088	.082	-.052	.073	-.061	.078	-.113	.081	.019	.079
Std. Oil (N. J.)	-.115	.057	-.164	.061	-.124	.057	-.008	.052	-.002	.048	-.051	.048	-.077	.043	-.102	.048
Swift & Co.	-.053	.035	-.049	.038	.039	.031	-.083	.027	-.079	.038	-.153	.044	-.121	.048	-.063	.070
Texaco	.070	.161	.005	.162	.140	.156	.048	.154	.069	.159	.023	.162	.061	.158	.057	.154
Union Carbide	.049	.034	.017	.035	-.005	.029	-.036	.040	.122	.049	.142	.048	.098	.042	.169	.039
United Aircraft	-.102	.051	-.050	.047	-.076	.052	-.128	.013	-.121	.018	.045	.016	-.017	.017	.098	.011
U.S. Steel	.018	.014	-.023	.013	.039	.014	.058	.024	.086	.031	.025	.029	.084	.014	-.090	.010
Westinghouse	-.060	.048	-.083	.048	-.084	.046	-.033	.057	-.016	.052	.014	.039	-.025	.036	.068	.042
Woolworth	-.092	.132	-.049	.145	.030	.153	.011	.153	.094	.153	.062	.151	.091	.150	.055	.153
Average	-.012	.099	-.019	.100	.013	.097	.008	.096	.017	.096	.019	.096	.030	.093	.053	.094

TABLE 1—(CONTINUED)

Security	0.140 F	0.140 B	0.160 F	0.160 B	0.180 F	0.180 B	0.200 F	0.200 B	0.250 F	0.250 B	0.300 F	0.300 B	0.400 F	0.400 B	0.500 F	0.500 B
Allied Chemical	-.017	.128	-.075	.119	-.047	.123	.036	.101	.067	.082	.037	.037	-.015	-.015		
Alcoa	-.082	-.022	-.169	-.036	.050	-.039	-.015	-.038	.001	-.050	-.112	-.047	-.040	-.053	-.129	-.129
American Can	.080	.035	.072	.031	.026	-.012	.001	-.015	-.065	-.013	-.160	-.004				
Amer. Tel. & Tel	.192	.183	.197	.197	.185	.185	.159	.159	.154	.153						
Amer. Tobacco	.221	.125	.229	.229	.223	.223	.218	.218	.193	.193	.174	.174	.134	.134		
Anaconda	.052	.099	-.044	.081	.007	.073	.102	.059	.029	.036	-.060	.004	-.251	.134		
Beth. Steel	-.039	.033	.072	.045	.036	.043	.021	.032	-.070	.001	-.158	-.008	-.034	-.034		
Chrysler	-.065	-.011	-.049	-.009	-.113	-.004	-.091	-.002	-.079	.011	-.142	-.032	-.376	-.021		
Dupont	.105	.067	.058	.070	.032	.071	.008	.078	-.093	.094	-.118	.111				
Eastman Kodak	.062	.162	.061	.162	.108	.168	.105	.152	.262	.262	.125	.125	-.015	-.015		
General Elec	.045	.045	-.001	.043	-.062	.046	-.135	.057	-.052	.050	-.017	.072	.200	.200		
General Foods	.321	.240	.309	.236	.291	.235	.283	.240	.270	.270	.250	.250				
General Motors	-.282	.097	.011	.081	-.058	.089	-.080	.064	-.094	.168						
Goodyear	-.063	.088	-.052	.081	-.048	.069	.083	.100	.007	.086	-.090	.072	.007	.007		
Int. Harvester	.097	.153	.152	.146	.123	.135	.094	.131	.041	.219						
Int. Nickel	.091	.109	.128	.093	.149	.135	.137	.141	.128	.128	.113	.113				
Int. Paper	.015	.029	-.006	.065	.032	.062	.002	.061	-.041	.004	-.116	.015	-.050	-.050		
Johns Manville	-.134	-.159	.032	.154	-.023	.144	.033	.131	.100	.100	.068	.068	.017	.017		
Owens-Illinois	.083	.080	.034	.078	-.038	.084	.030	.077	-.051	.069	.055	.055				
Procter & Ganble	.237	.234	.233	.233	.294	.230	.279	.228	.242	.242	.220	.220	.180	.180		
Sears	.116	.243	.150	.226	.245	.230	.224	.226	.166	.245	.204	.204				
Std. Oil (Calif.)	-.009	.079	-.024	.019	-.067	.021	-.130	.282	-.146	.037	-.095	.034				
Std. Oil (N.J.)	.004	.044	-.026	.045	-.051	-.030	-.076	-.035	-.161	-.019	-.285	.007				
Swift & Co.	-.092	.096	-.011	.084	-.056	.095	-.111	.106	.024	.095	-.036	.111				
Texaco	-.050	.159	-.049	.162	-.114	.167	-.124	.174								
Union Carbide	.108	.087	.071	.080	.022	.070	-.002	.055	-.090	.037	.004	.004	-.056	-.056		
United Aircraft	-.062	.016	-.099	.002	-.173	.010	-.174	.003	-.166	.008	-.127	-.175	.209	.209	-.670	.670
U.S. Steel	.091	.119	.036	.112	-.135	.009	.072	.083	.025	.047	-.107	.053	.001	.001	-.043	-.043
Westinghouse	.038	.034	-.031	.039	.076	.200	.175	.175	.128	.128	.111	.111	.061	.061	-.044	-.014
Woolworth	.111	.177	.063	.220	.166	.166	.162	.162	.137	.137	.121	.111				
Average	.039	.103	.042	.103	.036	.100	.043	.098	.027	.097	-.005	.064	-.027	.044	-.214	.121

Filter size

NOTES TO TABLE 1

In applying the filter technique, the data determine whether the first position taken will be long or short. With an x per cent filter, an initial position is taken as soon as there is an up-move or a down-move (whichever comes first) where the total price change is equal to or greater than x per cent. The position is assumed to be taken on the first day for which the price change equals or exceeds the x per cent limit. Any positions open at the end of the sampling period are disregarded. Thus only completed transactions are included in the calculations.

The closing price on the day a position is opened defines a reference price: a peak in the case of a long transaction and a trough in the case of a short transaction. On each subsequent day it is necessary to check whether the position should be closed, i.e., whether the current price is x per cent below the reference (peak) price in a long position or x per cent above the reference (trough) price if the open position is short. If the current position is not to be closed, it is then necessary to check whether the reference price must be changed. In a long position this will be necessary when the current price exceeds the reference price so that a new peak has been attained, whereas in a short position a new trough will be defined when the current price is below the reference price. Of course, when the reference price changes all subsequent testing uses the new value as base.

On ex-dividend days the reference price is adjusted by adding back the amount of the dividend. Such an adjustment is necessary in order to insure that the filter will not be triggered simply because the stock's price typically falls on an ex-dividend date. In addition, if a split occurs when a position is open, the price of the security subsequent to the split is adjusted upward by the appropriate factor until the position is closed.

With this background discussion we shall now consider the rate-of-return calculations summarized in Table 1. The following are the basic variables in the calculations:

$P_{ti}^{(j)}$ = the closing price of security j for the day on which transaction t for filter i was initiated.

$I_{ti}^{(j)}$ = the total dollar profit on transaction t of filter i when applied to security j. The profits are capital gains plus dividends, which are positive for long transactions and negative for short transactions.

$n_{ti}^{(j)}$ = the duration in terms of total trading days of transaction t for filter i when applied to security j.

$N_i^{(j)}$ = the total number of trading days during which positions were open under filter i when applied to security j. Thus

$$N_i^{(j)} = \sum_{t=1}^{T_i^{(j)}} n_{ti}^{(i)}$$

where $T_i^{(j)}$ is the total number of transactions initiated by filter i for security j.

$r_{ti}^{(j)}$ = the rate of return with daily compounding on transaction t of filter i when applied to security j. It is computed as

$$P_{ti}^{(j)}\left[1 + r_{ti}^{(j)}\right] n_{ti}^{(j)} = P_{ti}^{(j)} + I_{ti}^{(j)}$$

$r_i^{(j)}$ = the over-all rate of return with daily compounding provided by filter i when applied to security j. It is computed as

$$r_i^{(j)} = \left\{ \prod_{t=1}^{T^{(j)}} \left[1 + r_{ti}^{(j)}\right]^{n_{ti}^{(j)}} \right\}^{1/N_i^{(j)}} - 1$$

$R_i^{(j)}$ = the nominal annual rate of return for filter i when applied to company j. It is computed as

$$R_i^{(j)} = 260 r_i^{(j)}$$

A. ANALYSIS OF RESULTS BY SECURITY

Table 2 summarizes the filter results by security. For each security the table shows average returns per filter under both the filter rule and the buy-and-hold policy. The reported returns are variously adjusted for dividends and for commissions.

When commissions are taken into account the largest profits under the filter technique are those of the broker. Only four securities (American Tel. and Tel., General Foods, Procter & Gamble, and Sears) have positive average returns per filter when commissions are included (col. [2].) When commissions are omitted, the returns from the filter technique (col. [1].) are, of course, greatly improved but are still not as large as the returns from simply buying and holding. Comparison of the profits before commissions under the filter technique (col. [1]) and under a buy-and-hold policy (col. [6]) indicates that, even ignoring transactions costs, the filter technique is inferior to buy-and-hold for all but two securities: Alcoa and Union Carbide.

This last result is inconsistent with some of Alexander's latest empirical work [2, Tables 1 and 2]. When commissions are omitted, Alexander finds that the filter technique is typically superior to a buy-and-hold policy, at least for the period 1928–61. A bias in Alexander's computations, however, tends to overstate the actual profitability of the filter technique relative to buy-and-hold. This bias arises because using common price indices makes it impossible to adjust properly for dividends. Under a buy-and-hold policy the total profit is the price change for the time period plus any dividends that have been paid. Dividends simply increase the profitability of holding shares. Under the filter technique, however, the investor alternates between long and short positions. In a short sale the borrower of the securities typically reimburses the lender for any dividends that are paid while the short position is outstanding. Thus adjusting for dividends will reduce the profitability of short sales and thereby reduce the profitability of the filter technique relative to buy-and-hold.

NOTES TO TABLE 1—Continued

R_i^j are the returns shown for the filter technique (F) in Table 1.

$_bR_i^{(j)}$ = the nominal annual rate of return from buy-and-hold during the time period for which filter i had open positions in security j.

$$_bR_i^{(j)} = 260\ _br_i^{(j)}$$

where $_br_i^{(j)}$ is defined as

$$_br_i^{(j)} = \left\{ \prod_{t=1}^{T_i^{(j)}} [1 + _br_{ti}^{(j)}]^{n_{ti}^{(j)}} \right\}^{1/N_{ib}^{(j)}} - 1$$

where $_br_{ti}^{(j)} \neq r_{ti}^{(j)}$ if the corresponding filter is long, transaction and $_br_{ti}^{(j)} = -r_{ti}^{(j)}$ if the corresponding filter transaction is short. $_bR_i^{(j)}$ are the returns reported for the buy-and-hold policy (B) in Table 1.

This roundabout procedure for computing buy-and-hold returns is necessary to insure that the buy-and-hold returns cover exactly the same time periods and are computed on exactly the same basis as the returns under the filter technique.

Finally, it should also be noted that the results for the largest filters are probably not reliable since for these filters the number of transactions is very small. Cf. Table 3.

TABLE 2*

Nominal annual rates of return by company: averaged over all filters

Security	Average returns adj. for divds.		Breakdown of col. (1)		Average returns	Buy and hold returns not adj. for comm.		Profitable filters/ total filters: adj. for divds.	
	Not adj. for comm. (1)	Adj. for comm. (2)	Long (3)	Short (4)	Not adj. for divds. or comm. (5)	Adj. for divds. (6)	Not adj. for divds. (7)	Not adj. for comm. (8)	Adj. for comm. (9)
Allied Chemical ..	−.0079	−.2371	0486	−.1453	−.0221	.0712	.0384	9/23	4/23
Alcoa	.0664	−.1388	.0744	.0627	.0643	−.0064	−.0224	13/24	4/24
American Can ..	−.0489	−.3022	.0052	−.1347	−.0639	.0507	.0061	9/22	6/22
Amer Tel. & Tel ...	.1410	.0581	.2156	−.0727	.1221	.1824	.1484	21/21	17/21
Amer. Tobacco ..	.1095	−.0491	.1706	−.0724	.0814	.1704	.1307	18/23	12/23
Anaconda	−.0170	−.3091	.0398	−.1069	−.0255	.0540	.0125	8/23	4/23
Beth. Steel	−.0459	−.3214	−.0100	−.1282	−.0733	.0283	−.0266	7/23	3/23
Chrysler	−.0609	−.369£	−.0598	−.0643	−.0645	.0017	−.0311	8/23	2/23
Dupont. 0512		−.0164	.1135	−.0605	.0431	.0889	.0348	20/22	12/22
Eastman Kodak ..	.0757	−.0649	.1786	−.1761	.0653	.1756	.1555	21/22	12/22
General Elec	−.0125	−.1963	.0394	−.1079	−.0237	.0576	.0285	9/23	1/23
General Foods ...	.1740	.0103	.2780	−.0621	.1607	.2509	.2283	23/23	12/23
General Motors ..	−.0581	−.3420	.0337	−.1868	−.0708	.0956	.0500	7/21	1/21
Goodyear	−.0538	−.3501	.0179	−.1942	−.0731	.0843	.0467	10/23	2/23
Int. Harvester	−.0274	−.3474	.1020	−.2624	−.0410	.1677	.1192	7/21	6/21
Int. Nickel	.0776	−.0843	.1517	−.0895	.0632	.1395	.1104	20/22	7/22
Int. Paper	.0167	−.1654	.0346	−.0178	.0026	.0193	−.0238	13/23	2/23
Johns Manville....	−.0576	−.3577	.0157	−.2302	−.0707	0878	.0497	7/23	5/22
Owens-Illinois	.0056	−.1584	.0763	−.1401	−.0010	.0958	.0679	12/22	10/22
Procter & Gamble...	1847	.0480	.2736	−.0459	.1720	.2193	.1966	23/23	15/23
Sears	.1903	.0069	.2772	−.2014	.1735	.2396	.2154	22/22	16/22
Std. Oil (Calif.) ..	−.0756	−.3405	.0018	−.1941	−.0915	.0748	.0302	3/22	0/22
Std. Oil (NJ.)	−.0818	−.3020	−.0314	−.1670	−.0963	.0432	−.0033	2/22	0/22
Swift & Co	−.0542	−.3793	−.0028	−.2098	−.0623	.0553	.0095	4/22	1/22
Texaco	.0605	−.1516	.1828	−.3054	.0410	.1710	.1349	16/20	4/20
Union Carbide ...	.0649	−.0335	.0909	−.0031	.0533	.0421	.0133	18/23	9/23
United Afrcraft ..	−.1117	−.4478	−.0459	−.1500	−.1166	.0578	.0066	1/24	0/24
U.S. Steel	.0264	−.1622	.0467	−.0433	.0135	.0303	−.0087	18/24	7/24
Westinghouse	−.0186	−.2804	.0177	−.1164	−.0305	.0610	.0338	9/24	7/24
Woolworth	.0414	−.1491	.1296	−.2158	.0267	.1482	.1080	16/22	10/22
Average	.0185	−.1978	.0822	−.1279	.0032	.0986	.0620	12.5/ 22.5	6.4/225

* *See Notes to Table 2.*

The size of the bais introduced by omitting dividends from the calculations can be seen by comparing returns before commisssions under the filter technique and under the buy-and-hold policy, first for the case where the calculations are properly adjusted for dividends and second for the case where they are not. In our results adjusted for dividends (cols. [1] and [6] of Table 2) the filter technique only surpasses the buy-and-hold policy for two securities: The difference between the average return for all securities under the filter technique (0.185) and the average return from buy-and-hold (.0986) is 8.01 percentage points. On the other hand, when dividends are excluded (col. [5] and [7] of Table 2), average returns per filter for five securities are greater than the corresponding returns provided by buy-and-hold: The difference between the over-all average return under the filter rule (.0032) and the average return from buy-and-hold (.0620) is 5.9 percentage points. Thus adjustment for dividends increases the average advantage of buy-and-hold over the filter technique by at least 2 percentage points. If such an adjustment were applied to Alexander's data, it would prbably account for much of the favorable showing of the filter rule.[3]

NOTES TO TABLE 2

The numbers in columns (1), (2), and (5) are average returns per filter under different assumptions concerning what is included in computing dollar profits on individual transactions. The returns in column (2) are adjusted for both dividends and brokerage fees; those in column (1) are adjusted only for dividends; while those in column (5) are not adjusted for either dividends or commissions. The general formula for computing the average return per filter is

$$R^{(j)} = \frac{\sum_{i=1}^{24} R_i^{(j)}}{S^{(j)}}$$

where $S^{(j)}$ is the number of filters that resulted in completed transactions in security j and $R_i^{(j)}$ is the return from filter i when applied to security j. $R_i^{(j)} = 0$ for security j if the ith filter resulted in no completed transactions. The general procedure used in computing the $R_i^{(j)}$ is discussed in the Notes to Table 1.

Columns (6) and (7) of Table 2 show the average returns per filter from buy-and-hold. The returns in column (7) do not include either dividends or brokerage fees, while those in column (6) include only dividends. The general formula used in computing average returns per filter from buy-and-hold is

$$_bR^{(j)} = \frac{\sum_{i=1}^{24} {_bR_i^{(j)}}}{S^{(j)}}$$

where $_bR_i^{(j)}$ is the rate of return from buy-and-hold during the time period for which filter i resulted in open positions in security j. $_bR_i^{(j)} = 0$ for security j if the ith filter resulted in no completed transactions. The procedure for computing the $bR_i^{(j)}$ is discussed in the Notes to Table 1.

Columns (3) and (4) of Table 2 show the average returns per filter separately for long and short transactions. Although the returns in columns (3) and (4) are computed in the same way as those in column (1), it is important to note that the returns in column (1) are not a simple average of the returns on long and short positions. In order to use columns (3) and (4) to compute the returns in column (1), it is necessary to know the number of days that long and short positions are open.

[3] Another possible explanation of the differences between Alexander's results and ours is that there may be "dependence" in successive changes in a price index, even though successive price changes in the individual securities of the index are independent. This spurious dependence in index changes arises from lack of synchronization in the trading of individual securities in the index. The reasoning is as follows: Suppose there is a market factor which affects the behavior of all securities. When there is a change in the market factor, the prices of individual securities have also implicitly changed. All securities will not trade at precisely the time of the change in the market factor; thus for

The breakdown of returns before commissions for long and short transactions adds further evidence that the simple filter rule probably cannot be used to increase expected profits. Column (4) of Table 2 makes it clear that the short positions initiated by the filter rule are usually disastrous for the investor. Only one security, Alcoa, has positive average returns per filter on short transactions. For all securities, the average return on short transactions is −.1279, while the average return from buy-and-hold is .0986.

On long positions thirteen securities have greater average returns per filter (col. [3]) than the corresponding returns from buy-and-hold. Averaging over-all securities, the return on long transactions under the filter technique is .0822 while that from buy-and-hold is .0986. Thus even if the filter techique were restricted to long positions, it would not consistently outperform the buy-and-hold policy.[4]

B. ANALYSIS OF RESULTS BY FILTER

Although analysis of the filter results by security has not produced evidence of important dependence, this may not be conclusive. For example, even though the filter technique in general does not do better than a simple buy-and-hold policy, some filters may be consistently better than others and indeed better than buy-and-hold. This along with other possibilities will now be examined.

Table 3 shows the average returns per security provided by each of the different size filters. From column (2) it is evident that when brokerage fees are included none of the filters consistently produce large returns. All filters below 12 per cent and above 25 per cent produce negative average returns per security after commissions. Although filters between 12 per cent and 25 per cent yield positive returns, they are small when compared to .0986, the average return for

some securities the effect of the change on reported prices will only be recognized with some lag.

If successive changes in the market factor are independent, this lag in the adjustment of reported prices will not in itself produce positive dependence in successive price changes for individual securities. This is not true, however, for an average of, say, daily "closing" prices of a sample of individual securities. If the "closing" prices are really the prices on the last trade of the day, yesterday's "closing" price for some securities will not fully reflect all of yesterday's movement in the market factor since some securities will not have traded at exactly the end of yesterday's trading period. This means, of course, that the price changes today for such securities will be affected by yesterday's changes in the market factor, which in turn will tend to introduce persistence in successive changes in the average.

This line of reasoning was first suggested by Professor Lawrence Fisher. A more complete discussion, along with some empirical results, is provided in Fama [5, pp. 296–98].

[4] Even on extremely close scrutiny Table 2 does not yield evidence of dependence. For example, the average returns before commissions under the filter technique (col. [1]) are positive for fifteen securities and negative for fifteen. Col. (8) shows, for each security, the ratio of number of profitable filters to active filters. For fifteen securities, over half of all active filters for each security show positive returns, while for the other fifteen securities less than half of all the active filters are profitable. The average number of profitable filters for all securities is 12.5 while the average number of active filters is 22.5. Thus the ratio of profitable to active filters is slightly greater than one-half. But this discrepancy is not surprising since the securities do not in general follow driftless random walks.

TABLE 3*

Nominal annual rates of return by filter: averaged over all companies

	Average return per security		Breakdown of average return per security before commissions		No. of profitable securities per filter (5)	Total transactions (6)
	Before commissions (1)	After commissions (2)	Long (3)	Short (4)		
0.005	.1152	−1.0359	.2089	.0097	27/30	12,514
.010	.0547	− .7494	.1444	−.0518	20/30	8,660
.015	.0277	− .5614	.1143	−.0813	17/30	6,270
.020	.0023	− .4515	.0872	−.1131	16/30	4,784
.025	−.0156	− .3732	.0702	−.1378	13/30	3,750
.030	−.0169	− .3049	.0683	−.1413	14/30	2,994
.035	−.0081	− .2438	.0734	−.1317	13/30	2,438
.040	.0008	− .1950	.0779	−.1330	14/30	2,013
.045	−.0117	− .1813	.0635	−.1484	14/30	1,720
.050	−.0188	− .1662	.0567	−.1600	13/30	1,484
.060	.0128	− .0939	.0800	−.1189	18/30	1,071
.070	.0083	− .0744	.0706	−.1338	16/30	828
.080 ..	.0167	− .0495	.0758	−.1267	15/30	653
.090	.0193	− .0358	.0765	−.1155	17/30	539
.100	.0298	− .0143	.0818	−.1002	19/30	435
.120 :.......	.0528	.0231	.0958	−.0881	21/30	289
.140	.0391	.0142	.0853	−.1108	19/30	224
.160	.0421	.0230	.0835	−.1709	17/30	172
.180	.0360	.0196	.0725	−.1620	17/30	139
.200	.0428	.0298	.0718	−.1583	20/30	110
.250 ..	.0269	.0171	.0609	−.1955	15/29	73
.300	−.0054	− .0142	.0182	−.2264	12/26	51
.400	−.0273	− .0347	−.0095	−.0965	7/16	21
0.500	−.2142	− .2295	−.0466	−.1676	0/4	4

* *Cols. (1) and (2) show the average returns per security provided by each of the different filters. The figures in col. (2) are adjusted for both dividends and commissions while those in col. (1) are adjusted only for dividends. The general formula, in the notation of the Notes to Table 1, is*

$$R_i = \sum_{j=1}^{30} R_i^{(j)}/F_i$$

where $R_i^{(j)}$ is the return from filter i when applied to security j, and F_i is the number of securities that had at least one complete transaction under filter i. R^i is considered zero for security j if the ith filter resulted in no computed transactions.

all securities from a buy-and-hold policy. These results support the conclusion that the filter technique cannot be used to increase the expected profits of the investor who must pay the usual brokerage commissions.

Although the random-walk model is adequate for the average investor, close scrutiny of Table 3 indicates that there are very slight amounts of both positive and negative dependence in the price changes. Note that if successive price changes conformed strictly to the random-walk model, the average returns per security on long positions should be approximately equal to the average returns from buy-and-hold while the average returns on short positions should be approximately equal to the negative of the average returns from buy-and-hold.[5] In Table 3, however, for three filter sizes, 0.5, 1.0, and 1.5 per cent, the average returns per security on long positions (col. [3]) are greater than the average return from buy-and-hold, .0986. For the same filter sizes the losses on short positions are smaller than the gains from buy-and-hold. The returns on both long and short positions, however, fall dramatically as the filter size is increased.

This behavior of the returns on the smallest filters is evidence of persistence or positive dependence in very small movements of stock prices. The results indicate that the conditional probability of a positive (negative) change tomorrow, given a positive (negative) change today, is greater than the unconditional probability, but the effect of today's change on subsequent changes decreases very rapidly as one predicts further into the future. In this model the best way to utilize the dependence in the changes is to transact frequently, which is in effect what happens with the smallest filters.

On the other hand, there is also evidence in Table 3 of negative dependence in intermediate size price movements. No filter larger than 1.5 per cent produces an average return per security on long positions greater than the average return from buy-and-hold, and the returns on long positions fall fairly steadily up to a filter size of 5 per cent. Similarly, for filter sizes greater than 1.5 and less than 12 per cent the average losses on short positions are greater absolutely than the average return from buy-and-hold.[6] These results suggest that for values of x greater than 1.5, when the price level of a security has moved down (up) x per cent, the conditional probability that it will move down (up) x per cent further before it moves up (down) x per cent is lower than the unconditional probability. Or in other words, the average duration of intermediate size price movements is shorter than would be predicted under a pure random walk.

The question that now arises, of course, is whether either the positive dependence in extremely small price moves or the negative dependence in larger moves can be used to increase expected profits. The nature of the positive dependence in the price series suggests two possible trading procedures that would seem to produce greater expected profits than a simple buy-and-hold policy, at least for the floor trader who does not pay the usual brokerage fees. First, one could operate a 0.5 per cent filter, opening and closing long and short positions whenever such actions were signaled by the filter rule. Second, one could operate only the long positions triggered by the 0.5 per cent rule. With such a small filter, signals to open new long positions in some securities will usually occur very soon after receiving signals to close positions in others. Thus, if one follows the policy of investing all available funds in the security which triggers the next open position, capital should not be idle for a very large proportion of the time.

[5] In a random walk with positive drift, long positions will be open for longer periods than short positions. Thus, although the expected rate of return from short positions is just the negative of the expected return on long positions, the net expected return from the filter will be positive.

[6] The results for the largest filters are probably not reliable since the number of transactions per security is very small.

Yet because of out-of-pocket transactions costs which even the floor trader cannot avoid, neither of these policies can outperform buy-and-hold by any significant margin. The most important of these transactions costs is the clearinghouse fee which varies according to the price of the stock but averages approximately 0.1 per cent on each complete transaction (i.e., purchase plus sale or sale plus purchase). For our thirty securities and across a time period of approximately five years the 0.5 per cent filter initiated 12,514 transactions. This is an average of eighty-four transactions per security per year. The clearinghouse fees alone from this many transactions will reduce the average annual return per security from the 0.5 per cent filter by about 8.4 percentage points, which is more than sufficient to push the returns from the simple filter rule below those of a buy-and-hold policy.[7]

Let us now consider the policy of operating only the long positions initiated by the 0.5 per cent filter. If one succeeded in remaining fully invested nearly all of the time, the clearinghouse fees would be about as large as under the simple filter technique.[8] Thus taking only clearinghouse fees into account causes the average return per security from this modified filter rule to fall from .209 to .125, which is still about 2.5 percentage points in excess of the average return from the buy-and-hold policy, .0986.

There are other factors, however, which indicate that even the modified filter rule would not in practice be better than a simple buy-and-hold policy. First, the .209 annual average rate of return per security on long positions is computed under the implicit assumption that funds are never idle. In restricting oneself to long positions, however, even with a 0.5 per cent filter some funds will be idle part of the time, and this will reduce the return under the filter rule.[9] Second, since the filter rule is more complicated than a buy-and-hold policy, it will be more expensive to operate (e.g., costs of search, etc.). Finally, if the filter is allowed to trigger only long positions, in order to minimize the amount of time that funds are idle it will be necessary to follow closely the price movements

---

[7] Because it neglects the effects of discounting, however, this rough and ready adjustment for clearinghouse fees slightly overstates the effects of such fees on filter returns. For example, the clearinghouse fee incurred when a position is closed should be discounted back to the point in time when the position was opened. With the smallest filters, however, positions are open for such short periods of time (an average of about three days per transaction for the 0.5 per cent filter) that proper discounting of the fees would have little effect.

[8] In this refinement of the filter technique, when a long position is closed in one security, the proceeds from the sale of the stock are used to increase the investment base for the next long position that the filter signals for some other security. Thus, although only half as many transactions are triggered as under the simple filter rule, the average investment per transaction is twice as large, so that the clearing house fees under the two policies would be almost equal.

[9] For a given security and filter size, the "annual" rate of return on long positions is computed by first finding the rate of return with daily compounding on long positions and then multiplying this daily rate by the number of trading days in the year. For a given filter size the average "annual" rate of return per security on long positions is just a simple average of the "annual" returns for each security. Since long positions, of course, are not continuously open in a single security, this procedure implicitly assumes that when a position is closed in some security the funds can be *immediately* reinvested at the average return on long positions for all securities. In fact, however, this will not be the case since immediate reinvestment will not always be possible.

of many securities. In practice this will probably mean that to better the chances of getting in and out at the proper times, it will sometimes be necessary to place orders with specialists. Since the floor brokerage fees of the specialist are almost twice as large as clearinghouse charges, this alone will probably be sufficient to erase any remaining advantage of the filter rule over buy-and-hold.

We now wish to determine whether the negative dependence that is evident in the results for the intermediate and larger size filters can be used to increase expected profits. As noted earlier, for filter sizes larger than 1.5 per cent, average returns per security on long positions are less than the average return from buy-and-hold; thus the long signals for these filters should be ignored. On the other hand, for filter sizes larger than 1.5 per cent average losses on short positions exceed in absolute value the average returns from buy-and-hold; and up to a filter size of 5 per cent, the losses on short positions rise as the filter size is increased. This suggests that we pick a filter, say 5 per cent, and watch only for short signals, operating them in reverse (i.e., go long when the filter signals a short position). To go long when a short signal is received has the effect of reversing the signs of the returns from short positions. Thus the negative annual average return of –.160 on the short positions of the 5 per cent filters becomes a positive return of the same magnitude. This compares with the average return on buy-and-hold of .0986.

In practice, however, it is unlikely that this modified reverse filter rule would have any advantage over the buy-and-hold policy. First, clearinghouse fees would reduce the annual returns from the filter rule by about 1 percentage point. Second, the .160 average return per security that comes from operating the short signals of the 5 per cent filter as long signals implicitly assumes that funds are never idle. With a 5 per cent filter, however, funds will probably be idle a substantial fraction of the time even if we apply the filter rule to many securities and follow the policy of investing all available funds in the next security for which a position is signaled. Finally, if in order to minimize the time during which funds are idle the filter rule is applied to many securities, it will probably be necessary to place many orders with specialists. Specialists' commissions, of course, will further reduce the returns from the reverse filter rule.[10]

Thus if the costs of operating different versions of the filter rule are considered, it seems that even the floor trader cannot use it to increase his expected gains appreciably. Since the marginal transaction costs of the floor trader are the minimum trading costs under present institutional arrangements, our results also indicate that the market is working rather efficiently from an economic viewpoint. In conclusion, there appears to be both positive and negative dependence in price changes. The order of magnitude of the dependence is so small, however, that our results add further to the evidence that for practical purposes the random-walk model is an adequate description of price behavior.

---

[10] From the results in Table 3 it would seem that using short signals to initiate long positions would be even more profitable for the very largest filters than for the 5 per cent filter, especially since transactions costs will be very low for these filters. This cost savings, however, is probably more than counterbalanced by the fact that the proportion of time when funds are idle will be greater for the larger filters. That transactions are infrequent for the largest filters is a very mixed blessing, since it means that funds received when positions are closed may stand idle for long periods.

This concludes our discussion of the practical economic implications of the filter tests. The next and final section of the paper will be concerned with the more esoteric statistical implications of the empirical results.

III. THE FILTER RULE AND THE SERIAL CORRELATION MODEL: A COMPARISON

A major reason for studying the filter rule arises from the fear that the dependence in price changes is of such a complicated form that standard statistical tools, such as serial correlations, may provide misleading measures of the degree of dependence in the data. We shall now see, however, that for our samples this does not seem to be the case; the rather strong correspondence between the filter results and serial correlation tests indicates that, if indeed the serial correlations fail to uncover some of the dependence in the changes, this same dependence has also remained hidden from the scrutiny of the filter tests.

In another study [4, pp. 72, 73] one of the authors has computed serial correlation coefficients for the data used in this report. The first-order coefficients for the daily price changes of the individual securities are positive in twenty-two out of thirty cases, and the average value of the coefficients is .026. Such results are entirely consistent with the small degree of persistence on a very short-term basis that was uncovered by the filter tests. Similarly, for four-and nine-day price changes the first-order serial correlation coefficients are negative in twenty-one and twenty-four out of thirty cases. Again, however, the coefficients are extremely close to zero; for the four-and nine-day changes the average values are $-.038$ and -0.53, respectively. These results are entirely consistent with the small degree of negative dependence in intermediate size price movements that was uncovered by the filter results.[11]

Even though standard statistical tools such as serial correlations cannot provide exact estimates of the expected profits from mechanical trading rules such as the filter technique, the discussion above suggests that for measuring the direction and degree of dependence in price changes, the standard tools are probably as powerful as the Alexandrian filter rules.

REFERENCES

1. ALEXANDER, SIDNEY S. "Price Movements in Speculative Markets: Trends or Random Walks," *Industrial Management Review,* II (May, 1961), 7–26.

[11] In fact, there are indications that the relationships between the filter results and the serial correlations are even more formal than is implied by the discussion in the text. The rank correlation between the first-order daily serial correlations for the different securities and the returns before commissions from the 0.5 per cent filter is .76. Thus the small degree of persistence in very small price movements affects the serial correlations in the same direction as the filter results. For the different securities, the rank correlation between the first-order serial correlations for four-day price changes and the returns before commissions on the 5 per cent filter is .45. Although the formal relationship between the filter results and the serial correlations is not as strong for the intermediate size price movements, there is still a definite correspondence between the results provided by the two measures.

2. ———. "Price Movements in Speculative Markets: Trends or Random Walks, No. 2," *Industrial Management Review,* V (Spring, 1964), 26–46.
3. COOTNER, PAUL H. "Stock Prices: Random vs. Systematic Changes," *Industrial Management Review,* III (Spring, 1962), 25–45.
4. FAMA, EUGENE F. "The Behavior of Stock Market Prices," *Journal of Business,* XXXVIII (January, 1965), 34–105.
5. ———. "Tomorrow on the New York Stock Exchange," *Journal of Business,* XXXVIII (July, 1965), 285–99.
6. GODFREY, MICHAEL D., GRANGER, CLIVE, W. J., and MORGENSTERN, OSKAR. "The Random Walk Hypothesis of Stock Market Behavior," *Kyklos,* XVII (1964), 1–30.
7. GRANGER, CLIVE W. J., and MORGENSTERN, OSKAR. "Spectral Analysis of New York Stock Market Prices," *Kyklos,* XVI (1963), 1–27.
8. KENDALL, M. G. "The Analysis of Economic Time Series," *Journal of the Royal Statistical Society,* Ser. A., XCVI (1953), 11–25.
9. MANDELBROT, BENOIT. "Forecasts of Future Prices, Unbiased Markets, and 'Martingale' Models," *Journal of Business,* XXXIX, No. 1, Part II (Supplement, January, 1966).
10. ———. "The Variation of Certain Speculative Prices," *Journal of Business,* XXXVI (October, 1963), 394–419.
11. MOORE, ARNOLD. "A Statistical Analysis of Common Stock Prices" (unpublished Ph. D. dissertation, Graduate School of Business, University of Chicago, 1962).
12. SAMUELSON, PAUL A. "Proof That Properly Anticipated Prices Fluctuate Randomly," *Industrial Management Review,* VI (Spring, 1965), 41–49.

*Jensen and Bennington's article is a test of a widely publicized filter
rule formulated by Levy, as well as an excellent discussion of the methodology of testing filter rules. They examine the results produced by
filter rules against a buy-and-hold strategy, both with respect to risk
and to return. Since this represents one of the few examples of tests
utilizing both risk and return, the reader should note particularly the
alternative risk measures the authors employ. A detailed discussion of
risk–return performance measures can be found in Part II of this book.*

17

Random Walks and Technical Theories: Some Additional Evidence

Michael C. Jensen and George A. Benington*

This article is reprinted with permission from the Journal of Finance,
Vol. XXV, No. 2 (May, 1970), pp. 469–482.

I. INTRODUCTION

The random walk and martingale efficient market theories of security price
behavior imply that stock market trading rules based solely on the past price
series cannot earn profits greater than those generated by a simple buy-and-hold
policy.[1] A vast amount of statistical testing of the behavior of security prices
indicates very little evidence of any important dependencies in security price
changes through time.[2] Technical analysts or chartists, however, have insisted
that this evidence does not imply their methods are invalid and have argued
that the dependencies upon which their rules are based are much too subtle to
be captured by simple statistical tests. In an effort to meet these criticisms
Alexander (1961, 1964) and later Fama and Blume (1966) have examined the

* This Research was supported by the Security Trust Company, Rochester, New York.
We wish to express our appreciation to David Besenfelder for his help in the computer
programming effort.

[1] Cf. Cootner (1964), Fama (1965), Mandelbrot (1966) and Samuelson (1965).

[2] For example, cf. Fama (1965), Roll (1968), and the papers in Cootner (1964).

profitability of various "filter" trading rules based only on the past price series which purportedly capture the essential characteristics of many technical theories. These studies indicate the "filter" rules do not yield profits net of transactions costs which are higher than those earned by a simple buy-and-hold strategy. Similarly, James (1968) and Van Horne and Parker (1967) have found that various trading rules based upon moving averages of past prices do not yield profits greater than those of a buy-and-hold policy.

Robert A. Levy (1967a, b) has reported empirical results of tests of variations of a technical portfolio trading rule variously called the "relative strength" or "portfolio upgrading" rule. The rule is based solely on the past price series of common stocks, and yet his results seem to indicate that some of the variations of the trading rule perform "significantly" better than a simple buy-and-hold strategy. On the basis of this evidence Levy (1967a) concludes that ". . . the theory of random walks has been refuted." In an invited comment Jensen (1967) pointed out that Levy's results do not support a conclusion as strong as this. In that "Comment" it was pointed out that due to several errors the results reported by Levy overstated the excess returns earned by the profitable trading rules over the returns earned by the buy-and-hold comparison. (These arguments will not be repeated here; the interested reader may consult the original articles for the specific criticisms.) Nevertheless, even after correction for these errors Levy's results still indicated some of the trading rules earned substantially more than the buy-and-hold returns, and Jensen (1967) indicated that even these results were inconclusive because of the existence of a subtle form of selection bias.

In his Ph. D. thesis, Levy (1966) reports the results of tests of the profitability of some 68 variations of various trading rules of which very few that were based only on past information yielded returns higher than that given by a buy-and-hold policy.[3] All these rules were tested on the same body of data[4] used in showing the profitability of the additional rules reported by Levy (1967a). Likewise, given enough computer time, we are sure that we can find a mechanical trading rule which "works" on a table of *random numbers*—provided of course that we are allowed to test the rule on the *same* table of numbers which we used to discover the rule. We realize of course that the rule would prove useless on any other table of random numbers, and this is exactly the issue with Levy's results.

As pointed out in the "Comment," the only way to discover whether or not Levy's results are indicative of substantial dependencies in stock prices or are merely the result of this selection bias is to replicate the rules on a different body of data. In a "Reply" Levy (1968) states that additional testing of one of the rules on another body of data[5] yielded returns of 31% per annum. He did not report the buy-and-hold returns for this sample; he did report the returns on the S & P 500-stock index over the same period as slightly less than 10% per

---

[3] The results for 20 of these rules, none of which show higher returns after transactions costs than the (correct) buy-and-hold returns of 13.4% [cf. Jensen (1967)], are reported in another article by Levy (1967c).

[4] Weekly closing prices on 200 securities listed on the New York Stock Exchange in the 5-year period from October, 1960 to October, 1965.

[5] The daily closing prices of 625 New York Stock Exchange securities over the period July 1, 1962 to November 25, 1966.

annum, and claims the trading rule returns when adjusted[6] to a risk level equal to that of the S & P ". . . would have produced nearly 16% . . .".

The purpose of this paper is to report the results of an extensive set of tests of two of Levy's rules which seemed to earn substantially more than a buy-and-hold policy for his sample of 200 securities in the period 1960–1965.

II. THE TRADING RULE

The "relative strength" trading rule as defined by Levy is as follows:

> Define $\overline{P}_{jt}$ to be the average price of the j'th security over the 27 weeks prior to and including time t. Let $PR_{jt} = P_{jt}/\overline{P}_{jt}$ be the ratio of the price at time t to the 27-week average price at time t. (1) Define a percentage X $(0 < X < 100)$ and a "cast out rank" K, and invest an equal dollar amount in the $X\%$ of the securities under consideration having the largest ratio PR_{jt} at time t. (2) In weeks $t + \tau$ ($\tau = 1, 2, \ldots$) calculate $PR_{j, t+\tau}$ for all securities, rank them from low to high, and sell all securities currently held with ranks greater than K. (3) Immediately reinvest all proceeds from these sales in the $X\%$ of the securities at time $t + \tau$ for which $PR_{j, t+\tau}$ is greatest.

Levy found that the two policies with ($X = 10\%$, $K = 160$) and ($X = 5\%$, $K = 140$) yielded the maximum returns for his sample (20% and 26.1% unadjusted for risk, while the buy-and-hold returns were 13.4%). We have replicated his tests for these two rules for seven non-overlapping 5-year time periods and for 3 to 5 non-overlapping randomly chosen samples of securities within each time period. The results are presented below.

III. THE DATA

The data for this study were drawn from the University of Chicago Center for Research in Security Prices Monthly Price Relative File.[7] The file contains monthly closing prices, dividends and commission rates on every security on the New York Stock Exchange over the period January, 1926 to March, 1966. In total the file contains data on 1,952 securities and allows one to construct a complete series of (1) dividends and prices adjusted for all capital changes and (2) the actual round lot commission rate on each security for each month.

IV. THE ANALYSIS

In order to keep the broad parameters of our replication as close as possible to the original framework used by Levy, we divided the 40-year period covered by our file into the seven non-overlapping time periods (equal in length to Levy's) given in Table 1. (Note that the last period, October 1960–September 1965, is almost identical to Levy's.) After enumerating all securities listed on the

---

[6] No description of his adjustment method was provided.

N.Y.S.E. at the beginning of *each* of these periods (see Table 1) we randomly ordered them into subsamples of 200 securities each (the same size sample as that used by Levy).

TABLE 1

Sample intervals and number of securities listed on the N.Y.S.E. at the beginning of each time period

Time period*			Number of securities listed on N.Y.S.E. at beginning of period
(1)	Oct. 1930–Sept.	1935	733
(2)	Oct. 1935–Sept.	1940	722
(3)	Oct. 1940–Sept.	1945	788
(4)	Oct. 1945–Sept.	1950	866
(5)	Oct. 1950–Sept.	1955	1010
(6)	Oct. 1955–Sept.	1960	1044
(7)	Oct. 1960–Sept.	1965	1110

* *The first 7 months of these periods are used in establishing the initial rankings for the trading rules. Thus the first returns are calculated for May of the following year. All return data are reported for the interval May 1931 through September 1935, etc.*

Thus we obtained 29 separate samples of 200 securities each[8] for use in replicating the trading rule—where Levy had one observation on 200 securities we have 29 observations. These 29 independent samples allow us to obtain a very good estimate of the ability of the trading rules to earn profits superior to that of the buy-and-hold policy in any given time period and over many different time periods. Note also that we have eliminated one additional source of bias in Levy's procedure by not requiring (as he did) that the securities be listed over the entire 5-year sample period. No investor can possibly accomplish this when actually operating a trading rule since he cannot know ahead of time which firms will stay in business and which will not.

The Trading Profits vs. the B & H Returns.—The average returns earned over all seven time periods for all 29 samples by each of the trading rules and the buy-and-hold (B & H) policy are given in Table 2. The returns on the B & H policy given in Table 2 are the weighted average returns which would have been earned by investing an equal dollar amount in *every* security listed on the N.Y.S.E. at the beginning of each of the 7 periods under consideration (assuming that all dividends were reinvested in their respective securities when received).[9] The returns net of commissions account for the actual transactions

[7] Now distributed by Standard Statistics Inc.

[8] Except for the third time period in which there were only 788 securities listed giving us 4 samples for that time period of 197 securities each.

[9] If a security was delisted during a particular time period the proceeds were assumed to have been reinvested in the Fisher Investment Performance Index (cf. Fisher [1966]) which was constructed to approximate the returns from a buy-and-hold policy including all securities on the N.Y.S.E. This procedure is unlikely to cause serious bias and saves a considerable amount of computer time. The weights used in calculating the average

costs involved in the initial purchase and final sale (but ignore the transactions costs on the reinvestment of dividends as do the return calculations on the trading rule portfolios).

TABLE 2

Average returns and performance measures over all periods for various policies*

Policy	Average annual return**		Average performance measure $\bar{\delta}$
	Net of trans. costs	Gross of trans. costs	
(1)	(2)	(3)	(4)
Buy-and Hold***	.107	.111	−.0018
($X=10\%, K=160$)	.107	.125	−.0049
($X=5\%, K=140$)	.093	.124	−.0254

* *Calculated over all portfolios in Tables 4 and 5.*
** *Continuously compounded.*
*** *Weighted Average. Weights are proportional to number of trading rule portfolios in each period.*

We can see from Col. 3 of Table 2 that before allowance for commissions costs the trading rules earned approximately 1.4% more than the B & H policy. However, from Col. 2 of Table 2 we see that after allowance for commissions[10] the trading rules earned returns roughly equivalent to or less than the B & H policy. We shall see below however that the trading rules generate portfolios with greater risk than the B & H policy so that after allowance for the differential risk the rules performed somewhat worse than the B & H policy. Thus at first glance the results of Levy's trading rule simulation on 200 securities are not substantiated in our replication on 29 independent samples of 200 securities selected over a 35 year time interval.

Fama and Blume (1966) and more recently Smidt (1968) have argued persuasively that these results (the higher returns before allowance for transactions costs and returns comparable or lower than the B & H policy after allowance for transactions costs) are just what we would expect in an efficient market in which traders acting upon information are subject to transactions costs. We can expect outside traders to remove dependencies in security prices only up to the limits imposed by the transactions costs. Any dependencies which are not large enough to yield extraordinary profits after allowance for the costs of acting upon them are thus consistent with the economic meaning of the theory of random walks.

Tables 3 and 4 present the summary statistics of the replication of Levy's trading rules for each time period. Columns 3 and 4 contain the annual returns

---

B & H returns are proportional to the number of trading rule portfolios in each period. This procedure was followed in order to make the B & H average comparable to the trading rule average in which (due to the differing sample sizes) the time periods receive different weights. The simple averages for each time period are given in Tables 3 and 4.

[10] Calculated at the actual round lot rate applying to each security at the time of each trade.

TABLE 3

Summary statistics for B & H and trading rule portfolios for various time periods (trading rule is Levy's $(X=10\%, K=160)$ Policy)

		Continuously compounded annual rate of return				
Time period	Portfolio	Net of trans. costs	Gross of trans. costs	Std. dev.*	Beta	Delta
(1)	(2)	(3)	(4)	(5)	(6)	(7)
May 31	B & H	0.047	0.051	0.157	0.942	−0.017
to						
Sep 35	1.	0.088	0.100	0.137	0.774	0.027
	2.	−0.013	0.009	0.112	0.617	−0.066
[1]	3.	−0.032	−0.013	0.151	0.860	−0.093
Portfolio Average		0.014	0.032	0.133	0.750	−0.044
May 36	B & H	−0.031	−0.027	0.109	0.929	0.004
to	1.	−0.081	−0.067	0.095	0.769	−0.057
Sep 40	2.	−0.048	−.0032	0.106	0.802	−0.020
[2]	3.	−0.103	−0.085	0.104	0.829	−0.078
Portfolio Averge		−0.078	−0.062	0.101	0.800	−0.052
May 41	B & H	0.300	0.306	0.058	1.032	−0.043
to	1.	0.290	0.316	0.059	0.969	−0.032
Sep 45	2.	0.320	0.347	0.067	1.048	−0.032
	3.	0.237	0.260	0.056	0.881	−0.049
[3]	4.	0.259	0.290	0.071	1.178	−0.116
Portfolio Average		0.277	0.303	0.063	1.019	−0.057
May 46	B & H	0.032	0.036	0.049	0.950	0.012
to	1.	0.021	0.037	0.055	0.996	−0.000
Sep 50	2.	0.002	0.019	0.053	0.933	−0.017
	3.	0.031	0.047	0.054	0.983	0.010
[4]	4.	0.006	0.021	0.053	0.952	−0.014
Portfolio Average		0.015	0.031	0.054	0.966	−0.005
May 51	B & H	0.157	0.161	0.031	0.989	−0.004
to						
Sep 55	1.	0.164	0.179	0.039	1.139	−0.016
	2.	0.204	0.219	0.041	1.179	0.013
[5]	3.	0.150	0.170	0.041	1.162	−0.030
	4.	0.162	0.178	0.037	1.026	−0.002
	5.	0.179	0.196	0.033	0.919	0.026
Portfolio Average		0.172	0.188	0.038	1.085	−0.002

* *Standard deviation of the monthly returns.*

TABLE 3 (continued)

Time period	portfolio	Continuously compounded annual rate of return		Std. dev.	Beta	Delta
		Net of trans. costs	Gross of trans. costs			
(1)	(2)	(3)	(4)	(5)	(6)	(7)
May 56	B & H	0.090	0.095	0.033	0.968	0.012
to						
Sep 60	1.	0.272	0.281	0.048	0.829	0.174
	2.	0.125	0.141	0.046	1.067	0.040
[6]	3.	0.110	0.128	0.044	1.122	0.024
	4.	0.201	0.216	0.048	1.096	0.104
	5.	0.083	0.099	0.041	1.076	0.002
Portfolio Average		0.158	0.173	0.045	1.038	0.069
May 61	B & H	0.096	0.101	0.039	0.956	0.014
to						
Sep 65	1.	0.129	0.146	0.048	1.044	0.040
	2.	0.087	0.105	0.042	0.922	0.008
[7]	3.	0.101	0.120	0.051	1.161	0.010
	4.	0.063	0.081	0.046	1.032	−0.019
	5.	0.103	0.123	0.044	0.953	0.021
Portfolio Average		0.097	0.115	0.046	1.022	0.012

net and gross of actual transactions costs generated by the trading rule when applied to each sample of 200 securities[11] and for the buy-and-hold comparison. The last line of each panel gives the average values of the trading rule statistics for each sample for the period summarized in the panel.

After transactions costs the $(X = 10\%, K = 160)$ trading rule earned more than the B & H policy in only 13 of the 29 cases and the B & H policy showed higher returns in 16 of the 29 cases (see Col. 3 of Table 3). Thus, even ignoring the risk issues, the rule was not able to generate systematically higher returns than the B & H policy. Table 4 shows that the $(X = 5\%, K = 140)$ policy performed even less well, yielding a score of 12 to 17 in favor of the B & H policy.

Note also panel 7 of Tables 3 and 4 which gives the results for a time period almost identical to Levy's. The trading rule returns on all 5 portfolios are far smaller than the 20% and 26% respectively he reported. In fact 12.9% is the highest return we obtained in this period and 5 of the 10 rules earned less than the B & H policy. This is additional evidence that Levy's original high returns were spurious and probably attributable to the selection bias discussed earlier.

As before, gross of transactions costs, both trading rules performed much better relative to the B & H policy, with the $(X = 10\%, K = 160)$ policy

[11] The data is monthly. Thus the PR_{jt} is defined as the ratio of the price at the end of month t to the average of the closing prices for months $t-6$ through month t. The trading rule is then applied at one-month intervals for the remainder of the period.

earning higher returns than the B & H policy in 19 of the 29 cases and the ($X = 5\%$, $K = 140$) policy yielding higher returns in 18 of the 29 cases.

In addition comparison of the mean portfolio return (net of transactions costs) with the B & H return in each subperiod indicates that the B & H returns were higher in 4 out of the 7 periods for the ($X = 10\%$, $K = 160$) rule and 5 out of the 7 periods for the ($X = 5\%$, $K = 140$) rule. Gross of transactions costs the B & H policy yielded higher returns in 4 of 7 periods for the ($X = 10\%$, $K = 160$) policy and 3 of 7 periods for the ($X = 5\%$, $K = 140$) policy.

An Alternative Comparison and a Test of Significance.—Tables 3 and 4 contain the B & H returns calculated for an initial equal dollar investment in *every* security on the exchange at the beginning of each period. We have also calculated the B & H returns which would have been realized on *each sample* of 200 securities. The differences between these B & H returns and the trading rule returns for each sample in each time period are given in Table 5. The results are substantially the same as those reported in Tables 3 and 4 in terms of the number of instances in which the trading rules earned higher returns than the B & H policy (see last two lines of Table 5 for a summary).

The mean difference between the B & H and trading rule returns is given for each policy (both net and gross of transactions costs) in Table 5 along with the standard deviation of the differences. The "t" values given at the bottom of Table 5 (none of which is greater than 1.5) indicate that none of the differences is significantly different from zero. Thus even ignoring the issue of differential risk between the B & H and trading rule policies the trading rules do not earn significantly more than the B & H policy.

V. RISK AND THE PERFORMANCE OF THE TRADING RULES

In order to compare the riskiness of the portfolios generated by the trading rules with the risk of the B & H policy we have calculated the standard deviation of the monthly returns (after transactions costs), and these are given in column 5 of Tables 3 and 4. Except for the first two subperiods the standard deviations of the trading rule portfolios are uniformly higher than that for the B & H policy. Thus, for equal expected returns a risk averse investor choosing among portfolios on the basis of mean and standard deviation would not be indifferent between them. This brings us to a serious issue.

If securities markets are dominated by risk averse investors and risky assets are priced so as to earn more on average than less risky assets then any portfolio manager or security analyst will be able to earn above average returns if he systematically selects a portfolio with higher than average risk; so too will a mechanical trading rule. Jensen (1967) has pointed out that there is good reason to believe that Levy's trading rules will tend to select such an above average risk portfolio during time periods in which the market is experiencing generally positive returns. Thus it is important in comparing the returns of the trading rule to those of the B & H policy to make explicit allowance for any differential returns due solely to different degrees of risk.

A Portfolio Evaluation Model.—Jensen (1969) has proposed a model for evaluating the performance of portfolios which takes explicit account of the

TABLE 4

Summary statistics for B & H and trading rule portfolios for various time periods [Trading rule is Levy's $(X=5\%,\ K=160)$ policy]

Time period	Portfolio	Continuously Compounded annual rate of return		Std. dev.	Beta	Delta
		Net of trans. costs	Gross of trans. costs			
(1)	(2)	(3)	(4)	(5)	(6)	(7)
May 31 to	B & H	0.047	0.051	0.157	0.942	−0.017
Sep 35	1.	−0.154	−0.125	0.138	0.728	−0.223
	2.	−0.054	−0.017	0.128	0.672	−0.110
[1]	3.	−0.047	−0.017	0.151	0.822	−0.108
Portfolio Average		−0.085	−0.053	0.139	0.741	−0.147
May 36 to	B & H	−0.031	−0.027	0.109	0.929	0.004
Sep 40	1.	−0.142	−0.121	0.102	0.806	−0.124
	2.	−0.021	0.004	0.141	0.962	0.016
[2]	3.	−0.157	−0.127	0.103	0.761	−0.143
Portfolio Average		−0.107	−0.081	0.116	0.843	−0.083
May 41 to	B & H	0.300	0.306	0.058	1.032	−0.043
Sep 45	1.	0.309	0.352	0.072	1.094	−0.053
	2.	0.326	0.368	0.084	1.160	−0.059
[3]	3.	0.203	0.237	0.066	0.995	−0.110
	4.	0.246	0.292	0.081	1.329	−0.170
Portfolio Average		0.271	0.312	0.076	1.145	−0.098
May 46 to	B & H	0.032	0.036	0.049	0.950	0.012
Sep 50	1.	−0.021	0.005	0.056	1.004	−0.042
	2.	−0.004	0.016	0.056	0.958	−0.024
[4]	3.	0.038	0.060	0.059	1.021	0.017
	4.	−0.003	0.019	0.056	0.965	−0.023
Portfolio Average		0.002	0.025	0.057	0.987	−0.018
May 51 to	B & H	0.157	0.161	0.031	0.989	−0.004
Sep 55	1.	0.155	0.178	0.038	1.074	−0.015
	2.	0.155	0.178	0.042	1.136	−0.023
[5]	3.	0.188	0.213	0.046	1.228	−0.007
	4.	0.132	0.160	0.036	0.949	−0.019
	5.	0.221	0.241	0.039	0.868	0.067
Portfolio Average		0.170	0.194	0.040	1.051	0.001

TABLE 4 (continued)

Time period	Portfolio	Continuously compounded annual rate of return		Std. dev.	Beta	Delta
		Net of trans. costs	Gross of trans. costs			
(1)	(2)	(3)	(4)	(5)	(6)	(7)
May 56 to Sep 60	B & H	0.090	0.095	0.033	0.968	0.012
	1.	0.245	0.258	0.046	0.822	0.152
	2.	0.158	0.181	0.058	1.174	0.064
[6]	3.	0.135	0.159	0.051	1.205	0.043
	4.	0.242	0.263	0.056	1.170	0.135
	5.	0.080	0.106	0.046	1.139	−0.004
Portfolio Average		0.172	0.193	0.052	1.102	0.078
May 61 to Sep 65	B & H	0.096	0.101	0.039	0.956	0.014
	1.	0.101	0.130	0.053	1.087	0.013
	2.	0.091	0.119	0.047	0.956	0.010
[7]	3.	0.123	0.149	0.060	1.296	0.023
	4.	0.078	0.107	0.053	1.092	−0.009
	5.	0.073	0.104	0.052	1.019	−0.010
Portfolio Average		0.093	0.122	0.053	1.090	0.005

effects of differential riskiness in comparing portfolios. The model is based upon recent mean-variance general equilibrium models of the pricing of capital assets proposed by Sharpe (1964), Lintner (1965), Mossin (1966), and Fama (1968). The measure of performance, δ_j for any portfolio j in any given holding period suggested by Jensen is

$$\delta_j = R_j - [R_F + (R_M - R_F)\beta_j] \qquad (1)$$

where

R_j = the rate of return on portfolio j.
R_F = the riskless rate of interest.
R_M = the rate of return on a market portfolio consisting of an investment in each outstanding asset in proportion to its value.
$\beta_j = \dfrac{\text{cov }(R_j,\ R_M)}{\sigma^2(R_M)}$ = the systematic risk of the j'th portfolio.

We shall not review the details of the derivation of (1) here; the interested reader is referred to Jensen (1969). However, Figure 1 gives a graphical interpretation of the measure of performance δ_j. The point M represents the realized returns on the market portfolio and its "systematic" risk (which from the definition of β, can be seen to be unity). The point R_F is the riskless rate and the equation of the line $R_F M Q$ is

TABLE 5

Differences between B & H and trading returns. (B & H returns calculated for each subsample of 200 securities.)

| Period | B&H returns trading—rule returns | | | |
| | [X= 10%, K = 160] | | [X= 5%, K = 140.] | |
	Net of trans. costs	Gross of trans. costs	Net of trans. costs	Gross of trans. costs
(1)	(2)	(3)	(4)	(5)
1	−0.024	−0.032	0.218	0.193
	0.057	0.040	0.098	0.066
	0.079	0.065	0.094	0.069
2	0.035	0.024	0.096	0.078
	0.033	0.021	0.006	−0.015
	0.074	0.061	0.128	0.103
3	0.012	−0.008	−0.007	−0.044
	−0.013	−0.033	−0.019	−0.054
	0.039	0.021	0.073	0.044
	0.058	0.034	0.071	0.032
4	0.012	0.0	0.054	0.032
	0.030	0.016	0.036	0.019
	0.008	−0.004	0.001	−0.017
	0.020	0.008	0.029	0.010
5	−0.016	−0.027	−0.007	−0.026
	−0.032	−0.043	0.017	−0.002
	0.003	−0.012	−0.035	−0.055
	−0.012	−0.024	0.018	−0.006
	−0.017	−0.029	−0.059	−0.074
6	−0.177	−0.181	−0.150	−0.158
	−0.034	−0.045	−0.067	−0.085
	−0.022	−0.035	−0.047	−0.066
	−0.100	−0.110	−0.141	−0.157
	−0.004	−0.016	−0.001	−0.023
7	−0.033	−0.045	−0.005	−0.029
	0.002	−0.011	−0.002	−0.025
	0.003	−0.011	−0.019	−0.040
	0.035	0.022	0.020	−0.004
	0.005	−0.010	0.035	0.009
Mean Difference $= d$	.001	−.013	.015	−.008
Std. Dev. $=\sigma$ ($\tilde{d}$)	.050	.048	.075	.072
$t(\bar{d}) = \bar{d}/[\sigma(\tilde{d})/\sqrt{29}]$	1.07	−1.46	1.08	−.60
Number (−)	12	18	13	18
Number (+)	17	11	16	11

$$E(R \mid R_M, \beta) = R_F + (R_M - R_F)\beta. \tag{2}$$

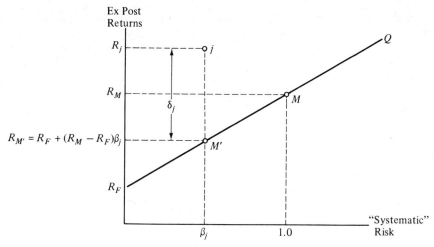

FIGURE 1

The measure of performance δ_j for a hypothetical portfolio.

If the asset pricing model is valid, the line R_FMQ given by eq. (2) gives us the locus of expected returns on any portfolio conditional on the ex post market returns and the systematic risk of the portfolio, β, in the absence of any forecasting ability by the portfolio manager. Thus the line R_FMQ represents the trade off between risk and return which existed in the market over this particular holding period. The point j represents the ex post returns R_j on a hypothetical portfolio j over this holding period, and β_j is its systematic risk. The vertical distance between the risk-return combination of any portfolio j and the line R_FMQ in Figure 1 is the measure of performance of portfolio j.

In the absence of any forecasting ability by the portfolio manager the expected value of δ_j is zero. That is we expect the realized returns of the portfolio to fluctuate randomly about the line R_FMQ through successive holding intervals. If $\delta_j > 0$ systematically, the portfolio has earned returns higher than that implied solely by its level of risk, and therefore the manager can be judged to have superior forecasting ability. If $\delta_j < 0$ systematically, the portfolio has earned returns less than that implied by its level of risk, and if the model is valid this can only be explained by the absence of forecasting ability and the generation of large expenses by the manager (see Jensen [1969, pp. 227f]).

The measure δ_j may also be interpreted in the following manner: Let M' be a portfolio consisting of a combined investment in the riskless asset and the market portfolio M such that its risk is equal to β_j. Now δ_j may be interpreted as the difference between the return realized on the j'th portfolio and the return R_M' which could have been earned on the equivalent risk market portfolio M'. If $\delta_j > 0$, the portfolio j has yielded the investor a return greater than the return on a combined investment in M and F with an identical level of systematic risk.

The measures of systematic risk for each of the portfolios generated by the trading rules and for the B & H policy are given in column 6 of Tables 3 and

4, and the measures of performance δ_j are given in column 7. The market returns and risk-free rates used in these estimates are given in Table 6. The average δ's for the B & H policy and the trading rule portfolios over all periods are given in column 4 of Table 2. The δ for the B & H policy (after transactions costs) over all 7 periods was $-.0018$; that is the B & H policy earned on average .18% per year (compounded continuously) less than that implied by its level of risk and the asset pricing model.

TABLE 6

Market and riskless returns used in estimating the performance measures δ_j

Period	Market return*	Riskless rate**
(1) May 1931–Sept. 1935	.064	.0334
(2) May 1936–Sept. 1940	−.039	.0108
(3) May 1941–Sept. 1945	.296	.0080
(4) May 1946–Sept. 1950	.020	.0104
(5) May 1951–Sept. 1955	.149	.0206
(6) May 1956–Sept. 1960	.075	.0296
(7) May 1961–Sept. 1965	.079	.0344

* *Continuously compounded returns on Fisher Investment Performance Index (Fisher [1966]), obtained from most recent Monthly Price Relative Tape distributed by Standard Statistics ,Inc.*
** *Continuously compounded yield to maturity (at the beginning of the period) of a government bond maturing at the end of the period estimated from yield curves presented in the U.S. Treasury Bulletin, except for the first two periods. The rate for the first period is the average yield on long-term government bonds at the beginning of the period taken from the Eighteenth Annual Report of the Federal Reserve Board—1931 (Washington, D.C., 1932), p. 79. The rate for the second period is the average yield on U.S. Treasury 3–5 year notes taken from the Twenty-Third Annual Report of the Board of Governors of the Federal Reserve System—1936 (Washington, D.C., 1937), p. 118.*

On the other hand the average δ for the trading rules (net of transactions cost) was $-.49\%$ and -2.54% respectively for the $(X = 10\%, K = 160)$ and $(X = 5\%, K = 140)$ policies. That is, after explicit adjustment for the systematic riskiness of the two policies, they earned $-.49\%$ and -2.54% less than that implied by their level of risk and the asset pricing model. In addition the average δ for the portfolios was greater than the δ for the B & H policy in only 2 periods for both of the trading rules (see Tables 3 and 4). Since the point at issue is whether or not the trading rules perform *significantly better* than the B & H policy the fact that they don't on the average even perform as well means we need not bother with any formal tests of significance.

VI. SUMMARY AND CONCLUSIONS

Our replication of two of Levy's trading rules on 29 independent samples of 200 securities each over successive 5-year time intervals in the period 1931 to 1965 does not support his results. After allowance for transactions costs the trading rules did not on the average earn significantly more than the B & H policy. Furthermore, since the trading rule portfolios were on the average more risky than the B & H portfolios this simple comparison of returns is biased in favor of the trading rules. After explicit adjustment for the level of risk it was shown that net of transactions costs the two trading rules we tested earned on average $-.31\%$ and -2.36% less than an equivalent risk B & H policy. Given these results we conclude that with respect to the performance of Levy's "relative strength" trading rules the behavior of security prices on the N.Y.S.E. is remarkably close to that predicted by the efficient market theories of security price behavior, and Levy's (1967a) conclusion that ". . . the theory of random walks has been refuted," is not substantiated.

REFERENCES

1. SIDNEY S. ALEXANDER. "Price Movements in Speculative Markets: Trends or Random Walks," *Industrial Management Review,* II (May 1961), 7–26.
2. SIDNEY S. ALEXANDER. "Price Movements in Speculative Markets: Trends or Random Walks, Number 2," *Industrial Management Review,* V (Spring, 1964), 25–46.
3. PAUL H. COOTNER (ed.). *The Random Character of Stock Market Prices.* (Cambridge, Mass: M.I.T. Press, 1964).
4. EUGENE FAMA. "The Behavior of Stock-Market Prices," *Journal of Business,* XXXVII (January, 1965), 34–105.
5. EUGENE FAMA, and MARSHALL BLUME. "Filter Rules and Stock Market Trading," *Journal of Business,* XXXIX (January, 1966), 226–41.
6. EUGENE FAMA. "Risk, Return, and Equilibrium: Some Clarifying Comments," *Journal of Finance* (March, 1968), 29–40.
7. LAWRENCE FISHER. "Some New Stock Market Indexes," *Journal of Business,* XXXIX, Part 2 (January, 1966), 191–225.
8. F. E. JAMES, Jr. "Monthly Moving Averages—An Effective Investment Tool?," *Journal of Financial and Quantitative Analysis* (September, 1968), 315–326.
9. MICHAEL C. JENSEN. "Random Walks: Reality or Myth—Comment," *Financial Analysts Journal* (November—December, 1967), 77–85.
10. MICHAEL C. JENSEN. "Risk, the Pricing of Capital Assets, and the Evaluation of Investment Portfolios," *Journal of Business,* XLII (April, 1969), 167–247.
11. ROBERT A. LEVY. "An Evaluation of Selected Applications of Stock Market Timing Techniques, Trading Tactics and Trend Analysis," (Unpublished Ph. D. dissertation, The American University, 1966).
12. ROBERT A. LEVY. "Random Walks: Reality or Myth," *Financial Analysts Journal* (November–December, 1967a).
13. ROBERT A. LEVY. "Relative Strength as a Criterion for Investment Selection," *Journal of Finance,* XXII (December, 1967b), 595–610.
14. ROBERT A. LEVY. "The Principle of Portfolio Upgrading," *The Industrial Management Review* (Fall, 1967c), 82–96.
15. ROBERT A. LEVY. "Random Walks: Reality or Myth—Reply," *Financial Analysts Journal,* (January–February, 1968), 129–132.
16. JOHN LINTNER. "Security Prices, Risk, and Maximal Gains from Diversification," *Journal of Finance,* XX (December, 1965), 587–616.
17. BENOIT MANDELBROT. "Forecasts of Future Prices, Unbiased Markets and 'Martingale' Models," *Journal of Business,* XXXIX, Part 2 (January, 1966), 242–55.
18. JAN MOSSIN. "Equilibrium in a Capital Asset Market," *Econometrica,* XXXIV (October, 1966), 768–83.
19. RICHARD ROLL. "The Efficient Market Model Applied to U.S. Treasury Bill Rates," (Unpublished Ph. D. dissertation, University of Chicago, 1968).

20. PAUL A. SAMUELSON. "Proof That Properly Anticipated Prices Fluctuate Random-ly," *Industrial Management Review,* VI (Spring, 1965), 41–49.
21. WILLIAM F. SHARPE. "Capital Asset Prices: A Theory of Market Equilibrium under Conditions of Risk," *Journal of Finance,* XIX (September, 1964), 425–42.
22. SEYMOUR SMIDT. "A New Look at the Random Walk Hypothesis," *Journal of Finance and Quantitative Analysis* (September, 1968), 235–261.
23. J. C. VAN HORNE and G. G. C. PARKER. "The Random Walk Theory: An Empiri-cal Test," *Financial Analysts Journal* (November–December, 1967), 87–92.

Breen demonstrates that a fundamental filter rule can outperform random selection. His article has several interesting aspects. First, it provides a measure of the risk as well as the return associated with a decision rule. Second, it provides some evidence as to the sensitivity of a filter rule to a change in its parameters. Third, it provides evidence that absolute rather than industry-relative measures may be a more meaningful way to examine stocks.

18

Low Price-Earnings Ratios and Industry Relatives

*William Breen**

This article is reprinted with permission from the Financial Analyst Journal, *Vol. 24 ,No. 4 (July–August, 1968), pp. 125–127.*

This study investigates an aspect of the low price-earnings ratio–high price performance discussion. Recent issues of the *Financial Analysts Journal* have contained several interesting examinations of the merits and drawbacks of low price-earnings (P/E) ratios as indicators of future high price performance of common stocks. These discussions are well summarized by Molodovsky in his article published in the *Journal's* May–June 1967 issue, and will not be re-examined here. One interesting question which has not arisen in the literature is whether a price-earnings ratio should be considered low relative to the whole market, or relative to the industry in which the company resides. This study will try to shed some light on that question.

METHOD OF ANALYSIS

In order to test whether a low price-earnings multiple is more properly an industry-relative concept, we have performed a straightforward simulation of

---

* The author is indebted to Standard Statistics for making the COMPUSTAT tapes available to him.

the performance of two portfolios. Each portfolio is chosen from the same population, and each consists of low P/E securities. In one portfolio price-earnings ratios are measured relative to the market, while in the second, securities are chosen whose price-earnings ratios are low relative to the average for the industry. Using this method, we hope to isolate the more productive definition of low P/E multiples. We will adjudge the portfolio with the consistently higher return, if one portfolio has a consistently higher return, to designate the more productive and useful definition of low price-earnings ratios.

Before we proceed with a detailed explanation of the selection and performance of the two portfolios, we must add several caveats and modifications. There are several reasons why price-earnings ratios may be low, as Molodovsky has pointed out. Low price-earnings multiples, or their inverse, high current earnings yields, may be due to the market anticipating poor earnings performance of a company. If this expectation proves to be correct, then the low P/E multiple is "justified." If this expectation is not correct, or if a company has been overlooked by the market in general, and does have a good potential for growth in earnings, it might be said that the low price-earnings multiple signifies that the company in question is undervalued by the market.

It is then within this context of apparent undervaluation that the concept of low price-earnings ratios presents itself as a logical guide to portfolio selection. It is also in this context that the question of low relative to market or low relative to industry arises. A company with a high P/E relative to the market as a whole might reside in an industry with an historically high average industry multiple, and in fact might have the lowest multiple in the industry, and the lowest percent of the industry average of any company in the sample. Then by one standard, this company would appear undervalued, and by the other not.

When we select the two portfolios, we would like some criteria to separate the securities which are potentially undervalued from those which the market correctly assesses as having a poor future earnings pattern. In actual investment situations, the analyst would consider a whole host of company characteristics to accomplish this separation. In the simulation study we perform, we are necessarily much more limited than the analyst. The prime limiting factor is our desire to avoid hindsight whenever possible. We therefore propose the simple criterion that a security will not be eligible for either portfolio unless its average compound growth in earnings over the five years preceding the selection year has been at least ten percent per year. This average compound growth rate in earnings is calculated in the familiar manner of computing the simple log-linear regression of earnings on time. We hope this simple criterion captures some of the flavor of potential unrecognized growth performance.

A second caveat which must be heeded pertains to the meaningfulness of the portfolio performance figures in general. We measure total portfolio return as the average percentage price appreciation plus percent dividend return over each portfolio. Suppose that this return were indistinguishable in a statistical sense from the returns from securities selected at random. In this case, comparisons between the "results" from the two portfolios would have no validity for making inferences concerning the underlying selection procedures, since both procedures could be considered nothing more than disguised random generators. Of course, if the results from only one of the portfolios seemed to arise from a non-chance mechanism, this portfolio would appear to dominate the second, and we could still make some sort of comparison. In either case, what is clearly needed is some method to ascertain, within a statistical framework, whether or not the results from any portfolio selection simulation was a non-chance phenomenon.

Statistical distributions of the results or returns from portfolios chosen by chance would provide one vehicle for the determination of randomness versus non-randomness of portfolio returns. In the forthcoming September issue of the *Journal of Finance,* I present a tabulation of such distributions, for the years 1952–1966. Given these distributions, and a particular portfolio return, the percent of randomly chosen portfolios which had a return less than or equal to the given portfolio return can be found. If this percentage is high, it can be said that the given portfolio is significantly different from a random portfolio. In the next section, we will report these percentages as well as the actual return figures.

SPECIFIC SELECTION PROCEDURES

The basic population from which portfolios will be selected is the Standard Statistics 1400 company annual COMPUSTAT population. For each year we first eliminate all companies whose average compound growth rate is less than ten percent for the immediately previous five-year period. We then construct a portfolio for each year which contains the ten securities which have the lowest absolute price-earnings ratios in the entire high growth rate population. We designate this portfolio number one. Portfolio two is similarly chosen, except that we chose the ten securities which have the lowest P/E multiples relative to their own industries. Each portfolio is assumed to be purchased during the first week in January, held one year, and sold the following January. Since we are using January to January figures, we also eliminate from the basic population all companies whose fiscal year ends in the months January through June. This elimination helps rid the analysis of some elements of hindsight. The one-year holding period, and the ten-security size of the portfolio are arbitrary, and are chosen to conform with the procedure used to calculate the distributions of random portfolio returns.

Before presenting numerical results, we should spell out in more detail the method of calculating the two definitions of low multiples. In the case of low relative-to-market P/E ratios, we should compute each company P/E as a percent of the average multiple, for that year, of the whole COMPUSTAT population. Since the selection procedure depends only on ordinal properties of this latter percent, we can alternatively make the selection on the basis of absolute price-earnings ratios. We follow this latter procedure.

For the industry-relative criterion, we first compute the average price-earnings multiple for each COMPUSTAT industry classification. Where there are but one or two companies comprising an industry sample, we throw out this industry classification. After computing these average industry multiples, we compute, for each company in the sample, the ratio of the company P/E to the average industry P/E. We then use this ratio as the measure of industry-relative undervalue. This method is followed for each year in question.

The basic comparisons will be made on a year-to-year basis. That is, we consider the basic observations to be returns from each portfolio over a one-year horizon. If a security were, in fact, undervalued and the market recognized this fact, the performance of that entrant in the portfolio will demonstrate this fact. If the market did not recognize a true undervalued security, the security should appear again the following year in the portfolio, and eventually it should produce favorable performance. If, on the other hand, a security "earned" its low multiple, there is a good chance that it disappears from the next year's portfolio, due to the growth rate screen imposed on the basic population. For this reason, the successive one-year holding periods seem reasonable.

NUMERICAL RESULTS

We are interested in which of two measures of low price-earnings ratios give better investment performance. If the results from either portfolio are clearly superior, it will be said that the method which gave rise to those results is superior. In Table I, the return from each of the two portfolios is given, for each year 1953–1966. The number in parentheses beside each return figure is the percent of randomly chosen portfolios in that particular year that had returns less than or equal to the given return. The bottom figure in each column is the average compound return, measured by the geometric mean of the total return associated with each column.

It should first be observed from the numbers in parentheses in Table I that for the most part, both portfolios yield returns which are significantly different from the returns from randomly chosen portfolios. Thus, it seems sensible to discuss comparisons of the two portfolio returns. We could apply many techniques for determining whether one of the two portfolios had the better all around performance, or whether there were no observable differences in their performance. If we say that one portfolio return is greater than the other if it

TABLE I

Year/return	Low market relatives Portfolio One	Low industry relatives Portfolio Two
1953	.1928 (95%)	.1328 (95%)
1954	.5751 (95%)	.9284 (95%)
1955	.4517 (95%)	.3554 (95%)
1956	.1940 (90%)	.0769 (65%)
1957	−.0986 (45%)	−.1564 (20%)
1958	1.1159 (95%)	.7263 (95%)
1959	1.0285 (95%)	.6108 (95%)
1960	.1370 (90%)	.1212 (90%)
1961	1.5519 (95%)	.3606 (70%)
1962	−.0419 (95%)	−.1982 (35%)
1963	.2554 (75%)	.3376 (90%)
1964	.2610 (80%)	.2672 (80%)
1965	.5050 (80%)	.2202 (15%)
1966	.0343 (85%)	.0608 (90%)
Mean Compound Return	.375	.239

"beats" five percent more of the randomly selected portfolios than the second, there are seven ties in the sample, portfolio one (market-relative low P/E) is higher by this measure in five years, and portfolio two (industry-relative low P/E) leads in two years. This, taken with the average annual compound rate suggests that portfolio one weakly dominates portfolio two. Other types of tests will give similar results. On this basis, it would seem that the more proper measure of low price-earnings ratios is relative to the whole sample of companies under consideration.

TABLE II

Year/return	Portfolio one	Portfolio two
1953	.0249	.0347
1954	.8897	.9015
1955	.3424	.3247
1956	.2160	.1549
1957	−.1178	−.1949
1958	1.2030	.8378
1959	.6101	.6088
1960	.0502	.1084
1961	.7334	.6633
1962	−0.903	−.1268
1963	.3672	.3708
1964	.2756	.2398
1965	.5112	.3741
1966	.0048	−.0264
Mean Compound Return	.301	.263

We can investigate further in two directions. First, let us extend the number of securities in the portfolio. Thus, we will repeat the simulation described above, except that we will include fifty securities in each portfolio. Unfortunately, distributions of fifty-stock random portfolio returns are not available, and so we cannot report the item in parentheses given in Table I. Table II gives the results of this second simulation.

Several interesting observations can be drawn from Table II and from a comparison of Tables I and II. When considering a portfolio comprised of fifty securities, the dominance of portfolio one over portfolio two is even less clear than in the ten-security case. But the average compound return, and the absolute number of years in which returns from portfolio one are larger than returns from portfolio two still indicate that the market relative concept is superior to the industry relative concept.

If one were asked to speculate about the results prior to the experiment, two considerations come to mind. The first is that when the market relatives are used, traditionally low P/E industries will dominate the portfolio. The second is that when using the industry relatives, large industries with large variance of company P/E's will dominate the portfolio. Examination of the makeup of the ten-security portfolios shows that the latter possibility proves to be much more in evidence than the former. To make a possible correction for this phenomenon, we have constructed one further simulation comparison.

A third portfolio has been constructed, which is a combination of low industry relatives and low market relatives. For this third portfolio we chose the ten securities with the lowest ratio of company P/E to average industry P/E, which also were among the fifty lowest absolute price-earnings ratios. The results from this simulation are presented in Table III. On the basis of percent above random, there is little to choose between this portfolio and portfolio one, although in terms of absolute yearly return, and compound return, portfolio one seems to dominate.

TABLE III

Composite portfolio

Year	Return	Percent of random less than return
1953	.1298	(95)
1954	.9264	(95)
1955	.3554	(95)
1956	.2274	(90)
1957	.1695	(15)
1958	.7480	(95)
1959	.5611	(95)
1960	.1443	(90)
1961	1.3842	(95)
1962	−.1832	(40)
1963	.3466	(90)
1964	.3027	(85)
1965	.2621	(25)
1966	.0866	(90)
Average Compound Return	.310	

CONCLUSIONS

There are several implications which may be drawn from this study. First, low price-earnings multiples, measured either relative to the whole population, or to industry classification, when combined with a control on average past growth in earnings, give portfolio performance which in most years is superior to the performance of randomly selected securities.

Second, the evidence seems to (weakly) support the hypothesis that the relevant measure of low price-earnings multiples is a comparison based on the whole market, rather than on an industry basis. Of course, strictly speaking, we should say that the analysis holds for the industry classification used in the compustat statistical service. This industry classification is, however, roughly equivalent to the Standard Industrial Classification, and can be taken as representative of commonly used industry definitions. Even in this light, we have not shown within the limited context of this study that some industry classification is not useful. We do show, however, that the standard industry definition is of less importance than a consideration of certain security characteristics relative to the whole security population. While it is dangerous to generalize results such as have been presented here, it is perhaps not too far out of bounds to suggest that these results give some credence to the assertion that in the future, industry specialists will be less important than "characteristics" specialists in the analytical assessment of common stocks.

The Shelton article is of interest for two reasons: First, it demonstrates the ability of a stock valuation model (used by Value Line) to select undervalued securities, and second, it demonstrates that a large, heterogeneous group of investors can produce results which are better than random selection.

19

The Value Line Contest: A Test of the Predictability of Stock-Price Changes

John P. Shelton

This article is reprinted with permission from the Journal of Business, *Vol. 40, No. 3 (July, 1967), pp. 251–269.*

Whether or not an individual, or a group of investors, can outperform the stock market is a question of considerable interest to professional investors and students of the security markets. On the surface, the question would seem to be fairly easy to answer, except in the case of private individuals, where it is nearly impossible to get accurate and complete records. But even pension and mutual funds, whose records are available for careful measurement, have found the problem nearly insuperable, as is indicated in a number of recent articles.[1]

* This study could not have been undertaken without financial support from the Ford Foundation, made available through the Graduate School of Business of the University of Chicago, and Arnold Bernhard & Co., Inc., which not only provided a part of the funds used during the study but gave, in a generous and unquestioning manner, complete assistance in providing any and all data requested. James Warren, UCLA doctoral student, competently programmed all the statistical analysis.

[1] See, e.g., Ira Horowitz, "A Model for Mutual Fund Evaluation" (Mutual Funds as Investment Alternatives), *Industrial Management Review*, Vol. VI, No. 2 (Spring, 1965); Randolph W. McCandish, Jr., "Some Methods for Measuring Performance of a

In this context, it becomes especially interesting to examine the results of a very large number of investment choices made under the well-defined conditions that governed the 1965–66 Value Line contest. In succeeding sections, this paper describes the contest, reviews the recent discussions concerning the random-walk hypothesis of stock-price behavior, and then presents and analyzes the results attained by the contest's 18,565 entrants.

I. THE CONTEST

In September, 1965, Value Line, an investment advisory service, announced a Contest in Stock Market Judgment. Though the Value Line management conceived the contest as a promotional device, it provided—as a by-product—an unusually good opportunity to test the stock-selecting ability of a large number of people. The contest required that the entrants supply merely their names and addresses; therefore little is known about them, but the participants are probably typical of individuals who feel they know enough about the stock market to make their own investment decisions.

The contestant was required to select a portfolio of 25 stocks from 350 that were ranked in categories IV and V by Value Line as of November 26, 1965. At that date, Value Line rated 1,072 stocks according to its expectation of their probable market performance in the next twelve months; it ranked 100 in Class I (highest), 259 in Class II (above average), 363 in Class III (average), 250 in Class IV (below average), and 100 in Class V (lowest). In order to administer the contest efficiently, each participant was required to print a specified code number for each stock in addition to printing the name of each stock he selected, and to return his challenge list to Value Line in an envelope postmarked no later than Sunday, December 5. The rules of the contest assumed that an equal amount was invested in each stock at the close of the market Friday, December 3, 1965. The contestant's entries were then keypunched with the stocks' names and related codes; in determining the accuracy of the entries, the computer program used by Value Line used the duplication of information (i.e., both stock name and code number) to double check the selection that was made.

When the contest ended, the closing prices as of Friday, June 3, 1966, for each of the 350 stocks, adjusted for stock splits, stock dividends, and other capital changes, were keypunched, and a computer calculated the percentage change in the price of each stock in every contestant's portfolio. The total change in each portfolio was also determined by averaging the percentage changes of all 25 stocks. Stating this in another way, for each portfolio the average price

Pension Fund," *Financial Analysts Journal,* Vol. XXI, No. 6 (November–December, 1965); William S. Gray, "Measuring the Analyst's Performance," *Financial Analysts Journal,* Vol. XXII, No. 2 (March–April, 1966); Frank E. Block, "Risk and Performance," *Financial Analysts Journal,* Vol. XXII, No. 2 (March–April, 1966); Peter O. Dietz, "Pension Fund Investment Performance—What Method To Use When," *Financial Analysts Journal,* Vol. XXII, No. 1 (January–February, 1966); John C. Sherman, "A Device To Measure Portfolio Performance," *Financial Analysts Journal,* Vol. XXII, No. 2 (January–February, 1966); John A. Sieff, "Measuring Investment Performance: The Unit Approach," *Financial Analysts Journal,* XXII, No. 4 (July–August, 1966), 93; Richard S. Bower and J. Peter Williamson, "Measuring Pension Fund Performance: Another Comment," *Financial Analysts Journal,* XXII, No. 3 (May–June, 1966), 143.

change was calculated, the average being based on an equal amount of money invested in each stock—not an equal number of shares of each stock being purchased (which would have given greater weight to high-priced stocks)—and the contestant was given a percentage score determined by dividing ending value by beginning value. For example, if the average price performance of the stocks in a portfolio were 90 per cent, it would mean that if $25,000 had been invested in the portfolio (placing $1,000 in each stock), the ending value would be $22,500, or the arithmetic mean of the individual price changes was –10 per cent.

The Value Line management also selected a list of twenty-five stocks from a universe of one hundred they had ranked in Class I as of November 26, 1965. The Value Line company mailed its list of twenty-six stocks to each contestant in an envelope postmarked prior to December 5, 1965.

The contestants were competing for a first prize of $5,000 that would be awarded to anyone whose challenge list of twenty-five stocks outperformed Value Line's list of twenty-five stocks by a greater margin than any other list submitted. A second prize of $2,500 was awarded for the next best list, third prize was $1,000, and fourth prize was $500. In addition, one hundred more prizes of $100 each were provided for contestants whose portfolio's performance exceeded the performance of Value Line's stock list. As it developed, only twenty contestants chose portfolios that did better than Value Line's, so that not all the prizes potentially available were earned.

For our purposes, however, little interest attaches to the contest winners alone or to their portfolios, because if there are "random" elements in stock-price behavior, some fraction of portfolios will perform very well, just as some others will perform very badly. But this may be only the result of chance factors. The likelihood of such an occurrence can be evaluated only by taking into account the performance of the entire list of entries, not just the best or the worst. This analysis does so.

Contest entrants were self-selected, but from a universe that should have included a high proportion of the well-qualified investors and advisors. Entrants could have learned about the contest from items that appeared in *The Wall Street Journal* and other financial publications; in addition, entry applications were mailed directly to all Value Line subscribers, all former Value Line subscribers, and others who were on Value Line's promotional mailing lists.

A brief review of the problems encountered in evaluating performance will help to show how unique was the opportunity provided by the Value Line contest for measuring performance. The problems include such questions as these:

What is the span over which performance should be measured?—The commonly employed calender year is arbitrary and may have no relation to the planning horizon the investor has in mind.

How should adjustment be made if a pension fund receives a sizable augmentation just before a major turn in the market?—Some funds receive quarterly or other lumped payments at times over which they have no control.

What yardstick should be used as a criterion for evaluating performance?—Among those available are the Dow-Jones Industrial Average, the Utilities Average, the Rail Average, the Standard & Poor 500 Stocks Index, the New York Stock Exchange Index, the Amex Index, any of the various over-the-counter indexes, and the Securities and Exchange Commission Index. Since the fund may own stocks that are traded on several exchanges and over the counter, there is no clear, defined, and easy-to-obtain performance measure for the appropriate universe.

Furthermore, it is difficult to obtain an unbiased measure of the performance of a fund, since the fund by its very act of taking a position may influence the performance of the stocks it buys or sells and thus affect the very criterion that was used for measurement. For example, in February, 1966, the newly created Manhattan Fund had nearly $300 million to invest. Before the year was ended, its fall in value closely matched the change in the Dow-Jones Industrial Average, but for several months after the fund began it fell less than the industrial average. It is possible that the purchasing power of the fund played some part in sustaining the prices of stocks on which it had concentrated purchases.

Another problem involves the issue of risk aversion. The trade-off between lower risk and reduced yield is well accepted in theory and is undoubtedly considered by the funds, but a difficulty in evaluating performance is the lack of a precise statement of how much return a fund is willing to forego in order to achieve how much stability; the task is further complicated by the lack of agreement on how to quantify risk.

In view of such problems it is not surprising that researchers who seek to understand the behavior of security markets have reached few, if any, widely accepted conclusions on how investors have actually performed in relation to the general market. Nonetheless, it is useful to summarize the previous studies in order to provide an intellectual frame of reference for this study.

The early work of Alfred Cowles, using forecasts published by a small number of professionals, led him to conclude that there was no "evidence of ability to predict successfully the future course of the stock market."[2]

H. K. Wu analyzed data for stock transactions of corporate insiders and concluded that "there is very little evidence that a definite relationship exists between insider transactions and subsequent price movements in relation to the general market trend."[3]

S. S. Colker evaluated the success of all brokerage houses' corporate analyses cited in *The Wall Street Journal* from June, 1960, to June, 1961, asking whether the stocks analyzed by the brokerage houses performed any better than the market as a whole. The author concluded, "the average businessman is probably expecting too much in anticipating that the stocks to which those in the business of buying and selling securities have invited public attention will appreciate to a markedly greater extent than the market as a whole."[4]

Perhaps the most conclusive study of actual performance was done by Irwin Friend and his Wharton colleagues in *A Study of Mutual Funds: Invest-*

[2] Alfred Cowles, "Stock Market Forecasting," *Econometrica,* Vol. XII, Nos. 3–4 (July–October, 1944); reprinted in E. B. Fredrickson (ed.), *Frontiers of Investment Analysis* (Scranton, Pa.: International Textbook Co., 1965), p. 480. See also Alfred Cowles, "Can Stock Market Forecasters Forecast?" *Econometrica,* I (July, 1933), 309–24.

[3] H. K. Wu, "Corporate Insider Trading Profits and the Ability to Forecast Stock Prices," in H. K. Wu and A. J. Zakon (eds.), *Elements of Investments* (New York: Holt, Rinehart & Winston, 1965), p. 448.

[4] S. S. Colker, "An Analysis of Security Recommendations by Brokerage Houses," *Quarterly Review of Economics and Business,* III (Summer, 1963), 21.

ment Policy and Investment Company Performance, which concludes that "when adjustments are made for this composition [of the portfolios proportions between bonds, preferred and common stocks, and other assets] the average performance by the funds did not differ appreciably from what would have been achieved by an unmanaged portfolio with the same division among asset types. About half the funds performed better, half worse, than such an unmanaged portfolio."[5]

These studies cast doubt on financial experts' ability to obtain better-than-average results. These doubts are reinforced by the experience of many academic researchers, who have looked for patterns or systematic behavior in the stock market, using sensitive tests for serial correlation, runs and reversals, and periodicity; all of these have failed to disclose any statistically significant market patterns.

Nonetheless, many people doubt that U.S. stock-price changes can accurately be characterized as random. Cowles' study, for example, suffered from trying to cope with vague and loosely worded predictions. Insiders may be buying and selling stock for reasons of control, personal financial requirements, or based on time spans longer than one or two years. Colker's study is based on analyses that may or may not be "buy" recommendations.

Finally, prior studies have been handicapped by inadequate numbers of observations, which, in the presence of random variation and under the usual tests of significance, have made it difficult to substantiate any other conclusion than that of random and unpredictable price changes.

In contrast to the problems that prior studies had to face, many aspects of the Value Line contest made it nearly ideal for evaluating the ability of individuals who are somewhat familiar with the securities market to select stocks that would outperform the market. For one thing, the Value Line contest had a specific time horizon so that all participants knew exactly the period over which they were being evaluated. Second, the entrants had risked nothing; therefore they were seeking to outperform the market without constraints that might be imposed by risk limitations. To put it another way, price changes were the only variable the contestants were trying to evaluate. In the third place, they were not investing money; thus their predictions could be tested against a market that was free from self-fulfilling disturbances. Also, for control purposes, it is extremely useful to have a specified universe of securities from which selections can be made. Such specification was not available in other studies. Finally, since dividends in the short span of six months have a high degree of certainty, the major element involved in the discussion about whether the stock market is predictable revolves around the question of price changes, which was the focus of this contest.

The author's interest in the contest had little to do with the competition between Value Line and the participants, but was focused on the unstated "contest" between the total performance of the entrants and the average performance of the universe of stocks from which they made their selections. It is valuable to

[5] Irwin Friend, F. E. Brown, Edward S. Herman, and Douglas Vickers, *A Study of Mutual Funds: Investment Policy and Investment Company Performance* (prepared for the Securities and Exchange Commission by the Wharton School of Finance and Commerce [Report of the Committee on Interstate and Foreign Commerce, House Report No. 2274, 87th Cong., 2d sess., August 28, 1962]), pp. 17–18.

have at least one report on precisely how a large group of people fared in selecting stocks, since this adds to the body of knowledge about securities and investor behavior. Moreover, it is possible to view the results of the contest as having implications regarding the random-walk hypothesis.

II. IMPLICATIONS FOR THE RANDOM WALK HYPOTHESIS

Discussions during the design and execution of the research on this paper made it clear that some who find statistical analysis of the contest, per se, worthwhile object if the data from the Value Line contest is used to support implications about the validity, or invalidity, of the random-walk hypothesis. The objections stem from some or all of the following points: The random-walk hypothesis relates only to short-term price movements, and six months is too long a period to be considered short term; the random-walk hypothesis states that expected price changes are random, conditional solely on prior prices and price changes, whereas the contestants undoubtedly took into consideration much more information; and the random-walk hypothesis should be interpreted to include not just price changes but the sum of price changes plus dividend income.

After considerable study the author is convinced not only that different writers have different interpretations of the random-walk hypothesis as related to the stock market but that the issue can eventually be pressed almost to a philosophical, or at least semantic, level primarily because the concept of randomness is so hard to quantify. For purposes of this paper the random-walk hypothesis will be defined as follows:

$$\epsilon(P_{t+1} \mid P_0, \ldots, P_t) = \epsilon(P_{t+1} \mid P_t). \tag{1}$$

In prose, the above equation says that tomorrow's expected price of a particular stock, given today's and all previous prices, is the same as the expectation of tomorrow's price given only today's price.[6]

Stated narrowly, as above, virtually all careful empirical studies thus far reported give strong support to the random-walk hypothesis.[7] But these analyses are of limited practical interest because they are constrained to utilize only price data. In the actual world of investing, no one makes decisions on the basis of only one kind of information. Whether the analyst be a "chartist," a "fundamentalist," or some other type of practitioner, he considers more information than is allowed in the hypothesis as narrowly defined above.

The question that is more relevant to the real world is whether price changes, given whatever knowledge the investor uses, behave randomly. Some of

---

[6] The random-walk hypothesis can also be modified to recognize the effects of earnings retention and the existence of a positive rate of interest. That modification would still be completely consistent with the interpretation presented in this paper.

[7] See, e.g., the numerous articles in Paul H. Cootner (ed.), *The Random Character of Stock Market Prices* (Cambridge, Mass.: M.I.T. Press, 1964), and such articles as Eugene F. Fama, "The Behavior of Stock Market Prices," *Journal of Business,* Vol. XXXVIII, No. 1 (January, 1965), and Michael D. Godfrey, Clive W. J. Granger, and Oskar Morgenstern, "The Random-Walk Hypothesis of Stock Market Behavior," *Kyklos,* XVII, Fase 1 (1964), 1–30.

the articles on the random-walk hypothesis explicitly cite this larger frame of reference. For example, consider the description given by Paul Cootner:

> The stock exchange is a well-organized, highly-competitive market. Assume that, in fact, it is a perfect market. While individual buyers or sellers may act in ignorance, taken as a whole, the prices set in the marketplace thoroughly reflect the best evaluation of currently available knowledge. If any substantial group of buyers thought prices were too low, their buying would force up the prices. The reverse would be true for sellers. Except for appreciation due to earnings retention, the conditional expectation of tomorrow's price, given today's price, is today's price.
>
> In such a world, the only price changes that would occur are those which result from new information. Since there is no reason to expect that information to be non-random in its appearance, the period-to-period price changes of a stock should be random movements, statistically independent of one another. The level of stock prices will, under these conditions, derscribe what statisticains call a random walk, and physicists call Brownian motion.[8]

With such authority for the position that the random-walk hypothesis need not be confined to the narrow view that price changes are conditional on no information except prior prices, this paper specifies one interpretation of the random-walk hypothesis, as follows, letting K_t stand for all knowledge possessed by the investor today, including the current price:

$$\epsilon[\Delta P_t \,|\, K_t] = 0. \tag{2}$$

This restatement of the random-walk concept, while it goes beyond the definition used by some investigators, is clearly of greater interest to the practitioners of investment and is consistent with the writings of some academicians.

Having established one interpretation of the random-walk hypothesis, we return to the line of reasoning involved in testing whether the Value Line contestants outperformed the list of stocks from which they could make their choices. Readers can decide for themselves whether they think the data are relevant to the random-walk hypothesis.

The first question raised in this study is the following: Did the 18,565 contestants[9] select portfolios, on average, that differed from the performance of the 350 stocks to which their selection was confined by enough to conclude that the result was not likely to have happened by chance? The null hypothesis being tested is this: The average score for all contestants did not differ from the

---

[8] Paul H. Cootner, "Stock Prices: Random vs. Systematic Changes," *Industrial Management Review*, III, No. 2 (Spring, 1962), 25. See also Sidney S. Alexander, "Price Movements in Speculative Markets: Trends of Random Walks," *Industrial Management Review*, II, No. 2 (May, 1961), 7-8, and Paul A. Samuelson, "Proof That Properly Anticipated Prices Fluctuate Randomly," *Industrial Management Review*, VI, No. 2 (Spring, 1965), 48.

[9] More than 25,000 people applied for contest entry blanks; 21,636 submitted selections, but because some of them chose stocks outside the universe of 350, did not choose exactly 25 stocks, did not write the correct code number beside each stock name, or failed to make the postmark deadline, the actual number of portfolios evaluated in the contest was 18,565.

average performance of the 350 stocks that constitute the underlying universe by more than could be attributed to the effects of sampling.

The mathematical and logical basis for our test is as follows:

1. Let the arithmetic mean and the standard deviation of the percentage change in prices for the stocks be designated M_{350} and σ_{350}.
2. Similarly, the mean and standard deviation of all possible single portfolios of 25 stocks selected from the universe of 350 will be designated $M_{P_{25}}$ and $\sigma_{P_{25}}$
3. Also, the mean and standard deviation of all possible means of 18,565 portfolios of twenty-five stocks will be designated M_{19} and σ_{19}.

(The subscript "19" is to remind the reader that this represents the theoretical mean and standard deviation of a large sample where each observation in the sample consists of the mean of almost 19,000 portfolios of twenty-five stocks each. The Value Line contest provides one specific example of such a group of portfolios.)

4. Finally, let the actual mean of the Value Line contestants be designated M_{VL}.

Since the mean of the sampling distribution of the mean equals the mean of the original population from which the samples are drawn, we know that

$$M_{350} = M_{P25} = M_{19}. \qquad \textbf{(a)}$$

Similarly, because the standard error of the sample mean in random samples of size n is equal to the standard deviation of the population divided by the square root of the sample size,

$$\sigma_{P25} = \frac{\sigma_{350}}{\sqrt{25}} \qquad \textbf{(b)}$$

and

$$\sigma_{19} = \frac{\sigma_{P25}}{\sqrt{18,565}} \qquad \textbf{(c)}$$

The null hypothesis is that:

$$M_{VL} = M_{19} \pm 3\sigma_{19}$$

Since $M_{19} = M_{P25} = M_{359}$, the null hypothesis can also be stated $M_{VL} = M_{350} \pm 3\sigma_{19}$.

Let H_0 symbolize that the average performance of the Value Line contestants is within three relevant standard deviations of M_{350}; this indicates the null hypothesis is supported. Let H_1, symbolize the average Value Line performance is more than three σ_{19} from M_{350}; this indicates the null hypothesis is denied.

To see the implications of accepting or rejecting H_0, note that the process that generates the percentage change in the prices can be categorized as (a) random or (b) non-random. Similarly, the process by which the contestants selected their portfolios can be characterized as (a) random or (b) non-random. (The last sentence is primarily an acknowledgement of the virtue of generality; in fact, it would be extremely unlikely if any significant number of contestants actually did make their choices by a random process, and an analysis of the actual selections made reveals that the number of times the various stocks were selected could hardly be explained by random selection.)

These possibilities can be summarized in the following matrix:

The selection process was	Price changes are			
	Random		Non-random	
Random ....H_0	(1)	H_0	(2)	
Non-random ....H_0	(3)	H_1	(4)	

If the price changes are random, then no selection technique will generate results to refute H_0. This is equivalent to saying that no technique for playing against a roulette wheel will produce results significantly better than random, even if the bettor uses such blatantly non-random techniques as betting only on red, odd numbers.

Similarly, if the selection process used by the contestants were random, the results would be consistent with H_0 regardless of the way price changes occur. These situations are indicated by cells (1), (2), and (3) of the matrix.

However, if the research shows that H_0 has to be rejected, then it has to be inferred that the investors chose non-randomly and that the price changes of 350 stocks from December, 1965 to June, 1966, were shown to be non-random, and by inference the whole random-walk hypothesis, as interpreted above, is cast in doubt.

One final caveat about the interpretation of the random-walk hypothesis presented above, which is essentially based on the analysis in the article by Paul Samuelson cited in note 8, is this: The view that changes in stock prices behave like a random walk does not mean that no expert can, with high regularity, make money by predicting stock-price changes. He might have foreknowledge about, or be able to predict, something that is highly correlated with the ex post behavior of stock prices. The essence of the random-walk hypothesis that no one can make consistently successful predictions about future price changes from past or present knowledge alone. Even if the stock market does change in a random fashion, it would be clearly profitable if one could know at least twenty-four hours in advance of all dividend declarations. However, it is doubtful if enough of the Value Line contestants had access to inside and future information to affect the average results significantly. The information they had when they made their selections was the sort of past or present knowledge that was generally available, and thus likely to have been fully accounted for in the prices at the time the selections were made. Consequently, the caveat cited in this paragraph can hardly apply.

Once again it should be emphasized that the results of the contest merit evaluation for what they contribute to our knowledge of the ability of a self-selected group of investors to outperform the market. Some may consider this has implications for the random-walk hypothesis, but the primary purpose of this paper is merely to report the empirical evidence and allow the reader to add his own implications.

III. RESULTS

This section presents and analyzes the results in the following order: (1) the behavior (mean, median, mode, and measures of dispersion) of the price changes of the 350 stocks available for selection, (2) the performance (mean and dispersion) of 18,565 randomly selected portfolios of 25 stocks (which can be used as an indication of how randomly selected portfolios would theoretically behave, given the actual price changes of the 350 stocks), (3) the performance (mean, median, mode, and measures of dispersion) of the 18,565 portfolios actually selected by contestants. Items 4–9 report on tests of the hypotheses of random price change and random selection followed by tests and discussion of a number of subsidiary questions.

1. *Behavior of the 350 stocks available for selection.*—The 350 stocks experienced over the twenty-six weeks an average loss in value of 5.957 per cent, or, in other words, they ended the contest with 94.043 per cent of their market value six months before. The standard deviation of the percentage price changes for the 350 stocks during the six months was 15.93 per cent. The range was from 202.5 per cent (1 stock, Vasco Metals, more than doubled in price) to 64.7 per cent (Consolidated Cigar lost more than one-third of its market value during the contest). The interquartile range was from 85.5 to 97.1 per cent.

When plotted in a histogram (Fig. 1) the stock-price changes were unimodal, but not normally distributed. They were skewed to the right, so that the median (90.75 per cent) was 21 per cent of one standard deviation less than the mean. The modal value was about 89 per cent. The distribution not only was skewed but also was leptokurtic; that is, it had a higher concentration around the mean and at the extremes than a normal curve would have. This distribution is consistent with most studies of stock-price changes.

2. *Performance of randomly selected portfolios.*—Despite the non-normality of the distribution of the individual price changes, the distribution of the performance of portfolios of 25 stocks selected at random from such a group should closely approximate a normal distribution. To demonstrate this, and for comparison with the portfolios actually selected by contestants, a computer program was written to select a portfolio of 25 stocks randomly from the 350 involved in the contest and to calculate that portfolio's performance; the selected stocks were then "replaced" and the process repeated many times, until 18,565 such portfolios had been selected.[10] The result simulates what would have happened if the contestants' stock selections had been random or if their selections—no matter how artful—had been made from stocks whose price changes were then generated by a truly random process.

The mean score of the 18,565 randomly selected portfolios was 94.05. This agrees closely, as it should, with the 350 stocks of 94.04. The standard deviation

---

[10] The possible number of different 25-stock portfolios selected from a universe of 350 stocks is 350!/325!25!, which turns out to be 107.1×10^{36}, or 107 trillion, trillion, trillion.

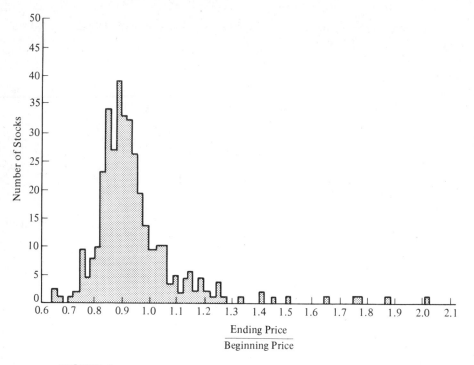

FIGURE 1

Distribution of price changes of 350 stocks

of the 18,565 portfolios was 3.08 per cent (vs. 3.18 per cent, which represents 15.93 per cent divided by $\sqrt{25}$).

3. *Performance of contestants' portfolios.*—The foregoing helps to show how it can be statistically significant when such a large group as our 18,565 contestants achieves average results that diverge from the mean of the 350 stocks by even a small amount. It is helpful here to recall the number of different possible portfolios of 25 stocks that could have been selected, namely, 107.1×10^{36}. Then imagine that these were lumped together by randomly chosen groups of 18,565 portfolios each! There would be

$$\frac{107.1 \times 10^{36}!}{(107.1 \times 10^{36} - 18,565)! \, 18,565!}$$

different ways to collect 18,565 portfolios, each containing 25 stocks from the 350. Clearly the mean score of all these would be extremely close to the mean score of the underlying stocks, and the vast majority would be quite close to that mean. In fact we would expect that approximately 68 per cent would lie within .00023 (or $\frac{23}{1000}$ of 1 per cent) on either side of the mean. (Remember that the score of the one random selection simulated on the computer was within $\frac{10}{1000}$ of 1 per cent of the mean.) Furthermore, all but 139 out of 100,000 such portfolio groupings would lie in a range of about $\frac{7}{100}$ of 1 per cent from the mean of the underlying 350 stocks. Thus, unless some non-random phenomenon were involved, the mean results of the 18,565 Value Line contestants should have equaled the mean of the 350 stocks, namely, .9404, or at least been in the range from .9397 to .9411.

In fact, the average score achieved by the 18,565 contestants, .9523, is about forty-nine relevant standard deviations greater than the expected mean. It is extremely unlikely that a difference as large as this would have occurred if the price changes during those six months were so truly random that investor selectivity would be of no value. That the contestants did not select randomly is a necessary, but not a sufficient, explanation for the observed difference. If the price changes were truly created by random behavior, the contestants could not have achieved significantly better-than-average results no matter how deliberately they made their selections. The results can only be explained by the additional hypothesis that the price changes were not generated by a random process.

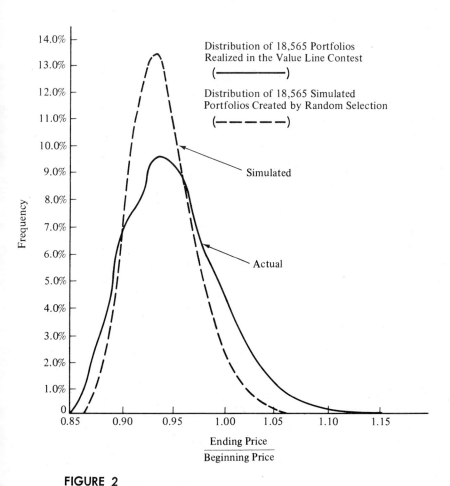

FIGURE 2

Distribution of actual versus randomly selected portfolios

The distribution of the 18,565 contest portfolios and the 18,565 randomly generated portfolios is pictured in Figure 2. The range of contest portfolio scores was .8425 to 1.1574. The interquartile range was .9105 to .9795. The median contestants' score was .9479, and the model score was in the .9300–.9399 bracket. The standard deviation of the 18,565 actual portfolios was 4.39 per cent.

After-the-fact data may seem obvious and perhaps uninteresting. The average score achieved by the contestants was only about 1.2 per cent above average results. Is this very noteworthy? The answer depends on what one expected, which makes it worth quoting the opinion of one professionally competent individual who was asked to review a request for financial support necessary to underwrite this study. He recommended against providing financial support, indicating, among other things, that the contestants should be characterized as uninformed investors, selecting among stocks they knew little about, using poorly formulated predictions. He concluded, "We would be astounded to find the null hypothesis rejected. . . . Considering the [very low] a priori probability of rejecting H_0, we do not think it would further our objectives to financially support your research."

The Value Line contest showed that contestants were able, as of December 5, 1965, to exercise selectivity among 350 stocks and achieve results that are not explainable unless subsequent price changes were predictable enough to rule out the conclusion that they could have been random.

4. *Effect of non-normality of the 350 individual stock-price changes.*—The difference of 1.2 per cent between the mean score of the 350 stocks and the 18,565 portfolios of 25 stocks appears to be extremely unlikely to arise from sampling error if the population of all samples of size 18,565 (where the item observed is the mean performance of a 25-stock portfolio) is normally distributed. It is highly probable that the sampling distribution of means of 18,565 portfolios would approximate normality because of the central-limit theorem, especially in view of the near-normality of the sampling distribution for means of single 25-stock portfolios, which would be the universe from which 18,565 portfolios would be chosen. Data for the randomly generated 25-stock portfolios (where $n = 18,565$) are shown in Figure 3, where the cumulative percentage distribution for that group of portfolios is plotted on probability (or normal curve) graph paper; the points lie close to a straight line. However, if we are willing to make an assumption about the size of the true standard deviation for the population of the means of all possible 18,565 25-stock portfolios, we can ignore the issue of whether the distribution is normal and use Tchebycheff's inequality. Assuming normality, we estimated that the standard deviation of the true distribution of 18,565 portfolios selected from the stocks in this contest should be close to $\frac{2}{100}$ of 1 per cent. But even if it were, in fact, as large as $\frac{1}{8}$ of 1 per cent (nearly six times greater than would be expected), then, regardless of the shape of the distribution, we would not expect a positive difference from the mean as large as 1.2 per cent to be actually achieved by the contestants more than one time in two hundred.

5. *Did contestants benefit by avoiding dividends?*—Several additional issues have to be evaluated before the above conclusion can be completely accepted. Probably the most important concerns the fact that the contest focuses solely on price changes, giving no credit to dividend income that might have been received

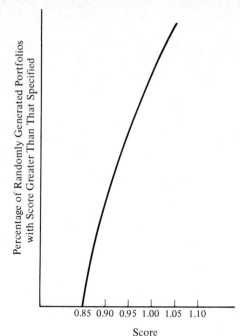

Percentage of Randomly Generated Portfolios with Score Greater Than That Specified

0.85 0.90 0.95 1.00 1.05 1.10

Score

FIGURE 3

Normal probability graph for performance
of randomly generated portfolio

during the six months. If it is assumed that for different stocks of equivalent risk and for a period such as six months, total expected return to the investor (dividends plus price change) will be approximately equal, then the lower the expected dividend yield, the more the expected capital gain. Consequently, the selectivity the contestants exhibited may have been only that amount necessary to choose stocks paying low dividends. To test whether the contestants' ability to outperform the market was simply associated with an avoidance of stocks yielding high dividends, a rank correlation was run between the frequency with which the stocks were selected by contestants and the estimated yield for the coming twelve months, as published in *The Value Line Investment Survey* on December 3, 1965. If the contestants' selectivity consisted of choosing low-dividend yielders, there should have been a statistically significant negative correlation between the number of times the stock was chosen and its yield. The actual rank correlation was –.006, which is in no way statistically significant. This indicated that the contestants' performance was based on something other than dividend avoidance.

6. *Was the contest period representative?*—Another possible objection arises because, instead of having a sample of 18,565 portfolios, there is only a sample of one contest with a particular set of beginning and ending dates. This would suggest there was some unusual phenomenon that prevailed as of early December, 1965, which the contestants took into consideration, consciously or not, but which the market had not already discounted. If such were the case, then the selectivity exhibited in the contest would not necessarily appear at other times. This question can be settled only if Value Line (or some other organization) holds similar contests in the future and the contestants' results are

repeatedly tested against the mean performance of the stocks in the contest universe. In that case, this paper can be viewed as the first report on a continuing area of research. Fortunately for the field of investment research, Value Line is scheduling a second contest for the spring and summer of 1967 and may conduct further ones from time to time.

7. *Were contestants simply "playing the long shots"?*—A final objection might be that the contestants were not really able to select individual stocks with better-than-average prospects, but that they were able to distinguish stocks with greater variance from those with less variance. (Some formulations of the random-walk hypothesis would permit such an ability to stratify securities by the amount of their price-change amplitude.) This would require that the contestants (or at least enough of them to affect the results) foresaw the market decline that actually occurred and selected stocks that would move (in this case, down) with *less* amplitude than the average security in the list. This argument, however, seems farfetched in view of the situation at the time of the contest. The market had been rising on a broad trend for nearly three years, with none but the most minor interruptions since July, and the general tone of forecasts was optimistic. It would be impossible to document the claim that most people were optimistic about the stock market at the time the contest began, but one piece of evidence comes from predictions by thirty-five faculty members of the UCLA School of Business Administration who participated during the last week of November, 1965, in the school's annual Business Forecasting Conference. Among other things, they predicted the Dow-Jones Industrial Index for 1966; the summation of their forecasts was for the index to range between 1,038 and 975, with a mean value of 960. Since the Dow Industrial stood at 948 on December 1, this was not a bearish forecast.

Another piece of evidence regarding the general outlook for the market at the time the contest began is obtained from the "Report of the Finance Committee of the American Economic Association," prepared in mid-December, 1965. "The Finance Committee remains mildly optimistic as to the trend of general business and corporate profits. . . . Therefore, the Committee believes that a fairly aggressive investment position is still desirable in spite of the high level of the stock market and long duration of the present period of business expansion."[11]

In short it is difficult to believe that the sharp downturn in the stock market that began in early February, 1966 was foreseen by many contestants. Furthermore, if they chosen stocks on the basis of selecting those that would change more than the market in either direction (because the rules of the contest did not penalize exaggerated downside performance, while exaggerated upside performance might win them a prize), then the over-all performance of the contestants should have been worse, not better, than the average of the 350 stocks, because the market was lower at the end of the contest than at the beginning.[12]

[11] "Report of the Finance Committee," *American Economic Review,* LVI, No. 2 (May, 1966), 623.

[12] Mr. Sam Eisenstadt, chief statistician for Value Line, commented on this point in a letter to the author: "the market was unique in this six months' interval. Although Standard & Poor's composite average declined 5.91%, Standard & Poor's index of low-priced stocks declined 2.31% in contrast to its index of high-priced stocks, which

8. *Some measures of selectivity of contestants' portfolios.*—The fact that contestants did not select securities at random in making their portfolio selections can be proved, though it is hardly conceivable that many contestants would be so flippant or casual about the contest as to select stocks randomly. Nonetheless, the number of times each security was selected in the contest was determined, and the frequency of actual selection was compared to the expected frequency that would be generated if stocks were selected randomly. A χ^2 test was applied to see if the actual frequency of selection differed from the expected by a statistically significant amount. The difference was in fact so great that the resulting χ^2 value was not given in tables, the statistical significance being beyond the .001 probability. One way to illustrate how non-random the selections actually were is to note the fact that when 18,565 portfolios were generated randomly, the five stocks that least frequently appeared in this random simulation showed up on an average of 1,239 times (the lowest one being 1,213 times). The five stocks that showed up the most times averaged 1,417 (the most frequent being 1,434). These numbers suggest the range around the average expected selection of 1,326 times that might occur if stocks had been selected randomly. In contrast, the five stocks selected least frequently in the contest appeared on the average 108 times (the lowest being 83 times), and the five stocks selected most frequently averaged 5,700 times (the highest being 7,413 times). Furthermore, the actual selections showed that 190 securities were selected fewer than 1,213 times, which was the least frequent when portfolios were generated randomly, and that 126 were selected more often than 1,434, which was the most frequent in the random selection. Table 1 shows data for the 10 per cent most frequently selected stocks.

The major goal of this study of Value Line's contest was to evaluate the performance of the contestants against the securities from which they had to select. It is clear that the average performance of the contestants was better than could have been expected if one believes that stock prices are utterly unpredictable. To the extent that the random-walk view hypothesizes that stock-price changes over a period such as six months are completely unpredictable, this study casts doubt on such a hypothesis.

9. *Comparison with a naïve, trend-extrapolation technique of selection.*—Perhaps the contestants selected their portfolios on the basis of the price performance of stocks in the prior six months under the assumption that trends tend to persist. To test this, the 350 stocks were ranked according to their price performance for the twenty-seven weeks prior to December 3, 1965, and fourteen portfolios were constructed placing the 25 stocks that did the best in the prior six months in portfolio 1, the 25 stocks that ranked 26–50 for the prior six months in portfolio 2, etc. The prices at the end of the contest were used to determine the performance of the fourteen trend-extrapolated portfolios; for example, the 25 stocks that had done the best the prior six months would, as a portfolio, have had a score of 96.9 per cent in the contest. The fourteen naïvely selected portfolios were then ranked according to their performance during the contest period. One measure of the consistency of past and future performance is the rank correlation between the achievement of the portfolios during the contest

---

declined 9.78%. To the extent one can classify low-priced stocks as volatile and high-priced stocks as being of high quality, the market was exceptional because it was a declining market in which the low-priced stocks outperformed the blue chips."

TABLE 1

Price performance of the thirty-five most frequently selected stocks over the duration of the contest

Name of stock	No. of contestants choosing the stock	Ratio of price at end of contest divided by price at beginning
1. Control Data	7,413	.794
2. Bell & Howell	5,817	1.065
3. Chrysler Corp	5,307	.811
4. Cenco Instruments	5,016	1.145
5. Caterpillar Tractor	4,940	.810
6. Brunswick Corp.	4,811	.973
7. Gillette Co.	4,593	.939
8. American Tel. & Tel	4,480	.880
9. Northrop Corp	4,372	.775
10. Parke-Davis	4,315	1.016
11. Columbia Broadcasting	4,021	1.320
12. Revlon	3,895	1.129
13. Monsanto Chemical	3,689	.917
14. United Nuclear Corp	3,659	1.000
15. High Voltage Engineer.	3,621	1.030
16. Curtiss-Wright	3,530	.796
17. American Enka	3,494	1.020
18. Gulf Oil Corp	3,449	.884
19. Texaco	3,338	.889
20. American Photocopy	3,293	.897
21. Western Union	3,252	.751
22. Singer Mfg	3,090	.917
23. Royal Dutch Petrol	2,994	.892
24. Transamerica	2,917	.818
25. Greyhound Corp.	2,901	.867
26. E. J. Korvette	2,886	.726
27. Gen. Portland Cement.	2,881	.867
28. Rayette, Inc.	2,874	.934
29. Lithium Corp.	2,850	.944
30. Sterling Drug	2,785	.919
31. Winn Dixie Stores	2,773	.886
32. Abbott Labs	2,772	.961
33. W. R. Grace & Co	2,665	.834
34. Standard Oil of N.J.	2,654	.905
35. Electric Storage Battery	2,638	.947

Note.—If all stocks had been chosen randomly, the expected number of times each stock would have been selected was 1,326. The average performance over the contest period for the ten most popular stocks was .921; for the next ten most popular stocks the performance was .988; for the thirty-five most frequently selected stocks the average price performance was .921, or a loss of 7.9 per cent. For all stocks in the universe, the average price ratio was 9.40.

TABLE 2

Consistency of performance of fourteen portfolios selected on basis of prior six month's performance*

Portfolios composed of stocks whose prior 6-months' performance ranked them:	Score achieved by the portfolio during the contest	Contest rank
1–25	.9692	5
25–50	.9884	3
51–75	.8871	14
76–100	.9987	1
101–125	.9320	7
126–150	.9079	13
151–175	.9148	9
176–200	.9184	8
201–225	.9099	10
226–250	.9602	6
251–275	.9711	4
276–300	.9083	12
301–325	.9915	2
326–350	.9091	11
Mean of:		
Top seven portfolios	.9426	
Bottom seven portfolios	.9384	

* *Rank correlation = + .12.*

time and their record for the prior six months. This is shown in Table 2; the rank correlation was + .12, which was not statistically significant.

10. *Did contestants profit from two days' more information?*—The rules of the contest created another possibility that warrants examination. The contestants were permitted to submit entries postmarked no later than Sunday, December 5, 1965, but their selections were priced as of the close of the market on Friday, December 3. The question arises, did a significant number of contestants utilize information that became available over the weekend to select stocks on Sunday that looked better than they might have at the close on Friday? Perhaps the use of two days' hindsight might explain how the contestants outperformed slightly, but significantly, the universe of stocks to which their selections were confined.

To test this possibility, the thirty-five most frequently chosen stocks were investigated to see how they performed, both over the weekend and over the entire period of the contest. If the most frequently selected stocks opened on Monday morning, December 6, at prices that were relatively favorable compared with Friday's close, it could be inferred that contestants took advantage of weekend news items in selecting their stocks. As it developed, the thirty-five most popular stocks in the contest opened on Monday at an average of 2.2 per cent below their Friday's close; this is compared to the Dow-Jones Industrial Average, which opened 1.6 per cent below its Friday close. By implication, any information obtained on Saturday or Sunday had little to do with guiding the most frequent selections.

A further point of some interest is whether the thirty-five most widely chosen stocks outperformed the universe during the entire contest, even if they might have done poorly at the very beginning. Table 1 lists the stocks in order of their popularity and shows the ratio of each one's price at the end of the contest to the opening price. On average, the thirty-five most popular stocks had an ending value of 92.1 per cent of their original prices, or a loss of 7.9 per cent, compared with a loss in the total list of nearly 6.0 per cent.

The investigation of the performance of the most frequently selected stocks shows that the contestants' superior performance is not explained either by knowledge they may have obtained over the weekend at the beginning of the contest or by the six months' performance of the stocks that ranked in the top 10 per cent in terms of popularity.

11. *Value Line's performance.*—Finally, in evaluating the predictability of the stock market it would be incomplete not to mention the performance of Value Line's own selections in the contest, although this is difficult to evaluate rigorously. Value Line's performance supports the view that stock-price changes have some degree of predictability, because it is difficult to ignore the fact that Value Line's score was exceeded by only twenty people out of nearly twenty thousand. If stock-price changes are truly random, there should be no significant distinction between the 100 stocks in Class I, which Value Line reserved for its universe, and the 350 that were provided for the contestants. Since the standard deviation of the 350 stocks was approximately 16 per cent and a standard deviation of a portfolio of 25 should be close to 2.3 per cent, we should expect that Value Line's performance would be within the range 94.04 per cent $\pm$ 6.9 per cent 986 times out of 1,000. The actual amount (nearly 17 per cent) by which Value Line outperformed the average of the contestants' stocks is clearly too great to explain by happenstance. Furthermore, it is certainly worth noting that the average performance during that six-month period for each of Value Line's categories was in the proper relationship according to the company's predictions. This information is found in Table 3. Even when the appropriate variances are considered, the performance of Value Line in the contest or in its general selectivity becomes significant by standard statistical tests. This conclusion, however, must be qualified by factors that are beyond the scope of this paper to evaluate. For one thing, there is the question of the extent to which Value Line's good results may have arisen from the phenomena of self-fulfilling predictions. There is no way of knowing how much influence Value Line has on the stock market through its subscribers, library readers, or others who may be affected by obtaining its recommendations secondhand from brokers or friends. Furthermore, Value Line manages three mutual funds and quite properly buys stocks for these funds that are given high ranking by its advisory service. It may be that Value Line in actuality has so little impact on the market that the performance of its recommendations can be tested against subsequent market performance without any allowance for the self-fulfilling aspect of its advice; on the other hand, it may be that a market where supply and demand are in close balance can be tilted by a significant amount when a well-regarded, widely distributed advisory service makes recommendations. This might be particularly

the case whne Value Line announced the 25 stocks it had selected for the contest, since this contest was unprecedented in the investment world and the significance of the contest to Value Line's reputation was so obvious that most people would believe the company had considerable confidence in the 25 stocks it had selected.[13]

TABLE 3

Performance of Value Line's portfolio and stock groupings during the contest period December 3, 1965–June 3, 1966

	Average of percentage changes in prices	S.D. of the price changes (per cent)	Percentage of stocks that rose in price	Percentage of stocks that went up more than the median of all 1, 072 stocks
Value Line defending list of 25 stocks	+10.984	25.25	48.0	68.0
All 100 stocks ranked in Class I	+5.105	19.40	53.0	70.0
All 259 stocks ranked in Class II	+3.101	19.00	45.6	62.5
All 363 stocks ranked in Class III	−0.774	17.48	40.5	52.3
All 250 stocks ranked in Class IV	−5.228	15.99	23.2	36.0
All 100 stocks ranked in Class V..........	−7.779	15.57	14.0	25.0
Average percentage changes of all stocks ranked I, II, III, IV, and V	−0.982			
Median change of all stocks	− 5.00			
Change in Dow-Jones Industrial Average	− 6.16			

A second qualification arises from the consideration, once again, of the representatives of the contest period. It is possible that Value Line's performance, even though it was apparently statistically superior, was unique to that contest period. But it is impressive that Value Line was willing to state and publicize so widely its expectations and their outcomes. Also, Value Line's willingness to conduct a second contest will provide another opportunity to evaluate its performance.

[13] Regarding the question of self-fulfilment, Arnold Bernhard made the following comment in a letter to the author: "I can understand how in a market where trading is evenly balanced, the recommendation of an influential service or the purchase by mutual funds might tilt the price upward for a brief time. But have you considered that the stocks Value Line selected for its list were selected from those ranked I before the contest list was published? If there had been self-fulfillment, it would have worked against us, it would seem. True, the thrust of a I rank on 100 stocks is not quite so vigorous as a I rank on 25. But still, insofar as our service has influence, you might want to take into consideration that we did recommend these stocks as I's before selecting them for our contest; and these ranks, in practically every case, were in being for weeks prior to the contest. Conversely, the stocks Value Line ranked IV and V were so ranked before the contest started. According to the self-fulfillment theory, that should have worked against us, too, because it should have artificially depressed stocks that contestants were eligible to choose. Much as I should like to believe it, I doubt that any service can influence the market over a period of six months."

IV. CONCLUSION

The evidence from this study indicates that the stock market, during at least the six months of the contest, had enough elements of predictability that it is difficult to believe the price changes were generated randomly. Since this conclusion differs from most of the prior, carefully conducted, statistical studies, it is worth asking why. Two answers suggest themselves. Most of the prior research was attempting to see if the market changes demonstrated predictable patterns conditional on fairly limited amounts of information, such as the most recent price change and the current volume. The contestants, however, used their full range of information in making selections. Second, prior studies, because of the data they used, were not able to demonstrate in a conclusive fashion that a moderate amount of predictability was statistically significant. If the price changes are close to random, but not quite, the results would normally fall in the range where the evidence of predictability would not be statistically significant. In contrast, because of the large number of stocks in the contest universe, the requirement for twenty-five stocks in each portfolio, and the large number of contestants, it was possible in this study to apply extremely precise standards for comparing observed versus expected performance.

The results of the contest still leave two questions unanswered: Was the predictability peculiar to this segment of time? Would the margin of predictability have been even greater if the contestants were somehow limited to investors with above-average qualifications of some sort, or ones who were motivated to spend more time and thought on their choices?

On the first of these questions, at least, we can hope that more information will become available from the second contest, now in process. The second question poses so many problems regarding the determination and measurement of qualifications that it is unlikely that empirical evidence will ever become available; nonetheless, it is hard to believe that the margin of predictive ability would not be greater for well-informed investors.

part two

PORTFOLIO ANALYSIS

A. Portfolio Theory

Markowitz, in this pioneering article, presents the foundation of modern portfolio analysis. He starts by examining and rejecting maximization of expected returns as a decision rule for portfolio analysis. After establishing the need to consider risk as well as expected return in portfolio construction, Markowitz turns to a detailed discussion of diversification. He demonstrates exactly how the risk of a portfolio of securities is different from the sum of the risks of the individual securities of which it is composed. Although risk can be reduced through the judicious choice of securities, risk reduction usually implies some reduction in expected return. The identification of those portfolios which represent the most efficient trade-off of risk and return (called the efficient frontier) is a key concept in this article. Markowitz presents both an algebraic and geometric interpretation of the portfolio problem and its solution.

20

Portfolio Selection

Harry Markowitz[*]

This article is reprinted with permission from the Journal of Finance
Vol. VII, No. 1 (March, 1952), pp. 77–91.

The process of selecting a portfolio may be divided into two stages. The first stage starts with observation and experience and ends with beliefs about the future performances of available securities. The second stage starts with the relevant beliefs about future performances and ends with the choice of portfolio. This paper is concerned with the second stage. We first consider the rule that the investor does (or should) maximize discounted expected, or anticipated, returns. This rule is rejected both as a hypothesis to explain, and as a maximum to guide investment behavior. We next consider the rule that the investor does (or should) consider expected return a desirable thing *and* variance of return an undesirable thing. This rule has many sound points, both as a maxim for, and hypothesis about, investment behavior. We illustrate geometrically relations between beliefs and choice of portfolio according to the "expected returns–variance of returns" rule.

One type of rule concerning choice of portfolio is that the investor does (or should) maximize the discounted (or capitalized) value of future returns.[1]

[*] This paper is based on work done by the author while at the Cowles Commission for Research in Economics and with the financial assistance of the Social Science Research Council. It will be reprinted as Cowles Commission Paper, New Series, No. 60.

Since the future is not known with certainty, it must be "expected" or "anticipated" returns which we discount. Variations of this type of rule can be suggested. Following Hicks, we could let "anticipated" returns include an allowance for risk.[2] Or, we could let the rate at which we capitalize the returns from particular securities vary with risk.

The hypothesis (or maxim) that the investor does (or should) maximize discounted return must be rejected. If we ignore market imperfections the foregoing rule never implies that there is a diversified portfolio which is preferable to all non-diversified portfolios. Diversification is both observed and sensible; a rule of behavior which does not imply the superiority of diversification must be rejected both as a hypothesis and as a maxim.

The foregoing rule fails to imply diversification no matter how the anticipated returns are formed; whether the same or different discount rates are used for different securities; no matter how these discount rates are decided upon or how they vary over time.[3] The hypothesis implies that the investor places all his funds in the security with the greatest discounted value. If two or more securities have the same value, then any of these or any combination of these is as good as any other.

We can see this analytically: suppose there are N securities; let r_{it} be the anticipated return (however decided upon) at time t per dollar invested in security i; let d_{it} be the rate at which the return on the ith security at time t is discounted back to the present; let X_i be the relative amount invested in security i. We exclude short sales, thus $X_i \geq 0$ for all i. Then the discounted anticipated return of the portfolio is

$$R = \sum_{t=1}^{\infty} \sum_{i=1}^{N} d_{it} r_{it} X$$

$$= \sum_{i=1}^{N} X_i \left(\sum_{t=1}^{\infty} d_{it} r_{it} \right)$$

$R_i = \sum_{t=1}^{\infty} d_{it} r_{it}$ is the discounted return of the ith security, therefore

$R = \sum X_i R_i$, where R_i is independent of X_i. Since $X_i \geq 0$ for all i and $\sum X_i = 1$, R is a weighted average of R_i with the X_i as non-negative weights. To maximize R, we let $X_i = 1$ for i with maximum R_i. If several $Ra_a, a = 1, \ldots, K$ are maximum then any allocation with

$$\sum_{a=1}^{K} Xa_a = 1$$

[1] See, for example, J. B. Williams, *The Theory of Investment Value* (Cambridge, Mass.: Harvard University Press, 1938), pp. 55–75.

[2] J. R. Hicks, *Value and Capital* (New York: Oxford University Press, 1939), p. 126. Hicks applies the rule to a firm rather than a portfolio.

[3] The results depend on the assumption that the anticipated returns and discount rates are independent of the particular investor's portfolio.

maximizes R. In no case is a diversified portfolio preferred to all non-diversified portfolios.[4]

It will be convenient at this point to consider a static model. Instead of speaking of the time series of returns from the ith security $(r_{i1}, r_{i2}, \ldots, r_{it}, \ldots)$ we will speak of "the flow of returns" (r_i) from the ith security. The flow of returns from the portfolio as a whole is $R = \sum X_i r_i$. As in the dynamic case if the investor wished to maximize "anticipated" return from the portfolio he would place all his funds in that security with maximum anticipated returns.

There is a rule which implies both that the investor should diversify and that he should maximize expected return. The rule states that the investor does (or should) diversify his funds among all those securities which give maximum expected return. The law of large numbers will insure that the actual yield of the portfolio will be almost the same as the expected yield.[5] This rule is a special case of the expected returns–variance of returns rule (to be presented below). It assumes that there is a portfolio which gives both maximum expected return and minimum variance, and it commends this portfolio to the investor.

This p esumption, that the law of large numbers applies to a portfolio of securities, cannot be accepted. The returns from securities are too intercorrelated. Diversification cannot eliminate all variance.

The portfolio with maximum expected return is not necessarily the one with minimum variance. There is a rate at which the investor can gain expected return by taking on variance, or reduce variance by giving up expected return.

We saw that the expected returns or anticipated returns rule is inadequate. Let us now consider the expected returns–variance of returns $(E-V)$ rule. It will be necessary to first present a few elementary concepts and results of mathematical statistics. We will then show some implications of the $E-V$ rule. After this we will discuss its plausibility.

In our presentation we try to avoid complicated mathematical statements and proofs. As a consequence a price is paid in terms of rigor and generality. The chief limitations from this source are (1) we do not derive our results analytically for the n security case; instead, we present them geometrically for the 3 and 4 security cases; (2) we assume static probability beliefs. In a general presentation we must recognize that the probability distribution of yields of the various securities is a function of time. The writer intends to present, in the future, the general, mathematical treatment which removes these limitations.

We will need the following elementary concepts and results of mathematical statistics:

Let Y be a random variable, i.e., a variable whose value is decided by chance. Suppose, for simplicity of exposition, that Y can take on a finite number of values $y_1, y_2, \ldots, y_n$. Let the probability that $Y = y_1$ be p_1, that $Y = y_2$ be p_2, etc. The expected value (or mean) of Y is defined to be

$$E = p_1 y_1 + p_2 y_2 + \ldots + p_N y_N$$

The variance of Y is defined to be

---

[4] If short sales were allowed, an infinite amount of money would be placed in the security with highest r.

[5] Williams, *op. cit.*, pp. 68, 69.

$$V = p_1(y_1 - E)^2 + p_2(y_2 - E)^2 + \ldots + p_N(y_N - E)^2$$

V is the average squared deviation of Y from its expected value. V is a commonly used measure of dispersion. Other measures of dispersion closely related to V are the standard deviation, $\sigma = \sqrt{V}$, and the coefficient of variation, σ/E.

Suppose we have a number of random variables: $R_1, \ldots, R_n$. If R is a weighted sum (linear combination) of the R_i

$$R = a_1 R_1 + a_2 R_2 + \ldots + a_n R_n$$

then R is also a random variable. (For example, R_1 may be the number which turns up on one die; R_2 that of another die, and R the sum of these numbers. In this case $n = 2$, $a_1 = a_2 = 1$).

It will be important for us to know how the expected value and variance of the weighted sum (R) are related to the probability distribution of the R_1, $\ldots$, R_n. We state these relations below; we refer the reader to any standard text for proof.[6]

The expected value of a weighted sum is the weighted sum of the expected values, i. e., $E(R) = a_1 E(R_1) + a_2 E(R_2) + \ldots + a_n E(R_n)$. The variance of a weighted sum is not as simple. To express it we must define "covariance." The covariance of R_1 and R_2 is

$$\sigma_{12} = \{E[R_1 - E(R_1)][R_2 - E(R_2)]\}$$

i.e., the expected value of [(the deviation of R_1 from its mean) times (the deviation of R_2 from its mean).] In general we define the covariance between R_i and R_j as

$$\sigma_{ij} = \{E[R_i - E(R_i)][R_j - E(R_j)]\}$$

σ_{ij} may be expressed in terms of the familiar correlation coefficient (ρ_{ij}). The covariance between R_i and R_j is equal to [(their correlation) times (the standard deviation of R_i) times (the standard deviation of R_j)]

$$\sigma_{ij} = \rho_{ij}\sigma_i\sigma_j$$

The variance of a weighted sum is

$$V(R) = \sum_{i=1}^{N} a_i^2 V(R_i) + 2 \sum_{i=1}^{N-1} \sum_{j=i+1}^{N} a_i a_j \sigma_{ij}$$

If we use the fact that the variance of R_i is σ_{ii} then

$$V(R) = \sum_{i=1}^{N} \sum_{j=1}^{N} a_i a_j \sigma_{ij}$$

Let R_i be the return on the ith security. Let μ_i be the expected value of R_i and

[6] E. g., J. V. Uspensky, *Introduction to Mathematical Probability* (New York: McGraw-Hill, 1937), Chapter 9, pp. 161–81.

σ_{ij}, be the covariance between R_i and R_j (thus σ_{ii} is the variance of R_i). Let X_i be the percentage of the investor's assets which are alocated to the ith security. The yield (R) on the portfolio as a whole is

$$R = \sum R_i X_i$$

The R_i (and consquently R) are considered to be random variables.[7] The X_i are not random variables, but are fixed by the investor. Since the X_i are percentages we have $\sum X_i = 1$. In our analysis we will exclude negative values of the X_i (i.e., short sales); therefore $X_i \geq 0$ for all i.

The return (R) on the portfolio as a whole is a weighted sum of random variables (where the investor can choose the weights). From our discussion of such weighted sums we see that the expected return E from the portfolio as a whole is

$$E = \sum_{i=1}^{N} X_i \mu_i$$

and the variance is

$$V = \sum_{i=1}^{N} \sum_{j=1}^{N} \sigma_{ij} X_i X_j$$

For fixed probability beliefs (μ_i, σ_{ij}) the investor has a choice of various combinations of E and V depending on his choice of portfolio $X_1, \ldots, X_N$. Suppose that the set of all obtainable (E, V) combinations were as in Figure 1. The E–V rule states that investor would (or should) want to select one of those portfolios which give rise to the (E, V) combinations indicated as efficient in the figure; i.e., those with minimum V for given E or more and maximum E for given V or less.

There are techniques by which we can compute the set of efficient portfolios and efficient (E, V) combinations associated with given μ_i and σ_{ij}. We will not present these techniques here. We will, however, illustrate geometrically the nature of the efficient surfaces for cases in which N (the number of available securities) is small.

The calculation of efficient surfaces might possibly be of practical use. Perhaps there are ways, by combining statistical techniques and the judgement of experts, to form reasonable probability beliefs (μ_i, σ_{ij}). We could use these beliefs to compute the attainable efficient combinations of (E, V). The investor,

---

[7] I.e., we assume that the investor does (and should) act as if he had probability beliefs concerning these variables. In general we would expect that the investor could tell us, for any two events (A and B), whether he personally considered A more likely than B, B more likely than A, or both equally likely. If the investor were consistent in his opinions on such matters, he would possess a system of probability beliefs. We cannot expect the investor to be consistent in every detail. We can, however, expect his probability beliefs to be roughly consistent on important matters that have been carefully considered. We should also expect that he will base his actions upon these probability beliefs—even though they be in part subjective.

This paper does not consider the difficult question of how investors do (or should) form their probability beliefs.

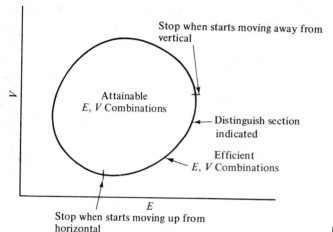

Stop when starts moving away from vertical

Attainable
E, V Combinations

Distinguish section indicated

Efficient
E, V Combinations

E

Stop when starts moving up from horizontal

FIGURE 1

being informed of what (E, V) combinations were attainable, could state which he desired. We could then find the portfolio which gave this desired combination.

Two conditions—at least—must be satisfied before it would be practical to use efficient surfaces in the manner described above. First, the investor must desire to act according to the E–V maxim. Second, we must be able to arrive at reasonable μ_i and σ_{ij}. We will return to these matters later.

Let us consider the case of three securities. In the three security case our model reduces to

$$1) \qquad E = \sum_{i=1}^{3} X_i \mu_i$$

$$2) \qquad V = \sum_{i=1}^{3} \sum_{j=1}^{3} X_i X_j \sigma_{ij}$$

$$3) \qquad \sum_{i=1}^{3} X_i = 1$$

$$4) \qquad X_i \geq 0 \qquad \text{for} \qquad i = 1, 2, 3 .$$

From (3) we get

$$3') \qquad X_3 = 1 - X_1 - X_2$$

If we substitute (3′) in equations (1) and (2) we get E and V as functions of X_1 and X_2. For example we find

$$1') \qquad E = \mu_3 + X_1(\mu_1 - \mu_3) + X_2(\mu_2 - \mu_3)$$

The exact formulas are not too important here (that of V is given below).[8] We can simply write

[8] $V = X_1^2(\sigma_{11} - 2\sigma_{13} + \sigma_{33}) + X_2^2(\sigma_{22} - 2\sigma_{23} + \sigma_{33}) + 2X_1 X_2 (\sigma_{12} - \sigma_{13} - \sigma_{23} + \sigma_{33}) + 2X_1(\sigma_{13} - \sigma_{33}) + 2X_2(\sigma_{23} - \sigma_{33}) + \sigma_{33}$

a) $E = E(X_1, X_2)$

b) $V = V(X_1, X_2)$

c) $X_1 \geq 0, X_2 \geq 0, 1 - X_1 - X_2 \geq 0$

By using relations (a), (b), (c), we can work with two dimensional geometry.

The attainable set of portfolios consists of all portfolios which satisfy constraints (c) and (3') [or equivalently (3) and (4)]. The attainable combinations of X_1, X_2 are represented by the triangle abc in Figure 2. Any point to the left of the X_2 axis is not attainable because it violates the condition that $X_1 \geq 0$. Any point below the X_1 axis is not attainable because it violates the condition that $X_2 \geq 0$. Any point above the line $(1 - X_1 - X_2 = 0)$ is not attainable because it violates the condition that $X_3 = 1 - X_1 - X_2 \geq 0$.

We define an *isomean* curve to be the set of all points (portfolios) with a given expected return. Similarly an *isovariance* line is defined to be the set of all points (portfolios) with a given variance of return.

An examination of the formulae for E and V tells us the shapes of the isomean and isovariance curves. Specifically they tell us that typically[9] the isomean curves are a system of parallel straight lines; the isovariance curves are a system of concentric ellipses (see Fig. 2). For example, if $\mu_2 \neq \mu_3$ equation (1') can be written in the familiar form $X_2 = a + bX_1$; specifically (1)

$$X_2 = \frac{E - \mu_3}{\mu_2 - \mu_3} - \frac{\mu_1 - \mu_3}{\mu_2 - \mu_3} X_1$$

Thus the slope of the isomean line associated with $E = E_o$ is $-(\mu_1 - \mu_3)/(\mu_2 - \mu_3)$ its intercept $(E_o - \mu_3)/(\mu_2 - \mu_3)$. If we change E we change the intercept but not the slope of the isomean line. This confirms the contention that the isomean lines from a system of parallel lines.

Similarly, by a somewhat less simple application of analytic geometry, we can confirm the contention that the isovariance lines form a family of concentric ellipses. The "center" of the system is the point which minimizes V. We will label this point X. Its expected return and variance we will label E and V. Variance increases as you move away from X. More precisely, if one isovariance curve, C_1, lies closer to X than another, C_2, then C_1 is associated with a smaller variance than C_2.

With the aid of the foregoing geometric apparatus let us seek the efficient sets.

X, the center of the system of isovariance ellipses, may fall either inside or outside the attainable set. Figure 4 illustrates a case in which X falls inside the attainable set. In this case, X is efficient, for no other portfolio has a V as low as X; therefore no portfolio can have either smaller V (with the same or greater E) or greater E with the same or smaller V. No point (portfolio) with expected return E less than E is efficient. For we have $E > E$ and $V < V$.

Consider all points with a given expected return E; i.e., all points on

---

[9] The isomean "curves" are as described above except when $\mu_1 = \mu_2 = \mu_3$. In the latter case all portfolios have the same expected return and the investor chooses the one with minimum variance.

As to the assumptions implicit in our description of the isovariance curves see footnote 12.

the isomean line associated with E. The point of the isomean line at which V takes on its least value is the point at which the isomean line is tangent to an isovariance curve. We call this point $\hat{X}(E)$. If we let E vary, $\hat{X}(E)$ traces out a curve.

Algebraic considerations (which we omit here) show us that this curve is a straight line. We will call it the critical line l. The critical line passes through X for this point minimizes V for all points with $E(X_1, X_2) = E$. As we go along l in either direction from X, V increases. The segment of the critical line from X

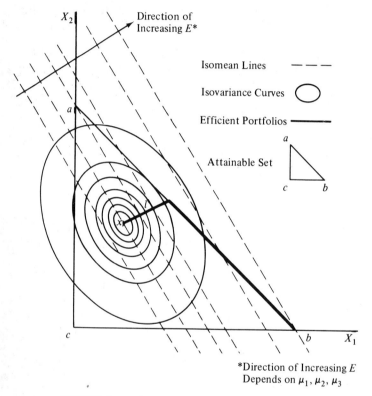

Direction of Increasing E^*

Isomean Lines

Isovariance Curves

Efficient Portfolios

Attainable Set

*Direction of Increasing E
Depends on μ_1, μ_2, μ_3

FIGURE 2

to the point where the critical line crosses the boundary of the attainable set is part of the efficient set. The rest of the efficient set is (in the case illustrated) the segment of the $\overline{ab}$ line from d to b. b is the point of maximum attainable E. In Figure 3, X lies outside the admissible area but the critical line cuts the admissible area. The efficient line begins at the attainable point with minimum variance (in this case on the $\overline{ab}$ line). It moves toward b until it intersects the critical line, moves along the critical line until it intersects a boundary and finally moves along the boundary to b. The reader may wish to construct and examine the following other cases: (1) X lies outside the attainable set and the critical line does not cut the attainable set. In this case there is a security which does not enter into any efficient portfolio. (2) Two securities have the same μ_i.

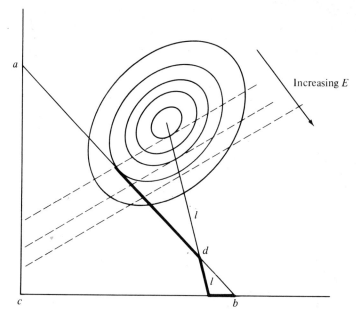

Increasing E

FIGURE 3

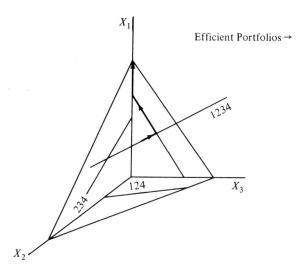

X_1

Efficient Portfolios →

1234

124

234

X_3

X_2

FIGURE 4

In this case the isomean lines are parallel to a boundary line. It may happen that the efficient portfolio with maximum E is a diversified portfolio. (3) A case wherein only one portfolio is efficient.

The efficient set in the 4 security case is, as in the 3 security and also the N security case, a series of connected line segments. At one end of the efficient set is the point of minimum variance; at the other end is a point of maximum expected return[10] (see Fig. 4).

[10] Just as we used the equation $\sum_{i=1}^{4} X_i = 1$ to reduce the dimensionality in the three

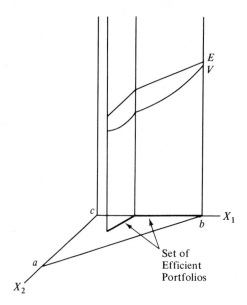

Set of
Efficient
Portfolios

FIGURE 5

Now that we have seen the nature of the set of efficient portfolios, it is not difficult to see the nature of the set of efficient (E, V) combinations. In the three security case $E = a_0 + a_1 X_1 + a_2 X_2$ is a plane; $V = b_0 + b_1 X_1 + b_2 X_2 + b_{12} X_1 X_2 + b_{11} X_1^2 + b_{22} X_2^2$ is a paraboloid.[11] As shown in Figure 5, the section of the E-plane over the efficient portfolio set is a series of connected line segments. The section of the V-paraboloid over the efficient portfolio set is a series of connected parabola segments. If we plotted V against E for efficient portfolios we would again get a series of connected parabola segments (see Fig. 6). This result obtains for any number of securities.

Various reasons recommend the use of the expected return–variance of return rule, both as a hypothesis to explain well-established investment behavior and as a maxim to guide one's own action. The rule serves better, we will see,

---

security case, we can use it to represent the four security case in 3 dimensional space. Eliminating X_i we get $E = E(X_1, X_2, X_3)$, $V = V(X_1, X_2, X_3,)$. The attainable set is represented, in three-space, by the tetrahedron with vertices $(0, 0, 0,), (0, 0, 1), (0, 1, 0),$ $(1, 0, 0)$, representing portfolios with, respectively, $X_4 = 1, X_3 = 1, X_2 = 1, X_1 = 1$. Let s_{123} be the subspace consisting of all points with $X_4 = 0$. Similarly we can define $s_{a1}, \ldots, a_a$ to be the subspace consisting of all points with $X_i = 0, t \neq a_1, \ldots, a.$ For each subspace $s_{a1}, \ldots, a_a$ we can define a *critical line* $la_1 \ldots .a_a$. This line is the locus of points P where P minimizes V for all points in $s_{a1} \ldots a_a$ with the same E as P. If a point is in $s_{a1}, \ldots, a_a$ and is efficient it must be on $a_1, \ldots, a_a$. The efficient set may be traced out by starting at the point of minimum available variance, moving continuously along various $la_1, \ldots, a_a$ according to definite rules, ending in a point which gives maximum E. As in the two dimensional case the point with minimum available variance may be in the interior of the available set or on one of its boundaries. Typically we proceed along a given critical line until either this line intersects one of a larger subspace or meets a boundary (and simultaneously the critical line of a lower dimensional subspace). In either of these cases the efficient line turns and continues along the new line. The efficient line terminates when a point with maximum E is reached.

[11] See footnote 8.

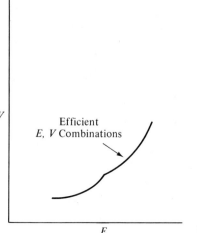

V

Efficient
E, V Combinations

E

FIGURE 6

as an explanation of, and guide to "investment" as distinguished from "spec-culative" behavior.

Earlier we rejected the expected returns rule on the grounds that it never implied the superiority of diversification. The expected return-variance of return rule, on the other hand, implies diversification for a wide range of μ_i, σ_{ij}. This does not mean that the $E\text{-}V$ rule never implies the superiority of an undiversified portfolio. It is conceivable that one security might have an extremely higher yield and lower variance than all other securities; so much so that one particular undiversified portfolio would give maximum E and minimum V. But of a large, presumably representative range of μ_i, σ_{ij} the $E\text{-}V$ rule leads to efficient port-folios almost all of which are diversified.

Not only does the $E\text{-}V$ hypothesis imply diversification, it implies the "right kind" of diversification for the "right reason." The adequacy of di-versification is not thought by investors to depend solely on the number of different securities held. A portfolio with sixty different railway securities, for example, would not be as well diversified as the same size portfolio with some railroad, some public utility, mining, various sort of manufacturing, etc. The reason is that it is generally more likely for firms within the same industry to do poorly at the same time than for firms in dissimilar industries.

Similarly in trying to make variance small it is not enough to invest in many securities. It is necessary to avoid investing in securities with high covari-ances among themselves. We should diversify across industries because firms in different industries, especially industries with different economic characteristics. have lower covariances than firms within an industry.

The concepts "yield" and "risk" appear frequently in financial writings. Usually if the term "yield" were replaced by "expected yield" or "expected return," and "risk" by "variance of return," little change of apparent mea-ning would result.

Variance is a well-known measure of dispersion about the expected. If instead of variance the investor were concerned with standard error, $\sigma = \sqrt{V}$, or with the coefficient of dispersion, σ/E, his choice would still lie in the set of efficient portfolios.

Suppose an investor diversifies between two portfolios (i.e., if he puts some of his money in one portfolio, the rest of his money in the other. An example of diversifying among portfolios is the buying of the shares of two different investment companies). If the two original portfolios have *equal* variance then typically[12] the variance of the resulting (compound) portfolio will be less than the variance of either original portfolio. This is illustrated by Figure 7. To interpret Figure 7 we note that a portfolio (P) which is built out of two portfolios $P' = (X_1', X_2')$ and $P'' = (X_1'', X_2'')$ is of the form $P = \lambda P' + (1-\lambda)P'' = (\lambda X_1' + (1-\lambda)X_1'', \lambda X_2' + (1-\lambda)X_2'')$ P is on the straight line connecting P' and P''.

The E-V principle is more plausible as a rule for investment behavior as distinguished from speculative behavior. The third moment[13] M_3 of the probability distribution of returns from the portfolio may be connected with a propensity to gamble. For example if the investor maximizes utility (U) which depends on E and V $[U=U(E, V), \partial U/\partial E > 0, \partial U/\partial E < 0]$ he will never accept an actuarially

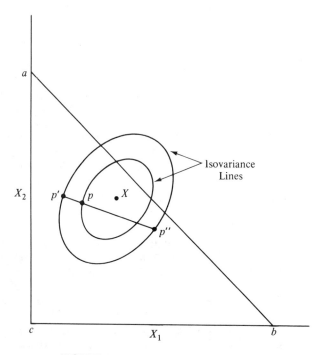

FIGURE 7

[12] In no case will variance be increased. The only case in which variance will not be decreased is if the return from both portfolios are perfectly correlated. To draw the isovariance curves as ellipses it is both necessary and sufficient to assume that no two distinct portfolios have perfectly correlated returns.

[13] If R is a random variable that takes on a finite number of values $r_1, \ldots, r_n$ with probabilities $p_1 \ldots, p_2$ respectively, and expected value E, then $M_3 = \sum_{i=1}^{n} P_i (r_i - E)^3$

fair [14] bet. But if $U = U(E, V, M_3)$ and if $\partial U/\partial M_3 \neq 0$ then there are some fair bets which would be accepted.

Perhaps—for a great variety of investing institutions which consider yield to be a good thing; risk, a bad thing; gambling, to be avoided—E, V efficiency is reasonable as a working hypothesis and a working maxim.

Two uses of the E–V principle suggest themselves. We might use it in theoretical analyses or we might use it in the actual selection of portfolios.

In theoretical analyses we might inquire, for example, about the various effects of a change in the beliefs generally held about a firm, or a general change in preference as to expected return versus variance of return, or a change in the supply of a security. In our analyses the X_i might represent individual securities or they might represent aggregates such as, say, bonds, stocks and real estate.[15]

To use the E–V rule in the selection of securities we must have procedures for finding reasonable μ_i and σ_{ij}. These procedures, I believe, should combine statistical techniques and the judgement of practical men. My feeling is that the statistical computations should be used to arrive at a tentative set of μ_i and σ_{ij}. Judgment should then be used in increasing or decreasing some of these μ_i and σ_{ij} on the basis of factors or nuances not taken into account by the formal computations. Using this revised set of μ_1 and σ_{ij}, the set of efficient E, V combinations could be computed, the investor could select the combination he preferred, and the portfolio which gave rise to this E, V combination could be found.

One suggestion as to tentative μ_i, σ_{ij} is to use the observed μ_i, σ_{ij} for some period of the past. I believe that better methods, which take into account more information, can be found. I believe that what is needed is essentially a "probabilistic" reformulation of security analysis. I will not pursue this subject here, for this is "another story." It is a story of which I have read only the first page of the first chapter.

In this paper we have considered the second stage in the process of selecting a portfolio. This stage starts with the relevant beliefs about the securities involved and ends with the selection of a portfolio. We have not considered the first stage: the formation of the relevant beliefs on the basis of observation.

---

[14] One in which the amount gained by winning the bet times the probability of winning is equal to the amount lost by losing the bet, times the probability of losing.

[15] Care must be used in using and interpreting relations among aggregates. We cannot deal here with the problems and pitfalls of aggregation.

Samuelson's article deals with the portfolio selection problem in a dynamic framework. Samuelson reexamines and expands the theory of portfolio selection when the elasticity of marginal utility is invariant with changes in wealth. He concludes that, under this class of utility functions and assuming frictionless markets, investment behavior should not be a function of age.

21

Lifetime Portfolio Selection by Dynamic Stochastic Programming

*Paul A. Samuelson**

This article is reprinted with permission from the Review of Economic and Statistics, *Vol. LI, No. 3 (August, 1969), pp. 139–246.*

INTRODUCTION

Most analyses of portfolio selection, whether they are of the Markowitz–Tobin mean-variance or of more general type, maximize over one period.[1] I shall here formulate and solve a many-period generalization, corresponding to lifetime planning of consumption and investment decisions. For simplicity of exposition I shall confine my explicit discussion to special and easy cases that suffice to illustrate the general principles involved.

* Aid from the National Science Foundation is gratefully acknowledged. Robert C. Merton has provided me with much stimulus. I owe thanks also to Stanley Fischer.

[1] See for example Harry Markowitz [5]; James Tobin [14]; Paul A. Samuelson [10]; Paul A. Samuelson and Robert C. Merton [13]. See, however, James Tobin [15], for a pioneering treatment of the multi-period portfolio problem; and Jan Mossin [7] which overlaps with the present analysis in showing how to solve the basic dynamic stochastic program recursively by working backward from the end in the Bellman fashion, and which proves the theorem that protfolio proportions will be invariant only if the marginal utility function is isoelastic.

As an example of topics that can be investigated within the framework of the present model, consider the question of a "businessman risk" kind of investment. In the literature of finance, one often reads: "Security A should be avoided by widows as too risky, but is highly suitable as a businessman's risk." What is involved in this distinction? Many things.

First, the "businessman" is more affluent than the widow; and being further removed from the threat of falling below some subsistence level, he has a high propensity to embrace variance for the sake of better yield.

Second, he can look forward to a high salary in the future; and with so high a present discounted value of wealth, it is only prudent for him to put more into common stocks compared to his present tangible wealth, borrowing if necessary for the purpose, or accomplishing the same thing by selecting volatile stocks that widows shun.

Third, being still in the prime of life, the businessman can "recoup" any present losses in the future. The widow or retired man nearing life's end has no such "second or n^{th} chance."

Fourth (and apparently related to the last point), since the businessman will be investing for so many periods, "the law of averages will even out for him," and he can afford to act almost as if he were not subject to diminishing marginal utility.

What are we to make of these arguments? It will be realized that the first could be purely a one-period argument. Arrow, Pratt, and others[2] have shown that any investor who faces a range of wealth in which the elasticity of his marginal utility schedule is great will have high risk tolerance; and most writers seem to believe that the elasticity is at its highest for rich—but not ultra-rich!—people. Since the present model has no new insight to offer in connection with statical risk tolerance, I shall ignore the first point here and confine almost all my attention to utility functions with the same relative risk aversion at all levels of wealth. Is it then still true that lifetime considerations justify the concept of a businessman's risk in his prime of life?

Point two above does justify leveraged investment financed by borrowing against future earnings. But it does not really involve any increase in relative risk-taking once we have related what is at risk to the proper larger base. (Admittedly, if market imperfections make loans difficult or costly, recourse to volatile, "leveraged" securities may be a rational procedure.)

The fourth point can easily involve the innumerable fallacies connected with the "law of large numbers." I have commented elsewhere[3] on the mistaken notion that multiplying the same kind of risk leads to cancellation rather than augmentation of risk. I.e., insuring many ships adds to risk (but only as $\sqrt{n}$); hence, only by insuring more ships and by *also* subdividing those risks among more people is risk on each brought down (in ratio $1/\sqrt{n}$).

However, before writing this paper, I had thought that points three and four could be reformulated so as to give a valid demonstration of businessman's risk, my thought being that investment for each period is akin to agreeing to take a $1/n^{th}$ interest in insuring n independent ships.

The present life time model reveals that investing for many periods does not *itself* introduce extra tolerance for riskness at early, or any, stages of life.

[2]   See K. Arrow [1]; J. Pratt [9]; P. A. Samuelson and R. C Merton [13].
[3]   P. A. Samuelson [11]

BASIC ASSUMPTIONS

The familiar Ramsey model may be used as a point of departure. Let an individual maximize

$$\int_0^T \rho^{-\rho t} U[C(t)]\, dt \tag{1}$$

subject to initial wealth W_0 that can always be invested for an exogeneously given certain rate of yield r; or subject to the constraint

$$C(t) = rW(t) - \dot{W}(t) \tag{2}$$

If there is no bequest at death, terminal wealth is zero.

This leads to the standard calculus-of-variations problem

$$J = \underset{\{W(t)\}}{\text{Max}} \int_0^T \rho^{-\rho t} U[rW - \dot{W}]\, dt \tag{3}$$

This can be easily related [4] to a discrete-time formulation

$$\text{Max} \sum_{t=0}^{T} (1 + \rho)^{-t} U[C_t] \tag{4}$$

subject to

$$C_t = W_t - \frac{W_{t+1}}{1 + r} \tag{5}$$

or,

$$\underset{\{W_t\}}{\text{Max}} \sum_{t=0}^{T} (1 + \rho)^{-t} U\left[W_t - \frac{W_{t+1}}{1 + r}\right] \tag{6}$$

for prescribed (W_o, W_{T+1}). Differentiating partially with respect to each W_t in turn, we derive recursion conditions for a regular interior maximum

[4] See P. A. Samuelson [12], p. 273 for an exposition of discrete-time analogues to calculus-of-variations models. Note: here I assume that consumption, C_t, takes place at the beginning rather than at the end of the period. This change alters slightly the appearance of the equilibrium conditions, but not their substance.

$$\frac{(1 + \rho)}{1 + r} U' \left[W_{t-1} - \frac{W_t}{1 + r} \right] = U' \left[W_t - \frac{W_{t+1}}{1 + r} \right] \qquad (7)$$

If U is concave, solving these second-order difference equations with boundary conditions (W_0, W_{T+1}) will suffice to give us an optimal lifetime consumption-investment program.

Since there has thus far been one asset, and that a safe one, the time has come to introduce a stochastically-risky alternative asset and to face up to a portfolio problem. Let us postulate the existence, alongside of the safe asset that makes \$1 invested in it at time t return to you at the end of the period \$1 $(1 + r)$, a risk asset that makes \$1 invested in, at time t, return to you after one period \$1Z_t, where Z_t is a random variable subject to the probability distribution

$$\text{Prob } \{Z_t \leq z\} = P(z), \qquad z \geq 0 \qquad (8)$$

Hence, $Z_{t+1} - 1$ is the percentage "yield" of each outcome. The most general probability distribution is admissible: i.e., a probability density over continuous z's, or finite positive probabilities at discrete values of z. Also I shall usually assume independence between yields at different times so that $P(z_0, z_1, \ldots, z_t, \ldots, z_T) = P(z_t) P(z_1) \ldots P(z_T)$

For simplicity, the reader might care to deal with the easy case

$$\text{Prob } \{Z = \lambda\} = 1/2 = \text{Prob } \{Z = \lambda^{-1}\}, \qquad \lambda > 1 \qquad (9)$$

In order that risk averters with concave utility should not shun this risk asset when maximizing the expected value of their portfolio, λ must be large enough so that the expected value of the risk asset exceeds that of the safe asset, i.e.,

$$\frac{1}{2} \lambda + \frac{1}{2} \lambda^{-1} > 1 + r, \quad \text{or}$$

$$\lambda > 1 + r + \sqrt{2r + r^2}.$$

Thus, for $\lambda = 1.4$, the risk asset has a mean yield of 0.057, which is greater than a safe asset's certain yield of $r = .04$.

At each instant of time, what will be the optimal fraction, w_t, that you should put in the risky asset, with $1 - w_t$ going into the safe asset? Once these optimal portfolio fractions are known, the constraint of (5) must be written

$$C_t = \left[W_t - \frac{W_{t+1}}{[(1 - w_t)(1 + r) + w_t Z_t]} \right] \qquad (10)$$

Now we use (10) instead of (4), and recognizing the stochastic nature of our problem, specify that we maximize the expected value of total utility over time. This gives us the stochastic generalizations of (4) and (5) or (6)

$$\underset{\{C_t, w_t\}}{\text{Max}} \ E \sum_{t=0}^{T} (1 + \rho)^{-t} U[C_t] \qquad (11)$$

subject to

$$C_t = \left[W_t - \frac{W_{t+1}}{(1+r)(1-w_t) + w_t Z_t} \right]$$

W_0 given, W_{T+1} prescribed.

If there is no bequeathing of wealth at death, presumably $W_{T+1} = 0$. Alternatively, we could replace a prescribed W_{T+1} by a final bequest function added to (11), of the form $B(W_{T+1})$, and with W_{T+1} a free decision variable to be chosen so as to maximize (11) + $B(W_{T+1})$. For the most part, I shall consider $C_T = W_T$ and $W_{T+1} = 0$.

In (11), E stands for the "expected value of," so that, for example,

$$EZ_t = \int_0^\infty z_t \, dP(z_t).$$

In our simple case of (9),

$$EZ_t = \frac{1}{2}\lambda + \frac{1}{2}\lambda^{-1}.$$

Equation (11) is our basic stochastic programming problem that needs to be solved simultaneously for optimal saving-consumption and portfolio-selection decisions over time.

Before proceeding to solve this problem, reference may be made to similar problems that seem to have been dealt with explicitly in the economics literature. First, there is the valuable paper by Phelps on the Ramsey problem in which capital's yield is a prescribed random variable. This corresponds, in my notation, to the $\{w_t\}$ strategy being frozen at some fractional level, there being no portfolio selection problem. (My analysis could be amplified to consider Phelps'[5] wage income, and even in the stochastic form that he cites Martin Beckmann as having analyzed.) More recently, Levhari and Srinivasan [4] have also treated the Phelps problem for $T = \infty$ by means of the Bellman functional equations of dynamic programming, and have indicated a proof that concavity of U is sufficient for a maximum. Then, there is Professor Mirrlees' important work on the Ramsey problem with Harrod-neutral technological change as a random variable.[6] Our problems become equivalent if I replace $W_t - W_{t+1}[(1+r)(1-w_t) + w_t Z_t]^{-1}$ in (10) by $A_t f(W_t/A_t) - nW_t - (W_{t+1} - W_t)$ let technical change be governed by the probability distribution

$$\text{Prob } \{A_t \le A_{t-1}Z\} = P(Z);$$

reinterpret my W_t to be Mirrlees' per capita capital, K_t/L_t, where L_t is growing at the natural rate of growth n; and posit that $A_t f(W_t/A_t)$ is a homogeneous

[5] E. S. Phelps [8].

[6] J. A. Mirrless [6]. I have converted his treatment into a discrete-time version. Robert Mertons's companion paper throws light on Mirrlees' Brownian-motion model for A_t.

first degree, concave, neoclassical production function in terms of capital and efficiency-units of labor.

It should be remarked that I am confirming myself here to regular interior maxima, and not going into the Kuhn–Tucker inequalities that easily handle boundary maxima.

SOLUTION OF THE PROBLEM

The meaning of our basic problem

$$J_T(Wo) = \underset{\{C_t, w_t\}}{\text{Max}} \ E \sum_{t=0}^{T} (1 + \rho)^{-t} U[C_t] \tag{11}$$

subject to $C_t = W_t - W_{t+1}[(1 - w_t)(1 + r) + w_t Z_t]^{-1}$ is not easy to grasp. I act now at $t = 0$ to select C_0 and w_0, knowing W_0 but not yet knowing how Z_0 will turn out. I must act now, knowing that one period later, knowledge of Z_0's outcome will be known and that W_1 will then be known. Depending upon knowledge of W_1, a new decision will be made for C_1 and w_1. Now I can only guess what this decision will be.

As so often is the case in dynamic programming, it helps to begin at the end of the planning period. This brings us to the well-known one-period portfolio problem. In our terms, this becomes

$$J_1(W_{T-1}) = \underset{\{C_{T-1}, w_{T-1}\}}{\text{Max}} \ U[C_{T-1}] + E(1 + \rho)^{-1} U[(W_{T-1} - C_{T-1}) \cdot$$

$$\{(1 - w_{T-1})(1 + r) + w_{T-1} Z_{T-1}\}^{-1}] \tag{12}$$

Here the expected value operator E operates only on the random variable of the next period since current consumption C_{T-1} is known once we have made our decision. Writing the second term as $EF(Z_T)$ this becomes

$$EF(Z_T) = \int_0^\infty F(Z_T) \, dP(Z_T | Z_{T-1}, Z_{T-2}, \ldots, Z_0)$$

$$= \int_0^\infty F(Z_T) \, dP(Z_T), \text{ by our independence postulate.}$$

In the general case, at a later stage of decision making, say $t = T - 1$, knowledge will be available of the outcomes of earlier random variables, $Z_{t-2}, \ldots$; since these might be relevant to the distribution of subsequent random variables, conditional probabilities of the form $P(Z_{T-1} | Z_{T-2}, \ldots)$ are thus involved. However, in cases like the present one, where independence of distributions is posited, conditional probabilities can be dispensed within favor of simple distributions.

Note that in (12) we have substituted for C_T its value as given by the constraint in (11) or (10).

To determine this optimum (C_{T-1}, w_{T-1}), we differentiate with respect to each separately, to get

$$0 = U'[C_{T-1}] - (1 + \rho)^{-1}EU'[C_T]\{(1 - w_{T-1})(1 + r) + w_{T-1}Z_{T-1}\} \quad \text{(12')}$$

$$0 = EU'[C_T](W_{T-1} - C_{T-1})(Z_{T-1} - 1 - r)$$

$$= \int_0^\infty U'[W_{T-1} - C_{T-1}]\{(1 - w_{T-1}(1 + r) - w_{T-1}Z_{T-1}\}]$$

$$\cdot (W_{T-1} - C_{T-1})(Z_{T-1} - 1 - r)\, dP\,(Z_{T-1}) \quad \text{(12'')}$$

Solving these simultaneously, we get our optimal decisions (C^*_{T-1}, w^*_{T-1}) as functions of initial wealth W_{T-1} were known, (12'') would by itself be the familiar one-period portfolio optimality condition, and could trivially be rewritten to handle any number of alternative assets.

Substituting (C^*_{T-1}, w^*_{T-1}) into the expression to be maximized gives us $J_1(W_{T-1})$ explicitly. From the equations in (12), we can, by standard calculus methods, relate the derivatives of U to those of J, namely, by the envelope relation

$$J_1'(W_{T-1}) = U'[C_{T-1}]. \quad \text{(13)}$$

Now that we know $J_1[W_{T-1}]$, it is easy to determine optimal behavior one period earlier, namely by

$$J_2(W_{T-2}) = \underset{\{C_{T-2}, w_{T-2}\}}{\text{Max}} \quad U[C_{T-2}] + E(1 + \rho)^{-1}J_1[(W_{T-2} - C_{T-2}) \cdot$$

$$\{(1 - w_{T-2})(1 + r) + w_{T-2}Z_{T-2}\}] \quad \text{(14)}$$

Differentiating (14) just as we did (11) gives the following equations like those of (12)

$$0 = U'[C_{T-2}] - (1 + \rho)^{-1}EJ_1'[W_{T-2}]\{(1 - w_{T-2})(1 + r) + w_{T-2}Z_{T-2}\}$$

$$\text{(15')}$$

$$0 = EJ_1'[W_{T-1}](W_{T-2} - C_{T-2})(Z_{T-2} - 1 - r)$$

$$= \int_0^\infty J_1'[(W_{T-2} - C_{T-2})\{(1 - w_{T-2})(1 + r) + w_{T-2}Z_{T-2}\}] \cdot$$

$$(W_{T-2} - C_{T-2})(Z_{T-2} - 1 - r)\, dP\,(Z_{T-2}). \quad \text{(15'')}$$

These equations, which could by (13) be related to $U'[C_{T-1}]$, can be solved simultaneously to determine optimal (C^*_{T-2}, w^*_{T-2}) and $J_2(W_{T-2})$.

Continuing recursively in this way for $T - 3$, $T - 4$, . . ., 2, 1, 0, we finally have our problem solved. The general recursive optimality equations can be written as

$$\begin{cases} 0 = U'[C_0] - (1 + \rho)^{-1}EJ'_{T-1}[W_0]\{(1 - w_0)(1 + r) + w_0 Z_0\} \\ 0 = EJ'_{T-1}[W_1](W_0 - C_0)(Z_0 - 1 - r) \end{cases}$$

$$\cdot \quad \cdot \quad \cdot \quad \cdot \quad \cdot \quad \cdot$$

$$0 = U'[C_{T-1}] - (1 + \rho)^{-1}EJ'_{T-t}[W_t]\{(1 - w_{t-1})(1 + r) + w_{t-1}Z_{t-1}\} \quad \text{(16')}$$

$$0 = EJ'_{T-t}[W_{t-1} - C_{t-1})(Z_{t-1} - 1 - r), \qquad (t = 1, \ldots, T - 1) \quad \text{(16'')}$$

In (16'), of course, the proper substitutions must be made and the E operators must be over the proper probability distributions. Solving (16'') at any stage will give the optimal decision rules for consumption-saving and for portfolio selection, in the form

$$C^*_t = f[W_t; Z_{t-1}, \ldots, Z_0]$$
$$= f_{T-t}[W_t] \text{ if the } Z\text{'s are independently distributed}$$
$$w^*_t = g[W_t; Z_{t-1}, \ldots, Z_0]$$
$$= g_{T-t}[W_t] \text{ if the } Z\text{'s are independently distributed}$$

Our problem is now solved for every case but the important case of infinite-time horizon. For well-behaved cases, one can simply let $T \to \infty$ in the above formulas. Or, as often happens, the infinite case may be the easiest of all to solve, since for it $C^*_t = f(W_t)$, $w^*_t = g(W_t)$, independently of time and both these unknown functions can be deduced as solutions to the following functional equations:

$$0 = U'[f(W)] - (1 + \rho)^{-1} \int_0^\infty J'[W - f(W))\{(1 + r)$$

$$- g(W)(Z - 1 - r)\}][(1 + r) - g(W)(Z - 1 - r)] \, dP(Z) \quad \text{(17')}$$

$$0 = \int_0^\infty U'[\{W - f(W)\} \{1 + r - g(W)(Z - 1 - r)\}][Z - 1 - r] \text{(17'')}$$

Equation (17'), by itself with $g(W)$ pretended to be known, would be equivalent, to equation (13) of Levhari and Srinivasan [4, p. f]. In deriving (17')–(17'') I have utilized the envelope relation of my (13), which is equivalent to Levarhi and Srinivasan's equation (12) [4, p. 5].

BERNOULLI AND ISOELASTIC CASES

To apply our results, let us consider the interesting Bernoulli case where $U = \log C$. This does not have the bounded utility that Arrow [1] and many writers have convinced themselves is desirable for an axiom system. Since I do not believe that Karl Menger paradoxes of the generalized St. Petersburg type hold any terrors for the economist, I have no particular interest in boundedness of utility and consider $\log C$ to be interesting and admissible. For this case, we have, from (12),

$$J_1(W) = \underset{\{C, w\}}{\text{Max}} \log C + E(1 + \rho)^{-1}\log[(W - C)\{(1 - w)(1 + r) + wZ\}]$$

$$= \underset{\{C\}}{\text{Max}} \log C + (1 + \rho)^{-1}\log[W - C]$$

$$+ \underset{\{w\}}{\text{Max}} \int_0^\infty \log[(1 - w)(1 + r) + wZ]\, d\,P\,(Z). \tag{18}$$

Hence, equations (12) and (16')–(16'') split into two independent parts and the Ramsey–Phelps saving problem becomes quite independent of the lifetime portfolio selection problem. Now we have

$$0 = (1/C) - (1 + \rho)^{-1}(W - C)^{-1} \text{ or}$$
$$C_{T-1} = (1 + \rho)(2 + \rho)^{-1}W_{T-1} \tag{19'}$$

$$0 = \int_0^\infty (Z - 1 - r)[(1 - w)(1 + r)$$

$$+ wZ]^{-1}\, dP\,(Z) \text{ or } w_{T-1} = w^* \text{ independently of } W_{T-1} \tag{19''}$$

These independence results, of the C_{T-1} and w_{T-1} decisions and of the dependence of w_{T-1} on W_{T-1}, hold for all U functions with isoelastic marginal utility. I.e., (16') and (16'') become decomposable conditions for all

$$U(C) = 1/\gamma C^\gamma, \qquad \gamma < 1 \tag{20}$$

as well as for $U(C) = \log C$, corresponding by L'Hôpital's rule to $\gamma = 0$.
To see this, write (12) or (18) as

$$J_1(W) = \underset{\{C, w\}}{\text{Max}} \frac{C^\gamma}{\gamma} + (1 + \rho)^{-1}\frac{(W - C)^\gamma}{\gamma}$$

$$\times \int_0^\infty [(1 - w)(1 + r) + wZ]^\gamma dP(Z) = \underset{\{C\}}{\text{Max}} \frac{C^\gamma}{\gamma} + (1 + \rho)^{-1}\frac{(W - C)^\gamma}{\gamma}$$

$$\times \underset{\{w\}}{\text{Max}} \int_0^\infty [(1 - w)(1 + r) + wZ]^\gamma\, dp\,(Z) \tag{21}$$

Hence, (12'') or (15'') or (16'') becomes

$$\int_0^\infty [(1 - w)(1 + r) + wZ]^{\gamma-1}(Z - r - 1)dP(Z) = 0, \tag{22''}$$

which defines optimal w^* and gives

$$\underset{\{w\}}{\text{Max}} \int_0^\infty [(1 - w)(1 + r) + wZ]^\gamma\, dP(Z)$$

$$= \int_0^\infty [(1 - w^*)(1 + r) + w^*Z]^\gamma\, dP\,(Z) = [1 + r^*]^\gamma, \text{ for short}$$

Here, r^* is the subjective or util-prob mean return of the portfolio, where diminishing marginal utility has been taken into account.[7] To get optimal consumption-saving, differentiate (21) to get the new form of (12'), (15'), or (16')

$$0 = C^{\gamma-1} - (1 + \rho)^{-1}(1 + r^*)^{\gamma}(W - C)^{\gamma-1} \tag{22'}$$

Solving, we have the consumption decision rule

$$C^*_{T-1} = \frac{a_1}{1 + a_1} W_{T-1} \tag{23}$$

where

$$a_1 = [(1 + r^*)^{\gamma} / (1 + \rho)]^{1/\gamma-1} \tag{24}$$

Hence, by substitution, we find

$$J_1(W_{T-1}) = b_1 W^{\gamma}_{T-1} / \gamma \tag{25}$$

where

$$b_1 = a_1^{\gamma}(1 + a_1)^{-\gamma} + (1 + \rho)^{-1}(1 + r^*)^{\gamma}(1 + a_1)^{-\gamma}. \tag{26}$$

Thus, $J_1(\cdot)$ is of the same elasticity form as $U(\cdot)$ was. Evaluating indeterminate forms for $\gamma = 0$, we find J_1 to be of log form if U was.

Now, by mathematical induction, it is easy to show that this isoelastic property must also hold for $J_2(W_{T-2})$, $J_3(W_{T-3})$, . . ., since, whenever it holds for $J_n(W_{T-n})$, it is deducible that it holds for $J_{n+1}(W_{T-n-1})$. Hence, at every stage, solving the general equations (16') and (16''), they decompose into two parts in the case of isoelastic utility. Hence,

Theorem:
For isoelastic marginal utility functions, $U'(C) = C^{\gamma-1}$, $\gamma < 1$, the optimal portfolio decision is independent of wealth at each stage and independent of all consumption-saving decisions, leading to a constant w^*, the solution to

$$0 = \int_0^{\infty} [(1 - w)(1 + r) + wZ]^{\gamma-1}(Z - 1 - r) \, dP(Z)$$

Then optimal consumption decisions at each stage are, for a no-bequest model, of the form

$$C^*_{T-i} = c_i W_{T-i}$$

where one can deduce the recursion relations

$$c_1 = \frac{a_2}{1 + w_1}$$

[7] See Samuelson and Merton for the util-prob concept [13].

$$a_1 = [(1 + \rho) / (1 + r^*)^\gamma]^{1/1-\gamma}$$

$$(1 + r^*)^\gamma = \int_0^\infty [(1 - w^*)(1 + r) + w^*Z]^\gamma dP(Z)$$

$$c_i = \frac{a_1 c_{i-1}}{1 + a_1 c_{i-1}}$$

$$= \frac{a_1^i}{1 + a_1 + a^2_1 + \ldots + a^i_1} < c_{i-1}$$

$$= \frac{a^i_1(a_1 - 1)}{a_1^{i+1} - 1}, \qquad a_1 \neq 1$$

$$= \frac{1}{1 + i}, \qquad a_1 = 1$$

In the limiting case, as $\gamma \to 0$ and we have Bernoulli's logarithmic function, $a_1 = (1 + \rho)$, independent of r^*, and all saving propensities depend on subjective time preference ρ only, being independent of technological investment opportunities (except to the degree that W_t will itself definitely depend on those opportunities).

We can interpret $1 + r^*$ as kind of a "risk-corrected" mean yield; and behavior of a long-lived man depends critically on whether

$$(1 + r^*)^\gamma \gtreqless (1 + \rho), \text{ corresponding to } a_1 \lesseqgtr 1$$

(i) For $(1 + r^*)^\gamma = (1+\rho)$, one plans always to consume at a uniform rate, dividing current W_{T-i} evenly by remaining life, $1/(1 + i)$. If young enough, one saves on the average; in the familiar "hump saving" fashion, one dissaves later as the end comes sufficiently close into sight.

(ii) For $(1 + r^*)^\gamma > (1 + \rho)$, $a_1 < 1$, and investment opportunities are, so to speak, so tempting compared to psychological time preference that one consumes nothing at the beginning of a long-long life, i.e., rigorously

$$\operatorname*{Lim}_{i \to \infty} c_i = 0, \quad a_1 < 1$$

and again hump saving must take place. For $(1 + r^*)^\gamma > (1 + \rho)$, the *perpetual* lifetime problem, with $T = \infty$, is divergent and ill-defined, i.e., $J_i(W) \to \infty$ as $i \to \infty$. For $\gamma \leq 0$ and $\rho > 0$, this case cannot arise.

(iii) For $(1 + r^*)^\gamma < (1 + \rho)$, $a_1 > 1$, consumption at very early ages drops only to a limiting positive fraction (rather than zero), namely

$$\operatorname*{Lim}_{i \to \infty} c_i = 1 - 1/a_1 < 1, \, a_1 > 1$$

Now whether there will be, on the average, initial hump saving depends upon the size of $r^* - c_\infty$, or whether

$$r^* - 1 - \frac{(1 + r^*)^{\gamma/1-\gamma}}{(1 + \rho)^{1/1-\gamma}} > 0$$

This ends the *Theorem*. Although many of the results depend upon the no-bequest assumption, $W_{T+1} = 0$, as Merton's companion paper shows (p. 247, this *Review*) we can easily generalize to the cases where a bequest function $B_T (W_{T+1})$ is added to $\sum_0^T (1 + \rho)^{-t}U(C_t)$. If B_T is itself of isoelastic form,

$$B_T \equiv b_T(W_{T+1})^\gamma / \gamma,$$

the algebra is little changed. Also, the same comparative statics put forward in Merton's continuous-time case will be applicable here, e.g., the Bernoulli $\gamma = 0$ case is a watershed between cases where thrift is enhanced by riskiness rather than reduced, etc.

Since proof of the theorem is straightforward, I skip all details except to indicate how the recursion relations for c_i and b_i are derived, namely from the identities

$$b_{i+1} W^\gamma / \gamma = J_{i+1}(W) = \underset{C}{\text{Max}} \{ C^\gamma / \gamma + b_i(1 + r^*)^\gamma (1 + \rho)^{-1}(W - C)^\gamma / \gamma \}$$

$$= \{ c^\gamma_{i+1} + b_i(1 + r^*)^\gamma(1 + \rho)^{-1}(1 - c_{i+1})^\gamma \} W^\gamma / \gamma$$

and the optimality condition

$$0 = C^{\gamma-1} - b_i(1 + r^*)^\gamma(1 + \rho)^{-1}(W - C)^{\gamma-1}$$

$$= (c_{i+1} W)^{\gamma-1} - b_i(1 + r^*)^\gamma(1 + \rho)^{-1}(1 - c_{i+1})^{\gamma-1} W^{\gamma-1}$$

which defines c_{i+1} in terms of b_i.

What if we relax the assumption of isoelastic marginal utility functions? Then w_{T-j} becomes a function of W_{T-j-1} (and, of course, of r, ρ, and a functional of the probability distribution P). Now the Phelps–Ramsey optimal stochastic saving decisions do interact with the optimal portfolio decisions, and these have to be arrived at by simultaneous solution of the nondecomposable e-quations (16') and (16'').

What if we have more than one alternative asset to safe cash? Then merely interpret Z_t as a (column) vector of returns $(Z_t^2, Z_t^3, \cdots)$ on the respective risky assets; also interpret w_t as a (row) vector $(w_t^2, w_t^3, \ldots)$, inter-pret $P(Z)$ as vector notation for

$$\text{Prob} \{ Z^2_t \leq Z^2, Z^3_t \leq Z^3, \ldots \} = P(Z^2, Z^3, \ldots) = P(Z),$$

interpret all integrals of the form $\int G(Z) \, dP(Z)$ as multiple integrals $\int G(Z^2, Z^3, \ldots) \, dP(Z^2, Z^3, \ldots)$. Then (16'') becomes a vector-set of equations, one for each component of the vector Z_t, and these can be solved simultaneously for the unknown w_t vector.

If there are many consumption items, we can handle the general problem by giving a similar vector interpretation to C_t.

Thus, the most general portfolio lifetime problem is handled by our equations or obvious extensions thereof.

CONCLUSION

We have now come full circle. Our model denies the validity of the concept of businessman's risk; for isoelastic marginal utilities, in your prime of life you have the same relative risk-tolerance as toward the end of life! The "chance to recoup" and tendency for the law of large numbers to operate in the case of repeated investments is not relevant. [Note: if the elasticity of marginal utility, $- U'(W)/WU''(W)$, rises empirically with wealth, and if the capital market is imperfect as far as lending and borrowing against future earnings is concerned, then it seems to me to be likely that a doctor of age 35–50 might rationally have his highest consumption then, and certainly show greatest risk tolerance then— in other words be open to a "businessman's risk." But not in the frictionless isoelastic model!]

As usual, one expects w^* and risk tolerance to be higher with algebraically large γ. One expects C_t to be higher late in life when r and r^* is high relative to ρ. As in a one-period model, one expects any increase in "riskiness" of Z_t, for the same mean, to decrease w^*. One expects a similar increase in riskiness to lower or raise consumption depending upon whether marginal utility is greater or less than unity in its elasticity.[8]

Our analysis enables us to dispel a fallacy that has been borrowed into portfolio theory from information theory of the Shannon type. Associated with independent discoveries by J. B. Williams [16], John Kelly [2], and H. A. Latané [3] is the notion that if one is investing for many periods, the proper behavior is to maximize the *geometric* mean of return rather than the arithmetic mean. I believe this to be incorrect (except in the Bernoulli logarithmic case where it happens[9] to be correct for reasons quite distinct from the Williams–Kelly– Latané reasoning).

These writers must have in mind reasoning that goes something like the following: If one maximizes for a distant goal, investing and reinvesting (all one's proceeds) many times on the way, then the probability becomes great that with a portfolio that maximizes the geometric mean at each stage you will end up with a larger terminal wealth than with any other decision strategy.

This is indeed a valid consequence of the central limit theorem as applied to the additive logarithms of portfolio outcomes. (I.e., maximizing the geometric mean is the same thing as maximizing the arithmetic mean of the logarithm of outcome at each stage; if at each stage, we get a mean log of $m^{**} > m^*$, then after a large number of stages we will have $m^{**}T >> m^*T$, and the properly normalized probabilities will cluster around a higher value.)

There is nothing wrong with the logical deduction from premise to theorem. But the implicit premise is faulty to begin with, as I have shown else-

---

[8] See Mertion's cited companion paper in this issue, for explicit discussion of the comparative statical shifts of (16)'s C^*_t and w^*_t functions as the parameters (ρ, γ, r, r^*, and $P(Z)$ or $P(Z_1,...)$ or $B(Wt)$ functions change. The same results hold in the discrete-and-continuous-time models.

[9] See Latané [3, p... 151] for explicit recognition of this point. I find somewhat mystifying his footnote there which says, "As pointed out to me by Professor L. J. Savage (in correspondence), not only is the maximization of G]the geometric mean] the rule for maximum expected utility in connection with Bernoulli's function but (in so far as approximations are permissible) this same rule is approximately valid for all utility functions." [Latané, p. 151 n. 13.]. The geometric mean criterion is definitely too conservative to maximize an isoelastic utility function corresponding to positive γ in my equation (20), and it is definitely too daring to maximize expected utility when $\gamma < 0$. Professor Saverge has informed me recently that his 1969 position differs from the view attributed to him in 1959.

where in another connection [Samuelson, 10, p. 3]. It is a mistake to think that, just because a w^{**} decision ends up with almost-certain probability to be better than a w^* decision, this implies that w^{**} must yield a better expected value of utility. Our analysis for marginal utility with elasticity differing from that of Bernoulli provides an effective counter example, if indeed a counter example is needed to refute a gratuitous assertion. Moreover, as I showed elsewhere, the ordering principle of selecting between two actions in terms of which has the greater probability of producing a higher result does not even possess the property of being transitive.[10] By that principle, we could have w^{***} better than w^{**}, and w^{**} better than w^*, and also have w^* better than w^{***}.

REFERENCES

1. ARROW, K. J., "Aspects of the Theory of Risk-Bearing" (Helsinki, Finland: Yrjö Jahnssonin Säätiö, 1965).
2. KELLY, J., "A New Interpretation of Information Rate," *Bell System Technical Journal* (Aug. 1956), 917–926.
3. LATANÉ, H. A., "Criteria for Choice Among Risky Ventures," *Journal of Political Economy* 67 (Apr. 1959), 144–155.
4. LEVHARI, D. and T. N. SRINIVASAN, "Optimal Savings Under Uncertainty," Institute for Mathematical Studies in the Social Sciences, Technical Report No. 8, Stanford University, Dec. 1967.
5. MARKOWITZ, H., *Portfolio Selection: Efficient Diversification of Investment* (New York: John Wiley & Sons, 1959).
6. MIRRLEES, J. A., "Optimum Accumulation Under Uncertainty," Dec. 1965, unpublished.
7. MOSSIN, J., "Optimal Multiperiod Portfolio Policies," *Journal of Business,* 41, 2 (Apr. 1968), 215–229.
8. PHELPS, E. S., "The Accumulation of Risky Capital: A Sequential Utility Analysis," *Econometrica,* 30, 4 (1962), 729–743.
9. PARTT J., "Risk Aversion in the Small and in the Large," *Econometrica,* 32 (Jan. 1964).
10. SAMUELSON, P. A., "General Proof that Diversification Pays," *Journal of Financial and Quantitative Analysis,* II (Mar. 1967), 1–13.
11. ———, "Risk and Uncertainty: A Fallacy of Large Numbers," *Scientia,* 6th Series, 57th year (April–May, 1963).
12. ———, "A Turnpike Refutation of the Golden Rule in a Welfare Maximizing Many-Year Plan," Essay XIV, *Essays on the Theory of Optimal Economic Growth,* Karl Shell (ed.) (Cambridge, Mass.: MIT Press, 1967).
13. ———, and R. C. MERTON, "A Complete Model of Warrant Pricing that Maximizes Utility," *Industrial Management Review* (in press).
14. TOBIN, J., "Liquidity Preference as Behavior Towards Risk," *Review of Economic Studies,* XXV, 67, (Feb. 1958) 65–86.
15. ———, "The Theory of Portfolio Selection," *The Theory of Interest Rates,* F. H. Hahn and F. P. R. Brechling (eds.) (London: Macmillan, 1965).
16. WILLIAMS, J. B., "Speculation and the Carryover," *Quarterly Journal of Economics,* 50 (May 1936), 436–455.

---

[10] See Samuelson [11].

Chen, Jen, and Zionts deal with the problem of portfolio revision over time. First they discuss the two-period case. If transaction costs are ignored, portfolio revision (in the two-period case) is identical to the problem of single-period portfolio selection. However, the presence of transaction costs necessitates the introduction of a new set of constraints into the portfolio revision problem.

Then the authors extend their analysis to the multi-period (multi) revision case and construct a dynamic model which can be used to select an optimum series of portfolios over time.

22

The Optimal Portfolio Revision Policy

Andrew H. Y. Chen, Frank C. Jen, and Stanley Zionts*

This article is reprinted with permission from the Journal of Business, *Vol. XLIV, No. 1 (January, 1971).*

In a dynamic setting, portfolio management is a portfolio revision process through which an investor revises his portfolio periodically to adapt to changing conditions either endogenous or exogenous to the portfolio. For example, an investor accepting an intrinsic value hypothesis may find it profitable to revise his portfolio when his expectations in returns and riskiness of some earning assets deviates significantly from those of the market. Likewise, an investor accepting the random walk hypothesis may find it profitable to revise his portfolio because of an exogenously determined cash demand (either inflow or outflow) or changes in portfolio value and proportions due to change in prices of earnings assets and cash earnings received. The problem is of considerable importance because investment decisions are usually made starting with a portfolio rather than cash and consequently some assets must be liquidated to permit investment in others. Despite its importance, the problem has received only limited attention in the literature. The paper seeks to address to this problem. After briefly reviewing a single-period and a multi-period portfolio selection models, we shall examine a revision procedure proposed by Smith [6], and

* The authors are indebted to the members of the Workshop in Finance, University of New York at Buffalo, as well as the referee for their comments.

illustrate its inadequacies. In Section Two, an alternative single-period portfolio revision model is formulated and compared with Smith's model. The model takes into consideration the expected transfer costs to be incurred in the transition. In Section Three, the model is extended to the multi-period case, and compared with the Mossin's dynamic portfolio selection model. Section Four summarizes the findings and indicates areas for further research.

I. PREVIOUS RESEARCH IN PORTFOLIO SELECTION AND PORTFOLIO REVISION

In a well-known work, *Portfolio Selection* [4], Harry Markowitz formulated a single-period portfolio selection model. The problem is to allocate certain initial wealth among alternative earning assets and is formulated as a quadratic programming problem. The objective function is to maximize the expected return with the constraint that all asset holdings must be non-negative.[1] Costs associated with buying or selling an earning asset (hereafter called transfer costs) are however ignored.

Mossin extended the Markowitz model to a multi-period case using a dynamic programming approach [5, pp. 221–23]. The approach calls for applying the Markowitz model as the decision model at the beginning of each period. Using the cash value of the portfolio (assuming no transfer costs) as the state variable, a dynamic programming recursive relationship is then developed. With this recursive procedure, an investor can select the optimal portfolio in the first period for a given initial wealth.

Neither the Mossin nor the Markowitz model can be used without modification to revise a portfolio. The reason is that the investors starting with a portfolio of earning assets are "locked-in" because of the transfer costs involved in changing the composition of a portfolio. Hence the development of a portfolio revision model is needed.

Smith [6, 7], on the other hand, used the Markowitz model to attack the problem of how to revise a portfolio in order to account for the locked-in effect. He recognized that if transfer costs are ignored, the portfolio revision problem is equivalent to the portfolio selection problem. He therefore proposed the use of the Markowitz model and the market value of the old portfolio to derive a "target" protfolio. Realizing that the target portfolio is not attainable because transfer costs cannot be ignored in real life, he suggests the intuitively appealing procedure of "controlled" transition by changing earning assets one at a time to move toward the "target" portfolio.

The suggested "controlled" transition approach is inefficient because the "true" optimal portfolio can be derived exactly. Further, Smith has not con-considered the multi-period aspect of the model and thus falls into the myopia trap. A single-period portfolio revision model that can be used to derive the "true" optimal portfolio is developed in the next section. The model will then be further extended to the multi-period case.

---

[1]   Markowitz' procedure ignores the possibility of liquidating part of the portfolio to meet future cash demands exogenous to the model. Jen and Zionts [1] consider this problem in some detail.

II. A SINGLE-PERIOD PORTFOLIO REVISION MODEL

THE MODEL

We will now formulate a single-period portfolio revision model. We assume, as did Markowitz, that there is no need to liquidate a part of the portfolio to meet an exogenous cash demand. The model differs from a portfolio selection model in that it can be used to determine the composition of the new optimal portfolio given that transfer costs are incurred in changing a portfolio. The following notation will be used:

R_k, $k=0, 1,\ldots,N$—The mean return of asset k.

σ_{kl}, $k,l=0,1, \ldots,N$—The covariance of returns of assets k and l. For $k=l$, the variance of the return of asset k.

α_k, $k=0,1, N$— The amount of the fund invested in the kth asset at the beginning of the first period. Asset zero is cash and hence, α_0 is the amount of cash held in the portfolio.

β_k, $k=0,1, \ldots,N$—The amount of kth asset held in the portfolio at the end of the first period *before* portfolio revision.

Note that for the kth asset, β_k (for $k \neq 0$) differs from α_k by the amount of capital appreciation or depreciation incurred in the first period. β_0 differs from α_0 by the *cash* return received on all earning assets. Hence, $\sum_k B_k = \sum_k (1 + y_k)\alpha_k$ where y_k is the total return on the kth asset for the first period. Further assume that y_k has two components: y_k^c representing the percent of cash dividend realized and y_k^g representing the percent of price appreciation (or depreciation) recorded.[2] Therefore:

$$\beta_0 = \alpha_0 + \sum_k y_k^c \alpha_k \quad \text{for} \quad k = 1, \ldots, N$$

$$\beta_k = (1 + y_k^g)\alpha_k$$

γ_k $k =0, 1, \ldots, N$—The amount of the kth asset held in the new portfolio *after* portfolio revision at the beginning of the second period. γ is the amount of cash in the new portfolio. Note that the γ's are decision variables.

δ_k $k =0, 1,\ldots,N$—The increase in the amount of the kth asset held from the existing portfolio to the new portolio.

ω_k $k =0, 1,\ldots, N$—The decrease in the amount of the kth asset held from the existing portfolio to the new portfolio.

B_k $k =0, 1,\ldots,N$—The buying transfer cost of the k-th asset, with B (buying transfer cost of cash) equal to zero.

---

[2] In this framework, one may think that returns in the model can be easily fromulated on an after-tax basis so that the difference in tax rates on capital gains and dividends (or interest) can be taken into account. Unfortunately, many aspects of the tax regulations are difficult to include because they create discontinuities in the various functions. For example the tax rate on capital gains is not only affected by the length of holding period, but also levied only on *realized* gains, losses are deductible only up to a certain amount; dividends are subject to special treatment. Further research is therefore needed.

S_k $k = 0, 1, \ldots N$—The selling transfer cost of the kth asset, with S_0 (selling transfer cost of cash equal to zero.

Both transfer costs are assumed to be proportional to the amount transferred. The assumption is used for mathematical simplicity. Following the Markowitz portfolio selection model, we assume that all asset holdings must be non-negative, that is:

$$\alpha_k, \beta_k, \gamma_k \geq 0, \quad k = 0, 1, \ldots, N \tag{2.1}$$

By definition, a change in the holding of the kth asset (δ_k or ω_k) equals the difference between the amount held in the old portfolio (β_k) and the amount held in the new portfolio (γ_k):

$$\delta_k - \omega_k = \gamma_k - \beta_k, \quad \delta_k, \omega_k \geq 0 \tag{2.2}$$

Note that an investor can either buy or sell or not change the amount of an asset held in the portfolio. Hence, either δ_k or ω_k or both will equal zero.

In addition, the market value of the new portfolio must equal the ending value of the old portfolio less the transfer costs incurred to change the old portfolio to the new one. Hence, the following indentity must hold:

$$\sum_{k=0}^{N} \gamma_k = \sum_{k=0}^{N} \beta_k - \sum_{k=0}^{N} (\delta_k B_k + \omega_k S_k) \tag{2.3}$$

Note that by combining (2.2) and (2.3), we obtain the reasonable result that the difference between proceeds from sales of assets and the value of purchases of other assets equals the total transaction costs. Further, as indicated by (2.3), the market value of the portfolio after transition will never exceed the market value before transition.

The object of the portfolio revision model is to maximize the following objective function, subject to the constraints of (2.1) through (2.3).

$$\text{Max}_{\gamma_k} \sum_{k=0}^{N} (1 + \bar{R}_k)\gamma_k - \lambda \left[\sum_{k=1}^{N} \sum_{l=1}^{N} \gamma_k \gamma_l \sigma_{kl} \right] \tag{2.4}$$

Equation (2.4) is in the same form as in the Markowitz model except that we are maximizing expected final wealth less a multiple of the variance of final wealth. However, constraints (2.2) and (2.3) are not present in the Markowitz model. These constraints define the relationship between the market value of the assets in the old and the new portfolios and the transfer costs to be incurred in such a transition. Thus, with a predetermined λ, the model can be used to find the composition of the new optimal portfolio after taking into consideration the transfer costs expected to be incurred in the transition. It can also be used for the case where an investor starts with cash and has to incur a transfer cost to purchase a portfolio. As to a method of solution, standard computational procedures applicable to quadratic programming problems can be used.[3]

---

[3] If the transfer costs are non-convex as they would be if the transfer costs consisted of a fixed as well as a variable component, then the solution cannot be found by usual quad-

The difference between Smith's and our procedure can be better seen geometrically (Figure 1). Point *A* is the old portfolio which is now in the interior
of a new feasible region because it is no longer optimal. *II'* is Smith's efficient
frontier unattainable because of the transfer costs, but the shaded area is the area
in which the new optimal portfolio is located.[4] *JJ'* is the investor's utility function[5] with a slope of λ. Hence, the tangent point *B* represents Smith's "target"
portfolio toward which Smith suggested that an investor should move. Using our
model, however, an investor can derive the attainable new efficient frontier
represented by *GG'*. Since *HH'* is the investor's utility function, the new tangent
point *C* represents the new optimal portfolio of the investor to which he should
move *directly* and *immediately*. Under Smith's procedure a point in the heavily
shaded area which is far from optimal would be reached.

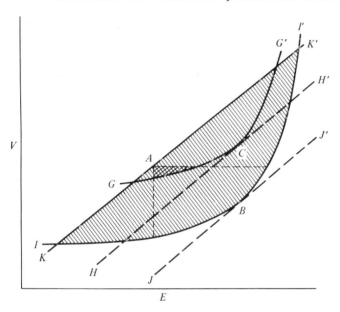

FIGURE 1

Locus of possible optimal transition
portfolios

---

ratic programming procedures. Instead, an integer–quadratic approach would have to
be used.

[4] Note that the shaded area is the locus of all possible optimal points as the transfer
costs range, asset by asset, from zero to 100%. As the transfer costs of all assets approach 100%, the initial point *A* becomes optimal.

Smith [7, p. 376] suggested that the new optimal portfolio must have either more
expected return or less variance or both. This statement is wrong since the new efficient
frontier could shift so drastically from Smith's new efficient frontier because of the
transfer costs that the new optimal portfolio may be higher or lower in either expected
return or variance or both. Hence the new optimal portfolio should be in the region
indicated in Figure 1.

[5] *JJ'* is the traditional quadratic utility function. That it appears linear on our graph is
due to the fact that the axes are labeled *E–V*, not *E–σ*.

Smith also raised the question of how often an investor should revise his portfolio. Because he proposed a heuristic procedure for moving toward an unattainable optimum, Smith had to undertake extensive empirical examinations to obtain some insights into the problem of finding how frequently investors should revise their portfolio. Our model is direct and includes the consideration of expected transfer costs. Thus, assuming that cost of reviewing the portfolio is zero and that information is free, a portfolio should be reviewed as soon as any new information becomes available. Further, an investor should revise his portfolio *as soon as* he finds his present portfolio is not the optimal one as dictated by our model. Indeed, conceptually speaking, an investor will always revise his portfolio up to the point that the marginal utility of revision equals the marginal cost of transition.

ANALYTICAL RESULTS FOR A TWO-ASSET CASE WITH SYMMETRIC TRANSFER COSTS

The difference between the composition of Smith's target portfolio and that of our optimal portfolio can be derived analytically for the case of two assets. These two assets are assumed respectively to have random returns R_1 and R_2 with means of $\bar{R}_1$ and $\bar{R}_2$ and variances of V_1 and V_2. The covariance between these two assets is assumed to be zero.

Using the framework developed earlier, the composition of Smith's target portfolio is the solution of the maximization problem:

$$\text{Max}_{r_1, r_2} U = (1 + \bar{R}_1)r_1 + (1 + \bar{R}_2)r_2 - \lambda(r_1^2 V_1 + r_2^2 V_2) \qquad \textbf{(2.5)}$$

Subject to:

$$r_1, \ r_2 \geq 0$$
$$r_1 + r_2 = W_0$$

where W_0 is the market value of the portfolio before revision. Solving via Lagrange multipliers yields the following solution:

$$r_1 = \frac{\bar{R}_1 - \bar{R}_2 + 2\lambda V_2 W_0}{2\lambda(V_1 + V_2)}$$
$$r_2 = \frac{\bar{R}_2 - \bar{R}_1 + 2\lambda V_1 W_0}{2\lambda(V_1 + V_2)} \qquad \textbf{(2.6)}$$

The composition of the optimal portfolio under our scheme is the solution of the maximization problem below, assuming a symmetric transfer cost ($B_i = S_i = C_i$) and further the optimal strategy calls for buying some asset 1 and selling some asset 2 (i.e., $\delta_1 > 0$ and $\omega_2 > 0$):

$$\text{Max}_{r_1, r_2} U = (1 + \bar{R}_1)r_1 + (1 + \bar{R}_2)r_2 - \lambda(r_1^2 V_1 + r_2^2 V_2) \qquad \textbf{(2.7)}$$

Subject to:

$$r_1, r_2, \delta_1, \omega_2 \geq 0$$

$$\delta_1 = r_1 - \beta_1$$

$$\omega_2 = \beta_2 - r_2$$

$$r_1 + r_2 = \beta_1 + \beta_2 - \delta_1 C_1 - \omega_2 C_2$$

$$= W_0 - \delta_1 C_1 - \omega_2 C_2$$

Solving via Lagrange multipliers yields the solution:

$$r_1 = \frac{(1 - C_2)[(1 + \bar{R}_1)(1 - C_2) - (1 + \bar{R}_2)(1 + C_1)]}{2\lambda[V_1(1 - C_2)^2 + V_2(1 + C_1)^2]}$$

$$+ \frac{V_2(1 + C_1)[(1 + C_1)\beta_1 + (1 - C_2)\beta_2]}{V_1(1 - C_2)^2 + V_2(1 + C_1)^2}$$

$$r_2 = \frac{(1 + C_1)[(1 + \bar{R}_2)(1 + C_1) - (1 + \bar{R}_1)(1 - C_2)]}{2\lambda[V_1(1 - C_2)^2 + V_2(1 + C_1)^2]}$$

$$+ \frac{V_1(1 - C_2)[(1 + C_1)\beta_1 + (1 - C_2)\beta_2]}{V_1(1 - C_2)^2 + V_2(1 + C_1)^2} \tag{2.8}$$

We can see that for the special case of no transfer costs (i.e., $C_1 = C_2 = 0$) the solution of our model in (2.8) becomes that of Smith's target portfolio in (2.6). For any positive C's including the case $C_1 = C_2 = C$, however, the two solutions are different.

Strictly speaking, we should also develop the reverse case, namely to sell asset 1 and buy asset 2. The solution is entirely symmetric to (2.8) and is found simply by interchanging subscripts there. In addition, there is also the case of investor not changing his portfolio at all, i.e., all δ's and ω's equal zero. An efficient quadratic programming algorithm can however be used to derive the optimum revision strategy in one step.

III. A MULTI-PERIOD PORTFOLIO REVISION MODEL

THE MODEL

The single-period portfolio revision model presented in the preceding section is now extended to a multi-period model using, like Mossin, a dynamic programming approach. The approach calls first for the determination of an optimal decision (or equivalently a decision rule) for all possible starting portfolios for the last (Tth) period of a finite planning horizon T. The result is then used to determine the optimal decision for the next to the last period and then recursively until the optimal decision for first period is derived.

At the *beginning* of the Tth period, an investor has a portfolio of assets represented by the β_{kT}'s. The problem is to change the portfolio to the optimal one having r_{kT}'s satisfying simultaneously the constraints in equations (2.1) through (2.3) and maximizing the expected utility of the market value of the portfolio at the *end* of the period.[6] Mathematically, the optimal portfolio

---

[6]   Market value is used because normally an investor will keep his portfolio far longer than its finite planning horizon. For those investors who *have* to liquidate the portfolio

revision at the beginning of the final period is to solve the foowing maximization problem (assuming, for convenience, $B_1 = S_i = C_i$).

$$\text{Max } E_T(U_T) = \sum_k (1 + \bar{R}_{kT}) \gamma_{kT} - \lambda [\sum_k \sum_l \gamma_{kT} \gamma_{lT} \sigma_{kT, lT}] \qquad \textbf{(3.1)}$$
$$\gamma_{kT}$$

Subject to constraints

$$\gamma_{kT}, \delta_{kT}, \omega_{kT} \geq 0 \qquad \textbf{(3.2)}$$

$$\delta_{kT} - \omega_{kT} = \gamma_{kT} - \beta_{kT} \qquad \textbf{(3.3)}$$

$$\sum_k \gamma_{kT} = \sum_k \beta_{kT} - \sum_k (\delta_{kT} + \omega_{kT}) C_k \qquad \textbf{(3.4)}$$

or alternatively in Mossin's simplified notation the objective is to:

$$\text{Max } E_T(U_T) = \phi_{T-1}(\beta_{0T}, \beta_{1T}, \ldots, \beta_{nT})$$
$$\gamma_{kT}$$

where ϕ_{T-1} is Mossin's derived utility function for the portfolio existing at the end of period T—1 to be determined from equations (3.1) to (3.4).

For period T–1, the objective is then to:

$$\text{Max } E_{T-1} [\phi_{T-1}(\beta_{0T}, \beta_{1T}, \ldots, \beta_{nT})]$$
$$\gamma_{kT-1}$$

$$= \text{Max } E_{T-1} \{\text{Max } E_T(U_T)$$
$$\gamma_{kT-1} \qquad \gamma_{kT}$$

subject to constraints similar to (3.2) to (3.4). The model is then recursively applied until the optimal decision is derived for the beginning of the initial period.

COMPUTATIONAL CONSIDERATIONS

The computational problem of solving our multiple-period portfolio revision problem is enormous. Each period's portfolio revision problem is a quadratic programming problem whose solution should be relatively easy to obtain given the initial portfolio. However, the initial portfolio of each period is not known *a priori* because it is only a stage in a dynamic programming framework. These portfolios can therefore only be treated as a vector with each component corresponding to the market value of the investment in the respective asset. The fact that we have to treat the state variable of a dynamic programming problem as a vector increases the computational requirements greatly (as compared to treating it as a scalar) because of the large number of optimization (quadratic programming) subproblems that must be solved.[7]

at the end of the planning horizon, the objective function can be reformulated to include expected liquidation cost. If the planning horizon is long, i.e., if T is large, both formulations will yield approximately the same initial decisions unless the transfer costs are very large.

[7]   See the subsection below for further discussion of this problem.

Certain special cases do appear to be computationally feasible, however. If it is assumed when making the first decision that the portfolio will be held for the entire planning horizon[8] the computational requirements simplify tremendously. The simplification is because no revision at the outset must be considered. But, of course, at the end of each period the portfolio is revised using the same assumption.

A second possibility that is somewhat cumbersome, but nonetheless considerably more computationally feasible than the original scheme, is to utilize the proposed portfolio revision framework for the first few periods (possibly only the first) and then assume zero transfer costs for subsequent periods. The subsequent periods would thereby use a model similar to that of Mossin [5]. The advantage of this procedure over the original one is that the state variable for the latter periods is a continuous scalar—the cash value of a portfolio. A number of quadratic programming problems would still have to be solved for each period, but by the use of parametric programming methods on the state variable,[9] all the solutions for a given stage may be found as a function of the parameter. There is no analogy to this for the originally proposed model. The recursive relations of the dynamic programming process is conceptually the same as that of Mossin and will be used to link the stages.

Each of the above alternatives has considerable merit. The choice appears to depend on the structure of the return, variance and transfer costs. Hence, this is clearly a fruitful area for future research.

COMPARISON WITH MOSSIN'S MODEL FOR A TWO-ASSET TWO-PERIOD CASE

Despite the computational difficulty, we will illustrate the difference between Mossin's model and ours by resorting to a two-asset two-period case. We will derive the solution for Mossin's model first.

The analytical result derived for Smith's two-asset single-period case is regarded as the equivalent of Mossin's single period model, except for the objective function.[10] Thus, at the beginning of the second (last) period, an investor using Mossin's model will allocate his wealth according to equation (2.6) which is:

$$\gamma_{12} = \frac{\bar{R}_{12} - \bar{R}_{22} + 2\lambda V_{22}W_1}{2\lambda(V_{12} + V_{22})}$$

$$\beta_{22} = \frac{\bar{R}_{22} - \bar{R}_{12} + 2\lambda V_{12}W_1}{2\lambda(V_{12} + V_{22})} \tag{3.5}$$

---

[8] We are suggesting this procedure only for the resulting computational simplification.

[9] See for example Hadley[1].

[10] Mossin's objective function is quadratic in wealth whereas the others are a linear function of the mean and variance of return or wealth. We continue using our objective function to be consistent with our earlier analysis which follows a utility function similar to Markowitz.

We agree with Mossin that the utility function used by us is not perfect. We note however that Mossin's $(U=W_1-\theta W_1^2)$ has flaws also because U is at its maximum when $W_1=1/2\theta$. The function is hardly meaningful in a dynamic framework unless W_1 is far from attainable. In the latter case however, utility is approximately linear in wealth over the relevant range.

where W_1 is the market value of the portfolio at the beginning of the second period and the second subscript denotes the time period. Assuming that the distributions of R's for the first and second periods are identical, the investor has this objective function at the beginning of the first period:

$$\underset{\gamma_{11},\,\gamma_{21}}{\text{Max}}\quad E_1(U_1) = E_1\,\{(1 + \bar{R}_1)\gamma_{12} + (1 + \bar{R}_2)\gamma_{22}$$

$$- \lambda\,(\gamma_{12}^2 V_1 + \gamma_{22}^2 V_2)\}\tag{3.6}$$

Subject to the constraints:

$$\gamma_{11} + \gamma_{21} = W_0 \tag{3.7}$$

$$\gamma_{11}(1 + R_1) + \gamma_{21}(1 + R_2) = W_1 \tag{3.8}$$

Note that W_1 in (3.8) is a stochastic variable because it is a linear combination of two stochastic variables R_1 and R_2. Further, this constraint represents one of the major differences between the model for the 1st period and that for the second period.[11]

Substituting into (3.6) the values of γ_{12} and γ_{22} derived in (3.5) and using Lagrange multipliers yields this analytic solution for Mossin's model:[12]

$$\gamma_{11} = \frac{(\bar{R}_1 - \bar{R}_2)[V_1(1 + \bar{R}_2) + V_2(1 + \bar{R}_1)]}{2\lambda V_1 V_2[\bar{R}_1 - \bar{R}_2)^2 + (V_1 + V_2)}$$

$$- \frac{W_0[(1 + \bar{R}_2)(\bar{R}_1 - \bar{R}_2) - V_2]}{[(\bar{R}_1 - \bar{R}_2)^2 + (V_1 + V_2)]}$$

$$\gamma_{21} = W_0 - \gamma_{11} \tag{3.9}$$

For some values of λ, it is possible that a corner solution for either $\gamma_{11} = W_0$ or $\gamma_{11} = 0$ will be reached. These values of λ can be found from (3.9) by setting $\gamma_{11} \leq 0$ and $\gamma_{11} \geq W_0$ given that $\bar{R}_2 > \bar{R}_1$:

for $\gamma_{11} \leq 0$:

$$\lambda \leq \frac{(\bar{R}_1 - \bar{R}_2)[V_1(1 + \bar{R}_2) + V_2(1 + \bar{R}_1)]}{2W_0 V_1 V_2[(1 + \bar{R}_2)(\bar{R}_1 - \bar{R}_2) - V_2)]}$$

for $\gamma_{11} \geq W_0$ (assuming that $|(1 + \bar{R}_1)(\bar{R}_1 - \bar{R}_2)| > V_1$):

$$\lambda \geq \frac{(\bar{R}_1 - \bar{R}_2)[V_1(1 + \bar{R}_2) + V_2(1 + \bar{R}_1)]}{2W_0 V_1 V_2[(1 + \bar{R}_1)(\bar{R}_1 - \bar{R}_2) + V_1]} \tag{3.10}$$

In other words, for a non-corner solution, λ has to have a value between the range specified in (3.10).

---

[11] If the assumption that distributions of R's for the first and second periods are identical does not hold, constraint (3.8) will be changed to:

$\gamma_{11}(1+R_{11})+\gamma_{21}(1+R_{21})=W_1$ (3.8). Further $\bar{R}_1, \bar{R}_2, V_1$ and V_2, in (3.6) will be changed. respectively to $\bar{R}_{12}, \bar{R}_{22}, V_{12}$, and V_{22}.

[12] In general we will be using quadratic programming methods. For this special case, however, it is useful to develop analytic results.

As to the solution for our model, *assuming* that the optimal decision for the second period calls for switching some asset 2 to asset 1, we shall have to solve a quadratic programming problem in order to obtain the solution for that case. In addition, we must also solve a second quadratic programming problem, one calling for switching some asset 1 to asset 2 at the beginning of period 2, in order to obtain a solution for that case. Thus, for a two-asset two-period model, we must solve two quadratic programming problems in order to derive a complete set of possible analytical solutions.[13] We, therefore, choose to compare the difference in structure between Mossin's and our dynamic model through two numerical problems presented in the Appendix. Both problems are two-period two-asset problems. The first problem assumes an investor starting with cash (a dynamic portfolio selection problem) whereas the second problem assumes an investor starting with a portfolio (a portfolio revision problem). In both problems, two quadratic programming problems must be solved. The results for Mossin's model are exactly the same (because of no transfer costs), but for our model, the results for the two cases are not only different from Mossin's but also different from each other.

IV. SUMMARY AND CONCLUSIONS

In this paper, we have formulated a single-period portfolio revision model by incorporating into the Markowitz model two constraints which specify the effect of transfer costs on portfolio revision. The model can be used to determine the optimal portfolio to which an investor should change his current portfolio immediately. Analytical results for our model are derived for a two-asset case and compared with Smith's target portfolio. A computationally feasible procedure is also suggested for the n-asset case.

The single-period portfolio revision model is then extended to the multi-period case using a dynamic programming framework. Although solving the general multi-period multi-asset case is computationally very difficult, we discussed ways in which the difficulties may be overcome. In the Appendix, two two-asset two-period problems are presented to illustrate the differences between the solutions of Mossin's multi-period model and our model.

In addition to the limitation that solving the general multi-period model is computationally difficult, the suggested single-period and multi-period models do not take into consideration the fact that there may be exogenous cash demands on the portfolio. In this connection, although Jen and Zionts [3] have presented elsewhere a single-period portfolio selection model that takes account of stochastic cash demands on the portfolio, further extension of that model to a multi-period portfolio revision model is necessary.

---

[13] To continue the reasoning, 2^3-2 quadratic programming problems need to be solved for a three-asset two-period case and 2^n-2 problems must be solved for an n-asset two-period case. More generally, for t periods, w have to solve $(2^n-2)^{t-1}$ quadratic programming problems for either the portfolio selection problem or the portfolio revision problem. Obviously, this is not a feasible procedure for large n and t.

APPENDIX

Two two-asset two-period portfolio problems are presented in order to facilitate comparing the solution of the portfolio selection case with that of the portfolio revision case. For both problems, the two assets are assumed to have the following characteristics:

	Asset 1	Asset 2
$\bar{R}_i$	0.1	0.5
V_i	0.1	1.0
$C_i = S_i = B_i$	0.05	0.3

Returns are assumed to be reflected in capital appreciation or depreciation and not paid in cash, and assume $\lambda = 0.008$.

Problem One: A Portfolio Selection Problem:

The investor is assumed to start with $200 cash.

Using equation (3.9) to derive the solution for Mossin's case yields $r_{11} = 5.95$ and $r_{21} = 194.05$. Further, the investor is expected to switch some asset 2 to asset 1 in the beginning of the second period.[14]

For our model, the result is the solution of the following maximization problem:

$$\text{Max}_{r_{11},\, r_{21}} \quad E\{(1 + \bar{R}_1)r_{12} + (1 + \bar{R}_2)r_{22} - \lambda[r_{12}^2 V_1 + r_{22}^2 V_2]\}$$

Subject to:

(1) $r_{11} + r_{21} = 200 - r_{11}C_1 - r_{21}C_2$

(2) $\beta_{12} = (1 + \bar{R}_1)r_{11}$

(3) $\beta_{22} = (1 + \bar{R}_2)r_{21}$

Equation (1) is a definitional equation relating portfolio values to transfer cost. Equations (2) and (3) are definitional equations relating β's to r's. The stochastic β_{12} and β_{22} are in turn related to r_{12} and r_{22} with the functional forms of the relationship determined by the direction the portfolio should be changed in the beginning of the second period. [Thus, analytical results in (2.8) will be applicable if, in the second period, investors should switch some asset 2 to asset 1.] Solving both possible combinations of the maximization problem yields this optimal solution for this portfolio selection problem: $r_{11} = 153.60$ and $r_{21} = 29.78$ where, at the beginning of the second period, we expect to switch some of asset 1 to asset 2. The expected amount of asset 1 to be switched to asset 2

---

[14] The expected value of r_{12} is $247.84 while that of r_{22} is $49.78. These values can be derived by using (3. 5) and the fact that the expected value of W_1 is $297.62.

($\bar{\omega}_{12}$ and $\bar{\delta}_{22}$) is however related to stochastic variables β_{12}, β_{22}, γ_{12} and γ_{22} according to equation (3.3). In practice, of course, the *actual* outcome of the first period and the changing expectations on returns and riskness of assets will force an investor to use the model to optimize again at the end of the first period. Thus, the action taken at that time may differ significantly from the action anticipated at the beginning of the first period even if the latter will affect the former. The reason is that both Mossin's and our models have certainty equivalents which enable us to treat certain decision variables as if they are known or certain.

Thus, applying Mossin's model directly, the optimal decision for the investor at the beginning of the first period is to allocate about 3 per cent of his cash in asset 1 and the remainder in asset 2. Applying our model with transfer costs, the optimal decision is to buy about 77 per cent asset 1, 15 per cent asset 2 and spend 8 per cent as transfer cost.[15] Hence, introducing the concept of transfer cost in a portfolio selection model can change the composition of a portfolio significantly. The significant difference can be attributed however, to the significant differences in return, risk and transfer cost in assets 1 and 2.

Problem Two: A Portfolio Revision Problem:

The investor is assumed to start with a portfolio consisting of asset 1 having a market value of $100 and asset 2 having a market value of $100.

For Mossin's model, solution to the portfolio revision problem is the same as that of the portfolio selection problem, becuase he ignores the costs to be incurred in buying and selling an earning asset. Thus, the optimal portfolio at the beginning of the first period is again $\gamma_{11} = 5.95$ and $\gamma_{21} = 194.05$.

For our model, even solving the numerical quadratic programming problems by hand is sufficiently cumbersome. Hence, we choose to illustrate the structure of the model by assuming that the investor will switch some asset 2 to asset 1 in the beginning of the first period and will not change the portfolio in the beginning of the second period. The necessary portfolio revision at the beginning of the first period is then to solve the following maximization problem.

$$\underset{\gamma_{11}, \gamma_{21}}{\text{Max}} \quad E\{(1 + \bar{R}_1)\gamma_{12} + (1 + \bar{R}_2)\gamma_{22} - \lambda[\gamma_{12}{}^2 V_1 + \gamma_{22}{}^2 V_2]\}$$

Subject to:

(1) $\delta_{11} = \gamma_{11} - 100$, $\omega_{21} = 100 - \gamma_{21}$

(2) $\gamma_{11} + \gamma_{21} = 200 - \delta_{11}C_1 - \omega_{21}C_2$

(3) $\beta_{12} = (1 + R_1)\gamma_{11} = \gamma_{12}$

(4) $\beta_{22} = (1 + R_2)\gamma_{21} = \gamma_{22}$

Note that the constraint in equation (1) is an addition to those used in the portfolio selection problem above. In addition, the form of the constraint in

---

[15] It is interesting to note that should an investor using Mossin's model start with cash in the amount of $183.38, the total market value of the portfolio in the first period for our model, he will invest all the wealth in asset 2 (i. e., $\gamma_{11} = 0$, $\gamma_{21} = 183.38$).

equation (2) is slightly different from its corresponding constraint in Problem 1, while constraints (3) and (4) specify that assets 1 and 2 are not to be changed in the beginning of the second period. This problem yields the following solution: $r_{11} = 74.82$, $r_{21} = 118.40$. That is, the investor will switch immediately 25.08 of asset 1 to 18.40 of asset 2.

Whether the solution is an optimal one is unknown to us because we have not exhausted all possible combinations of switching strategies for the first and second period. It is clear however that the composition of the new portfolio at the beginning of the first period will be different from both that using Mossin's model and that of the portfolio selection problem in our framework.

REFERENCES

1. HADLEY, G., *Non-Linear and Dynamic Programming, Readings:* Mass., Addison-Wesley, 1964.
2. HADLEY, G. and WHITIN, T.M., *Analysis of Inventory Systems,* Englewood Cliffs, N.J., Prentice-Hall, 1963.
3. JEN, FRANK C. and STANLEY ZIONTS, "Effects of Liquidity Needs on Portfolio Planning," Working Paper Series Number 8, State University of New York at Buffalo.
4. MARKOWITZ, HARRY, *Portfolio Selection: Efficient Diversification of Investments,* New York: John Wiley & Sons, Inc., 1959.
5. MOSSIN, JAN, "Optimal Multi-period Portfolio Policies," *Journal of Business,* Vol. 41, No. 2 (April 1869), pp. 215–229.
6. SMITH, KEITH V., "A Transition Model for Portfolio Revision," *Journal of Finance,* vol. 22 (September 1967), pp. 425–439.
7. SMITH, KEITH V., "Alternative Procedures for Revising Investment Portfolios," *Journal of Financial and Quantitative Analysis,* Vol. III, No. 4 (December 1968), pp. 371–403.

Sharpe presents a model that relates the return of a security to a market index. This model assumes that the comovement of securities depends solely on their response to the common market index. The model vastly reduces the data requirements of the Markowitz model. It also reduces computation time due to the simplified form of the variance–covariance matrix. As Cohen and Pogue show in the next article (24), the simplification of the covariance structure made by Sharpe is extremely sensible and leads to the selection of very desirable portfolios. When one also considers the increase in accurancy of inputs which can be achieved because of the reduced data requirements, the Sharpe model becomes very competitive indeed.

23

A Simplified Model For Portfolio Analysis

William F. Sharpe*

This article is reprinted with permission from Management Science, *Vol. 9, No. 2 (January, 1963), pp. 277–293.*

This paper describes the advantages of using a particular model of the relationships among securities for practical applications of the Markowitz portfolio analysis technique. A computer program has been developed to take full advantage of the model: 2,000 securities can be analyzed at an extremely low cost—as little as 2% of that associated with standard quadratic programming codes. Moreover, preliminary evidence suggests that the relatively few parameters used by the model can lead to very nearly the same results obtained with much larger sets of relationships among securities. The possibility of low-cost analysis, coupled with a likelihood that a relatively small amount of information need be sacrificed make the model an attractive candidate for initial practical applications of the Markowitz technique.

* The author wishes to express his appreciaion for the cooperation of the staffs of both the Western Data Processing Center at UCLA and the Pacific Northwest Research Computer Laboratory at the University of Washington where the program was tested. His greatest debt, however, is to Dr. Harry M. Markowitz of the RAND Corporation, with whom he was privileged to have a number of stimulating conversations during the past year. It is no longer possible to segregate the ideas in this paper into those which were his, those which were the author's, and those which were developed jointly. Suffice it to say that the only accomplishments which are unquestionably the property of the author are those of authorship–first of the computer program and then of this article.

1. INTRODUCTION

Markowitz has suggested that the process of portfolio selection be approached by (1) making probabilistic estimates of the future performances of securities, (2) analyzing those estimates to determine an *efficient set* of portfolios, and (3) selecting from that set the portfolios best suited to the investor's preferences [1, 2, 3]. This paper extends Markowitz' work on the second of these three stages –*portfolio analysis*. The preliminary sections state the problem in its general form and describe Markowitz' sloution technique. The remainder of the paper presents a simplified model of the relationships among securities, indicates the manner in which it allows the portfolio analysis problem to be simplified, and provides evidence on the costs as well as the desirability of using the model for practical applications of the Markowitz technique.

2. THE PORTFOLIO ANALYSIS PROBLEM

A security analyst has provided the following predictions concerning the future returns from each of N securities:

> $E_i \equiv$ the expected value of R_i (the return from security i)
> C_{i_1} through C_{in}: C_{ij} represents the covariance between R_i and R_j (as usual, when $i = j$ the figure is the variance of R_i)

The portfolio analysis problem is as follows. Given such a set of predictions, determine the set of *efficient portfolios;* a portfolio is efficient if none other gives either (a) a higher expected return and the same variance of return or (b) a lower variance of return and the same expected return.

Let X_i represent the proportion of a portfolio invested in security i. Then the expected return (E) and variance of return (V) of any portfolio can be expressed in terms of (a) the basic data (E_i-values and C_{ij}-values) and (b) the amounts invested in various securities:

$$E = \sum_i X_i E_i$$

$$V = \sum_i \sum_j X_i X_j C_{ij}.$$

Consider an objective function of the form:

$$\phi = \lambda E - V$$
$$= \lambda \sum_i X_i E_i - \sum_i \sum_j X_i X_j C_{ij}.$$

Given a set of values for the parameters (λ, E_i's and C_{ij}'s), the value of ϕ can be changed by varying the X_i values as desired, as long as two basic restrictions are observed:

> 1. The entire portfolio must be invested[1]:

---

[1] Since cash can be included as one of the securities (explicitly or implicitly) this assumption need cause no lack of realism.

$$\sum_i X_i = 1$$

and 2. no security may be held in negative quantities[2]:

$$X_i \geq 0 \text{ for all } i$$

A portfolio is described by the proportions invested in various securities –in our notation by the values of X_i. For each set of admissable values of the X_i variables there is a corresponding predicted combination of E and V and thus of ϕ. Figure 1 illustrates this relationship for a particular value of λ. The line ϕ shows the combinations of E and V which give $\phi = \phi_1$, where $\phi = \lambda_k E - V$; the other lines refer to larger values of $\phi(\phi_3 > \phi_2 > \phi_3)$. Of all possible portfolios, one will maximize the value of ϕ; in Figure 1 it is portfolio C.[3] The relationship between this solution and the portfolio analysis problem is obvious. The E, V combination obtained will be on the boundary of the set of attainable combinations; moreover, the objective function will be tangent to the set at that point. Since this function is of the form

$$\phi = \lambda E - V$$

the slope of the boundary at the point must be λ; thus, by varying λ from $+ \infty$ to 0, every solution of the portfolio analysis problem can be obtained.

For any given value of λ the problem described in this section requires the maximization of a quadratic function, ϕ (which is a function of X_i, X_i^2, and $X_i X_j$ terms) subject to a linear constraint ($\sum_i X_i = 1$), with the variables restricted to non-negative values. A number of techniques have been developed to solve such *quadratic programming problems*. The critical line method, developed by Markowitz in conjunction with his work on portfolio analysis, is particularly suited to this problem and was used in the program described in this paper.

3. THE CRITICAL LINE METHOD

Two important characteristics of the set of efficient portfolios make systematic solution of the portfolio analysis problem relatively straightforward. The first concerns the relationships among portfolios. Any set of efficient portfolios can be described in terms of a smaller set of *corner portfolios*. Any point on the E, V curve (other than the points associated with corner portfolios) can be obtained with a portfolio constructed by dividing the total investment between the two adjacent corner portfolios. For example, the portfolio which gives E, V combination C in Figure 1 might be some linear combination of the two corner portfolios with E, V combinations shown by points 2 and 3. This characteristic allows the analyst to restrict his attention to corner portfolios rather than the complete

---

[2] This is the standard formulation. Cases in which short sales are allowed require a different approach.

[3] This fact is crucial to the critical line computing procedure described in the next section.

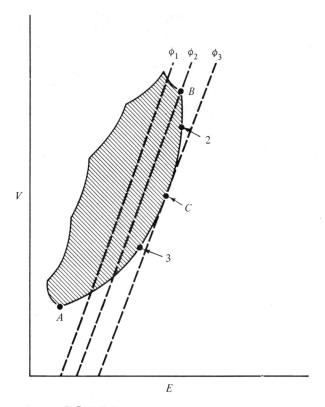

FIGURE 1

set of efficient portfolios; the latter can be readily derived from the former.

The second characteristic of the solution concerns the relationships among corner portfolios. Two corner portfolios which are adjacent on the E, V curve are related in the following manner: one portfolio will contain either (1) all the securities which appear in the other, plus one additional security, or (2) all but one of the securities which appear in the other. Thus in moving down the E, V curve from one corner portfolio to the next, the quantities of the securities in efficient portfolios will vary until either one drops out of the portfolio or another enters. The point at which a change takes place marks a new corner portfolio.

The major steps in the critical line method for solving the portfolio analysis problem are:

1. The corner portfolio with $\lambda = \infty$ is determined. It is composed entirely of the one security with the highest expected return.[4]
2. Relationships between (a) the amounts of the various securities contained in efficient portfolios and (b) the value of λ are computed. It is possible to derive such relationships for any section of the E, V curve between adjacent corner portfolios. The relationships which apply to one section of the curve

---

[4] In the event that two or more of the securities have the same (highest) expected return, the first efficient portfolios is the combination of such securities with the lowest variance.

will not, however, apply to any other section.
3. Using the relationships computed in (2), each security is examined to determine the value of λ at which a change in the securities included in the portfolio would come about:
   a. securities presently in the portfolio are examined to determine the value of λ at which they would drop out, and
   b. securities not presently in the portfolio are examined to determine the value of λ at which they would enter the protfolio.
4. The next largest value of λ at which a security either enters or drops out of the protfolio is determined. This indicates the location of the next corner portfolio.
5. The composition of the new corner portfolio is computed, using the relationships derived in (2). However, since these relationships held only for the section of the curve between this corner portfolio and the preceding one, the solution process can only continue if new relationships are derived. The method thus returns to step (2) unless $\lambda = 0$, in which case the analysis is complete.

The amount of computation required to complete a portfolio analysis using this method is related to the following factors:

1. The number of securities analyzed
   This will affect the extent of the computation in step (2) and the number of computations in step (3).
2. The number of corner portfolios
   Steps (2) through (5) must be repeated once to find each corner portfolio.
3. The complexity of the variance-covariance matrix
   Step (2) requires a matrix be inverted and must be repeated once for each corner portfolio.

The amount of computer memory space required to perform a portfolio analysis will depend primarily on the size of the variance-covariance matrix. In the standard case, if N securities are analyzed this matrix will have $\frac{1}{2}(N^2 + N)$ elements.

4. THE DIAGONAL MODEL

Portfolio analysis requires a large number of comparisons; obviously the practical application of the technique can be greatly facilitated by a set of assumptions which reduces the computational task involved in such comparisons. One such set of assumptions (to be called the diagonal model) is described in this article. This model has two virtues: it is one of the simplest which can be constructed without assuming away the existence of interrelationships among securities and there is considerable evidence that it can capture a large part of such interrelationships.

The major characteristic of the diagonal model is the assumption that the returns of various securities are related only through common relationships with some basic underlying factor. The return from any security is determined solely by random factors and this single outside element; more explicitly:

$$R_i = A_i + B_i I + C_i$$

where A_i and B_i are parameters, C_i is a random variable with an expected value of zero and variance Q_i, and I is the level of some index. The index, I, may be the level of the stock market as a whole, the Gross National Product, some price index or any other factor thought to be the most important single influence on the returns from securities. The future level of I is determined in part by random factors:

$$I = A_{n+1} + C_{n+1}$$

where A_{n+1} is a parameter and C_{n+1} is a random variable with an expected value of zero and a variance of Q_{n+1}. It is assumed that the covariance between C_i and C_j is zero for all values of i and $j(i \neq j)$.

Figure 2 provides a graphical representation of the model. A_i and B_i serve to locate the line which relates the expected value of R_i to the level of I. Q_i indicates the variance of R_i around the expected relationship (this variance is assumed to be the same at each point along the line). Finally, A_{n+1} indicates the expected value of I and Q_{n+1} the variance around that expected value.

The diagonal model requires the following predictions from a security analyst:

1) values of A_i, B_i and Q_i for each of N securities
2) values of A_{n+1} and Q_{n+1} for the index I.

The number of estimates required from the analyst is thus greatly reduced: from 5,150 to 302 for an analysis of 100 securities and from 2,003,000 to 6,002 for an analysis of 2,000 securities.

Once the parameters of the diagonal model have been specified all the inputs required for the standard portfolio analysis problem can be derived. The relationships are:

$$E_i = A_i + B_i(A_{n+1})$$
$$V_i = (B_i)^2(Q_{n+1}) + Q_i$$
$$C = (B_i)(B_j)(Q_{n+1})$$

A portfolio analysis could be performed by obtaining the values required by the diagonal model, calculating from them the full set of data required for the standard portfolio analysis problem and then performing the analysis with the derived values. However, additional advantages can be obtained if the portfolio analysis problem is restated directly in terms of the parameters of the diagonal model. The following section describes the manner in which such a restatement can be performed.

5. THE ANALOGUE

The return from a portfolio is the weighted average of the returns from its component securities:

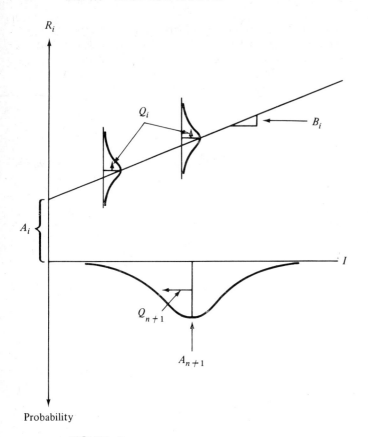

FIGURE 2

$$R_p = \sum_{i=1}^{N} X_i R_i.$$

The contribution of each security to the total return of a portfolio is simply $X_i R_i$ or, under the assumptions of the diagonal model:

$$X_i(A_i + B_i I + C_i).$$

The total contribution of a security to the return of the portfolio can be broken into two components: (1) an investment in the "basic characteristics" of the security in question and (2) an "investment" in the index:

$$X_i(A_i + B_i I + C_i) = X_i(A_i + C_i) \tag{1}$$

$$+ X_i B_i I. \tag{2}$$

The return of a portfolio can be considered to be the result of (1) a series of investments in N "basic securities" and (2) an investment in the index:

$$R_p = \sum_{i=1}^{N} X_i(A_i + C_i) + \left[\sum_{i=1}^{N} X_i B_i\right] I$$

Defining X_{n+1} as the weighted average responsiveness of R_p to the level of I:

$$X_{n+1} \equiv \sum_{i=1}^{N} X_i B_i$$

and substituting this variable and the formula for the determinants of I, we obtain:

$$R_p = \sum_{i=1}^{N} X_i(A_i + C_i) + X_{n+1}(A_{n+1} + C_{n+1})$$

$$= \sum_{i=1}^{N+1} X_i(A_i + C_i).$$

The expected return of a portfolio is thus:

$$E = \sum_{i=1}^{N+1} X_i A_i$$

while the variance is[5]:

$$V = \sum_{i=1}^{N+1} X_i^2 Q_i$$

This formulation indicates the reason for the use of the parameters A_{n+1} and Q_{n+1} to describe the expected value and variance of the future value of I. It also indicates the reason for calling this the "diagonal model." The variance-covariance matrix, which is full when N securities are considered, can be expressed as a matrix with non-zero elements only along the diagonal by including an $(n + 1)$st security defined as indicated. This vastly reduces the number of computations required to solve the portfolio analysis problem (primarily in step 2 of the critical line method, when the variance-covariance matrix must be inverted) and allows the problem to be stated directly in terms of the basic parameters of the diagonal model:

$$\text{Maximize: } \lambda E - V$$

$$\text{Where: } E = \sum_{i=1}^{N+1} X_i A_i$$

$$V = \sum_{i=1}^{N+1} X_i^2 Q_i$$

[5] Recall that the diagonal model assumes cov $(C_i, C_j) = 0$ for all i and j $(i \neq j)$

Subject to: $X_i \geq 0$ for all i from 1 to N

$$\sum_{i=1}^{N} X_i = 1$$

$$\sum_{i=1}^{N} X_i B_i = X_{n+1}.$$

6. THE DIAGONAL MODEL PORTFOLIO ANALYSIS CODE

As indicated in the previous section, if the portfolio analysis problem is expressed in terms of the basic parameters of the diagonal model, computing time and memory space required for solution can be greatly reduced. This section describes a machine code, written in the FORTRAN language, which takes full advantage of the characteristics of the diagonal model. It uses the critical line method to solve the problem stated in the previous section.

The computing time required by the diagonal code is considerably smaller than that required by standard quadratic programming codes. The RAND QP code[6] required 33 minutes to solve a 100-security example on an IBM 7090 computer; the same problem was solved in 30 seconds with the diagonal code. Moreover, the reduced storage requirements allow many more securities to be analyzed: with the IBM 709 the RAND QP code can be used for no more than 249 securities, while the diagonal code can analyze up to 2,000 securities.

Although the diagonal code allows the total computing time to be greatly reduced, the cost of a large analysis is still far from insignificant. Thus there is every incentive to limit the computations to those essential for the final selection of a portfolio. By taking into account the possibilities of borrowing and lending money, the diagonal code restricts the computations to those absolutely necessary for determination of the final set of efficient portfolios. The importance of these alternatives, their effect on the portfolio analysis problem and the manner in which they are taken into account in the diagonal code are described in the remainder of this section.

A. THE "LENDING PORTFOLIO"

There is some interest rate (r_l) at which money can be lent with virtual assurance that both principal and interest will be returned; at the least, money can be buried in the ground $(r_l = 0)$. Such an alternative could be included as one possible security $(A_i = 1 + r_l, B_i = 0, Q_i = 0)$ but this would necessitate some needless computation.[7] In order to minimize computing time, lending at

---

[6] The program is described in [4]. Several alternative quadratic programming codes are available. A recent code, developed by IBM, which uses the critical line method is likely to prove considerably more efficient for the portfolio analysis problem. The RAND code is used for comparison since it is the only standard program with which the author has had experience.

[7] Actually, the diagonal code cannot accept non-positive values of Q_i; thus if the lending alternative is to be included as simply another security, it must be assigned a very small value of Q_i. This procedure will give virtually the correct solution but is inefficient.

some pure interest rate is taken into account explicitly in the diagonal code.

The relationship between lending and efficient portfolios can best be seen in terms of an E, σ curve showing the combinations of expected return and standard deviation of return $(= \sqrt{V})$ associated with efficient portfolios. Such a curve is shown in Figure 3 (FBCG) ; point A indicates the E, σ combination attained if all funds are lent. The relationship between lending money and purchasing portfolios can be illustrated with the portfolio which has the E, σ combination shown by point Z. Consider a portfolio with X_z invested in portfolio Z and the remainder $(1 - X_z)$ lent at the rate r_l. The expected return from such a portfolio would be:

$$E = X_z E_z + (1 - X_z)(1 + r_l)$$

and the variance of return would be:

$$V = X_z^2 V_z + (1 - X_z)^2 V_l + 2X_z(1 - X_z)(\text{cov}_{zl}).$$

But, since V_l and cov_{zl} are both zero:

$$V = X_z^2 V_z$$

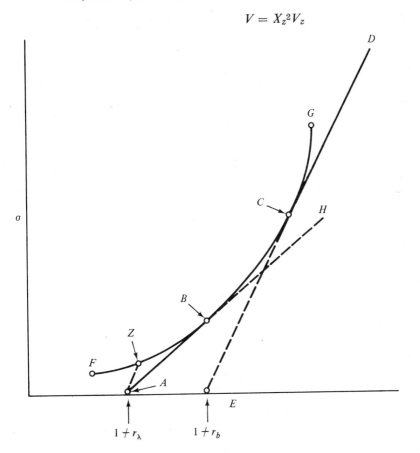

FIGURE 3

and the standard deviation of return is:

$$\sigma = X_z \sigma_z.$$

Since both E and σ are linear functions of X_z, the E, σ combinations of all portfolios made up of portfolio Z plus lending must lie on a straight line connecting points Z and A. In general, by splitting his investment between a portfolio and lending, an investor can attain any E, σ combination on the line connecting the E, σ combinations of the two components.

Many portfolios which are efficient in the absence of the lending alternative becomes inefficient when it is introduced. In Figure 3, for example, the possibility of attaining E, σ combinations along the line AB makes all portfolios along the original E, σ curve from point F to point B inefficient. For any desired level of E below that associated with portfolio B, the most efficient portfolio will be some combination of portfolio B and lending. Portfolio B can be termed the "lending portfolio" since it is the appropriate portfolio whenever some of the investor's funds are to be lent at the rate r_l. This portfolio can be found readily once the E, a curve is known. It lies at the point on the curve at which a ray from $(E = 1 + r_l, \sigma = 0)$ is tangent to the curve. If the E, σ curve is not known in its entirety it is still possible to determine whether or not a particular portfolio is the lending portfolio by computing the rate of interest which *would* make the portfolio in question the lending portfolio. For example, the rate of interest associated in this manner with portfolio C is r_b, found by extending a tangent to the curve down to the E-axis. The diagonal code computes such a rate of interest for each corner portfolio as the analysis proceeds; when it falls below the previously stated lending rate the code computes the composition of the lending portfolio and terminates the analysis.

B. THE "BORROWING PORTFOLIO"

In some cases an investor may be able to borrow funds in order to purchase even greater amounts of a portfolio than his own funds will allow. If the appropriate rate for such borrowing were r_b, illustrated in Figure 3, the E, σ combinations attainable by purchasing portfolio C with both the investor's funds and with borrowed funds would lie along the line CD, depending on the amount borrowed. Inclusion of the borrowing alternative makes certain portfolios inefficient which are efficient in the absence of the alternative; in this case the affected portfolios are those with E, σ combinations along the segment of the original E, σ curve from C to G. Just as there is a single appropriate portfolio if any lending is contemplated, there is a single appropriate portfolio if borrowing is contemplated. This "borrowing portfolio" is related to the rate of interest at which funds can be borrowed in exactly the same manner as the "lending portfolio" is related to the rate at which funds can be lent.

The diagonal code does not take account of the borrowing alternative in the manner used for the lending alternative since it is necessary to compute all previous corner portfolios in order to derive the portion of the E, σ curve below the borrowing portfolio. For this reason all computations required to derive the full E, σ curve above the lending portfolio must be made. However, the code does allow the user to specify the rate of interest at which funds can be borrowed. If this alternative is chosen, none of the corner portfolios which will be inefficient when borrowing is considered will be printed. Since as much as 65% of the total computer time can be spent recording (on tape) the results of the analysis this is not an insignificant saving.

7. THE COST OF PORTFOLIO ANALYSIS WITH THE DIAGONAL CODE

The total time (and thus cost) required to perform a portfolio analysis with the diagonal code will depend upon the number of securities analyzed, the number of corner portfolios and, to some extent, the composition of the corner portfolios. A formula which gives quite an accurate estimate of the time required to perform an analysis on an IBM 709 computer was obtained by analyzing a series of runs during which the time required to complete each major segment of the program was recorded. The approximate time required for the analysis will be[8]:

Number of seconds $= .6$

$+ .114 \times$ number of securities analyzed

$+ .54 \times$ number of corner portfolios

$+ .0024 \times$ number of securities analyzed $\times$ number of corner portfolios.

Unfortunately only the number of securities analyzed is known before the analysis is begun. In order to estimate the cost of portfolio analysis before it is performed, some relationship between the number of corner portfolios and the number of securities analyzed must be assumed. Since no theoretical relationship can be derived and since the total number of corner portfolios could be several times the number of securities analyzed, it seemed desirable to obtain some crude notion of the typical relationship when "reasonable" inputs are used. To accomplish this, a series of portfolio analyses was performed using inputs generated by a Monte Carlo model.

Data were gathered on the annual returns during the period 1940-1951 for 96 industrial common stocks chosen randomly from the New York Stock Exchange. The returns of each security were then related to the level of a stock market index and estimates of the parameters of the diagonal model obtained. These parameters were assumed to be samples from a population of A_i, B_i, and Q_i triplets related as follows:

$$A_i = \bar{A} + r_1$$
$$B_i = \bar{B} + \psi A_i + r_2$$

---

[8] The computations in this section are based on the assumption that no corner portfolios prior to the lending portfolio are printed. If the analyst chooses to print all preceding portfolios, the estimates given in this section should be multiplied by 2.9; intermediate cases can be estimated by interpolation.

$$Q_i = \bar{Q} + \theta A_i + \gamma B_i + r_3$$

where r_1, r_2 and r_3 are random variables with zero means. Estimates for the parameters of these three equations were obtained by regression analysis and estimates of the variances of the random variables determined.[9] With this information the characteristics of any desired number of securities could be generated. A random number generator was used to select a value for A_i; this value, together with an additional random number determined the value of B_i; the value of Q_i was then determined with a third random number and the previously obtained values of A_i and B_i.

Figure 4 shows the relationship between the number of securities analyzed and the number of corner portfolios with interest rates greater than 3% (an

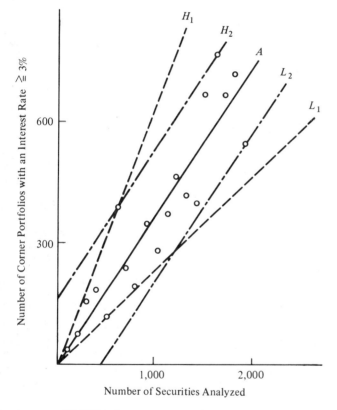

FIGURE 4

approximation to the "lending rate"). Rather than perform a sophisticated analysis of these data, several lines have been used to bracket the results in

[9] The random variables were considered normally distributed; in one case, to better approximate the data, two variances were used for the distribution—one for the portion above the mean and another for the portion below the mean.

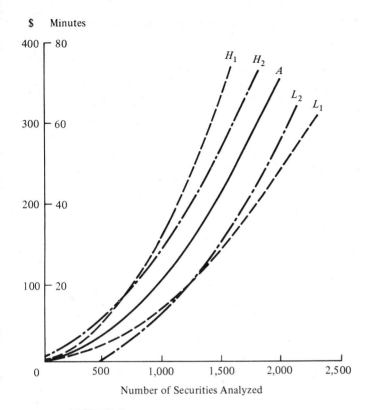

FIGURE 5

various ways. These will be used subsequently as extreme cases, on the presumption that most practical cases will lie within these extremes (but with no presumption that these limits will never be exceeded). Curve A indicates the average relationship between the number of portfolios and the number of securities: average $(N_p/N_3) = .37$. Curve H_2 indicates the highest such relationship: maximum $(N_p/N_3) = .63$; the line L_2 indecates the lowest: minimum $(N_p/N_3) = .24$ The other two curves, H_2 and L_2, indicate respectively the maximum deviation above (155) and below (173) the number of corner portfolios indicated by the average relationship $N_p = .37 N_3$.

In Figure 5 the total time required for a portfolio analysis is related to the number of securities analyzed under various assumptions about the relationship between the number of corner portfolios and the number of securities analyzed. Each of the curves shown in Figure 5 is based on the corresponding curve in Figure 4; for example, curve A in Figure 5 indicates the relationship between total time and number of securities analyzed on the assumption that the relationship between the number of corner portfolios and the number of securities is that shown by curve A in Figure 4. For convenience a second scale has been provided in Figure 5, showing the total cost of the analysis on the assumption that an IBM 709 computer can be obtained at a cost of $300 per hour.

8. THE VALUE OF PORTFOLIO ANALYSIS BASED ON THE DIAGONAL MODEL

The assumptions of the diagonal model lie near one end of the spectrum of possible assumptions about the relationships among securities. The model's extreme simplicity enables the investigator to perform a portfolio analysis at a very small cost, as we have shown. However, it is entirely possible that this simplicity so restricts the security analyst in making his predictions that the value of the resulting portfolio analysis is also very small.

In order to estimate the ability of the diagonal model to summarize information concerning the performance of securities a simple test was performed. Twenty securities were chosen randomly from the New York Stock Exchange

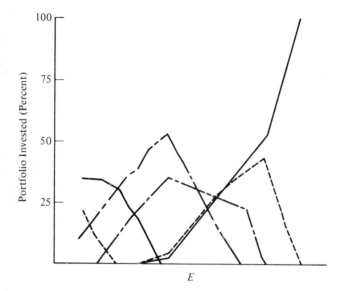

FIGURE 6a

Composition of efficient portfolios
derived from the analysis of the
diagonal model

and their performance during the period 1940–1951 used to obtain two sets of data: (1) the actual mean returns, variances of returns and covariances of returns during the period, and (2) the parameters of the diagonal model, estimated by regression techniques from the performance of the securities during the period. A portfolio analysis was then performed on each set of data. The results are summarized in Figures 6a and 6b. Each security which entered any of the efficient portfolios in significant amounts is represented by a particular type of line; the height of each line above any given value of E indicates the percentage of the efficient portfolio with that particular E composed of the security in question. The two figures thus indicate the compositions of all the efficient portfolios chosen from the analysis of the historical data (Figure 6b) and the compositions of all the portfolios chosen from the analysis of the parameters

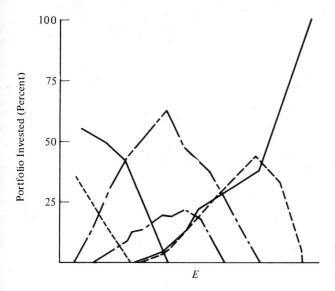

FIGURE 6b

Composition of efficient portfolios derived from the analysis of historical data

of the diagonal model (Figure 6a). The similarity of the two figures indicates that the 62 parameters of the diagonal model were able to capture a great deal of the information contained in the complete set of 230 historical relationships. An additional test, using a second set of 20 securities, gave similar results.

These results are, of course, far too fragmentary to be considered conclusive but they do suggest that the diagonal model may be able to represent the relationships among securities rather well and thus that the value of portfolio analyses based on the model will exceed their rather nominal cost. For these reasons it appears to be an excellent choice for the initial practical applications of the Markowitz technique.

REFERENCES

1. MARKOWITZ, HARRY M., *Portfolio Selection, Efficient Diversification of Investments,* New York, John Wiley and Sons, Inc., 1959.
2. MARKOWITZ, HARRY M., "Portfolio Selection," *The Journal of Finance,* Vol. 12 (March 1952), 77–91.
3. MARKOWITZ, HARRY M., "The Optimization of a Quadratic Function Subject to Linear Constraints," *Naval Research Logistics Quarterly,* Vol. 3 (March and June, 1956), 111–133.
4. WOLFE, PHILIP, "The Simplex Method for Quadratic Programming," *Econometrica,* Vol. 27 (July 1959), 382–398.

Cohen and Pogue present two new model structures that share with the Sharpe model a vast reduction in both data requirements and computational time. However, their models allow more sources of interaction between securities than does Sharpe's. The authors explore the structure of their models along with Sharpe's, and examine how well these models perform in the selection of portfolios. The ability of these models to select portfolios that perform better than random portfolios and at least as well as (or better) than mutual funds should be noted.

Also, the reader should note the tests performed in this article. This is one of the best examples in this volume of careful and imaginative testing of some alternative hypotheses.

24

An Empirical Evaluation of Alternative Portfolio-Selection Models

*Kalman J. Cohen and Jerry A. Pogue**

This article is reprinted with permission from the Journal of Business, *Vol. 40, No. 1 (April, 1967), pp. 166–193.*

I. INTRODUCTION

The approach currently regarded as providing the best analytical framewrok for selecting securities for an investment portfolio was first set forth by Markowitz and is described in detail in his 1959 book.[1] The Markowitz approach, however, has not as yet led to satisfactory solutions to the major problems of a real-world portfolio manager. One reason is that, like its predecessors, the Markowitz model greatly simplifies reality at a number of points, for example, by treating portfolio selection as a one-time act rather than as a continuous process of review and reallocation, subject to transactions and information costs. In addition, the full Markowitz model, with its more explicit recognition of the possible interrelationships among the performances of different securities, imposes new esti-

---

* The research for this paper was supported by National Science Foundation grant GS-597. The authors wish to thank Professor Marshall Blume, Lawrence Fisher, and William Shape for helpful comments and suggestions.

[1] Harry M. Markowitz, *Portfolio Selection: Efficient Diversification of Investment* (Cowles Foundation Monograph No. 16 [New York: John Wiley & Sons, 1959].

mating demands on the security analyst and computational demands on the computer, demands which rise very rapidly as the number of securities to be considered rises toward any realistic level.

The purpose of the research reported here was empirically to evaluate the ex ante and ex post performances of a number of single-period portfolio-selection models based upon the Markowitz formulation but representing successive steps toward simpler (but less rigorous) models which pose fewer problems of data preparation and computation. These simpler models represent the covariance relationships between individual securities and one or more indexes of industry or market performance.

For the securities and period studied, our results indicate that the ex post performance of the index models is not dominated by the Markowitz formulation. It also indicates that, for strictly common stock universes, the performance of the multi-index models is not superior to that of the single-index formulation, indicating the secondary importance of industry considerations for common stock portfolios.

The ex post performance of the efficient sets was compared to that of randomly selected portfolios and actual performance of seventy-eight common stock mutual funds. The results indicate that, even with a naïve security evaluation model, the efficient sets dominate the random portfolios and are not dominated by the mutual funds.

II. FEATURES OF ALTERNATIVE PORTFOLIO-SELECTION MODELS

In order to apply the Markowitz technique, the investor must form expectations about the future performance of all securities in his universe. These expectations include not only the expected return and variance of return for each security but also the covariances between all possible pairs of returns. This requirement tends to be very large for security universes of practical size.

For example, in applying the Markowitz technique in a straightforward manner, 5,150 items of input data are required for an analysis of a 100-security universe. These data, in an operational situation, must be supplied almost entirely by the security analyst.

A large amount of computation time is required to handle an analysis of of practical size. For example, an analysis of a 150–security universe using an existing computer program[2] required ninety minutes of IBM 7090 processing time. At the current commercial rate, the cost for this run is $600.

The index models incorporate extensions of the basic Markowitz framework, having been developed to simplify the data preparation problem and to allow the use of efficient computational algorithms which take advantage of the special properties of the index structure.

Algebraic expressions for the return and variance of a portfolio as a function of the component security data are developed in the Appendix for each

---

[2] IBM Portfolio Selection Program (IB PS90), IBM 7090 Program No. 7090-FI03X. Subsequent to completing most of the computations with this program, an improved Quadratic Programming Code was made available through the Share General Program Library. This program (RS-QPF4) considerably reduces the computation time required to generate an efficient set.

model. In addition, the implicit correlation between individual securities in the universe implied by each of the models is derived. The notation to be used throughout the paper will now be developed, followed by a brief discussion of each of the portfolio-selection models and the assumptions that each makes about the interactions among securities.

N = number of securities in the universe considered;

M = number of industry classifications into which the universe of N securities has been divided;

N_j = the *set* of securities in classification J, that is

$$\{i \mid i \epsilon N_j\}, \; j=1\cdots,M,$$

R_i = a random variable, the distribution of which defines the possible retruns on security i during some fixed time period where $i = 1, \dots N$;

$E(R_i)$ = expected value of R_i;

σ_{ii} = variance of the distribution of R_j;

σ_{ij} = covariance between returns R_i and R_j;

X_i = the proportion of the portfolio invested in security i where $X_i > 0$ for all i

$$\sum_{i=1}^{N} X_i = 1$$

For compactness of notation, the following vector quantities are defined

X' = portfolio vector $= (X_i, \dots, X_N)$;

R' = return vector $= (R_i, \dots, R_N)$;

E' = expected value of return vector $= [E(R_i), \dots, E(R_N)]$;

Σ_N = covariance matrix for security returns

$\quad R_i, \dots, R_N = E\{[R - E(R)][R' - E(R')]\} = ||\sigma_{ij}||, i=1,\dots,N, j=1,\dots,N$;

R_p = a random variable representing the return on a portfolio during a specified time period

$\quad = R'X$;

$E = E(R_p)$ = expected value of $R_p = E'X$;

$V = VAR(R_p)$ = variance of $R_p = X'\Sigma_N X$

THE MARKOWITZ MODEL[4]

This model requires the following data for each component of the security universe considered.

1. The expected return, $E(R_i)$, i=1, $\dots$, N.
2. The variance of return, σ_{ii}, i=1,$\dots$, N.
3. The covariance of return between R_i and R_i' for all pairs of securities, σ_{ii}', $i \neq i'$, i=1,..., N, i'=1,..., N.

[3] Once the parameters for an index model have been obtained, the expressions for the implicit covariability between the returns of each pair of securities could be used to derive the necessary inputs for the Markowitz model. Identical results would then be achieved by both formulations. This approach was originally suggested by Markowitz (*op. cit.*, pp. 96–101) as a method of reducing the data input requirements for his formulating.

[4] For a more detailed description, see H. M. Markowitz, "Portfolio Selection," *Journal of Finance*, III, No. 1 (March, 1952), 77–91.

In effect, the investor must supply the expected return vector E and the covariance matrix $\sum_N$.

The expected return and variance of any portfolio can be expressed in terms of the basic data [$E(R_i)$ and σ_{ij} values] and the amounts invested in various securities:

$$E = \sum_i X_i E(R_i) = X'E,$$

$$V = \sum_i \sum_j X_i X_j \sigma_{ij} = X'\sum_N X.$$

Given the above data, the model generates efficient portfolios which have minimum risk for any given level of return. Note that in this model no simplifying assumptions have been made regarding the relationships among securities. For an analysis of N securities, the analyst must provide estimates of N expected returns, N variances of return, and $N(N—1)/2$ covariances of return.

SINGLE-INDEX MODEL

The practical application of the above technique would be greatly facilitated by a set of assumptions which would reduce the estimation task. One such set of assumptions is the *single-index model*. This approach, first suggested by Markowitz as a method of preparing input for the first model described, was later developed by Sharpe in a way that took computational advantage of the structure of the data.[5]

The major characteristic of the single-index model is the assumption that the various securities are relatied only through common relationships with an index of general market performance. In this model, the reutrn from any security is determined by random factors and a linear relationship with the market index:

$$R_i = A_i + B_i I + C_i,$$

where A_i and B_i are parameters which can be determined for each security by least-squares regression analysis. C_i is a random element. I is the level of some index, such as the Dow-Jones Industrial Average, GNP or any specially constructed index that is more closely aligned with the specific purposes of the analysis. The future level of the market index is given by

$$I = A_{N+1} + C_{N+1},$$

where

$$E(I) = A_{N+1},$$

$$E(C_{N+1}) = 0,$$

$$VAR(I) = E(C^2_{N+1}) = Q_{N+1}.$$

These relationships imply that the parameter A_{N+1} is an unbiased estimate of the market level in the time period considered. The possible values of I are

[5] William F. Sharpe, "A Simplified Model for Portfolio Analysis," *Management Science*, IX, No. 2 (January, 1963), 277–93.

thus distributed symmetrically about A_{N+1} with variance Q_{N+1}. In this formulation, the following assumptions are made

$$E(C_i) = 0, \qquad i = 1, \ldots, N \,; \tag{1}$$

that is for each security we have an unbiased estimate of the mean return during the time horizon given by

$$
\begin{aligned}
E(R_i) &= A_i + B_i E(I) = A_i + B_i A_{N+1}. \\
VAR(C_i) &= E(C_i^2) = Q_i, \qquad i = 1, \ldots, N \,, \\
E(C_{N+1} \cdot C_i) &= 0, \qquad\qquad i = 1, \ldots, N \,;
\end{aligned}
\tag{2}
$$

that is, for any given value of I, the return on security i is distributed about $A_i + B_i I$. Q_i, the variance of the residual return C_i, is independent of the level of I.

$$
\begin{aligned}
E(C_i C_{i'}) = 0, \qquad i = i', \qquad &i = 1, \ldots, N \,, \\
&i' = 1, \ldots, N \,;
\end{aligned}
\tag{3}
$$

that is, the yield residuals are uncorrelated. This assumption states that the returns on any two securities i and i' are related only through the relationship with the market index I.

The contribution made by Sharpe was to show that, if you start out with the linear relationships defined above, then by appropriately introducing a new variable, a dummy $N + 1^{ST}$ security, a special type of covariance matrix is obtained. The covariance matrix, which is full in the N securities Markowitz formulation, contains non-zero elements only along the $N + 1$ diagonal positions for the single-index model. Everywhere off the main diagonal $\sum_{N+1}$ has zero elements. This vastly reduces the amount of computation required to generate the efficient set of portfolios, as the process requires repeated inversion of the covariance matrix. When a computational algorithm is used which takes advantage of the diagonal form of the covariance matrix, the efficient set of portfolios can be obtained at approximately 1 per cent of the computation cost required for the full Markowitz formulation.

The dummy $N + 1^{ST}$ security can be considered as a weighted responsiveness of security returns to movements in the market level I, as

$$X_{N+1} = \sum_{i=1}^{N} X_i B_i.$$

As shown in the Appendix, the return and variance of a portfolio are given by

$$E(R_p) = \sum_{i=1}^{N+1} X_i A_i = X'A,$$

where

$$X' = (X_i, \ldots, X_{N+1}),$$

and

$$A' = (A_i, \ldots, A_{N+1}).$$

$$VAR(R_p) = \sum_{i=1}^{N+1} X^2{}_i Q_i = X' \sum_{N+1} X.$$

While reduction in computation time is an important factor in the research and development phases of portfolio-selection models, the most important characteristic of this model with regard to operational application is the reduction in security data required. Only three estimates are required for each security, A_i, B_i, Q_i, and two for the market index, A_{N+1}, Q_{N+1}, rather than estimates of each element in the variance-covariance matrix. Thus the number of estimates required is reduced from $N(N + 3)/2$ in the Markowitz-model formulation to $3N + 2$ in the single-index formulation.

MULTI-INDEX MODELS

The single-index model presents a great simplification, in terms of both necessary inputs and computation, over the original Markowitz formulation. The question arises, however, as to whether this formulation is an oversimplification. In tying the variability of security yield only to a general market index, some of the important relationships among securities—originally expressed in the Markowitz formulation as independently determined covariances between each pair of securities—may be lost. It is hence possible that the original single-index model does not generate a truly efficient set of portfolios.

This potential deficiency would be particularly acute when several classes of securities are being considered for inclusion in the same portfolio. It would not appear realistic that a single index of market performance would provide an adequate base for expectation about the future performance of common stocks, preferred shares, bonds, and other types of assets.

Part of the purpose of this research is to investigate empirically the differences in the results from the Markowitz and single-index Sharpe formulations for universes of common stocks. Given the wide gap between the relatively rigorous method by which the traditional Markowitz technique treats the relationships between securities and the very simplified way this is done in the single-index model, it seemed appropriate to consider other models of intermediate complexity between these two extremes. This would allow us to capture the covariance relationships in a potentially more efficient manner than the single-index model, while at the same time achieving some computational savings over the general Markowitz approach.

To this end, we have developed two multi-index models; one we call the *covariance form of the multi-index model;* the other, the *diagonal form* of the *multi-index model.*

All of the index models are similar in that they relate the return for any security as a linear function of some index. However, in the multi-index model, rather than using a general market index we use a number of class or industry indexes. In the case of strictly common stock universes, the class indexes can be thought of as industry indexes. In dealing with different classes of securities, such as preferred stocks, common stocks, government bonds, corporate bonds, and so on, a special appropriate index could be defined for each of these classes of securities.

The first multi-index model, the covariance form, maintains the single-index type of formulation within each security class. It allows, however, for the full covariability among class indexes, in much the same manner as between securities in the Markowitz formulation.

The second model, the diagonal form, employs a hierarchy of indexes. The first group of indexes relates directly to the yields of the securities in their respective classes of industry groupings, in the same manner as the covariance model. An additional index is then used as a medium for expressing the relationships among the various industry or class indexes. The structures and assumptions of these models will now be discussed in more detail.

Multi-index model—covariance form.—In this model we assume that the universe of securities is composed of components from M classes or industries. The return on each security is assumed to be linearly related to the level of the index of the industry or class to which it belongs.

$$R_i = A_i + B_i J_j + C_i, \qquad \{i \,|\, i\epsilon N_j\},$$

where $N_j =$ the *set* of securities in class j, $j = 1, \ldots, M$. J_j is the future level of jth industry index, where $J_j = A_{N+j} + C_{N+j}$, $j = 1, \ldots, M$. As in the single-index model, the following assumptions are made

$$E(C_i) = 0, \qquad i = 1, \ldots, N. \tag{1}$$

$$\begin{aligned} E(C_i \cdot C_i) = Q_i, \quad & i = i', \qquad i = 1, \ldots, N, \\ = 0, \quad & i \neq i', \qquad i = 1, \ldots, N. \end{aligned} \tag{2}$$

$$E(C_{N+j}) = 0, \qquad j = 1, \ldots, M. \tag{3}$$

$$E(C_{N+j}^2) = Q_{N+j}, \, j = 1, \ldots, M. \tag{4}$$

$$E(C_{N+j} C_i) = 0, \qquad i = 1, \ldots, N, \qquad j = 1, \ldots, M. \tag{5}$$

Thus far the assumptions *within* each class are similar to those in the single-index model. To express the relationships among the M industry subuniverses, we introduce the covariance matrix of the industry indexes

$$\Sigma_M = ||\sigma_{jj'}|| = ||COV\, J_j \cdot J_{j'}||,$$
$$j = 1, \ldots, M, \qquad j' = 1, \ldots, M.$$

As shown in the Appendix, the expressions for the expected return and variance of a portfolio are given by

$$E(R_p) = \sum_{i=1}^{N+M} X_i A_i = X'A,$$

where

$$X_{N+j} = \sum_{\{i \,|\, i\epsilon N_j\}} X_i B_i, \qquad j = 1, \ldots, M,$$

$$X' = (X_1, \ldots, X_{N+M}),$$
$$A' = (A_1, \ldots, A_{N+M}).$$

$$VAR(R_p) = \sum_{i=1}^{N} X_i^2 Q_i + \sum_{j=1}^{M} \sum_{j'=1}^{M} X_{N+j} X_{N+j'} \sigma_{jj'}$$

$$= X'_N \Sigma_N X_N + X'_M \Sigma_M X_M = X' \Sigma_{N+M} X,$$

where

$$\Sigma_{N+M} = \begin{vmatrix} \Sigma_N & O \\ O & \Sigma_M \end{vmatrix}.$$

The covariance matrix (Σ_{N+M}), which must be repeatedly inverted in generating the efficient frontiers, can be partitioned into four submatrixes, only two of which have non-zero elements.

The first submatrix (Σ_N) is a diagonal matrix because of the single-index assumptions within each industry. The second matrix (Σ_M) is not simplified at all because we have made *no* simplifying assumptions regarding the covariances among industry indexes. However, a great deal of computational saving will be realized in a realistic application, since the number of industry indexes (M) will be much fewer than the number of securities (N). Thus when the total covariance matrix Σ_{N+M} is inverted using partitioning techniques, the only matrix which must be inverted using general techniques is the smaller Σ_M matrix. The inverse of Σ_N, being a diagonal matrix, is easily and quickly obtained.

Multi-index model—diagonal form.—This model has the same basic structure as the covariance form, with the additional assumption that each industry index is itself linearly related to an over-all market index. This involves the definition of a further dummy security (the $N + M + 1^{ST}$) which is related to the responsiveness of the industry indexes to the general market index.

The future levels of the industry indexes are thus assumed to be given by: $J_j = A_{N+j} + B_{N+j} I + C_{N+j}, j = 1, \ldots, M$, where we make similar assumptions to those made in the single-index formulation or within an industry group as in the covariance model:

$$E(C_{N+j}) = 0, \qquad j = 1, \ldots, M,$$
$$E(C^2_{N+j}) = Q_{N+j}, \quad j = 1, \ldots, M,$$
$$E(C_{N+j} C_i) = 0, \qquad i = 1, \ldots, N, \qquad j = 1, \ldots, M,$$
$$E(C_{N+j} C_{N+j'}) = 0, \qquad j \neq j'.$$

The level of the general market index, I, is defined as in the single-index model $I = A_{N+M+1} + C_{N+M+1}$, where A_{N+M+1} is the expected value of I and C_{N+M+1} is a random variable with mean zero and variance Q_{N+M+1}. C_{N+M+1} is assumed to be uncorrelated with any of the other security or index residuals; that is, $E(C_{N+M+1} C_i) = 0, i = 1, \ldots, N + M$. As developed in the Appendix, the expressions for the return and variance of a portfolio are given by

$$E(R_p) = \sum_{i=1}^{N+M+1} X_i A_i = \boldsymbol{X'A},$$

where

$$X_{N+j} = \sum_{\{i\,|\,i\epsilon N_j\}} X_i B_i,$$

$$X_{N+M+1} = \sum_{j=1}^{M} X_{N+j} B_{N+j},$$

$$\boldsymbol{X'} = (X_1, \ldots, X_{N+M+1}),$$
$$\boldsymbol{A'} = (A_1, \ldots, A_{N+M+1}).$$

$$VAR(R_p) = \sum_{i=1}^{N} X_i^2 Q_i + \sum_{j=1}^{M} X^2_{N+j} Q_{N+j} + X^2_{N+M+1} Q_{N+M+1}$$

$$= \sum_{i=1}^{N+M+1} X_i^2 Q_i = \boldsymbol{X'} \Sigma_{M+N+1} \boldsymbol{X}$$

where $X' = (X_1, \cdots, X_N, X_{N+1}, \cdots, X_{N+M+1})$

When the form of the covariance matrix $\sum_{N+M+1}$ is examined, it is found to be completely diagonal, as it was in the case of the single-index model. It is not the same covariance matrix, however, because even though we are in a sense relating each security ultimately to a market index, due to the differences in the assumptions about the properties of the yield and index residuals, the covariance matrixes will be different.[6]

COMPARISONS OF THE MODEL FORMULATIONS

To summarize at this point, it is seen that we will be considering four different versions of the efficient frontier. The four models theoretically form a decreasing sequence with respect to the completeness by which each model represents the true covariability between the securities of the universe. Starting with the complete Markowitz fromulation, we have an exact representation of the covariance relationships.

Next we have the multi-index model, covariance form, where the universe has been divided into classes or industries. The relationships among the industry indicators are completely maintained in this model by the inclusion of a full variance-covariance matrix for these indexes.

In the next model, the diagonal form of the multi-index model, we attempt to relate the levels of the industry indexes through their relationship with a common index of market level. Thus instead of an exact representation of the covariability of the the indexes, we are now using a linear model, with its inherent assumptions about homogeneity of variance and non-correlation of residuals. Hence this is a less complete representation than the preceding model.

---

[6] This can be seen by comparing the algebaraic expressions for the implicit correlation between pains of returns for both models (refer to the Appendix).

In the final model, the single-index formulation, we have made the assumption that the returns on all securities in the universe are related only through their common dependence on the general market index. However, along with this decreasing ability to represent the true covariance matrix, comes increasing ease of computation or decreasing of computation costs because each of these models generates a covariance matrix that is successively easier to invert.

Rather than developing specific computationally efficient programs for each of the index models, we have used an existing general-purpose portfolio-selection computer program[7] to in effect simulate the structure of each of our models. The program, being very general in nature, does not make use of computational efficiencies which are inherent in the data structure of the various index models. Thus we cannot make statements about the computational properties of the index models other than to specify a computational ranking based on our knowledge of the structures of the models. We are more concerned at this time with empirically investigating the relative performance of these models. Given the superiority of one formulation in a particular circumstance, it would then be appropriate to develop an efficient, computational code, if one does not already exist.[8]

III. DATA AND TESTS USED

The test samples of 75-and 150-security universes have been prepared using yearly price and yield data for the periods 1947–57 (ex ante) and 1958–64 (ex post).

The ex ante efficient portfolios generated by each of the four models have been examined to compare (1) the location of the ex ante efficient frontiers; (2) the composition of the efficient portfolios; (3) the performance of the ex ante efficient portfolios during the ex post period.

In addition, the ex post performance of the efficient sets has been compared to that of randomly generated portfolios and the actual performance of seventy-eight basically common stock mutual funds.

In order that the results of the research be more meaningful to the institutional investor, we have placed upper-bound constraints in the amount of any security which càn be contained in an efficient portfolio. In practice, many institutional investors have legal restrictions on the proportion of their portfolio which can be invested in any one security. Others adhere heuristically to such restrictions to avoid becoming formally involved as major shareholders in the companies in which they invest. In other cases, it may still be desirable to employ upper-bound restrictions as a method of hedging against the risk of biases in the input data.

Formally, these limits can be considered to be upper-bound constraints on the variables X_i. Such upper bounds have been introduced into all four of the portfolio-selection models with which we deal in this paper. When efficient portfolios have been generated from a universe of seventy-five common stocks, the upper-bound constraints have all been set equal to 0.05, insuring that a mini-

---

[7] IBM Portfolio Selection Program, *op. cit.*

[8] IBM has developed a 1401 computer code for the single-index model: 1401 Portfolio Selection Program (1401—FI-04 X).

mum of twenty securities appears in each portfolio; when a universe of 150 stocks has been used, all the upper bounds have been equated to 0.025, so that the minimum number of securities in a portfolio is forty.

Before presenting a description of the empirical findings, some of the considerations involved in developing input data for the study will now be discussed.

DEVELOPMENT OF INPUT DATA

Yearly security data for the period 1947–64 were used to develop input for the portfolio selection and evaluation phases of the study. The source of this information was the Standard and Poor's Compustat Industrial Service. Although this included over nine hundred common stocks, only 543 had the necessary continuous price and dividend histories over the full 1947–64 period. The data were arbitrarily divided into two groups, 1947–57 and 1958–64. Security information from the initial eleven-year period was used to develop the required estimates for each portfolio-selection model. Data from the final seven-year period were used to evaluate the ex post performances of the sets of efficient portfolios.

To measure the yield for a security in any year, both capital gains and dividends were considered.[9] For simplicity, tax effects were not considered. Yields were computed for each of the 543 securities in each year of the 1947–64 period. These yields were then used to develop market and industry indexes for the index models.

Rather than using any of the standard published indexes, an aggregate performance index was computed which was more pertinent to the investment performance of our security universe. This index used is an unweighted arithmetic average of yields of all securities in the 543–security universe.[10] The universe of securities was divided into ten industry subgroupings, and similar industry indexes were computed for each industry.

In order to generate the expected values of returns for the Markowitz model and the expected value of the indexes for the index models, the following assumptions were made:

1. The expected return for each security for the period 1958–64 was assumed to be an arithmetic average[11] of the yearly returns in the initial period.
2. Similarly, the expected value (A_{N+1}) for each industry or general index was assumed to be an average of the actual levels in the 1947–57 period.
3. Similar assumptions were made regarding variability and covariability of security yield and index level. Estimates of future variability were assumed to be equal to those computed for the initial period.
4. The expected future values of the parameters for the index models $(A_i, B_i, Q_i,)$ were assumed to be equal to the values developed in the 1947–57 period using least-squares regression techniques.

[9] Yields were calculated for each year in the following manner: $R_i(t) = $ [Price$_i$ $(t)+$ Dividends $(t)-$Price$_i$ $(t-1)$]/[Price$_i$ $(t-1)$] where $R_i(t)$ is the yield on security i in year t. For the rationale underlying this type of index, see Kalman. J. Cohen and Bruce P.

[10] Fitch, "The Average Investment Performance Index," *Management Science,* Series B, XII, No. 6 (February, 1966), B-195-B-215.

[11] We use the arithmetic rather than geometric average here because we are not interested

In effect, we are assuming that performance in our seven-year evaluation period can be adequately predicted from the performance during the eleven-year base period. In order to avoid possible misunderstandings, we must stress that in an operational situation we would definitely *not* advocate any method of forming future expectations which is based strictly on historical data. We have adopted such a method in this study because we are concerned at this time with only a part of the portfolio-analysis process. The naiveté of our security-evaluation model should not change any conclusions we may wish to make about the *relative* performance of various portfolio-selection techniques.

When the efficient frontiers had been generated, the yield data from the 1958–64 period were used to calculate the *true* ex post return and variance of the efficient portfolios. The computation method for all models was that specified for the Markowitz formulation, using the true covariance matrix.

All calculations were carried out for both 150–and 75–security universes. The 150–security universe is a randomly chosen subset of the 543 common stokcs available. The 75–security universe is a randomly chosen subset of the 150–security universe. This nesting of the universes was established so that the comparisons of the results obtained from the 75–security and the 150–security universes would primarily portray the effects of universe size rather than of differences in the nature of the securities.

To provide a basis for an objective comparison of the ex post performance of the efficient sets, the actual performances of randomly generated portfolios and some common-stock mutual funds were considered.

Two groups of sixty random portfolios were chosen, one group to correspond to each universe size, that is, such that the random portfolios would have approximately the same numbers of securities per portfolio as efficient portfolios selected from the respective universes.[12]

The seventy-eight mutual funds were selected from Table 19 of Arthur Wiesenberger's *Investment Companies*.[13] Those selected include all growth, growth and income, and income with growth funds which have continuous histories for 1958–64. The basic yearly "return" for the mutual funds used is defined

in the average compounded rate of growth of a portfolio over a successive number of years. Rather since we are dealing with static selection models, in which the definition of time horizons is arbitrary, we prefer to consider our ex post and ex ante periods as effective "single-year" periods in which the return vectors $R = (R_1, \ldots, R_N)$ are independently distributed according to the probability distributions $fi (R_1, \ldots, R_N)$, $i =$ 1 (ex ante period), 2 (ex post period).

Thus the eleven observations arbitrarily allocated to the ex ante "period" can be assumed to be random and independent observations from the population of "one-year" returns. As such we use a least-squares, or arithmetic averaging, technique to estimate the mean of the ex ante distribution $f_i (R_1, \ldots, R_N)$.

As of the end of 1957, when the portfolios are selected, the moments of $f_1 (R_1, \ldots, R_N)$ are asumed to be the best estimates of the unknown moments of $f_2 (R_1, \ldots, R_N)$. In developing the actual moments of $f_2 (R_1, \ldots, R_N)$ for evaluating the ex post performance of the ex ante efficient portfolios, a similar argument applies, i.e., the seven years of data can be assumed to be seven random and independent observations from $f_2 (R_1 \ldots, R_N)$.

[12] For comparison with the 75-security universe efficient portfolios, the random portfolios were selected to contain 20 securities. For the 150-security universe, each random portfolio consisted of 40 randomly selected securities. Equal dollar weights were given to the securities contained in each random portfolio.

[13] A. Wiesenberger, *Investment Companies* (Port Washington, N.Y.: Kennikat Press, 1965).

as the percentage change in net-asset value per share plus capital gains distributions plus income dividends. The average return and variance of return for each mutual fund over the seven-year ex post period was computed in a straightforward fashion consistent with previous ex post calculations. In effect, each mutual fund was treated as a separate portfolio for evaluation purposes.

ANALYSIS OF THE CORRELATION ASSUMPTIONS IN THE INDEX MODEL

If the returns of all securities in the universe were related in such a manner that the various yield *and* index residuals in each model were absolutely uncorrelated, that is, $E(C_i \cdot C_j) = 0$, for $i \neq j$, over the time horizon considered, then the index models would represent the true covariability of the securities indentically. However, the assumption that the residuals are uncorrelated is an approximation. By assuming the various residuals to be uncorrelated for the purpose of model formulation, the *implied* covariances among securities in the index models will differ from the true covariance as defined by the Markowitz model.

Table 1 shows the distributions of correlation coefficients among the *yield* residuals $(C_i, i = 1, \ldots, 150)$ for the single-index and multi-index models for the 1947–57 period. These distributions, while centered about zero, have reasonably wide dispersion. By assuming away this yield correlation, we are in

TABLE 1

Distributions of correlation coefficients of yield residuals, 150-security universe, 1947–57

Correlation coefficient	Single-index model		Multi-model (covariance form)	
	Relative frequency	Cumulative frequency	Relative frequency	Cumulative frequency
−1.000 to −.900	.001	.001	.000	.000
−.899 to −.800	.004	.005	.002	.002
−.799 to −.700	.013	.018	.009	.011
−.699 to −.600	.027	.045	.023	.034
−.599 to −.500	.041	.086	.037	.071
−.499 to −.400	.058	.144	.058	.129
−.399 to −.300	.077	.221	.076	.205
−.299 to −.200	.089	.310	.090	.295
−.199 to −.100	.089	.399	.098	.393
−.099 to .000	.101	.500	.104	.497
.000 to .099	.101	.601	.105	.602
.100 to .199	.093	.694	.104	.706
.200 to .299	.086	.780	.086	.792
.300 to .399	.073	.853	.076	.868
.400 to .499	.058	.911	.054	.922
.500 to .599	.042	.953	.039	.961
.600 to .699	.028	.981	.024	.985
.700 to .799	.015	.966	.012	.997
.800 to .899	.004	1.000	.003	1.000
.900 to 1.000	.000	1.000	.000	1.000

effect reducing the covariability between securities, which in turn will cause the "reduced" covariance matrixes implied by these models to understate the variance of efficient portfolios generated by them. It is interesting to note that the distribution of correlation coefficients for the multi-index model is only slightly less dispersed than that for the single-index model. Thus the structuring of the models to include a number of indexes has not had as major an effect on reducing the covariability among yield residuals for the universe of common stocks considered as might have been expected.

Table 2 summarizes the distribution of correlation coefficients among the ten industry indexes for the period 1947–57. The very high interrelations among industries is very evident from this table. This high interindex correlation would not be as predominant if we were dealing with a wider class of securities than just common stocks.

TABLE 2

Distribution of correlation coefficients between indexes, multi-index model, covariance form, 1947–57

Correlation coefficient	Relative frequency	Cumulative frequency
.000 to .099	.000	.000
.100 to .199	.000	.000
.200 to .299	.000	.000
.300 to .399	.000	.000
.400 to .499	.000	.000
.500 to .599	.045	.045
.600 to .699	.045	.090
.700 to .799	.244	.334
.800 to .899	.333	.667
.900 to 1.000	.333	1.000

The structure of the covariance form of the multi-index model includes a 10×10 covariance matrix to account exactly for the correlations among industry indexes. In the diagonal form, each industry index is assumed to be linearly related to the general market index. As in the single-index model, the index residuals (C_{N+j}, $j = 1, \ldots, M$) are assumed to be mutually uncorrelated. Table 3 indicates the empirical results of this assumption. While a large amount of the covariability between industry indexes is explained by their common dependence on the general market index, the assumption does not fit the facts as well as in the yield residuals case. The dispersion of the correlation coefficient distribution is wider and somewhat skewed.

While Tables 1, 2, and 3 are interesting insofar as they indicate how well some of our individual assumptions are satisfied, a more aggregate measure, which is perhaps more meaningful to the final selection performance of the models, is how well the models are able to reproduce the true covariances between individual security returns. To obtain a measure of this relative ability, the correlation matrix implied by each of the index models was compared with

TABLE 3

Distribution of correlation coefficients of index residuals, multi-index model, diagonal form, 1947–57

Correlation coefficient	Relative frequency	Cumulative frequency
−1.000 to −.900	.000	.000
−.899 to −.800	.089	.089
−.799 to .700	.000	.089
−.699 to −.600	.067	.156
−.599 to −.500	.089	.245
−.499 to −.400	.111	.356
−.399 to −.300	.022	.378
−.299 to −.200	.067	.445
−.199 to −.100	.111	.556
−.099 to .000	.044	.600
.000 to .099	.022	.622
.100 to .199	.089	.711
200 to .299	.067	.778
.300 to .399	.089	.867
.400 to .499	.000	.867
.500 to .599	.067	.934
.600 to .699	.022	.956
.700 to .799	.022	.978
.800 to .899	.022	1.000
.900 to 1.000	.000	1.000

the true correlation matrix used in the Markowitz model.[14] While the multi-index models most closely represented the true correlations among securities within the same industries, the relationships among securities in different industries were somewhat better represented by the single-index model. Because of the much larger number of interindustry as opposed to intraindustry comparisons, the single-index model was found, on the average, to better represent the true correlation matrix. Table 4 indicates the distributions of coefficient differences for the single and multi-index (covariance form) models for the 75–security universe for the period 1947–57.

[14] The true correlation matrix, as used in the Markowitz formulation, was compared with the implicit correlation matrix of each of the index models for the 75-security universe. Each matrix consisted of 2,775 coefficients above the main diagonal, of which 2,484 had been generated by interindustry security correlations, and only 291 coefficients were the result of correlations among securities in the same industries.

Differences were taken between the true correlation coefficients and the equivalent correlation coefficients generated by each index model. The distributions of intraindustry and interindustry differences were then compared.

The distribution of differences for the 291 intraindustry correlations was more tightly distributed about zero for the multi-index model. However, the distribution of the 2,482 interindustry differences was slightly more centralized for the single index model. Thus, when the differences for the total matrix were examined, the single-index model was found, on the average, to better represent the true correlation matrix (see Table 4).

TABLE 4

Distribution of correlation coefficient error, 75-security universe, 1947–57

Correlation coefficient error	Single-index model		Multi-index model (covariance form)	
	Relative frequency	Cumulative frequency	Relative frequency	Cumulative frequency
−1.000 to −.900	.000	.000	.000	.000
−.899 to −.800	.000	.000	.000	.000
−.799 to −.700	.000	.000	.000	.000
−.699 to −.600	.001	.001	.003	.003
−.599 to −.500	.003	.004	.006	.009
−.499 to −.400	.013	.017	.020	.029
−.399 to −.300	.034	.051	.042	.071
−.299 to −.200	.074	.125	.080	.151
−.199 to −.100	.124	.249	.117	.268
−.099 to .000	.204	.453	.176	.444
.000 to .099	.221	.674	.186	.630
.100 to .199	.156	.830	.163	.793
.200 to .299	.092	.922	.103	.896
.300 to .399	.044	.966	.064	.960
.400 to .499	.020	.986	.024	.984
.500 to .599	.011	.997	.014	.998
.600 to .699	.003	1.000	.002	1.000
.700 to .799	.000	1.000	.000	1.000
.800 to .899	.000	1.000	.000	1.000
.900 to 1.000	.000	1.000	.000	1.000

The reason for this slight superiority is that the compound assumptions required to introduce the multi-index structure appear to introduce more error into the implicit correlation between two securities in different industries than the single-index model. This is felt to be the result of dealing with strictly common stock universes, in which the industries tend to be strongly interrelated and amenable to the single-index type of assumptions. If a wider class of securities had been included, it is felt that the multi-index formulation would tend to dominate in interindustry as well as intraindustry comparisons.

When the implied correlation matrixes of the covariance and diagonal forms of the multi-index model are compared, the former is found to dominate slightly the latter in its ability to reproduce the true correlations, as would be expected.

IV. RESULTS AND ANALYSIS

Figures 1 and 2 illustrate the ex ante efficient frontiers for the two security universes considered.

Figure 1 shows the efficient frontiers as specified by the selection models. In the index-model cases, the standard deviation levels associated with the frontiers are understated to varying degrees, having been computed by the "reduced" covariance matrixes implicit in these models. The amounts by which the risk levels have been understated can be seen by comparing Figure 1 with Figure 2. In Figure 2 the actual ex ante standard deviations associated with the various efficient portfolios have been calculated using the true ex ante covariance matrix (as developed for the Markowitz model).

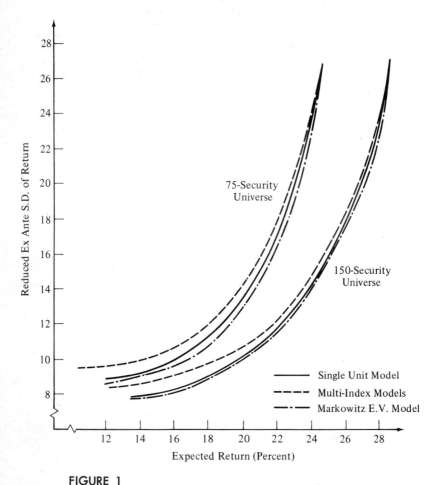

FIGURE 1

Comparison of efficient frontiers

The results in Figure 2 allow direct comparisons between models, showing the relative optimization ability of each of the models for the security universes considered. While the performance of the covariance form of the multi-index model was found to dominate that of the diagonal model, the dominance was so slight that the curves have been combined.

The interesting feature of Figures 1 and 2 is the relative locations of the single-and multi-index frontiers. The single-index frontier tends to dominate

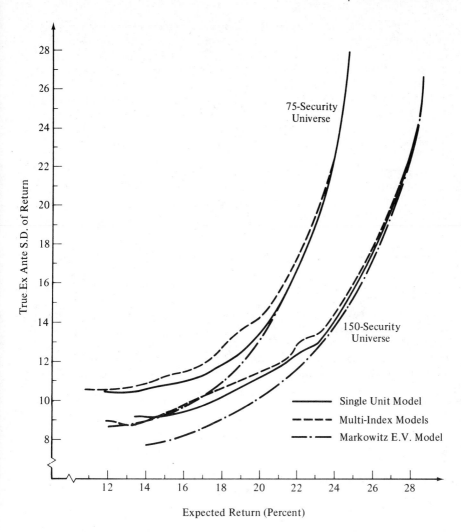

FIGURE 2

Comparison of efficient frontiers

those of the multi-index models over a wide range of expected returns. This is related to the ability of the single-index model to represent large parts of the true covariance matrix more effectively than do the multi-index models, for universes of strictly common stocks. As previously discussed, if we were dealing with a wider class of securities, one would expect this result to be reversed.

It is also noted that the single-index model tends to understate the standard deviations of efficient portfolios to a greater extent than the multi-index models. This is seen by comparing the relative upward shifts in proceeding from Figures 1 to 2. As seen from Figure 1, the dominance of the single-index model over the multi-index formulations is not nearly so clearly defined as in Figure 2.

These figures also illustrate the combined effects of jointly changing the universe size and the upper-bound restrictions. Increasing the universe size from 75 to 150 securities gives the models greater opportunity to increase return for the same level of risk. Hence we would expect that increasing the universe size should shift the efficient frontiers to the right. Conversely, decreasing the upper-bound restrictions for some given universe size should have the opposite effect. The results shown in these figures illustrate that, for the security sample considered, doubling the universe size had a much stronger effect than halving the upper-bound restrictions. In this case, it would be necessary to more than halve the upper-bound constraints to balance doubling the universe size. On the basis of this limited sample, we might conjecture that the ex ante expectations may be more sensitive to decisions which restrict the universe size than to decisions regarding the size of the upper-bound restrictions to be placed on the proportion of the portfolio that can be invested in any one security.

COMPOSITION OF THE EFFICIENT PORTFOLIOS

The efficient portfolios generated by each index model were compared to the Markowitz portfolios for equivalent levels of ex ante expected return. The comparisons between the non-optimal index portfolios and the optimal Markowitz portfolios consisted of computing the square root of the average sum of squared deviations between the investment proportions of the index-model portfolios and the investment proportions held by the optimal Markowitz portfolios; that is, the goodness of fit was measured by

$$D_{iE} = \sqrt{\frac{1}{N} \sum_{j=1}^{N} (X_{ij} - X_{4j})^2}$$

where

i = model number, $i=1$ single index model,
                          $i=2$ diagonal model,
                          $i=3$ covariance model,
                          $i=4$ Markowitz model;
j = security number, $j=1,\ldots, N$ for $N=75,150$;
E = level of expected return at which the portfolios are being compared;
X_{ij} = proportion of the portfolio with E expected return invested in jth security by model i;
D_{iE} = a goodness-of-fit measure between two multivariate portfolios. It is analogous to the standard deviation of the portfolio composition of the ith model (at level E) when the optimal Markowitz portfolio ($i=4$) is used as a standard of comparison.

The goodness-of-fit indexes have been plotted in Figure 2 for both universe sizes. The superior ex ante performance of the single-index relative to the multi-index model is explained by observing how much more closely the single-index portfolios "fit" the Markowitz portfolios over the whole range of returns, for both universe sizes.

At the highest possible level of return, in both universes, the portfolios of the four models are identical, each consisting of the minimum number of securities allowed by the constraints having the highest expected returns. As the level of return decreases, the portfolios tend to become less similar as more opportunities for substitution at the same level of portfolio return become available.

Table 5 summarizes the average composition of the efficient portfolios across the range of expected returns. Note that, on the average, the optimal

TABLE 5

Summary of composition statistics

	75 securities				150 securities			
	Single	Diagonal	Covari-ance	Expected return variance	Single	Diagonal	Covari-ance	Expected return variance
Average number of securities in portfolio	24.3	23.7	23.5	22.6	44.7	44.3	44.3	42.9
Average number of securities at upper bound	16.0	16.6	16.9	18.3	35.2	35.9	35.9	37.6
Average percentage at upper bound	65.9	70.5	71.8	81.1	78.8	80.9	81.0	87.7

Markowitz portfolios tend to contain the fewest securities of which the highest percentage are at their upper bounds. As we proceed through the multi-index to the single-index models, the portfolios tend to contain more securities, of which a progressively higher percentage are at fractional or unconstrained levels. Thus the multi-index portfolios tend to be structurally more similar to the optimal portfolios, but as seen from Figure 3, they have a greater compositional variance.

In Tables 6 and 7 the composition of the ex ante portfolios is summarized at specific levels of expected return, showing the number of securities and the percentage of the portfolio invested in each industry grouping. These tables indicate how the composition of the efficient portfolios vary over the attainable range of expected returns.

COMPARISON OF EX POST PERFORMANCE

Figures 4 and 5 show the ex post results for a sample of efficient portfolios, plotted on the same diagram as the ex ante expectations, for the diagonal form of the multi-index model. In addition, the ex post performance of the randomly selected portfolios and seventy-eight mutual funds have been included for comparison. The general pattern of relationships shown also holds true for similar comparisons using any of the other three models. The other graphs have not been included, however, for the sake of brevity.

From Figures 4 and 5 it is observed that the ex post results of the efficient

TABLE 6

Comparison of efficient portfolios by industry groupings, 75-security universe

A. Number of securities in each industry

Industry	No.	12.5%				14.0%				16.0%				18.0%				20.0%				22.0%				24.0%			
		1	2	3	4	1	2	3	4	1	2	3	4	1	2	3	4	1	2	3	4	1	2	3	4	1	2	3	4
Mines	5	1	1	1	0	1	1	1	1	1	1	1	1	1	0	1	1	1	1	1	1	1	1	1	1	2	2	2	2
Foods	12	7	7	6	4	7	6	6	4	6	5	5	4	4	5	5	5	4	4	4	3	4	4	4	4	3	3	3	3
Textiles	2	1	0	0	1	1	0	0	1	1	0	1	0	1	0	0	1	1	1	0	1	1	1	1	1	1	0	0	1
Paper	5	1	1	1	1	1	1	2	1	1	2	2	2	2	1	2	2	2	1	2	2	2	2	2	2	2	2	2	1
Chemicals	8	4	3	2	3	4	2	2	2	4	2	2	3	4	2	2	3	2	2	2	3	2	2	3	2	1	1	1	1
ORSGC*	8	2	3	3	2	2	3	3	3	3	4	4	2	4	4	4	3	5	5	5	4	3	3	3	2	2	1	1	2
Metals	7	0	0	0	1	1	1	1	1	1	1	1	1	1	1	1	1	1	1	1	1	2	2	2	2	2	2	2	2
Electricals	13	5	4	6	5	5	6	6	5	5	6	6	6	5	5	6	6	4	4	4	6	6	6	6	6	6	6	6	5
Transport	7	0	0	0	1	0	0	0	0	0	0	0	0	0	0	0	0	0	0	0	0	1	1	1	3	2	2	2	2
Retail	8	6	5	5	5	6	6	5	5	6	5	5	5	5	4	4	4	5	2	2	2	3	2	2	2	2	2	2	2
No. in portfolio	27	25	25	22	26	26	26	24	24	27	25	23	24	24	22	24	24	24	22	21	21	22	23	22	21	21	21	21	21
No. at upper bound	13	16	17	18	14	13	15	18	15	16	16	17	16	16	17	19	17	17	19	19	17	18	19	19	19	19	18	17	19
% at upper bound	48.2	64.0	68.0	81.8	53.9	60.0	75.0	55.0	66.7	64.0	73.9	66.7	77.3	66.7	77.3	81.0	90.5	77.3	79.2	77.3	81.0	90.5	77.3	73.9	78.3	86.4	90.5	85.8	81.0 90.5

B. Percentage of portfolio invested in each industry

Industry	12.5%				14.0%				16.0%				18.0%				20.0%				22.0%				24.0%			
	1	2	3	4	1	2	3	4	1	2	3	4	1	2	3	4	1	2	3	4	1	2	3	4	1	2	3	4
Mines	3.2	5.0	5.0	0	1.9	4.8	5.0	2.2	2.8	4.7	3.6	0	1.2	5.0	5.0	5.0	3.4	3.2	5.0	5.0	5.0	5.0	5.0	5.0	6.6	7.4	7.5	6.7
Foods	25.8	26.1	24.0	16.2	16.1	22.8	21.4	22.8	22.5	20.0	16.4	22.0	22.0	21.7	16.6	15.4	20.0	20.0	15.0	19.6	15.2	15.2	15.0	18.1	15.0	15.0	15.0	13.3
Textiles	2.7	0	0	5.0	4.7	0	0	5.0	0.4	0	0	5.0	3.5	0	5.0	5.0	0.1	0	0	5.0	1.2	1.2	1.2	5.0	5.0	5.0	5.0	5.0
Paper	5.0	5.0	4.6	4.6	5.0	4.6	7.6	5.0	4.2	4.9	10.0	10.0	4.9	3.5	5.0	10.0	5.0	5.0	5.0	5.0	5.0	5.0	5.0	5.0	5.0	10.0	10.0	5.0
Chemicals	12.6	6.6	5.8	12.1	11.3	11.8	7.2	7.7	8.4	7.8	10.0	10.0	9.7	9.7	11.6	10.0	10.0	10.0	10.0	10.0	10.0	10.0	11.2	10.0	3.4	3.9	3.6	5.0
ORSGC*	10.0	11.2	12.1	10.0	12.2	11.2	13.4	12.3	13.7	15.2	15.3	10.0	19.9	18.3	19.9	20.0	22.6	18.1	20.0	22.6	11.3	11.2	11.2	10.0	10.0	10.0	3.6	10.0
Metals	0	0	0	5.0	0	4.8	5.0	1.7	0.9	1.5	0.9	5.0	5.0	5.0	5.0	5.0	9.0	9.2	5.0	5.0	10.0	11.3	10.0	5.0	10.0	10.0	5.0	5.0
Electricals	13.6	16.7	18.1	21.7	20.5	19.9	20.9	25.0	22.1	22.4	22.9	29.6	20.1	20.7	25.5	20.4	20.0	20.0	26.9	20.0	27.7	28.0	28.6	26.1	25.0	28.7	28.9	25.0
Transport	0	0	0	5.0	0	0.4	0	0	0	0	0	0	0	0	0	0	0	0	0	0	4.5	4.5	4.5	5.0	10.0	10.0	10.0	10.0
Retail	27.0	25.0	25.0	25.0	25.7	25.0	23.2	22.5	25.7	23.8	22.8	21.4	23.5	19.7	18.3	16.3	14.3	10.0	10.0	10.0	10.0	10.0	10.0	10.0	15.0	10.0	10.0	10.0

Note.—1 = Single-index model; 2 = multi-index model, covariance form; 3 = multi-index model, diagonal form; 4 = Markowitz E.V. model.
* Oil, rubber, stone, glass and clay.

TABLE 7

Comparison of efficient portfolios by industry grouping, 150-security universe

A. Number of securities in each industry

Industry No.	14.25%				16.0%				18.0%				20.0%				22.0%				24.0%				26.0%				28.0%			
	1	2	3	4	1	2	3	4	1	2	3	4	1	2	3	4	1	2	3	4	1	2	3	4	1	2	3	4	1	2	3	4
Mines 10	2	2	2	2	2	1	—	1	2	2	1	1	2	1	1	2	2	2	2	2	2	2	2	2	2	2	2	2	3	4	4	3
Foods 23	8	12	8	6	9	8	8	6	9	7	7	7	8	7	7	6	7	7	7	5	5	5	5	5	5	5	5	5	4	4	4	4
Textiles ...5	1	2	2	2	1	—	—	—	1	—	—	1	1	—	—	1	1	—	—	1	1	—	—	1	1	—	—	1	1	—	—	1
Paper 9	2	2	2	3	2	2	2	3	2	2	2	2	2	2	2	2	2	2	2	2	2	2	2	2	2	2	2	2	3	3	3	3
Chemicals 16	7	5	5	4	9	5	6	6	6	6	6	6	6	6	6	6	6	5	5	6	5	5	5	6	5	6	6	6	3	2	2	3
ORSGC* .16	5	5	5	4	4	5	5	4	4	4	4	3	5	5	6	5	7	8	8	7	8	8	9	7	6	6	6	6	2	2	2	2
Metals ...14	3	3	3	3	3	3	3	3	2	2	2	4	2	2	2	4	2	2	2	4	3	3	3	4	2	3	4	2	6	6	6	3
Electrical 26	5	6	6	6	7	7	7	7	7	8	8	8	9	9	9	7	8	8	9	7	9	9	9	9	11	11	11	9	10	11	11	10
Transport 14	2	2	2	3	2	2	2	2	2	3	3	3	3	3	3	2	2	2	2	1	1	1	1	2	3	3	3	3	4	4	4	5
Retail ...17	11	11	11	11	15	12	11	11	14	11	10	11	11	9	9	9	10	10	7	9	8	7	7	7	6	5	5	5	3	4	4	3
No. in portfolio....	46	49	46	43	52	47	46	44	51	45	46	45	44	43	44	43	44	46	43	42	42	42	43	44	41	42	43	43	41	41	41	41
No. at upper bound....	30	34	34	37	33	35	38	38	33	30	33	38	35	37	37	37	35	37	38	37	38	38	38	38	39	36	35	37	39	39	38	39
% at upper bound....	65.2	69.4	73.9	86.0	63.5	74.5	76.1	86.4	64.7	66.7	71.8	84.4	79.6	86.0	84.1	86.0	80.4	88.4	88.1	90.5	90.5	88.4	86.4	95.2	95.2	85.8	81.4	86.0	95.2	95.2	92.7	95.2

B. Percentage of portfolio invested

Industry	14.25%				16.0%				18.0%				20.0%				22.0%				24.0%				26.0%				28.0%			
	1	2	3	4	1	2	3	4	1	2	3	4	1	2	3	4	1	2	3	4	1	2	3	4	1	2	3	4	1	2	3	4
Mines	3.6	5.0	5.0	2.5	5.0	5.0	5.0	2.5	2.5	4.4	5.0	2.5	3.1	2.5	2.5	3.4	5.0	2.9	3.8	3.4	5.0	5.0	5.0	5.9	5.0	5.0	5.0	7.1	7.5	8.6	8.8	7.5
Foods	18.0	19.6	16.8	13.8	18.4	15.6	15.6	12.9	18.9	16.4	15.6	15.6	17.6	15.7	15.1	14.6	13.1	15.2	15.5	10.9	10.0	12.5	12.5	10.0	10.5	12.5	12.5	10.4	10.0	10.0	10.0	10.0
Textiles.	2.2	3.5	3.7	3.5	17.8	2.5	2.5	2.5	2.5	1.7	1.6	2.5	2.5	0	0	2.5	2.5	0.1	0	2.5	2.5	0	0	2.5	2.5	0	0	2.5	2.5	0	0	1.2
Paper.......	5.0	5.0	5.0	7.5	5.0	5.0	5.6	5.6	2.7	3.6	3.4	3.2	2.5	2.5	2.5	2.5	3.4	5.0	5.0	5.0	5.0	5.0	5.0	5.0	5.0	5.0	5.0	7.3	7.3	7.5	7.5	7.5
Chemicals...	13.6	10.4	9.2	11.3	12.0	10.2	10.8	11.8	13.9	14.6	14.0	13.6	16.3	15.0	15.0	15.0	12.5	12.5	12.5	15.0	14.6	12.5	12.5	15.0	12.5	11.9	11.7	13.7	6.2	5.0	5.0	7.5
ORSGC*	7.3	8.2	9.9	9.9	9.2	8.6	9.9	9.1	6.3	9.6	10.0	7.5	8.6	11.3	11.9	9.9	12.5	17.5	17.5	14.8	17.5	19.7	19.8	17.5	15.0	15.0	15.0	15.0	15.0	15.0	15.0	15.0
Metals	5.0	5.6	6.5	7.5	5.2	5.1	5.9	4.5	4.0	5.0	5.2	8.6	3.5	5.0	5.0	10.0	3.3	5.0	5.0	7.5	9.0	7.5	7.5	5.0	5.0	7.1	8.1	7.5	15.0	15.0	15.0	7.5
Electrical ...	9.2	10.4	11.4	11.8	12.4	13.1	14.1	16.2	15.0	14.4	14.5	17.8	16.4	18.2	18.2	16.5	17.8	17.8	18.2	17.5	18.9	19.3	19.0	22.1	25.0	24.0	23.4	22.5	25.0	27.5	27.1	25.0
Transport ...	0.8	5.0	5.0	7.5	2.4	5.0	5.0	5.0	2.7	5.4	6.2	5.0	2.5	7.5	7.5	5.0	2.5	4.8	5.0	2.5	2.5	2.5	2.6	3.0	7.0	7.0	6.8	7.5	11.3	10.0	10.0	11.3
Retail	35.2	27.5	27.5	27.5	35.8	25.4	25.2	27.5	31.6	24.9	23.4	23.5	27.0	22.4	21.5	20.6	24.7	19.3	17.5	20.3	18.6	16.4	16.1	15.6	15.0	12.5	12.5	11.2	7.5	8.9	9.2	7.5

Note.—1 = Single-index model; 2 = multi-index model, covariance form; 3 = multi-index model, diagonal form; 4 = Markowitz E.V. model.
* Oil, rubber, stone, glass, and clay.

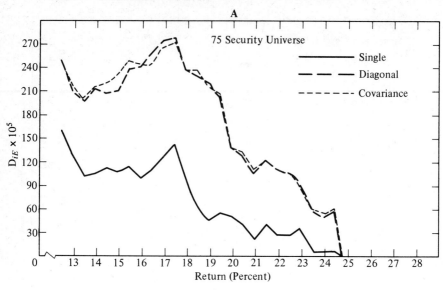

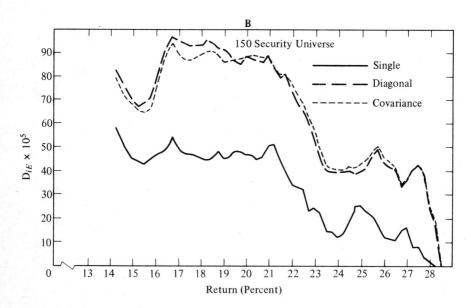

FIGURE 3

Goodness-of-fit test—efficient portfolios,
Markowitz versus index models

portfolios tend to be grouped together. This is due in part to the naïveté of the method by which expectations about security returns were formed. In addition, the ex post results tend to be grouped further from the efficient frontier when the security universe size is increased.

As noted from Figures 4 and 5, the portfolios selected by the diagonal multi-index model tend to dominate the random portfolios. The mutual funds,

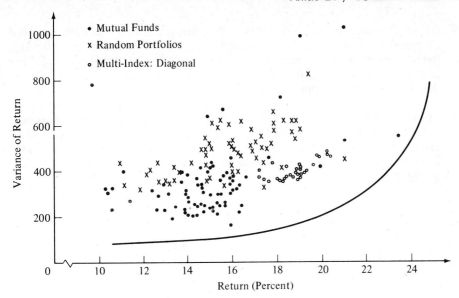

FIGURE 4

Comparison of ex post performance of 78 mutual
funds and 60 randomly selected portfolios with the
multi-index (diagonal form) model: 75-security universe.

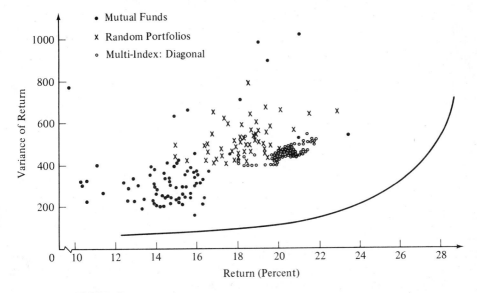

FIGURE 5

Comparison of ex post performance of 78 mutual funds
and 60 randomly selected portfolios with the multi-
index (diagonal form) model: 150-security universe.

however, are *not* dominated ex post by either the random- or model-selected
portfolios, but tend to be more conservative, accepting less risk and a lower

return. It should be pointed out that the mutual fund returns have not been corrected for management fees; hence they appear in a slightly less favorable light. Correction for the management fee (which is approximately 0.5–1.0 per cent per annum) would tend to shift the distribution of mutual funds in the direction of higher ex post return.

Figure 6 shows the ex post results for the multi-index model (diagonal form) for both security universe sizes. It is seen that the levels of both ex post risk and return have increased for the larger universe size. The average ex post return per portfolio has increased from 18.8 per cent to 20.3 per cent, while the average standard deviation of return has increased from 20.0 per cent to 21.4 per cent.

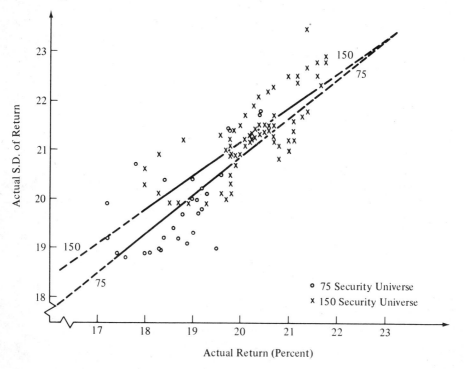

FIGURE 6

Ex-post performance, multi-index model
(diagonal form)

The lines drawn through the two groups of points represent risk-return trade-off relationships. The slopes of these lines define the increase in risk that must be accepted to increase return by 1 per cent.[15]

---

[15] A statistical comment should be made with regard to these risk-return relationships. It is possible to obtain a positive relationship between sample portfolio mean returns and variances of returns even though all of the samples were drawn from the same underlying density function $f(R_1, \ldots, R_N)$. This would result if the single underlying distribution was positively skewed, in which case the covariance of sample means and variances would equal the third population moment about the mean divided

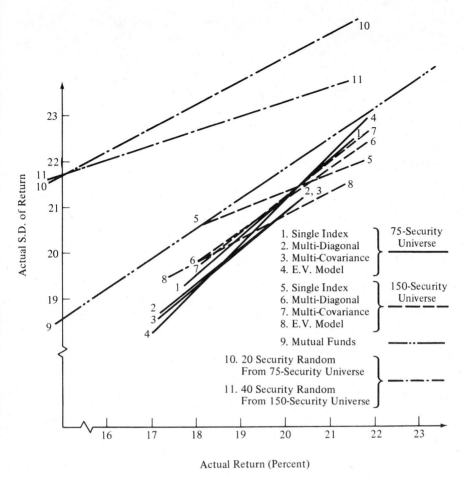

Actual S.D. of Return

Actual Return (Percent)

1. Single Index
2. Multi-Diagonal
3. Multi-Covariance
4. E.V. Model
} 75-Security Universe

5. Single Index
6. Multi-Diagonal
7. Multi-Covariance
8. E.V. Model
} 150-Security Universe

9. Mutual Funds

10. 20 Security Random From 75-Security Universe

11. 40 Security Random From 150-Security Universe

FIGURE 7

Comparison of ex post performance
risk-return trade-off relationships

Figure 7 shows the risk-return trade-off relationships for each of the models considered for each universe size. In addition, the diagram shows the relationships inherent in the ex post performance of the two groups of random port-

by the number of observations in each sample (i, e., $COV[m_1, m_2] = \mu_3/N$). If this were the case, then the slope coefficient observed would only be a function of the skewness of the underlying distribution.

Evidence from various researchers has indicated that security-yield distributions tend to be positively skewed. In this case, the above statistical problems would arise in attempting to correlate the mean annual returns of different securities with the variances of their annual returns. In our case, however, we are dealing with portfolio-yield distributions rather than security-yield distributions. Since we have an average of 23 securities in each of the 75-security universe portfolios and 43 securities in each of the 150-securities universe portfolios (see Table 5), the Central Limit Theorem should insure that the portfolio yield distributions are reasonably symmetric. Hence we can

folios and the group of mutual funds. The ordering of these lines indicates dominance relationships among the ex post performances of various methods of portfolio selection. However, while its lines appear distinct in the diagram, it is not obvious whether the observed orderings are statistically significant. This is due to the incomplete fulfilment by the ex post data of various statistical assumptions implicit to the linear regression model.

When statistical tests are made to determine the significance of the observed differences among the regression lines, the following conclusions can be drawn:

1. The ex post performance of the efficient portfolios selected by the models and portfolios selected by the models and the mutual funds clearly dominates that of the random portfolios.
2. The ex post performance of the efficient portfolios tends to dominate the performance of the mutual funds for higer levels of actual return (above 15 per cent).
3. The performances of the mutual funds with returns less than 15 per cent are not dominated by the efficient portfolios.
4. There is no strong evidence (at the 5 per cent level of significance) for the absolute dominance of any of the portfolio selection models over the total range of returns available. There is a tendency for the Markowitz model to perform most effectively over more restricted ranges, followed by the covariance form of the multi-index model.

V. CONCLUDING REMARKS

On the basis of empirical evidence provided in the study, the single-index model is seen to have more desirable ex ante properties than the more elaborate multi-index formulations. In particular, the ex ante efficient portfolios produced by the single-index model have lower expected risks than those of the multi-index formulations for equivalent levels of return, and the former are computationally less costly to obtain than are the latter. The ex post picture is not clear. The lack of clearer ex post differentiation is due in part to the naïveté of our security model and in part to the fact that only common stocks are included in the universes of securities considered. It thus does not appear worthwhile at this time to devote effort to developing an efficient computational algorithm for one of the multi-index models, if our primary interest is in common-stock universes. When broader universes of securities are considered (e.g., when various types of bonds and preferred stocks are included along with common stocks), it is expected that the richer representation of the variance-covariance matrix permitted by the multi-index models in comparison with the single-index model will become more relevant and more necessary. If such is the case, then, as shown in this paper, the diagonal form of the multi-index model would be the most useful. This model's ex ante and ex post performances are almost identical with the covariance form, while it has more desirable computational pro-

conclude that the positive sloping relationships obtained from the ex post performances of the various models are for the most part inherently due to differences in the portfolio-yield distributions $f_i(R_1, \ldots, R_N)$ and not statistical artifacts induced by the skewness of a single underlying distribution $f(R_1, \ldots, R_N)$.

perties. The computational requirements for this model are only slightly more complex than those of the Sharpe single-index model. (As with the single-index model, the diagonal multi-index model has a "diagonal" form covariance matrix.)

Despite the admittedly naïve security-evaluation model which provided the input data to the four models considered in this paper, it is encouraging that the ex post performance of the efficient portfolios selected by each of these models clearly dominated the ex post performance of randomly selected portfolios. The actual performance of the mutual funds during the ex post period also clearly dominates the performance of both sets of random portfolios.[16]

It is also interesting to note that the ex post performance of the efficient portfolios was not dominated by (and if anything was superior to) the ex post performance of the mutual funds. This result is particularly striking, since the mutual funds were fully managed during the 1958–64 evaluation periods, while efficient portfolios were unchanged after their initial selection. Furthermore, the mutual funds presumably employed a more sophisticated (and certainly a more expensive)method of security evaluation than the naïve procedure employed by us in generating efficient portfolios. Finally, the mutual funds were able to invest a much broader universe of common stocks than we employed in our analysis.

In the light of all these factors, the results we have obtained definitely suggest that formal models for selecting efficient portfolios must be considered as very relevant components in the development of improved normative procedures for investment management.

APPENDIX

MARKOWITZ MODEL

$$R_p = \boldsymbol{R}'\boldsymbol{X}.$$

$$E = E(R_p) = \boldsymbol{E}'\boldsymbol{X} = \sum_{i=1}^{N} X_i E(R_i).$$

$$V = VAR(R_p) = \boldsymbol{X}'\Sigma_N\boldsymbol{X} = \sum_{i=1}^{N} \sum_{j=1}^{N} X_i X_j \sigma_{ij}.$$

---

[16] In a recently published paper, Friend and Vickers stated: "We conclude, therefore, that there is still no evidence–either in our new or old tests, or in the tests so far carried out by others—that mutual fund performance is any better than that realizable by random or mechanical selection of stock issues" (Irwin Friend and Douglas Vickers, "Portfolio Selection and Investment Performance," *Journal of Finance,* XX, No. 3 [September, 1965], 412). The evidence that we have obtained in our study stands in clear disagreement with their conclusion, even though the time periods considered for the ex post evaluations are almost identical. Friend and Vickers did not use the actual investment returns achieved by mutual funds, as we did; furthermore, their random portfolio returns were based not upon random portfolios of actual common stocks, as were ours, but rather, upon random portfolios invested in composite industry indexes. Since mutual funds in fact reconstitute their portfolios when their managers feel that this will improve investment performance, and since neither mutual funds nor individual investors can in fact invest in composite industry indexes rather than individual securities, we feel that the methods of comparison employed by us are more relevant than those utilized by Friend and Vickers. *(cont.)*

SINGLE-INDEX MODEL

$$R_i = A_i + B_i I + C_i, \qquad i = 1, \dots, N.$$
$$I = A_{N+1} + C_{N+1}.$$

$$R_p = \sum_{i=1}^{N} X_i(A_i + B_i I + C_i)$$

$$= \sum_{i=1}^{N} X_i(A_i + C_i) + \left[\sum_{i=1}^{N} X_i B_i \right] I.$$

Let $X_{N+1} = \sum_{i=1}^{N} X_i B_i,$

$$\therefore R_p = \sum_{i=1}^{N} X_i(A_i + C_i) + X_{N+1}(A_{N+1} + C_{N+1})$$

$$= \sum_{i=1}^{N+1} X_i(A_i + C_i).$$

Let $\boldsymbol{R'} =$ the $N + 1$ security return vector

$$= (A_1 + C_1, A_2 + C_2, \dots, A_{N+1} + C_{N+1}),$$
$$\boldsymbol{X'} = (X_1, \dots, X_{N+1}),$$
$$\boldsymbol{E'} = (A_1, \dots, A_{N+1}), \qquad E(C_i) = 0.$$
$$\boldsymbol{R_p} = \boldsymbol{R'X},$$

$$E = E(R_p) = E(\boldsymbol{R'X}) = \boldsymbol{E'X} = \sum_{i=1}^{N+1} X_i A_i.$$
$$V = VAR(R_p)$$
$$= E[\boldsymbol{R'X} - E(\boldsymbol{R'X})]^2$$
$$= E\left[\sum_{i=1}^{N+1} X_i C_i \right]^2$$
$$= E\left[\sum_{i=1}^{N+1} X_i^2 C_i^2 \right], \qquad \text{as} \, E(C_i \cdot C'_i) = 0. \quad i \neq i, i = 1, \dots, N + 1$$
$$= \sum_{i=1}^{N+1} X_i^2 Q_i, \, \text{as} \, E(C_i^2) = Q_i$$
$$= \boldsymbol{X'}\Sigma_{N+1}\boldsymbol{X}.$$

In the same paper (p. 413), Friend and Vickers also state: "This paper, in addition, points up the dangers of using past measures of return and variance as a basis for portfolio selection, or of assuming that the procedures for portfolio selection outlined by Markowitz provide any clues to future investment performance." We wish to stress that the conclusions we have reached in this study strongly contradict this statement by Friend and Vickers.

Implicit covariance between returns R_i and $R_{i'}$

$$
\begin{aligned}
COV(R_i R_{i'}) &= E\{[R_i - E(R_i)][R_{i'} - E(R_{i'})]\} \\
&= E[(B_i C_{N+1} + C_i)(B_{i'} C_{N+1} + C_{i'})] \\
&= E[B_i B_{i'} C_{N+1}^2] + E[C_i C_{i'}], \quad \text{as } E(C_{N+1} \cdot C_i) = 0, \quad i = 1, \ldots, N \\
&= B_i^2 Q_{N+1} + Q_i, \quad \text{if } i = i' \\
&= B_i B_{i'} Q_{N+1}, \quad \text{if } i \neq i', \quad \text{as } E(C_i C_i') = 0.
\end{aligned}
$$

MULTI-INDEX MODEL—COVARIANCE FORM

$$
R_i = A_i + B_i J_j + C_i, \qquad \{i \mid i \epsilon N_j\},
$$

where $N_j = $ the set of securities in class j,

$$
\begin{aligned}
J_j &= A_{N+j} + C_{N+j}, \qquad j = 1, \ldots, M. \\
R_p &= \sum_{i=1}^{N} X_i R_i \\
&= \sum_{j=1}^{M} \left[\sum_{\{i \mid i \epsilon N_j\}} X_i (A_i + B_i J_j + C_i) \right] \\
&= \sum_{j=1}^{M} \sum_{\{i \mid i \epsilon N_j\}} X_i (A_i + C_i) + \sum_{j=1}^{M} \left[\sum_{\{i \mid i \epsilon N_j\}} X_i B_i \right] J_j.
\end{aligned}
$$

Let $X_{N+j} = \displaystyle\sum_{\{i \mid i \epsilon N_j\}} X_i B_i,$

$$
\therefore R_p = \sum_{j=1}^{M} \sum_{\{i \mid i \epsilon N_j\}} X_i (A_i + C_i) + \sum_{j=1}^{M} X_{N+j} J_j.
$$

Note that the first term on the right-hand side implies summation over all N securities.

$$
\begin{aligned}
\therefore R_p &= \sum_{i=1}^{N} X_i (A_i + C_i) + \sum_{j=1}^{M} X_{N+j} (A_{N+j} + C_{N+j}) \\
&= \sum_{i=1}^{N+M} X_i (A_i + C_i).
\end{aligned}
$$

Let $\boldsymbol{R}' = (A_1 + C_1, \ldots, A_N + C_N, A_{N+1} + C_{N+1}, \ldots, A_{N+M} + C_{N+M}),$
$\boldsymbol{X}' = (X_1, \ldots, X_N, X_{N+1}, \ldots, X_{N+M}),$
$\boldsymbol{E}' = (A_1, \ldots, A_N, A_{N+1}, \ldots, A_{N+M}),$

$$
\therefore E = E(R_p) = \boldsymbol{E}' \boldsymbol{X} = \sum_{i=1}^{N+M} X_i A_i, \quad \text{as } E(C_i) = 0, i = 1, \ldots, N + M.
$$

$$
\begin{aligned}
V &= VAR(R_p) \\
&= E[\boldsymbol{R}' \boldsymbol{X} - E(\boldsymbol{R}' \boldsymbol{X})]^2
\end{aligned}
$$

$$= E\left[\sum_{i=1}^{N+M} X_i C_i\right]^2$$

$$= E\left[\sum_{i=1}^{N} X_i^2 C_i^2\right] + E\left[\sum_{j=1}^{M}\sum_{j'=1}^{M} X_{N+j} X_{N+j'} C_{N+j} C_{N+j'}\right],$$

$$\text{as } E(C_{N+j} C_i) = 0, i = 1, \ldots, N, j = 1, \ldots, M$$

$$= \sum_{i=1}^{N} X_i^2 Q_i + \sum_{j=1}^{M}\sum_{j'=1}^{M} X_{N+j} X_{N+j'} \sigma_{jj'}$$

where $\sigma_{jj'}$ is the covariance between the levels of industry indexes J_j and $J_{j'}$. When $j = j'$, $\qquad \sigma_{jj'} = Q_{N+j}$.

$$\therefore V = X'_N \Sigma_N X_N + X'_M \Sigma_M X_M$$
$$= X' \Sigma_{N+M} X.$$

Implicit covariance between returns R_i and $R_{i'}$

$$COV(R_i R_{i'}) = E\{[R_i - E(R_i)][R_{i'} - E(R_{i'})]\}$$
$$= E[(B_i C_{N+j} + C_i)(B_{i'}' C_{N+j} + C_{i'}')]$$
$$= E[B_i B_{i'}' C_{N+j} C_{N+j}'] + E[C_i C_{i'}'], \qquad \text{as} \qquad E(C_{N+j}' C_i) = 0,$$
$$i = 1, \ldots, N, \qquad j = 1, \ldots, M.$$

$$COV(R_i R_{i'}) = B_i^2 Q_{N+j} + Q_i, \qquad \text{if} \qquad i = i'$$

$$= B_i B_{i'}' \sigma_{jj'}, \qquad \text{if } i \neq i', \qquad \text{as} \qquad E(C_i C_{i'}') = 0, \qquad i = 1, \ldots, N.$$

MULTI-INDEX MODEL—DIAGONAL FORM

In this model an additional index is used as a medium for expressing the relationship between the industry indexes.

$$J_j = A_{N+j} + B_{N+j} I + C_{N+j}, \qquad j = 1, \ldots, M,$$

where

$$I = A_{N+M+1} + C_{N+M+1}.$$

As in the covariance form of the multi-index model.

$$R_p = \sum_{i=1}^{N} X_i(A_i + C_i) + \sum_{j=1}^{M} X_{N+j} J_j.$$

Consider the second term on the right-hand side, and let $J_j = A_{N+j} + B_{N+j} I + C_{N+j}$,

$$\therefore \sum_{j=1}^{M} X_{N+j} J_j = \sum_{j=1}^{M} X_{N+j}(A_{N+j} + B_{N+j} I + C_{N+j})$$

$$= \sum_{j=1}^{M} X_{N+j} (A_{N+j} + C_{N+j}) + \left[\sum_{j=1}^{M} X_{N+j} B_{N+j} \right] I.$$

Let $X_{N+M+1} = \sum_{j=1}^{M} X_{N+j} B_{N+j},$

$$\therefore \sum_{j=1}^{M} X_{N+j} J_j = \sum_{j=1}^{M+1} X_{N+j} (A_{N+j} + C_{N+j}).$$

$$\therefore R_p = \sum_{i=1}^{N} X_i (A_i + C_i) + \sum_{j=1}^{M+1} X_{N+j} (A_{N+j} + C_{N+j}),$$

$$R_p = \sum_{i=1}^{N+M+1} X_i (A_i + C_i).$$

Let $\qquad \boldsymbol{R}' = (A_1 + C_1, \ldots, A_N + C_N, A_{N+1} + C_{N+1}, \ldots, A_{N+M+1}$
$$+ C_{N+M+1}),$$
$$\boldsymbol{X}' = (X_1, \ldots, X_N, X_{N+1}, \ldots, X_{N+M}, X_{N+M+1}),$$
$$\boldsymbol{E}' = (A_1, \ldots, A_N, A_{N+1}, \ldots, A_{N+M}, A_{N+M+1}).$$

$$\therefore E = E(R_p) = \boldsymbol{E}'\boldsymbol{X} = \sum_{i=1}^{N+M+1} X_i A_i, \text{ as } E(C_i) = 0, i = 1, \ldots, N+M+1.$$

$$V = VAR(R_p)$$
$$= E[\boldsymbol{R}'\boldsymbol{X} - E(\boldsymbol{R}'\boldsymbol{X})]^2$$

$$= E \left(\sum_{i=1}^{N+M+1} X_i C_i \right)^2$$

$$= \sum_{i=1}^{N+M+1} X_i^2 Q_i, \text{ as } E(C_i C_i) = 0, i \neq i' \ i = 1, \ldots, N+M+1,$$

$$= \boldsymbol{X}' \Sigma_{N+M+1} \boldsymbol{X}.$$

Implicit covariance between returns R_i and R_i'

$$COV(R_i R_i') = E\{[R_i - E(R_i)][R_i' - E(R_i')]\}$$
$$= E[B_i \{B_{N+j} C_{N+M+1} + C_{N+j}\} + C_i)(B_i' \{B_{N+j}' C_{N+M+1}$$
$$+ C_{N+j'}\} + C_i')]$$
$$= B_i B_i' B_{N+j} B_{N+j}' Q_{N+M+1}, \quad \text{if} \quad i \neq i', \quad \text{and} \quad j \neq j'.$$
$$= B_i B_i' B^2_{N+j} Q_{N+M+1} + B_i B_i' Q_{N+j}, \quad \text{for} \quad i \neq i', \quad \text{and} \quad j = j'.$$
$$= B_i^2 B^2_{N+j} Q_{N+M+1} + B_i^2 Q_{N+j} + Q_i, \quad \text{for} \quad i = i'. \quad \text{and} \quad j = j'.$$

C. Choosing an Efficient Portfolio

As discussed in the introduction, the choice between portfolio A, with high risk and variance, and portfolio B, with low risk and variance, can be fairly transparent. It is transparent if the return of A is so much higher than B that under almost any circumstances it returns more than portfolio B. Baumol presents this idea in a more precise and quantifiable fashion. In particular, he argues that portfolio A is preferable to portfolio B if the mean return of A less some number of standard deviations is greater than the mean return of B less the same number of standard deviations and A has a higher mean return: The number of standard deviations depends on the risk aversion of the individual. In other words, Baumol reformulates risk in terms of a lower limit.

25

An Expected Gain-Confidence Limit Criterion For Portfolio Selection

William J. Baumol*

This article is reprinted with permission from Management Science, *Vol. 10, No. 1 (October, 1963), pp. 174–182.*

A new efficiency criterion is proposed for the Markowtiz portfolio selection approach. It is shown that the use of standard deviation as a measure of risk in the original Markowitz analysis and elsewhere in economic theory is sometimes unreasonable. An investment with a relatively high standard deviation (σ) will be relatively safe if its expected value (E) is sufficiently high. For the net result may be a high expected floor, $E-K\sigma$, beneath the future value of the investment (where K is some constant). The revised efficient set is shown to eliminate paradoxical cases arising from the Markowitz calculation. It also simplifies the task left to the investor. For it yields a smaller efficient set (which is a subset of the Markowitz efficient set) and therefore reduces the range of alternatives from among which the investor must still select his portfolio. The proposed criterion may also be somewhat more easily understood by the nonprofessional.

[1] The author is grateful for their helpful comments to E. J. Kane, B. K. Malkiel and Harry Markowitz, to E. Zinbarg of the Prudential Insurance Company for first calling the problem to his attention, and to the National Science Foundation whose grant was so helpful in the completion of this paper.

The economic literature has frequently sought to explain[2] and set up norms[3] for the selection of portfolios of stocks, bonds and other securities in terms of two standard statistical concepts which are taken to indicate the value of the portfolio to the investor. These variables are the expected return, E, representing the most likely net yield of the investment, and the standard deviation of that return, σ, representing, in some sense, the degree of undependability of the yield. The greater the standard deviation of the return the more risky the portfolio is generally assumed to be and, consequently, the less desirable from the investor's viewpoint.[4] This premise has led to the argument that, given the value of E, any *ceteris paribus* increase in σ is undesirable.

More specifically, in his pathbreaking work on portfolio selection, Markowitz has on this basis defined a portfolio to be *efficient* if ". . . it is impossible to obtain a greater average [expected] return without incurring greater standard deviation; it is impossible to obtain smaller standard deviation without giving up return on the average." ([5] p. 22.) He goes on to imply that, in the absence of specific knowledge of the investor's preference structure one cannot say that one efficient portfolio is better than another. Only "judgment" can be "employed in choosing one of the set of all efficient portfolios" (*loc. cit.*)

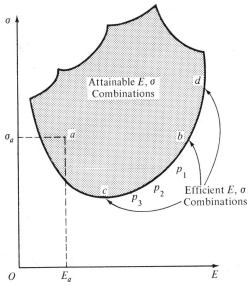

FIGURE 1

2   See, e. g., Tobin [8] p. 71 ff. and Lintner [2] pp. 254–261 and 264–266. Both of these authors use variance rather than standard deviation, but the latter concept is more convenient for present purposes.

3   See Markowitz [4] and [5].

4   Because of the observed rate of increases of sample variances with the size of sample, and on a number of other statistical and heuristic grounds, some of the students of the data have recently come to feel that many economic series, and particularly security yield and price statistics, are drawn from a sample of infinite variance. If this is so, the standard deviation of a sample, while necessarily finite, is not very meaningful and is certainly a poor measure of risk. This criticism is equally applicable to the Markowitz construction and to the alternative which is proposed in this paper. For a detailed

Markowitz uses a diagram similar to Figure 1 to illustrate the point.

Suppose some portfolio, A, offers an expected return E and a standard deviation σ_a. Then this portfolio can be represented by point a in the diagram. Assume all portfolios available with a fixed amount of money to be invested have been represented similarly and that the dots describing them constiture the shaded region in the figure. We see then that A is not an efficient portfolio because c which lies below and to the right of a offers a higher expected yield and a lower standard deviation. The locus of all efficient portfolios is the lower right-hand segment of the boundary of the shaded region because these points represent all lowest σ-highest E combinations. This locus is the heavy arc cbd.

Now I shall argue that this efficient set is very likely to contain portfolios which, many investors would agree, should be rejected out of hand. I shall suggest that the expected yield-standard deviation investment criterion [henceforth referred to as the (E, σ) criterion] does not accomplish quite what it is designed to do, and should be replaced by another closely related standard.[6] Fortunately, the criterion I shall propose calls for no extensive modifications of the arguments of the current literature. Indeed, all of the standard Markowitz analysis remains equally applicable, except that some unacceptable portfolios which do not satisfy the criterion have to be culled out of the Markowitz (E, σ) efficient set.

Before going further I must emphasize that my criticism of Markowitz's work is in no way meant to detract from his very significant contribution. Rather, I intend it to be regarded as an amendment which adds somewhat to the applicability of his approach, and which calls for no major change in his analytic and computational machinery.

1. UNACCEPTABLE (E, σ) EFFICIENT PORTFOLIOS

Consider two portfolios A and B which have the expected values and standard deviations shown in Table 1. Note that A and B may both be efficient—neither "dominates" the other because B has the better expected return but the poorer standard deviation. Yet we see that if we take $E + \sigma$ and $E - \sigma$ as a sort of upper and lower confidence limit, that is, if $E - \sigma$ is considered the (equally likely) lowest plausible outcome for each investment and $E + \sigma$ is the highest plausible outcome for each investment, it may well be questioned whether anyone in his right mind would ever choose portfolio A. For the worst anticipated outcome associated with B, $E_b - \sigma_b = 11$ is better than the highest plausible outcome for $A = E_a + \sigma_a = 10$!

What has gone wrong here? The difficulty is that the investor is not interested in σ per se. He would prefer the danger of coming out $10 short on a $100 expected return as against an $8 shortfall below a $50 expected return. That is,

---

discussion of the implications for economics of distributions with nonfinite variances by the leading investigator of the subject, see Mandelbrot [3].

5   Markowitz points out ([5] pp. 152–3) that the efficient locus, cbd, will, in fact, be made up of arcs of hyperbolas.

6   It should be mentioned that Markowitz does consider several other criteria. See, e. g., [5], pp. 15 and 187. However, he does not seem to think highly of them and does not pursue their analysis very deeply.

while *for a given value* of $E\sigma = \$10$ is always worse than $\sigma = \$8$ this need no longer be the case when the value of E varies.

TABLE 1

	A	B
E	8	15
σ	2	4
$E + \sigma$	10	19
$E - \sigma$	6	11

2. AN ALTERNATIVE EFFICIENT PORTFOLIO CRITERION

What alternative measure, then, should be employed to represent the investor's risk? One possibility is suggested by standard probability theory which tells us the following: If our basic random variable (the return on our investment) is normally distributed,[7] then there is only about a 16 percent probability that the realized return will ever fall below $E-\sigma$, there is only a 2 percent probability that it will ever be lower than $E-2\sigma$, no more than a 0.1 percent probability that it will fall below $E-3\sigma$, etc. Thus we may say that the risk involved in a given portfolio is represented by $E-K\sigma$ for some appropriately chosen value of K. Here $E-K\sigma$ may be considered the lower confidence limit for the investor's return.[8]

The situation may perhaps be made clearer with the aid of the following diagram (Figure 2). On the horizontal axis we represent the expected values, E, of various efficient portfolios and on the vertical axis we represent the values of $E+K\sigma$, E and $E-K\sigma$ corresponding to these same portfolios.[9] Here the 45° line, as usual, describes the identity $E \equiv E$ so by adding or subtracting $K\sigma$ from the 45° line we obtain, respectively, the $E + K\sigma$ and $E-K\sigma$ curves.

Now, even though these portfolios are all efficient on the Markowitz (E, σ) criterion it is easy to see that the investor may readily reject some of them. For example, he will generally prefer portfolio A to portfolio C because

[7] Markowitz ([5], p(51–52) does consider some alternative efficiency concepts and recognizes their relationship in the normal distribution case. However, (though his concept is not clearly defined) he seems to be in error in arguing that a portfolio is (E, σ) efficient *if* and only *if* it is what he calls "mean-probability of loss efficient." The "only if" is valid, but the "if" is not, if I interpret him correctly.

[8] For a somewhat similar approach to utility theory, see Quandt [6]. Cf. also Roy [7]. The reader may prefer a decision theoretic approach to the matter in which the value of K is determined in terms of the *cost* of an erroneous choice, but this would complicate matters excessively for present purposes. Note also that this confidence limit approach, by ignoring all contingencies more remote than K standard deviations from the expected value, implicitly assumes a rather simple minded investor utility function.

[9] That is, the (E, σ) efficient locus *cbd* in Figure 1 may be described by the equation $\sigma = f(E)$. The equation for the upper curve in Figure 2 is then $L = E + kf(E)$, where E is the abscissa of any point on the curve and L is its ordinate. A similar equation, equation (1) below, holds for the lower curve in the figure.

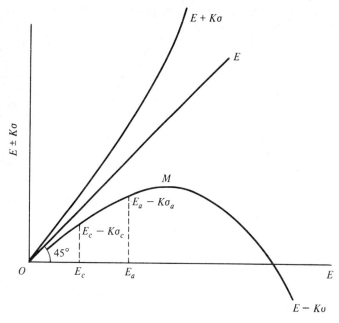

FIGURE 2

$E_a > E_c$ and $E_a - K\sigma_a > E_c - K\sigma_c$. That is, portfolio A offers both a higher expected return and a higher floor on earnings $(E - K\sigma)$. This is so because our $E - K\sigma$ curve has a positive slope between E_c and E_a —over this range of the curve portfolios with higher expected returns are also safer! Only to the right of point M, where the $E - K\sigma$ curve begins to turn down, do we get to portfolios which are efficient in terms of our alternative (E, L) criterion (where for brevity I write $L = E - K\sigma$ to designate the *lower* confidence limit). For only in this negatively sloping segment does the investor have to make up his mind in trading off greater expected return against reduced safety.[10]

3. RELATIONSHIP BETWEEN (E, L) EFFICIENCY AND $(E, \tilde{\sigma})$ EFFICIENCY

Let us see now how the set of (E, L) efficient portfolios is related to the Markowitz (E, σ) efficient set. It is easy to argue that *the former is a subset of the latter*.[11] That is, no portfolio can be (E, L) efficient without being (E, σ) efficient. For suppose portfolio A were not (E, σ) efficient because it is "(E, σ) dominated" by portfolio B, that is, because $E_b \geq E_a$ and $\sigma_b \leq \sigma_a$. Then we must have for our L figures $L_b \geq L_a$ since $L_b = E_b - K\sigma_b \geq E_b - K\sigma_a \geq E_a - K\sigma_a = L_a$.

---

[10]   Of course, I am defining a portfolio to be *(E, L)* efficient if there exists no other portfolio which offers a higher value of E without any reduction in L.

[11]   Indeed, one may helpfully describe the *(E, L)* investment procedure as follows: the investor chooses on the basis of E and σ, but from his calculated *(E, σ)* efficient points he excludes from consideration all portfolios dominated in the *(E, L)* plane, i.e., he excludes all portfolios like portfolio A in Table 1.

Hence (E, σ) inefficient portfolio A cannot be (E, L) efficient either, because as compared with B it involves both a lower expected return, E, and a smaller lower confidence limit, L.

We can go further and determine what portion of the (E, σ) efficient set cbd in Figure 1 is also (E, L) efficient. For this purpose let the equation of the curve cbd be represented by $\sigma = f(E)$. Then we have

$$L = E - K\sigma = E - Kf(E). \tag{1}$$

But we have seen that for (E, L) efficient portfolios, portfolios offering larger expected values of E must be characterized by less high values of L, i.e., such efficient portfolios are represented by the negatively sloping segment of the $L = E - K\sigma$ curve in Figure 2. Hence, (E, L) efficiency requires $dL/dE < 0$, so that, differentiating (1), we obtain

$$dL \,/\, dE = 1 - Kf'(E) < 0$$

or

$$f'(E) > 1 \,/\, K. \tag{2}$$

To see what this implies, in Figure 1 let P_1, P_2, and P_3 represent the points on the (E, σ) efficiency locus cbd where the curve has slope unity, $\frac{1}{2}$ and $\frac{1}{3}$ respectively. Then since as the diagram is drawn, the slope of arc P_1bd is greater than unity throughout, (2) tells us that it is the locus of the (E, L) efficient set for $K = 1$. Similarly, arc P_2bd is the (E, L) efficiency locus for $K = 2$, etc. Thus we see that, normally,[12] *the (E, L) efficient set will be a proper subset of the (E, σ) set*, i.e., there will be many Markowitz efficient portfolios which are not efficient on the proposed (E, L) criterion. However, it is to be noted that the Markowitz (E, σ) efficient set is the limit of the (E, L) efficient set as K becomes larger and larger, i.e., as K approaches infinity. In other words the more conservative our confidence limit criterion—the more standard deviations below our expected outcome which we consider plausible, the more closely our (E, L) efficient set will approximate the Markowitz (E, σ) set.

This result is really not difficult to explain. The basic objection to the Markowitz criterion is that in the expression $L = E - K\sigma$ an increasing E may more than counterbalance an increase in σ, so that despite greater variability in the return from the portfolio with the larger E, it may be considered relatively safe because the lower confidence limit L is relatively high. But the larger the value of K in $E - K\sigma$ the more of a rise in E it will take to compensate[13] for a given fall in σ. When K is very large the $K\sigma$ becomes the overwhelmingly important term in $L = E - K\sigma$ and so the behavior of L will be almost

---

[12] The only exception occurs if arc cbd in Figure 1 is of slope greater than, say, unity throughout its length, with a kink at point c. In that case the (E, L) efficiency locus for $K > 1$ will also be cbd so that it will coincide with the (E, σ) efficient set.

[13] For example, in the case shown in Table 1, with a sufficiently large K investment B would yield a smaller value of L than does investment A. The borderline occurs where $K = 3.5$, at which $L_a = L_b = 1$.

perfectly correlated with that of σ. Hence an (E, L) criterion will then not differ significantly from an (E, σ) criterion.[14]

4. THE (E,L) CRITERION IN APPLIED PORTFOLIO SELECTION

It can be claimed for the (E, L) criterion that it is a somewhat more easily interpreted measure of risk than is (E, σ). In fact, it is possible with the former to take explicit account of differing atitudes toward risk and to examine their consequences. Figure 3 shows a family of different $L = E - K\sigma$ curves for different

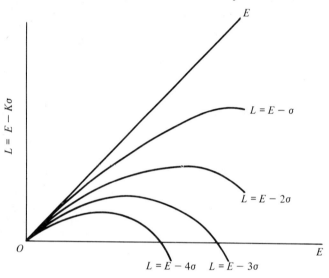

FIGURE 3

values of K, and indicates the alternative (E, L) combinations which are available with different selections of the value of K. The higher the value of K chosen by the investor, the more conservative he must be considered since he must then be taking into account far less likely possibilities of loss. As is to be expected, Figure 3 shows that an investor whose K is 4, and who must surely be considered extremely conservative on almost any standards, may plausibly be expected to accept relatively low values of E. For his is the lowest curve shown in the figure, and the points where it turns down and crosses the E axis are well to the left of the corresponding points on the other curves shown in the diagram. This relationship is mentioned merely to illustrate the ready interpretability of our diagram.[15]

---

[14] An alternative way of looking at the entire matter is to say that the choice of K depends on the investor's attitude toward risk, and that this psychological element determines the region within which one can expect to find points of tangency between the investor's indifference curves and the (E, σ) efficiency locus. The smaller the value of K the greater, *ceteris paribus*, will be the slopes of the indifference curves and, therefore, the further to the right on arc *cbd* must the possible tangency points lie.

[15] Another example of the interpretation which may be given Figure 3 follows from our observation that *(E, L)* efficient points must lie on negatively sloping segments of our

One disadvantage of the (E, L) appoach is that is imposes on the user of the analysis yet another explicit judgment which takes a form to which he is little habituated.[16] For, to employ the method, the investor must first express his risk preferences by choosing a specific value for K. But even where the distribution cannot be assumed to be approximately normal this requirement is not totally unreasonable, because, with the aid of Chebyshev's inequality[17] any value of K can be assigned an interpretation in terms of the likelihood that observations will fall beyond $E \pm K\sigma$.

The preceding remarks are somewhat peripheral to the basic question of application to which this section is addressed. The purpose of the Markowitz analysis may be described in general terms as a procedure whereby, from among the astronomical number[18] of candidate portfolios, the vast majority of possibilities can be ruled out because they are not worth the investor's consideration (they are not in the efficient set). The goal of the approach is to present the investor (or his counsellor) with a much smaller and more tractable list of alternatives from among which he must still make up his mind, perhaps partly with the help of the E, σ data used in the calcuation. The (E, L) procedure which has been proposed in this note, besides providing data which may be more meaningful intuitively and ruling out confusing paradoxical cases such as that

---

curves. We see in the diagram that, as K increases, the positively sloping (inefficient) segment of the curve grows shorter and shorter so that the efficient set grows more and more extensive, as we have already seen. In the limit, as K approaches infinity, the slope of the corresponding curve will be negative even at the origin, and every point on the curve will be *(E, L)* efficient.

16 Here it may be appropriate to remark briefly on Markowitz' apparent reluctance to use historical data as a basis for estimation of the E and σ values needed in his calculation. No doubt it is true that extrapolation of these values from past history is a risky business and when there is specific information indicating changes in the operations of a particular company or in the performance of the economy as a whole, this should clearly be taken into account. But, particularly because investment management is not habituated to translating its experience into the language of expected values, variances, and covariances required for the computation, there is surely much to be said for providing these measures routinely by more or less mechanical statistical calculation, *but then having them examined and modified by the professional investors before they are used in the portfolio selection procedure.*
For this purpose it is probably not desirable to proceed as Markowitz does in his illustrative calculations ([5] Chapter 2) by dealing with a time series of annual returns data. This implies that investors are typically concerned with a one year experience and perhaps even that portfolios will characteristically be held for one year periods. Since securities will be held for varying lengths of time, it may well be preferable to collect data for much shorter time periods (say monthly) and then select a sample of time periods for the calculation of mean variances and covariances with the aid of a table of random numbers. That is, if one employs data about a security extending over a 36 month period, this approach might, for example, have us dealing with the return from month 3 to month 12, the return from month 8 to month 24, etc. Such a random sample of possible investor experience in holding the security in question may well be helpful to a potential purchaser who does not know in advance for how long a period he will keep it in his portfolio.

17 Chebyshev's inequality (whose proof is quite elementary) states that for *any* distribution with given mean and variance, the probability of observations outside the range $E \pm K\sigma$ will be no greater than $1/K^2$! See, e.g., Feller [1], pp. 183–4.

18 I assume here that expenditures on any security can be made only in discrete amounts so that the number of possible portfolios will be finite.

described in Table 1, is helpful because it yields a smaller efficient set. This means that far fewer (and only more clearly relevant) alternatives are likely to be offered to the investor for comparison in the difficult and complex selection process. In effect, then, the proposed (E, L) approach may add efficacy to the pruning procedure which is the basic application of the Markowitz analysis.

REFERENCES

1. FELLER, WILLIAM, *An Introduction to Probability Theory and Its Applications,* Vol. I, Wiley, New York, 1950.
2. LINTNER, JOHN, "Dividends, Earnings, Leverage, Stock Prices and the Supply of Capital to Corporations," *Review of Economics and Statistics,* Vol. XLIV, August, 1962.
3. MANDELBROT, BENOIT, "The Variation of Certain Speculative Prices," I.B.M. Research Note NC-87, March 26, 1962.
4. MARKOWITZ, HARRY, "Portfolio Selection," *Journal of Finance,* Vol. VII, March, 1952.
5. _____, *Portfolio Selection,* Cowles Foundation Monograph 16, Wiley, New York, 1959.
6. QUANDT, RICHARD E., "A Contribution to the Pathology of Gambling," *Zeitschrift Für Nationalökonomie,* Vol. XX, 1960.
7. ROY, A. D., "Safety First and the Holding of Assets," *Econometrica,* Vol. 20, July, 1952.
8. TOBIN, JAMES, "Liquidity Preference as Behavior Toward Risk," *Review of Economic Studies,* Vol. XXV, February, 1958.

Tobin's article is one of the pioneering articles in portfolio selection. Of particular note is the discussion of the assumptions underlying a mean variability approach to portfolio selection and the discussion of the properties of the portfolios selected by particular utility functions.

26

Liquidity Preference as Behavior Towards Risk

James Tobin[1]

This article is reprinted with permission from The Review of Economics Studies, *Vol. XXV, No. 67 (February, 1958), pp. 65–87.*

One of the basic functional relationships in the Keynesian model of the economy is the liquidity preference schedule, an inverse relationship between the demand for cash balances and the rate of interest. This aggregative function must be derived from some assumptions regarding the behavior of the decision-making units of the economy, and those assumptions are the concern of this paper. Nearly two decades of drawing downward-sloping liquidity preference curves in textbooks and on classroom blackboards should not blind us to the basic implausibility of the behavior they describe. Why should anyone hold the non-interest bearing obligations of the government instead of its interest bearing obligations? The apparent irrationality of holding cash is the same, moreover, whether the interest rate is 6%, 3% or $\frac{1}{2}$ of 1%. What needs to be explained is not only the existence of a demand for cash when its yield is less than the yield on alternative assets but an inverse relationship between the aggregate demand for cash and the size of this differential in yields.[2]

[1] I am grateful to Challis Hall, Arthur Okun, Walter Salant, and Leroy Webrle for helpful comments on earlier drafts of this paper.
[2] " . . . in a world involving no transaction friction and no uncertainty, there would be no reason for a spread between the yield on any two assets, and hence there would be

1. TRANSACTIONS BALANCES AND INVESTMENT BALANCES

Two kinds of reasons for holding cash are usually distinguished: transactions reasons and investment reasons.

1.1 TRANSACTIONS BALANCES: SIZE AND COMPOSITION

No economic unit—firm or household or government—enjoys perfect synchronization between the seasonal patterns of its flow of receipts and its flow of expenditures. The discrepancies give rise to balances which accumulate temporarily, and are used up later in the year when expenditures catch up. Or, to put the same phenomenon the other way, the discrepancies give rise to the need for balances to meet seasonal excesses of expenditures over receipts. These balances are *transactions balances*. The aggregate requirement of the economy for such balances depends on the institutional arrangements that determine the degree of synchronization between individual receipts and expenditures. Given these institutions, the need for transactions balances is roughly proportionate to the aggregate volume of transactions.

The obvious importance of these institutional determinants of the demand for transactions balances has led to the general opinion that other possible determinants, including interest rates, are negligible.[3] This may be true of the size of transactions balances, but the composition of transactions balances is another matter. Cash is by no means the only asset in which transactions balances may be held. Many transactors have large enough balances so that holding part of them in earning assets, rather than in cash, is a relevant possibility. Even though these holdings are always for short periods, the interest earnings may be worth the cost and inconvenience of the financial transactions involved. Elsewhere[4] I have shown that, for such transactors, the proportion of cash in transactions balances varies inversely with the rate of interest; consequently this source of interest-elasticity in the demand for cash will not be further discussed here.

1.2 INVESTMENT BALANCES AND PORTFOLIO DECISIONS

no difference in the yield on money and on securities . . . in such a world securities themselves would circulate as money and be acceptable in transactions; demand bank deposits would bear interest, just as they often did in this country in the period of the twenties." Paul A. Samuelson, *Foundations of Economic Analysis* (Cambridge: Harvard University Press, 1947), p. 123. The section, pp. 122–124, from which the passage is quoted makes it clear that liquidity preference must be regarded as an explanation of the existence and level not of the interest rate but of the differential between the yield on money and the yields on other assets.

[3] The traditional theory of the velocity of money has, however, probably exaggerated the invariance of the institutions determining the extent of lack of synchronization between individual receipts and expenditures. It is no doubt true that such institutions as the degree of vertical integration of production and the periodicity of wage, salary, dividend, and tax payments are slow to change. But other relevant arrangements can be adjusted in response to money rates. For example, there is a good deal of flexibility in the promptness and regularity with which bills are rendered and settled.

[4] "The Interest Elasticity of the Transactions Demand for Cash," *Review of Economics and Statistics,* vol. 38 (August 1956), pp. 241–247.

In contrast to transactions balances, the investment balances of an economic unit are those that will survive all the expected seasonal excesses of cumulative expenditures over cumulative receipts during the year ahead. They are balances which will not have to be turned into cash within the year. Consequently the cost of financial transactions–converting other assets into cash and vice versa—does not operate to encourage the holding of investment balances in cash.[5] If cash is to have any part in the composition of investment balances, it must be because of expectations or fears of loss on other assets. It is here, in what Keynes called the speculative motives of investors, that the explanation of liquidity preference and of the interest-elasticity of the demand for cash has been sought.

The alternatives to cash considered, both in this paper and in prior discussions of the subject, in examining the speculative motive for holding cash are assets that differ from cash only in having a variable market yield. They are obligations to pay stated cash amounts at future dates, with no risk of default. They are, like cash, subject to changes in real value due to fluctuations in the price level. In a broader perspective, all these assets, including cash, are merely minor variants of the same species, a species we may call monetary assets —marketable, fixed in money value, free of default risk. The differences of members of this species from each other are negligible compared to their differences from the vast variety of other assets in which wealth may be invested: corporate stocks, real estate, unincorporated business and professional practice, etc. The theory of liquidity preference does not concern the choices investors make between the whole species of monetary assets, on the one hand, and other broad classes of assets, on the other.[6] Those choices are the concern of other branches of economic theory, in particular theories of investment and of consumption. Liquidity preference theory takes as given the choices determining how much wealth is to be invested in monetary assets and concerns itself with the allocation of these amounts among cash and alternative monetary assets.

Why should any investment balances be held in cash, in preference to other monetary assets? We shall distinguish two possible sources of liquidity preference, while recognizing that they are not mutually exclusive. The first is inelasticity of expectations of future interest rates. The second is uncertainty about the future of interest rates. These two sources of liquidity preference will be examined in turn.

2. INELASTICITY OF INTEREST RATE EXPECTATIONS

2.1 SOME SIMPLIFYING ASSUMPTIONS

To simplify the problem, assume that there is only one monetary asset other than cash, namely consols. The current yield of consols is r per "year".

---

[5] Costs of financial transactions have the effect of deterring changes from the existing portfolio, whatever its composition; they may thus operate against the holding of cash as easily as for it. Because of these costs, the *status quo* may be optimal even when a different composition of assets would be preferred if the investor were starting over again.

[6] For an attempt by the author to apply to this wider choice some of the same theoretical

$1 invested in consols today will purchase an income of $r per "year" in perpetuity. The yield of cash is assumed to be zero; however, this is not essential, as it is the current and expected differentials of consols over cash that matter. An investor with a given total balance must decide what proportion of this balance to hold in cash, A_1, and what proportion in consols, A_2. This decision is assumed to fix the portfolio for a full "year."[7]

2.2 FIXED EXPECTATIONS OF FUTURE RATE

At the end of the year, the investor expects the rate on consols to be r_e. This expectation is assumed, for the present, to be held with certainty and to be independent of the current rate r. The investor may therefore expect with certainty that every dollar invested in consols today will earn over the year ahead not only the interest $r, but also a capital gain or loss g:

$$g = \frac{r}{r_e} - 1 \tag{2.1}$$

For this investor, the division of his balance into proportions A_1 of cash and A_2 of consols is a simple all-or-nothing choice. If the current rate is such that $r + g$ is greater than zero, then he will put everything in consols. But if $r + g$ is less than zero, he will put everything in cash. These conditions can be expressed in terms of a critical level of the current rate r_c, where:

$$r_c = \frac{r_e}{1 + r_e} \tag{2.2}$$

At current rates above r_c, everything goes into consols; but for r less than r_c, everything goes into cash.

2.3 STICKY AND CERTAIN INTEREST RATE EXPECTATIONS

So far the investor's expected interest-rate r_c has been assumed to be completely independent of the current rate r. This assumption can be modified

---

tools that are here used to analyze choices among the narrow class of monetary assets, see "A Dynamic Aggregative Model", *Journal of Political Economy*, vol. 63 (April 1955), pp. 103–115.

[7] As noted above, it is the costs of financial transactions that impart inertia to portfolio composition. Every reconsideration of the portfolio involves the investor in expenditure of time and effort as well as of money. The frequency with which it is worthwhile to review the portfolio will obviously vary with the investor and will depend on the size of his portfolio and on his situation with respect to costs of obtaining information and engaging in financial transactions. Thus the relevant "year" ahead for which portfolio decisions are made is not the same for all investors. Moreover, even if a decision is made with a view to fixing a portfolio for a given period of time, a portfolio is never so irrevocably frozen that there are no conceivable events during the period which would induce the investor to reconsider. The fact that this possibility is always open must influence the investor's decision. The fiction of a fixed investment period used in this paper is, therefore, not a wholly satisfactory way of taking account of the inertia in portfolio composition due to the costs of transactions and of decision making.

so long as some independence of the expected rate from the current rate is maintained. In Figure 2.1, for example, r_e is shown as a function of r, namely $\varphi(r)$. Correspondingly $r_e/(1+r_e)$ is a function of r. As shown in the figure, this function $\varphi/(1+\varphi)$ has only one intersection with the 45° line, and at this intersection its slope $\varphi'/(1+\varphi)^2$ is less than one. If these conditions are met, the intersection determines a critical rate r_c such that if r exceeds r_c the investor holds no cash, while if r is less than r_c he holds no consols.

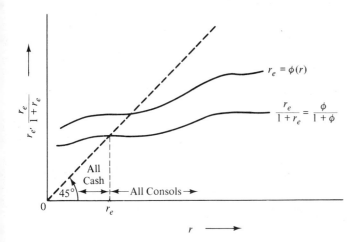

FIGURE 2.1

Stickiness in the relation between expected and current interest rate.

2.4 DIFFERENCES OF OPINION AND THE AGGREGATE DEMAND FOR CASH

According to this model, the relationship of the individual's investment demand for cash to the current rate of interest would be the discontinuous step function shown by the heavy vertical lines $LMNW$ in Figure 2.2. How then do we get the familiar Keynesian liquidity preference function, a smooth, continuous inverse relationship between the demand for cash and the rate of interest? For the economy as a whole, such a relationship can be derived from individual behaviour of the sort depicted in Figure 2.2 by assuming that individual investors differ in their critical rates r_c. Such an aggregate relationship is shown in Figure 2.3.

At actual rates above the maximum of individual critical rates the aggregate demand for cash is zero, while at rates below the minimum critical rate it is equal to the total investment balances for the whole economy. Between these two extremes the demand for cash varies inversely with the rate of interest r. Such a relationship is shown as $LMN\sum W$ in Figure 2.3. The demand for cash at r is the total of investment balances controlled by investors whose critical rates r_c exceed r. Strictly speaking, the curve is a step function, but, if the number of investors is large, it can be approximated by a smooth curve. Its shape depends on the distribution of dollars of investment balances by the

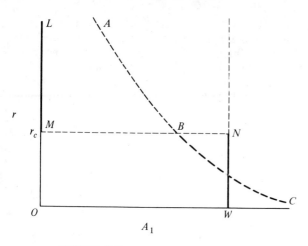

FIGURE 2.2

Individual demand for cash assuming
certain but inelastic rate expectations

critical rate of the investor controlling them; the shape of the curve in Figure
2.3 follows from a unimodal distribution.

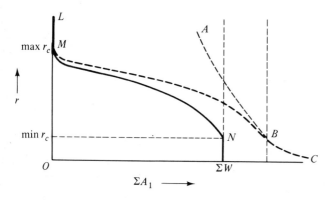

FIGURE 2.3

Aggregate demand for cash assuming
differences among individuals in interest
rate expections.

2.5 CAPITAL GAINS OR LOSSES AND OPEN MARKET OPERATIONS

In the foregoing analysis the size of investment balances has been taken as
independent of the current rate on consols r. This is not the case if there are
already consols outstanding. Their value will depend inversely on the current
rate of interest. Depending on the relation of the current rate to the previously
fixed coupon on consols, owners of consols will receive capital gains or losses.
Thus the investment balances of an individual owner of consols would not be
constant at W but would depend on r in a manner illustrated by the curve

ABC in Figure 2.2.[8] Similarly, the investment balances for the whole economy would follow a curve like *ABC* in Figure 2.3, instead of being constant at $\sum W$. The demand for cash would then be described by *LMBC* in both figures. Correspondingly the demand for consols at any interest rate would be described by the horizontal distance between *LMBC* and *ABC*. The value of consols goes to infinity as the rate of interest approaches zero; for this reason, the curve *BC* may never reach the horizontal axis. The size of investment balances would be bounded if the monetary assets other than cash consisted of bonds with definite maturities rather than consols.

According to this theory, a curve like *LMBC* depicts the terms on which a central bank can engage in open-market operations, given the claims for future payments outstanding in the form of bonds or consols. The curve tells what the quantity of cash must be in order for the central bank to establish a particular interest rate. However, the curve will be shifted by open-market operations themselves, since they will change the volume of outstanding bonds or consols. For example, to establish the rate at or below *min* r_c, the central bank would have to buy all outstanding bonds or consols. The size of the community's investment balances would then be independent of the rate of interest; it would be represented by a vertical line through, or to the right of, *B*, rather than the curve *ABC*. Thus the new relation between cash and interest would be a curve lying above *LMB*, of the same general contour as $LMN\sum W$.

2.6 KEYNESIAN THEORY AND ITS CRITICS

I believe the theory of liquidity preference I have just presented is essentially the original Keynesian explanation. The *General Theory* suggests a number of possible theoretical explanations, supported and enriched by the experience and insight of the author. But the explanation to which Keynes gave the greatest emphasis is the notion of a "normal" long-term rate, to which investors expect the rate of interest to return. When he refers to uncertainty in the market, he appears to mean disagreement among investors concerning the future of the rate rather than subjective doubt in the mind of an individual investor.[9] Thus Kaldor's correction of Keynes is more verbal than substantive when he says, "It is . . . not so much the *uncertainty* concerning future interest rates as the *inelasticity* of interest expectations which is responsible for Mr. Keynes' 'liquidity preference function,' . . ."[10]

[8] The size of their investment balances, held in cash and consols, may not vary by the full amount of these changes in wealth; some part of the changes may be reflected in holdings of assets other than monetary assets. But presumably the size of investment balances will reflect at least in part these capital gains and losses.

[9] J. M. Keynes, *The General Theory of Employment, Interest, and Money* (New York: Harcourt Brace, 1936), Chapters 13 and 15, especially pp. 168–172 and 201–203. One quotation from p. 172 will illustrate the point: " . . . It is interesting that the stability of the system and its sensitiveness to changes in the quantity of money should be so dependent on the existence of a *variety* of opinion about what is uncertain. Best of all that we should know the future. But if not, then, if we are to control the activity of the economic system by changing the quantity of money, it is important that opinions should differ."

[10] N. Kaldor, "Speculation and Economic Stability," *Review of Economic Studies,* vol. 7 (1939), p. 15.

Keynes' use of this explanation of liquidity preference as a part of his theory of under employment equilibrium was the target of important criticism by Leontief and Fellner. Leontief argued that liquidity preference must necessarily be zero *in equilibrium,* regardless of the rate of interest. Divergence between the current and expected interest rate is bound to vanish as investors learn from experience; no matter how an interest rate may be, it can be accepted as "normal" if it persists long enough. This criticism was a part of Leontief's general methodological criticism of Keynes, that unemployment was not a feature of equilibrium, subject to analysis by tools of static theory, but a phenomenon of disequilibrium requiring analysis by dynamic theory.[11] Fellner makes a similar criticism of the logical appropriatenesss of Keynes' explanation of liquidity preference for the purposes of his theory of underemployment equilibrium. Why, he asks, are interest rates the only variables to which inelastic expectations attach? Why don't wealth owners and others regard pre-depression price levels as "normal" levels to which prices will return? If they did, consumption and investment demand would respond to reductions in money wages and prices, no matter how strong and how elastic the liquidity preference of investors.[12]

These criticisms raise the question whether it is possible to dispense with the assumption of stickiness in interest rate expectations without losing the implication that Keynesian theory drew from it. Can the inverse relationship of demand for cash to the rate of interest be based on a different set of assumptions about the behavior of individual investors? This question is the subject of the next part of the paper.

3. UNCERTAINTY, RISK AVERSION, AND LIQUIDITY PREFERENCE

3.1 THE LOCUS OF OPPORTUNITY FOR RISK AND EXPECTED RETURN

Suppose that an investor is not certain of the future rate of interest on consols; investment in consols then involves a risk of capital gain or loss. The higher the proportion of his investment balance that he holds in consols, the more risk the investor assumes. At the same time, increasing the proportion in consols also increases his expected return. In the upper half of Figure 3.1, the vertical axis represents expected return and the horizontal axis risk. A line such as OC_1 pictures the fact that the investor can expect more return if he assumes more risk. In the lower half of Figure 3.1, the left-hand vertical axis measures the proportion invested in consols. A line like OB shows risk as proportional to the share of the total balance held in consols.

The concepts of expected return and risk must be given more precision.

The individual investor of the previous section was assumed to have, for any current rate of interest, a definite expectation of the capital gain or loss g [defined in expression (2.1) above] he would obtain by investing one dollar in

[11] W. Leontief, "Postulates: Keynes' General Theory and the Classicists", Chapter XIX in S. Harris, editor, *The New Economics* (New York: Knopf, 1947), pp. 232–242. Section 6, pp. 238–239, contains the specific criticism of Keynes' liquidity preference theory.

[12] W. Fellner, *Monetary Policies and Full Employment* (Berkeley: University of California Press, 1946), p. 149.

consols. Now he will be assumed instetad to be uncertain about g but to base his actions on his estimate of its probability distribution. This probability distribution, it will be assumed, has an expected value of zero and is independent of the level of r, the current rate on consols. Thus the investor considers a doubling of the rate just as likely when rate is 5% as when it is 2%, and a halving of the rate just as likely when it is 1% as when it is 6%.

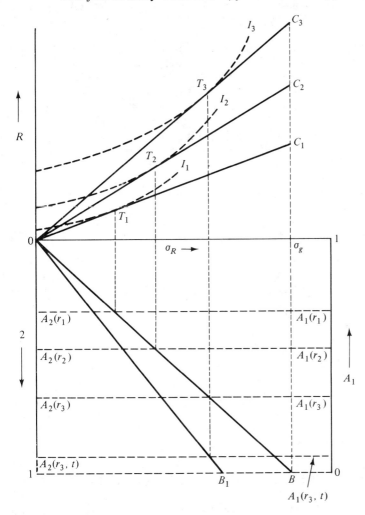

FIGURE 3.1

A portfolio consists of a proportion A_1 of cash and A_2 of consols, where A_1 and A_2 add up to 1. We shall assume that A_1 and A_2 do not depend on the absolute size of the initial investment balance in dollars. Negative values of A_1 and A_2 are excluded by definition; only the government and the banking system can issue cash and government consols. The return on a portfolio R is:

$$R = A_2(r + g) \qquad 0 \le A_2 \le 1. \qquad (3.1)$$

Since g is a random variable with expected value zero, the expected return on the portfolio is:

$$E(R) = \mu_R = A_2 r. \qquad (3.2)$$

The risk attached to a portfolio is to be measured by the standard deviation of R, σ_R. The standard deviation is a measure of the dispersion of possible returns around the mean value μ_R. A high standard deviation means, speaking roughly, high probability of large deviations from μ_R, both positive and negative. A low standard deviation means low probability of large deviations from μ_R; in the extreme case, a zero standard deviation would indicate certainty of receiving the return μ_R. Thus a high-σ_R portfolio offers the investor the chance of large capital gains at the price of equivalent chances of large capital losses. A low-σ_R portfolio protects the investor from capital loss, and likewise gives him little prospect if unusual gains. Although it is intuitively clear that the risk of a portfolio is to be identified with the dispersion of possible returns, the standard deviation is neither the sole measure of dispersion nor the obviously most relevant measure. The case for the standard deviation will be further discussed in section 3.3. below.

The standard deviation of R depends on the standard deviation of g, σ_g, and on the amount invested in consols:

$$\sigma_R = A_2 \sigma_g \qquad 0 \le A_2 \le 1. \qquad (3.3)$$

Thus the proportion the investor holds in consols A_2 determines both his expected return μ_R and his risk σ_R. The terms on which the investor can obtain greater expected return at the expense of assuming more risk can be derived from (3.2) and (3.3):

$$\mu_R = \frac{r}{\sigma_g} \sigma_R \qquad 0 \le \sigma_R \le \sigma_g. \qquad (3.4)$$

Such an *opportunity locus* is shown as line OC_1 (for $r = r_1$) in Figure 3.1. The slope of the line is r_1/σ_g. For a higher interest rate r_2, the opportunity locus would be OC_2; and for r_3, a still higher rate, it would be OC_3. The relationship (3.3) between risk and investment in consols is shown as line OB in the lower half of the figure. Cash holding A_1 ($= 1 - A_2$) can also be read off the diagram on the right-hand vertical axis.

3.2 LOCI OF INDIFFERENCE BETWEEN COMBINATIONS OF RISK AND EXPECTED RETURN

The investor is assumed to have preferences between expected return μ_R and risk σ_R that can be represented by a field of indifference curves. The *investor is indifferent between all pairs* (μ_R, σ_R) that *lie on a curve such as I_1 in Figure 3.1* Points on I_2 are preferred to those on I_1; for given risk, an investor always prefers a greater to a smaller expectation of return. Conceivably, for some investors, *risk-lovers,* these indifference curves have negative slopes. Such individuals are willing to accept lower expected return in order to have the chance of unusually high capital gains afforded by high values of σ_R. *Risk-averters,* on the other hand, will not be satisfied to accept more risk unless they can also expect greater expected return. Their indifference curves will be positively sloped. Two kinds of risk-averters need to be distinguished. The first type, who may be called *diversifiers* for reasons that will become clear below, have indifference curves that are concave upward, like those in Figure 3.1. The second type, who may be called *plungers* have indifference curves that are upward sloping, but either linear or convex upward.

3.3 INDIFFERENCE CURVES AS LOCI OF CONSTANT EXPECTED UTILITY OF WEALTH

The reader who is willing to accept the indifference fields that have just been introduced into the analysis may skip to section 3.4 without losing the main thread of the argument. But these indifference curves need some explanation and defence. Indifference curves between μ_R and σ_R do not neccessarily exist. It is a simplification to assume that the investor chooses among the alternative probability distributions of R available to him on the basis of only two parameters of those distributions. Even if this simplification is accepted, the mean and standard deviation may not be the pair of parameters that concern the investor.

3.3. 1. One justification for the use of indifference curves between μ_R and σ_R would be that the investor evaluates the future of consols only in terms of some two-parameter family of probability distributions of g. For example, the investor might think in terms of a range of equally likely gains or losses, centered on zero. Or he might think in terms that can be approximated by a normal distribution. Whatever two-parameter family is assumed—uniform, normal, or some other—the whole probability distribution is determined as soon as the mean and standard deviation are specified. Hence the investor's choice among probability distributions can be analyzed by $\mu_R - \sigma_R$ indifference curves; any other pair of independent parameters could serve equally well.

If the investor's probability distributions are assumed to belong to some two-parameter family, the shape of his indifference curves can be inferred from the general characteristics of his utility-of-return function. This function will be assumed to relate utility to R, the percentage growth in the investment balance by the end of the period. This way of formulating the utility function makes the investor's indifference map, and therefore his choices of proportions cash and consols, independent of the absolute amount of his initial balance.

On certain postulates, it can be shown that an individual's choice among probability distributions can be described as the maximization of the expected value of a utility function.[13] The ranking of probability distributions with respect to the expected value of utility will not be changed if the scale on which utility is measured is altered either by the addition of a constant or by multiplication by

[13] See Von Neumann, J. and Morgenstern, O., *Theory of Games and Economic Behavior*, 3rd Edition (Princeton: Princeton University Press, 1953), pp. 15–30, pp. 617–632; Herstein, I. N. and Milnor, J., "An Axiomatic Approach to Measurable Utility", *Econometrica*, vol. 23 (April 1953), pp. 291–297; Marschak, J., "Rational Behavior, Uncertain Prospects, and Measurable Utility", *Econometrica*, vol. 18 (April 1950), pp. 111–141; Friedman, M. and Savage, L. J., "The Utility Analysis of Choices Involving Risk", *Journal of Political Economy*, vol. 56 (August 1948), pp. 279–304, and "The Expected Utility Hypothesis and the Measurability of Utility", *Journal of Political Economy*, vol. 60 (December 1952), pp. 463–474. For a treatment which also provides an axiomatic basis for the subjective probability estimates here assumed, see Savage, L. J., *The Foundations of Statistics* (New York: Wiley, 1954).

a positive constant. Consequently we are free to choose arbitrarily the zero and unit of measurement of the utility function $U(R)$ as follows:

$U(0) = 0;\ U(-1) = -1$

Suppose that the probability distribution of R can be described by a two-parameter density function $f(R;\ \mu_R, \sigma_R)$. Then the expected value of utility is:

$$E[U(R)] = \int_{-\infty}^{\infty} U(R)f(R;\ \mu_R, \sigma_R)\ dR. \tag{3.5}$$

$$\text{Let } z = \frac{R - \mu_R}{\sigma_R}.$$

$$E[U(R)] = E(\mu_R, \sigma_R) = \int_{-\infty}^{\infty} U(\mu_R + \sigma_R z)f(z;\ 0, 1)\ dz. \tag{3.6}$$

An indifference curve is a locus of points (μ_R, σ_R) along which expected utility is constant. We may find the slope of such a locus by differentiating (3.6) with respect to σ_R:

$$0 = \int_{-\infty}^{\infty} U'(\mu_R + \sigma_R z)\left[\frac{d\mu_R}{d\sigma_R} + z\right] f(z;\ 0, 1)\ dz.$$

$$\frac{d\mu_R}{d\sigma_R} = -\frac{\displaystyle\int_{-\infty}^{\infty} zU'(R)f(z;\ 0, 1)\ dz}{\displaystyle\int_{-\infty}^{\infty} U'(R)f(z;\ 0, 1)\ dz} \tag{3.7}$$

$U'(R)$, the marginal utility of return, is assumed to be everywhere non-negative. If it is also a decreasing function of R then the slope of the indifference locus must be positive; an investor with such a utility function is a risk-averter. If it is an increasing function of R, the slope will be negative; this kind of utility function characterizes a risk-lover.

Similarly, the curvature of the indifference loci is related to the shape of the utility function. Suppose that (μ_R, σ_R) and (μ'_R, σ'_R) are on the same indifference locus, so that $E(\mu_R, \sigma_R) = E(\mu_R, \sigma_R)$. Is $[(\mu_R + \mu'_R)/2, (\sigma_R + \sigma'_R)/2]$ on the same locus, or on a higher or a lower one? In the case of declining marginal utility we know that for every z:

$$\tfrac{1}{2}U(\mu_R + \sigma_R z) + \tfrac{1}{2}U(\mu'_R + \sigma'_R z)$$
$$< U\left(\frac{\mu_R + \mu'_R}{2} + \frac{\sigma_R + \sigma'_R}{2}\, z\right)$$

Consequently $E[(\mu_R + \mu'_R)/2, (\sigma_R + \sigma'_R)/2]$ is greater than $E(\mu_R, \sigma_R)$ or $E(\mu'_R, \sigma'_R)$, and $[(\mu_R + \mu'_R)/2, (\sigma_R + \sigma'_R)/2]$, which lies on a line between (μ_R, σ_R) and (μ'_R, σ'_R), is in a higher locus than those points. Thus it is shown that a risk-averter's indifference curve is necessarily concave upwards, provided it is derived in this manner from a two-parameter family of probability distributions and declining marginal utility of return. All risk-averters are diversifiers; plungers do not exist. The same kind of argument shows that a risk-lower's indifference curve is concave downwards.

3.3.2. In the absence of restrictions on the subjective probability distributions of the investor, the parameters of the distribution relevant to his choice can be sought in parametric restrictions on his utility-of-return function. Two parameters of the utility function are determined by the choice of the utility scale. If specification of the utility function requires no additional parameters, one parameter of the probability distribution summarizes all the information relevant for the investor's choice. For example, if the utility function is linear [$U(R) = R$], then the expected value of utility is simply the expected value of R, and maximizing expected utility leads to the same behaviour as maximizing return in a world of certainty. If, however, one additional parameter is needed to specify the utility function, then two parameters of the probability distribution will be relevant to the choice; and so on. Which parameters of the distribution are relevant depends on the form of the utility function.

Focus on the mean and standard deviation of return can be justified on the assumptions that the utility function is quadratic. Following our conventions as to utility scale, the quadratic function would be:

$$U(R) = (1 + b)R + bR^2. \tag{3.8}$$

Here $0 < b < 1$ for a risk-lover, and $-1 < b < 0$ for a risk-averter. However (3.8) cannot describe the utility function for the whole range of R, because marginal utility cannot be negative. The function given in (3.8) can apply only for:

$$(1 + b) + 2bR \geq 0;$$

that is, for:

$$R \geq - \left(\frac{1+b}{2b} \right) (b > 0) \quad \text{(Risk-lover)}$$

$$R \leq - \left(\frac{1+b}{2b} \right) (b < 0) \quad \text{(Risk-averter).} \tag{3.9}$$

In order to use (3.8), therefore, we must exclude from the range of possibility values of R outside the limits (3.9). At the maximum investment in consols ($A_2 = 1$), $R = r + g$. A risk-averter must be assumed therefore, to restrict the range of capital gains g to which he attaches non-zero probability so that, for the highest rate of interest r to be considered:

$$r + g \leq - \left(\frac{1+b}{2b} \right). \tag{3.10}$$

The corresponding limitation for a risk-lover is that, for the lowest interest rate r to be considered:

$$r + g \geq - \left(\frac{1+b}{2b} \right). \tag{3.11}$$

Given the utility function (3.8), we can investigate the slope and curvature of the indifference curves it implies. The probability density function for R, f

(R), is restricted by the limit (3.10) or (3.11); but otherwise no restriction on its shape is assumed.

$$E[U(R)] = \int_{-\infty}^{\infty} U(R)f(R)dR = (1 + b)\mu_R + b(\sigma_R^2 + \mu_R^2). \tag{3.12}$$

Holding $E[U(R)]$ constant and differentiating with respect to or σ_R obtain the slope of an indifference curve, we have:

$$\frac{d\mu_R}{d\sigma_R} = \frac{\sigma_R}{-\left(\dfrac{1+b}{2b}\right) - \mu_R}. \tag{3.13}$$

For risk-averter, $-(1 + b)/2b$ is positive and is the upper limit for R, according to (3.9); $-(1 + b)/2b$ is necessarily larger than μ_R. Therefore the slope of an indifference locus is positive. For a risk-lover, on the other hand, the corresponding argument shows that the slope is negative.

Differentiating (3.13) leads to the same conclusions regarding curvature as the alternative approach of section 3.3.1. namely that a risk-averter is necessarily a diversifier.

$$\frac{d^2\mu_R}{d\sigma_R} = \frac{1 + \left(\dfrac{d\mu_R{}^2}{d\sigma_R}\right)}{\left(-\dfrac{(1+b)}{2b} - \mu_R\right)^2}. \tag{3.14}$$

For a risk-averter, the second derivative is positive and the indifference locus is concave upwards; for a risk-lover, it is concave downward.

3.4 EFFECTS OF CHANGES IN THE RATE OF INTEREST

In section 3.3 two alternative rationalizations of the indifference curves introduced in section 3.2 have been presented. Both rationalizations assume that the investor (1) estimates subjective probability distributions of capital gain or loss in holding consols, (2) evaluates his prospective increase in wealth in terms of a cardinal utility function, (3) ranks alternative prospects according to the expected value of utility. The rationalization of section 3.3.1 derives the indifference curves by restricting the subjective probability distributions to a two-parameter family. The rationalization of section 3.3.2 derives the indifference curves by assuming the utility function to be quadratic within the relevant range. On either rationalization, a risk-averter's indifference curves must be concave upwards, characteristic of the diversifiers of section 3.2, and those of a risk-lover concave downwards. If the category defined as *plungers* in 3.2 exists at all, their indifference curves must be determined by some process other than those described in 3.3.

The opportunity locus for the investor is described in 3.1 and summarized in equation (4.3). The investor decides the amount to invest in consols so as to reach the highest indifference curve permitted by his opportunity-locus. This maximization may be one of three kinds:

I. Tangency between an indifference curve and the opportunity locus, as illustrated by points T_1, T_2, and T_3 in Figure 3.1. A regular maximum of this kind can occur only for a risk-averter, and will lead to diversification. Both A_1, cash holding, and A_2, consol holding, will be positive. They too are shown in Figure 3.1, in the bottom half of the diagram, where, for example, $A_1(r_1)$ and $A_2(r_1)$ depict the cash and consol holdings corresponding to point T_1.

II. A corner maximum at the point $\mu_R = r$, $\sigma_R = \sigma_g$, as illustrated in Figure 3.2. In Figure 3.2 the opportunity locus is the ray OC, and point C represents the highest expected return and risk obtainable by the investor i.e. the expected return and risk from holding his entire balance in consols. A utility mxaimum at C can occur either for a risk-averter or for a risk-lover. I_1 and I_2 represent indifference curves of a diversifier; I_2 passes through C and has a lower slope, both at C and everywhere to the left of C, than the opportunity locus. I_1' and I_2' represent the indifference curves of a risk-lover, for whom it is clear that C is always the optimum position. Similarly, a plunger may, if his indifference curves stand with respect to his opportunity locus as in Figure 3.3 (OC_2) plunge his entire balance in consols.

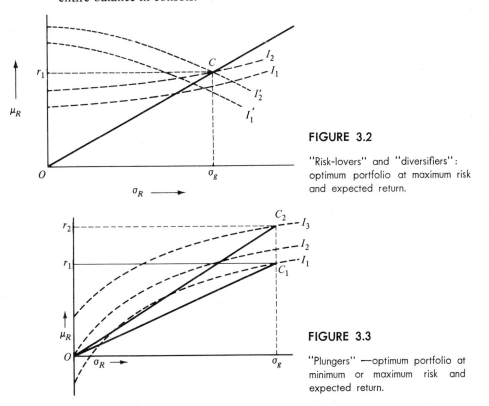

FIGURE 3.2

"Risk-lovers" and "diversifiers": optimum portfolio at maximum risk and expected return.

FIGURE 3.3

"Plungers" —optimum portfolio at minimum or maximum risk and expected return.

III. A corner maximum at the origin, where the entire balance is held in cash. For a plunger, this case is illustrated in Figure 3.3 (OC_1). Conceivably it could also occur for a diversifier, if the slope of his indifference curve at the origin exceeded the slope of the opportunity locus. However, case III is entirely excluded for investors whose indifference curves represent the constant-expected-utility loci of section 3.3. Such investors, we have already noted, cannot be plungers. Furthermore, the slope of all constant expected-utility loci at $\sigma_R = 0$ must be zero, as can be seen from (3.7) and (3.13).

We can now examine the consequences of a change in the interest rate r, holding constant the investor's estimate of the risk of capital gain or loss. An increase in the interest rate will rotate the opportunity locus OC to the left. How will this affect the investor's holdings of cash and consols? We must consider separately the three cases.

I. In Figure 3.1, OC_1, OC_2, and OC_3 represent opportunity loci for successively higher rates of interest. The indifference curves I_1, I_2, and I_3 are drawn so that the points of tangency T_1, T_2, and T_3, correspond to successively higher holdings of consols A_2. In this diagram, the investor's demand for cash depends inversely on the interest rate.

This relationship is, of course, in the direction liquidity preference theory has taught us to expect, but it is not the only possible direction of relationship. It is quite possible to draw indifference curves so that the point of tangency moves left as the opportunity locus is rotated counter-clockwise. The ambiguity is a familiar one in the theory of choice, and reflects the ubiquitous confllict between income and substitution effects. An increase in the rate of interest is an incentive to take more risk; so far as the substitution effect is concerned, it means a shift from security to yield. But an increase in the rate of interest also has an income effect, for it gives the opportunity to enjoy more security along with more yield. The ambiguity is analogous to the doubt concerning the effect of a change in the interest rate on saving; the substitution effect argues for a positive relationship, the income effect for an inverse relationship.

However, if the indifference curves are regarded as loci of constant expected utility, as derived in section 3.3, part of this ambiguity can be resolved. We have already observed that these loci all have zero slopes at $\sigma_R = 0$. As the interest rate r rises from zero, so also will consul holding A_2. At higher interest rates, however, the inverse relationship may occur.

This reversal of direction can be, however, virtually excluded in the case of the quadratic utility function (section 3.3.2). The condition for a maximum is that the slope of an indifference locus as given by (3.13) equal the slope of the opportunity locus (3.4).

$$\frac{r}{\sigma_g} = \frac{A_2 \sigma_g}{-\left(\frac{1+b}{2b}\right) - A_2 r} \; ; \quad A_2 = \frac{r}{r^2 + \sigma_g^2}\left(-\frac{1+b}{2b}\right). \tag{3.15}$$

Equation (3.15) expresses A_2 as a function of r and differentiating gives:

$$\frac{dA_2}{dr} = \frac{\sigma_g^2 - r^2}{(\sigma_g^2 + r^2)^2}\left(-\frac{1+b}{2b}\right); \; \frac{r}{A_2}\frac{dA_2}{dr} = \frac{\sigma_g^2 - r^2}{\sigma_g^2 + r^2} \tag{3.16}$$

Thus the share of consols in the portfolio increases with the interest rate for r less than σ_g. Moreover, if r exceeds σ_g, a tangency maximum cannot occur unless r also exceeds g_{max}, the largest capital gain the investor conceives possible (see

3.10).[14] The demand for consols is less elastic at high interest rates than at low, but the elasticity is not likely to become negative.

II and III. A change in the interest rate cannot cause a risk-lover to alter his position, which is already the point of maximum risk and expected yield. Conceivably a "diversifier" might move from a corner maximum to a regular interior maximum in response either to a rise in the interest rate or to a fall. A "plunger" might find his position altered by an increase in the interest rate, as from r_1 to r_2 in Figure 3.3; this would lead him to shift his entire balance from cash to consols.

3.5 EFFECTS OF CHANGES IN RISK

Investor's estimates σ_g of the risk of holding monetary assets other than cash, "consols," are subjective. But they are undoubtedly affected by market experience, and they are also subject to influence by measures of monetary and fiscal policy. By actions and words, the central bank can influence investor's estimates of the variability of interest rates; its influence on these estimates of risk may be as important in accomplishing or preventing changes in the rate as open-market operations and other direct interventions in the market. Tax rates, and differences in tax treatment of capital gains, losses, and interest earnings, affect in calculable ways the investor's risks and expected returns. For these reasons it is worth while to examine the effects of a change in an investor's estimate of risk on his allocation between cash and consols.

In Figure 3.4, T_1 and $A_2(r_1, \sigma_g)$ represent the initial position of an investor, at interest rate r_1 and risk σ_g. OC_1 is the opportunity locus (3.4), and OB_1 is the

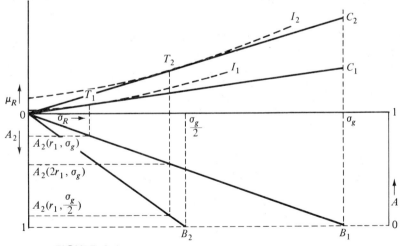

FIGURE 3.4

Comparison of effects of changes in interest rate (r) and in "risk" (σ_g) on holding of consols.

[14] For this statement and its proof, I am greatly indebted to my colleague Arthur Okun. The proof is as follows:

risk-consols relationship (3.3). If the investor now cuts his estimate of risk in half, to $\sigma_g/2$, the opportunity locus will double in slope, from OC_1 to OC_2, and the investor will shift to point T_2. The risk-consols relationship will have also doubled in slope, from OB_1 to OB_2. Consequently point T_2 corresponds to an investment in consols of A_1 $(r_1, \sigma_g/2)$. This same point T_2 would have been reached if the interest rate had doubled while the investor's risk estimate σ_g remained unchanged. But in that case, since the risk-consols relationship would remain at OB_1, the corresponding investment in consols would have been only half as large, i.e., A_2 $(2r_1, \sigma_g)$. In general, the following relationship exists between the elasticity of the demand for consols with respect to risk and its elasticity with respect to the interest rate:

$$\frac{\sigma_g}{A_2}\frac{dA_2}{d\sigma_g} = -\frac{r}{A_2}\frac{dA_2}{dr} - 1. \tag{3.17}$$

The implications of this relationsip for analysis of effects of taxation may be noted in passing, with the help of Figure 3.4. Suppose that the initial position of the investor is T_2 and $A_2(2r_1, \sigma_g)$. A tax of 50% is now levied on interest income and capital gains alike, with complete loss offset provisions. The result of the tax is to reduce the expected net return per dollar of consols from $2r_1$ to r_2 and to reduce the risk to the investor per dollar of consols from σ_g to $\sigma_g/2$. The opportunity locus will remain at OC_2, and the investor will still wish to obtain the combination of risk and expected return depicted by T_2. To obtain this combination, however, he must now double his holding of consols, to A_2 $(r_1, \sigma_g/2)$; the tax shifts the risk-consols line from OB_1 to OB_2. A tax of this kind, therefore, would reduce the demand for cash at any market rate of interest, shifting the investor's liquidity preference schedule in the manner shown in Figure 3.5. A tax on interest income only, with no tax on capital gains and no offset privileges for capital losses, would have quite different effects. If the Treasury began to split the interest income of the investor in Figure 3.4 but not to share the risk, the investor would move from his initial position, T_2 and A_2 $(2r_1, \sigma_g)$, to T_1 and A_2 (r_1, σ_g). His demand for cash at a given market rate of interest would be increased and his liquidity preference curve shifted to the right.

3.6 MULTIPLE ALTERNATIVES TO CASH

So far it has been assumed that there is only one alternative to cash, and A_2 has represented the share of the investor's balance held in that asset, "consols."

If $r^2 \geq \sigma_g^2$, then by (3.15) and (3.10):

$$1 \geq A_2 \geq \frac{r}{2r^2}\left(-\frac{1+b}{2b}\right) \geq \frac{1}{2r}\ (r + g_{max}).$$

From the two extremes of this series of inequalities it follows that $2r \geq r + g_{max}$ or $r \geq g_{max}$. Professor Okun also points out that this condition is incompatible with a tangency maximum if the distribution of g is symmetrical. For then $r \geq g_{max}$ would imply $r \geq g_{max} \geq 0$. There would be no possibility of net loss on consols and thus no reason to hold any cash.

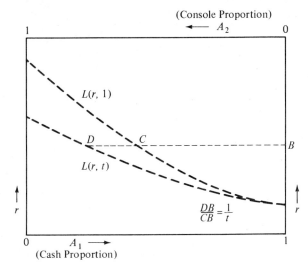

(Console Proportion)

←— A_2 0

$L(r, 1)$

D C B

$L(r, t)$

$\dfrac{DB}{CB} = \dfrac{1}{t}$ r

r

0   A_1 —→   1
(Cash Proportion)

FIGURE 3.5

Effect of tax (at rate $1-t$) on liquidity preference function

The argument is not essentially changed, however, if A_2 is taken to be the aggregate share invested in a variety of non-cash assets, e.g., bonds and other debt instruments differing in maturity, debtor, and other features. The return R and the risk σ_g on "consols" will then represent the average return and risk on a composite of these assets.

Suppose that there are m assets other than cash, and let x_i ($i = 1,2, \ldots, m$) be the amount invested in the ith of these assets. All x_i are non-negative, and $\sum_{i=1}^{m} x_i = A_2 \leq 1$. Let r_i be the expected yield, and let g_i be the capital gain or loss, per dollar invested in the ith asset. We assume $E(g_i) = 0$ for all i. Let v_{ij} be the variance or covariance of g_i and g_j as estimated by the investor.

$$v_{ij} = E(g_i g_j), \quad (i, j, = 1, 2, \ldots, m). \tag{3.18}$$

The over-all expected return is:

$$\mu_R = A_2 r = \sum_{i=1}^{m} x_i r_i. \tag{3.19}$$

The over-all variance of return is:

$$\sigma_R^2 = A_2^2 \sigma_g^2 = \sum_{i=1}^{m} \sum_{j=1}^{m} x_i x_j v_{ij}. \tag{3.20}$$

A set of points x_i for which $\sum_{i=1}^{m} x_i r_i$ is constant may be defined as a *constant-return locus*. A constant-return locus is linear in the x_i. For two assets x_1 and x_2, two loci are illustrated in Figure 3.6. One locus of combinations of x_1 and x_2 that give the same expected return μ_R is the line from μ_R/r_2 to μ_R/r_1, through C; another locus, for a higher constant, μ'_R, is the parallel line from μ_R'/r_2 to μ_R'/r through C'.

A set of point x_i for which σ_R^2 is constant may be defined as a *constant-risk locus*. These loci are ellipsoidal. For two assets x_1 and x_2, such a locus is illustrated by the quarter-ellipse from $\sigma_R/\sqrt{v_{22}}$ to, $\sigma_R/\sqrt{v_{11}}$ through point C. The equation of such an ellipse is:

$$x_1^2 \, v_{11} + 2x_1 \, x_2 \, v_{12} + x_2^2 \, v_{22} = \sigma_R^2 = \text{constant.}$$

Another such locus, for a higher risk level, σ_R, is the quarter-ellipse from $\sigma_R' / \sqrt{v_{22}}$ to $\sigma_R' / \sqrt{v_{11}}$ through point C'.

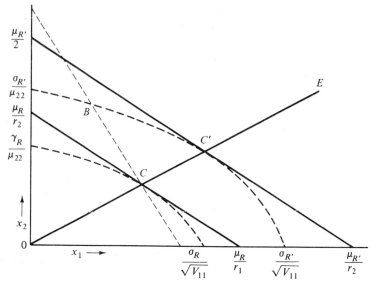

FIGURE 3.6

Dominant combinations of two
assets.

From Figure 3.6 it is clear that C and C' exemplify *dominant* combinations of x_1 and x_2. If the investor is incurring a risk of σ_2 somewhere on the ellipse through C, he will expect to have the highest possible expectation of return available to him at that level of risk. The highest available expected return is represented by the constant-expected-return line tangent to the ellipse at C. Similarly C' is a dominant point: it would not be possible to obtain a higher expected return than at C' without incurring additional risk, or to diminish risk without sacrificing expected return.

In general, a dominant combination of assets is defined as a set x_i which minimizes σ_R^2 for μ_R constant:

$$\sum_i \left(\sum_j v_{ij} \, x_j \right) x_i - \lambda \left(\sum_i r_i x_i - \mu_R \right) = \min \tag{3.21}$$

where λ is a Lagrange multiplier. The conditions for the minimum are that the x_i satisfy the constraint (3.19) and the following set of m simultaneous linear equations, written in matrix notation:

$$[v_{ij}] \, [x_i] = [\lambda r_i]. \tag{3.22}$$

All dominant sets lie on a ray from the origin. That is if $[x_i^{(0)}]$ and $[x_i^{(1)}]$ are dominant sets, then there is same non-negative scalar κ such that $[x_i^{(1)}] = [\kappa x_i^{(0)}]$. By definition of a dominant set, there is some $\lambda^{(0)}$ such that:

$$[v_{ij}][x_i^{(0)}] = [\lambda^{(0)} r_i],$$

and some $\lambda^{(1)}$ such that:

$$[v_{ij}][x_i^{(1)}] = [\lambda^{(1)} r_i].$$

Take $k = \lambda^{(1)}/\lambda^{(0)}$. Then:

$$[v_{ij}][\kappa x_i^{(0)}] = [\kappa \lambda^{(0)} r_i] = [\lambda^{(1)} r_i] = [v_{ij}][x_i^{(1)}].$$

At the same time, $\sum_i r_i x_i^{(0)} = \mu_R^{(0)}$ and $\sum_i r_i x_i^{(1)} = \mu_R^{(1)}$. Hence, $\mu_R^{(1)} = \kappa \mu_R^{(0)}$. Conversely every set on this ray is a dominant set. If $[x_{(i)}^{(0)}]$ is a dominant set, then so is $[\kappa x_i^{(0)}]$ for any non-negative constant κ. This is easily proved. If $[x_i^{(0)}]$ satisfies (3.19) and (3.22) for $\mu_R^{(0)}$ and $\lambda^{(0)}$, then $[\kappa x_i^{(0)}]$ satisfies (3.19) and (3.22) for $\lambda^{(\kappa)} = \kappa \lambda^{(0)}$ and $\mu_R^{(\kappa)} = \kappa \mu_R^{(0)}$. In the two-dimensional case pictured in Figure 3.6, the dominant pairs lie along the ray $OCC'E$.

There will be some point on the ray (say E in Figure 3.6) at which the investor's holdings of non-cash assets will exhaust his investment balance $(\sum_i x_i = 1)$ and leave nothing for cash holding. Short of that point the balance will be divided among cash and non-cash assets in proportion to the distances along the ray; in Figure 3.6 at point C for example, OC/OE of the balance would be non-cash, and CE/OE cash. But the convenient fact that has just been proved is that the proportionate composition of the non-cash assets is independent of their aggregate share of the investment balance. This fact makes it possible to describe the investor's decisions as if there were a single non-cash asset, a composite formed by combining the multitude of actual non-cash assets in fixed proportions.

Corresponding to every point on the ray of dominant sets is an expected return μ_R and risk σ_R; these pairs (μ_R, σ_R) are the opportunity locus of sections 3.1 and 3.4. By means of (3.22), the opportunity locus can be expressed in terms of the expected return and variances and covariances of the non-cash assets: Let:

$$[V_{ij}] = [V_{ij}]^{-1}.$$

Then:

$$\mu_R = \lambda \sum_i \sum_j r_i r_j V_{ij} \tag{3.23}$$

$$\sigma_R^2 = \lambda^2 \sum_i \sum_j r_i r_j V_{ij}. \tag{3.24}$$

Thus the opportunity locus is the line:

$$\mu_R = \sigma_R \sqrt{\sum_i \sum_j r_i r_j V_{ij}} = \sigma_R \frac{r}{\sigma_g}. \tag{3.25}$$

This analysis is applicable only so long as cash is assumed to be a riskless asset. In the absence of a residual riskless asset, the investor has no reason to confine his choices to the ray of dominant sets. This may be easily verified in the two-asset case. Using Figure 3.6 for a different purpose now, suppose that the entire investment balance must be divided between x_1 and x_2. The point (x_1, x_2) must fall on the line $x_1 + x_2 = 1$, represented by the line through BC in the diagram. The investor will not necessarily choose point C. At point B, for example, he would obtain a higher expected yield as well as a higher risk; he may prefer B to C. His opportunity locus represents the pairs (μ_R, σ_R) along the line through BC $(x_1 + x_2 = 1)$ rather than along the ray OC, and is a hyperbola rather than a line. It is still possible to analyze portfolio choices by the apparatus of (μ_R, σ_R) indifference and opportunity loci, but such analysis is beyond the scope of the present paper.[15]

It is for this reason that the present analysis has been deliberately limited, as stated in section 1.2, to choices among monetary assets. Among these assets cash is relatively riskless, even though in the wider context of portfolio selection, the risk of change in purchasing power, which all monetary assets share, may be relevant to many investors. Breaking down the portfolio selection problem into stages at different levels of aggregation —allocation first among, and then within, asset categories—seems to be a permissible and perhaps even indispensable simplification both for the theorist and for the investor himself.

4. IMPLICATIONS OF THE ANALYSIS FOR LIQUIDITY PREFERENCE THORY

The theory of risk-avoiding behaviour has been shown to provide a basis for liquidity preference and for an inverse relationship between the demand for cash and the rate of interest. This theory does not depend on inelasticity of expectations of future interest rates, but can proceed from the assumption that the expected value of capital gain or loss from holding interest-bearing assets is always zero. In this respect, it is a logically more satisfactory foundation for liquidity preference than the Keynesian theory described in section 2. Moreover, it has the empirical advantage of explaining diversification—the same individual holds both cash and "consols"—while the Keynesian theory implies that each investor will hold only one asset.

The risk aversion theory of liquidity preference mitigates the major logical objection to which, according to the argument of section 2.6, the Keynesian theory is vulnerable. But it cannot completely meet Leontief's position that in a strict stationary equilibrium liquidity preference must be zero unless cash and consols bear equal rates. By their very nature consols and, to a lesser degree, all time obligations contain a potential for capital gain or loss that cash and other demand obligations lack. Presumably, however, there is some length of

---

[15] A forthcoming book by Harry Markowitz, *Techniques of Portfolio Selection*, will treat the general problem of finding dominant sets and computing the corresponding opportunity locus, for sets of securities all of which involve risk. Markowitz's main interest is prescription of rules of rational behaviour for investors; the main concern of this paper is the implications for economic theory, mainly comparative statics that can be derived from assuming that investors do in fact follow such rules. For the general nature of Markowitz's approach, see his article, "Portfolio Selection", *Journal of Finance*, Vol. VII, No. 1 (March 1952), pp. 77–91.

experience of constancy in the interest rate that would teach the most stubbornly
timid investor to ignore that potential. In a pure stationary state, it could be
argued, the interest rate on consols would have been the same for so long that
investors would unanimously estimate σ_g to be zero. So stationary a state is of
very little interest. Fortunately the usefulness of comparative statics does not
appear to be confined to comparisons of states each of which would take a generation or more to achieve. As compared to the Keynesian theory of liquidity
preference, the risk aversion theory widens the applicability of comparative
statics in aggregative analysis; this is all that need be claimed for it.

The theory, however, is somewhat ambiguous concerning the direction of
relationship between the rate of interest and the demand for cash. For low interest rates, the theory implies a negative elasticity of demand for cash with
respect to the interest rate, an elasticity that becomes larger and larger in absolute value as the rate approaches zero. This implication, of course, is in accord
with the usual assumptions about liquidity preference. But for high interest
rates, and especially for individuals whose estimates σ_g of the risk of capital
gain or loss on "consols" are low, the demand for cash may be an increasing,
rather than a decreasing, function of the interest rate. However, the force of this
reversal of direction is diluted by recognition, as in section 2.5, that the size of
investment balances is not independent of the current rate of interest r. In section
3.4 we have considered the proportionate allocation between cash and "consols"
on the assumption that it is independent of the size of the balance. An increase
in the rate of interest may lead an investor to desire to shift towards cash. But to
the extent that the increase in interest also reduces the value of the investor's
consol holdings, it automatically gratifies this desire, at least in part.

The assumption that investors expect on balance no change in the rate of
interest has been adopted for the theoretical reasons explained in section 2.6
rather than for reasons of realism. Clearly investors do form expectations of
changes in interest rates and differ from each other in their expectations. For
the purposes of dynamic theory and of analysis of specific market situations, the
theories of sections 2 and 3 are complementary rather than competitive. The
formal apparatus of section 3 will serve just as well for a non-zero expected
capital gain or loss as for a zero expected value of g. Stickiness of interest rate
expectations would mean that the expected value of g is a function of the rate
of interest r, going down when r goes down and rising when r goes up. In addition to the rotation of the opportunity locus due to a change in r itself, there
would be a further rotation in the same direction due to the accompanying
change in the expected capital gain or loss. At low interest rates expectation of
capital loss may push the opportunity locus into the negative quadrant, so that
the optimal position is clearly no consols, all cash. At the other extreme, expectation of capital gain at high interest rates would increase sharply the slope
of the opportunity locus and the frequency of no cash, all consols positions,
like that of Figure 3.3. The stickier the investor's expectations, the more sensitive his demand for cash will be to changes in the rate of interest.

*Given an efficient frontier, we have the problem of picking which of the
efficient portfolios we desire to hold. Pratt discusses the properties of
various utility functions that might be used to select such a portfolio. In
particular, the reader should note the discussion of the properties of the
quadratic utility function, since the quadratic utility function is often
employed in conjunction with the portfolio problem. As an example of
this use, see Don Farrar*, The Investment Decision Under Uncertainty: Portfolio Selection, *Prentice-Hall, Englewood Cliffs, New Jersey,
1962.*

27

Risk Aversion in the Small and in the Large

John W. Pratt[1]

This article is reprinted with permission from Econometrica, *Vol. XXXII,
No. 1–2 (January–April, 1964), pp. 122–136.*

This paper concerns utility functions for money. A measure of risk aversion
in the small, the risk premium or insurance premium for an arbitrary risk,
and a natural concept of decreasing risk aversion are discussed and related
to one another. Risks are also considered as a proportion of total assets.

1. SUMMARY AND INTRODUCTION

Let $u(x)$ be a utility function for money. The function $r(x) = -u''(x)/u'(x)$
will be interpreted in various ways as a measure of local risk aversion (risk
aversion in the small); neither $u''(x)$ nor the curvature of the graph of u is an
appropriate measure. No simple measure of risk aversion in the large will be
introduced. Global risks will, however, be considered, and it will be shown that
one decision maker has greater local risk aversion $r(x)$ than another at all x
if and only if he is globally more risk-averse in the sense that, for every risk, his
cash equivalent (the amount for which he would exchange the risk) is smaller

---

[1]   This research was supported by the National Science Foundation (grant NSF-G24035).
Reproduction in whole or in part is permitted for any purpose of the United States
Government.

than for the other decision maker. Equivalently, his risk premium (expected monetary value minus cash equivalent) is always larger, and he would be willing to pay more for insurance in any situation. From this it will be shown that a decision maker's local risk aversion $r(x)$ is a decreasing function of x if and only if, for every risk, his cash equivalent is larger the larger his assets, and his risk premium and what he would be willing to pay for insurance are smaller. This condition, which many decision makers would subscribe to, involves the third derivative of u, as $r' \leq 0$ is equivalent to $u'''u' \geq u''^2$. It is not satisfied by quadratic utilities in any region. All this means that some natural ways of thinking casually about utility functions may be misleading. Except for one family, convenient utility functions for which $r(x)$ is decreasing are not so very easy to find. Help in this regard is given by some theorems showing that certain combinations of utility functions, in particular linear combinations with positive weights, have decreasing $r(x)$ if all the functions in the combination have decreasing $r(x)$.

The related function $r^*(x) = xr(x)$ will be interpreted as a local measure of aversion to risks measured as a proportion of assets, and monotonicity of $r^*(x)$ will be proved to be equivalent to monotonicity of every risk's cash equivalent measured as a proportion of assets, and similarly for the risk premium and insurance.

These results have both descriptive and normative implications. Utility functions for which $r(x)$ is decreasing are logical candidates to use when trying to describe the behavior of people who, one feels, might generally pay less for insurance against a given risk the greater their assets. And consideration of the yield and riskiness per investment dollar of investors' portfolios may suggest, at least in some contexts, description by utility functions for which $r^*(x)$ is first decreasing and then increasing.

Normatively, it seems likely that many decision makers would feel they ought to pay less for insurance against a given risk the greater their assets. Such a decision maker will want to choose a utility function for which $r(x)$ is decreasing, adding this condition to the others he must already consider (consistency and probably concavity) in forging a satisfactory utility from more or less malleable preliminary preferences. He may wish to add a further condition on $r^*(x)$.

We do not assume or assert that utility may not change with time. Strictly speaking, we are concerned with utility at a specified time (when a decision must be made) for money at a (possibly later) specified time. Of course, our results pertain also to behavior at different times if utility does not change with time. For instance, a decision maker whose utility for total assets is unchanging and whose assets are increasing would be willing to pay less and less for insurance against a given risk as time progresses if his $r(x)$ is a decreasing function of x. Notice that his actual expenditure for insurance might nevertheless increase if his risks are increasing along with his assets.

The risk premium, cash equivalent, and insurance premium are defined and related to one another in Section 2. The local risk aversion function $r(x)$ is introduced and interpreted in Sections 3 and 4. In Section 5, inequalities concerning global risks are obtained from inequalities between local risk aversion functions. Section 6 deals with constant risk aversion, and Section 7 demonstrates the equivalence of local and global definitions of decreasing (and increasing) risk aversion. Section 8 shows that certain operations preserve the property of decreasing risk aversion. Some examples are given in Section 9. Aversion to proportional risk is discussed in Sections 10 to 12. Section 13 concerns some related work of Kenneth J. Arrow.[2]

Throughout this paper, the utility $u(x)$ is regarded as a function of total assets rather than of changes which may result from a certain decision, so that $x = 0$ is equivalent to ruin, or perhaps to loss of all readily disposable assets. (This is essential only in connection with proportional risk aversion.) The symbol $\sim$ indicates that two functions are equivalent as utilities, that is, $u_1(x) \sim u_2(x)$ means there exist constants a and b (with $b > 0$) such that $u_1(x) = a + bu_2(x)$ for all x. The utility functions discussed may, but need not, be bounded. It is assumed, however, that they are sufficiently regular to justify the proofs; generally it is enough that they be twice continuously differentiable with positive first derivative, which is already required for $r(x)$ to be defined and continuous. A variable with a tilde over it, such as z, is a random variable. The risks z considered may, but need not, have "objective" probability distributions. In formal statements, z refers only to risks which are not degenerate, that is, not constant with probability one, and interval refers only to an interval with more than one point. Also, increasing and decreasing mean nondecreasing and nonincreasing respectively; if we mean strictly increasing or decreasing we will say so.

2. THE RISK PREMIUM

Consider a decision maker with assets x and utility function u. We shall be interested in the *risk premium* π such that he would be indifferent between recieving a risk z and receiving the non-random amount $E(z)-\pi$, that is, π less than the actuarial value $E(z)$. If u is concave, then $\pi \geq 0$, but we don't require this. The risk premium depends on x and on the distribution of z, and will be denoted $\pi(x,z)$. (It is not, as this notation might suggest, a function $\pi(x,z)$ evaluated at a randomly selected value of z, which would be random.) By the properties of utility,

$$u(x + E(z) - \pi(x,z)) = E\{u(x + z).\} \tag{1}$$

We shall consider only situations where $E[u(x + z)]$ exists and is finite. Then $\pi(x,z)$ exists and is uniquely defined by (1), since $u(x + E(z) - \pi)$ is a strictly decreasing, continuous function of π ranging over all possible values of u. It follows immediately from (1) that, for any constant u,

$$\pi(x,z) = \pi(x + \mu, z - \mu). \tag{2}$$

---

[2] The importance of the function $r(x)$ was discovered independently by Kenneth J. Arrow and by Robert Schlaifer, in different contexts. The work presented here was, unfortunately, essentially completed before I learned of Arrow's related work. It is, however, a pleasure to acknowledge Schlaifer's stimulation and participation throughout, as well as that of John Bishop at certain points.

Addendum (1969). In retrospect, I wish footnote 2 had made clear that Robert Schlaifer's contribution included formulating originally the concept of decreasing risk aversion in terms of the probability premium and proving that it implies $r(x)$ is decreasing, i.e., that (c') implies (a') in Theorem 2.

By choosing $\mu = E(z)$ (assuming it exists and is finite), we may thus reduce consideration to a risk $z - u$ which is actuarially neutral, that is, $E(z - u) = 0$.

Since the decision maker is indifferent between receiving the risk z and receiving for sure the amount $\pi_a(x,z) = E(z) - \pi(x,z)$, this amount is sometimes called the cash equivalent or value of z. It is also the asking price for π, the smallest amount for which the decision maker would willingly sell z if he had it. It is given by

$$u(x + \pi_a(x,z)) = E\{u(x + z)\}. \tag{3a}$$

It is to be distinguished from the bid price $\pi_b(x,z)$, the largest amount the decision maker would willingly pay to obtain z, which is given by

$$u(x) = E\{u(x + z - \pi_b(x,z))\}. \tag{3b}$$

For an unfavorable risk z, it is natural to consider the insurance premium $\pi_I(x,z)$ such that the decision maker is indifferent between facing the risk z and paying the nonrandom amount $\pi_I(x,z)$. Since paying π_I is equivalent to receiving $- \pi_I$, we have

$$\pi_I(x,z) = - \pi_a(x,z) = \pi(x,z) - E(z) \tag{3c}$$

If z is actuarially neutral, the risk premium and insurance premium coincide.

The results of this paper will be stated in terms of the risk premium π, but could equally easily and meaningfully be stated in terms of the cash equivalent or insurance premium.

3. LOCAL RISK AVERSION

To measure a decision maker's local aversion to risk, it is natural to consider his risk premium for a small, actuarially neutral risk z. We therefore consider $\pi(x,z)$ for a risk z with $E(z) = 0$ and small variance σ_z^2; that is, we consider the behavior of $\pi(x,z)$ as $\sigma_z^2 \to 0$. We assume the third absolute central moment of z is of smaller order than σ_z^2. (Ordinarily it is of order σ_z^3). Expanding u around x on both sides of (1), we obtain under suitable regularity conditions[3]

$$u(x - \pi) = u(x) - \pi u'(x) + O(\pi^2), \tag{4a}$$

$$E\{u(x + z)\} = E\{u(x) + zu'(x) + \tfrac{1}{2}z^2 u''(x) + O(z^3)\} \tag{4b}$$

$$= u(x) + \tfrac{1}{2}\sigma_z^2 u''(x) + o(\sigma_z^2).$$

Setting these expressions equal, as required by (1), then gives

$$\pi(x,z) = \tfrac{1}{2}\sigma_z^2 r(x) + o(\sigma_z^2), \tag{5}$$

---

[3] In expansions, $O(\ )$ means "terms of order at most" and $o(\ )$ means "terms of smaller order than."

where

$$r(x) = -\frac{u''(x)}{u'(x)} = -\frac{d}{dx} \log u'(x).$$ (6)

Thus the decision maker's risk premium for a small, actuarially neutral risk z is approximately $r(x)$ times half the variance of z; that is, $r(x)$ is twice the risk premium per unit of variance for infinitesimal risks. A sufficient regularity condition for (5) is that u have a third derivative which is continuous and bounded over the range of all z under discussion. The theorems to follow will not actually depend on (5), however.

If z is not actuarially neutral, we have by (2), with $\mu = E(z)$, and (5):

$$\pi(x,z) = \tfrac{1}{2}\sigma_z^2 r(x + E(z)) + o(\sigma_z^2).$$ (7)

Thus the risk premium for a risk z with arbitrary mean $E(z)$ but small variance is approximately $r(x + E(z))$ times half the variance of z. It follows also that the risk premium will just equal and hence offset the actuarial value $E(z)$ of a small risk (z); that is, the decision maker will be indifferent between having z and not having it, when the actuarial value is approximately $r(x)$ times half the variance of z. Thus $r(x)$ may also be interpreted as twice the actuarial value the decision maker requires per unit of variance for infinitesimal risks.

Notice that it is the variance, not the standard deviation, that enters these formulas. To first order any (differentiable) utility is linear in small gambles. In this sense, these are second order formulas.

Still another interpretation of $r(x)$ arises in the special case $z = \pm h$, that is, where the risk is to gain or lose a fixed amount $h > 0$. Such a risk is actuarially neutral if $+ h$ and $-h$ are equally probable, so $P(z = h) - P(z = -h)$ measures the *probability premium* of z. Let $p(x,h)$ be the probability premium such that the decision maker is indifferent between the status quo and a risk $z = \pm h$ with

$$P(z = h) - P(z = -h) = p(x,h).$$ (8)

Then $P(z = h) = \tfrac{1}{2}[1 + p(x,h)]$, $p(z = -h) = \tfrac{1}{2}[1-p(x,h)]$, and $p(x,h)$ is defined by

$$u(x) = E\{u(x + z)\} = \tfrac{1}{2}[1 + p(x,h)]u(x + h) + \tfrac{1}{2}[1 - p(x,h)]u(x - h).$$ (9)

When u is expanded around x as before, (9) becomes

$$u(x) = u(x) + hp(x,h)u'(x) + \tfrac{1}{2}h^2u''(x) + O(h^3).$$ (10)

Solving for $p(x,h)$, we find

$$p(x,h) = \tfrac{1}{2}hr(x) + O(h^2).$$ (11)

Thus for small h the decision maker is indifferent between the status quo and a risk of $\pm h$ with a probability premium of $r(x)$ times $\tfrac{1}{2} h$; that is, $r(x)$ is twice the probability premium he requires per unit risked for small risks.

In these ways we may interpret $r(x)$ as a measure of the *local risk aversion* or *local propensity to insure* at the point x under the utility function $u;$ $-r(x)$ would measure locally liking for risk or propensity to gamble. Notice that we have not introduced any measure of risk aversion in the large. Aversion to ordinary (as opposed to infinitesimal) risks might be considered measured by $\pi(x,z)$, but π is a much more complicated function than r. Despite the absence of any simple measure of risk aversion in the large, we shall see that comparisons of aversion to risk can be made simply in the large as well as in the small.

By (6), integrating $-r(x)$ gives $\log u'(x) + c;$ exponentiating and integrating again then gives $e^c u(x) + d$. The constants of integration are immaterial because $e^c u(x) + d \sim u(x)$. (Note $e^c > 0$.) Thus we may write

$$u \sim \int e^{-\int r},\tag{12}$$

and we observe that the local risk aversion function r associated with any utility function u contains all essential information about u while eliminating everything arbitrary about u. However, decisions about ordinary (as opposed to "small") risks are determined by r only through u as given by (12), so it is not convenient entirely to eliminate u from consideration in favor of r.

4. CONCAVITY

The aversion to risk implied by a utility function u seems to be a form of concavity, and one might set out to measure concavity as representing aversion to risk. It is clear from the foregoing that for this purpose $r(x) = -u''(x)/u'(x)$ can be considered a measure of the concavity of u at the point x. A case might perhaps be made for using instead some one-to-one function of $r(x)$, but it should be noted that $u''(x)$ or $-u''(x)$ is not in itself a meaningful measure of concavity in utility theory, nor is the curvature (reciprocal of the signed radius of the tangent circle) $u''(x) (1 + [u'(x)]^2)^{-3/2}$. Multiplying u by a positive constant, for example, does not alter behavior but does alter u'' and the curvature.

A more striking and instructive example is provided by the function $u(x) = -e^{-x}$ As x increases, this function approaches the asymptote $u = 0$ and looks graphically less and less concave and more and more like a horizontal straight line, in accordance with the fact that $u'(x) = e^{-x}$ and $u''(x) = -e^{-x}$ both approach 0. As a utility function, however, it does not change at all with the level of assets x, that is, the behavior implied by $u(x)$ is the same for all x, since $u(k + x) = -e^{-k-x} \sim u(x)$. In particular, the risk premium $\pi(x,z)$ for any risk z and the probability premium $p(x,h)$ for any h remain absolutely constant as x varies. Thus, regardless of the appearance of its graph, $u(x) = -e^{-x}$ is just as far from implying linear bahavior at $x = \infty$ as at $x = 0$ or $x = -\infty$. All this is duly reflected in $r(x)$, wihch is constant: $r(x) = -u''(x)/u'(x) = 1$ for all x.

One feature of $u''(x)$ does have a meaning, namely its sign, which equals that of $-r(x)$. A negative (positive) sign at x implies unwillingness (willingness) to accept small, actuarially neutral risks with assets x. Furthermore, a negative (positive) sign for all x implies strict concavity (convexity) and hence unwillingness (willingness) to accept any actuarially neutral risk with any assets. The absolute magnitude of $u''(x)$ does not in itself have any meaning in utility theory, however.

5. COMPARATIVE RISK AVERSION

Let u_1 and u_2 be utility functions with local risk aversion functions r_1 and r_2, respectively. If, at a point x, $r_1(x) > r_2(x)$, then u_1 is locally more risk-averse than u_2 at the point x; that is, the corresponding risk premiums satisfy π_1 $(x,z) > \pi_2(x,z)$ for sufficiently small risks z, and the corresponding probability premiums satisfy $p_1(x,h) > p_2(x,h)$ for sufficiently small $h > 0$. The main point of the theorem we are about to prove is that the corresponding global properties also hold. For instance, if $r_1(x) \gneq r_2(x)$ for all x, that is, u_1 has greater local risk aversion than u_2 everywhere, then $\pi_1(x,z) > \pi_2(x,z)$ for every risk z, so that u_1 is also globally more risk-averse in a natural sense.

It is to be understood in this section that the probability distribution of z, which determines $\pi_1(x,z)$ and $\pi_2(x,z)$, is the same in each. We are comparing the risk premiums for the same probability distribution of risk but for two different utilities. This does not mean that when Theorem 1 is applied to two decision makers, they must have the same personal probability distributions, but only that the notation is imprecise. The theorem could be stated in terms of $\pi_1(x,z_1)$ and $\pi(x,z)$ where the distribution assigned to z by the first decision maker is the same as that assigned to z_2 by the second decision maker. This would be less misleading, but also less convenient and less suggestive, expecially for later use. More precise notation would be, for instance, $\pi_1(x,F)$ and $\pi_2(x,F)$, where F is a cumulative distribution function.

Theorem 1: Let $r_i(x)$, π_i (x,z), and $p_i(x)$ be the local risk aversion, risk premium, and probability premium corresponding to the utility function $\tilde{\mu}_1$, $i=1,2$. Then the following conditions are equivalent, in either the strong form (indicated in brackets), or the weak form (with the bracketed material omitted)

(a) $r_1(x) \geq r_2(x)$ for all x [and $>$ for at least one x in every interval]

(b) $\pi_1(x,z) \geq [>] \pi_2(x,z)$ for all x and z

(c) $P_1(x,h) \geq [>] P_2(x,h)$ for all x and all $h > 0$

(d) $u_1 (u_2^{-1}(t))$ is a [strictly] concave function of t.

(e) $\dfrac{u_1(y)-u_1(x)}{u_1(w)-u_1(v)} \leq [<] \dfrac{u_2(y)-u_2(x)}{u_2(w)-u_2(v)}$ for all v,w,x,y with $v < w \leq x < y$

The same equivalences hold if attention is restricted throughout to an interval, that is, if the requirement is added that $x, x + z, x + h, x-h, u_2^{-1}(t), v, w$, and y, all lie in a specified interval.

Proof: We shall prove things in an order indicating somewhat how one might discover that (a) implies (b) and (c).

To show that (b) follows from (d), solve (1) to obtain

$$\pi_i(x,z) = x + E(z) - u_i^{-1}(E\{u_i(x + z)\}). \tag{13}$$

Then

$$\pi_1(x,z) - \pi_2(x,z) = u_2^{-1}(E\{u_2(x+z)\}) - u_1^{-1}(E\{u_1(x+z)\})$$
$$= u_2^{-1}(E\{t\}) - u_1^{-1}(E\{u_1(u_2^{-1}(t))\}), \tag{14}$$

where $t = u_2(x+z)$. If $u_1(u_2^{-1}(t))$ is [strictly] concave, then (by Jensen's inequality)

$$E\{u_1(u_2^{-1}(t))\} \leq [<] u_1(u_2^{-1}(E\{t\})). \tag{15}$$

Substituting (15) in 14), we obtain (b).

To show that (a) implies (d), note that

$$\frac{d}{dt} u_1(u_2^{-1}(t)) = \frac{u'_1(u_2^{-1}(t))}{u'_2(u_2^{-1}(t))}, \tag{16}$$

which is [strictly] decreasing if (and only if) log $u'_1(x)/u_2(x)$ is. The latter follows from (a) and

$$\frac{d}{dx} \log \frac{u'_1(x)}{u'_2(x)} = r_2(x) - r_1(x). \tag{17}$$

That (c) is implied by (e) follows immediately upon writing (9) in the form

$$\frac{1 - p_i(x,h)}{1 + p_i(x,h)} = \frac{u_i(x+h) - u_i(x)}{u_i(x) - u_i(x-h)}. \tag{18}$$

To show that (a) implies (e), integrate (a) from w to x, obtaining

$$-\log \frac{u'_1(x)}{u'_1(w)} \geq [>] -\log \frac{u'_2(x)}{u'_2(w)} \quad \text{for} \quad w < x, \tag{19}$$

which is equivalent to

$$\frac{u'_1(x)}{u'_1(w)} \leq [<] \frac{u'_2(x)}{u'_2(w)} \quad \text{for} \quad w \leq x \tag{20}$$

This implies

$$\frac{u_1(y) - u_1(x)}{u'_1(w)} \leq [<] \frac{u_2(y) - u_2(x)}{u'_2(w)} \quad \text{for} \quad w \leq x < y, \tag{21}$$

as may be seen by applying the Mean Value Theorem of differential calculus to the difference of the two sides of (21) regarded as a function of y. Condition (e) follows from (21) upon application of the Mean Value Theorem to the difference of the reciprocals of the two sides of (e) regarded as a function of w.

We have now proved that (a) implies (d) implies (b), and (a) implies (e) implies (c). The equivalence of (a)–(e) will follow if we can prove that (b) implies (a), and (c) implies (a), or equivalently that not (a) implies not (b) and not (c). But this follows from what has already been proved, for if the weak, [strong] form of (a) does not hold, then the strong [weak] form of (a) holds on some interval with u_1 and u_2 interchanged. Then the strong [weak] forms of (b) and (c) also hold on this interval with u_1 and u_2 interchanged, so the weak [strong] forms of (b) and (c) do not hold. This completes the proof.

We observe that (e) is equivalent to (20), (21), and

$$\frac{u_1(w) - u_1(v)}{u'_1(x)} \geq [>] \frac{u_2(w) - u_2(v)}{u'_2(x)} \quad \text{for} \quad v < w \leq x. \tag{22}$$

6. CONSTANT RISK AVERSION

If the local risk aversion function is constant, say $r(x) = c$, then by (12):

$$u(x) \sim x \qquad \text{if} \quad r(x) = 0; \tag{23}$$
$$u(x) \sim -e^{-cx} \quad \text{if} \quad r(x) = c > 0; \tag{24}$$
$$u(x) \sim e^{-cx} \qquad \text{if} \quad r(x) = c < 0. \tag{25}$$

these utilities are, respectively, linear, strictly concave, and strictly convex.

If the risk aversion is constant locally, then it is also constant globally, that is, a change in assets makes no change in preference among risks. In fact, for any k, $u(k + x) \sim u(x)$ in each of the cases above, as is easily verified. Therefore it makes sense to speak of "constant risk aversion" without the qualification "local" or "global."

Similar remarks apply to constant risk aversion on an interval, except that global consideration must be restricted to assets x and risks z such that $x + z$ is certain to stay within the interval.

7. INCREASING AND DECREASING RISK AVERSION

Consider a decision maker who (i) attaches a positive risk premium to any risk, but (ii) attaches a smaller risk premium to any given risk the greater his assets x. Formally this means

(i) $\pi(x,z) > 0$ for all x and z;
(ii) $\pi(x,z)$ is a strictly decreasing function of x for all z.

Restricting z to be actuarially neutral would not affect (i) or (ii), by (2) with $\mu = E(z)$.

We shall call a utility function (or a decision maker possessing it) *risk-averse* if the weak form of (i) holds, that is, if $\pi(x,z) \geq 0$ for all x and z; it is well known that this is equivalent to concavity of u, and hence to $u'' \leq 0$ and to $r \geq 0$. A utility function is *strictly risk-averse* if (i) holds as stated; this is equivalent to strict concavity of u and hence to the existence in every interval of at least one point where $u'' < 0, r > 0$.

We turn now to (ii). Notice that it amounts to a definition of strictly decreasing risk aversion in a global (as opposed to local) sense. On would hope that decreasing global risk aversion would be equivalent to decreasing local risk aversion $r(x)$. The following theorem asserts that this is indeed so. Therefore it makes sense to speak of "decreasing risk aversion" without the qualification "local" or "global." What is nontrivial is that $r(x)$ decreasing implies $\pi(x,z)$ decreasing, inasmuch as $r(x)$ pertains directly only to infinitesimal gambles. Similar considerations apply to the probability premium $p(x,h)$.

Theorem 2: The following conditions are equivalent.
(a') The local risk aversion function $r(x)$ is [strictly] decreasing.
(b') The risk premium $\pi(x,z)$ is a [strictly] decreasing function of x for all z.
(c') The probability premium $p(x,h)$ is a [strictly] decreasing function of x for all $h > 0$.

   The same equivalences hold if "increasing" is substituted for "decreasing" throughout and/or attention is restricted throughout to an interval, that is, the requirement is added that x, $x+z, x+h$ and $x-h$ all lie in a specified interval.

Proof: This theorem follows upon application of Theorem 1 to $u_1(x) = u(x)$ and $u_2(x) = u(x + k)$ for arbitrary x and k.
It is easily verified that (a') and hence also (b') and (c') are equivalent to (d')
$u'(u^{-1}(t))$ is a [strictly] convex function of t.
This corresponds to (d) of Theorem 1. Corresponding to (e) of Theorem 1 and (20)-(22) is
   (e') $u'(x)u'''(x) \geq (u''(x))^2$ *[and $>$ for at least one x in every interval]*.
The equivalence of this to (a')–(c') follows from the fact that the sign of $r'(x)$ is the same as that of $(u''(x))^2 - u'(x)u'''(x)$. Theorem 2 can be and originally was proved by way of (d') and (e'), essentially as Theorem 1 is proved in the present paper.

8. OPERATIONS WHICH PRESERVE DECREASING RISK AVERSION

We have just seen that a utility function evinces decreasing risk aversion in a global sense if and only if its local risk aversion function $r(x)$ is decreasing. Such a utility function seems of interest mainly if it is also risk-averse (concave, $r \geq 0$). Accordingly, we shall now formally define a utility function to be [strictly] *decreasingly risk-averse* if its local risk aversion function r is [strictly] decreasing and nonnegative. Then by Theorem 2, conditions (i) and (ii) of Section 7 are equivalent to the utility's being strictly decreasingly risk-averse.

   In this section we shall show that certain operations yield decreasingly risk-averse utility functions if applied to such functions. This facilitates proving that functions are decreasingly risk-averse and finding functions which have this property and also have reasonably simple formulas. In the proofs, $r(x)$, $r_1(x)$, etc., are the local risk aversion functions belonging to $u(x)$, $u_1(x)$, etc.

Theorem 3: Suppose $a > 0$: $u_1(x) = u(ax + b)$ is [strictly] decreasingly risk-averse for $x_0 \leq x \leq x_1$ if and only if $u(x)$ is [strictly] decreasingly risk-averse for $ax_0 + b \leq x \leq ax_1 + b$.

Proof: This follows directly from the easily verified formula:

$$r_1(x) = ar(ax + b). \tag{26}$$

Theorem 4: If $u_1(x)$ is decreasingly risk-averse for $x_0 \leq x \leq x_1$, and $u_2(x)$

is decreasingly risk-averse for $u_1(x_0) \le x \le u_1(x_1)$, then $u(x) = u_2(u_1(x))$ is decreasingly risk averse for $x_0 \le x \le x_1$, and strictly so unless one of u_1 and u_2 is linear from some x on and the other has constant risk aversion in some interval.

Proof: We have $\log u'(x) = \log u_2'(u_1'(x)) + \log u_1'(x)$, and therefore

$$r(x) = r_2(u_1(x))u'_1(x) + r_1(x). \tag{27}$$

The functions $r_2(u_1(x))$, $u_1'(x)$, and $r_1(x)$ are > 0 and decreasing, and therefore so is $r(x)$. Furthermore, $u_1'(x)$ is strictly decreasing as long as $r_1(x) > 0$, so $r(x)$ is strictly decreasing as long as $r_1(x)$ and $r_2[u_1(x)]$ are both > 0. If one of them is 0 for some x, then it is 0 for all larger x, but if the other is strictly decreasing, then so is r.

Theorem 5: If $u_1, \ldots, u_n$ are decreasingly risk-averse on an interval $[x_0, x_1]$ and $c_1, \ldots, c_n$ are positive constants, then $u = \sum_1^n c_i u_i$ is decreasingly risk-averse on $[x_0, x_1]$, and strictly so except on subintervals (if any) where all u_i have equal and constant risk aversion.

Proof: The general statement follows from the case $u = u_1 + u_2$. For this case

$$r = -\frac{u''_1 + u''_2}{u'_1 + u'_2} = \frac{u'_1}{u'_1 + u'_2} r_1 + \frac{u'_2}{u'_1 + u'_2} r_2; \tag{28}$$

$$r' = \frac{u'_1}{u'_1 + u'_2} r'_1 + \frac{u'_2}{u'_1 + u'_2} r'_2 + \frac{u''_1 u'_2 - u'_1 u''_2}{(u'_1 + u'_2)^2} (r_1 - r_2) \tag{29}$$

$$= \frac{u'_1 r'_1 + u'_2 r'_2}{u'_1 + u'_2} - \frac{u'_1 u'_2}{(u'_1 + u'_2)^2} (r_1 - r_2)^2.$$

We have $u'_1 > 0$, $u'_2 > 0$, $r'_1 \le 0$, and $r'_2 \le 0$. Therefore $r' \le 0$, and $r' < 0$ unless $r_1 = r_2$ and $r'_1 = r'_2 = 0$. The conclusion follows.

9. EXAMPLES

9.1. *Example 1.* The utility $u(x) = -(b - x)^c$ for $x \le b$ and $c > 1$ is strictly increasing and strictly concave, but it also has strictly *increasing* risk aversion: $r(x) = (c - 1)/(b - x)$. Notice that the most general concave quadratic utility $u(x) = \alpha + \beta x - \gamma x^2$, $\beta > 0$, $\gamma > 0$, is equivalent as a utility to $-(b - x)^c$ with $c = 2$ and $b = \frac{1}{2}\beta/\gamma$. Therefore a quadratic utility cannot be decreasingly risk averse on any interval whatever. This severely limits the usefulness of quadratic utility, however nice it would be to have expected utility depend only on the mean and variance of the probability distribution. Arguing "in the small" is no help: decreasing risk aversion is a local property as well as a global one.

9.2 *Example 2.* If

$$u'(x) = (x^a + b)^{-c} \quad \text{with} \quad a > 0, c > 0, \tag{30}$$

then $u(x)$ is strictly decreasingly risk averse in the region

$$x > [\max\{0, -b, b(a - 1)\}]^{1/a}. \tag{31}$$

To prove this, note

$$r(x) = -\frac{d}{dx}\log u'(x) = \frac{ac}{x + bx^{1-a}}, \tag{32}$$

which is ≥ 0 and strictly decreasing in the region where the denominator $x + bx^{1-a}$ is ≥ 0 and strictly increasing, which is the region (30). (The condition $x \geq 0$ is included to insure that x^a is defined; for $a \geq 1$ it follows from the other conditions.)

By Theorem 3, one can obtain a utility function that is strictly decreasingly risk-averse for $x > 0$ by substituting $x + d$ for x above, where d is at least the right hand side of (31). Multiplying x by a positive factor, as in Theorem 3, is equivalent to multiplying b by a positive factor.

Given below are all the strictly decreasingly risk-averse utility functions $u(x)$ on $x > 0$ which can be obtained by applying Theorem 3 to (30) with the indicated choices of the parameters a and c:

$a = 1, 0 < c < 1$: $\quad u(x) \sim (x + d)^q$ $\qquad$ with $d \geq 0, 0 < q < 1$; (33)

$a = 1, c = 1$: $\qquad u(x) \sim \log(x + d)$ $\qquad$ with $d \geq 0$; $\qquad\qquad$ (34)

$a = 1, c > 1$: $\qquad u(x) \sim -(x + d)^{-q}$ $\qquad$ with $d \geq 0, q > 0$; $\qquad$ (35)

$a = 2, c = .5$: $\qquad u(x) \sim \log(x + d +$
$\qquad\qquad\qquad\qquad [(x + d)^2 + b])$ $\qquad$ with $d \geq |b|^{1/2}$; $\qquad\quad$ (36)

$a = 2, c = 1$: $\qquad u(x) \sim \arctan(\alpha x + \beta)$ or
$\qquad\qquad\qquad\qquad \log(1 - (\alpha x + \beta)^{-1})$ $\quad$ with $\alpha > 0, \beta \geq 1$; $\quad$ (37)

$a = 2, c = 1.5$: $\quad u(x) \sim [1 + (\alpha x + \beta)^{-2}]^{-1/2}$ or
$\qquad\qquad\qquad\qquad -[1 - (\alpha x + \beta)^{-2}]^{-1/2}$ $\quad$ with $\alpha > 0, \beta \geq 1$. $\quad$ (38)

9.3 *Example* 3. Applying Theorems 4 and 5 to the utilities of Example 2 and Section 6 gives a very wide class of utilities which are strictly decreasingly risk averse for $x > 0$, such as

$$u(x) \sim -c_1 e^{-cx} - c_2 e^{-dx} \qquad \text{with } c_1 > 0, c_2 > 0, c > 0, d > 0. \tag{39}$$

$$u(x) \sim \log(d_1 + \log(x + d_2)) \quad \text{with } d_1 \geq 0, d_2 \geq 0, d_1 + \log d_2 \geq 0. \tag{40}$$

10. PROPORTIONAL RISK AVERSION

So far we have been concerned with risks that remained fixed while assets varied. Let us now view everything as a proportion of assets. Specifically, let $\pi^*(x,z)$ be the *proportional risk premium* corresponding to a proportional risk z; that is, a decision maker with assets x and utility function u would be indifferent between receiving a risk xz and receiving the nonrandom amount $E(xz) - x\pi^*(x,z)$. Then $x\pi^*(x,z)$ equals the risk premium $\pi(x,xz)$, so

$$\pi^*(x,z) = \frac{1}{x}\pi(x, xz). \tag{41}$$

For a small, actuarially neutral, proportional risk z we have; by (5),

$$\pi^*(x,z) = \tfrac{1}{2}\sigma_z^2 r^*(x) + o(\sigma_z^2), \tag{42}$$

where

$$r^*(x) = xr(x). \tag{43}$$

If z is not actuarially neutral, we have, by (7),

$$\pi^*(x,z) = \tfrac{1}{2}\sigma_z^2 r^*(x + xE(z)) + o(\sigma_z^2). \tag{44}$$

We will call r^* the *local proportional risk aversion* at the point x under the utility function u. Its interpretation by (42) and (44) is like that of r by (5) and (7).

Similarly, we may define the *proportional probability premium* $p^*(x,h)$, corresponding to a risk of gaining or losing a proportional amount h, namely

$$p^*(x,h) = p(x,xh). \tag{45}$$

Then another interpretation of $r^*(x)$ is provided by

$$p^*(x,h) = \tfrac{1}{2}hr^*(x) + O(h^2), \tag{46}$$

which follows from (45) and (11).

11. CONSTANT PROPORTIONAL RISK AVERSION

If the local proportional risk aversion function is constant, say $r^*(x) = c$, then $r(x) = c/x$, so the utility is strictly decreasingly risk-averse for $c > 0$ and has negative, strictly increasing risk aversion for $c < 0$. By (12), the possibilities are:

$$u(x) \sim x^{1-c} \qquad \text{if} \quad r^*(x) = c < 1, \tag{47}$$
$$u(x) \sim \log x \qquad \text{if} \quad r^*(x) = 1, \tag{48}$$
$$u(x) \sim -x^{-(c-1)} \text{ if} \quad r^*(x) = c > 1. \tag{49}$$

If the proportional risk aversion is constant locally, then it is constant globally, that is, a change in assets makes no change in preferences among proportional risks. This follows immediately from the fact that $u(kx) \sim u(x)$ in each of the cases above. Therefore it makes sense to speak of "constant proportional risk aversion" without the qualification "local" or "global." Similar remarks apply to constant proportional risk aversion on an interval.

12. INCREASING AND DECREASING PROPORTIONAL RISK AVERSION

We will call a utility function [strictly] increasingly or decreasingly proportionally risk-averse if it has a [strictly] increasing or decreasing local proportional risk aversion function. Again the corresponding local and global properties are equivalent, as the next theorem states.

Theorem 6: The following conditions are equivalent.
(a") The local proportional risk aversion function $r^*(x)$ is [strictly] decreasing.
(b") The proportional risk premium $\pi^*(x,z)$ is a [strictly] decreasing function of x for all z.
(c") The proportional probability premium $p^*(x,h)$ is a [strictly] decreasing function of x for all $h > 0$.

    The same equivalences hold if "increasing" is substituted for "decreasing" throughout and/or attention is restricted throughout to an interval, that is, if the requirement is added that x, $x + xz$, $x + xh$, and $x - xh$ all lie in a specified interval.

Proof: This theorem follows upon application of Theorem 1 to $u_1(x) = u(x)$ and $u_2(x) = u(kx)$ for arbitrary x and k.

    A decreasingly risk-averse utility function may be increasingly or decreas - ingly proportionally risk-averse or neither. For instance, $u(x) \sim - \exp[-q^{-1}(x + b)^q]$, with $b \geq 0$, $q < 1$, $q \neq 0$, is strictly decreasingly risk-averse for $x > 0$ while its local proportional risk aversion function $r^*(x) = x(x + b)^{-1}[(x + b)^q + 1 - q]$ is strictly increasing if $0 < q < 1$, strictly decreasing if $q < 0$ and $b = 0$, and neither if $q < 0$ and $b > 0$.

13. RELATED WORK OF ARROW

Arrow[4] has discussed the optimum amount to invest when part of the assets x are to be held as cash and the rest invested in a specified, actuarially favorable risk. If i is the return per unit invested, then investing the amount a will result in assets $x + ai$. Suppose $a(x,i)$ is the optimum amount to invest, that is $a(x,i)$ maximizes $E\{u(x+ai)\}$. Arrow proves that if $r(x)$ is [strictly] decreasing, increasing, or constant for all x, then $a(x,i)$ is [strictly] increasing, decreasing, or constant, respectively, except that $a(x,i) = x$ for all x below a certain value (depending on i). He also proves a theorem about the asset elasticity of the demand for cash which is equivalent to the statement that if $r^*(x)$ is [strictly] decreasing, increasing, or constant for all x, then the optimum proportional investment $a^*(x,i) = a(x,i)/x$ is [strictly] increasing, decreasing, or constant, respectively, except that $a^*(x,i) = 1$ for all x below a certain value. In the present framework it is natural to deduce these results from the following theorem, whose proof bears essentially the same relation to Arrow's proofs as the proof of Theorem 1 to direct proofs of Theorems 2 and 6. For convenience we assume that $a_1(x,i)$ and $a_2(x,i)$ are unique.

Theorem 7: Condition (a) of Theorem 1 is equivalent to (f) $a_1(x,i) \leq a_2(x,i)$ for all x and i [and $<$ if $0 < a_1(x,i) < x$].
The same equivalence holds if attention is restricted throughout to an interval, that is, if the requirement is added that x and $x + ix$ lie in a specified interval.

PROOF: To show that (a) implies (f), note that $a_j(x,i)$ maximizes

$$v_j(a) = \frac{1}{u'_j(x)} E\{u_j(x + ai)\}, \qquad j = 1, 2. \tag{50}$$

---

[4] Kenneth J. Arrow, "Liquidity Preference," Lecture VI in "Lecture Notes for Economics 285, The Economics of Uncertainty," pp. 33–53, undated, Stanford University.

Therefore (f) follows from

$$\frac{d}{da}\{v_1(a) - v_2(a)\} = E\left\{i\left(\frac{u'_1(x + ai)}{u'_1(x)} - \frac{u'_2(x + ai)}{u'_2(x)}\right)\right\} \leq [<] 0, \qquad (51)$$

which follows from (a) by (20).

If, conversely, the weak [strong] form of (a) does not hold, then its strong [weak] form holds on some interval with u_1 and u_2 interchanged, in which case the weak [strong] form of (f) cannot hold, so (f) implies (a). [The fact must be used that the strong form of (f) is actually stronger than the weak form, even when x and $x + ix$ are restricted to a specified interval. This is easily shown.]

Assuming u is bounded, Arrow proves that (i) it is impossible that $r^*(x) \leq 1$ for all $x > x_0$, and he implies that (ii) $r^*(0) \leq 1$. It follows, as he points out, that if u is bounded and r^* is monotonic, then r^* is increasing. (i) and (ii) can be deduced naturally from the following theorem, which is an immediate consequence of Theorem 1 (a) and (e).

Theorem 8: If $r_1(x) \geq r_2(x)$ for all $x > x_0$ and $u_1(\infty) = \infty$, then $u_2(\infty) = \infty$. If $r_1(x) \geq r_2(x)$ for all $x < \epsilon$, $\epsilon > 0$, and $u_2(0) = -\infty$, $+$ then $u_1(0) = -\infty$. This gives (i) when $r_1(x) = 1/x$, $r_2(x) = r(x)$, $u_1(x) = \log x$, $u_2(x) = u(x)$. It gives (ii) when $r_1(x) = r(x)$, $r_2(x) = c/x$, $c > 1$, $u_1(x) = u(x)$, $u_2(x) = -x^{1-c}$.

This section is not intended to summarize Arrow's work,[4] but only to indicate its relation to the present paper. The main points of overlap are that Arrow introduces essentially the functions r and r^* (actually their negatives) and uses them in significant ways, in particular those mentioned already, and that he introduces essentially $p^*(x,h)$, proves an equation like (46) in order to interpret decreasing r^*, and mentions the possibility of a similar analysis for r.

In this article, Sharpe uses modern portfolio theory to derive the equilibrium yield for a risky asset. As might be expected, this return depends on the asset's covariance with the market index (since the covariance affects portfolio risk). The reader should study footnote 22, which contains the derivation of the relationship between the return on a risky asset and the return on the market portfolio.

28

Capital Asset Prices:
A Theory of Market Equilibrium
Under Conditions of Risk

William F. Sharpe[*]

This article is reprinted with permission from the Journal of Finance, *Vol. XIX, No. 3 (September, 1964), pp. 425–442.*

I. INTRODUCTION

One of the problems which has plagued those attempting to predict the behavior of capital markets is the absence of a body of positive microeconomic theory dealing with conditions of risk. Although many useful insights can be obtained from the traditional models of investment under conditions of certainty, the pervasive influence of risk in financial transactions has forced those working in this area to adopt models of price behavior which are little more than assertions. A typical classroom explanation of the determination of capital asset prices, for example, usually begins with a careful and relatively rigorous description of

[*] A great many people provided comments on early versions of this paper which led to major improvements in the exposition. In addition to the referees, who were most helpful, the author wishes to express his appreciation to Dr. Harry Markowitz of the RAND Corporation, Professor Jack Hirshleifer of the University of California at Los Angeles, and to Professors Yoram Barzel, George Brabb, Bruce Johnson, Walter Oi and R. Haney Scott of the University of Washington.

the process through which individual preferences and physical relationships interact to determine an equilibrium pure interest rate. This is generally followed by the assertion that somehow a market risk-premium is also determined, with the prices of assets adjusting accordingly to account for differences in their risk.

A useful representation of the view of the capital maket implied in such discussions is illustrated in Figure 1. In equilibrium, capital asset prices have adjusted so that the investor, if he follows rational procedures (primarily diversification), is able to attain any desired point along a *capital market line*.[1] He may obtain a higher expected rate of return of his holdings only by incurring additional risk. In effect, the market presents him with two prices: the *price of time,* or the pure interest rate (shown by the intersection of the line with the horizontal axis) and the *price of risk,* the additional expected return per unit of risk borne (the reciprocal of the slope of the line).

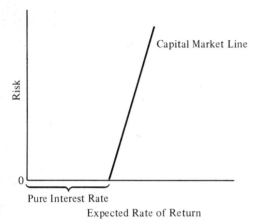

Risk

0

Pure Interest Rate

Expected Rate of Return   **FIGURE 1**

Capital Market Line

At present there is no theory describing the manner in which the price of risk results from the basic influences of investor preferences, the physical attributes of capital assets, etc. Moreover, lacking such a theory, it is difficult to give any real meaning to the relationship between the price of a single asset and its risk. Through diversification, some of the risk inherent in an asset can be avoided so that its total risk is obviously not the relevant influence on its price; unfortunately little has been said concerning the particular risk component which is relevant.

In the last ten years a number of economists have developed *normative* models dealing with asset choice under conditions of risk. Markowitz,[2] following Von Neumann and Morgenstern, developed an analysis based on the expected utility maxim and proposed a general solution for the portfolio selection problem. Tobin[3] showed that under certain conditions Markowitz's model implies

[1] Although some discussions are also consistent with a non-linear (but monotonic) curve.

[2] Harry M. Markowitz, *Portfolio Selection, Efficient Diversification of Investments* (New York: John Wiley and Sons, Inc., 1959). The major elements of the theory first appeared in his article "Portfolio Selection," *The Journal of Finance,* XII (March 1952), 77–91.

[3] James Tobin, "Liquidity Preference as Behavior Towards Risk," *The Review of Economic Studies,* XXV (February, 1958), 65–86.

that the process of investment choice can be broken down into two phases: first, the choice of a unique optimum combination of risky assets; and second, a separate choice concerning the allocation of funds between such a combination and a single riskless asset. Recently, Hicks[4] has used a model similar to that proposed by Tobin to derive corresponding conclusions about individual investor behavior, dealing somewhat more explicitly with the nature of the conditions under which the process of investment choice can be dichotomized. An even more detailed discussion of this process, including a rigorous proof in the context of a choice among lotteries has been presented by Gordon and Gangolli.[5]

Although all the authors cited use virtually the same model of investor behavior,[6] none has yet attempted to extend it to construct a *market* equilibrium theory of asset prices under conditions of risk.[7] We will show that such an extension provides a theory with implications consistent with the assertions of traditional financial theory described above. Moreover, it sheds considerable light on the relationship between the price of an asset and the various components of its overall risk. For these reasons it warrants consideration as a model of the determination of capital asset prices.

Part II provides the model of individual investor behavior under conditions of risk. In Part III the equilibrium conditions for the capital market are conisidered and the capital market line derived. The implications for the relationship between the prices of individual capital assets and the various components of risk are described in Part IV.

II. OPTIMAL INVESTMENT POLICY FOR THE INDIVIDUAL

THE INVESTOR'S PREFERENCE FUNCTION

Assume that an individual views the outcome of any investment in probabilistic terms; that is, he thinks of the possible results in terms of some probability distribution. In assessing the desirability of a particular investment, however, he is willing to act on the basis of only two parameters of this distribu-

---

[4] John R. Hicks, "Liquidity," *The Economic Journal*, LXXII (December, 1962), 787–802.

[5] M. J. Gordon and Ramesh Gangolli, "Choice Among and Scale of Play on Lottery Type Alternatives," College of Business Administration, University of Rochester, 1962. For another discussion of this relationship see W. F. Sharpe, "A Simplified Model for Portfolio Analysis," *Management Science*, Vol. 9, No. 2 (January 1963), 277–293. A related discussion can be found in F. Modigliani and M. H. Miller, "The Cost of Capital, Corporation Finance, and the Theory of Investment," *The American Economic Review*, XLVIII (June 1958), 261–297.

[6] Recently Hirshleifer has suggested that the mean-variance approach used in the articles cited is best regarded as a special case of a more general formulation due to Arrow. See Hirshleifer's "Investment Decision Under Uncertainty," *Papers and Proceedings of the Seventy-Sixth Annual Meeting of the American Economic Association*, Dec. 1963, or Arrow's "Le Role des Valeurs Boursieres pour la Repartition la Meilleure des Risques," *International Colloquium on Econometrics*, 1952.

[7] After preparing this paper the author learned that Mr. Jack L. Treynor, of Arthur D. Little, Inc., had independently developed a model similar in many respects to the one described here. Unfortunately Mr. Treynor's excellent work on this subject is, at present, unpublished.

tion—its expected value and standard deviation.[8] This can be represented by a total utility function of the form:

$$U = f(E_w, \sigma_w)$$

where E_w indicates expected future wealth and σ_w the predicted standard deviation of the possible divergence of actual future wealth from E_w.

Investors are assumed to prefer a higher expected future wealth to a lower value, ceteris paribus $(dU/dE_w > 0)$. Moreover, they exhibit risk-aversion, choosing an investment offering a lower value of σ_w to one with a greater level, given the level of E_w $(dU/d\sigma_w < 0.)$ These assumptions imply that indifference curves relating E_w and σ_w will be upward-sloping.[9]

To simplify the analysis, we assume that an investor has decided to commit a given amount (W_i) of his present wealth to investment. Letting W_t be his terminal wealth and R the rate of return on his investment:

$$R \equiv \frac{W_t - W_i}{W_i},$$

we have

$$W_t = RW_i + W_i.$$

This relationship makes it possible to express the investor's utility in terms of R, since terminal wealth is directly related to the rate of return:

$$U = g(E_R, \sigma_R).$$

Figure 2 summarizes the model of investor preferences in a family of indifference curves; successive curves indicate higher levels of utility as one moves down and/or to the right.[10]

---

[8] Under certain conditions the mean-variance approach can be shown to lead to unsatisfactory predictions of behavior. Markowitz suggests that a model based on the semi-variance (the average of the squared deviations below the mean) would be preferable; in light of the formidable computational problems, however, he bases his analysis on the variance and standard deviation.

[9] While only these characteristics are required for the analysis, it is generally assumed that the curves have the property of diminishing marginal rates of substitution between E_w and σ_w, as do those in our diagrams.

[10] Such indifference curves can also be derived by assuming that the investor wishes to maximize expected utility and that his total utility can be represented by a quadratic function of R with decreasing marginal utility. Both Markowitz and Tobin present such a derivation. A similar approach is used by Donald E. Farrar in *The Investment Decision Under Uncertainty* (Prentice-Hall, 1962). Unfortunately Farrar makes an error in his derivation; he appeals to the Von Neumann–Morgenstern cardinal utility axioms to transform a function of the form:

$$E\ (U) = a + bE_R - cE_R^{\,2} - c\sigma_R^2$$

into one of the form:

$$E(U) = k_1\ E_R - k_2\sigma_R^2$$

That such a transformation is not consistent with the axioms can readily be seen in this form, since the first equation implies non-linear indifference curves in the E_R, σ_R^2 plane while the second implies a linear relationship. Obviously no three (different) points can lie on both a line and a non-linear curve (with a monotonic derivative). Thus

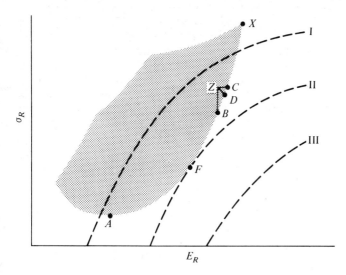

FIGURE 2

THE INVESTMENT OPPORTUNITY CURVE

　　　The model of investor behavior considers the investor as choosing from a set of investment opportunities that one which maximizes his utility. Every investment plan available to him may be represented by a point in the E_R, σ_R plane. If all such plans involve some risk, the area composed of such points will have an appearance similar to that shown in Figure 2. The investor will choose from among all possible plans the one placing him on the indifference curve representing the highest level of utility (point F). The decision can be made in two stages: first, find the set of efficient investment plans and, second choose one from among this set. A plan is said to be efficient if (and only if) there is no alternative with either (1) the same E_R and a lower σ_R,(2) the same σ_R and a higher E_R or (3) a higher E_R and a lower σ_R. Thus investment Z is inefficient since investments B, C, and D (among others) dominate it. The only plans which would be chosen must lie along the lower right-hand boundary $(AFBDCX)$—the *investment opportunity curve.*

　　　To understand the nature of this curve, consider two investment plans— A and B, each including one or more assets. Their predicted expected values and standard deviations of rate of return are shown in Figure 3. If the proportion a of the individual's wealth is placed in plan A and the remainder $(1-a)$ in B, the expected rate of return of the combination will lie between the expected returns of the two plans:

$$E_{Rc} = \alpha E_{Ra} + (1 - \alpha)E_{Rb}$$

The predicted standard deviation of return of the combination is:

---

the two functions must imply different orderings among alternative choices in at least some instance.

$$\sigma_{Rc} = \sqrt{\alpha^2\sigma_{Ra}^2 + (1-\alpha)^2\sigma_{Rb}^2 + 2r_{ab}\alpha(1-\alpha)\sigma_{Ra}\sigma_{Rb}}$$

Note that this relationship includes r_{ab}, the correlation coefficient between the predicted rates of return of the two investment plans. A value of $+1$ would indicate an investor's belief that there is a precise positive relationship between the outcomes of the two investments. A zero value would indicate a belief that the outcomes of the two investments are completely independent and -1 that the investor feels that there is a precise inverse relationship between them. In the usual case r_{ab} will have a value between 0 and $+1$.

Figure 3 shows the possible values of E_{Rc} and σ_{Rc} obtainable with different

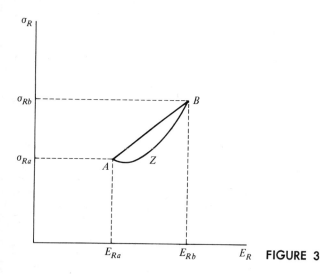

FIGURE 3

combinations of A and B under two different assumptions about the value of r_{ab}. If the two investments are perfectly correlated, the combinations will lie along a straight line between the two points, since in this case both E_{Rc} and σ_{Rc} will be linearly related to the proportions invested in the two plans.[11] If they are less than perfectly positively correlated, the standard deviation of any combination must be less than that obtained with perfect correlation (since r_{ab} will be less); thus the combinations must lie along a curve below the line AB.[12] AZB shows such a curve for the case of complete independence ($r_{ab}=0$); with negative correlation the locus is even more U-shaped.

[11]
$$E_{Rc} = \alpha E_{Ra} + (1-\alpha) E_{Rb} = E_{Rb} + (E_{Ra} - E_{Rb})\alpha$$
$$\sigma_{Rc} = \sqrt{\alpha^2\sigma_{Ra}^2 + (1-\alpha)^2\sigma_{Rb}^2 + 2r_{ab}\alpha(1-\alpha)\sigma_{Ra}\sigma_{Rb}}$$
but $r_{ab} = 1$, therefore the expression under the square root sign can be factored:
$$\sigma_{Rc} = \sqrt{\alpha\sigma_{Ra}+(1-\alpha)\sigma_{Rb}]^2}$$
$$= \alpha\sigma_{Ra}+(1-\alpha)\sigma_{Rb}$$
$$= \sigma_{Rb}+(\sigma_{Ra}-\sigma_{Rb})\alpha$$

[12] This curvature is, in essence, the rationale for diversification.

[13] When $r_{ab} = 0$, the slope of the curve at point A is $-\sigma_{Ra}/(E_{Rb}-E_{Ra})$, at point B it is $\sigma_{Rb}/(E_{Rb}-E_{RA})$. When $r_{ab}=-1$, the curve degenerates to two straight lines to a point on the horizontal axis.

The manner in which the investment opportunity curve is formed is relatively simple conceptually, although exact solutions are usually quite difficult.[14] One first traces curves indicating E_R, σ_R values available with simple combinations of individual assets, then considers combinations of combinations of assets. The lower right-hand boundary must be either linear or increasing at an increasing rate $d^2\sigma_R/dE^2_R > 0$). As suggested earlier, the complexity of the relationship between the characteristics of individual assets and the location of the investment opportunity curve makes it difficult to provide a simple rule for assessing the desirability of individual assets, since the effect of an asset on an investor's over-all investment opportunity curve depends not only on its expected rate of return (E_{Ri}) and risk (σ_{Ri}), but also on its correlations with the other available opportunities (r_{i1}, r_{i2},..., r_{in}). However, such a rule is implied by the equiliburium conditions for the model, as we will show in part IV.

THE PURE RATE OF INTEREST

We have not yet dealt with riskless assets. Let P be such an asset; its risk is zero ($\sigma_{Rp} = 0$) and its expected rate of return, E_{Rp}, is equal (by definition) to the pure interest rate. If an investor places α of his wealth in P and the remainder in some risky asset A, would obtain an expected rate of return:

$$E_{Rc} = \alpha E_{Rp} + (1 - \alpha)E_{Ra}$$

The standard deviation of such a combination would be:

$$\sigma_{Rc} = \sqrt{\alpha^2\sigma^2_{Rp} + (1 - \alpha)^2\sigma_{Ra}^2 + 2r_{pa}\alpha(1 - \alpha)\sigma_{Rp}\sigma_{Ra}}$$

but since $\sigma_{Rp} = 0$, this reduces to:

$$\sigma_{Rc} = (1 - \alpha)\sigma_{Ra}.$$

This implies that all combinations involving any risky asset or combination of assets plus the riskless asset must have values of E_{Rc} and σ_{Rc} which lie along a straight line between the points representing the two components. Thus in Figure 4 all combinations of E_R and σ_R lying along the line PA are attainable if some money is loaned at the pure rate and some placed in A. Similarly, by lending at the pure rate and investing in B, combinations along PB can be attained. Of all such possibilities, however, one will dominate: that investment plan lying at the point of the original investment opportunity curve where a ray from point P is tangent to the curve. In Figure 4 all investments lying along the original curve from X to ϕ are dominated by some combination of investment in ϕ and lending at the pure interest rate.

Consider next the possibility of borrowing. If the investor can borrow

14   Markowitz has shown that this is a problem in parametric quadratic programming. An efficient solution technique is described in his article, "The Optimization of a Quadratic Function Subject to Linear Constraints," *Naval Research Logistics Quarterly,* Vol. 3 (March and June, 1956), 111–133. A solution method for a special case is given in the author's "A Simplified Model for Portfolio Analysis," *op. cit.*

at the pure rate of interest, this is equivalent to disinvesting in *P*. The effect of borrowing to purchase more of any given investment than is possible with the given amount of wealth can be found simply by letting α take on negative values in the equations derived for the case of lending. This will obviously give points lying along the extension of line *PA* if borrowing is used to purchase more of *A*; points lying along the extension of *PB* if the funds are used to purchase *B*, etc.

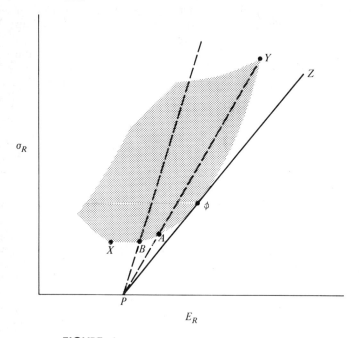

FIGURE 4

As in the case of lending, however, one investment plan will dominate all others when borrowing is possible. When the rate at which funds can be borrowed equals the lending rate, this plan will be the same one which is dominant if lending is to take place. Under these-conditions, the investment opportunity curve becomes a line (*PφZ* in Figure 4). Moreover, if the original investment opportunity curve is not linear at point *φ*, the process of investment choice can be dichotomized as follows: first select the (unique) optimum combination of risky assets (point *φ*), and second borrow or lend to obtain the particular point on *PZ* at which an indifference curve is tangent to the line.[15]

Before proceeding with the analysis, it may be useful to consider alter-

---

[15]   This proof was first presented by Tobin for the case in which the pure rate of interest is zero (cash). Hicks considers the lending situation under comparable conditions but does not allow borrowing. Both authors present their analysis using maximization subject to constraints expressed as equalities. Hicks' analysis assumes independence and thus insures that the solution will include no negative holdings of risky assets; Tobin's covers the general case, thus his solution would generally include negative holdings of some assets. The discussion in this paper is based on Markowitz' formulation, which includes non-negativity constraints on the holdings of all assets.

native assumptions under which only a combination of assets lying at the point of tangency between the orginal investment opportunity curve and a ray from P can be efficient. Even if borrowing is impossible, the investor will choose ϕ (and lending) if his risk-aversion leads him to a point below ϕ on the line $P\,\phi$. Since a large number of investors choose to place some of their funds in relatively risk-free investments, this is not an unlikely possibility. Alternatively, if borrowing is possible but only up to some limit, the choice of ϕ would be made by all but those investors willing to undertake considerable risk. These alternative paths lead to the main conclusion, thus making the assumption of borrowing or lending at the pure interest rate less onerous than it might initially appear to be.

III. EQUILIBRIUM IN THE CAPITAL MARKET

In order to derive conditions for equilibrium in the capital market we invoke two assumptions. First, we assume a common pure rate of interest, with all investors able to borrow or lend funds on equal terms. Second, we assume homogeneity of investor expectations[16]: investors are assumed to agree on the prospects of various investments—the expected values, standard deviations and correlation coefficients described in Part II. Needless to say, these are highly restrictive and undoubtedly unrealistic assumptions. However, since the proper test of a theory is not the realism of its assumptions but the acceptability of its implications, and since these assumptions imply equilibrium conditions which from a major part of classical financial doctrine, it is far from clear that this formulation should be rejected—especially in view of the dearth of alternative models leading to similar results.

Under these assumptions, given some set of capital asset prices, each investor will view his alternatives in the same manner. For one set of prices the alternatives might appear as shown in Figure 5. In this situation, an investor with the preferences indicated by indifference curves A_1 through A_4 would seek to lend some of his funds at the pure interest rate and to invest the remainder in the combination of assets shown by point ϕ, since this would give him the preferred over-all position A^*. An investor with the preferences indicated by curves B_1 through B_4 would seek to invest all his funds in combination ϕ, while an investor with indifference curves C_1 through C_2 would invest all his funds plus additional (borrowed) funds in combination ϕ in order to reach his preferred position (C^*). In any event, all would attempt to purchase only those risky assets which enter combination ϕ.

The attempts by investors to purchase the assets in combination ϕ and their lack of interest in holding assets not in combination ϕ would, of course, lead to a revision of prices. The prices of assets in ϕ will rise and, since an asset's expected return relates future income to present price their expected returns will fall. This will reduce the attractiveness of combinations which include such assets; thus point ϕ (among others) will move to the left of its initial position.[17]

---

[16]   A term suggested by one of the referees.

[17]   If investors consider the variability of future dollar returns unrelated to present price, both E_R and σ_R will fall; under these conditions the point representing an asset would move along a ray through the origin as its price changes.

On the other hand, the prices of assets not in ϕ will fall, causing an increase in their expected returns and a rightward movement of points representing combinations which include them. Such price changes will lead to a revision of investors' actions; some new combination or combinations will become attractive, leading to different demands and thus to further revisions in prices. As the process continues, the investment opportunity curve will tend to become more linear, with points such as ϕ moving to the left and formerly inefficient points (such as F and G) moving to the right.

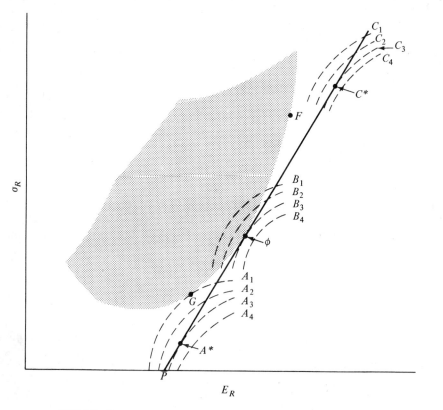

FIGURE 5

Capital asset prices must, of course, continue to change until a set of prices is attained for which every asset enters at least one combination lying on the capital market line. Figure 6 illustrates such an equilibrium condition.[18] All possibilities in the shaded area can be attained with combinations of risky assets, while points lying along the line PZ can be attained by borrowing or lending at the pure rate plus an investment in some combination of risky assets. Certain possibilities (those lying along PZ from point A to point B) can be obtained in either

18   The area in Figure 6 representing E_R, σ_R values attained with only risky assets has been drawn at some distance from the horizontal axis for emphasis. It is likely that a more accurate representation would place it very close to the axis.

manner. For example, the E_R, σ_R values shown by point A can be obtained solely by some combination of risky assets; alternatively, the point can be reached by a combination of lending, and investing in combination C of risky assets.

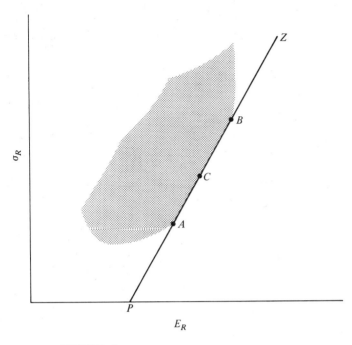

FIGURE 6

It is important to recognize that in the situation shown in Figure 6 many alternative combinations of risky assets are efficient (i.e., lie along line PZ), and thus the theory does not imply that all invetors will hold the same combination.[19] On the other hand, all such combinations must be perfectly (positively) correlated, since they lie along a linear border of the E_R, σ_R region.[20] This provides a key to the relationship between the prices of capital assets and different types of risk.

---

[19] This statement contradicts Tobin's conclusion that there will be a unique optimal combination of risky assets. Tobin's proof of a unique optimum can be shown to be incorrect for the case of perfect correlation of efficient risky investment plans if the line connecting their E_R, σ_R points would pass through point P. In the graph on page 83 of this article *(op. cit.)* the constant-risk locus would, in this case, degenerate from a family of ellipses into one of straight lines parallel to the constant-return loci, thus giving multiple optima.

[20] E_R, σ_R values given by combinations of any two combinations must lie within the region and cannot plot above a straight line joining the points. In this case they cannot plot below such a straight line. But since only in the case of perfect correlation will they plot along a straight line, the two combinations must be perfectly correlated. As shown in Part IV, this does not necessarily imply that the individual securities they contain are perfectly correlated.

IV. THE PRICES OF CAPITAL ASSETS

We have argued that in equilibrium there will be a simple linear relationship between the expected return and standard deviation of return for efficient combinations of risky assets. Thus far nothing has been said about such a relationship for individual assets. Typically the E_R, σ_R values associated with single assets will lie above the capital market line, reflecting the inefficiency of undiversified holdings. Moreover, such points may be scattered throughout the feasible region, with no consistent relationship between their expected return and total risk (σ_R). However, there will be a consistent relationship between their expected returns and what might best be called *systematic risk,* as we will now show.

Figure 7 illustrates the typical relationship between a single capital asset (point i) and an efficient combination of assets (point g) of which it is a part. The curve igg' indicates all E_R, σ_R values which can be obtained with feasible combinations of asset i and combination g. As before, we denote such a combination in terms of a proportion α of asset i and $(1-\alpha)$ of combination g. A value of $\alpha = 1$ would indicate pure investment in asset i while $\alpha = 0$ would imply investment in combination g. Note, however, that $\alpha = .5$ implies a total investment of more than half the funds in asset i, since half would be invested in i itself and the other half used to purchase combination g, which also includes some of asset i. This means that a combination in which asset i does not appear at all must be represented by some negative value of α. Point g' indicates such a combination.

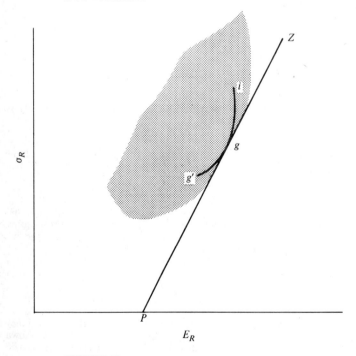

FIGURE 7

In Figure 7 the curve *igg'* has been drawn tangent to the capital market line (*PZ*) at point *g*. This is no accident. All such curves must be tangent to the capital market line in equilibrium, since (1) they must touch it at the point representing the efficient combination and (2) they are continuous at that point.[21] Under these conditions a lack of tangency would imply that the curve intersects *PZ*. But then some feasible combination of assets would lie to the right of the capital market line, an obvious impossibility since the capital market line represents the efficient boundary of feasible values of E_R and σ_R.

The requirement that curves such as *igg'* be tangent to the capital market line can be shown to lead to a relatively simple formula which relates the expected rate of return to various elements of risk for all assets which are included in combination *g*.[22] Its economic meaning can best be seen if the relationship betwee the return of asset *i* and that of combination *g* is viewed in a manner similar to that used in regression analysis.[23] Imagine that we were given a number of (ex post) observations of the return of the two investments. The points might plot as shown in Fig. 8. The scatter of the R_i observations around their mean (which will approximate E_{Ri}) is, of course, evidence of the

[21] Only if $r_{ig} = -1$ will the curve be discontinuous over the range in question.

[22] The standard deviation of a combination of *g* and *i* will be:

$$\sigma = \sqrt{\alpha^2 \sigma_{Ri}^2 + (1-\alpha)^2 \sigma_{Rg}^2 + 2r_{ig}\alpha(1-\alpha)\sigma_{Ri}\sigma_{Rg}}$$

at $\alpha = 0$:

$$\frac{d\sigma}{d\alpha} = -\frac{1}{\sigma}[\sigma_{Rg}^2 - r_{ig}\sigma_{Ri}\sigma_{Rg}]$$

but $\sigma = \sigma_{Rg}$ at $\alpha = 0$. Thus:

$$\frac{d\sigma}{d\alpha} = -[\sigma_{Rg} - r_{ig}\sigma_{Ri}]$$

The expected return of a combination will be:

$$E = \alpha E_{Ri} + (1-\alpha)E_{Rg}$$

Thus, at all values of α:

$$\frac{dE}{d\alpha} = -[E_{Rg} - E_{Ri}]$$

and, at $\alpha = 0$:

$$\frac{d\sigma}{dE} = \frac{\sigma_{Rg} - r_{ig}\sigma_{Ri}}{E_{Rg} - E_{Ri}}$$

Let the equation of the capital market line be:

$$\sigma_R = s(E_R - P)$$

where *P* is the pure interest rate. Since *igg'* is tangent to the line when $\alpha = 0$, and since (E_{Rg}, σ_{Rg}) lies on the line:

$$\frac{\sigma_{Rg} - r_{ig}\sigma_{Ri}}{E_{Rg} - E_{Ri}} = \frac{\sigma_{Rg}}{E_{Rg} - P}$$

or:

$$\frac{r_{ig}\sigma_{Ri}}{\sigma_{Rg}} = -\left[\frac{P}{E_{Rg} - P}\right] + \left[\frac{1}{E_{Rg} - P}\right]E_{Ri}.$$

[23] This model has been called the diagonal model since its portfolio analysis solution can be facilitated by rearranging the data so that the variance-covariance matrix becomes diagonal. The method is described in the author's article, cited earlier.

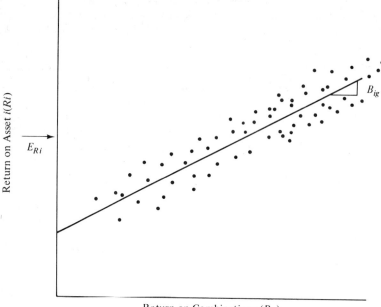

FIGURE 8

total risk of the asset—σ_{ri}. But part of the scatter is due to an underlying relationship with the return on combination g, shown by B_{ig}, the slope of the regression line. The response of R_i to changes in R_g (and variations in R_g itself) account for much of the variation in R_i. It is this component of the asset's total risk which we term the *systematic* risk. The remainder,[24] being uncorrelated with R_g, is the unsystematic component. This formulation of the relationship between R_i and R_g can be employed *ex ante* as a predictive model. B_{ig} becomes the *predicted* response of R_i to changes in R_g. Then, given σ_{Rg} (the predicted risk of R_g), the systematic portion of the predicted risk of each asset can be determined.

This interpretation allows us to state the relationship derived from the tangency of curves such as *igg'* with the capital market line in the form shown in Figure 9. All assets entering efficient combination g must have (predicted) B_{ig} and E_{Ri} values lying on the line PQ.[25] Prices will adjust so that assets which are

---

[24] Ex post, the standard error.

$$r_{ig} = \sqrt{\frac{B_{ig}{}^2\sigma_{Rg}{}^2}{\sigma_{Ri}{}^2}} = \frac{B_{ig}\sigma_{Rg}}{\sigma_{Ri}}$$

and:

$$B_{ig} = \frac{r_{ig}\sigma_{Ri}}{\sigma_{Rg}}$$

[25] The expression on the right is the expression on the left-hand side of the last equation in footnote 22. Thus:

$$B_{ig} = - \left[\frac{P}{E_{Rg} - P}\right] + \left[\frac{1}{E_{Rg} - P}\right] E_{Ri}.$$

more responsive to changes in R_g will have higher expected returns than those which are less responsive. This accords with common sense. Obviously the part of an asset's risk which is due to its correlation with the return on a combination cannot be diversified away when the asset is added to the combination. Since B_{ig} indicates the magnitude of this type of risk it should be directly related to expected return.

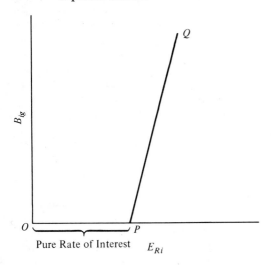

Pure Rate of Interest E_{Ri} **FIGURE 9**

The relationship illustrated in Figure 9 provides a partial answer to the question posed earlier concerning the relationship between an asset's risk and its expected return. But thus far we have argued only that the relationship holds for the assets which enter some particular efficient combination (g). Had another combination been selected, a different linear relationship would have been derived. Fortunately this limitation is easily overcome. As shown in the footnote,[26] we may arbitrarily select *any* one of the efficient combinations,

[26] Consider the two assets i and i^*, the former included in efficient combination g and the latter in combination g^*. As shown above:

$$B_{ig} = -\left[\frac{P}{E_{Rg} - P}\right] + \left[\frac{1}{E_{Rg} - P}\right]E_{Ri}$$

and:

$$B_{i^*g^*} = -\left[\frac{P}{E_{Rg^*} - P}\right] + \left[\frac{1}{E_{Rg^*} - P}\right]E_{Ri^*}.$$

Since R_g and R_g^* are perfectly correlated:

$$r_{i^*g^*} = r_{i^*g}$$

Thus:

$$\frac{B_{i^*g^*}\sigma_{Rg^*}}{\sigma_{Ri^*}} = \frac{B_{i^*g}\sigma_{Rg}}{\sigma_{Ri^*}}$$

and:

$$B_{i^*g^*} = B_{i^*g}\left[\frac{\sigma_{Rg}}{\sigma_{Rg^*}}\right]$$

Since both g and g^* lie on a line which intercepts the E-axis at P:

$$\frac{\sigma_{Rg}}{\sigma_{Rg^*}} = \frac{E_{Rg} - P}{E_{Rg^*} - P}$$

then measure the predicted responsiveness of *every* asset's rate of return to that of the combination selected; and these coefficients will be related to the expected rates of return of the assets in exactly the manner pictured in Figure 9.

The fact that rates of return from all efficient combinations will be perfectly correlated provides the justification for arbitrarily selecting any one of them. Alternatively we may choose instead any variable perfectly correlated with the rate of return of such combinations. The vertical axis in Figure 9 would then indicate alternative levels of a coefficient measuring the sensitivity of the rate of return of a capital asset to changes in the variable chosen.

This possibility suggests both a plausible explanation for the implication that all efficient combinations will be perfectly correlated and a useful interpretation of the relationship between an individual asset's expected return and its risk. Although the theory itself implies only that rates of return from efficient combinations will be perfectly correlated, we might expect that this would be due to their common dependence on the over-all level of economic activity. If so, diversification enables the investor to escape all but the risk resulting from swings in economic activity—this type of risk remains even in efficient combinations. And, since all other types can be avoided by diversification, only the responsiveness of an asset's rate of return to the level of economic activity is relevant in assessing its risk. Prices will adjust until there is a linear relationship between the magnitude of such responsiveness and expected return. Assets which are unaffected by changes in economic activity will return the pure interest rate; those which move with economic activity will promise appropriately higher expected rates of return.

This discussion provides an answer to the second of the two questions posed in this paper. In Part III it was shown that with respect to equilibrium conditions in the capital market as a whole, the theory leads to results consistent with classical doctrine (i.e., the capital market line). We have now shown that with regard to capital assets considered individually, it also yields implications consistent with traditional concepts: it is common practice for investment counselors to accept a lower expected return from defensive securities (those which respond little to changes in the economy) than they require from aggressive securities (which exhibit significant response). As suggested earlier, the familiarity of the implications need not be considered a drawback. The provision of a logical framework for producing some of the major elements of traditional financial theory should be a useful contribution in its own right.

---

and:

$$B_i{^*}_g{^*} = B_i{^*}_g \left[\frac{E_{Rg} - P}{E_{Rg}{^*} - P} \right]$$

Thus:

$$-\left[\frac{P}{E_{Rg}{^*} - P} \right] + \left[\frac{1}{E_{Rg}{^*} - P} \right] E_{Ri}{^*} = B_i{^*}_g \left[\frac{E_{Rg} - P}{E_{Rg}{^*} - P} \right]$$

from which we have the desired relationship between $R_i{^*}$ and g:

$$B_i{^*}_g = -\left[\frac{P}{E_{Rg} - P} \right] + \left[\frac{1}{E_{Rg} - P} \right] E_{Ri}{^*}$$

$B_i{^*}_g$ must therefore plot on the same line as does B_{ig}.

The price of a risky asset can be determined from market equilibrium theory based on modern portfolio theory. This theory has been developed by Sharpe in the previous article (28) and by Lintner (see the references in article 29). Fama discusses the derivations presented by Sharpe and Lintner and shows that they are consistent. In addition, Fama shows that the assumptions of Sharpe's single-index model are inconsistent with his derivation of the price of a risky asset and therefore can be considered only as an approximation of the true model (albeit a very good approximation).

29

Risk, Return, and Equilibrium: Some Clarifying Comments

*Eugene F. Fama**

This article is reprinted with permission from the Journal of Finance, *Vol. XXIII, No. 1 (March, 1968), pp. 29–40.*

Sharpe [12] and Lintner [7] have recently proposed models directed at the following questions: (a) What is the appropriate measure of the risk of a capital asset? (b) What is the equilibrium relationship between this measure of the asset's risk and its one-period expected return?[1] Lintner contends that the measure of risk derived from his model is different and more general than that proposed by Sharpe. In his reply to Lintner, Sharpe [13] agrees that their results are in some ways conflicting and that Lintner's paper supersedes his.

This paper will show that in fact there is no conflict between the Sharpe–Lintner models. Properly interpreted they lead to the same measure of the risk of an individual asset and to the same relationship between an asset's risk and its one-period expected return. The apparent conflicts discussed by Sharpe and Lintner are caused by Sharpe's concentration on a special stochastic process for describing returns that is not necessarily implied by his asset pricing

* In preparing this paper I have benefited from discussions with members of the Workshop in Finance of the Graduate School of Business. The comments of M. Blume, P. Brown, M. Jensen, M. Miller, H. Roberts, R. Roll, M. Scholes and A. Zellner were especially helpful. The research was supported by a grant from the Ford Foundation.

[1] The terms "capital asset" and "one-period return" will be defined below.

model. When applied to the more general stochastic processes that Lintner treats, Sharpe's model leads directly to Lintner's conclusions.

I. EQUILIBRIUM IN THE SHARPE MODEL

The Sharpe capital asset pricing model is based on the following assumptions:

(a) The market for capital assets is composed of risk averting investors, all of whom are one-period expected-utility-of-terminal-wealth maximizers (in the von Neumann-Morgenstern [16] sense) and find it possible to make optimal portfolio decisions solely on the basis of the means and standard deviations of the probability distributions of terminal wealth associated with the various available portfolios.[2] If the one-period return on an asset or portfolio is defined as the change in wealth during the horizon period divided by the initial wealth invested in the asset or portfolio, then the assumption implies that investors can make optimal portfolio decisions on the basis of means and standard deviations of distributions of one-period portfolio returns.[3]

(b) All investors have the same decision horizon, and over this common horizon period the means and variances of the distributions of one-period returns on assets and portfolios exist.

(c) Capital markets are perfect in the sense that all assets are infinitely divisible, there are no transactions costs or taxes, information is costless and available to everybody, and borrowing and lending rates are equal to each other and the same for all investors.

(d) Expectations and portfolio opportunities are "homogenous" throughout the market. That is, all investors have the same set of portfolio opportunities, and view the expected returns and standard deviations of return[4] provided by the various portfolios in the same way.

Assumption (a) places the analysis within the framework of the Markowitz [10] one-period mean-standard deviation portfolio model. Tobin [15] shows that the mean-standard deviation framework is appropriate either when probability distributions of portfolio returns are normal or Gaussian[5] or when

[2] In the one-period expected utility of terminal wealth model, the objects of choice for the investor are the probability distributions of terminal wealth provided by each asset and portfolio. Each "portfolio" represents a complete investment strategy covering all assets (e.g., bonds, stocks, insurance, real estate, etc.) that could possibly affect the investor's terminal wealth. That is, at the beginning of the horizon period the investor makes a single portfolio decision concerning the allocation of his investable wealth among the available terminal wealth producing assets. All terminal wealth producing assets are called capital assets.

[3] The one-period return defined in this way is just a linear transformation of the units in which terminal wealth is measured; an investor's utility function can be defined in terms of one-period return just as well as in terms of terminal wealth. Note that the one-period return involves no compounding; it is just the ratio of the change in terminal wealth to initial wealth, even though the horizon period may be very long.

Though the remainder of the analysis will be in terms of the one-period return, we should keep in mind that the objects being priced in the market are the probability distributions of terminal wealth associated with each of the available capital assets.

[4] Henceforth the terms "return" and "one-period return" will be used synonymously.

[5] Tobin claims (and properly so) that the mean-standard deviation framework is appropriate whenever distributions of returns on all assets and portfolios are of the same

investor utility of return functions are well approximated by quadratics. In either case the optimal portfolio for a risk averter will be a member of the mean-standard deviation efficient set, where an efficient portfolio must satisfy the following criteria: (1) If any other portfolio provides lower standard deviation of one-period return, it must also have lower expected return; and (2) if any other portfolio has greater expected return, it must also have greater standard deviation of return.[6]

Assumptions (b), (c) and (d) of the Sharpe model standardize the picture of the portfolio opportunity set available to each investor. Assumption (b) implies that the portfolio decisions of all investors are made at the same point in time, and the horizon considered in making these decisions is the same for

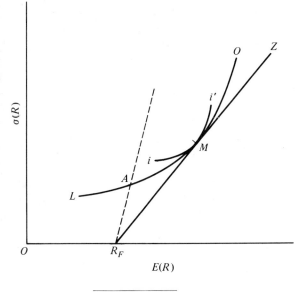

FIGURE 1

type and can be fully described by two parameters. If the distribution of the return on a portfolio is always of the same type as the distributions of the returns on the individual assets in the portfolio, then that distribution must be a member of the stable (or stable Paretian) class. But the only stable distribution whose variance exists is the normal.

[6] The mean-standard deviation model presupposes, of course, the existence of means and variances for all distributions of one-period returns. The work of Mandelbrot [9], Fama [2], and Roll [11] suggests, however, that this assumption may be inappropriate, at least with respect to the standard deviation. Distributions of returns on common stocks and bonds apparently conform better to members of the stable or stable Paretian family for which the variance does not exist than to the normal distribution (the only member of the family for which the variance does exist). This does not mean that mean-standard deviation portfolio models are useless. Fama [3] has shown that insights into the effects of diversification on dispersion of return that are derived from the mean-standard deviation model remain valid when the model is generalized to include the entire stable family. In a later paper [4] it is shown that much of the Sharpe–Lintner mean-standard deviation capital asset pricing model can also be generalized to include the non-normal members of the stable family. Thus it is not inappropriate to reconsider the Sharpe–Lintner models, since resolution of the apparent conflicts between them has implications for the more general model of [4].

all. Assumptions (c) and (d) standardize both the set of available portfolios and investors' evaluations of the combinations of expected return and standard deviation provided by each member of the set.[7]

The situation facing each investor can be represented as in Figure 1. The horizontal axis of the figure measures expected return $E(R)$ over the common horizon period, while the vertical axis measures standard deviation of return, $\sigma(R)$. If attention is restricted to portfolios involving only risky assets, Sharpe [12] shows that the set of mean-standard deviation efficient portfolios will fall along a curve convex to the origin, like LMO in Figure 1.[8]

The model assumes, however, that in addition to the opportunities presented by portfolios of risky assets, there is a riskless asset F which will provide the sure return R_F over the common horizon period; it is assumed that the investor can both borrow and lend at the riskless rate R_F. Consider portfolios C involving combinations of the riskless asset F and an arbitrary portfolio A of risky assets. The expected return and standard deviation of return provided by such combinations are

$$E(R_C) = xR_F + (1-x)E(R_A) \qquad x \le 1. \tag{1}$$
$$\sigma(R_C) = (1-x)\sigma(R_A), \tag{2}$$

where x is the proportion of available funds invested in the riskless asset F, so that $(1-x)$ is invested in A. Applying the chain rule,

$$\frac{d\sigma(R_C)}{dE(R_C)} = \frac{d\sigma(R_C)}{dx} \cdot \frac{dx}{dE(R_C)} = \frac{\sigma(R_A)}{E(R_A) - R_F} . \tag{3}$$

This implies that the combinations of expected return and standard deviation provided by portfolios involving F and A must fall along a straight line through R_F and A in Figure 1.

It is now easy to determine the effects of borrowing-lending opportunities on the set of efficient portfolios. In Figure 1 consider the line R_FMZ, touching LMO at M. This line represents the combinations of expected return and standard deviation associated with portfolios where the proportion x ($x \le 1$) is invested in the riskless asset F and $1-x$ in the portfolio of risky assets M. At the point R_F, $x = 1$, while at the point M, $x = 0$. Points below M along R_FMZ correspond to lending portfolios ($x > 0$), while points above M cor-

---

[7] Lintner [7, pp. 600–01] considers an extension of the asset pricing model to the case where investors disagree on the expected returns and standard deviations provided by portfolios. The results are essentially the same as those derived under the assumption of "homogenous expectations." Since Lintner's criticism of Sharpe does not depend on this part of his work, our discussion will use the simpler "homogeneous expectations" version of the model. Most of Lintner's discussion is also within this framework, and in all other respects his assumptions are identical to those of Sharpe.

It is important to emphasize that the Sharpe–Lintner asset pricing models, like the Markowitz–Tobin portfolio models, present one-period analyses. For a more complete discussion of the one-period framework see [4].

[8] Strictly speaking this result presupposes that there are at least two portfolios in the efficient set. That is, there is no portfolio which has both higher expected return and lower standard deviation of return than *any* other portfolio. In a market of risk averters with "homogeneous expectations" this is not a strong presumption.

respond to borrowing portfolios $(x < 0)$. At given levels of $\sigma (R)$ there are portfolios along $R_F MZ$ which provide higher levels of $E (R)$ than the corresponding portfolios along LMO. Thus (except for M) the portfolios along LMO are dominated by portfolios along $R_F MZ$, which is now the efficient set.

The conditions necessary for equilibrium in the asset market can now be stated. Since all investors have the same horizon and view their portfolio opportunities in the same way, the Sharpe model implies that everybody faces the same picture of the set of efficient portfolios. If the relevant picture is Figure 1, then all efficient portfolios for all investors will lie along $R_F MZ$. More risky efficient portfolios involve borrowing $(x < 0)$ and investing all available funds (including borrowings) in the risky combination M. Less risky efficient portfolios involve lending $(x > 0)$ some funds at the rate R_F and investing remaining funds in M. The particular portfolio that an investor chooses will depend on his attitudes toward risk and return, but optimum portfolios for all investors will involve some combination of the riskless asset F and the portfolio of risky assets M[9]. There will be no incentive for anyone to hold risky assets not included in M. If M does not contain all the risky assets in the market, or if it does not contain them in exactly the proportions in which they are outstanding, then there will be some assets that no one will hold. This is inconsistent with equilibrium, since in equilibrium all assets must be held.

Thus, if Figure 1 is to represent equilibrium, M must be the market portfolio; that is, M consists of all risky assets in the market, each weighted by the ratio of its total market value to the total market value of all assets.[10] In addition, the riskless rate R_F must be such that net borrowing in the market is 0; that is, at the rate R_F the total quantity of funds that people want to borrow is equal to the quantity that others want to lend.

As a description of reality, this view of equilibrium has an obvious short-

[9] As noted earlier, Tobin [15] shows that the mean-standard deviation portfolio model is appropriate either when probability distributions of returns on portfolios are normal or when investor utility of return functions are well approximated by quadratics. In either case the indifference curves (i.e., loci of constant expected utility) of a risk averter will be positively sloping and concave to the origin in the $E(R)$, $\sigma(R)$ plane of Figure 1, with expected utility increasing as we move on to indifference curves further to the right in the plane. Since the efficient set of portfolios is linear, equilibrium for the investor (i.e., the point of maximum attainable expected utility) will occur at a point of tangency between an indifference curve and the efficient set or at the point R_F. The degree of the investor's risk aversion will determine whether this will be a point above or below M along $R_F MZ$ in Figure 1.

[10] Figure 1 itself does not tell us that the market portfolio M is the only combination of risky assets with expected return and standard deviation $E(R_M)$ and $\sigma(R_M)$. Suppose there is another portfolio G such that $E(R_G) = E(R_M)$ and $\sigma(R_G) = \sigma(R_M)$. Consider portfolios C where the proportion x $(0 < x < 1)$ is invested in G and $(1-x)$ in M. Then

$$E(R_C) = xE(R_G) + (1-x)E(R_M) = E(R_M)$$

$$\sigma(R_C) = [x^2\sigma^2(R_G) + (1-x)^2\sigma^2(R_M) + 2x (1-x) \text{ corr } (R_G, R_M) \sigma(R_G) \sigma(R_M)]^{1/2}$$

It follows that $\sigma (R_C) < \sigma(R_M)$ unless corr$(R_G, R_M) = 1$, that is, unless the returns on portfolios G and M are perfectly correlated. The condition $\sigma(R_C) < \sigma (R_M)$ is inconsistent with equilibrium, since in equilibrium M must be a member of the efficient set. Thus, if there is a portfolio with the same expected return and standard deviation as the market portfolio M, its returns must be *perfectly* correlated with those of M, an unlikely situation. In any case, such a portfolio would be a perfect substitute for M.

coming. In particular, all investors hold only combinations of the riskless asset F and M. The market portfolio M is the only efficient portfolio of all risky assets.[11] This result follows from the assumed existence of the opportunity to borrow or lend indefinitely at the riskless rate R_F. Fortunately, in [4] it is shown that the measure of the risk of an individual asset and the equilibrium relationship between risk and expected return derived from the capital asset pricing model will be essentially the same whether or not it is assumed that such riskless borrowing-lending opportunities exist.

II. THE MEASUREMENT OF RISK AND THE RELATIONSHIP BETWEEN RISK AND RETURN

We consider now the major problems of the Sharpe capital asset pricing model: that is, (a) determination of a measure of risk consistent with the portfolio and expected utility models, and (b) derivation of the equilibrium relationship between risk and expected return. It is important to note that the development of the Sharpe model to this point is completely consistent with Lintner [7]. In particular, the two models are based on the same set of assumptions, and the resulting views of equilibrium are the same. Thus it seems unlikely that the implications of the two models for the measurement of risk and the relationship between risk and return can be different. In fact it will now be shown that Sharpe's approach leads to exactly the same conclusions as Lintner's. The "conflicts" which they find in their respective results will be shown to arise from the fact that both misinterpret the implications of the Sharpe model.

For any risky asset i there will be a curve, like $i\,M\,i'$ in Figure 1, which shows the combinations of $E(R)$ and $\sigma(R)$ that can be attained by forming

---

[11] Sharpe [12] himself proposes a slightly different version of equilibrium, one which does not imply that the market portfolio M is the *only* efficient portfolio of risky assets. He argues that in equilibrium an entire segment of the right boundary of the set of feasible risky portfolios may be tangent to a straight line through R_F. He further shows that the returns on all portfolios along such a segment must be perfectly correlated. Since ex post returns on portfolios of different risky assets are never perfectly correlated, it is unlikely that investors will expect them to be perfectly correlated ex ante, and so multiple tangencies would seem to represent an uninteresting case.

Note, though, that if a segment of the right boundary of the set of feasible risky portfolios is tangent to a line through R_F, to be consistent with equilibrium the market, portfolio M must be one of the tangency points along the segment. This is an implication of the fact that when the portfolios of individuals are aggregated, the aggregate is just the market portfolio with zero net borrowing. Thus, it must be possible to obtain the market portfolio by taking weighted combinations of portfolios along the tangency segment.

In sum, given the assumptions of the Sharpe model, equilibrium can be associated (a) with a situation where the market portfolio is the only efficient combination of risky assets or (b) with a situation where there are many efficient combinations of risky assets, one of which is the market portfolio. Fortunately, Sharpe shows that in using the portfolio model to develop the relationship between risk and expected return on individual assets, it does not matter which of these representations of equilibrium is adopted. Because it simplifies the exposition of the model and also seems to be more realistic, we shall concentrate on the case where the market portfolio is the only efficient combination of risky assets. This is also the case dealt with by Lintner [7].

portfolios of asset i and the market portfolio M. If x is the proportion of av ble funds invested in asset i, the returns on such portfolios (C) can be expre as[12]

$$R_C = xR_i + (1 - x)R_M \qquad (x \le 1). \qquad (4)$$

Now consider portfolios (D) where the proportion x is invested in riskless asset F and $(1-x)$ in the market portfolio M. The returns on such p folios will be given by

$$R_D = xR_F + (1 - x)R_M. \qquad (5)$$

As noted earlier, the combinations of expected return and standard devi of return provided by such portfolios fall along the efficient set line $R_F M$ Figure 1. It is easy to show that the functions underlying $i\,M\,i'$ and LMC both differentiable at the point M. Since $R_F MZ$ is the efficient set, $i\,M\,i$ LMO must be tangent at M. That is,

$$\frac{d\sigma(R_C)}{dE(R_C)} = \frac{d\sigma(R_D)}{dE(R_D)}, \quad \text{when} \quad x = 0. \qquad (6)$$

The economic interpretation of (6) is familiar. $d\sigma(R_D)/d\,E(R_D)$ marginal rate of exchange of standard deviation for expected return the efficient set $R_F MZ$. Since all investors have the same view of the ef set, $d\sigma(R_D)/dE\,(R_D)$ is in fact the market rate of exchange. On the hand, $d\sigma(R_C)/dE(R_C)$ is the marginal rate of exchange of standard dev for expected return in the market portfolio as the proportion of asset i market portfolio is changed. In equilibrium excess demand for asset i m 0. But this will only be the case if when $x = 0$ in (4), the expected reti asset i is such that the marginal rate of exchange $d\sigma\,(R_C)/dE\,(R_C)$ is eq the market rate of exchange $d\sigma(R_D)/dE(R_D)$.

Sharpe's insight was in noting that the equilibrium condition (6) both a measure of the risk of asset i and the equilibrium relationship b the risk and the expected return on the asset. Using the chain rule to expressions for $d\sigma\,(R_C)/dE(R_C)$ and $d\sigma\,(R_D)/dE\,(R_D)$, and then eva these derivatives at $x = 0$, (6) becomes

$$\frac{\text{cov}(R_i, R_M) - \sigma^2(R_M)}{[E(R_i) - E(R_M)]\sigma(R_M)} = \frac{\sigma(R_M)}{E(R_M) - R_F}.$$

[12] When $0 \le x \le 1$ portfolios along $i\,M\,i'$ between i and M are obtained. At . market portfolio M is obtained. Since M contains asset i, even when $x = 0$ the C will contain some of i. When $x < 0$, so that there is a short position in ass folios along the segment Mi' are obtained.
Though the discussion in the text is phrased in terms of individual assets, the applies directly to the case where i is a portfolio.

[13] That is,

$$\frac{d\sigma(R_C)}{dE(R_C)} = \frac{d\sigma(R_C)}{dx} \cdot \frac{dx}{dE(R_C)}, \quad \text{and} \quad \frac{d\sigma(R_D)}{dE(R_D)} = \frac{d\sigma(R_D)}{dx} \cdot \frac{dx}{dE(R_D)}$$

To get an expression for the expected return on asset i, it suffices to solve (7) for $E(R_i)$, leading to

$$E(R_i) = R_F + \frac{[E(R_M) - R_F]}{\sigma^2(R_M)} \operatorname{cov}(R_i, R_M), \qquad i = 1, 2, \ldots, N, \qquad (8)$$

where N is the total number of assets in the market. Alternatively, the "risk premium" in the expected return on asset i is

$$E(R_i) - R_F = \left[\frac{E(R_M) - R_F}{\sigma^2(R_M)}\right] \operatorname{cov}(R_i, R_M) = \lambda \operatorname{cov}(R_i, R_M),$$
$$i = 1, 2, \ldots, N. \qquad (9)$$

Now (9) applies to each of the N assets in the market, and the value of λ, the ratio of the risk premium in the expected return on the market portfolio to the variance of this return, will be the same for all assets. Thus the differences between the risk premiums on different assets depend entirely on the covariance term in (9). The coefficient λ can be thought of as the market price per unit of risk so that the appropriate measure of the risk of asset i is cov (R_i, R_M). Thus this term certainly deserves closer study. In the process we shall find that (9), which is just a rearrangement of the last expression in Sharpe's [12] footnote 22, is exactly Lintner's [7] expression for the risk premium.

Note that by definition R_M, the return on the market portfolio, is just the weighted average of the returns on all the individual assets in the market. That is,

$$R_M = \sum_{j=1}^{N} X_j R_j, \qquad (10)$$

where X_j is the proportion of the total market value of all assets that is accounted for by asset j. It follows that

$$\operatorname{cov}(R_i, R_M) = E\{[R_M - E(R_M)][R_i - E(R_i)]\}$$
$$= E\left\{\sum_{j=1}^{N} X_j[R_j - E(R_j)][R_i - E(R_i)]\right\}$$
$$= \sum_{j=1}^{N} X_j \operatorname{cov}(R_j, R_i). \qquad (11)$$

Substituting (11) into (9) yields

$$E(R_i) - R_F = \lambda \sum_{j=1}^{N} X_j \operatorname{cov}(R_j, R_i) \qquad i = 1, 2, \ldots N, \qquad (12)$$

which is exactly Lintner's [7, p. 596] equation (11) but derived from Sharpe's model.[14]

[14] Lintner [7,8] makes much of the fact that

$$\operatorname{cov}(R_i, R_M) = \sum_{j \ne i} x_j \operatorname{cov}(R_j, R_i) + x_i \sigma^2(R_i)$$

$$j \ne i$$

Within the context of the Sharpe model (12) is quite reasonable. From (10)

$$\sigma^2(R_M) = \sum_{k=1}^{N} \sum_{j=1}^{N} X_k X_j \operatorname{cov}(R_j, R_k) = \sum_{k=1}^{N} X_k \sum_{j=1}^{N} X_j \operatorname{cov}(R_j, R_k). \qquad (13)$$

Now the term for $k = i$ in (13) is just

$$X_i \sum_{j=1}^{N} X_j \operatorname{cov}(R_j, R_i) = X_i \operatorname{cov}(R_i, R_M).$$

Thus $X_i \operatorname{cov}(R_i, R_M)$ measures the contribution of asset i to the variance of the return on the market portfolio. Since this contribution is proportional to $\operatorname{cov}(R_i, R_M)$ and since the market portfolio is the only stochastic component in all efficient portfolios, it is not unreasonable that the risk premium on asset i is proportional to $\operatorname{cov}(R_i, R_M)$.

Note that (9) and (12) allow us to rank the risk premiums in the expected returns on different assets, but they provide no information about the magnitudes of the premiums. These depend on the difference $E(R_M)-R_F$, which in turn depends on the attitudes of all the different investors in the market toward risk and return. Without knowing more about attitudes toward risk, all we can say is that $E(R_M)-R_F$ must be such that in equilibrium all risky assets are held and the borrowing-lending market is cleared.

Thus, properly interpreted, the models of Sharpe and Lintner lead to identical conclusions concerning the appropriate measures of the risk of an individual asset and the equilibrium relationship between the risk of the asset and its expected return. What, then, is the source of the "conflict" between the two models which both authors apparently feel exists? Unfortunately Sharpe puts the major results of his paper in his footnote 22 [12, p. 438]; in the text he concentrates on applying these results to the market or "diagonal" model of the behavior of asset returns which he proposed in an earlier paper [14]. But the market model that he uses contains inconsistent constraints which lead to misinterpretation of the capital asset pricing model. Lintner, in his turn, does not appreciate the generality of Sharpe's results, and accepts (and in some ways misinterprets) Sharpe's treatment of the market model.

III. THE RELATIONSHIP BETWEEN RISK AND RETURN IN THE MARKET MODEL

In the "market model" which Sharpe [12, pp. 438–42] uses to illustrate his asset pricing model, it is assumed that there is a linear relationship between the one-period return on an individual asset and the return on the market portfolio M. That is,

$$R_i = \alpha_i + \beta_i R_M + \varepsilon_i \qquad i = 1, 2, \ldots, N, \qquad (15)$$

---

contains a term for the variance of asset i. He stresses the importance of the variance term in empirical studies concerned with measuring the riskiness of an individual asset. Recall, however, that X_i is the total market value of all outstanding units of asset i divided by the total market value of *all* assets. Thus the variance term in (14) is likely to be trivial relative to the weighted sum of covariances—a familiar result in portfolio models.

where α_i and β_i are parameters specific to asset i. It is further assumed that the random disturbances ϵ_i have the properties,

$$E(\varepsilon_i) = 0 \qquad i = 1, 2, \ldots, N \tag{16a}$$

$$\text{cov}(\varepsilon_i, \varepsilon_j) = 0 \qquad i, j = 1, 2, \ldots, N, \quad i \neq j, \tag{16b}$$

$$\text{cov}(\varepsilon_i, R_M) = 0 \qquad i = 1, 2, \ldots, N. \tag{16c}$$

Thus the assumption is that the only relationships between the returns on individual risky assets arise from the fact that the return on each is related to the return on the market portfolio M via (15).

Applying the market model of (15) and (16) to the equivalent risk premium expressions (9) and (12) will allow us to pinpoint the apparent source of conflict between the results of Sharpe and Lintner. From (15) and (16)

$$\text{cov}(R_i, R_M) = E\{(\beta_i [R_M - E(R_M)] + \varepsilon_i)[(R_M - E(R_M)]\} \tag{17a}$$

$$= \beta_i \sigma^2(R_M) + \text{cov}(\varepsilon_i, R_M) \tag{17b}$$

$$= \beta_i \sigma^2(R_M). \tag{17c}$$

Substituting (17c) into (9) yields

$$E(R_i) - R_F = \lambda \beta_i \sigma^2(R_M) = [E(R_M) - R_F]\beta_i, \qquad i = 1, 2, \ldots, N. \tag{18}$$

Thus when the stochastic process generating returns is as described by the market model of (15) and (16), the risk premium in the expected return on a given asset is proportional to the slope coefficient β for that asset. The more sensitive the asset is to the return on the market portfolio, the larger its risk premium.

In discussing the implications of his capital asset pricing model Sharpe concentrates on (18). But it is important to remember that the market model assumes a very special stochastic process for asset returns which was not assumed in the derivation of the general expressions (9) and (12) for the risk premium in the capital asset pricing model. The asset pricing model itself, as summarized by expressions (9) and (12), applies to much more general stochastic processes than those assumed in the market model and thus in (18). This point is especially crucial since we shall now see that the market model, as defined by (15) and (16), is inconsistent.

Expression (18) was obtained by applying the market model to (9). Since (12) and (9) are equivalent expressions for the risk premium in the expected return on asset i, it should be possible to apply the market model to (12) and obtain (18):

$$E(R_i) - R_F = \lambda \sum_{j=1}^{N} X_j \, \text{cov}(R_j, R_i) \tag{19}$$

$$= \lambda \left\{ \beta_i \sum_{j=1}^{N} X_j \beta_j \sigma^2(R_M) + X_i \sigma^2(\varepsilon_i) \right\} \tag{20}$$

which is exactly Lintner's [7, p. 605] expression (24). It will presently be shown that the market model implies $\sum X_j B_J = 1$. Thus (20) reduces to

$$E(R_i) - R_F = \lambda[\beta_i \sigma^2(R_M) + X_i \sigma^2(\varepsilon_i)] \tag{21}$$

or

$$E(R_i) - R_F = [E(R_M) - R_F]\left[\beta_i + \frac{X_i \sigma^2(\varepsilon_i)}{\sigma^2(R_M)}\right]. \tag{22}$$

But (22) includes a term involving $\sigma^2(\varepsilon_i)$ which does not appear in (18), and this is the major source of controversy between Lintner and Sharpe. In applying the asset pricing model to the market model, Sharpe arrives at (18) while Lintner derives (20) or its equivalent (22). Lintner [7, pp. 607–08] presumes that Sharpe is considering the case where all residual variances [the $\sigma^2(\varepsilon_i)$] are 0. But Sharpe clearly did not intend to impose this restriction on his model.[15] In addition, (18) is derived directly from (9), (15), and (16), and there is no presumption in the derivation that the residual variances are 0.

In fact the discrepancy between (18) and (22) arises from an inconsistency in the specification of the market model; neither of these expressions for the risk premium is correct. Note that (10) and (15) together imply

$$R_M = \sum_{j=1}^{N} X_j R_j = \sum_{j=1}^{N} X_j [\alpha_j + \beta_j R_M + \varepsilon_j]. \tag{23}$$

Thus, since ε_i is one of the terms in R_M, (16c) is inconsistent with the remaining assumptions of the market model. Since (16c) is used in deriving both (18) and (22), these are both incorrect expressions for the risk premium in the market model.

Unfortunately, (16c) is not the only inconsistency in the market model of (15), (16) and (23); it is also easy to show that (15), (16b) and (23) cannot hold simultaneously. Recalling that α_j and β_j are constants, (23) implies

$$\sum_{j=1}^{N} X_j \alpha_j = 0, \quad \sum_{j=1}^{N} X_j \beta_j = 1, \tag{24a}$$

$$\sum_{j=1}^{N} X_j \varepsilon_j = 0. \tag{26b}$$

The constraints of (24a) pose no problem; (24b), however, is inconsistent with (16b)—we cannot assume that the disturbances are independent and then constrain their weighted sum to be 0.

One possible specification of the market model which does not lead to the problems discussed above is as follows.

$$R_i = \alpha_i + \beta_i r_M + \varepsilon_i \quad i = 1, 2, \ldots, N, \tag{25a}$$

[15] Cf., Sharpe [12, pp. 438–39]. "The response of R_i to changes in R_g (our R_M) (and variations in R_g itself) account for much of the variation of R_i. It is this component of the asset's total risk which we term the *systematic* risk. The remainder, being uncorrelated with R_g, is the "unsystematic component." Though Sharpe does not explicitly specify the version of the market model he is considering, it seems clear from this quotation and the remainder of his discussion that, for his purposes, [15] and [16] represent the relevant model.

$$E(\varepsilon_i) = 0 \qquad\qquad i = 1, 2, \ldots, N, \qquad\qquad \text{(25b)}$$

$$\text{cov}(\varepsilon_i, \varepsilon_j) = 0 \qquad\qquad i, j = 1, 2, \ldots, N, \quad i \neq j, \qquad \text{(25c)}$$

$$\text{cov}(\varepsilon_i\, r_M) = 0 \qquad\qquad i = 1, 2, \ldots, N. \qquad\qquad \text{(25d)}$$

In this model r_M is interpreted as a common underlying market factor which affects the returns on all assets. The relationship between r_M and the return on the market portfolio is then

$$R_M = \sum_{j=1}^{N} X_j R_j = \sum_{j=1}^{N} X_j[\alpha_j + \beta_j r_M + \varepsilon_j]. \qquad \text{(26)}$$

From either (9) or (12) it follows that in this model the risk premium on asset i is

$$E(R_i) - R_F = \lambda \sum_{j=1}^{N} X_j \,\text{cov}(R_j, R_i)$$

$$= \lambda \sum_{j=1}^{N} X_j E\{(\beta_j[r_M - E(r_M)] + \varepsilon_j)(\beta_i[r_M - E(r_M)] + \varepsilon_i)\}$$

$$E(R_i) - R_F = \lambda \left\{ \beta_i \sum_{j=1}^{N} X_j \beta_j \sigma^2(r_M) + X_i \sigma^2(\varepsilon_i) \right\} \qquad \text{(27)}$$

which is equivalent to Lintner's [7, equation (23)] expression for the risk premium in this more general version of the market model. But it is again important to note that Lintner's results follow directly from (9) and (12), the *general* expressions for the risk premium developed in Sharpe's model.

Finally, though the issues discussed above are certainly interesting from a theoretical viewpoint, from a practical viewpoint (18), (22) and (27) are nearly equivalent expressions for the risk premium in the market model. The empirical evidence of King [6] and Blume [1] suggests that, on average, $\sigma^2(\varepsilon_i)$ and $\sigma^2(R_M)$ in (22) are about equal. Thus the size of the residual term in (22) will be determined primarily by X_i, the proportion of the total value of all assets accounted for by asset i, which will usually be quite small relative to β_i (which is on average 1). The risk premiums given by (18) and (22), then, will be nearly equal.

Next note that it is always possible to scale r_M in (26) so that $\sum X_j \alpha_j = 0$ and $\sum X_j \beta_j = 1$. Then

$$\sigma^2(R_M) = \sigma^2(r_M) + \sum_{j=1}^{N} X_j^2 \sigma^2(\varepsilon_j). \qquad \text{(28)}$$

But again the weighted sum of residual variances will be small relative to $\sigma^2(r_M)$ so that $\sigma^2(R_M) \cong \sigma^2(r_M)$, which implies that the risk premiums given by (22) and (27) are almost equal.

IV. CONCLUSIONS

In sum, then, there are no real conflicts between the capital asset pricing models of Sharpe [12] and Lintner [7, 8]. When they apply their general results to the market model, both make errors which turn out to be unimportant from a practical viewpoint. The important point is that their general models represent equivalent approaches to the problem of capital asset pricing under uncertainty.

REFERENCES

1. Marshall E. Blume. "The Assessment of Portfolio Performance," unpublished Ph. D. dissertation, Graduate School of Business, University of Chicago, 1967.
2. Eugene F. Fama. "The Behavior of Stock-Market Prices," *Journal of Business* (January, 1965), pp. 34–105.
3. ———. "Portfolio Analysis in a Stable Paretian Market," *Management Science* (January, 1965), pp. 404–19.
4. ———. "Risk, Return, and Equilibrium in a Stable Paretian Market," unpublished manuscript (October, 1967).
5. Michael Jensen. "Risk, the Pricing of Capital Assets, and the Evaluation of Investment Portfolios," unpublished Ph. D. dissertation, Graduate School of Business, University of Chicago, 1967.
6. Benjamin F. King. "Market and Industry Factors in Stock Price Behavior," *Journal of Business,* Supplement (January, 1966), pp. 139–90.
7. John Lintner. "Security Prices, Risk, and Maximal Gains from Diversification," *Journal of Finance* (December, 1965), pp. 587–615.
8. ———. "The Valuation of Risk Assets and the Selection of Risky Investments in Stock Portfolios and Capital Budgets," *Review of Economics and Statistics* (February, 1965), pp. 13–37.
9. Benoit Mandelbrot. "The Variation of Certain Speculative Prices," *Journal of Business* (October, 1963), pp. 394–419.
10. Harry Markowitz. *Portfolio Selection: Efficient Diversification of Investments.* New York: John Wiley and Sons, Inc., 1959.
11. Richard Roll. "The Efficient Market Model Applied to U.S. Treasury Bill Rates" unpublished Ph. D. thesis, Graduate School of Business, University of Chicago, 1968.
12. William F. Sharpe. "Capital Asset Prices: A Theory of Market Equilibrium under Conditions of Risk," *Journal of Finance* (September, 1964), pp. 425–42.
13. ———. "Security Prices, Risk, and Maximal Gains from Diversification: Reply," *Journal of Finance* (December, 1966), pp. 743–44.
14. ———. "A Simplified Model for Portfolio Analysis," *Management Science* (January, 1963), pp. 277–93.
15. James Tobin. "Liquidity Preference as Behavior Towards Risk," *Review of Economic Studies* (February, 1958), pp. 65–86.
16. John von Neumann and Oskar Morgenstern. *Theory of Games and Economic Behavior,* Princeton: Princeton University Press, third edition, 1953.

E. Evaluation of Investment Performance

In this article, Sharpe examines the performance of mutual funds using both a criteria which he develops and one proposed by Treynor. This article is important both for the discussion of ways to evaluate mutual funds and for the result of the evaluation itself. Sharpe's finding that mutual funds have not consistently outperformed the market is consistent with most other evidence and with the ñypothesis that markets are efficient.

30

Mutual Fund Performance

*William F. Sharpe**

This article is reprinted with permission from the Journal of Business: A Supplement, *No. 1, Part 2 (January, 1966), pp. 119–138.*

I. INTRODUCTION

Within the last few years considerable progress has been made in three closely related areas—the theory of portfolio selection, the theory of the pricing of capital assets under conditions of risk,[2] and the general behavior of stock-market prices.[3] Results obtained in all three areas are relevant for evaluating mutual fund performance. Unfortunately, few of the studies of mutual funds have taken advantage of the substantial backlog of theoretical and empirical material

* I am grateful to Norman H. Jones, of the RAND Corporation, and Eugene F. Fama, of the University of Chicago, for helpful comments and suggestions. Any views expressed in this paper are those of the author. They should not be interpreted as reflecting the views of the RAND Corporation or the official opinion or policy of any of its governmental or private research sponsors.

[1] The original work in the field was that of H. Markowitz; see his "Portfolio Selection", *Journal of Finance,* XII (March, 1952), 71–91, or the subsequent expanded version, *Portfolio Selection, Efficient Diversification of Investments* (New York: John Wiley & Sons, 1959). For extensions see my "A Simplified Model for Portfolio Analysis," *Management Science,* IX (January, 1963), 277–93, and Eugene F. Fama, "Portfolio Analysis in a Stable Paretian Market," *Management Science,* XI (January, 1965), 404–19.

[2] See, e.g., my "Capital Asset Prices: A Theory of Market Equilibrium under Conditions of Risk," *Journal of Finance,* XIX (September, 1964), 425–42.

[3] For a summary of this work see Eugene F. Fama, "The Behavior of Stock-Market Prices," *Journal of Business,* XXXVIII (January, 1965), 34–405.

made available by recent studies in these related areas. However, one paper pointing the direction for future studies of mutual fund performance has appeared. Drawing on results obtained in the field of portfolio analysis, Jack L. Treynor has suggested a new predictor of mutual fund performance[4]—one that differs from virtually all those used previously by incorporating the volatility of a fund's return in a simple yet meaningful manner.

This paper attempts to extend Treynor's work by subjecting his proposed measure to empirical test in order to evaluate its predictive ability. But we will also attempt to do something more—to make explicit the relationships between recent developments in capital theory and alternative models of mutual fund performance and to subject these alternative models to empirical test.

II. IMPLICATIONS OF RECENT DEVELOPMENTS IN CAPITAL THEORY

A. PORTFOLIO ANALYSIS THEORY[5]

The theory of portfolio analysis is essentially normative; it describes efficient techniques for selecting portfolios on the basis of predictions about the performance of individual securities. The key element in the portfolio analyst's view of the world is his emphasis on both expected return and risk. The selection of a preferred combination of risk and expected return must, in the final analysis, depend on the preferences of the investor and cannot be made solely by the technician. However, the technician can (and should) attempt to find *efficient* portfolios—those promising the greatest expected return for any given degree of risk. The *portfolio analyst's* tasks are thus (1) translating predictions about security performance into predictions of portfolio performance, and (2) selecting from among the large number of possible portfolios those that are efficient. The *security analyst's* task is to provide the required predictions of security performance (including the interrelationships among the performances of securities) The *investor's* task is to select from among the efficient portfolios the one that he considers most desirable, based on his particular feelings regarding risk and expected return.

What tasks are implied for the mutual fund by this view of the investment process? Certainly those of security analysis and portfolio analysis. The emphasis in mutual fund advertising on diversification and the search for incorrectly priced securities reflects the importance accorded these aspects of the process. Portfolio analysis theory, unfortunately, does not make clear the manner in which the third function should be performed. A mutual fund cannot practically determine the preference patterns of its investors directly. Even if it could, there might be substantial differences among them. The process must work in the other direction, with the mutual fund management selecting an attitude toward risk and expected return and then inviting investors with similar preferences to purchase shares in the fund. At one extreme, the fund might attempt to describe

---

[4] "How To Rate Management of Investment Funds," *Harvard Business Review*, XLIII (January–February, 1965), 63–75.

[5] The material in this section is based on the references given in n. 1.

an entire pattern of relative preference for expected return vis-a-vis risk (i.e., a pattern of indifference curves). A much more likely method, and one that seems to be followed in practice, involves merely a description of the general degree of risk planned for the fund's portfolio; the fund then simply attempts to select the efficient portfolio for that degree of risk (i.e., the one with the greatest expected return).

Portfolio analysis theory per se makes no assumptions about the pattern of security prices or the skill of investment managers. Thus few implications can be drawn concerning the results obtained by different mutual funds. Performance ex post might vary in two respects. First, different funds could exhibit different degrees of variability in return, due either to conscious selection of different degrees of risk or to erroneous predictions of the risk inherent in particular portfolios. Second, funds holding portfolios with similar variability in return might exhibit major differences in average return, due to the inability of some managers to select incorrectly priced securities and/or to diversify their holdings properly. In short, if sound mutual fund management requires the selection of incorrectly priced securities, effective diversification, and the selection of a portfolio in the chosen risk class, there is ample room for major and persisting differences in the performance of different funds.

B. THE BEHAVIOR OF STOCK-MARKET PRICES[6]

Recent work on the general behavior of stock-market prices has raised serious questions concerning the importance of one of the functions of mutual fund management. The theory of random walks asserts that the past behavior of a security's price is of no value in predicting its future price. The impressive evidence supporting this theory suggest that it may be very difficult (and very expensive) to detect securities that are incorrectly priced. If so, it is not because security analysts are not doing their job properly, but because they are doing it very well. However, if this is the case, it may not pay the manager of a particular fund to devote extensive resources to the search for incorrectly priced securities; and the fund that does so may provide its investors a poorer net performance (after costs) than one that does not.

Under these conditions, what are the tasks of the mutual fund? Broadly defined, they still include security analysis, portfolio analysis, and the selection of a portfolio in the desired risk class. But the emphasis is changed. Security analysis is directed more toward evaluating the interrelationships among securities—the extent to which returns are correlated. And portfolio analysis is concerned primarily with diversification and the selection of a portfolio of the desired risk. In a perfect capital market, any properly diversified portfolio will be efficient; the mutual fund manager must select from among alternative diversified portfolios the one with the appropriate degree of risk.

Strictly speaking, the implications of this view of the world for mutual fund performance do not differ from those of the theory of portfolio analysis. Ex post, funds can be expected to exhibit differences in variability of return, due to intentional or unintentional selection of different risk classes. And the port-

---

[6] The material in this section is based on Fama's "The Behavior of Stock-Market Prices," *op. cit.*

folios of some funds may be more efficient than others (i.e., give greater average return at the same level of variability) if managers differ in their ability to diversify effectively. However, the likelihood that persistent differences in efficiency will occur is greatly reduced. Recent work has shown that the task of diversification may be much simpler than formerly supposed, requiring only the spreading of holdings among standard industrial classes.[7] If so, most funds are likely to hold portfolios that are efficient ex ante. Any differences in efficiency ex post are thus probably transitory. The only basis for persistently inferior performance would be the continued expenditure of large amounts of a fund's assets on the relatively fruitless search for incorrectly valued securities.

C. THE THEORY OF CAPITAL-ASSET PRICES UNDER CONDITIONS OF RISK

Empirical work on the behavior of stock-market prices supports the view that the market responds very rapidly to new information affecting the value of securities. A natural reaction to these results is the construction of a model of a perfectly informed market in which each participant used his information in the manner suggested by portfolio analysis theory. Such an approach has been described elsewhere[8]; only the major features will be given here.

The predicted performance of a portfolio is described with two measures: the expected rate of return (E_i) and the predicted variability or risk, expressed as the standard deviation of return (σ_i). All investors are assumed to be able to invest funds at a common risk-free interest rate and to borrow funds at the same rate (at least to the desired extent). At any point of time, all investors share the same predictions concerning the future performance of securities (and thus portfolios). Under these conditions all efficient portfolios will fall along a straight line of the form[9]

$$E_i = p + b\sigma_i,$$

where p is the pure (riskless) interest rate and b is the risk premium. Since investors are assumed to be risk-averse, b will be positive.

These results follow immediately from a relationship first described by James Tobin.[10] If an investor can borrow or lend at some riskless interest rate p and/or invest in a portfolio with predicted performance (E_i, σ_i), then by allocating his funds between the portfolio and borrowing or lending he can attain any point on the line

$$E = p + \left(\frac{E_i - p}{\sigma_i}\right)\sigma.$$

Any portfolio will thus give rise to a complete (linear) boundary of E, σ combinations. The best portfolio will be the one giving the best boundary;

---

[7] See Benjamin F. King, "Market and Industry Factors in Stock Price Behavior," *Journal of Business*, XXXIX, No. 1, Part II (Supplement, January, 1966).

[8] In my "Capital Asset Prices . . . ," *op. viti*

[9] By definition, for inefficient portfolios: $E_i < p + b\sigma_i$.

[10] In his "Liquidity Preference as Behavior towards Risk," *Review of Economic Studies,* XXV (February, 1958), 65–86.

clearly it is the one for which $(E_i - p)/\sigma_i$ is the greatest. If more than one portfolio is to be efficient, all must lie along a common line and give identical values of this ratio.

The capital-market model described here deals with predictions of future performance. Since the predictions cannot be obtained in any satisfactory manner, the model cannot be tested directly. Instead, ex post values must be used—the average rate of return of a portfolio must be substituted for its expected rate of return, and the actual standard deviation of its rate of return for its predicted risk. We denote these measures by A_i and V_i (the latter for variability).

The capital-market model implies that ex post values for A_i and V_i for efficient portfolios should lie along a straight line, with higher values of V_i associated with higher values of A_i. Because there is risk in the stock market, the points will not lie precisely along such a line, even if the model is completely correct. But the relationship should be present, visible, and statistically significant.

The implications of this model for mutual fund performance are relatively straightforward. If all funds hold properly diversified portfolios and spend the appropriate amount for analysis and administration, they should provide rates of return giving A_i, V_i values lying generally along a straight line. Points that diverge from the underlying relationship should reflect only transitory effects and not persistent differences in performance. On the other hand, if some funds fail to diversify properly, or spend too much on research and/or administration, they will persistently give rates of return yielding inferior A_i, V_i values. Their performance will be poorer and can be expected to remain so

III. PERFORMANCE OF 34 OPEN-END MUTUAL FUNDS, 1954-63

To test some of the implications drawn in the previous section, the annual rates of return for thirty-four open-end mutual funds[11] during the period 1954–63 were analyzed in the manner described above. The annual rate of return for a fund is based on the sum of dividend payments, capital gains distributions, and changes in net asset value; it is thus a measure of *net* performance—gross yield less the expenses of management and administration. The latter range from 0.25 per cent of net assets per year to 1.5 per cent per year. Most funds also charge an initial fee of approximately 8.5 per cent for selling costs when shares are purchased; annual rates of return are *not* net of such costs.

The average annual rate of return (A_i) and the standard deviation of annual rate of return (V_i) for each fund are shown in Figure 1; the values are listed in Table 1. The relationship predicted by the theory of capital asset prices is clearly present—funds with large average returns typically exhibit greater variability than those with small average returns. Moreover, the relationship is approximately linear and significant.[12] However, there are differences in

[11] The funds used for this and all subsequent analyses were those for which annual rates of return were given by Weisenberger for at least the last 20 years. All data are from Arthur Weisenberger & Co., *Investment Companies* (1953, 1962, 1964 eds.).

[12] The results of statistical tests on these data are reported in my "Risk Aversion in the

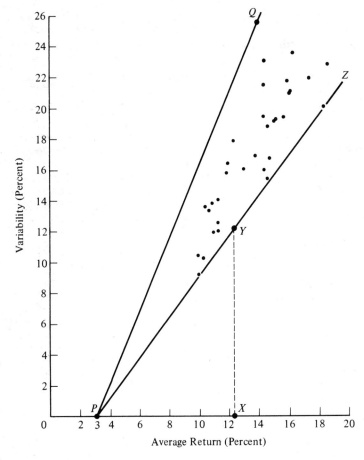

FIGURE 1

Average return and variability, 34
open-end mutual funds, 1954–63

efficiency; a number of funds are actually dominated (i.e., some other fund provided both a greater value of A_i and a smaller value of V_i). To analyze the differences, we need a single measure of performance; once such a measure is specified, any persistent differences can be investigated by testing alternative measures for predicting performance.

An intuitively appealing and theoretically meaningful measure of performance is easily derived from the Tobin effect. With substitution of the ex post measures (A and V) for the ex ante measures (E and σ), the formula described in Section II becomes

$$A = p + \left[\frac{A_i - p}{V_i}\right]V.$$

Stock Market: Some Empirical Evidence," *Journal of Finance*, September, 1965, pp. 416–22.

TABLE 1

Performance of 34 mutual funds, 1954–63

Mutual fund	Average annual return (per cent)	Variability of annual return (per cent)	Reward-to-variability ratio (R/V)*
Affiliated Fund	14.6	15.3	0.75896
American Business Shares	10.0	9.2	.75876
Axe-Houghton, Fund A	10.5	13.5	.55551
Axe-Houghton, Fund B	12.0	16.3	.55183
Axe-Houghton, Stock Fund	11.9	15.6	.56991
Boston Fund	12.4	12.1	.77842
Broad Street Investing	14.8	16.8	.70329
Bullock Fund	15.7	19.3	.65845
Commonwealth Investment Company	10.9	13.7	.57841
Delaware Fund	14.4	21.4	.53253
Dividend Shares	14.4	15.9	.71807
Eaton and Howard, Balanced Fund	11.0	11.9	.67399
Eaton and Howard, Stock Fund	15.2	19.2	.63486
Equity Fund	14.6	18.7	.61902
Fidelity Fund	16.4	23.5	.57020
Financial Industrial Fund	14.5	23.0	.49971
Fundamental Investors	16.0	21.7	.59894
Group Securities, Common Stock Fund	15.1	19.1	.63316
Group Securities, Fully Administered Fund	11.4	14.1	.59490
Incorporated Investors	14.0	25.5	.43116
Investment Company of America	17.4	21.8	.66169
Investors Mutual	11.3	12.5	.66451
Loomis-Sales Mutual Fund	10.0	10.4	.67358
Massachusetts Investors Trust	16.2	20.8	.63398
Massachusetts Investors—Growth Stock	18.6	22.7	.68687
National Investors Corporation	18.3	19.9	.76798
National Securities—Income Series	12.4	17.8	.52950
New England Fund	10.4	10.2	.72703
Putnam Fund of Boston	13.1	16.0	.63222
Scudder, Stevens & Clark Balanced Fund	10.7	13.3	.57893
Selected American Shares	14.4	19.4	.58788
United Funds—Income Fund	16.1	20.9	.62698
Wellington Fund	11.3	12.0	.69057
Wisconsin Fund	13.8	16.9	0.64091

* R/V ratio = (average return−3.0 per cent)/variability. The ratios shown were computed from original data and thus differ slightly from the ratios obtained from the rounded data shown in the table.

By investing in fund i and borrowing or lending at the riskless rate p, an investor could have attained any point along the line given by this formula. In 1953 it was possible to purchase a ten-year U.S. government bond at a price that would have guaranteed a return of slightly less than 3 per cent if held to maturity. Using 3 per cent as the estimate of p for the period, Boston Fund, shown by point Y in Figure 1, plus borrowing or lending could have provided any combination of average return and variability lying along line PYZ. Incorporated

Investors, shown by point Q, could have provided any combination lying along line PQ. Clearly the former is better than the latter, since for *any* level of risk it offered a greater average return. Indeed, the steepness[13] of the line associated with a fund provides a useful measure of performance—one that incorporates both risk and average return. We define this as the reward-to-variability ratio: For Boston Fund the ratio is equal to the distance XP on Figure 1 divided by the distance XY. The larger the ratio, the better the performance.

An alternative interpretation of the ratio gives rise to the name—reward-to-variability ratio (R/V). The numerator shows the difference between the fund's average annual return and the pure interest rate; it is thus the *reward* provided the investor for bearing risk. The denominator measures the standard deviation of the annual rate of return; it shows the amount of risk actually borne. The ratio is thus the reward per unit of variability.

The final column of Table 1 shows the values of the R/V ratio for the thirty-four funds. They vary considerably—from almost 0.78 (the Boston Fund) to slightly over 0.43 (Incorporated Investors). Those who view the market as nearly perfect and managers as good diversifiers would argue that the differences are either transitory or due to excessive expenditures by some funds. Others would argue that the differences are persistent and can be attributed (at least partially) to differences in management skill. The remainder of this paper attempts to test these alternative explanations, using pre-1954 data to predict performance from 1954 to 1963, and in the tradition of empirical studies of mutual funds, provides comparisons with the performance of the securities used to compute the Dow-Jones Industrial Average.

IV. THE PERSISTENCE OF DIFFERENCES IN PERFORMANCE

To determine the extent to which differences in performance continue through time, the returns from the thirty-four funds during the period 1944–53 were used to compute R/V ratios for the decade preceding the one previously investigated.[14] The funds were ranked in each period, from 1—the fund with the highest (best) R/V ratio, to 34—the fund with the lowest (worst) R/V ratio. Figure 2 plots the rankings in the two periods. Although the relationship is far from perfect, there is a general upward trend, suggesting that funds ranking low in the early period tend to rank low in the later period while those ranking high in the early period tend to rank high in the later period. The value of Spearman's rank correlation coefficient $(+.360)$ bears this out[15] as does the count of points

---

[13] The contangent of the angle made by the line with the horizontal axis is equal to the R/V ratio. Putting it another way, the reciprocal of the slope of the line (dA/dV) equals the R/V ratio.

[14] Since the long-term interest rate during this period was somewhat lower than that prevailing in the latter period, a pure interest rate of 2.5 per cent was used in the calculations (this was approximately the yield on a ten-year U.S. government bond in 1943). Although different assumptions regarding the pure interest rates in the two periods would substantially affect the rankings of individual funds, the relative predictive ability of the measures considered in this paper is not significantly affected by altering the assumed rates over a considerable range.

[15] The standard error for the sample size used in this and all subsequent calculations is 0.174.

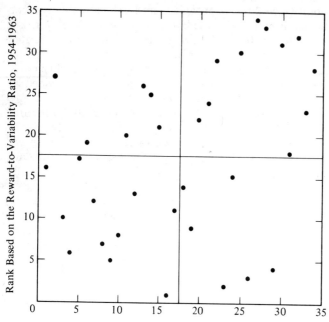

Rank Based on the Reward-to-Variability Ratio, 1944-1953

Rank Correlation Coefficient = 0.360

	Best	Worst
Worst	6	11
Best	11	6
	Best	Worst

FIGURE 2

Predictions based on the reward-
to-variability ratio

in the four quadrants (shown in the lower portion of the figure). Put rather crudely, the latter shows that an investor selecting one of the seventeen best funds in the first period would have an 11:6 chance of holding one of the seventeen best in the second period. Conversely, if he had selected one of the seventeen worst in the first period he would have an 11:6 chance of holding one of the seventeen worst in the second period. Simple regression analysis using the actual values of the R/V ratios gives similar results: the correlation coefficient is + .3157 and the t-value for the slope coefficient +1.88.

These results show that differences in performance can be predicted, although imperfectly. However, they do not indicate the sources of the differences. Equally important, there is no assurance that past performance is the best predictor of future performance. We consider next the alternative measure proposed by Treynor.

V. THE TREYNOR INDEX

In a perfect capital market no securities would be incorrectly priced. Thus one function of the mutual fund (finding such securities) would be eliminated, leaving only the tasks of diversification and selecting the appropriate risk class. Moreover, under such conditions it has been shown[16] that all truly diversified portfolios will move with the over-all market, giving high returns when the market in general provides high returns and low returns when the market provides low returns. The data bear out this hypothesis. During the period 1954–63, almost 90 per cent of the variance of the return on the typical fund in our sample was due to its comovement with the return on the thirty securities

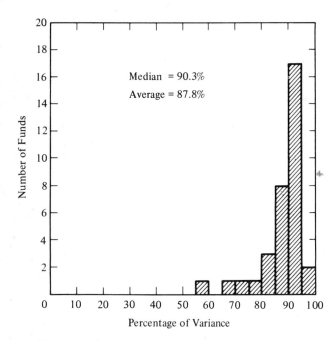

FIGURE 3

Percentage of variance due to co-movement with the Dow-Jones Industrial Average, 34 open-end mutual funds, 1954–63

used to compute the Dow-Jones Industrial Average moreover, as shown in Figure 3, the percentage was quite similar for most of the thirty-four funds.

[16] In my "Capital Asset Prices . . . ," *op. cit.*

Treynor has taken advantage of this relationship by using the *volatility* of a fund as a measure of its risk instead of the total *variability* used in the R/V ratio. Since the returns on all diversified portfolios move with the market, the extent to which changes in the market are reflected in changes in a fund's rate of return can stand as a good measure of the total variability of the fund's return over time. By observing this relationship over some past period, a reasonably good estimate of volatility—the change in the rate of return on a fund associated with a 1 per cent change in the rate of return on, say, the Dow-Jones portfolio— can be obtained. We will use B_i to represent this value for the ith fund.[17]

The measure that we will term the Treynor Index (TI) can be obtained by

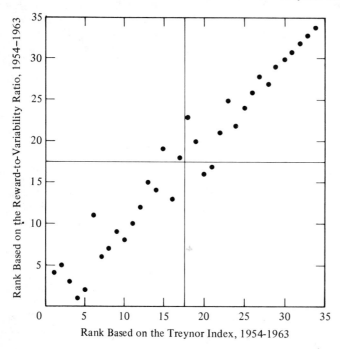

Rank Correlation Coefficient = 0.974

Worst	2	15
Best	15	2
	Best	Worst

FIGURE 4

Correlation between ranks, reward-to-variability ratio versus Treynor index

[17] To be consistent with the notation in my "A Simplified Model for Portfolio Analysis," *op. cit.*

simply substituting volatility for variability in the formula for the R/V ratio:

$$TI = \frac{A_i - p}{B_i} .$$

Stated in this manner, the relationship between the two measures is clear. And the extent of the contribution of volatility to over-all variability makes the ranking of funds on the basis of the Treynor Index very close to that based on the R/V ratio. Figure 4 shows the rankings using the two measures for the period 1954–63. Since the mutual funds in our sample all hold highly diversified portfolios, the similarity of the rankings is not surprising. And the cost of uing the Treynor Index as a measure of past performance is relatively slight[18] since it mirrors the R/V ratio quite well. However, if some relatively undiversified funds (or more likely, privately held portfolios) had been included, the results could have been significantly different, since the Treynor Index cannot capture the portion of variability that is due to lack of diversification. For this reason it is an inferior measure of *past* performance. But for this reason it may be a superior measure for predicting *future* performance.

If mutual funds hold well-diversified portfolios, any major discrepancies between the variability of their returns and that portion due to movements in the market are likely to be due to transitory effects. By concentrating on the systematic part of a fund's variability—that is, its volatility—we can avoid paying attention to these transitory effects and concern ourselves with the more permanent relationships. Thus, given some reasonable assurance that a fund will perform its diversification function well, the Treynor Index may provide better predictions of future performance than the R/V ratio.

As Figure 5 shows, the data bear out this suspicion. Using the rankings of funds based on the Treynor Index computed from 1944–53 data to predict rankings based on the performance (measured by the R/V ratio) in the subsequent ten years gives somewhat better results than those obtained before. The odds of remaining in the selected half are now 12 to 5 (instead of 11 to 6) and the rank correlation coefficient is substantially higher—.454 instead of .360. Simple regression using actual values gives similar results—the correlation coefficient is + .4008 and the t-value for the slope coefficient + 2.47. While the differences between these results and those based on the R/V ratio are far from overwhelming, the Treynor Index does appear to be the better predictor.

Before turning to other methods for predicting performance, the relationship between the measure we have termed the Treynor Index and that suggested by Treynor needs to be clarified. Our measure (TI) is similar in form to the R/V

---

[18] Treynor apparently intended that his index be used both for measuring a fund's performance after the fact and for predicting its performance in the future: "When one talks about the historical performance pattern of a fund, he is looking at the past; but when he considers the preferences of individual investors and their choices among funds, he is talking about their appraisal of the future. We shall continue to talk about the performance of funds in terms of historical performance patterns, even though actual investor choices among funds are necessarily based on expectations regarding future performance patterns. The implication is that a good historical performance pattern is one which, if continued into the future, would cause investors to prefer it to others" (Treynor, *op. cit.,* p. 67).

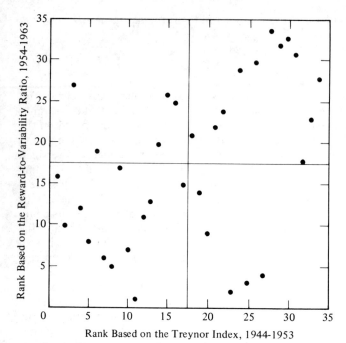

Rank Correlation Coefficient = 0.454

	Best	Worst
Worst	5	12
Best	12	5

FIGURE 5

Predictions based on the Treynor
index

ratio. One measure proposed by Treynor[19] was simply the negative of ours:

$$\text{Slope angle} = -TI.$$

This form has a major advantage, since it can be transformed into a rather different quantity—the rate of return on a market portfolio (e.g., the Dow-Jones portfolio) that would cause the fund in question to provide a rate of return equal to the pure interest rate.[20] This substitute measure has considerable intui-

[19] Described on p. 69 in Treynor, *op. cit.*:

$$a = \frac{(\mu - \mu^*)}{\sigma}$$

[20] The original index ("*SA*" for slope angle) is

$$SA_i = -TI_i = -\left(\frac{A_i - p}{B_i}\right) = \frac{p - A_i}{B_i}$$

tive appeal. Moreover, if predictions are to be made subjectively (using some judgment) rather than objectively (solely on the basis of historical data), the advantages of this alternative index are substantial. For the purposes of this paper, however, such considerations are relatively unimportant, since we are dealing only with objective methods of prediction. Accordingly we will continue to state the Treynor Index in the form directly comparable to the R/V ratio.

VI. EXPENSE RATIOS AND SIZE

Past performance appears to provide a basis for predicting future performance, especially when measured with the Treynor Index. But this does not necessarily imply that differences in performance are due to differences in management skill. The high correlation among mutual fund rates of return suggests that most accomplish the task of diversification rather well. Differences in performance are thus likely to be due to either differences in the ability of management to find incorrectly priced securities or to differences in expense ratios. If the market is very efficient, the funds spending the least should show the best (net) performance. If it is not, funds devoting more resources to management may gain enough to more than offset the increased expenditure and thus show better net performance. Intimately related with such considerations is the impact of size. A fund with substantial assets can obtain a given level of security analysis by spending a smaller percentage of its income than can a smaller fund; alternatively, by spending the same percentage it can obtain more (and/or better) analysis.

If the relationship between the rate of return on the fund (r_i) and that on the Dow-Jones portfolio (D) is

$$r_i = a_i + B_i D$$

then the average return on the fund is related to that on the Dow-Jones portfolio (D) by

$$A_i = a_i + B_i D.$$

Thus

$$SA_i = \frac{p - A_i}{B_i} = \frac{-p - (a_i + B_i D)}{B_i} = \left(\frac{p - a_i}{B_i}\right) - D$$

D_i *—the return on the Dow-Jones portfolio required to make the return on the fund equal to the pure interest rate (p) is

$$p = r_i = a_i + B_i D_i^*, \quad D_i^* = \frac{p - a_i}{B_i}$$

Therefore,

$$SA_i = D^* - D.$$

Clearly, if the slope angle for one fund is higher than that of another, the return on the Dow-Jones required to make it yield the pure interest rate will be also. Since D_i * is simply the slope angle plus a constant $(\bar{D})$, both measures will give the same ranking. The advantage of using D_i^* lies in its intuitive appeal and the fact that if future values are being estimated directly, no prediction about market performance is required. The insensitivity of Treynor's rankings (using either of the two measures) to predictions about market behavior follows directly from his assumption that variability is due *only* to the response of the fund's return to changes in the market. If there is another source of variability, the rankings of funds (using the R/V ratio) will depend to some extent on the behavior of the market.

On the other hand, more analysis may be required for a large fund than for a smaller one. In any event, both influences should be considered.

Figure 6 shows the relationship between the expenses incurred by the thirty-four funds and their performance. Since we are concerned with prediction, the funds were ranked on the basis of the ratio of expenses to net assets during 1953 (needless to say, expense ratios changed somewhat during the subsequent ten years). Expenses ranged from 0.27 per cent of net assets (rank 1) to 1.49 per cent of net assets (rank 34).

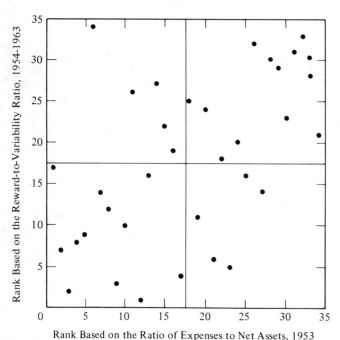

Rank Based on the Ratio of Expenses to Net Assets, 1953

Rank Correlation Coefficient = 0.505

	Lowest	Highest
Worst	5	12
Best	12	5

FIGURE 6

Predictions based on the ratio of expenses to net assets

The results tend to support the cynics: good performance is associated with low expense ratios. One of our summary measures (the rank correlation coefficient)[21] suggests that expense ratios provide somewhat better predictions than the Treynor Index; another suggests that the two are equally good (the odds of remaining in the selected half are 12 to 5 in both cases). The third suggests that the expense ratio is a slightly poorer predictor than the Treynor Index: Simple regression using actual values gave a correlation coefficient of −.3746 (the Treynor Index gave + .4008) with a t-value of −.229 (instead of +2.47). Selecting a fund with a low ratio of expense to net assets may not be as foolish as some have suggested.

Figure 7 provides information concerning the predictive ability of the

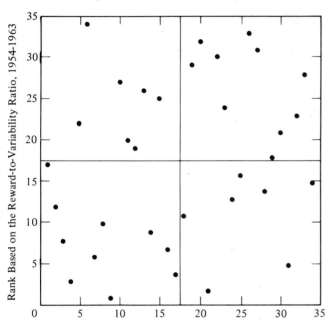

Rank Based on Net Asset Value, December 1953

Rank Correlation Coefficient = 0.234

	Largest	Smallest
Worst	7	10
Best	10	7

FIGURE 7

Predictions based on size

[21] Some of the funds had equal expense ratios (to the accuracy of two decimal places, as computed by Weisenberger). In such cases ranks were assigned alphabetically. For this reason the rank correlation coefficient is not as trustworthy as those computed for the other comparisons.

amount of a fund's asets. Size, measured by net asset value at the end of 1953, ranged from $522 million (rank 1) to $5.26 million (rank 34). Although the data show some correlation—with the larger funds exhibiting somewhat better performance—the relationship is marginal at best. This is borne out by the correlation cofficient based on actual values; it is $+.1523$, with a t-value of $+0.87$.

Multiple correlations, using actual values of the variables, gave the results shown in Table 2. The extremely small t-values for the slope coefficients relating R/V ratios to size, plus the fact that the signs differ from case to case, support the assertion that size per se is an unimportant factor in predicting future performance. The t-values for the Treynor Index and the expense ratio support the assertion that both are useful for such predictions (although neither is highly significant).

TABLE 2

Dependent variable: R/V ratio, 1953–63

Multiple correlation coefficients	t-values for slope coefficients		
	Treynor index, 1944–53	Expense/NAV 1953	Size (NAV) Dec. 1953
.4633	+1.67	−1.43	−0.46
.4572	+1.64	−1.38	......
.4015	+2.26	......	+.15
.3767	......	−2.07	−0.24

Unfortunately, the results do not provide strong confirmation for either of the views of mutual fund management described in the earlier sections of this paper. Expense ratios account for a substantial portion of the differences in performance, but so does another measure (the Treynor Index). Thus differences in management skill may be important. However, one reservation is in order. Expense ratios as reported do not include all expenses; brokers' fees are omitted. Thus the expense ratio does not capture all the differences in expenses among funds. It is entirely possible that funds with performance superior to that predicted by the traditional expense ratio engage in little trading, thereby minimizing brokerage expense. It was not feasible to attempt to measure total expense ratios for this study; had such ratios been used, a larger portion of the difference in performance might have been explained in this manner, and the apparent differences in management skill might have been smaller. Clearly, more work is needed before the traditional view of the importance of the search for incorrectly priced securities can be accepted.

VII. THE RELATIVE RISK OF MUTUAL FUNDS

All the calculations presented thus far deal with a measure of performance (the R/V ratio) that disregards risk per se, concentrating instead on the relationship between the reward obtained from the fund and the risk actually experienced. As shown earlier, the investor should be most concerned with this relationship, if he can arrange his other commitments (either by borrowing additional funds or by investing in some riskless security) to complement the risk inherent in a particular fund in any manner he desires. However, to do this he must have some idea of the variability the fund will actually experience. If mutual fund managers do not perform the second of the three tasks we have outlined(staying in a selected risk class), investors will find it difficult to arrange their over-all holdings in the most desirable manner. Holders of mutual fund shares presumably expect that funds will show reasonable consistency over time with regard to the variability of returns.

Figure 8 provides some evidence on this point. The funds were ranked in

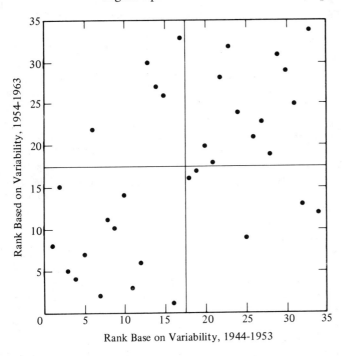

Rank Correlation Coefficient = 0.528

	Smallest	Largest
Largest	5	12
Smallest	12	5

Smallest   Largest

FIGURE 8

Consistency of risk class

each of the two periods studied (1944–53 and 1954–63) on the basis of variability —rank 1 indicating the smallest amount and rank 34 the largest. A reasonable amount of consistency between periods is evident, but a number of major shifts appear.[22] In some cases this may have been due to announced changes in management philosophy; in others it was probably inadvertent. Whatever the cause, the prevalence of such shifts in our sample is likely to disappoint some investors. On the other hand, there is no well-defined standard against which the results can be compared; given the difficulties involved,[23] one might reasonably argue that the data show that mutual fund managers fulfill remarkably well the obligation to stay within their selected risk classes.

VIII. MUTUAL FUNDS VERSUS THE DOW-JONES INDUSTRIAL AVERAGE

We have dealt at length with comparisons among mutual funds but have not considered an alternative strategy—investing directly in a reasonably diversified group of securities. To investigate such an alternative we must specify the portfolio to be held; following tradition, the thirty securities used to compute the Dow-Jones Industrial Average will be used.

When calculating the returns from the Dow Jones portfolio, no costs (brokerage, management, or administrative) are deducted. To some extent this overstates the performance available from such a direct investment. On the other hand, the initial selling (load) charge is not deducted when determining the returns from mutual funds; thus the results from both types of investments are overstated. The magnitudes of the differences between the measures we use and those relevant for a particular investor depend on a number of factors,[24] but for most investors the comparison made here should give results similar to those obtained if all the relevant costs had been considered.

Figure 9 shows the distribution of the R/V ratios for the thirty-four funds (based on their performance during the period 1954–63). The vertical line represents the R/V ratio for the Dow-Jones portfolio—its return average 16.3 per cent during the period with a variability of 19.94 per cent, giving an R/V ratio of 0.667. The average R/V ratio for the funds in our sample was 0.633—considerably smaller than that of the Dow-Jones Average. Although another group of mutual funds would give different results, the odds are greater than 100 to 1 against the possibility that the average mutual fund did as well as the Dow-Jones portfolio from 1954 to 1963.[25] In this group, only eleven funds did better than the Dow-Jones portfolio, while twenty-three did worse.

[22] Simple regression analysis using actual values gave a correlation coefficient of $+.4518$ and a t-value of $+2.86$.

[23] In "The Variation of Certain Speculative Prices," *Journal of Business,* XXXVI (October, 1963), 394–419, B. Mandelbrot has shown that predicting the variability of the changes in security prices is very difficult indeed. Presumably the law of large numbers cannot be relied upon to eliminate enough of the difficulty to make predictions of variability of the return on portfolios relatively simple.

[24] For example, the amount to be invested, the number of years the portfolio is to be held, and the extent to which dividends are to be reinvested.

[25] The standard deviation of the R/V values for the 34 funds was 0.08067. If the population of mutual funds had a mean of 0.667 and a standard deviation of 0.08067, the distri-

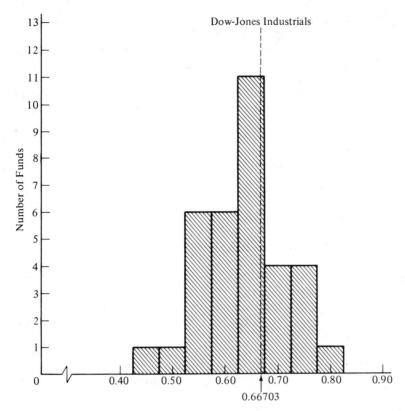

Reward-to-Variability Ratio, 1954-1963

FIGURE 9

Mutual fund performance versus Dow–
Jones Industrials, 1954–63

From the standpoint of the investor the comparison shown in Figure 9 is the most relevant. But to account for the relatively poor performance of most mutual funds it is instructive to compare *gross* performance (i.e., before deducting expenses) with that of the Dow-Jones portfolio. Such a comparison[26] shows that nineteen funds did better than the Dow-Jones portfolio, and only fifteen did worse. Although another group of funds would give different results,

---

bution of sample means for groups of 34 would have a standard deviation of 0.01383 $(0.08067/\sqrt{34})$ and be roughly normally distributed. The observed mean of 0.633 is 2.46 standard deviations below the assumed mean of 0.667; the odds are 144 to 1 that under the hypothesized conditions a sample of 34 funds would have an average R/V value as low as 0.633.

[26] The comparison was made by assuming that each fund maintained its 1953 ratio of expenses to net assets throughout the subsequent ten years. Under these conditions the only change required to compute the R/V ratios for gross performance was to add each fund's expense ratio to its average return before the R/V ratio was computed.

it is unlikely that the gross performance of the average mutual fund was worse than that of the Dow-Jones portfolio from 1954 to 1963.[27]

While it may be dangerous to generalize from the results found during one ten-year period, it appears that the average mutual fund manager selects a portfolio at least as good as the Dow-Jones Industrials, but that the results actually obtained by the holder of mutual fund shares (after the costs associated with the operation of the fund have been deducted) fall somewhat short of those from the Dow-Jones portfolio. This is consistent with our previous conclusion that, all other things being equal, the smaller a fund's expense ratio, the better the results obtained by its stockholders.

IX. CONCLUSIONS

This paper represents an attempt to bring to bear on the measurement and prediction of mutual fund performance some of the results of recent work in capital theory and the behavior of stock-market prices. We have shown that performance can be evaluated with a simple yet theoretically meaningful measure that considers both average return and risk. This measure precludes the "discovery" of differences in performance due solely to differences in objectives (e.g., the high average returns typically obtained by funds who consciously hold risky portfolios). However, even when performance is measured in this manner there are differences among funds; and such differences do not appear to be entirely transitory. To a major extent they can be explained by differences in expense ratios, lending support to the view that the capital market is highly efficient and that good managers concentrate on evaluating risk and providing diversification, spending little effort (and money) on the search for incorrectly priced securities. However, past performance per se also explains some of the differences. Further work is required before the significance of this result can be properly evaluated. But the burden of proof may reasonably be placed on those who argue the traditional view—that the search for securities whose prices diverge from their intrinsic values is worth the expense required, even for a mutual fund operating under severe constraints on the proportion of funds invested in any single security.[28] Fortunately many who hold this view have both the means and the data required to perform extensive analyses; we will all look forward to their results.

[27] The standard deviation of the gross R/V values for the 34 funds was 0.08304. If the population of mutual funds had a mean of 0.667 and a standard deviation of 0.08304, the distribution of sample means for groups of 34 would have a standard deviation of 0.01424 ($= 0.08304/\sqrt{34}$) and be roughly normally distributed. The observed mean of 0.677 is 0.74 standard deviations above the assumed mean of 0.667; the odds are 3.36 to 1 that under the hypothesized conditions a sample of 34 funds would have an average gross R/V value as high as 0.677.

[28] By law, no more than 5 per cent of the assets of a fund may be invested in any given security, and no more than 10 per cent of the assets of a given firm may be held by the fund. Moreover, the very size of many mutual funds makes it impossible to invest even the legal maximum in a security without driving its price up to a point substantially above the original (bargain) amount.

*If a portfolio consisted of a constant proportion of common stocks, then
there would be a linear relationship between the return on the portfolio
and the market's return [this comes from general equilibrium theory,
see Sharpe (30) and Fama (31)]. However, if a portfolio manager
were able to anticipate changes in the stock market, he would not
maintain a constant proportion of stocks but rather would decrease his
common stock holdings when a market was declining and increase it
when the market was improving. This would lead to a curved relationship between a mutual fund's rate of return and the market rate of return. A curved relationship is therefore a test of the ability of mutual
funds to anticipate market movements and is the subject of Treynor and
Mazuy work.*

31

Can Mutual Funds Outguess the Market?

Jack L. Treynor and Kay K. Mazuy

This article is reprinted with permission from the Harvard Business
Review, *Vol. 44, No. 4 (July–August, 1966), pp. 131–136, by the President and Fellows of Harvard College; all rights reserved.*

Are mutual fund managers successfully anticipating major turns in the stock
market? There is a widely held belief that they are. Whether investment managers themselves actually share this belief is hard to say. At one time or another in
promoting their services, however, a number of mutual funds have used the
claim that they can anticipate major stock market movements.

We have devised a statistical test of mutual funds' historical success in
anticipating major turns in the stock market. Applying this test to the performance record of 57 open-end mutual funds (as reported in this article), we
find no evidence to support the belief that mutual fund managers can outguess
the market.

DEBATED RESPONSIBILITIES

The question we have studied has an important bearing on the responsibilities
which investment managers can properly be asked to assume. For instance,
today almost everyone agrees that the market was dangerously high in early
1929 and that stocks were a bargain in the 1950's. On hindsight, laymen are

tempted to think that these extremes should have been "obvious" to fund managers at the time, and that they should have sold or bought common stocks accordingly. In actuality, of course, fund managers did *not* always sell in 1929 and buy in the 1950's.

What position should the fund manager take to protect himself against accusations that he should have anticipated market movements in this way? More broadly, what does the shareholder have a right to expect from the fund manager? Is the fund manager speculating if he attempts to anticipate major market movements? Or is he negligent if he fails to try? It seems to us that the answers to these questions depend in part on whether or not investment managers actually have the *ability* to anticipate major turns in the stock market.

Because a mutual fund's performance in each succeeding year is readily measured, widely published, and easily compared with that of other mutual funds, managers in this industry are perhaps particularly sensitive to the effect on their funds' performance of a market decline or market rise during the year. We believe that our findings may have significance not only for mutual fund managers, but also for pension, trust, and endowment fund managers—despite the fact that their objectives vary widely. If it is generally true that investment managers cannot outguess the market, then it may be necessary to revise certain conceptions about the responsibilities of investment management across the board.

ANALYTICAL APPROACH

It is well known that there is a definite tendency for the prices of most common stocks to move up and down together. Because this tendency exists, it is meaningful to talk about fluctuations in the "market." It is also well known that some common stocks are more volatile (i.e., sensitive to market fluctuations) than others.

Thus, when we talk about investment managers outguessing the market, we mean anticipating whether the general stock market is going to rise or fall and adjusting the composition of their portfolios accordingly. That is, if they think the market is going to fall, they shift the composition of the portfolios they manage from more to less volatile securities (including bonds). If they think the market is going to rise, they shift in the opposite direction. The result of such shifts is a change in effective *portfolio* volatility. (A simple graphical measure of portfolio volatility was developed by one of the authors in a previous HBR article,[1] and is reviewed in some detail later in this article.)

In order to test whether or not a mutual fund manager has actually outguessed the market, we ask, in effect: *Is there evidence that the volatility of the fund was higher in years when the market did well than in years when the market did badly?* This is the question that was applied to the 57 funds we studied. Of course, we did not know that *all* of them were trying to outguess the market, but that does not matter. Unquestionably, some of them were trying to do this and thought they had the ability.

[1] Jack L. Treynor, "How to Rate Management of Invest Funds, "HBR January–February 1965, p. 63.

PERFORMANCE DATA USED

Data for the mutual funds in our sample were obtained from *Investment Companies 1963,* by Arthur Wiesenberger Company.[2] For open-end investment companies, Wiesenberger employs the following formula to compute rate of return: "To asset value per share at the end of the period, adjusted to reflect reinvestment of all capital gains distributions, add dividends per share paid during the period from investment income, similarly adjusted; divide the total by the starting per share asset value."[3]

The resulting rate-of-return figure is only approximate, since it disregards subtleties relating to (1) the timing within the period of dividend distributions and (2) the relative after-tax value to the shareholder of market appreciation, on the one hand, and of dividend-interest income, on the other. We feel, however, that the measure is probably adequate for our purpose, even though these effects are disregarded.

THE CHARACTERISTIC LINE

If, year by year, the rate of return for a managed fund is plotted against the rate of return, similarly defined, for a suitable market average—such as the Dow-Jones Industrial Average or the Standard & Poor's 500–Stock Index—the result is the kind of patterns shown in Exhibit I. A line fitting the pattern is called the characteristic line. If the line has the same slope for years in which the market goes up as for years in which the market goes down, the slope of the line is constant; the line is straight. When this is so, a single number—the tangent of the slope angle of the line—is sufficient to characterize the sensitivity of the fund in question to market fluctuations, and we can talk meaningfully about "the" volatility of the line.

The fund shown in Part A of Exhibit I has kept a constant volatility over the years included in the sample. For such funds, the degree of scatter around the characteristic line is a measure of how well diversified the fund is. The more nearly perfect the diversification of the fund, the less scatter around the characteristic line, because the more accurately the fund reflects the stocks in the market average.

OUTGUESSING THE MARKET

What happens, however, if a fund management tries continually to outguess the market by oscillating between two characteristic lines, one of which has a high volatility and the other, a low volatility? ·

Part B of Exhibit I illustrates the extreme case in which management is able to outguess the market at every turn. Whenever management has elected the highly volatile composition demonstrated by characteristic line CD, the market has risen; whenever management has elected the low-volatility line

2 Port Washington, New York, Kennikat Press, Inc., 1963.
3 Ibid., p.99.

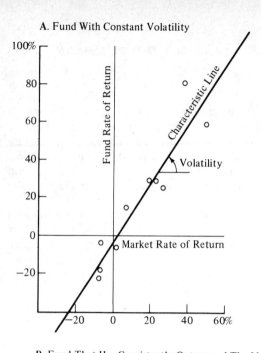

A. Fund With Constant Volatility

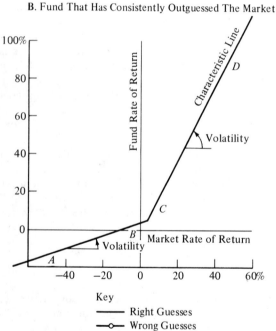

B. Fund That Has Consistently Outguessed The Market

Key
——— Right Guesses
—o— Wrong Guesses

EXHIBIT I

Illustrative characteristic lines

AB, the market has fallen. It is clear in this case that the characteristic line is no longer straight.

If, on the other hand, fund management guesses wrong as often as it guesses right, then we have the kind of picture shown as Part C of Exhibit I. Here the fund's performance traces out the undesirable points *H, G, F,* and *E* as frequently as it traces out the desirable points *A, B, C,* and *D.* The result is considerable scatter in the characteristic-line pattern, *but no curvature.*

C. Fund That Has Guessed Both Right and Wrong

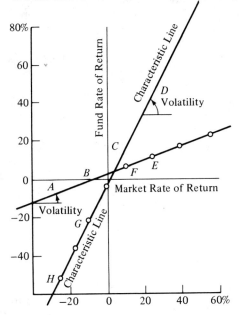

D. Fund That Has Outguessed The Market
With Better-Than-Average Success

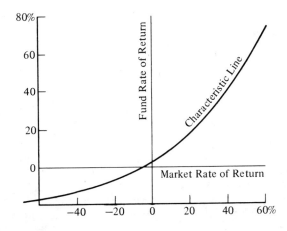

Probably no fund management would claim to be able to anticipate the market perfectly. Let us assume, however, that management has some prediction powers. Then, the better the market performs, the more likely management is to have anticipated good performance and to have increased fund volatility appropriately; and the larger, on the average, the chosen volatility is likely to be. The result will be a gradual transition of fund volatility from a flat slope at the extreme left of the characteristic-line diagram to a steep slope at the extreme right, with the slope varying more or less continuously in between, producing a smoothly curved characteristic line pattern with a certain amount of scatter resulting from management's bad predictions (see Part D of Exhibit I) rather than the kinked pattern associated with the policy illustrated in Exhibit IB.

The key to our test for successful anticipation is simple: the only way in which fund management can translate ability to outguess the market into a benefit to the shareholder is to vary the fund volatility systematically in such a fashion that the resulting characteristic line is concave upward, as in Exhibit ID. If fund management has correctly anticipated the market more often than not, then the characteristic line will no longer be straight. (And we can add, for the more mathematically inclined reader, that whether the characteristic line is smoothly curved or kinked, a least-squares statistical fit of a characteristic line to the performance data for the fund will be improved by inclusion of a quadratic term in the fitting formula.)

CHOICE OF FUNDS

If the management of a balanced fund elects to change the fund's volatility, it can shift the relative proportions of debt and equity, or change the average volatility of the equity portion, or both. However, stock funds and growth funds, which are commonly considered to consist primarily of equity securities, are obviously not free to alter their volatilities by shifting the relative proportions of debt and equity (although they can alter the average volatility of the common stocks held). For this reason, it is sometimes argued that a balanced fund is more likely to make frequent changes in fund volatility. To allow for this possibility, we divided our sample in roughly equal proportions between balanced and growth funds.

EXHIBIT II

Breakdown of sample by size and type of fund

| Market value | Number of funds | | |
of assets	Growth	Balanced	Total
Less than $20	7	10	17
$20–$99	7	13	20
$100–$500	10	7	17
More than $7,500	1	2	3
Total	25	32	57

* *In millions of dollars as of December 31, 1962.*

   In addition, it is sometimes argued that smaller funds will have less difficulty in changing their portfolio composition quickly when a change in volatility is desired. To account for this, we included in our sample of 57 mutual funds a wide range of fund sizes. Exhibit II shows the distribution of our sample among fund sizes and between balanced funds and growth funds.

TIME PERIOD STUDIED

   The period covered in the study includes the ten years beginning in 1953 and ending in 1962. One may ask if our findings would have been different if another time period had been selected for study. We do not think so. Subject to the various sources of random scatter in characteristic-line patterns discussed previously, the characteristic-line pattern remains invariant over time, regardless of the behavior of the market, unless and until basic management policies or abilities change. (In fact, management policies and abilities are probably drifting slowly as individual men in the management team mature and as the composition of the management team changes, but these effects are usually small, compared to the effects on the year-to-year rate of return caused by market fluctuations.)

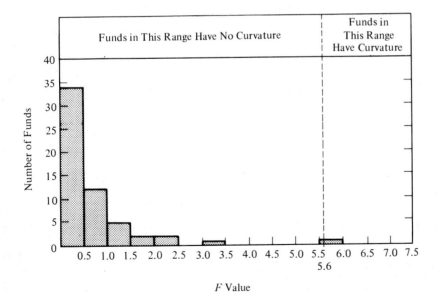

EXHIBIT III

Distribution of funds according to
F value

As mentioned earlier, if management is right more often than wrong in its attempts to outguess the market, the characteristic-line pattern will be curved. The degree of curvature depends on how heavily management bets on its expectations—that is, the degree to which management changes fund volatility when its expectations regarding the market change. So long as management policy continues roughly constant in this regard, the degree of curvature manifested in the characteristic line will remain unchanged.

The only criterion for the time period selected for a curvature study is that during the period the market should have exhibited wide and frequent swings both upward and downward, so that the characteristic-line data are not confined to a segment in the middle of the pattern which, because of its shortness, is indistinguishable from a straight line.

The period 1953–1962 contains one year in which the Dow-Jones Industrials demonstrated a rate of return of 50% and three years in which the return was negative by substantial amounts. We feel that this is a suitable period for our study because it is long enough to cover a variety of ups and downs in the general market, short enough to avoid serious problems resulting from the gradual drift of fund policies over time, and recent enough to reflect modern mutual fund management practices and policies. The fact that the market was generally rising throughout the period has no effect on the characteristic line, and hence in no way invalidates our findings.

We have used yearly data because we feel that even the smaller mutual funds would be reluctant to make the changes in portfolio composition necessary to change fund volatility much more often than once a year. Based as it is on yearly data, however, the study cannot detect any success that fund managements may have had with more frequent changes in volatility.

FINDINGS

What does the study show? It shows no statistical evidence that the investment managers of any of the 57 funds have successfully outguessed the market. More precisely, we find no evidence of curvature of the characteristic lines of any of the funds.

Here are some of the more technical aspects of our study:

> In order to test for the presence of curvature, we used the methods mentioned earlier. (A least-squares regression technique was employed to fit characteristic-line data for the 57 open-end mutual funds in our sample. That is, for each of the funds we calculated the constants for the equation which "best" describes the performance data of the mutual fund for the Standard & Poor's Composite Price Index as a quadratic function of the performance.)
>
> Exhibit III summarizes our results. The value of the F statistic, plotted along the horizontal axis, is a measure of the degree of curvature of the fund (and is normalized to allow for variations in the amount of random scatter observed). The vertical axis shows the number of funds which had F values equal to the F value given on the horizontal axis. As the magnitude of an F value increases, the higher the probability that the amount of curvature seen for the fund is real, i.e., is greater than we would expect by random chance. The vertical dotted line marks the F value (5.6) corresponding to the amount of apparent

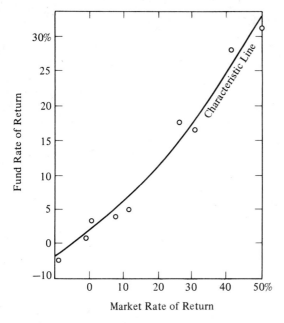

EXHIBIT IV

Characteristic line of the fund
which has the greatest value

curvature which even those funds that have no real curvature would display one time in twenty. A fund should show an *F* value greater than 5.6 in order to be considered to have real curvature.

In our sample of 57 managed funds, only one displayed even an *F* value of 5.6. This fund's curve and also the actual data points are given in Exhibit IV.

In other words, our findings show that for the mutual funds in our sample, at least, it is safe to assume that their characteristic lines are straight. Actual funds tend to resemble the fund in Exhibit I-A rather than the funds in Exhibits I-B and I-D. Our results suggest that an investor in mutual funds is completely dependent on fluctuations in the general market. This is not to say that a skillful fund management cannot provide the investor with a rate of return that is higher in both bad times and good than the return provided by the market averages, but it does suggest that the improvement in rate of return will be due to the fund manager's ability to identify underpriced industries and companies, rather than to any ability to outguess turns in the level of the market as a whole.

The fact that only one of the 57 mutual funds in our sample has a characteristic line suggesting curvature indicates that perhaps no investor—professional or amateur—can outguess the market. This finding has clear significance for the man in the street managing his own portfolio, for the man with fiduciary responsibility for a private estate, for the president of a manufacturing company responsible for its pension fund, and for a college treasurer managing an endowment. It means that probably the best assumption they can make is that investment managers have no ability to outguess the market and should not try to. It also means they should not hold fund managers responsible for failing to foresee changes in market climate.